Astoria in 1811.

A HISTORY

OF

OREGON,

1792—1849,

DRAWN FROM PERSONAL OBSERVATION AND AUTHENTIC INFORMATION.

BY

W. H. GRAY,

OF

ASTORIA.

PUBLISHED BY THE AUTHOR FOR SUBSCRIBERS.

PORTLAND, OREGON: HARRIS & HOLMAN.
SAN FRANCISCO: H. H. BANCROFT & CO.
NEW YORK: THE AMERICAN NEWS COMPANY.
1870.

ALVORD
PRINTER
N.Y.

INTRODUCTORY.

The reader will observe that when we commenced furnishing the historical articles for the *Marine Gazette*, we did not know that they would be of sufficient interest to justify arranging them in book form; but few articles had been given, however, before there was a call for back numbers of the paper, which were not on hand. It was then decided to continue the articles, giving an opportunity to correct errors in statement of historical facts, and collect such as were printed, with all just criticisms, review the whole, and complete the manuscript for publication.

As will be seen, we have endeavored to narrate events in plain language, and as nearly in the order of occurrence as possible.

We make no claim to literary merit or attractive style; the facts we have collected, the proofs we are able to give of the policy and practices of one of the most gigantic frauds ever continued for a series of years by one professedly civilized and Christian nation upon another, in chartering and continuing to license a monster monopoly; and the manner in which they have sought for a series of years to prevent American trade and settlement of the western portion of our country, is contained in the following pages. We can only give the principal events, which in the future may be better arranged in an interesting and authentic history, which we must leave for others to write. The reader will find in the following pages:—

I. The American history of the Hudson's Bay and Puget Sound Agricultural companies.

II. The causes of failure of the Protestant missions, the causes of Indian wars, and the causes that must tend to the utter destruction of the Indian race on the American continent.

III. The adverse influences that the early settlers had to contend with in coming to and settling in the country, fully explained.

IV. A concise history of the early settlement of the country, a short sketch of many of the public men in it, their public character and proceedings, and the organization of the provisional government.

V. The mining and agricultural interests of the country.

There are two grounds upon which every fact is based:—

1. Personal knowledge, observation, and participation in what is stated for one-third of a century.

2. The written and printed statements of others, so compared that conclusions are intended to be without a possibility of truthful contradiction; thus making this a standard history of the country for the time included within the period from its discovery by Captain Robert Gray to 1849.

ERRATA.

Page 526, 11th line from top, for "becamed," read "became."

Page 568, 6th line from bottom, for "Moxon," read "Maxon." Also on pages 570 and 573 the same error occurs.

Page 583, 19th line from top, for "that British," read "that the British."

Page 592, 7th line from bottom, for "propriety," read "propensity."

Page 602, 7th line from top, for "where," read "when."

Page 613, 4th line from bottom, for "ten," read "one hundred."

CONTENTS.

CHAPTER I.

CHAPTER II.

CHAPTER III.

CHAPTER IV.

CHAPTER V.

CHAPTER VI.

CHAPTER VII.

CHAPTER VIII.

CHAPTER IX.

CHAPTER X.

CHAPTER XI.

CHAPTER XII.

CHAPTER XIII.

CHAPTER XIV.

CHAPTER XV.

CHAPTER XVI.

CHAPTER XVII.

CHAPTER XVIII.

CHAPTER XIX.

CHAPTER XX.

CHAPTER XXI.

CHAPTER XXII.

CHAPTER XXIII.

CHAPTER XXIV.

CHAPTER XXV.

CHAPTER XXVI.

CHAPTER XXVII.

CHAPTER XXVIII.

CHAPTER XXIX.

CHAPTER XXX

CHAPTER XXXI.

CHAPTER XXXII.

CHAPTER XXXIII.

CHAPTER XXXIV.

CHAPTER XXXV.

CHAPTER XXXVI.

CHAPTER XXXVII.

CHAPTER XXXVIII.

CHAPTER XXXIX.

CHAPTER XL.

CHAPTER XLI.

CHAPTER XLII.

CHAPTER XLIII.

CHAPTER XLIV.

CHAPTER XLV.

CHAPTER XLVI.

CHAPTER XLVII.

CHAPTER XLVIII.

CHAPTER XLIX.

CHAPTER L.

CHAPTER LI.

CHAPTER LII.

CHAPTER LIII.

CHAPTER LIV.

CHAPTER LV.

CHAPTER LVI.

CHAPTER LVII.

CHAPTER LVIII.

CHAPTER LIX.

CHAPTER LX.

CHAPTER LXI.

CHAPTER LXII.

CHAPTER LXIII.

CHAPTER LXIV.

CHAPTER LXV.

HISTORY OF OREGON.

CHAPTER I.

First discovery of the river.—Natives friendly.—British ship.—Brig *Jennet.*—Snow *Sea Otter.*—The *Globe.*—*Alert.*—*Guatimozin.*—*Atahualpa.*—Lewis and Clarke.—Vancouver.—Hamilton.—Derby.—*Pearl.*—*Albatross.*—First house built in 1810.—Astor's settlement.—The *Tonquin.*—Astor's Company betrayed to the Northwest Company.

IN all countries it is difficult to trace the history of their early discovery and settlement. That of Oregon is no exception. The Spanish claim, and it is generally conceded, that they were the discoverers of the coast, and gave names to the principal capes and to Fuca's Straits. No evidence can be found in national archives, or among the native tribes of the country, that gives the discovery of the Columbia River to any civilized people but to the Bostons (Americans); so that, so far as civil history or national testimony is concerned, we are without any, except the conjectures of men as ignorant as ourselves. Hence we are left to the alternative of searching the old logs of vessels and such old books as have been written, and, in connection with the legends and statements of the aborigines of the country, form an opinion as to its discovery, and from such dates and conclusions commence its civil history. That of Oregon begins eight years previous to the commencement of the present century.

A ship, owned by Messrs. Barrell, Bulfinch & Co., of Boston, and commanded by Captain Robert Gray, discovered and entered the mouth of the third great river upon the American continent. It then had no name known to the civilized world. This unselfish American, instead of following the example of many contemporary British navigators by giving his own name to the majestic river he had discovered, gave it that of his noble ship, *Columbia.*

On the 7th of May, 1792, he discovered and ran in abreast of Cape Hancock, and anchored, and on the 11th ran ten miles up this river on the north side, which is now known as a little above Chinook Point, and at 1 P. M. they came to anchor. On the 14th they weighed anchor and ran, according to the ship's log, fifteen miles, which would bring them up abreast of Tongue Point, where their ship grounded upon a sand bar for a short time, but they backed her off into three fathoms of water and anchored. By sounding they discovered that there was not sufficient water to pass up the river in their present channel. Having filled all their water-casks, repaired, painted, and calked the ship, and allowed the vast numbers of Indians that thronged around them in the most peaceable and friendly manner, to visit and traffic with them, on the 20th of May, 1792, they went to sea again.

On the 20th of October of this year, the *Chatham*, commanded by Captain Broughton, of the British navy, entered the river. He grounded his ship on what is now called the Sulphur Spit, and found in the bay the brig *Jennet*, Captain Baker, from Bristol, Rhode Island. Captain Broughton explored the river in his small boat as high up as the present site of Vancouver, and left the river with his ship on the 10th of November.

In 1797, five years later, the snow *Sea Otter*, Captain Hill, from Boston, visited the river.

In 1798, the ship *Hazard*, Swift, master, owned by Perkins, Lamb & Co., Boston, visited the river. This same ship visited the river again in 1801.

In 1802, this same Boston company sent the ship *Globe*, Magee, master, to the river.

During the year 1802, a brisk, and something like a permanent American trade appears to have been in contemplation by this Boston company. They sent the ship *Caroline*, Derby, master, from Boston, and the ship *Manchester*, Brice, master, from Philadelphia.

In 1803, Lamb & Company sent the ship *Alert*, Ebbets, master; also the ship *Vancouver*, Brown, master. This year, the ship *Juno*, Kendricks, master, from Bristol, Rhode Island, owned by De Wolf, entered the Columbia River for trade.

In the year 1804, Theodore Lyman sent the ship *Guatimozin*, Bumsted, master, from Boston. The Perkins Company sent the ship *Hazard*, Swift, master, to the river the same year.

In 1805, Lyman & Company sent the ship *Atahualpa*, O. Potter, master, from Boston. Lamb & Company sent the ship *Caroline*, Sturges, master, from the same place.

On the 15th of November, 1805, Lewis and Clarke, with their party, having crossed the Rocky Mountains under the direction of President Jefferson, of the United States, arrived at Cape Hancock; remaining but a few days, they crossed the Columbia River and encamped near the mouth of a small river still bearing the name of these two explorers.

They left their encampment in March, 1806, and returned across the continent and reported the result of their expedition to the government.

This expedition consisted of one hundred and eighty soldiers or enlisted men. On arriving at the Mandan Village, on the Missouri River, in 1804, they encountered the influence of the Northwest British Fur Company, who, on learning their object, at once made arrangements to follow and get possession of the country at the mouth of the Columbia River.

In 1806, soon after Lewis and Clarke left their encampment on their return to the United States, the ship *Vancouver*, Brown, master, entered the river, having been sent out by Thomas Lyman, of Boston, in expectation of meeting Lewis and Clarke's party at the mouth of the river. The Lamb Company sent the ship *Pearl* the same year, under the command of Captain Ebbets. Lyman, in addition to the *Vancouver*, sent the brig *Lydia*, Hill, master, to the river, making three American ships from Boston in the year 1806.

In 1807, the ship *Hamilton* arrived in the river, sent by Thomas Lyman, of Boston, L. Peters, master. The Perkins Company sent the *Hazard*, Smith, master.

In 1808, the ship *Derby*, Swift, master, sent by the Perkins Company. Lyman sent the ship *Guatimozin*, Glanville, master; both made successful trips in and out of the river.

In 1809, the Perkins Company sent the ships *Pearl* and *Vancouver* into the river, the former commanded by Smith, the latter by Whittimore.

In 1810, the ship *Albatross*, from Boston, T. Winship, master, entered the river and sailed as high up as Oak Point, where the captain erected a house, cleared a piece of land for cultivation, and planted a garden. This year, John Jacob Astor, of New York, organized the Pacific Fur Company, in connection with Wilson Price Hunt, of New Jersey. These two gentlemen admitted as partners in the fur trade, Messrs. McKay, McDougal, and David and Robert Stewart. These four last-mentioned partners, with eleven clerks and thirteen Canadian voyageurs, and a complete outfit for a fort, with cannon and small-arms, stores, shops, and houses, with five mechanics, were all embarked on the ship *Tonquin*, Captain Jonathan Thorn, master, in September, 1810, and sailed for the Columbia River, where they arrived, March 24, 1811.

The present site of the town of Astoria was selected as the principal depot for this American Fur Company, and called by them, in honor of the originator of the company, ASTORIA. This establishment was soon in full operation. The timber and thick undergrowth within musket range of the establishment were cleared away, and a kitchen-garden planted outside the stockade.

In the highly-interesting narrative of Gabriel Franchere, we read that, "in the month of May, 1811, on a rich piece of land in front of our establishment [at Astoria], we put into the ground twelve potatoes, so shriveled up during the passage from New York that we despaired of raising any from the few sprouts that still showed signs of life. Nevertheless, we raised one hundred and nineteen potatoes the first season. And, after sparing a few plants to our inland traders, we planted fifty or sixty hills, which produced five bushels the second year; about two of these were planted, and gave us a welcome crop of fifty bushels in the year 1813."

They were cultivated at Astoria, by the old Northwest and Hudson's Bay companies, in their little fort gardens. A few Indian chiefs were presented with the seed, but no general distribution was made among them, as they were considered as the Bostons' root, and no better than those of the Indians, abounding in the country, which required less labor to cultivate. Up to the time of the arrival of the American missionaries, there never was an extra supply of potatoes in the country. In other words, the potato was a luxury enjoyed by none except the highest grades of the Fur Company's servants and distinguished visitors; its cultivation was not generally encouraged by the company.

In October, 1810, after dispatching the *Tonquin*, Mr. Astor fitted out the ship *Beaver*, twenty guns, Captain Sowles, master, with Mr. Clark, six clerks, and a number of other persons, to join the establishment at Astoria. The ship touched at the Sandwich Islands; Mr. Clark engaged twenty-six Kanakas as laborers for the establishments on the Columbia River, where the ship arrived, May 5, 1812.

On the 15th of July, 1813, Mr. David Thompson, under the direction of the Northwest Canadian British Company, arrived at Astoria. I use the word Canadian, as applied to the Northwest Fur Company, that was established by the charter of Louis XIII. of France, 1630, in what was then called Acadia, or New France, forty years before Charles of England gave his charter to the Hudson's Bay Company. This Northwest Fur Company, in the transfer of the sovereignty of Acadia, or New France, to England, in 1714, at the treaty of Utrecht, was acknowledged as having a legal existence, by both nations, and was allowed to transfer its allegiance and continue its trade under the protection of the British sovereign, as it had done under that of France.

As soon as the government and people of the United States entered upon active measures to explore and occupy the country west of the Rocky Mountains, this Canadian Northwest Fur Company dispatched

Mr. Thompson to explore the Columbia River, and make an establishment at its mouth; but, on account of delays and mistaking the course of the various rivers through which the party traveled, Mr. Thompson did not arrive at Mr. Astor's American establishment till in July, 1813; his object was to forestall Mr. Astor in the settlement of the country. He was received, kindly treated, and furnished with such goods and supplies as he and his party required, by Mr. McDougal, who was then in charge of Fort Astor, and, in company with David Stewart, returned as high up the Columbia as the Spokan,—Mr. Greenhow says Okanagon,—and established a trading-post, while Mr. Thompson went among the Kootenai and Flathead tribes, and established a trading-hut. It is due to those parties to state that as late as 1836, a square, solid, hewed log bastion, erected by Stewart's party, was still standing at Spokan, while no vestige of the Thompson huts could be found in the Flathead country. At Spokan, garden vegetables were produced about the fort, which the Indians in that vicinity learned to appreciate, and continued to cultivate after the fort was abandoned in 1825, having been occupied by the Northwest and Hudson's Bay companies till that time.

In the spring of 1811, the chief agent of the Pacific Fur Company, Mr. Hunt, with other partners, Crooks, McKenzie, and McClellen, with a party of sixty men, started across the continent. They were extremely annoyed by the opposition fur traders on their route, and also by hostile Indians. Such of the party as did not perish by famine and hostile Indians, and British fur traders, arrived at Astoria on the 28th of January, 1812.

On the 5th of May following the arrival of Mr. Hunt's party, the ship *Beaver* arrived with the third installment of traders, clerks, and Kanaka laborers. In consequence of the loss of the ship *Tonquin*, and all on board except the Indian interpreter, in the Cliquot Bay, near the entrance of the Straits of Fuca, by the treachery of the Indians in the vicinity, Mr. Hunt embarked in the *Beaver* for the Russian establishment in August, 1812, effected an arrangement of trade with them, and dispatched the ship to China. He continued in her till she reached the Sandwich Islands, where he remained until June, 1813, when the ship *Albatross* arrived from Canton, and brought the news of the war between the United States and Great Britain, and also that the ship *Beaver* was blockaded at Canton by a British ship of war. Mr. Hunt at once chartered the *Albatross* and sailed for the Columbia River, where he arrived on the 4th of August, 1813.

On his arrival at Astoria he learned that it was the intention of his partners, all of whom claimed to be British subjects (McDougal and

McKenzie having formerly been in the employ of the Northwest Company), to sell to McTavish, of that company. Hunt embarked in the *Albatross* for the Sandwich Islands, and from thence to the Washington Islands, where he learned from Commodore Porter, then at those Islands, in the frigate *Essex*, of the design of the British to seize all American property on the Pacific coast. From thence he returned to the Sandwich Islands, and chartered the brig *Pedler*, and arrived at Astoria in February, 1814, and learned that soon after his departure in the *Albatross*, in August, 1813, McTavish, with a party of the servants of the Northwest Company, had arrived at Astoria, and, in connection with McDougal, McKenzie, and Clarke, on the part of the American Pacific Fur Company, and McTavish and Alexander Stewart, on the part of the Canadian Northwest Company, had completed the sale of Astoria to that company, and secured for themselves important positions in the service of the latter company.

As a matter of fact and general historical interest, the amount and value of property thus transferred is here given: Eighteen thousand one hundred and seventy and one-fourth pounds of beaver, at two dollars per pound, selling in Canton at that time at from five to six dollars per pound; nine hundred and seventy otter skins, at fifty cents each, selling at that time in Canton for five and six dollars per skin.

The expense of building Mr. Astor's establishment at Astoria, including those at Okanagon and Spokan, with boats, *bateaux*, tools, cannon, munitions, goods, transportation and salaries of clerks and men, etc., etc., was near two hundred thousand dollars, for which he received in bills on Montreal about forty thousand, including the appraised value of the furs at the fort, which was thirty-six thousand eight hundred and thirty-five dollars and fifty cents; this would leave less than three thousand one hundred and sixty-four dollars and fifty cents for the improvements, boats, munitions, cannon, etc., for which the Hudson's Bay Company, in 1865, claims of our government, for the old, rotten, and abandoned post at Okanagon, nineteen thousand four hundred and sixty-six dollars and sixty-seven cents; the post at Colville, still held in place of the one built by Astor's company at Spokan, eighty thousand three hundred dollars; the post at Fort George (Astoria), abandoned in 1849, four thousand one hundred and thirty-six dollars and sixty-seven cents; in all, for the three establishments, one hundred and three thousand nine hundred and three dollars and thirty-four cents,—quite a contrast between the valuation of American property when in possession of British fur traders, having been used for forty years by British subjects, and abandoned as of little or no use to their trade, and that of American property but lately brought into the country. It will be remembered that Mr. Astor's Pacific Fur Company was commenced in 1810; that at the time it was betrayed into the possession of this Canadian Northwest Fur Company it had been in operation but two years, hence was new, and but just ready to commence a profitable trade in the country.

The contract transferring this valuable property from American to British owners, was signed on the 16th day of October, 1813, by Duncan McDougal, J. G. McTavish, and J. Stewart, and witnessed by the principal clerks of the establishment. On the 1st of December following, the British sloop of war *Raccoon*, Captain Black, arrived in the river, and proceeded to take formal possession of Astoria, by lowering the American flag and hoisting that of Great Britain in its place, and changing the name of the fort to that of Fort George.

Previous to the landing of the British soldiers, or King George's warriors, an interview took place (as related by Ross Cox) between the Indian warriors, with Concomly, their chief, at their head, and McDougal and McTavish. On the arrival of the British war vessel in Baker's Bay, the Indians, having learned that there was war between the King George people and Bostons (Americans), they said, as they had always found the Bostons friendly and liberal toward them, they were their friends, and were ready to fight for them, to prevent the King George men from making them slaves. They proposed to conceal themselves behind the rocks and trees outside of the fort and to kill the King George soldiers with their arrows and spears, while the men of the fort fought the ship and small boats which they came in, with their big guns and rifles. McDougal assured them that the King George warriors would not hurt them, and advised them to be friendly with them, as they would do the people of the fort no harm. Concomly and his warriors were only convinced that the Bostons would not be made slaves by the King George warriors when they saw the sloop leave the river without taking any of them away as prisoners or slaves.

The treachery of the Canadian part of Astor's company, which was not known to Mr. Astor, but provided for by the Northwest Canadian Company before the party left Montreal, and consummated by McDougal and his associates, in the absence of the American partners from the post, is proved by journals, letters, and facts still extant.

CHAPTER II.

The country restored.—The order.—Description of Astoria.—Different parties.—Northwest Fur Company.—Astor's plan.—Conflict of the two British fur companies.—The treaties.—The Selkirk settlement.—Its object.—The company asserts chartered rights as soon as united.

As stated in our first chapter, the English government, by its Canadian Northwest Fur Company, and the arrival of the British sloop of war, *Raccoon*, during the war of 1812–13, took possession of Oregon, and held it as British territory till it was formally restored to the United States on the 6th of October, 1818, in these words:—

We, the undersigned, do, in conformity to the first article of the treaty of Ghent, restore to the government of the United States, through its agent, J. P. Provost, Esq., the settlement of Fort George, on the Columbia River.

Given under our hands in triplicate, at Fort George (Columbia River), this 6th day of October, 1818.

F. Hickey, Captain H. M. Ship *Blossom.*
J. Keith, of the N. W. Co.

The order from the Prince Regent of England to the Northwest Company to deliver up the country to the American government, was issued on January 27, 1818, and complied with as above.

On the 17th of April, 1814, the Canadian Northwest Fur Company's ship, *Isaac Todd*, reached Astoria, called Fort George.

According to the description sent to Washington by Mr. Provost, it consisted of a stockade made of fir-logs, twenty feet high above the ground, inclosing a parallelogram of one hundred and fifty by two hundred and fifty feet, extending in its greatest length from northwest to southeast, and defended by bastions, or towers, at two opposite angles. Within this inclosure were all the buildings of the establishment, such as dwelling-houses, magazines, storehouses, mechanics' shops, etc.

The artillery were two heavy 18-pounders, six 6-pounders, four 4-pounders, two 6-pound coehorns, and seven swivels, all mounted.

The number of persons attached to the place besides the few native women and children, was sixty-five; of whom twenty-three were white, twenty-six Kanakas, and the remainder of mixed blood from Canada.

Of the party that crossed the Rocky Mountains with Mr. Hunt in 1811–12, six remained in the country, and but five returned to the United States; the remaining forty-five that started with him in his first expedition were mostly destroyed by the influence of the two British fur companies acting upon the Indians for that object.

These men, as independent trappers and petty traders among the Indians, were considered by those companies as intruders and trespassers upon their French and British chartered rights; hence none were allowed to remain in the country but such as were under their control, or subject to their rule.

From the time the Northwest Fur Company took possession of the country, with few exceptions, we have no authentic account of the number of vessels of any nation that visited the river, but we have reason to believe that they would average two each year; and, from known facts, we conclude that as soon as the post at Astoria was betrayed into the possession of the Canadian Northwest Fur Company by McDougal and associates, and the British government had taken formal possession of the country, this Northwest Company, with McDougal and others equally prominent, commenced to instill into the minds of the Indians a strong hatred of American traders by sea or land, and to change as much, and as fast as possible, the friendly feeling of the former toward the latter, so as to continue to hold the permanent and absolute sovereignty of the country, and make the Indians subservient to their commercial interests.

Mr. Astor says: "The plan by me adopted was such as must materially have affected the interests of the Northwest and Hudson's Bay companies, and it was easy to be foreseen that they would employ every means to counteract my operations, and which, as my impression, I stated to the executive of your department as early as February, 1813." This hatred of Americans had been so assiduously impressed upon the minds of the Indians, that one of their own vessels arriving in the river, being cast away on Sand Island, all on board were murdered by the Indians, who mistook them for Americans. The company sent a vessel from Vancouver (to which place they had removed their stores and principal depot) to punish the Indians, who had secured most of the wrecked property. The vessel came down and sent shell and grape-shot into the Indian village, destroying men, women, and children, landed their men and took such of their goods as they could find, having gained satisfactory evidence of the murder of the crew of the ship.

This view of the policy and practice of this Northwest and Hudson's Bay Company, is further sustained by the inquiries which Mr. Keith felt it incumbent on him to make of Mr. Provost, on the restoration of Astoria to the Americans by the British authorities.

Mr. Keith was anxious to learn the extent of the rights of his company to remain and trade in the country. It would seem, from the whole history of these companies, that they felt their rights in the country to be but temporary, that they were trespassers upon American interests, and shaped all their arrangements accordingly.

It is an admitted historical fact that, while the Northwest Fur Company of Montreal was extending its trade across the Rocky Mountains and supplanting the American Pacific Fur Company of Mr. Astor, the Hudson's Bay Company, with the assistance of Lord Selkirk's Red River settlement, was cutting off their communication with these western establishments, and that, in consequence of this Red River interference with their trade, a deadly feud sprang up between the rival companies, in which both parties enlisted all the men and Indians over whom they had any influence, and frequently met in drunken and deadly strife, till they had quite destroyed all profits in their trade, and rendered the Indians hostile alike to friend and foe of the white race. So that, in 1821, the British Parliament was compelled to notice their proceedings, and, on the 2d of July, 1821, in an act bearing date as above, says of them :—

"Whereas, the competition in the fur trade between the governor and company of adventurers of England trading into Hudson's Bay, and certain associations of persons trading under the name of the Northwest Company of Montreal, has been found, for some years past, to be productive of great inconvenience and loss, not only to the said company and association, but to the said trade in general, and also of *great injury to the native Indians*, and of other persons subjects of *his Majesty;* and whereas, the *animosities* and *feuds* arising from such competition have also, for some years past, kept the interior of America, to the northward and westward of the provinces of Upper and Lower Canada, and of the *Territories of the United States of America*, in a state of *continual disturbance;* and whereas, many breaches of the peace and violence extending to the *loss of lives* and considerable destruction of property have continually occurred therein," etc. (See Greenhow's History of Oregon, p. 467.)

The broad policy of British fur traders is here stated in plain language by their own government in a manner not to be mistaken. Their influence upon the Indians was injurious. Their policy toward each other was war and destruction to all opponents. The life and property of an opposing trader must not come in competition with the profits of their trade with Indians in any country.

How absurd it is for our government to spend millions of dollars to form treaties with Indians who are constantly visited by these foreign Indian traders and teachers, emissaries of a foreign power, who never breathed an honest breath or spoke a truthful word! Feeble and insignificant as they were, from 1813 to 1821 the whole Indian country of North America fell under their blighting and withering influence. Divided as they were, they were able to crush all honest competition, and *combine* in deadly combat against their own countrymen for the supremacy of the Indian trade. Have they lost their power and influence by uniting the elements of opposition in one vast fur monopoly? Nay, verily, as we shall see.

To gain a correct understanding of the foreign policy relative to the western portion of our country, it will be necessary to refer to the early history of the two fur companies, and trace their connection with France and England, which, notwithstanding the English government had given up the country to France in 1696 in the treaty of Ryswick, and no reservation was made on account of the Hudson's Bay Company—as they did Oregon to the United States in the treaty of Ghent, in 1815, and made no reservation on account of the Northwest Fur Company—still the Hudson's Bay Company held on to a single post, called Albany, on the southwest part of James Bay, for twenty-six years, as the Northwest and Hudson's Bay fur companies did to Astoria and Oregon for forty-nine years.

In the wording of the treaty of Utrecht, in 1714, in which the country was given back to England by France, there is one proviso that is not to be overlooked, viz.: "It is, however, provided, that it may be entirely free for the company of Quebec, and all others the subjects of the most Christian king whatsoever, to go, by land or by sea, whithersoever they please, out of the lands of the said bay, together with all their goods, merchandise, arms, and effects, of what nature or condition soever, except such things as are above reserved in this article," etc., the exceptions referring to forts, cannon, and permanent war materials.

This French stipulation in the treaty of Utrecht, in 1714, is repeated by the English diplomatist upon the Americans, in the third article of the treaty of June 15, 1846, forming the basis of the claim urged against our government in the treaty of 1864.

In the treaty stipulations between France and England in 1714, the commercial rights of the French company of Quebec were secured to them. From that time forward, the aggressive and oppressive policy of the British Hudson's Bay Company was brought into collision, not only with the French Northwest Fur Company, but with the United States and all American fur companies and missionary and commercial enterprises coming within their fur-trade influence.

It will be remembered that the Hudson's Bay Company, who claim their existence and privileges from the charter of Charles II., as early as 1670, had, in forty-four years' time, only established (as Mr. Fitzgerald says) "four or five insignificant forts on the shores of Hudson's Bay to carry on a trade in furs with those Indians who resorted thither;" while the French, for many years previous, had carried on an active trade with the Indians, and had explored the country and extended their posts up to the shores of the Saskatchewan, and over the Rocky Mountains, on to the waters of the Columbia. The French carried on the traffic by way of the St. Lawrence and the lakes to Fort William, on Lake Superior, and through the Lake of the Woods into Lake Winnipeg, or further south along the plains, crossing the course of the Red River; this being the direct and only line of posts kept up by the French Northwest Company, by which their food, goods, and furs were transported. The Hudson's Bay Company carried theirs by way of Hudson's Straits, around the coast of Labrador. In order to destroy and cut off as much as possible the trade of this Northwest Company, Lord Selkirk, in 1811–12, became a shareholder, and was allowed to claim, through the directors of the company, sixteen thousand square miles of territory in the Red River country, for the professed purpose of colonization.

This colony was planted directly in the line of the fur traffic of the Northwest Company, against which the Hudson's Bay Company had encouraged and carried on the most bitter hostility, enlisting both men and Indians in a deadly feud between the two rival companies.

Our English writer remarks on page 57: "To those who had read the mutual recriminations that had been bandied between these two bodies, it was a strange sight to see the names of Messrs. McGillivray and Edward Ellice associated with that of the Hudson's Bay Company,—to see men going hand-in-hand who had openly accused one another of the foulest crimes, *of wholesale robbery*, *of allowing their servants to instigate the Indian tribes to* MURDER *the servants of their rivals*,—this was a strange sight. And to see gentlemen who had publicly denied the validity of the company's charter, who had taken the opinion of the leading counsel of the day against it, who had tried every means, lawful and unlawful, to overthrow it, to see these same men range themselves under its protection, and, asserting all that they had before denied, proclaim its validity as soon as they were admitted to share its advantages; who, without its pale, asserted the rights of British subjects against its monopoly, and, within its pale, asserted its monopoly against the rights of British subjects,—this, too, was a strange sight. Yet to all this did the Hudson's Bay Company submit, rather than subject their charter and their claims to the investigation of a court of law."

The Hudson's Bay Company, one hundred and fifty years from the date of its charter, asserted its right to the country, and, by virtue of the privileges conferred in that charter, seized the supplies and goods of the Northwest French Canadián Company, and confiscated them to its own use. This resulted in a deadly war between the two companies, and was carried on, neither party applying to the courts of the mother country for a settlement of their difficulties; in fact, as has been shown by reference to the charter of the Hudson's Bay Company, they had no legal rights, because none were in existence at the date of their charter; but, from the maneuvering of the company and the plausible efforts of Lord Selkirk to colonize, civilize, and settle the Red River country, they entered into his schemes, in order to crush the rival company and secure the whole country to themselves. It is unnecessary to detail any accounts of the horrid murders and infamous transactions that were put on foot and perpetrated by these two companies. After a furious contention, carried on for several years, "they bribed rivals whom they could not defeat, and the two companies united and agreed to carry on the fur trade together, to the exclusion of all others."

The Selkirk settlement was soon made to feel the withering influence of the company that had located it in the country for a specific purpose. *Neither, however, was there any compromise* till its inhabitants had been driven from their homes, its Governor (Semple) and seventeen of his followers killed. Then a compromise was effected between the rival companies, and they were united by an act of Parliament, under the title of Honorable Hudson's Bay Company, in 1821,—a license given to Messrs. William and Simon McGillivray, of the Northwest Company, and Edward Ellice, of the Hudson's Bay Company. These corporate members and their associates "were to share the profits arising from the fur trade, not only from the Indian territories, but also from the Hudson's Bay Company's proper territories of Rupert's Land." The privileges of this company were limited to seven years. This carried them forward to 1828, in which year their license (called a charter) was renewed for ten years.

Our Indian missionary and American history commences in 1832, six years before this combined Northwest and Hudson's Bay Company's license of exclusive privileges to trade in British Indian Territory, and, jointly, in the Oregon Territory, would expire. Our English historian and Sir Edward Belcher are both mistaken when they attribute to the company the asking for, or in any way encouraging, the American missionaries to come to the country. This was an event wholly unknown to them, and brought about by the Indians themselves, by sending a delegation of four of their number to St. Louis, in 1832, to ask of the American people a religious teacher. Lee, Parker, and Whitman heard the request, and volunteered to make the effort to establish missions among them.

These missionaries all came across the Rocky Mountains unasked and uninvited by any one in the service of that company.

CHAPTER III.

English Hudson's Bay effort to secure Oregon.—British claim to Oregon.—Dr. McLaughlin's relation to the company.—Treatment of Red River settlers.—A mistake.—Sir Edward Belcher.—Duplicity of the Hudson's Bay Company.—A noble man.—An Englishman's opinion of the Hudson's Bay Company.—Sir James Douglas's testimony.—J. Ross Browne.—Duty of an historian.—Cause and effect.

SINCE commencing this work we have, by the kindness of friends who have taken a deep interest in all that relates to this country, been furnished with many valuable and important statements, documents, pamphlets, papers, and books, all relating to its early history.

Of the whole catalogue, the most valuable information is contained in a work entitled "An Examination of the Charter and Proceedings of the Hudson's Bay Company, with Reference to the Grant of Vancouver's Island. By James Edward Fitzgerald. London." Published in 1849.

The author of this book, though not having the personal knowledge of the company, the Indians, and the country about which he writes requisite to a complete history, has shown a correctness of statistical facts, a comprehensive knowledge of his subject, an enlarged view of the British colonial system, and a correct idea of the debasing practices and utterly false positions of the Hudson's Bay Company not found in any other writer.

Up to the time that this book of 293 pages fell into my hands, I did not know that any writer entertained similar views with myself in relation to this monstrous imposition upon the British and American people.

Mr. Fitzgerald has fortified his statements by his knowledge of the English people, their laws and usages, and the casual outcroppings of a system of unparalleled selfishness and despotism, carried on under the guise of a Christian commercial company, whose professed object was to extend commerce, and civilize and christianize the savage tribes of North America, yet who have invariably held up their Christian chartered privileges for the sole purpose of carrying on the most degrading and inhuman practices with not only the savages, but with all civilized and Christian men who have attempted to expose or even investigate their conduct.

As we proceed with our history, we feel confident that we shall be able to enlighten our readers on many dark subjects and transactions, and to fully prove every statement we have made, or may yet make. Mr. Fitzgerald has given us clearly and truthfully the English side of our history as connected with this Hudson's Bay Company. The American part of it the writer is gathering up, and, in giving it to the public, will discard every statement that does not bear the impress of truth.

The reader will notice that our subject is extensive, that England and America, commerce and Christianity, civilization and savagism, are all involved and interested in it, and that Oregon, California, and British and Russian America have all participated in it during the past and present century; that we are tracing cause and effect and bringing to light influences that, while producing their legitimate results, were strange and unaccountable, because always kept under the selfish and unscrupulous policy of this English corporation of fur traders.

By referring to the charter of the Hudson's Bay Company, we find that it was given by Charles II., in 1670, granting to the "governor and company and their successors the exclusive right to trade, fish, and hunt in the waters, bays, rivers, lakes, and creeks entering into Hudson's Straits, together with all the lands and territories not already occupied or granted to any of the king's subjects, or possessed by the subjects of any other Christian prince or State."

Forty years previous to the giving of this charter by Charles II., of England, Louis XIII., of France, gave a charter to a French company, who occupied the country called Acadia, or New France.

In 1632, Charles I., of England, resigned to Louis XIII., of France, the sovereignty of the country then called Acadia, or New France.

Forty years after Louis XIII., of France, had given his charter, and thirty-eight years after Charles I., of England, had given up his right to the country, Charles II., of England, imitating the example of him who wished to give the world and all its glory to obtain the worship of the Saviour of mankind, gave to the Hudson's Bay Company what he had not the shadow of a title to, as in the treaty of Ryswick, in 1697, twenty-seven years after this charter of the Hudson's Bay Company had been given, the whole country was confirmed to France, and no reservation made on account of the Hudson's Bay Company.

Mr. Fitzgerald, on his 12th page, says: "It has often been asserted, and is to a great extent believed, because there is very little general information on this subject, that the *claim which Great Britain made to the Oregon Territory was dependent upon, or, at any rate, strength-*

ened, by the settlement of the Hudson's Bay Company on the Columbia River.

"Those who hold such an opinion will be surprised to learn that there are many, and they well acquainted with the country itself, who assert that the conduct and policy of the Hudson's Bay Company in the Oregon Territory formed the chief part of the title which the United States had to the country, which was gratuitously given to her by the settlement of the boundary. What the United States owe to the company for its policy on the west side of the Rocky Mountains is a question to which the English public will some day demand a satisfactory answer.

"Dr. McLaughlin was formerly an agent in the Northwest Fur Company of Montreal; he was one of the most enterprising and active in conducting the war between that association and the Hudson's Bay Company. In the year 1821, when the rival companies united, Dr. McLaughlin became a factor of the Hudson's Bay Company. But his allegiance does not appear to have been disposed of along with his interests, and his sympathy with any thing other than British, seems to have done justice to his birth and education, which were those of a French Canadian. This gentleman was appointed governor of all the country west of the Rocky Mountains, and is accused, by those who have been in that country, of having uniformly encouraged the emigration of settlers from the United States, and of having discouraged that of British subjects. *While the company in this country (England) were asserting that their settlements on the Columbia River were giving validity to the claim of Great Britain to the Oregon Territory*, it appears that their chief officer on the spot was doing all in his power to facilitate the operations of those whose whole object it was to annihilate that claim altogether."

Mr. Fitzgerald has given us in the above statement an important fact, and one that reveals to an American the deep-laid schemes of the English government, which, by the influence of the Hudson's Bay Company, sought to secure the Oregon Territory to itself. He also explains the conduct of Dr. McLaughlin in his treatment of emigrants, as well as the relation he sustained to that company. While, as Americans, we can admire and applaud the conduct of a noble and generous "*Canadian-born*" *citizen*, we at the same time can see the low, debasing, and mean spirit of the Englishman, as manifested in the attempt to deprive the American Republic of its rightful domain.

We shall have occasion to refer to the bringing into Oregon of the Red River settlers, and as the result of that move, the unparalleled effort of Dr. Whitman to defeat the British designs upon the country.

Mr. Fitzgerald explains that matter so well, that we could not do justice to the truth of history not to quote him. He says, on the 14th page of his work: "There is one story told, about which it is right that the truth should be ascertained. It is said that a number of half-breeds from the Red River settlement were, in the year of 1841–2, induced by the company's officers to undertake a journey entirely across the continent, with the object of becoming settlers on the Columbia River. It appears that a number went, but on arriving in the country, so far from finding any of the promised encouragement, the treatment they received from Dr. McLaughlin was such, that, after having been nearly starved under the paternal care of that gentleman, they all went over to the American settlement in the Wallamet Valley."

This statement, while it affirms an important fact, gives a false impression as regards Dr. McLaughlin. He, to our certain knowledge, extended to the Red River settlers every facility within his power, and all of those emigrants to this day speak of his kindness in the highest terms. But not so of other leading or controlling members, who really represented the English part and policy of that company. Those settlers complained of the domineering and tyrannical treatment of their English overseers, which was the cause of their leaving what they supposed would eventually be the English part of Oregon Territory. They also became sensible that the Hudson's Bay Company in Oregon was a different concern from the Hudson's Bay Company in Rupert's Land; that, however small their privileges were there, they were less on Puget Sound; and being near an American settlement, they naturally sought its advantages and protection.

Mr. Fitzgerald informs us that "these emigrants became citizens of the United States, and it is further said were the first to memorialize Congress to extend the power of the United States over the Oregon Territory. For the truth of these statements we do not, of course, vouch, but we do say they demand inquiry."

This statement of Mr. Fitzgerald entitles him to be considered a candid and fair writer, and one who is seeking for truth in reference to the subject he is investigating. He has naturally imbibed the feelings of an Englishman against Dr. McLaughlin, under the strong effort made by the English Hudson's Bay Company to suppress and supersede the French Canadian influence in it.

He says, on page 15: "Dr. McLaughlin's policy was so manifestly American that it is openly canvassed in a book written by Mr. Dunn, one of the servants of the company, and written for the purpose of praising their system and policy."

Sir Edward Belcher also alludes to this policy. He says: "Some few years since, the company determined on forming settlements on the rich lands situated on the Wallamet and other rivers, and for providing for their retired servants, by allotting them farms, and further aiding them by supplies of cattle, etc. That on the Wallamet was a field too inviting for missionary enthusiasm to overlook, but instead of selecting a British subject to afford them spiritual assistance, recourse was had to Americans, a course pregnant with evil consequences, and particularly in the political squabble pending, as will be seen by the result. No sooner had the American and his allies fairly squatted (which they deem taking possession of the country), than they invited their brethren to join them, and called on the American government for laws and protection."

The American reader will smile at Sir Edward's little fling at the *squatters* in Oregon. He asserts a great truth in the same sentence that he utters a positive falsehood. No member of the Hudson's Bay Company, nor the whole company together, ever encouraged a single American missionary to come to the country. Revs. Lee and Parker and Dr. Whitman came without their invitation or aid. They were entirely independent of the company, and were only suffered to remain, the company not daring to drive them from the country on their first arrival, as they all held the protection of the American government, as Indian teachers, under the great seal of the Secretary of War. This English fling at their own company is evidence of a jealousy existing which could not be satisfied short of the utter extermination of all American influence on this coast, and is further illustrated by this same Sir Edward Belcher, in contrasting the treatment of Captain Wilkes and his party with that of his own. He says (vol. 1, p. 297): "The attention of the chief to myself and those immediately about me, particularly in sending down fresh supplies, previous to my arrival, I feel fully grateful for; but I can not conceal my disappointment at the want of accommodation exhibited toward the crews of the vessels under my command in a *British possession*." We old Oregonians are amused at Sir Edward's ignorance of the Hudson's Bay Company's treatment of the *crews* of vessels, and servants of the company. We all know his crew were allowed to associate freely with the native women in the country and to distribute their rations of rum, and any other supplies they might have, without any remonstrance from the company. Sir Edward continues: "We certainly were not distressed, nor was it imperatively necessary that fresh beef and vegetables should be supplied, or I should have made a formal demand. But as regarded those who might come after, and not improbably myself among the number, I inquired in direct terms what facilities her Majesty's ship of war might expect, in the event of touching at this port for bullocks, flour, vegetables, etc. I certainly was extremely surprised at the reply that they were not in a condition to supply. As any observation here would be useless, and I well knew this point could be readily settled where authority could be referred to, I let the matter rest. But having been invited to inspect the farm and dairy, and been informed of the quantity of grain, and the means of furnishing flour, and notwithstanding the profusion of cattle and potatoes, no offer having been made for our crew, I regretted that I had been led into the acceptance of private supplies; although, at that time, the other officers of the establishment had told my officers that supplies would of course be sent down."

Mr. Fitzgerald says "*the American policy of the Hudson's Bay Company* would seem, from the above facts, to be more than a matter of suspicion," while we Americans are only disposed to regard them as a part of the *duplicity* of that company in their effort *to deceive their own countrymen* as to the value of the country over which they had ruled so long.

They had been too successful in deceiving all American writers to allow their own countrymen to understand their secret policy. Sir Edward Belcher and our English historian were equally misled in relation to the *American policy of the Hudson's Bay Company.* It is true that Dr. McLaughlin, though he was a French Canadian subject, had not lost his American soul. The British iron had not driven the last noble sentiment of humanity from his heart, nor his connection with that polluted corporation of iniquity which pervades half the continent of North America; for when he found that this Hudson's Bay Company was utterly lost to humanity, he tells them to their teeth: "*Gentlemen, I will serve you no longer.*"

No true American historian will allow, without contradiction, that corrupt company to hand down to future infamy the name of a noble and generous servant, because their infamous policy was defeated by the establishment of the American missions in the country. Dr. McLaughlin did all that he could, honorably, to comply with their "system of iniquity."

Our English author says, on page 19, in reference to the conduct of the company: "They are convictions which have strengthened and deepened at every step of the inquiry; convictions that the Hudson's Bay Company has entailed misery and destruction upon thousands throughout the country which is withering under its curse; that it has cramped and crippled the energies and enterprise of England, which might have found occupation in the directions from which they are now excluded; that it has stopped the extension of civilization, and has *excluded the light of religious truth;* that it has alienated the hearts of all under its oppression, and made them hostile to their country; above all, that the whole and entire fabric is built upon utterly false and fictitious grounds; that it has not one shadow of reality in law or in justice; that there is not the smallest legal authority for any one of the rights which this corporation claims. It is this conviction which has urged me to submit the statements and arguments contained in the following pages to the consideration of the public; and to arraign before that tribunal, from which in these days there is no escape,—the judgment of public opinion,—*a corporation who, under the authority of a charter which is invalid in law,* hold a monopoly in commerce, and exercise *a despotism in government, and have so used that monopoly and wielded that power as to shut up the earth from the knowledge of man, and man from the knowledge of God.*"

With the statements and convictions of this English author before us, we will add a statement of Sir James Douglas, given in answer to interrogatory 11 in the case of Hudson's Bay Company's Claim *v.* United States, to give the reader a better idea of the power and influence of that company in Oregon, in 1846.

Sir James says: "The Honorable Hudson's Bay Company had fifty-five officers and five hundred and thirteen articled men. The company having a large, active, and experienced force of servants in their employ, and holding establishments judiciously situated in the most favorable portions for trade, forming, as it were, a net-work of posts aiding and supporting each other, *possessed an extraordinary influence with the natives*, and in 1846 practically enjoyed a monopoly of the fur trade in the country west of the Rocky Mountains, north and south of the forty-ninth parallel of latitude. The profits of their trade," says this witness, "from 1841 to 1846 were at least seven thousand pounds sterling annually."

The fifty-five officers and five hundred and thirteen articled men of the company, with their eight hundred half-breeds, and the Indians they could command by the judicious position of their respective posts, were deemed by them sufficient security for their trade, and a substantial reason why they should not give up the country without making another direct effort to drive the missionary and American settlements from it, notwithstanding all their pretension to join in the provisional government organized by the pioneer Americans in 1843.

The reader is referred to the discussion on the liquor question between Judge Sir James Douglas and Mr. Samuel Parker, as found in the tenth and eleventh numbers, first volume, of the *Spectator*, published June 11 and 25, 1845, and in another chapter of this work, and requested to keep all these facts before the mind, so as not to lose sight of the commanding influence, or, in other words, the commander, when we enter upon the preliminary and immediate causes of the Whitman massacre, and the Indian war that followed.

We have before us the original depositions in reference to the facts stated, and also the attempt to excuse the principal actors in that horrible transaction, as given by Brouillet in justification of the course pursued by the Jesuit missionaries.

We have also the superficial and bombastic report of J. Ross Browne, special agent of the Treasury Department, dated December 4, 1857, containing a copy of this Jesuit history of the murder of Dr. Whitman. In his remarks previous to giving Brouillet's history, he says: "In view of the fact, however, that objections might be made to any testimony coming from the citizens of the Territories, and believing also that it is the duty of a public agent to present, as far as practicable, *unprejudiced statements*, I did not permit myself to be governed by any representations unsupported by reliable historical data." * * * * "The fact also is shown that, as far back as 1835, the Indians west of the Rocky Mountains protested against the taking away of their lands by the white race. That this was one of the alleged causes of the murder of Dr. Whitman and family."

There are sixty-six pages in this report. Twelve of them are Mr. Browne's, one page of official acknowledgment, and fifty-three from the parties implicated.

The statements of Mr. Browne, of Mr. Fitzgerald, and the oath of Mr. Douglas, are sufficient to show the ignorance, stupidity, and falsehood incorporated in his report, were there no other historical facts to convict him of ignorance in allowing such representations to be made in an official document. In the proper place we will bring this report into our history, with both sides of the question.

Were we to express an opinion of Mr. J. Ross Browne's report, with our personal knowledge of what he pretends to relate, we would say he ignored the people, the country, and the government whose agent he claimed to be, and was reporting for the special benefit of the Roman religion and British government, as these are extensively quoted as historical data from which his report and conclusions are drawn.

The reader will understand our main object to be to give a full history of all influences and prominent transactions and events that have occurred in Oregon from 1792 to 1849.

To understand cause and effect, and the true history of the country, we have to examine the facts as connected with actions, and also to trace back the history of the actors, in order to see how far they may be made responsible for the result of their actions.

Oregon, from the time of its discovery, has been a field where all the influences of which we are writing have been living, active influences; and they are by no means inactive or dead at the present time. Some of them are more active now than they were in 1836.

A full knowledge of the past will enable us to guard the present and the future. Our English writer has gathered his facts and drawn his conclusions in London. We, upon this, our western coast, are witnesses of the cause and results of his conclusions, and any statement he makes we feel ourselves abundantly able to corroborate or correct.

As we proceed with our history we shall have frequent occasion to quote Mr. Fitzgerald, as the best English evidence, in favor of our American statements or positions. Since writing the above we have noticed a lengthy article in the Edinburgh *Westminster Review* for July, 1867, giving a concise history of the Hudson's Bay Company, under the heading, "The Last Great Monopoly." In that article the author has shown extensive historical knowledge of the operations and influences of that monopoly in that portion of our continent over which they have held exclusive control.

He regards them as a blight upon the country, and an "incubus" to be removed by national legislation. If our work had been published, we should conclude that he must have drawn many of his facts from our own observations. But this is not the case; hence the value to us of his corroboration of the facts we affirm from personal knowledge.

CHAPTER IV.

Care of Great Britain for her fur companies.—Columbia Fur Company.—Astor's second fur company.—Major Pilcher's fur company.—Loss of the ship *Isabel.*—Captain Bonneville's expedition.—Cause of his failure.—Captain Wyeth's, 1832.—Indians ask for missionaries in 1833.—Methodist Mission.—Fort Hall established.—Fort Boise.

By reference to the act of the British Parliament of June 2, 1821, it will be seen that the affairs of the North American British Fur companies were in a fair way to defeat all British interests in America. To suppress these feuds among their own people became a matter of national importance and policy.

To accomplish so desirable an object, Parliament, in the act above referred to, extended the civil and criminal jurisdiction of Canada over all the territories of the Hudson's Bay Company; in the thirteenth article of the act, and in the fourteenth, repealed all that was before taken away from that company, and confirmed absolutely all the rights supposed to have been given by the original charter, as follows:—

Section 14. "And be it further enacted, that nothing in this act contained shall be taken or construed to affect any right or privilege, authority or jurisdiction, which the governor and company of adventurers trading to Hudson's Bay are by law entitled to claim and exercise under their charter; but that all such rights, privileges, authorities, and jurisdictions, shall remain in as full force, virtue, and effect, as if this act had never been made; any thing in this act to the contrary notwithstanding."

This act, however just it may have been considered, certainly embodied a large amount of national prejudice against the people of French or Canadian birth, in exempting the territory of the Hudson's Bay Company from its influence. It had a twofold effect: the one, to check feuds among British subjects; the other, to unite them in one vast Indian monopoly,—to license this united company to go forward with their Indian political arrangements unmolested,—to punish and dispose of all intruders upon their supposed, or asserted rights, as they might deem for the interest of their trade, which, according to the charter of Charles II., bearing date May 2, 1670, they were "at all times hereafter to be personable and capable in law, to have, purchase, receive, possess, enjoy, and retain lands, rents, privileges, liberties, jurisdiction, franchises, and hereditaments of what kind, nature, or quality soever they be, to them and their successors."

The whole trade, fisheries, navigation, minerals, etc., of the countries, are granted to the company exclusively; all other of the king's subjects being forbidden to *visit*, *hunt*, *frequent*, *trade*, *traffic*, or *adventure* therein, under heavy penalties; and the company is moreover empowered to send *ships*, and to build *fortifications* for the defense of its possessions, as well as to *make war or peace with all nations or peoples* not Christian, inhabiting those territories, *which are declared to be henceforth reckoned* and *reputed* as one of *his Majesty's* plantations or colonies in America, called Rupert's Land.

It will be remembered that as early as 1818, a question arose between the United States and Great Britain, as to which was the rightful owner of the Oregon country. The Northwest Fur Company were the only subjects of Great Britain that had competed with the American fur companies in the discovery or trade of the country. To ignore that company altogether would weaken the British claim to Oregon by right of prior discovery and occupancy. Hence, by uniting the two companies under an ancient English charter, combining their united capital and numerical strength, discarding all doubtful subjects, and confirming the absolute power of their own British company, they could easily secure Oregon as British territory. The wisdom and effect of this policy will be developed as we proceed.

By the third article of the convention between the United States and Great Britain, signed October 20, 1818, "it is agreed that any country that may be claimed by either party on the northwest coast of America, westward of the Stony Mountains, shall, together with its harbors, bays, and creeks, and the navigation of all rivers within the same, be free and open for the term of ten years from the date of the signature of the present convention, to the vessels, citizens, and subjects of the two powers; it being well understood that this agreement is not to be construed to the prejudice of any claim which either of the two high contracting parties may have to any part of said country, nor shall it be taken to affect the claims of any other power or state to any part of the said country; the only object of the high contracting parties, in that respect, being to prevent disputes and differences among themselves."

This convention secured at that time the Northwest Fur Company's existence in the country, by the act uniting the two British fur companies three years later. In 1821, the privileges here secured were transferred and confirmed to the Hudson's Bay Company, who at once took the most active and efficient measures to guard against any future competition, by assessing and setting apart ten per cent. on their capital stock, which was counted at £200,000, as a sinking fund for the special purpose of opposing all competition in the fur trade by land or water.

The convention above referred to shows that Great Britain held a watchful eye over her fur traders in this distant country; and the act of her Parliament in 1821, that she was disposed, in a direct manner, to secure to her own people, as traders, the absolute sovereignty of the country. While Great Britain was protecting and strengthening her fur traders in North America, the American government was simply asserting its prior rights to the Oregon country, founded upon its discovery and subsequent purchase in what is termed the Louisiana purchase, from France; the treaties and conventions only serving to encourage and strengthen the British claim, while they used their influence, capital, and power against all American competition and settlement in the country.

In 1821, as was to be expected by the union of the two great British fur companies, under the license of the British Parliament, and absolute charter of Charles II., many of the servants, and especially such as were found favorable to the American fur traders, or violently opposed to the Hudson's Bay Company, were thrown out of employment. They naturally sought to continue their wild Indian trade and habits, and formed a company under the name of the Columbia Fur Company, extending their operations up the Mississippi, Missouri, and Yellowstone rivers. In 1826, they transferred their interests to Astor's second North American Fur Company, of which John Jacob Astor was the head. This company appears to have been commenced or organized in connection with Mr. W. H. Ashley, in 1823, and under his direction extended its trade to the south and west, along the Platte River, and passed into the Rocky Mountains as far as Green River, being the first to discover its sources, making a successful trading expedition that year.

In 1824, another expedition under Mr. Ashley explored the Rocky Mountains as far south as Salt Lake, and built a fort on the borders of a small lake, to which he gave his own name. In 1826, Mr. Ashley transported a 6-pound cannon to his establishment near Salt Lake, through what has since been termed Fremont's, or the south pass of the Rocky Mountains, in a wagon. This establishment had in its employ over one hundred men, and was remarkably successful and profitable to the partners.

In 1826, Mr. Ashley sold all his interest to the Rocky Mountain Fur Company, composed of Smith, Jackson, and Subleth, who extended their trade into California, and as far north as the Umpqua River, in Oregon; where Smith and his party were met by a professedly friendly party of Indians, who murdered his men, seized his furs, and delivered them to a party of men sent by the Hudson's Bay Company, under Mr. John McLeod and Thomas McKay, to receive the furs and pay the Indians for their services—as learned by the writer from eye-witnesses.

During this same year, 1827, Major Pilcher, with forty-five men, crossed the Rocky Mountains, and, in 1828–9, traversed the western portion of them as far north as Fort Colville. This fort had been established, and farming operations commenced, in 1825. This party of Major Pilcher were all cut off but two men, besides himself; his furs, as stated by himself to the writer, found their way into the forts of the Hudson's Bay Company.

In 1828, the brig *Owyhee*, Captain Demenses, and the schooner *Cowrey*, Captain Thompson, entered and remained nearly a year in the Columbia River, trading with the Indians. They were owned in Boston.

In 1830, the British ship *Isabel* was lost on Sand Island—the second known to have been wrecked on the bar, or in attempting to enter the river. The crew were all saved, and it was the opinion of the company at Vancouver that, had the crew remained with the ship, no great loss would have been sustained.

In 1832, Captain Bonneville, of the United States army, on furlough, started, with over one hundred men, on an expedition into the Rocky Mountains. He crossed the mountains, and reached the Wallawalla Valley, on the Columbia River; but, through the influence of the Hudson's Bay Company, his men were nearly all induced to leave him, so that he was obliged to abandon his property, and his expedition was a total failure, except the little scientific knowledge of the country gained by it.

To charge the failure of Captain Bonneville directly to the Hudson's Bay Company would not be strictly true; but their great influence over the Indians was sufficient to prevent them from furnishing his party with food or horses, while he was within reach of their forts. Hence, many of his men became dissatisfied, and left him, till his party became too weak to effect their return to the States with their valuable furs and property. These eventually were lost, or fell into the hands of the Indians, and through them, his furs reached the Hudson's Bay traders' establishments.

This same year, 1832, Captain Nathaniel Wyeth, of Massachusetts, started on an exploring expedition to the mouth of the Columbia River, with a view of establishing a permanent trade in the Oregon country. He traveled across the continent and gathered all the information requisite for the undertaking, and returned to Boston in 1833; and in 1834, having completed his arrangements, chartered the brig *May Dacre*, and dispatched her with his own, and the goods of the Methodist Mission, for the Columbia River.

The same year, some Flathead Indians, from a tribe in the midst of the Rocky Mountains, went to St. Louis, and, through Mr. Catlin, an American artist, made known their object, which was to know something more of the white man's God and religion. Through the representations of these Indians, the Methodist Episcopal Society in the United States established their missions in Oregon, and the American Board sent their missionaries among the Nez Percés, which, as will be seen, was the commencement of the permanent settlement of the country. It appears from the facts, briefly stated, that there had been eleven different trading expeditions and companies, besides the Northwest and Hudson's Bay companies, that had sought for wealth by making fur-trading establishments in Oregon. All of them, including the Northwest and Hudson's Bay companies, have retired from it, but the American missionaries are residents of the country, and their influence and labors are felt, notwithstanding other influences have partially supplanted and destroyed the good impressions first made upon the natives of the country by them. Still civilization, education, and religion, with all the improvements of the age, are progressing, and the old pioneer missionaries and settlers that were contemporary with them, with a few exceptions, are foremost in every laudable effort to benefit the present and rising generation.

In the month of March, 1833, a Japanese junk was wrecked near Cape Flattery, in the then Territory of Oregon, and all on board, except three men, were lost. Those three were received by Captain McNeal on board the British ship *Lama;* taken to Vancouver, and thènce sent to England. Rev. Mr. Parker gives this, and another similar wreck on the Sandwich Islands, as evidence of the origin of the natives of those countries. But we give it for another object. The three Japanese were taken to England, and, during their stay, learned the English language, were sent back to Macao, and became the assistant teachers of Mr. Gutzlaff, the English missionary at that place, and were the means of opening their *own* country to missionary and commercial relations with other nations.

Captain Wyeth, with Revs. Jason and Daniel Lee, Cyrus Shepard, and P. L. Edwards, the first missionary party, together with Doctor Nutall, a naturalist, and J. K. Townsend, an ornithologist, sent out by a literary society in Philadelphia, all under the escort furnished by Captain Wyeth, crossed the mountains and reached the plain formed by the Portneuf and Snake rivers. At their junction Captain Wyeth stopped, and established Fort Hall, while the missionaries and scientific men of his party, in company with an Englishman by the name of Captain Stewart, and a party of Hudson's Bay traders, under the direction of Mr. McLeod and McKay, proceeded to Fort Nez Percés (present name, Wallula). Thence they traveled in Hudson's Bay *bateaux* to Vancouver.

Captain Wyeth established his post on the Snake River, by erecting a stockade of logs, and quarters for his men, and then proceeded to the lower Columbia to receive his goods, which arrived in the *May Dacre*, Captain Lambert, from Boston, about the time he reached Fort William, on what is now known as Sauvies Island, a few miles below the mouth of the Multnomah River, now called the Wallamet.

Rev. Mr. Lee and party made their first location about sixty miles from the mouth of the Wallamet, near what is now called Wheatland, ten miles below Salem.

Captain Wyeth received his goods, and commenced his trading establishment, but found that, notwithstanding he was personally treated by the principal officers of the Hudson's Bay Company with great courtesy, yet it was evident that every possible underhanded and degrading device was practiced, both with the Indians and with his men, to destroy, as much as was possible, the value and profits of his trade. In the spring and summer of 1835 he supplied his Fort Hall establishment with goods.

During the year 1835, the Hudson's Bay Company erected a temporary post about twelve miles up the Boise River, designed to counteract and destroy as much as possible the American fur trade established by Captain Wyeth, who continued his efforts less than three years; and, having lost of the two hundred men who had been in his employ *one hundred and sixty* (as stated to Rev. Samuel Parker), and finding himself unable to compete with this powerful English company, he accepted Dr. McLaughlin's offer for his establishments, and left the country in 1836.

In 1835, the American Board of Commissioners for Foreign Missions sent Rev. Samuel Parker and Dr. Marcus Whitman to explore the Oregon country, with a view of establishing missions among the Indians west of the Rocky Mountains.

These two missionaries reached the American rendezvous on Green River, in company with the Rocky Mountain Fur Company's traders, under the direction of Captains Drips and Fitzpatrick. From the American rendezvous Mr. Parker continued his explorations in company with, and under the protection of the Nez Percé Indians, till he reached old Fort Wallawalla, now called Wallula; thence he continued in canoes to Vancouver, while Dr. Whitman returned to the United States to procure associates to establish the Nez Percé mission.

CHAPTER V.

Extent and power of Hudson's Bay Company.—Number of forts.—Location.—Policy.—Murder of Mr. Black.—McKay.—Manner of dealing with Indians.—Commander of fort kills an Indian.—Necessity of such a course.—Hudson's Bay Company not responsible for what their servants do.

HAVING briefly traced the operations of the two foreign fur companies in Oregon, a knowledge of the location of their several trading establishments will enable the reader to comprehend their power and influence in the country.

Fort Umpqua was located in the extreme southwestern part of Oregon, near the mouth of the river bearing that name. It was a temporary stockade built of logs, overlooking a small farm in its immediate vicinity, was generally occupied by a clerk and from four to eight Frenchmen.

Fort George (Astoria) already described.

They had a farm and small establishment at the mouth of the Cowlitz, and a more extensive farm some twenty-five miles up that river.

Fort Vancouver,—a stockade, six miles above the mouth of the Multnomah, or Wallamet River. This fort was the general depot for the southwestern department, at which their goods for Indian trade were landed, and their furs and peltries collected and shipped to foreign markets. There was also a trading-house at Champoeg, some thirty-five miles up the Wallamet River.

On the left bank of the Columbia River, near the 46° of north latitude, stood Fort Nez Percés, called Wallawalla, now Wallula,—a stockade, accidentally burned in 1841, and rebuilt with adobes in 1841–2.

On the left bank of the south branch of the Columbia, or Snake River, at the junction of the Boise, was located Fort Boise, built formerly, in 1834, with poles; later, with adobes.

Continuing up Snake River to the junction of the Portneuf, on its left bank we find Fort Hall, built by Captain Wyeth; a stockade in 1834; rebuilt by the Hudson's Bay Company, with adobes, in 1838.

Thence up the Columbia, Fort Okanagon, at the mouth of Okanagon River, formerly a stockade, latterly a house or hut; and up the Spokan some twenty miles, was the old Spokan Fort, built by Astor's Company, a stockade with solid bastions.

Continuing up the Columbia to Kettle Falls, and two miles above, on the left bank is Fort Colville, formerly a stockade, still occupied by the Hudson's Bay Company.

Thence up the Columbia to the mouth of the Kootanie River, near the forty-ninth parallel of latitude, is the trading establishment called Kootanie House. Thence returning south, and ascending the Flathead (Clark's) and Kootanie rivers, into what is now Montana Territory, is, or was, the hut called Flathead House. Still higher up on the Columbia was a small establishment, called the boat encampment, or Mountain House.

Entering the country by the Straits of Juan de Fuca and Puget Sound, we find Fort Nasqualla, formerly a stockade. Proceeding up Frazer River to near the forty-ninth parallel, upon the left or south bank of the river is Fort Langley, an extensive stockade. Thence up that river about ninety miles, half a mile below the mouth of the Coquehalla, is Fort Hope, a stockade. On the right bank of the Frazer, sixteen miles above, is Fort Yale, a trading-house.

Thence proceeding up the Frazer, and on to the waters of Thompson River, is Fort Kamloops; still further north and east, extending into New Caledonia, are Forts Alexander, William, Garey, and Abercrombie.

On the southeastern part of Vancouver Island is Fort Victoria, formerly a stockade. On the north side of the island is Fort Rupert, a stockade, still in good repair.

On the mainland, near Portland Channel, is Fort Simpson. At the mouth of the Stiken River, on Dundas Island, was formerly Fort Wrangle, a stockade. Recently the establishment has been removed some sixty miles up the Stiken River, and called Fort Stiken.

This, as will be seen, gives the company twenty-three forts and five trading-stations. In addition to these they had trading-parties extending south to California, southeast to Fort Hall and into Utah and Arizona, east into the Blackfoot country (Montana) and the Rocky Mountains, and north into New Caledonia and along the northwestern watershed of the Rocky Mountains.

They also had two steamers, the *Beaver* and *Otter*, to enter all the bays, harbors, rivers, and inlets along the western coast of our country, from Mexico on the south, to Russian America on the north, employing fifty-five officers and five hundred and thirteen articled men, all bound, under the strictest articles of agreement, to subserve the interests of that company under all circumstances; being strictly forbidden to acquire any personal or real estate outside of their stipulated pay as servants of the company, and were subject to such punishment for deficiency of labor or neglect of duty as the officer in charge might see fit to impose, having no appeal to any source for redress, as the original charter of Charles II., confirmed by act of Parliament in 1821, clearly conferred on the company absolute control over the country they occupied, and all in it.

As a matter of romance and adventure, many statements are made of conflicts with Indians and with wild animals, all terminating favorably to the interests of the company, confirming and strengthening their absolute power over all their opponents; but as they do not properly belong to a work of this character, they will be omitted, except where they may be brought to illustrate a fact, or to prove the principles and policy of the company.

As in the case of Mr. Black, a chief trader at Fort Kamloops, who had offended an Indian, the Indian disguised his resentment, entered the fort as a friend, and while Mr. Black was passing from the room in which the Indian had been received, he was deliberately shot by him, and fell dead. The Indian fled, and the fort was closed against the tribe. Not a single article of trade or supplies was allowed to the tribe till the murderer was given up, and hung by the company's men, when the fort was opened and trade resumed.

In another case, near the mouth of the Columbia, a trader by the name of McKay was killed in a drunken row with the Indians at a salmon fishery. A friendly Indian gave information at head-quarters, when an expedition was fitted out and sent to the Indian camp. The murderer, with a few other Indians, was found in a canoe, but escaped to shore. They were fired at, and one woman was killed and others wounded. Dr. McLaughlin, being in command of the party, informed the Indians that if the murderer was not soon given up, he would punish the tribe. They soon placed the murderer in the hands of the party, who were satisfied of the guilt of the Indian, and at once hung him, as an example of the punishment that would be inflicted upon murderers of white men belonging to the company.

One other instance of daring and summary punishment is related as having been inflicted by Mr. Douglas, while in charge of a fort in the midst of a powerful tribe of Indians. A principal chief had killed one of the company's men. Mr. Douglas, learning that he was in a lodge not far from the fort, boasting of his murderous exploit, armed himself, went to the lodge, identified the murdering chief, and shot him dead; then walked deliberately back to the fort.

A compliance with licensed parliamentary stipulations would have required the arrest of the murderers in all these cases, and the testimony and criminals to be sent to Canada for conviction and execution.

These cases illustrate, whether just or otherwise, the absolute manner of dealing with Indians by the company. The following chapter gives us the particulars of an aggravated case of brutal murder of the person in charge of one of their extreme northwestern forts by the men under his charge.

CHAPTER VI.

Murder of John McLaughlin, Jr.—Investigation by Sir George Simpson and Sir James Douglas.

VERY different was the course pursued by Sir George Simpson and Mr. (now Sir James) Douglas in the case of conspiracy and murder of John McLaughlin, Jr., at Fort Wrangle, near the southern boundary of Russian America.

In this case, Sir George Simpson went into a partial examination of the parties implicated, and reported that Dr. John McLaughlin, Jr., was killed by the men in self-defense. This report, from the known hostility of Sir George to the father and son, was not satisfactory, and Esquire Douglas was dispatched to Fort Wrangle, and procured the following testimony, which, in justice to the murdered man and the now deceased father, we will quote as copied from the original documents by Rev. G. Hines.

Pierre Kanaquassee, one of the men employed in the establishment at the time of the murder, and in whose testimony the gentlemen of the company place the utmost reliance, gives the following narrative, in answer to questions proposed by James Douglas, Esq., the magistrate that examined him:—

Q. Where were you on the night of the murder of the late Mr. John McLaughlin?

A. I was in my room, in the lower part of the main house, where I lived with George Heron, in an apartment in the lower story, immediately under the kitchen. My door opened into the passage which led to the apartment of Mr. John McLaughlin in the second story.

Q. What occurred on the night of the murder?

A. I will tell you the whole story, to the best of my recollection.

A few days preceding the murder, five Indians from Tako, with letters from Dr. Kennedy, arrived at the fort about midnight. The watchmen, hearing the knocking, called Mr. John. When he got up, he mustered a few hands to defend the gates, in case of any treacherous attack from the Indians, whom they did not, as yet, know. They were then admitted into the fort, delivered up their arms, according to custom, and were lodged in a small room in the lower story of the main house. A day or two after this, he beat, and put one of these Indians, a native of Nop, in irons, as Peter was told, for having committed some theft in Tako. About eight o'clock of the evening of the 20th of April, Mr. John gave liquor to the Indians, and made them drunk; after which he called the white men, viz., Laperti, Pripe, Lulaire, Heroux Bellinger, Simon, Fleury, McPherson, Smith, and Antoine Kawanope. During this time, Peter was in his own, which was the adjoining room, lying awake in bed, and overheard all that passed. He heard Mr. John say to McPherson, "Peter is not among us. Where is he?" McPherson replied, that he was in bed, and he was sent for him by Mr. John. Peter, in consequence, went into the room, and saw all the men seated in a ring, on the floor, around a number of bottles standing within the ring, and the Indians lying dead drunk on another part of the floor. Mr. John himself was standing outside of the ring, and McPherson placed himself on the opposite side of the ring; neither of them appeared to be partaking of the festivities of the evening, but were looking on, and forcing the people to drink. Antoine Kawanope was seated on his bed, apart from the other men, perfectly sober, as he told Peter afterward. Mr. John had ordered him not to drink, observing, "You are not to drink at this time, as I am going to die to-night, and you will help me in what I am going to do." On entering the room, Mr. John told Peter to sit down with the other people, and ordered his servant, Fleury, to give him a good dram, which he did, in a tin pan. Peter could not drink the whole, and was threatened by Mr. John with violence if he did not finish it. He succeeded in emptying the pan, by allowing the liquor to run into the bosom of his shirt. Mr. John, in doing this, did not appear to be angry, but in a half-playful mood. Peter remained there about a quarter of an hour, during which time he was careful not to drink too much, as a few hours previously Antoine had called at his room and said, "My uncle, take care of yourself to-night; the master is going to die." Peter said, "Who is going to kill him?" and Antoine said, "The Bluemen," meaning the Kanakas, "are going to kill him." This, Peter thought, was likely to be the case, as the men, some time before Christmas preceding, had agreed among themselves to murder him, and had signed a paper, which McPherson drew up, to that effect. Every one of the men of the place agreed to the commission of this deed, Smith and Heron as well as the others. Peter's name was signed by McPherson, and he attested it by his cross. This paper was signed in Urbaine's house, where the men severally repaired by stealth for the purpose, as Mr. John kept so vigilant a watch upon them, that they were afraid he might suspect their intentions if they were there in a body. The same impression made him also remark, in a low tone of voice, to Laperti, on his first entering the room, when he observed Mr. John forcing the people to drink, "I really believe our master feels his end near, as he never used to act in this manner." As above mentioned, after Peter had been about fifteen minutes in the room where the men were drinking, Mr. John retired, followed by Antoine. Mr. John had not on that occasion drank any thing with the men, neither did he (Peter) ever see him, at any time preceding, drink in their company. He, however, supposed that he must have taken something in his own room, as he appeared flushed and excited, but not sufficiently so as to render his gait in the least unsteady. McPherson also did not taste any thing in the room. As soon as Mr. John was gone, Peter also left the room, and went to bed in his own room.

Peter was informed by Antoine that Mr. John, on leaving the room where the men were drinking, went up-stairs to his own apartment, and he heard him say to his wife, "I am going to die to-night." And he and his wife both began to cry. Mr. John soon rallied, and observed, "Very well; if I die, I must fall like a man." He then told Antoine to load his rifles and pistols, and ordered him also to arm himself with his own gun. He and Antoine then went out, and Peter thinks he heard the report of more than fifteen shots. Antoine afterward told Peter that Mr. John fired at Laperti, but missed him, and afterward ordered Antoine to fire at Laperti. Antoine refused to do so, until his own life was threatened by Mr. John, when he fired in the direction, without aiming at Laperti. He also told the Kanakas to kill the Canadians, and it was in part they who fired the shots that he (Peter) had heard. Peter then got up and placed himself behind his door, and saw Mr. John come in and go up-stairs with Antoine, when he took the opportunity of going out, armed with his gun and a stout bludgeon, and found the men standing here and there on the gallery watching an opportunity to shoot Mr. John. Laperti's position on the gallery was fronting the door of the main house, toward which he had his gun pointed; when Peter saw him, he was on his knees, the small end of the gun resting on the top rail of the gallery, in readiness to fire. Laperti exclaimed, on seeing Peter, "I must kill him now, as he has fired two shots at me." Peter objected to this, and proposed to take and tie him. Nobody answered him. At that moment, Smith came up to Laperti and told him to hide himself or he would certainly be killed. Laperti said, "Where can I hide myself?" and Smith said, "Come with me and I will show you a place in the bastion where you can hide yourself," and they went off together in the direction of the bastion at the corner of Urbaine's house. Peter, after a few minutes' stay on the gallery, returned to his house, as he had previously agreed upon with George Hebram, who was lying sick in bed, and who had entreated him not to leave him alone. At the door of the main house, he met Mr. John coming out, followed by Antoine, who was carrying a lamp. Mr. John said to Peter, "Have you seen Laperti?" Peter answered, "No, I have not seen him;" and then Mr. John said, "Have you seen Urbaine?" And Peter again answered that he had not. The minute before this, as he (Peter) was returning from the gallery, he had seen Urbaine standing at the corner of the main house, next to Urbaine's own dwelling, in company with Simon. Urbaine said, "I don't know what to do; I have no gun, and do not know where to hide myself." Simon said, "I have a gun, if he comes I will shoot him, and will be safe." Mr. John, after Peter passed him, said to Antoine, "Make haste, and come with the lamp," and proceeded with a firm step to Urbaine's house, as Peter, who continued watching at the door, saw.

After he saw them go to Urbaine's house, he proceeded toward his own room, and he and Antoine called out, "Fire! fire!" The report of several shots, probably five, immediately followed, and he heard Antoine exclaiming, "Stop! stop! stop! He is dead now." Antoine afterward related to Peter, that on reaching Urbaine's house, Mr. John ordered him to go round by one corner, while he went round by the other, directing Antoine to shoot any of the Canadians he might meet. Mr. John then proceeded in a stooping position, looking very intently before him, when a shot was fired from the corner of the house toward which he was going, which caused his death, the ball having entered at the upper part of the breast-bone, a little below the gullet, and come out a little below the shoulder, having broken the spine in its passage. Peter was also told by one of the Kanakas, that as soon as Mr. John fell, Urbaine sprung forward from the corner of the house within a few paces of the body, and put his foot savagely on his neck, as if to complete the act, should the ball have failed in causing death. The Kanakas immediately asked Urbaine who had killed the master. Urbaine replied, "It is none of your business who has killed him!" Peter, who during this time had removed to his house, seeing Heron go out without his gun, went out round the body, and said, "My friend, we have now done what we long intended to do; let us now carry the body back to the house." Urbaine, Laperti, Bellinger, and other white men who were present replied, "When we kill a dog, we let him lie where we kill him." And Antoine told him they had previously given him the same reply to a similar proposition from him. Peter then approached the body, and, with one hand under the neck, raised the head and trunk, when a deep expiration followed, which was the last sign of animation. He had previously perceived no signs of life, nor did he hear any one say that any appeared after the deceased fell. The white men being unwilling to assist him, he carried the body, with the aid of the Kanakas, into the main house, where he had it stripped, washed clean, decently dressed, and laid out. In doing so he received no help from any but the Kanakas. The wounds made by the balls were very large, both openings being circular, and severally three inches in diameter. The body bled profusely, there being a deep pool of blood found around it, which was washed away afterward by the Kanakas. Peter never heard that he spoke or moved after he fell. There was a perpendicular cut on the forehead, skin-deep, in a line with the nose, which Peter thinks was caused by his falling on the barrel of his rifle, though Urbaine said that he had received it from an Indian with his dog. It was, as Peter supposes, about eleven o'clock, P. M., when he had done washing and laying out the body; the watches had not then been changed, therefore he thinks it could not be midnight. The people continued coming and going during the night, to see the body, and Peter proposed praying over the body, as is customary in Canada; but they objected, saying they did not wish to pray for him. He did sit up with the body all night, having soon after gone, first to Urbaine's and then to Lulaire's house, who each gave him a dram, which he took, saying, "There is no need of drinking now; they might drink their fill now." He soon afterward went to bed.

He inquired of Martineau, who also lived in the same room, if he had fired at the deceased. He replied, that he had fired twice. He then asked him if it was he that had killed him, and he said, "I do not know if it was me or not." He (Peter) put the same question to several of the other men whom he saw afterward; they all said that they had not shot him, and Martineau afterward said that he had not directed his gun at him, but had fired in the air.

The following morning he asked Antoine Kawanope if he knew who had killed the deceased. He replied, "I know who killed him, but I am not going to tell you, or any one else. When the governor comes, I will tell him." He asked Antoine why he would not tell; he said he was afraid it might cause more quarrels, and lead to other murders. He then advised Antoine not to conceal it from him, as he would tell no one. Antoine then said, he thought it was Urbaine who had done the deed. Peter observed that Urbaine had no gun. Antoine replied, "I think it was Urbaine, because as soon as the deceased fell, Urbaine rushed out from his lurking-place at the corner of the house, where, I was informed by the people, he always kept his gun secreted, with the intention of shooting the deceased." Peter says Laperti, Urbaine, and Simon were all concealed in the corner whence the shot came, and he thinks it to be one of the three who fired it. Urbaine always denied having committed the murder, and said, "I am going to the Russian fort for trial, and will be either banished or hung. I will let the thing go to the end, and will then inform upon the murderers."

Simon always said that he was never in the corner from whence the shot was fired, and knew nothing about the matter; but Peter thinks that he must have been there, as he saw him, as before related, at the corner of the main house, when he promised to protect Urbaine; and from the situation of the fort, he must have passed that spot with Urbaine, as there was no other passage from the place where they had been standing. Laperti also said he never fired at all. When Peter, as before related, went upon the gallery after the first firing had ceased, while Mr. John and Antoine had gone into the house, he saw all the men on the gallery, except Pripe, Lulaire, and McPherson, and he asked each of them, respectively, if they were going to shoot the master that night, and they all answered (as well as himself), they would do so at the first chance, except Pehou, a Kanaka, who would not consent to the murder. Smith was then without a gun.

Before the Christmas preceding, Peter put the question to Smith, how he should like to see him kill Mr. John? He replied, "I should like it very well; I would have no objection, because his conduct is so very bad that he can never expect to be protected by the company." Peter Manifree says that Mr. John appeared to be aware of the plot formed by the men against his life; as he supposes, through the information of Fleury, his servant, who was aware of every thing that passed among them. Mr. John had often said to the men, "Kill me, if you can. If you kill me, you will not kill a woman—you will kill a man." And he kept Antoine as a sentinel to watch his room. One evening George Heron proposed taking his life, and said if he could find a man to go with him, he would be the first to shoot him. Peter refused to go, and Heron watched a great part of the night in the passage leading to Mr. John's room, holding his gun pointed toward its door, with the object of shooting Mr. John if he appeared, as he usually did at night when going to visit the watchmen; but he did not go out that night, or Peter thinks that he would have been shot by Heron. The following morning Peter asked Antoine if he would defend Mr. John were he attacked by the people. Antoine said he would not, and would be the first man to seize or shoot him, should any attempt be made against his life or liberty. He put the same question to McPherson; but McPherson said, "No, do not kill him till the governor comes, by and by, and then we shall have redress."

Peter also says that all the unmarried men were in the habit of secretly going out of the fort at night, contrary to order, to visit the Indian camp, and that one evening, when he wished to go out, he met George

Heron on the gallery, who showed him where a rope was slung to the picket, by which he might let himself down to the ground outside of the fort, saying, "This is the way I and others get out, and you may do the same without fear of detection." On the morning after the murder he went into Urbaine's and Lulaire's house and got a dram in each of them, out of two bottles of rum which he saw there. He said, "Now Mr. John is dead, I shall go out of the fort and spend the day with my wife." Urbaine replied, "No: no one shall go out of the fort. We keep the keys, and we shall keep the gates shut." Peter was angry at this, and said to Antoine, "When Mr. John was alive, he kept us prisoners, and would not allow us to run after women; and now that we have killed him, the Canadians wish to keep us as close as he did. I see we must raise the devil again with these Canadians, before we can get our liberty."

Peter also says that one principal cause of their dislike to John, and their plots against his life, was the strictness with which he prevented their sallying from the fort in quest of women; that he flogged Martineau for having given his blanket to a woman with whom he maintained illicit commerce, and he also flogged Lamb and Kakepe for giving away their clothes in the same manner. This, Peter says, exasperated the men.

The day after the murder many of the men went up to Mr. John's room to see the body, and McPherson remarked to them, that when the master was living they were not in the habit of coming up there; but they did so now that he was dead. On hearing this, Peter and Urbaine went away and never returned. On their way to their own house, they met Pripe and Bellinger.

Urbaine told them what McPherson had said, and in a threatening manner said, "McPherson is getting as proud as the other, and will be telling tales about us. We will not murder him, but we will give him a sound thrashing." And Peter says that he soon after went to Smith and told him to put McPherson on his guard, as the Canadians intended to attack him. Smith asked Peter what he would do, now the master was dead, and Peter said he would obey McPherson's orders. Smith replied, "That is good, Peter. If we do not do so, we shall lose all our wages." All the Canadians, and, he thinks, Simon, continued drinking the whole of the day following the murder; the other men of the fort did not drink. He thinks it was the remains of the liquor they had been drinking the preceding night. Peter also says that, for a month previous to the murder, Urbaine, Laperti, and Simon, were in the habit of getting drunk every night on rum purchased from the Indians. Peter told them to take care of themselves, because Mr. John would be angry if he knew it. Mr. John took no notice of their conduct, because, as Peter thinks, he knew of the plot against his life, and felt intimidated. He also says that Laperti was excited against Mr. John on account of a suspected intrigue which he carried on with his wife. The night following the murder, they all went to bed quietly. The next day all was also quiet, and all work suspended, except watching the Indians, which they did very closely, as they were afraid they might be induced to attack the fort, on learning that the master was no more. They continued watching, turn about. The second day a coffin was made, and the corpse removed from the main house to the bath, when McPherson gave the men a dram. The third day the corpse was buried and the men had another dram. He does not know whether the men asked for the dram, or whether McPherson gave it of his own accord. The corpse was carried to the grave by Laperti, Pripe, Lulaire, and some Kanakas, but Urbaine did not touch it; does not think it was through fear. Peter often heard Laperti say, "I wish the governor was here, to see what he would do." He also says there was no quarrel in the room where they were drinking on the night of the murder; but he thinks there might have been a quarrel after they left, as Pripe was put in irons after that time. He also says that the Canadians must have fixed on that night to murder him, and that Fleury told him so, which accounts for his apparent dejection of mind, and of his having shed tears in presence of his wife and Antoine, when he said, "I know that I am going to die this night." He also thinks this might have led to the outbreak, but of this he is not sure. It is a mere matter of opinion. Mr. John was a little in liquor, but knew perfectly well what he was about. He never saw him so far gone with liquor as not to be able to walk actively about, except on one occasion, the preceding Christmas Eve, when he appeared to walk unsteady, but nevertheless could mount the gallery. They only knew he had tasted liquor from the excitement and changed appearance of his countenance. He does not know who first suggested the idea of murdering Mr. John.

Since the above disclosures were made, a few other facts have come to light, which, however, do not materially affect the character of these atrocities. Mr. John McLaughlin, Jr., was doubtless intemperate, reckless, and tyrannical, and often unnecessarily cruel in the punishments inflicted upon his men; but he was surrounded by a set of desperadoes, who, for months before the arrival of the night, during the darkness of which the fatal shot ushered him into the presence of his Judge, had been seeking an opportunity to rob him of life. Some time before this event, he flogged Peter for the crime of stealing fish. Peter was exceedingly angry, and resolved upon the destruction of his master.

At a time to suit his purpose, he went to the bastion, where were fire-arms, loaded to his hands, and rung the bell of alarm, with the intention of shooting Mr. McLaughlin when he should make his appearance. A man by the name of Perse came out to see what was the matter, instead of the intended victim, when Peter fired, but missed him, the ball hitting a post near his head. For this offense, Peter was again seized, put in irons, and subsequently severely flogged, and liberated. Nearly all the men had been flogged from time to time, for various offenses, and all conspired against the life of their master. As might have been expected, when the case was examined by Sir George Simpson, the murderers attempted to cast all the odium upon Mr. McLaughlin, doubtless for the purpose of exculpating themselves, in which attempt they but too well succeeded, in the estimation of Sir George. Whether the persons who procured his death would be pronounced, by an intelligent jury, guilty of willful murder, or whether, from the mitigating circumstances connected with these transactions, the verdict should assume a more modified form, is not for me to determine. But it can not be denied by any one, that the circumstances must be indeed extraordinary that will justify any man, or set of men, to cut short the probation of an immortal being, and usher him, with all his unrepented sins, into the presence of his God.

This account illustrates English and Hudson's Bay Company's dealings with Indians, and their treatment of men and murderers, both among the Indians and their own people.

We are forced to acknowledge that we can not see the correctness of moral principle in Mr. Hine's conclusions. There was unquestionably a premeditated and willful murder committed by the men at that fort. We can understand the motives of Sir George Simpson and Mr. Douglas, in allowing those men to escape the penalty of their crime, from the amount of pecuniary interests involved, and the personal jealousy existing against Dr. McLaughlin and his sons, in the company's service. We know of jealousies existing between Mr. Simpson and John McLaughlin, Jr., on account of statements made in our presence at the breakfast-table, that were only settled temporarily, while at Vancouver. These statements, and the placing of this young son of the doctor's at that post, we are satisfied had their influence in acquitting his murderers, if they did not in bringing about the murder, which to us appears plain in the testimony; and we so expressed our opinion, when the father requested us (while in his office) to examine a copy of those depositions. We have no hesitancy in saying, that we believe it to have been a malicious murder, and should have sent the perpetrators to the gallows. We have never been able to learn of the trial of any one implicated.

CHAPTER VII.

Treatment of Indians.—Influence of Hudson's Bay Company.—Rev. Mr. Barnley's statement.—First three years.—After that.—Treatment of Jesuits.—Of Protestants.—Of Indians.—Not a spade to commence their new mode of life.—Mr. Barnley's statement.—Disappointed.—His mistake.—Hudson's Bay Company disposed to crush their own missionaries.

REV. MR. BEAVER says of them: "About the middle of the summer of 1836, and shortly before my arrival at Fort Vancouver, six Indians were wantonly and gratuitously murdered by a party of trappers and sailors, who landed for the purpose from one of the company's vessels, on the coast somewhere between the mouth of the river Columbia and the confines of California. Having on a former occasion read the particulars of this horrid massacre, as I received them from an eye-witness, before a meeting of the Aborigines Society, I will not repeat them. To my certain knowledge, the circumstance was brought officially before the authorities of Vancouver, by whom no notice was taken of it; and the same party of trappers, with the same leader, one of the most infamous murderers of a murderous fraternity, are annually sent to the same vicinity, to perform, if they please, other equally tragic scenes. God alone knows how many red men's lives have been sacrificed by them since the time of which I have been speaking. *He also knows that I speak the conviction of my mind, and may he forgive me if I speak unadvisedly when I state my firm belief that* THE LIFE OF AN INDIAN WAS NEVER YET, BY A TRAPPER, PUT IN COMPETITION WITH A BEAVER'S SKIN."

One other case we will give to illustrate the conduct and treatment of this company toward the Indians under their "*mild and paternal care*," as given, not by a chaplain, or missionary, but by Lieut. Chappel, in his "Voyage to Hudson's Bay in H. M. S. *Rosamond*." He relates that on one occasion, an English boy having been missed from one of the establishments in Hudson's Bay, the company's servants, in order to recover the absent youth, made use of the following stratagem:—

"Two Esquimaux Indians were seized and confined in separate apartments. A musket was discharged in a remote apartment, and the settlers, entering the room in which one of the Esquimaux was confined, informed him by signs that his companion had been put to death for decoying away the boy; and they gave him to understand at the same time that he must prepare to undergo the same fate, unless he would faithfully pledge himself to restore the absentee. The Esquimaux naturally promised every thing, and, on being set at liberty, made the best of his way into the woods, and, of course, was never afterward heard of. They kept the other a prisoner for some time. At length he tried to make his escape by boldly seizing the sentinel's firelock at night; but the piece going off accidentally, he was so terrified at the report, that they easily replaced him in confinement; yet either the loss of liberty, a supposition that his countryman had been murdered, or that he was himself reserved for some cruel death, deprived the poor wretch of reason. As he became exceedingly troublesome, the settlers held a conference as to the most eligible mode of getting rid of him; *and it being deemed good policy to deter the natives from similar offenses by making an example, they accordingly shot the poor maniac in cold blood,* without having given themselves the trouble to ascertain whether he was really guilty or innocent" (p. 156). We have quoted these two examples, from two British subjects, to show the Hudson's Bay Company's manner of treating the Indians, who were under their absolute control from the mouth of the Umpqua River, in the extreme southwestern part of Oregon, to the extreme northern point on the coast of Labrador, including a country larger in extent than the whole United States.

This country had for two hundred and thirty years been in possession of these two powerful and equally unprincipled companies, who had kept it, as Mr. Fitzgerald says, "*so as to shut up the earth from the knowledge of man, and man from the knowledge of God.*"

But, we are asked, what has this to do with the history of Oregon, and its early settlement? We answer, it was this influence, and this overgrown combination of iniquity and despotism—this monster monopoly, which England and America combined had failed to overcome,—that was at last, after a conflict of thirty years, forced to retire from the country, by the measures first inaugurated by Lee, Whitman, and the provisional government of Oregon; and now this same monopoly seeks to rob the treasury of our nation, as it has for ages robbed the Indians, and the country of its furs.

They may succeed (as they have heretofore, in obtaining an extension of their licensed privileges with the English government), and obtain from the American government what they now, by falsehood, fraud, and perjury, claim to be their just rights. If they do, we shall be satisfied that we have faithfully and truly stated facts that have come to our knowledge while moving and living in the midst of their operations, and that we are not alone in our belief and knowledge of the events and influences of which we write.

Before closing this chapter we will quote one other witness (a British subject), the Rev. Mr. Barnley, a missionary at Moose Factory, on the southwestern part of James Bay, to show the full policy of that company toward British missionaries, and also to prove the assertion we make that the Hudson's Bay Company, as such, is, in a measure, guilty of and responsible for the Whitman and Frazer River massacres, and for the Indian wars and the murder of American citizens contiguous to their territory.

The missionary above referred to says: "My residence in the Hudson's Bay territory commenced in June, 1840, and continued, with the interruption of about eight months, until September, 1847." The Whitman massacre was in November, 1847. Mr. Barnley continues: "My letter of introduction, signed by the governor of the territory, and addressed 'To the Gentlemen in charge of the Honorable Hudson's Bay Company's Districts and Posts in North America,' in one of its paragraphs ran thus: 'The governor and committee feel the most lively interest in the success of Mr. Barnley's mission, and I have to request you will show to that gentleman every personal kindness and attention in your power, and facilitate by every means the promotion of the very important and interesting service on which he is about to enter;' and, consequently, whatsoever else I might have to endure, I had no reason to anticipate any thing but cordial co-operation from the officers of the company.

"*For the first three years* I had no cause of complaint. The interpretation was, in many cases, necessarily inefficient, and would have been sometimes a total failure, but for the kindness of the wives of the gentlemen in charge, who officiated for me; but I had the best interpreters the various posts afforded, the *supply of rum* to Indians was restricted, and the company, I believe, fulfilled both the spirit and the letter of their agreement with us, as far as that fulfillment was then required of them, and their circumstances allowed.

"In giving, however, this favorable testimony, so far as the first three years are concerned, I must say, that in my opinion we should have been informed, before commencing our labors, that the interpreters at some of the posts would be found so inefficient as to leave us dependent on the kindness of private individuals, and reduce us to the very unpleasant necessity of taking mothers from their family duties, that they might become the only available medium for the communication of Divine truth.

"But after the period to which I have referred, a very perceptible change, *i. e.*, in 1845, took place. [The company had decided to introduce the Roman Jesuits to aid them in expelling all Protestant missionaries and civilization from the Indian tribes.] There was no longer that hearty concurrence with my views, and co-operation, which had at first appeared so generally. The effect was as if the gentleman in charge of the southern department had discovered that he was expected to afford rather an external and professed assistance than a real and cordial one; and, under his influence, others, both of the gentlemen and servants, became cool and reluctant in those services of which I stood in need, until at length the letter as well as the spirit of the company's engagement with me failed." The reader will remember that while Mr. Barnley was receiving this treatment at the Hudson's Bay Company's establishment at Moose Factory, James Douglas and his associates were combining and training the Indians in Oregon for the purpose of relieving, or, to use the language of the Jesuit De Smet, "to rescue Oregon from Protestant and American influence."

Mr. Barnley continues: "I was prohibited from entertaining to tea two persons, members of my congregation, who were about to sail for England, because I happened to occupy apartments in the officer's residence, and was told that it could not be made a rendezvous for the company's servants and their families." P. J. De Smet, S. J., on the 113th page of his book, says: "*The Canadian-French and half-breeds who inhabit the Indian territory treat all the priests who visit them with great kindness and respect.*" On page 313, he says of the Hudson's Bay Company, just about this time: "In what manner can we testify our gratitude in regard to the two benefactors [Douglas and Ogden] who so generously charged themselves with the care of *transporting and delivering* to us our cases, without consenting to accept the slightest recompense? * * How noble the sentiments which prompted them gratuitously to burden themselves and their boats with the charitable gifts destined by the faithful to the destitute missionaries of the Indians!" These last quotations are from letters of Jesuit missionaries, who were brought to the Indian country by this same Hudson's Bay Company, and furnished transportation and every possible facility to carry on their missions among the Indians all over the American Indian country.

These missionaries have made no attempt to improve the condition of the Indians, but have impressed upon their ignorant minds a reverence for themselves and their superstitions. See Bishop Blanchet's reply to Cayuse Indians, November 4, 1847, page 44 of Brouillet's "Protestantism in Oregon;" also pages 34–5, Executive Doc. No. 38, J. Ross Browne, as given below:—

"The bishop replied that it was the pope who had sent him; that he had not sent him to take their land, but only for the purpose of saving their souls; that, however, having to live, and possessing no wealth, he had asked of them a piece of land that he could cultivate for his support; that in his country it was the faithful who maintained the priests, but that here he did not ask so much, *but only a piece of land*, and that the priests themselves would do the rest. He told them that he would not make presents to Indians, that he would give them nothing for the land he asked; that, in case they worked for him, he would pay them for their work, and no more; that he would assist them neither in plowing their lands nor in building houses, nor would he feed or clothe their children," etc.

At Moose Factory, Mr. Barnley says: "A plan which I had devised for educating and training to some acquaintance with *agriculture* native children *was disallowed*, but permission was given me by the governor in council to collect seven or eight boys from various parts of the surrounding country, to be clothed, and at the company's expense. A proposal made for forming a small Indian village near Moose Factory *was not acceded to;* and, instead, permission only given to attempt the location of one or two old men who were no longer fit for engaging in the chase, *it being very carefully and distinctly stated by Sir George Simpson that the company would not give them even a spade toward commencing their new mode of life.* When at length a young man was found likely to prove serviceable as an interpreter, every impediment was interposed to prevent his engaging in my service, although a distinct understanding existed that neither for food nor wages would he be chargeable to the company. And the pledge that I should be at liberty to train up several boys for future usefulness, though not withdrawn, was treated as if it had never existed at all; efforts being made to produce the impression on the mind of my general superintendent that I was, most unwarrantably, expecting the company to depart from their original compact, when I attempted to add but two of the stipulated number to my household. * * * * *

"At Moose Factory, where the resources were most ample, and where was the seat of authority in the southern department of Rupert's Land, the hostility of the company (and not merely their inability to aid me, whether with convenience or inconvenience to themselves) was most manifest.

"The Indians were compelled, in opposition to their convictions and desires, to labor on the Lord's day. They were not permitted to purchase the food required on the Sabbath, that they might rest on that day while voyaging, although there was no necessity for their proceeding, and their wages would have remained the same. * * *

"At length, *disappointed, persecuted, myself and wife broken in spirit,* and almost ruined in constitution by months of anxiety and suffering, a return to England became the only means of escaping a premature grave; and we are happy in fleeing from the *iron hand of oppression,* and bidding farewell to that which had proved to us a land of darkness and of sorrow.

"From the above statements you will perceive that if true in some cases, it is not in all, that the company have furnished the 'means of conveyance from place to place.' They have not done so, at all events, in the particular case mentioned, nor would they let me have the canoe, lying idle as it was, when they knew that I was prepared to meet 'the expense.'

"And equally far from the truth is it, that the missionaries have been '*boarded, lodged, provided with interpreters and servants free of charge.*'"

In this last statement, Mr. Barnley is mistaken, for, to our certain knowledge, and according to the voluntary statement of the Roman Jesuits, Revs. Bishop Blanchet, Demer, P. J. De Smet, Brouillet, and many other Jesuit missionaries, they received from the Hudson's Bay Company *board and lodging, and were provided with interpreters,* catechist, transportation, and even houses and church buildings.

The only mistake of Mr. Barnley was, that he was either an Episcopal or Wesleyan missionary or chaplain, like Mr. Beaver, at Fort Vancouver, and he, like Mr. Beaver, was a little too conscientious as to his duties, and efforts to benefit the Indians, to suit the policy of that company. The Roman Jesuitical religion was better adapted to their ideas of Indian traffic and morals; hence, the honorable company chose to get rid of all others, as they had done with all opposing fur traders. What was a civilized Indian worth to that company? Not half as much as a common otter or beaver skin. As to the soul of an Indian, he certainly could have no more than the gentlemen who managed the affairs of the honorable company.

CHAPTER VIII.

Petition of Red River settlers.—Their requests, from 1 to 14.—Names.—Governor Christie's reply.—Company's reply.—Extract from minutes.—Resolutions, from 1 to 9.—Enforcing rules.—Land deed.—Its condition.—Remarks.

BEFORE closing this subject we must explain our allusion to the Red River settlement, and in so doing illustrate and prove beyond a doubt the settled and determined policy of that organization to crush out their own, as well as American settlements,—a most unnatural, though true position of that company. It will be seen, by the date of the document quoted below, that, four years previous, that company, in order to deceive the English government and people in relation to the settlement on the Columbia River, and also to diminish the number of this Red River colony, had, by direction of Sir George Simpson, sent a part of it to the Columbia department. The remaining settlers of Rupert's Land (the Selkirk settlement) began to assert their right to cultivate the soil (as per Selkirk grant), as also the right to trade with the natives, and to participate in the profits of the wild animals in the country. The document they prepared is a curious, as well as important one, and too interesting to be omitted. It reads as follows:—

"RED RIVER SETTLEMENT,
August 29, 1845.

"SIR,—Having at this moment a very strong belief that we, as natives of this country, and as half-breeds, have the right to hunt furs in the Hudson Bay Company's territories whenever we think proper, and again sell those furs to the highest bidder, likewise having a doubt that natives of this country can be prevented from trading and trafficking with one another, we would wish to have your opinion on the subject, lest we should commit ourselves by doing any thing in opposition either to the laws of England or the honorable company's privileges, and therefore lay before you, as governor of Red River settlement, a few queries, which we beg you will answer in course.

"*Query* 1. Has a half-breed, a settler, the right to hunt furs in this country?

"2. Has a native of this country, not an Indian, a right to hunt furs?

"3. If a half-breed has the right to hunt furs, can he hire other half-breeds for the purpose of hunting furs?

"4. Can a half-breed sell his furs to any person he pleases?

"5. Is a half-breed obliged to sell his furs to the Hudson's Bay Company at whatever price the company may think proper to give him?

"6. Can a half-breed receive any furs, as a present, from an Indian, a relative of his?

"7. Can a half-breed hire any of his Indian relatives to hunt furs for him?

"8. Can a half-breed trade furs from another half-breed, in or out of the settlement?

"9. Can a half-breed trade furs from an Indian, in or out of the settlement?

"10. With regard to trading or hunting furs, have the half-breeds, or natives of European origin, any rights or privileges over Europeans?

"11. A settler, having purchased lands from Lord Selkirk, or even from the Hudson's Bay Company, without any conditions attached to them, or without having signed any bond, deed, or instrument whatever, whereby he might have willed away his right to trade furs, can he be prevented from trading furs in the settlement with settlers, or even out of the settlement?

"12. Are the limits of the settlement defined by the municipal law, Selkirk grant, or Indian sale?

"13. If a person can not trade furs, either in or out of the settlement, can he purchase them for his own and family use, and in what quantity?

"14. Having never seen any official statements, nor known, but by report, that the Hudson's Bay Company has peculiar privileges over British subjects, natives, and half-breeds, resident in the settlement, we would wish to know what those privileges are, and the penalties attached to the infringement of the same.

"We remain your humble servants,

"JAMES SINCLAIR,	ALEXIS GAULAT,
BAPTIST LA ROQUE,	LOUIS LETENDE DE BATOCHE,
THOMAS LOGAN,	WILLIAM MCMILLAN,
JOHN DEASE,	ANTOINE MORRAN,
BAT. WILKIE,	JOHN ANDERSON,
JOHN VINCENT,	THOMAS MCDERMOT,
WILLIAM BIRD,	ADALL TROTTIER,
PETER GARIOCH,	CHARLES HOLE,
HENRY COOK,	JOSEPH MONKMAN,
JOHN SPENCE,	BAPTIST FARMAN.

"ALEXANDER CHRISTIE, Esq.,
"Governor of Red River Settlement."

Governor Christie's reply to these inquiries was so mild and conciliatory that it will not add materially to our knowledge of the company to give it. But the eight rules adopted by the company in council let us into the secret soul of the *monstrosity*, and are here given, that Americans may be informed as to its secret workings, and also to show what little regard an Englishman has for any but an aristocratic or moneyed concern.

"*Extracts from minutes of a meeting of the Governor and Council of Rupert's Land, held at the Red River settlement, June* 10, 1845.

"*Resolved*, 1st, That, once in every year, any British subject, if an actual resident, and not a fur trafficker, may import, whether from London or from St. Peter's, stores free of any duty now about to be imposed, on declaring truly that he has imported them at his own risk.

"2d. That, once in every year, any British subject, if qualified as before, may exempt from duty, as before, imports of the local value of ten pounds, on declaring truly that they are intended exclusively to be used by himself within Red River settlement, and have been purchased with certain specified productions or manufactures of the aforesaid settlement, exported in the same season, or by the latest vessel, at his own risk.

"3d. That, once in every year, any British subject, if qualified as before, who may have personally accompanied both his exports and imports, as defined in the preceding resolution, may exempt from duty, as before, imports of the local value of fifty pounds, on declaring truly that they are either to be consumed by himself, or to be sold by himself to actual consumers within the aforesaid settlement, and have been purchased with certain specified productions or manufactures of the settlement, carried away by himself in the same season, or by the latest vessel, at his own risk.

"4th. That all other imports from the United Kingdon for the aforesaid settlement, shall, before delivery, pay at York Factory a duty of twenty per cent. on their prime cost; provided, however, that the governor of the settlement be hereby authorized to exempt from the same all such importers as may from year to year be reasonably believed by him to have neither trafficked in furs themselves, since the 8th day of December, 1844, nor enabled others to do so by illegally or improperly supplying them with trading articles of any description.

"5th. That all other imports from any part of the United States shall pay all duties payable under the provisions of 5 and 6 Vict., cap. 49, the Imperial Statute for regulating the foreign trade of the British possessions in North America; provided, however, that the governor-in-chief, or, in his absence, the president of the council, may so modify the machinery of the said act of Parliament, as to adapt the same to the circumstances of the country.

"7th. That, henceforward, no goods shall be delivered at York Factory to any but persons duly licensed to freight the same; such licenses being given only in cases in which no fur trafficker may have any interest, direct or indirect.

"8th. That any intoxicating drink, if found in a fur trafficker's possession, beyond the limits of the aforesaid settlement, may be seized and destroyed by any person on the spot.

"Whereas the intervention of middle men is alike injurious to the honorable company and to the people; it is resolved,

"9th. That, henceforward, furs shall be purchased from none but the actual hunters of the same.

"FORT GARRY, July 10, 1845."

Copy of License referred to in Resolution 7.

"On behalf of the Hudson's Bay Company, I hereby license A. B. to trade, and also ratify his having traded in English goods within the limits of Red River settlement. This ratification and this license to be null and void, from the beginning, in the event of his hereafter trafficking in furs, or generally of his usurping any whatever of all the privileges of the Hudson's Bay Company."

It was to save Oregon from becoming a den of such oppressors and robbers of their own countrymen, that Whitman risked his life in 1842–3, that the provisional government of the American settlers was formed in 1843, that five hundred of them flew to arms in 1847, and fought back the savage hordes that this same Hudson's Bay Company had trained, under the teaching of their half-breeds and Jesuit priests, to sweep them from the land. Is this so? Let us see what they did just across the Rocky Mountains with their own children, as stated by their own witnesses and countrymen.

Sir Edward Fitzgerald says of them, on page 213:—

"But the company do not appear to have trusted to paper deeds to enforce their authority.

"They were not even content with inflicting fines under the form of a hostile tariff; but, as the half-breeds say, some of the fur traders were imprisoned, and all the goods and articles of those who were *suspected of an intention to traffic in furs* were seized and confiscated.

"But another, and even more serious attack, was made on the privileges of the settlers.

"The company being, under their charter, nominal owners of the soil, dispose of it to the colonists in any manner they think best. A portion of the land in the colony is held from Lord Selkirk, who first founded the settlement.

"Now, however, the company drew up a new *land deed*, which all were compelled to sign who wished to hold any land in the settlement."

This new land deed, above referred to, is too lengthy and verbose to be given entire; therefore we will only copy such parts as bind the settlers not to infringe upon the supposed chartered rights of the Hudson's Bay Company.

The first obligation of the person receiving this deed was to settle upon the land within forty days, and, within five years, cause one-tenth part of the land to be brought under cultivation.

The second: "He, his executors, administrators, and assigns, shall not, directly or indirectly, mediately or immediately, *violate* or *evade* any of the chartered or licensed privileges of the said governor and company, or any restrictions on trading or dealing with Indians or others, which have been or may be imposed by the said governor and company, or by any other competent authority, *or in any way enable* any person or persons to *violate or evade*, or to persevere in violating or evading the same; and, in short, *shall obey all such laws and regulations* as within the said settlement now are, or hereafter may be in force." * * * * Here are enumerated a long list of political duties pertaining to the citizen.

The deed in its third condition says: "And also that he [the said receiver of the deed], his executors, administrators, and assigns, shall not nor will, without the license or consent of the said governor and company for that purpose first obtained, carry on or establish, in *any part* of North America, any trade or traffic in, or relating to, any kind of skins, furs, peltry, or *dressed leather*, nor in any manner, directly or indirectly, aid or abet any person or persons in carrying on such trade or traffic." * * * Here follows a long lingo, forbidding the settler to buy, make, or sell liquors in any shape on his lands, and requiring him, under pain of forfeiture of his title, *to prevent others from doing so*, and binding the settler, under all the supposed and unsupposed conditions of obligation, *not to supply* or allow to be supplied any articles of trade to any unauthorized (by the company) person supposed to violate their trade, including companies "corporate or incorporate, prince, power, potentate, or state whatsoever, who shall infringe or violate, or who shall set about to infringe or violate the exclusive rights, powers, privileges and immunities of commerce, trade, or traffic, or all or any other of the exclusive rights, powers, privileges, and immunities of, or belonging, or in any wise appertaining to, or held, used, or enjoyed by the said governor and company, and their successors, under their charter or charters, without the license or consent of the said governor and company and their successors, for the time being, first had and obtained.

"And, lastly,"—here follows a particular statement asserting that for the violation of any one of the thousand and one conditions of that deed, the settler forfeits to the company his right to the land, which reverts back to the company.

Our country delights to honor the sailor and soldier who performs a good, great, or noble act to save its territory from becoming the abode of despotism, or its honor from the taunt of surrounding nations. In what light shall we regard the early American missionaries and pioneers of Oregon?

It is true they heard the call of the oppressed savage for Christian light and civilization. They came in good faith, and labored faithfully, though, perhaps, mistaking many of the strict duties of the Christian missionary; and some, being led astray by the wiles and cunning of an unscrupulous fur monopoly, failed to benefit the Indians to the extent anticipated; yet they formed the nucleus around which the American pioneer with his family gathered, and from which he drew his encouragement and protection; and a part of these missionaries were the leaders and sustainers of those influences which ultimately secured this country to freedom and the great Republic.

The extracts from the deed above quoted show what Oregon would have been, had the early American missionaries failed to answer the call of the Indians, or had been driven from the country; or even had not Whitman and his associates separated, the one to go to Washington to ask for delay in the settlement of the boundary question, the others to the Wallamet Valley to aid and urge on the organization of the provisional government.

CHAPTER IX.

Puget Sound Agricultural Company.—Its original stock.—A correspondence.—No law to punish fraud.—A supposed trial of the case.—Article four of the treaty.—The witnesses.—Who is to receive the Puget Sound money.—Dr. Tolmie, agent of the company.—The country hunted up.—Difficult to trace a fictitious object.—Statement of their claim.—Result of the investigation.

The Puget Sound Agricultural Company, now claiming of our government the sum of $1,168,000, was first talked of and brought into existence at Vancouver in the winter of 1837, in consequence of, and in opposition to, the Wallamet Cattle Company, which was got up and successfully carried through by the influence and perseverance of Rev. Jason Lee, superintendent of the Methodist Mission. This Nasqualla and Puget Sound Company was an opposing influence to Mr. Lee and his mission settlement, and was also to form the nucleus for two other British settlements in Oregon, to be under the exclusive control of the Hudson's Bay Company.

The original stock of the company was nominally £200,000. The paid-up capital upon this amount was supposed to be ten per cent., which would give £20,000, or $96,800, at $4.84 per pound. From the most reliable information we can get, this amount was taken from a sinking fund, or a fund set apart for the purpose of opposing any opposition in the fur trade. About the time this Puget Sound Company came into existence, the American fur companies had been driven from the country, and the fund was considered as idle or useless stock; and as the question of settlement of the country would in all probability soon come up, Rev. Mr. Lee having taken the first step to the independence of his missionary settlement in the Wallamet, this Puget Sound Company was gotten up to control the agricultural and cattle or stock interests of the country. It was in existence in name some two years before its definite arrangements were fixed by the Hudson's Bay Company, through the agency of Dr. W. F. Tolmie, who went to to London for that purpose, and by whom they were concluded, "with the consent of the Hudson's Bay Company, who stipulated that an officer connected with the fur-trade branch of the Hudson's Bay Company should have supreme direction of the affairs of the Puget Sound Company in this country. It was also stipulated that the

Puget Sound Company should be under bonds *not to permit any of its employés* to be in any way concerned in the fur trade, in opposition to the Hudson's Bay Company."

It is easy to be seen by the above-stated condition, that the Hudson's Bay Company were not willing to allow the least interference with their fur trade by any one over whom they had any control or influence; that their design and object was to control the trade of the whole country, and that they had no intention in any way to encourage any American settlement in it, as shown by the arrangements made as early as 1837.

There had been a correspondence with the managing directors of the company in London previous to Dr. Tolmie's visit. The directors had discouraged the proposed enlargement of their business, but it seems from the statement of Dr. Tolmie, and the arrangements he made, that they acceded to his plans, and constituted him their special agent. There was at the time a question as to a separate charter for that branch of their business. It was finally conceded that a separate charter would enable this agricultural and cattle company to become independent of the fur branch, and thus be the means of establishing an opposition by the use of the funds appropriated to prevent any thing of this kind, and decided that as the company had stipulated that they were to have the "*supreme direction* of the Puget Sound Agricultural Company," no charter was necessary, and hence any arrangements to that effect were withdrawn. It was from a knowledge of the fact that that company had not even the Parliamentary acknowledgment of its separate existence from the Hudson's Bay Company, that all their land claims were at once taken; and upon that ground they have not dared to prosecute their claims, only under the wording of the treaty with the United States, which is the only shadow of a legal existence they have, and which, there is no question, would have been stricken from the treaty, except through the fur influence of the company to increase the plausibility of their claims against our government.

If there was any law to punish a fraud attempted to be committed by a foreign company upon a friendly nation, this would be a plain case; as the Hudson's Bay Company, they claim $3,822,036.37; as the Puget Sound Company, $1,168,000. The original stock of the Hudson's Bay Company was £10,500, or $50,820. In 1690 the dividends upon this capital invested were so enormous that the company voted to treble their stock, which was declared to be £31,500, or $152,460, In 1720 the capital was again declared trebled, and to be £94,500, or $457,380, while the only amount paid was £10,500, or $50,820. It was then proposed to add three times as much to its capital stock by subscription; each subscriber paying £100 was to receive £300 of stock, so that the nominal stock should amount to £378,000, or $1,820,520—the real additional sum subscribed being £94,500, and the amount of real stock added or paid but £3,150. In 1821, the Hudson's Bay Company and Northwest Company, of Montreal, were united. The Hudson's Bay Company called £100 on each share of its stock, thus raising it nominally to £200,000, or $958,000. The Northwest Company called theirs the same. The two companies combined held a nominal joint stock of £400,000, or $1,916,000, while we have reason to suppose that the original stock of the two companies, admitting that the Northwest French Company had an equal amount of original capital invested, would give £37,300, or $135,134, as the capital upon which they have drawn from our country never less than ten per cent. per annum, even when counted at £400,000, or $1,916,000; and what, we would ask, has America received in return for this enormous drain of her wealth and substance?

Have the Indians in any part of the vast country occupied by that company been civilized or bettered in their condition? Have the settlements under their fostering care been successful and prosperous? Have they done any thing to improve any portion of the country they have occupied, any further than such improvements were necessary to increase the profits of their fur trade?

To every one of these questions we say, emphatically, No, not in a single instance. On the contrary, they have used their privileges solely to draw all the wealth they could from the country, and leave as little as was possible in return.

The British author, from whose book we have drawn our figures of that company's stock, says of them: "To say, then, that the trade of this country (England) has been fostered and extended by the monopoly enjoyed by the company, is exactly contrary to the truth."

We come now to learn all we can of a something that has assumed the name of Puget Sound Agricultural Company, and under that name, through the paternal influence of a bastard corporation, presumes to ask an immense sum of the American government, whose country they have used all their power and influence to secure to themselves, by acting falsely to their own. We do not claim to be learned in the law of nations, therefore we can only express such an opinion in this case as we would were the case argued before a learned court and we one of the jurors, giving our opinion as to the amount the parties were entitled to receive. We will suppose that the lawyers have made their pleas, which would, when printed, with the testimony on both sides, make a volume of the usual size of law books of one thousand pages. Of course the fourth article of the treaty would be read to us by both the lawyers, and explained by the judge, who would doubtless say to the jury the first question to decide is, whether there is sufficient evidence to convince you that the company claiming this name have any legal existence outside the wording of the fourth article of this treaty. Our answer would be: "Your honor, there is not the least word in a single testimony presented before us to show that they ever had any existence, only as they assumed a name to designate the place a certain branch of the Hudson's Bay Company's business, outside of its legitimate trade; that this being a branch legitimately belonging to a settlement of loyal citizens of the country, we find that this Hudson's Bay Company, in assuming the *supreme direction*, as per testimony of Dr. Tolmie, superseded and usurped the prerogatives of the State; that the claim of this company, as set up in the wording of the treaty, is for the benefit of a company having no natural or legal right to assume *supreme direction* of the soil or its productions. Hence any improvement made, or stock destroyed, was at the risk of the individual owning, or making, or bringing such stock or improvements into the country, and subject exclusively to the laws of the country in which the trespass occurred. The claiming a name belonging to no legal body cannot be made legal by a deception practiced upon the persons making the treaty, as this would be equivalent to pledging the nation to the payment of money when no cause could be shown that money was justly due, as neither nation (except by a deception brought to bear upon commissioners forming the treaty by the mere assertion of an interested party) acknowledged the reported existence of such a corporation, thereby creating a corporate body by the wording of a treaty." This, to a common juror, we confess, would look like removing the necessity of a common national law, in relation to all claims of foreigners who might feel disposed to come over and trespass upon our national domain. A word in this treaty does not settle the matter, and the claim should not be paid. The article above referred to is commented upon by Mr. Day as follows:—

"That by article four of the treaty concluded between the United States of America and Great Britain, under date of the 15th day of June, 1864, it was provided that the farms, lands, and other property, of every description, belonging to the Puget Sound Agricultural Company, on the north side of the Columbia River [they should have included those in the French possession, and added another million to their claim; but we suppose they became liberal, and consented to take half of the country their servants had settled upon], should be confirmed to the said company; but that in case the situation of those farms and lands should be considered by the United States to be of public and political importance, and the United States government should signify a desire to obtain possession of the whole, or of any part thereof, the property so required should be transferred to the said government at a proper valuation, to be agreed upon between the parties.

"That the government of the United States has not, at any time, signified to the company a desire that any of the said property should be transferred to the said government at a valuation as provided by the treaty, nor has any transfer thereof been made [this was a great misfortune. Uncle Sam had so much land of his own he did not want to buy out this bastard company right away after the treaty was made]; but the company have ever since continued to be the rightful owners of the said lands, farms, and other property, and entitled to the free and undisturbed possession and enjoyment thereof. [True; so with all bastards. They live and die, and never find a father to own them, except they come up with a big pile of money, which in your claim is a case of *clonas* (don't know.)]

"That, by a convention concluded between the two governments on the 1st day of July, 1863, it was agreed that all questions between the United States authorities on the one hand, and the Puget Sound Agricultural Company on the other, with respect to the rights and claims of the latter, should be settled by the transfer of such rights and claims to the government of the United States for an adequate money consideration.

"And the claimants aver that the rights and claims of the Puget Sound Agricultural Company, referred to and intended in and by the said convention, are their rights and claims in and upon the said lands, farms, and other property of every description which they so held and possessed within the said territory, and which, by reason of the said treaty of the 15th of June, 1846, and according to the terms of the fourth article thereof, the United States became and were bound to confirm. And of the said farms and other property, they now submit to the honorable the commissioners a detailed statement and valuation, as follows."

There have been twenty-seven witnesses examined to prove the claims above set forth, and not a single one of them testified or gave the least intimation that there ever was any such company as here set forth in existence, only as connected with and subject to the control and management of the Hudson's Bay Company, the same as their farming operations at Vancouver or Colville, or any other of their posts. The claim is so manifestly fictitious and without foundation, that the learned attorney for the company bases his whole reliance upon the wording of the treaty, and in consequence of the wording of that treaty, "and according to the terms of the fourth article thereof, he says the United States *became* and *were bound* to confirm." So we suppose any other monstrous claim set up by a band of foreign fur traders having influence enough to start any speculation on a nominal capital in our country and failing to realize the profits anticipated, must apply for an acknowledgment of their speculation, be mentioned in a treaty, and be paid in proportion to the enormity of their demands. We are inclined to the opinion that so plain a case of fraud will be soon disposed of, and the overgrown monster that produced it sent howling after the Indians they have so long and so successfully robbed, as per their own admission, of £20,000,000 sterling. (See Mr. M. Martin's Hudson's Bay Company's Territory, etc., p. 131.)

There is another question arising in this supposed Puget Sound concern. Suppose, for a moment, the commissioners decide to pay the whole or any part of this demand, who will be the recipients of this money? We doubt whether the learned commissioners or the counsel of the supposed company could tell, unless it is to be his fee for prosecuting the case.

Doctor William Fraser Tolmie and Mr. George B. Roberts are the only two witnesses that appear to know much about the matter, and Mr. Roberts' information seems to be derived from the same source as our own, so that the writer, though not a member of the company, has about as good a knowledge of its object and organization as Mr. Roberts, who was connected with the Hudson's Bay Company, and also an agent of this Puget Sound Company.

Dr. Tolmie says: "The Puget Sound Company *acquired*, or purchased from the Hudson's Bay Company, all its improvements at Cowlitz and Nasqualla, with its lands, live stock, and agricultural implements, all of which were transferred, in 1840 or 1841, by the Hudson's Bay Company to the Puget Sound Company."

As we understand this matter, it amounts to just this, and no more: The Hudson's Bay Company had consented to enlarge their business by employing an outside capital or sinking fund they had at their disposal; they instructed Dr. Tolmie, their special agent for that purpose, to receive all the property at the two stations or farms named, to take possession of them, and instead of opening an account with their opposition sinking fund, they called it the Puget Sound Agricultural Company. This explains the ten per cent. paid stock into that company. Now, if this venture is profitable, nothing is lost; if it is not, it does not interfere with the legitimate business of the fur company—hence the distinct claim under this name.

"The Puget Sound Company charged the Hudson's Bay Company for all supplies furnished, and paid the Hudson's Bay Company for all goods received from them."

This was exactly in the line of the whole business done throughout the entire Hudson's Bay Company, with all their forts, and other establishments.

"Were not the accounts of the Puget Sound Company always forwarded to the Hudson's Bay Company's depot?" "*They were*," says Dr. Tolmie; and so were all the accounts of all the posts on this coast sent to the depot at Vancouver, and thence to head-quarters on the other side of the Rocky Mountains.

We have shown, by reference to the capital stock of the Hudson's Bay Company, that, in 1821, it was counted at £200,000. From this sum ten per cent., or £20,000, was set apart as a sinking fund to oppose any fur company or traders on the west side of the mountains, and an equal sum for the same purpose on the east.

This western amount, being placed under the direction of Dr. Tolmie and his successors, produced in seven years £11,000 sterling, equal to $53,240. This transaction does not appear, from the testimony adduced in the case, to have interfered in the least with the fur trade carried on at these stations, and by the same officers or clerks of the Hudson's Bay Company; hence, we are unable, from the whole catalogue of twenty-seven witnesses in the case, to find out who is to receive this nice little sum of $1,168,000 or £240,000—only £40,000 more than the mother had to trade upon when she produced this beautiful full-grown child, the Puget Sound Agricultural Company,—having had an abortion on the other side of the continent in the loss, without pay, of a large portion of the Red River or Selkirk country. Uncle Sam was ungenerous there.

This is truly an age of wonders, and this Hudson's Bay Company and its productions are entitled to some consideration for their ingenuity, if not for their honesty. It will be interesting to look at our British cousins and see what is said about this "*itself* and *its other self.*" Mr. Fitzgerald says, page 260: "It is a matter of importance to know whether the Hudson's Bay Company is about to submit itself and *its other self*—the Puget Sound Association—to the same regulations which are to be imposed on other settlers of Vancouver Island and British Columbia."

On page 287, he further states: "The Oregon Territory was peopled, under the influence of the company, with subjects of the United

States. (Since writing the former chapter, I have heard this account given of the conduct of the Hudson's Bay Company, in regard to the Oregon boundary, which offers still stronger ground for inquiry. The country south of the 49th parallel, it seems, was hunted up—therefore the posts of the Hudson's Bay Company were become of no value at all. By annexing all that country to the United States, and inserting in the treaty a clause that the United States should pay the company for all its posts if it turned them out, the company were able to obtain from the Americans a large sum of money for what would have been worth nothing had the territory remained British.) That lost us the boundary of the Columbia River. That is one specimen of the colonization of the Hudson's Bay Company. The boundary westward from the Lake of the Woods, we have seen, gave to the United States land from which the company was engaged, at the very time, in driving out British subjects, on the plea that it belonged to the company; and now that the boundary has been settled only a few years, we learn that the settlers on our side are asking the United States to extend her government over that country."

If this does not show a clear case of abortion on the part of that *honorable* Hudson's Bay Company east of the Rocky Mountains, tell us what does. But it is interesting to trace a little further the British ideas and pretensions to this Pacific coast. Our British author says, page 288:—

"Make what lines you please in a map and call them boundaries, but it is mockery to do so as long as the inhabitants are alienated from your rule, as long as you have a company in power whose policy erases the lines which treaties have drawn.

"Forasmuch, then, as these things are so, it becomes this country [Great Britain] to record an emphatic protest against the recent policy of the Colonial Office in abandoning the magnificent country on the shores of the Pacific Ocean to the Hudson's Bay Company.

"The blindest can not long avoid seeing the immense importance of Vancouver Island to Great Britain. Those who, two years ago [1846], first began to attract public attention to this question, are not the less amazed at the unexpected manner and rapidity with which their anticipations have been realized.

"Six months ago it was a question merely of colonizing Vancouver Island; now it is a question involving the interests of the whole of British North America, and of the empire of Great Britain in the Pacific Ocean."

It is always more or less difficult to trace the course of a false or fictitious object. It becomes peculiarly so when two objects of the same character come up; the one, by long practice and experience, assuming a fair and honorable exterior, having talent, experience, and wealth; the other, an illegitimate production, being called into existence to cripple the energies of two powerful nations, and living under the supreme control of the body, having acquired its position through the ignorance of the nations it seeks to deceive. It is out of the question to separate two such objects or associations. The one is the child of the other, and is permitted to exist while the object to be accomplished remains an opponent to the parent association.

The opposition to the fur monoply having ceased west of the Rocky Mountains, a new element of national aggrandizement and empire comes within the range of this deceitful and grasping association. Its child is immediately christened and set to work under its paternal eye. We have the full history of the progress made by this *Mr. Puget Sound Agricultural Company* in the testimony of the twenty-seven witnesses summoned to prove his separate existence from that of the *Hudson's Bay Company.*

We find, in tracing the existence of these two children of the British empire in North America, that they have established themselves in an island on the Pacific coast called Vancouver. In this island they are more thrifty and better protected than they were in the dominions of Uncle Samuel. Notwithstanding they are comfortably located, and have secured the larger part of that island and the better portion of British Columbia, there is occasionally a British subject that grumbles a little about them in the following undignified style:—

"If the company were to be destroyed to-morrow, would England be poorer? Would there not rather be demanded from the hands of our own manufacturers ten times the quantity of goods which is sent abroad, under the present system, to purchase the skins?" My dear sir, this would make the Indians comfortable and happy. "We boast [says this Englishman] that we make no slaves, none at least that can taint our soil, or fret our sight; but we take the child of the forest, whom God gave us to civilize, and commit him, bound hand and foot, to the most iron of all despotisms—*a commercial monoply.*

"Nor, turning from the results of our policy upon the native population, to its effect upon settlers and colonists, is there greater cause for congratulation.

"The system which has made the native a slave is making the settler a rebel.

"Restrictions upon trade, jealousy of its own privileges, interference with the rights of property, exactions, and all the other freaks in which monopoly and despotism delight to indulge, have, it appears, driven the best settlers into American territory, and left the rest, as it were, packing up their trunks for the journey."

This, so far as relates to the proceedings, policy, and influence of that company upon the settlement of Vancouver Island and British Columbia, is verified by the facts now existing in those British colonies. Their whole system is a perfect mildew and blight upon any country in which they are permitted to trade or to do business.

We have little or no expectation that any thing we may write will affect in the least the decision of the commissioners, whose business it is to decide this Puget Sound Company's case; but, as a faithful historian, we place on record the most prominent facts relating to it, for the purpose of showing the plans and schemes of an English company, who are a nuisance in the country, and a disgrace to the nation under whose charters they profess to act. Up to the time we were permitted to examine the testimony they have produced in support of their monstrous claims, we were charitable enough to believe there were some men in its employ who could be relied upon for an honest and truthful statement of facts in relation to the property and improvements for which these claims are made; but we are not only disappointed, but forced to believe the truth is not in them,—at least in any whose testimony is before us in either case. Our English author says:—

"It does not appear that the interposition of '*an irresponsible company*' can be attended with benefit to the colony. * * * A company whose direction is in London, and which is wholly *irresponsible*, either to the colonists or to the British Parliament. * * * There is ample evidence in the foregoing pages that it would be absurd to give this company credit for *unproductive patriotism*. * * * Considering the identity existing between this association [the Puget Sound Association] and the Hudson's Bay Company, in whose hands the whole management of the colonization of Vancouver Island is placed, there is a very strong reason to fear that the arrangements which have been made will, for some years at any rate, utterly ruin that country as a field for colonial enterprise. There is a strong inducement for the company to grant all the best part of the island to themselves, under the name of the Puget Sound Association; and to trust to the settlements which may be formed by that association as being sufficient to satisfy the obligation to colonize which is imposed by the charter.

"There is a strong inducement to discourage the immigration of independent settlers; first, because when all the colonists are in the position of their own servants, they will be able much more readily to prevent interference with the fur trade· and secondly, *because the presence of private capital in the island could only tend to diminish their own gains, derived from the export of agricultural produce.*

"And, on the other hand, there will be every possible discouragement to emigrants of the better class to settle in a colony where a large part of the country will be peopled only by the lowest order of workmen, where they may have to compete with the capital of a wealthy company, and that company not only their rival in trade, but at the same time possessed of the supreme power, and of paramount political influence in the colony.

"There is a reason, more important than all, why the Hudson's Bay Company will never be able to form *a colony*. An agricultural settlement they may establish; a few forts, where Scotchmen will grumble for a few years before they go over to the Americans, but never a community that will deserve the name of a British colony. THEY DO NOT POSSESS PUBLIC CONFIDENCE.

"But the Hudson's Bay Company—the colonial office of this unfortunate new colony—*has positive interests* antagonistic to those of an important settlement.

"It is a body whose history, tendency, traditions, and prospects are *equally and utterly opposed* to the existence, within its hunting-grounds, of an active, wealthy, independent, and flourishing colony," (we Americans say settlements) "with all the destructive consequences of ruined monopoly and wide-spread civilization."

Need we stop to say the above is the best of British testimony in favor of the position we have assumed in relation to a company who will cramp and dwarf the energies of their own nation to increase the profits on the paltry capital they have invested.

Have the Americans any right to believe they will pursue any more liberal course toward them than they have, and do pursue toward their own countrymen? As this writer remarks, "civilization ruins their *monopoly*." The day those two noble and sainted women, Mrs. Spalding and Mrs. Whitman, came upon the plains of the Columbia, they could do no less than allow England's banner to do them reverence, for God had sent and preserved them, as emblems of American civilization, religious light, and liberty upon this coast. One of them fell by the ruthless hand of the sectarian savages, pierced by Hudson's Bay balls from Hudson's Bay guns. The other was carried, in a Hudson's Bay boat, to the protecting care of the American settlement; and for what purpose? That the savage might remain in barbarism; that the monster monopoly might receive its profits from the starving body and soul of the Indian; that civilization and Christianity, and the star of empire might be stayed in their westward course.

Not yet satisfied with the blood of sixteen noble martyrs to civilization and Christianity, quick as thought their missives are upon the ocean wave. Wafted upon the wings of the wind, a foul slander is sent by the representatives of that monopoly all over the earth, to blast her (Mrs. Whitman's) Christian and missionary character with that of her martyred husband. And why?

Because that husband had braved the perils of a winter journey to the capital of his country, to defeat their malicious designs, to shut up the country and forever close it to American civilization and religion. And now, with an audacity only equaled by the arch-enemy of God and man, they come to our government and demand five millions of gold for facilitating the settlement of a country they had not the courage or power to prevent.

This, to a person ignorant of the peculiar arrangements of so monstrous a monopoly, will appear strange—that they should have an exclusive monopoly in trade in a country, and have not the courage or power to prevent its settlement, especially when such settlement interferes with its trade. So far as American territory was concerned, they were only permitted to have a joint occupancy in trade. The sovereignty or right of soil was not settled; hence, any open effort against any settler from any country was a trespass against the rights of such settler. They could only enforce their chartered privileges in British territory. The country, under these circumstances, afforded them a vast field in which to combine and arrange schemes calculated to perpetuate their own power and influence in it. The natives of the country were their trading capital and instruments, ready to execute their will upon all opponents. The Protestant missionaries brought an influence and a power that at once overturned their licensed privileges in trade, because with the privilege of trade, they had agreed, in accepting their original charter, to civilize and Christianize the natives of the country. This part of their compact the individual members of the company were fulfilling by each taking a native woman, and rearing as many half-civilized subjects as was convenient. This had the effect to destroy their courage in any investigation of their conduct. As to their power, as we have intimated above, it was derived from the capacity, courage, prejudices, and ignorance of the Indians, which the American missionary, if let alone, would soon overcome by his more liberal dealings with them, and his constant effort to improve their condition, which, just in proportion as the Indians learned the value of their own productions and labor, would diminish the profits in the fur trade.

This increase of civilization and settlement, says chief-trader Anderson, "had been foreseen on the part of the company, and to a certain extent provided for. The cession of Oregon, under the treaty of 1846, and the consequent negotiations for the transfer to the American government of all our rights and possessions in their territory, retarded all further proceedings."

In this statement of Mr. Anderson, and the statement of Mr. Roberts, an old clerk of the company, and from our own observations, this "foreseeing" on the part of the company was an arrangement with the Indians, and such as had been half civilized by the various individual efforts of the members and servants of the company, to so arrange matters that an exterminating war against the missionary settlements in the country should commence before the Mexican difficulty with the United States was settled.

This view of the question is sustained by the reply of Sir James Douglas to Mr. Ogden, by Mr. Ogden's course and treatment of the Indians on his way up the Columbia River, his letters to Revs. E. Walker and Spalding, his special instructions to the Indians, and payment of presents in war materials for their captives, and the course pursued by Sir James Douglas in refusing supplies to the provisional troops and settlers, and the enormous supplies of ammunition furnished to the priests for the Indians during the war of 1847–8.

We are decidedly of the same opinion respecting that company as their own British writer, who, in conclusion, after giving us a history of 281 pages, detailing one unbroken course of oppression and cruelty to all under their iron despotism, says:—

"The question at issue is a serious one,—whether a valuable territory shall be given up to an *irresponsible corporation*, to be colonized or not, as it may suit their convenience; or whether that colonization shall be conducted in accordance with any principles which are recognized as sound and right?"

We can easily see the connection in the principle of right in paying any portion of either of the monstrous claims of that company, which never has been responsible to any civilized national authority.

"The foregoing exposure of the character and conduct of the company has been provoked. When doubts were expressed whether the company were qualified for fulfilling the tasks assigned to them by the Colonial Minister, and when they appealed to their character and history, it became right that their history should be examined, and their character exposed.

"The investigation thus provoked has resulted in the discovery that their *authority is fictitious, and their claims invalid.* As their power is illegal, so the exercise of it has been mischievous; it has been mischievous to Great Britain, leaving her to accomplish, at a vast national expense, discoveries which the company undertook, and were paid to perform; and because our trade has been *contracted* and crippled, without any advantage, political or otherwise, having been obtained in return; it has been mischievous to the native Indians, cutting them off from all communication with the rest of the civilized world, depriving them of the fair value of their labor, keeping them in a condition of slavery, and leaving them in the same state of poverty, misery, and paganism in which it originally found them; it has been mischievous to the settlers and colonists under its influence, depriving them of their liberties as British subjects, frustrating, by exactions and arbitrary regulations, their efforts to advance, and, above all, undermining their loyalty and attachment to their mother country, and fostering, by bad government, a spirit of discontent with their own, and sympathy with foreign institutions."

This writer says: "This is the company whose power is now [in 1849] to be strengthened and consolidated!—to whose dominion is to be added the most important post which Great Britain possesses in the Pacific, and to whom the formation of a new colony is to be intrusted."

And, we add, this is the power that has succeeded in forcing their infamous claims upon our government to the amount above stated, and by the oaths of men trained for a long series of years to rob the Indian of the just value of his labor, to deceive and defraud their own nation as to the fulfillment of chartered stipulations and privileges.

The facts developed by our history may not affect the decision of the commissioners in their case, but the future student of the history of the settlement of our Pacific coast will be able to understand the influences its early settlers had to contend with, and the English colonist may learn the secret of their failure to build up a wealthy and prosperous colony in any part of their vast dominion on the North American continent.

CHAPTER X.

Case of The Hudson's Bay Company *v.* The United States.—Examination of Mr. McTavish.—Number of witnesses.—Their ignorance.—Amount claimed.—Original stock.—Value of land in Oregon.—Estimate of Hudson's Bay Company's property.—Remarks of author.

I HAVE carefully reviewed all the testimony in the above case, on both sides, up to May 1, 1867. On April 12, the counsel on the part of the United States having already spent twenty-five days in cross-examining Chief-Factor McTavish, so as to get at the real expenditures of the Hudson's Bay Company, and arrive at a just conclusion as to the amount due them,—Mr. McTavish having frequently referred to accounts and statements which he averred could be found on the various books of the company,—gave notice to the counsel of the company in the following language:—

"The counsel for the United States require of Mr. McTavish, who, as appears from his evidence, is a chief factor of the Hudson's Bay Company, and its agent in the prosecution of this claim, to produce here for examination by the United States or their counsel, all accounts, account-books, and letter-books of said company, together with the regulations under which their books were kept, and the various forms of contracts with servants of the company, all of which books, rules, and forms contain evidence pertinent to the issue in this case, as appears from the cross-examination of Mr. McTavish, and suspends the further cross-examination of this witness until he shall produce such books, accounts, rules, and forms."

On the 1st of May Mr. McTavish's examination was resumed.

Int. 952.—"Will you please produce here for examination by the United States or their counsel, all accounts, account-books, and letter-books of the Hudson's Bay Company which were kept at the various posts of that company south of the 49th parallel of north latitude during their occupation by the company, together with the regulations under which their books were kept, and the regular forms of contracts with the company's servants?"

Ans.—"I can not say whether I will produce them or not."

(The above question was objected to as incompetent, and as asking the witness, not as to what he knows of the subject, but as to what his future course of action will be, over which, as witness, he can have no control.)

During the examination of Mr. McTavish it was evident that he was the main prosecuting witness, and considerably interested in the results of the claim, or suit.

It would doubtless be interesting to most of our readers to see a review of the testimony, or at least a summary of the evidence presented on both sides in this case. There are now printed about one thousand pages of documents and depositions. That relating particularly to the Hudson's Bay Company comprises about two-thirds of the whole amount. The balance relates more particularly to the Puget Sound Agricultural Company's claim. This claim, the company have not been able, by any testimony yet presented, to separate from that of the Hudson's Bay Company; so that there is no prospect of their receiving one dollar on that account. There have been examined on the part of the Puget Sound Company, to prove its separate existence from the Hudson's Bay Company, thirty witnesses; on the part of the United States, twenty-one. On the part of the Hudson's Bay Company's claim as separate from the Puget Sound Company, nineteen witnesses; on the part of the United States, thirty. On both sides not far from forty-five witnesses have been called upon the stand to testify in this important case. The company in London have been requested to furnish evidence of the separate organization or independent existence of the two companies; and with all this evidence produced, nothing definite or certain is shown, except that the concern was gotten up to deceive the English people and rob the American government, and to counteract and oppose the American settlement of this country.

As a looker-on and an observer of events in this country, I must confess my astonishment at the ignorance, perverseness, and stupidity of men whom I have ever heretofore regarded as honorable and truthful.

From the testimony before me of the twenty odd English witnesses, it really appears as though they felt that all they had to do was to ask their pay, and our government would give it to them; or, in other words, they, as Englishmen and British subjects, are prepared to compel the payment of any sum they demand.

There are many interesting developments brought out in this case relative to the early history of this country, which renders the depositions in the case, though voluminous and tedious in the main, yet interesting to the close and careful student of our history.

If time and opportunity is given, I will review this whole testimony as a part of the history of this country, and, in so doing, will endeavor to correct an erroneous impression that will result from the testimony as now before us.

The amount claimed in this case is four million nine hundred and ninety thousand thirty-six dollars and sixty-seven cents, or, nine hundred and eighty-five thousand three hundred and fifty pounds sterling, in gold coin.

I now have before me, including the Hudson's Bay Company's memorial, eleven hundred and twenty-six pages of printed documents and depositions relating to this case. I also have what may properly be termed British testimony, bearing directly upon this case, which is entitled to its full weight in a proper and just decision as to the amount of compensation this Hudson's Bay Company is entitled to receive from our government.

I do not propose to review all the one thousand four hundred and nineteen pages of statements and depositions in detail; that would be too tedious, though I might be able to make it interesting to the general reader, as it develops the whole history of that portion of our continent that has for one hundred and ninety-seven years been under the exclusive jurisdiction of a monopoly that effectually closed it to all outside influences up to the year A. D. 1834.

According to our British testimony, it was originally £10,500. In 1690, in consequence of the enormous profits upon this small capital, it was increased threefold, making it £31,500. In 1720 it was declared to be £94,500. In this year the stock was (as is termed) *watered.* The then proprietors each subscribed £100, and received £300 of stock, calling the whole nominal stock £378,000, while the actual subscription was but £94,500, and only £3,150 was paid. The stock was ordered to reckon at £103,500, while the actual total amount paid was but £13,650.

In 1821, there was another "watering" of the stock, and a call of £100 per share on the proprietors, which raised their capital to £200,000. The Northwest Fur Company joined the Hudson's Bay Company in this year, and the joint stock was declared to be £400,000.

We are ready to admit, in fact, the testimony in the case goes to prove, that the French Northwest Company brought into the concern an equal amount of capital with that of the Hudson's Bay Company. This would give the present Hudson's Bay Company a real capital of £27,300, a nominal capital of £400,000.

By reference to the memorial of the company, we find they claim, on the 8th of April, 1867, of our government:—

For the right to trade, of which the settlement of the country and removal of Indians to reservations has deprived them, £200,000.

For the right of the free navigation of the Columbia River, £300,000.

For their forts, farms, posts, and establishments, with the buildings and improvements, £285,350, making, in all, £785,350, or $3,822,036.67, or £385,350 more than the whole amount of nominal stock which they claim to have invested in their entire trade.

We will not stop to speak of the morality of this claim; it is made in due form, and this with the claim as set forth in the same document, to wit: For lands, farms, forts, and improvements, £190,000; loss of live stock and other losses, £50,000; total, £240,000—equal to $1,188,000, to be paid in gold. In British money these two sums amount to £1,025,350 sterling, in American dollars to $4,990,036.67; or £625,350 sterling money more than their nominal stock, and £998,050 sterling more than all their real stock invested.

It will be remembered that this demand is simply on account of the settlement of Oregon by the Americans. A part of the posts for which this demand is made are still in their undisputed possession, and a large portion of the claim is set up in consequence of the loss of the profits of the fur trade, of that portion of their business as conducted in territory that originally belonged to the United States, and was actually given up to them by the treaty of December 24, 1814.

The reader will bear in mind, that in the review or discussion of this Hudson's Bay Company's claim on our government, we only refer to that part of their trade, and the rights or privileges they were permitted to enjoy, jointly with Americans, in what is now absolutely American territory. Over two-thirds of their capital has always been employed in territory that the American has not been permitted to enter, much less to trade and form a settlement of any kind.

The witnesses on the part of the Hudson's Bay Company have been forty-one in number. Of this number fifteen are directly interested in the results of the award. Fourteen were brought to the country by, and remained in the service of the company till they left the country; and were all British, though some of them have become naturalized American citizens. Twelve are American citizens, and are supposed to have no particular interest in the results of the case; in fact, their statements are all of a general and very indefinite character. Having come to the country since 1850, they know but little or nothing about the Hudson's Bay Company, its rights, policy, or interests there. Not one of them appears, from the testimony given, to understand the justness of the company's claim, or the injustice there would be in allowing any part of it. Their testimony appears to be given under the impression that because the treaty stipulated that the possessory rights of the company were acknowledged and to be respected, that therefore full payment must be paid the company for the right of trade, and the prospective profits in trade, and the increased value of assessable property for an indefinite period in the future. As, for example, a witness is asked:—

"What is the present value per acre of the company's claims at Cowlitz and Nasqualla, for farming and grazing purposes?"

Ans.—"Supposing both claims to belong to the same person or company, having a clear and undisputed title, and perfectly exempt from molestation in the transaction of business, I think the Cowlitz claim worth to-day thirty dollars an acre, and the Nasqualla claim five dollars an acre, for farming and grazing purposes."

The fifteen interested witnesses all testify to about the same thing, asserting positively as to the real value of the company's supposed rights. One of the chief factors, in answer to the interrogatory, "State the value of the post at Vancouver, as well in 1846 as since, until the year 1863; give the value of the lands and of the buildings separately; and state also what was the value of the post in relation to the other posts, and as a center of trade," said:—

"It being the general depot for the trade of the company west of the Rocky Mountains, in 1846 the establishment at Vancouver, with its out-buildings, was in thorough order, having been lately rebuilt; taking into account this post" (a notorious fact that but two new buildings were about the establishment and in decent repair), "together with the various improvements at the mill, on the mill plain, on the lower plain, and at Sauvies Island, I should estimate its value then to the company at from five to six hundred thousand dollars."

The value of the land used by the company, at Fort Vancouver, in 1846, say containing a frontage of twenty-five miles on the Columbia, by ten miles in depth, in all two hundred and fifty square miles, or about 160,000 acres, I should calculate as being worth then, on an average, from $2.50 to $3 an acre (at $2.50 would give us $400,000); this, with the improvements, say $500,000, gives us, at this witness's lowest estimate, $900,000 for the company's possessory rights.

This witness goes into an argument stating surrounding and probable events, and concludes in these words: "I am clearly of opinion that had the company entire control to deal with it as their own, without any question as to their title, from the year 1846 and up to 1858, when I left there, taking the fort as a center point, the land above and below it, to the extent of three square miles, or 1,920 acres, with frontage on the Columbia River, could have been easily disposed of for $250 per acre ($480,000). The remainder of the land claim of the company at

Vancouver is more or less valuable, according to its locality; thus, I consider the land on the lower plain, having frontage on the river for a distance of five miles, or 3,200 acres, as worth $100 per acre ($320,000). Below that, again, to the Cathlapootl, a distance of probably ten miles, with a depth of two miles, or 12,800 acres, is worth $25 an acre ($320,000). Going above the fort plain, and so on to the commencement of the claim, two miles above the saw-mill on the Columbia River, say a distance of six or seven miles and back three miles, or about 13,500 acres, should be worth from $10 to $15 per acre" ($135,000, at $10, his lowest estimate). "The remainder of the claim is worth from $1.50 to $3 per acre." It being 128,580 acres, at $1.50 per acre, $192,580. This would make for the Vancouver property, as claimed, and several witnesses have sworn the value to amount, as per summary of a chief factor's testimony—

For the fort, buildings, farm and mill improvements....................	$500,000
" 1,920 acres of land about the fort, at $250 per acre....................	400,000
" 3,200 " below the fort, at $100 " "	320,000
" 12,800 " on lower plain, at $25 " "	320,000
" 13,500 " above the saw-mill, at $10 " "	320,000
" 128,580 " balance of claim, at $1.50 " "	192,580

This gives us the sum of $1,947,580 in gold coin, as the value of the possessory rights of the honorable the Hudson's Bay Company to Fort Vancouver and its immediate surroundings.

This chief factor's oath and estimate of the property is sustained by the estimates and oaths of three other chief factors, amounting to about the same sum. This one, after answering in writing, as appears in his cross-examination, twenty sworn questions affirming to the facts and truth of his knowledge of the claims and business of the company, etc., is cross-questioned (Interrogatory 477), by the counsel for the United States, as follows: "Can you not answer the last interrogatory more definitely?" The 476th interrogatory was: "Have you not as much knowledge of what the company claimed in this direction as any other?" The answer to the 477th interrogatory is: "Referring to my answer to the last interrogatory, it will be at once seen that *I have no personal knowledge* as to what land the company actually claimed on that line *or any other*, as regards the land in the neighbor hood of Fort Vancouver. This answer embraces even the present time."

There are several American witnesses introduced to prove this monstrous claim, and to show the reasonableness and justness of their demand. I will give a specimen of an answer given by one of them. After estimating the amount of land in a similar manner to the witness above referred to, calculating the land in four divisions, at $50, $10, and

$1.25 per acre, and 161,000 acres amounting to $789,625, without any estimate upon the buildings or improvements, the following question was put to him: "Have you any knowledge of the market value of land in the vicinity of Vancouver, at any time since 1860?"

Ans.—"I only heard of one sale, which was near the military reserve; I think this was of 100 acres, and I understand brought $100 an acre. I heard of this within the last few months, but nothing was said, that I remember, about the time when the sale was made."

From the intelligence and official position of this American witness, we are forced to the conclusion that the enriching effects of old Hudson's Bay rum must have made him feel both wealthy and peculiarly liberal in estimating the possessory rights of his Hudson's Bay Company friends.

There is one noticeable fact in relation to quite a number of the witnesses called, and that have testified in behalf of the company's claim. It is their ignorance—we may add, total ignorance—of the general business, profits, and policy of the company. This remark will apply to every witness whose deposition has been taken, including their bookkeepers and clerks in London, and their chief factors in Oregon. Dr. McLaughlin seems to have been the only man upon this coast that knew, or that could give an intelligent account of its policy or its proceedings.

The whole Hudson's Bay Company concern appears like a great barrel, bale, or box of goods, put up in London, and marked for a certain district, servants and clerks sent along with the bales, and boxes, and barrels of rum, to gather up all the furs and valuable skins they can find all over the vast country they occupy, then bale up these furs and skins and send them to London, where another set of clerks sell them and distribute the profits on the sale of the furs.

As to the value of the soil, timber, minerals, or any improvements they have ever seen or made in the country, they are as ignorant as the savages of the country they have been trading with. *This ignorance is real or willful.* The oaths of the two witnesses to which I have referred show this fact beyond a doubt, they having been the longest in the service, and attained a high position, and should know the most of its business and policy.

There is one other American witness that has given his testimony in the case of Puget Sound Agricultural Company *v.* United States. He came to this country in 1853. In cross-interrogatory 55, he is asked: "In your opinion, did not the agents of this company afford great protection to the first settlers of this section of country by the exercise of their influence over the different Indian tribes?"

Ans.—"In my opinion, the officers of the company, being *educated gentlemen*, have always exerted whatever influence they might have had with the Indians to protect the whites of all nations in the early settlement of the country."

This opinion is expressed by a gentleman having no knowledge of the policy and proceedings of the company in relation to all American settlers previous to his arrival in the country. He concludes that because he, in his official transactions, having no occasion to ask or receive the company's protection, was treated kindly, all others must have been, as the company's officers were, in his opinion, "educated gentlemen."

In answer to this last official American gentleman and his officious opinion, as expressed on oath in this case, I will quote a statement, under oath, of one of our old *bed-rock* settlers, who came on to the west side of the Rocky Mountains in 1829, twenty-four years previous to the last witness, who pretends to know so much.

Int. 7.—"What influence did the Hudson's Bay Company exercise over the Indians in the section where you operated, with reference to the American trappers and traders? State such facts as occur to you in this connection."

Ans.—"The Hudson's Bay Company exercised a great influence over the western Indians; that is, the Cayuses, Nez Percés, Flatheads, and Spokans, and others through these; they had no influence over the Indians east of the Rocky Mountains at all, and away south they could do almost any thing with the Indians. I know of one party that was robbed by order of one of the Hudson's Bay Company men, the commander of Fort Wallawalla (Wallula); the party was robbed, and the fur brought back to the fort and sold. I was not with the party; that was my understanding about the matter; and that was what the Indians said, and what the whites said that were robbed." (A fact known to the writer.)

Int. 13.—"Was it not generally understood among the American trappers that the Hudson's Bay Company got a very large quantity of Jedediah Smith's furs, for which he and they failed to account to the company to which they belonged?" (Objected to, because it is leading, immaterial, and hearsay.)

Ans.—"It used to be said so among the trappers in the mountains," (and admitted by the company, as no correct account was ever rendered.)

Int. 14.—"If you remember, state the quantity which was thus reported." (Objected to as before.)

Ans.—"It was always reported as about forty packs."

Int. 15.—"Give an estimate of the value of forty packs of beaver at that time."

Ans.—"Forty packs of beaver at that time, in the mountains, was worth about $20,000. I do not know what they would be worth at Vancouver."

Int. 16.—"State whether the dispute about this matter was the cause of the dissolution of the firm of Smith, Jackson & Sublet, to which you refer in your cross-examination." (Objected to as above.)

Ans.—"I do not know; that was the report among mountain men."

With these specimens of testimony on both sides, I will venture a general statement drawn from the whole facts developed.

About the time, or perhaps one year before, the notice that the joint occupancy of the country west of the Rocky Mountains was given by the American government to that of the British, the Hudson's Bay Company, as such, had made extensive preparations and arrangements to hold the country west of the Rocky Mountains. This arrangement embraced a full and complete organization of the Indian tribes under the various traders and factors at the various forts in the country.

The probability of a Mexican war with the United States, and such influences as could be brought to bear upon commissioners, or the treaty-making power of the American government, would enable them to secure this object. In this they failed. The Mexican war was successfully and honorably closed. The Hudson's Bay Company's claims are respected, or at least mentioned as in existence, in the treaty of 1846, that the 49th parallel should be the boundary *of the two national dominions.*

On the strength of their supposed possessory right, they remain quietly in their old forts and French pig-pens, take a full inventory of their old Indian salmon-houses, and watch the progress of American improvement upon this coast, till 1863, when the American people are in the midst of a death struggle for its civil existence. They then for the third time "water" this monstrosity under the name of "'The International Financial Society, limited,' are prepared to receive subscriptions for the issue at par of capital stock in the Hudson's Bay Company, incorporated by royal charter, 1670," fixing the nominal stock of the Hudson's Bay Company at £2,000,000; and taking from this amount £1,930,000, they offer it for sale under this new title in shares of £20 each, claiming as belonging to them [*i. e.*, the Hudson's Bay Company] 1,400,000 square miles, or upward of 896,000,000 acres of land, and, after paying all expenses, an income of £81,000 in ten years, up to the 31st of May—over four per cent. on the £2,000,000." This vast humbug is held up for the English public to invest in,—a colonization scheme to enrich the favored shareholders of that old English aristocratic humbug chartered by Charles II. in 1670.

In the whole history of that company there has never been any investigation of its internal policy so thorough as in the present proceedings. In fact, this is the first time they have ventured to allow a legal investigation into their system of trade and their rights of property. They have grown to such enormous proportions, and controlled so vast a country, that the government and treasury of the United States has become, in their estimation, a mere appendage to facilitate their Indian trade and financial speculations. From our recent purchases of Russian territory, it becomes an important question to every American citizen, and especially our statesmen, to make himself familiar with so vast an influence under the British flag, and extending along so great an extent of our northern frontier. Should they establish, by their own interested and ignorant testimony, their present claims, there will be no end to their unreasonable demands, for they have dotted the whole continent with their trading-posts. They claim all that is supposed to be of any value to savage and civilized man. The English nation without its Hudson's Bay Company's old traps and hunting-parties would have no claim west of the Rocky Mountains, yet, for the sake of these, it has almost ventured a third war with our American people in sending from its shores, instead of land pirates, under the bars and stars, the red flag of the Hudson's Bay Company. The two flags should be folded together and laid up in the British Museum, as a lasting monument of British injustice.

I apprehend, from a careful review of all this testimony of the forty-one witnesses who were on the part of the Hudson's Bay Company, and the forty-two on the part of the United States, that the whole policy of the company has been thoroughly developed; yet, at the same time, without a long personal acquaintance with their manner of doing business, it would be difficult to comprehend the full import of the testimony given, though I apprehend the commissioners will have no very difficult task to understand the humbuggery of the whole claim, as developed by the testimony of the clerks in London and the investigation at head-quarters. As to the amount of award, I would not risk one dollar to obtain a share in all they get from our government. On the contrary, a claim should be made against them for damages and trespass upon the American citizens, as also the lives of such as they have caused to be murdered by their influence over the Indians.

The telegraph has informed us that the commissioners have awarded to the Hudson's Bay Company, $450,000, and to the Puget Sound concern, $200,000. We have no change to make in our opinion of the commissioners previously expressed, as they must have known, from the testimony developed in the Puget Sound concern, that that part of the claim was a fictitious one, and instituted to distract the public and divide the pretensions to so large an amount in two parts. That the commissioners should allow it can only be understood upon the principle that the Hudson's Bay Company were entitled to that amount as an item of costs in prosecuting their case.

No man at all familiar with the history of this coast, and of the Hudson's Bay Company, can conscientiously approve of that award. Our forefathers, in 1776, said "millions for defense, but not one cent for tribute," which we consider this award to be,—for the benefit of English duplicity and double-dealing, in the false representations they made at the making of the treaty, and the perjury of their witnesses.

CHAPTER XI.

Quotation from Mr. Swan.—His mistake.—General Gibbs' mistake.—Kamaiyahkan.—Indian agent killed.—I. I. Stevens misjudged.

THE gigantic fraud of slavery fell, in our own land, in the short space of four years; but that of this company—holding and destroying as many lives as the African slave trade—holds its own, and still lifts its head, under the patronage of a professed Christian nation; and claims to be an honorable company, while it robs and starves its unnumbered benighted Indians, and shuts up half of North America from civilization. At the same time it has obtained $650,000 for partially withdrawing its continued robberies of the American Indians within the United States, after implanting in the savage mind an implacable hatred against the American people.

While we have our own personal knowledge on this point, we will give a quotation from Mr. Swan's work, written in 1852, page 381, showing his views of the subject, which are mostly correct; but, in speaking of the trade of the Americans and of the Hudson's Bay Company, he says: "The Indians preferred to trade with the Americans, for they kept one article in great demand, which the Hudson's Bay people did not sell, and that was whisky."

In this Mr. Swan is entirely mistaken. The Hudson's Bay people always had liquor, and let the Indians have all they could pay for, as proved by their own writer, Mr. Dunn. (See 12th chapter.) Mr. S. continues: "Reckless, worthless men, who are always to be found in new settlements, would give or sell whisky to the Indians, and then, when drunk, abuse them. If the injury was of a serious nature, the Indian was sure to have revenge; and should he kill a white man, would be certainly hanged, if caught; but, although the same law operated on the whites, I have never known an instance where a white man has been hanged for killing an Indian." This has been my experience, Mr. Swan, for more than thirty years, with the Hudson's Bay Company, or English. When a white man kills an Indian, the tribe, or his friends, are satisfied with a present, instead of the life of the murderer. It has been invariably the practice with the Hudson's Bay Company to pay, when any of their people kill an Indian, and to kill the Indian murderer; not so when an American is killed. Says

Mr. Swan: "The ill-feelings thus engendered against the Americans, by this, and other causes, was continually *fanned and kept alive by these half-breeds and old servants of the company*, whose feelings were irritated by what they considered an unwarrantable assumption on the part of these settlers, in coming across the mountains to squat upon lands they considered theirs by right of prior occupancy. *The officers of the company* also sympathized with their old servants in this respect, and a *deadly feeling of hatred has existed* between these officers and the American emigrant, for their course in taking possession of the lands claimed by the Puget Sound Agricultural Company, and other places on the Sound and the Columbia River; and there is not a man among them who would not be glad to have had every American emigrant driven out of the country." It is unnecessary to add examples of this kind to prove to any reasonable mind the continued hostility of that company, and all under its influence, to the American government and people.

Can their friendship be bought by paying them the entire sum they claim? We think not.

Whatever sum is given will go to enrich the shareholders, who will rejoice over their success, as an Indian would over the scalp of his enemy. The *implacable hatred will remain*, and nothing but extermination, or a complete absorption of the whole continent into the American republic, will close up the difficulty, and save a remnant of the Indian tribes. This, to some, may not be desirable; but humanity and right should, and will, eventually, prevail over crime, or any foreign policy.

The American people are taunted by the Roman Jesuits and English with having driven the Indian from his lands, and having occupied it themselves; but how is it with the English? While the American has attempted to gather the Indians into convenient communities, and spent millions of dollars to civilize and better their condition, the English nation, as such, has never given one dollar, but has chartered company after company of merchants, traders, and explorers, who have entered the Indian country under their exclusive charters, or license to trade, and shut it up from all others. They have, in the profitable prosecution of their trade, so managed as to exterminate all surplus and useless Indians, and reduce them to easy and profitable control. Should one of their half-breed servants, or a white man, attempt to expose their system, or speak of their iniquitous policy, a great hue and cry is raised against him, both in England and America, and he must fall, either by a misinformed public or by savage hands, while they triumphantly refer to the ease with which they exercise absolute control over the Indians in their jurisdiction, as a reason why they should be permitted to continue their exclusive occupation and government of the country. Thus, for being forced partially to leave that portion of Oregon south of the 49th parallel, they presumed to make a claim against our government three times larger than the whole capital stock of the two companies combined.

This hue and cry, and the public sentiment they have continued to raise and control, has its double object. The one is to continue their exclusive possession of, and trade in the country, the other is to obtain all the money they can from the American government for the little part of it they have professedly given up.

It will be remembered that in the investigation of their claims, and the depositions given, it was stated that Forts Okanagon, Colville, Kootanie, and Flathead, were still in their possession in 1866; that Wallawalla, Fort Håll, and Boise were given up because they were prohibited by the government from trading ammunition and guns to the Indians. This means simply that the last-named posts were too far from their own territory to enable them to trade in these prohibited articles, and escape detection by the American authorities. The northern posts, or those contiguous to the 49th parallel, are still occupied by them. From these posts they supply the Indians, and send their emissaries into the American territory, and keep up the "*deadly hatred*," of which Mr. Swan speaks, and about which General Gibbs, in his letter explaining the causes of the Indian war, is so much mistaken.

There is one fact stated by General Gibbs, showing the continued combination of the Roman priests with the Hudson's Bay Company, which we will give in this connection. He says: "The Yankamas have always been opposed to the intrusion of the Americans." This is also a mistake of Mr. Gibbs, as we visited that tribe in the fall of 1839, and found them friendly, and anxious to have an American missionary among them. At that time there had been no priest among them, and no combined effort of the company to get rid of the American missionary settlements. Kamaiyahkan, the very chief mentioned by General Gibbs as being at the head of the combination against the Americans, accompanied us to Dr. Whitman's station, to urge the establishment of an American mission among his people.

General Gibbs says, that, "as early as 1853, Kamaiyahkan had projected a war of extermination. Father Pandosa, the priest at Atahnam (Yankama) mission, in the spring of that year, wrote to Father Mesplie, the one at the Dalls, desiring him to inform Major Alvord, in command at that post, of the fact. Major Alvord reported it to General Hitchcock, then in command on this coast. Hitchcock *cen-*

sured him as an *alarmist*, and Pandosa was *censured* by his superiors, who forthwith placed a priest of higher rank over him."

The next year, Indian agent Bolon was killed, and the war commenced. How did General Hitchcock learn that Pandosa, a simple-hearted priest, and Major Alvord were alarmists? The fact of the censure, and placing a priest of higher rank over Pandosa at the Yankama station (the very place we selected in 1839 for an American station), is conclusive evidence on this point.

"The war of extermination," that General Gibbs, in his mistaken ideas of Hudson's Bay policy and Indian character, attributes to the policy of Governor I. I. Stevens, was commenced in 1845. At that time, it was supposed by James Douglas, Mr. Ogden, and the ruling spirits of that company, that all they had to do was to withhold munitions of war from the Americans, and the Indians would do the balance for them.

The Indian wars that followed, and that are kept up and encouraged along our borders, and all over this coast, are the legitimate fruits of the "DEADLY HATRED" implanted in the mind and soul of the Indian BY THE HUDSON'S BAY COMPANY AND THEIR ALLIES, THE PRIESTS. There is an object in this: while they teach the Indians to believe that the Americans are robbing them of their lands and country, they at the same time pretend that they do not want it.

Like Bishop Blanchet with the Cayuses, they "only want a small piece of land to raise a little provisions from," and they are continually bringing such goods as the Indians want; and whenever they are ready to join their forces and send their war-parties into American territory, this company of *honorable English fur traders* are always ready to supply them with arms and ammunition, and to purchase from them the goods or cattle (including scalps, in case of war between the two nations) they may capture on such expeditions.

The more our government pays to that company, or their fictitious agent, the more means they will have to carry on their opposition to American commerce and enterprise on this coast. Should they obtain but one-third of their outrageous claim, it is contemplated to invest it, with their original stock, in a new company, under the same name, Honorable Hudson's Bay Company, and to extend their operations so as to embrace not only the fur, but gold and grain trade, over this whole western coast.

Will it be for the interests of this country to encourage them? Let their conduct and proceeding while they had the absolute control of it answer, and prove a timely warning to the country before such vampires are allowed to fasten themselves upon it.

CHAPTER XII.

Review of Mr. Greenhow's work in connection with the conduct and policy of the Hudson's Bay Company.—Schools and missionaries.—Reasons for giving extracts from Mr. Greenhow's work.—Present necessity for more knowledge about the company.

As stated by General Gibbs, Mr. Greenhow has given us a complete history of the discovery of Oregon. At the point where he leaves us the reader will observe our present history commences. We did not read Mr. Greenhow's very elaborate and interesting history till ours had been completed in manuscript. On reading it, we found abundant proof of statements we have made respecting the policy of the British government to hold, by the influence of her Hudson's Bay Company, the entire country west of the Rocky Mountains that was not fully occupied by the Russian and Spanish governments.

This fact alone makes our history the more important and interesting to the American reader. Mr. Greenhow, upon pages 360 and 361 of his work, closes the labors of the eleven different American fur companies with the name of Captain Nathaniel Wyeth, and upon these two pages introduces the American missionaries, with the Roman Jesuits, though the latter did not arrive in the country till four years after the former.

On his 388th page, after speaking of various transactions relative to California, the Sandwich Islands, and the proceedings in Congress relative to the Oregon country, he says: "In the mean time, the Hudson's Bay Company had been doing all in its power to extend and confirm its position in the countries west of the Rocky Mountains, from which its governors felicitated themselves with the idea that they had expelled the Americans entirely."

Page 389. "The object of the company was, therefore, to place a large number of British subjects in Oregon within the shortest time, and, of course, to exclude from it as much as possible all people of the United States; so that when the period for terminating the convention with the latter power should arrive, Great Britain might be able to present the strongest title to the possession of the whole, on the ground of actual occupation by the Hudson's Bay Company. To these ends the efforts of that company had been for some time directed. The immigration of British subjects was encouraged; the Americans were by all means excluded; *and the Indians were brought as much as possible into friendship with, and subject to, the company, while they were taught to regard the people of the United States as enemies!*"

In a work entitled "Four Years in British Columbia," by Commander R. C. Mayne, R. N., F. R. G. S., page 279, this British writer says: "I have also spoken of the intense hatred of them all for the Boston men (Americans). This hatred, although nursed chiefly by the cruelty with which they are treated by them, is also owing in a great measure to the system adopted by the Americans of removing them away from their villages when their sites become settled by whites. The Indians often express dread lest we should adopt the same course, and have lately petitioned Governor Douglas on the subject."

Commander Mayne informs us, on his 193d page, that in the performance of his official duties among the Indians, "recourse to very strong expressions was found necessary; and they were threatened with the undying wrath of Mr. Douglas, whose name always acts as a talisman with them."

We shall have occasion to quote statements from members of the Hudson's Bay Company, and from Jesuit priests, further confirming the truth of Mr. Greenhow's statement as above quoted. It would be gratifying to us to be able, from our long personal experience and observations relative to the policy and conduct of the Hudson's Bay Company, to fully confirm the very plausible, and, if true, honorable treatment of the aborigines of these countries; but truth, candor, observation, our own and other personal knowledge, compel us to believe and know that Mr. Greenhow is entirely mistaken when he says, on his 389th page, speaking of the Hudson's Bay Company:—

"In the treatment of the aborigines of these countries, the Hudson's Bay Company *admirably combined and reconciled humanity with policy.* In the first place, its agents were strictly prohibited from furnishing them with ardent spirits; and there is reason to believe that the prohibition has been carefully enforced.

"Sunday, March 11, 1852," says Mr. Dunn, one of their own servants, "Indians remained in their huts, perhaps praying, or more likely singing over the *rum* they had traded with us on Saturday. * * Tuesday, April 26.—Great many Indians on board. * * Traded a number of skins. They seem to like *rum* very much. * * May 4.—They were all *drunk;* went on shore, made a fire about 11 o'clock; being then all drunk began firing on one another. * * June 30.—The Indians are bringing their blankets—their skins are all gone; they seem very fond of *rum.* * * July 11.—They traded a quantity of *rum* from us."

The Kingston *Chronicle*, a newspaper, on the 27th of September, 1848, says: "The Hudson's Bay Company have, in some instances *with their rum*, traded the goods given in presents to the Indians by the Canadian government, and afterward so traded the same with them at an advance of little short of a thousand per cent."

Question asked by the Parliamentary Committee: "Are intoxicating liquors supplied in any part of the country—and where?" The five witnesses answered:—

1st. "At every place where he was."

2d. "All but the Mandan Indians were desirous to obtain intoxicating liquor; *and the company supply them with it freely.*"

3d. "At Jack River I saw liquor given for furs."

4th. "At York Factory and Oxford House."

5th. The fifth witness had seen liquor given "at Norway House only."

The writer has seen liquor given and sold to the Indians at every post of the company, from the mouth of the Columbia to Fort Hall, including Fort Colville, and by the traveling traders of the company; so that whatever pretensions the company make to the contrary, the proof is conclusive, that they traffic in liquors, without any restraint or hinderance, all over the Indian countries they occupy. That they charge this liquor traffic to renegade Americans I am fully aware; at the same time I know they have supplied it to Indians, when there were no Americans in the country that had any to sell or give.

In the narrative of the Rev. Mr. King, it is stated that "the agents of the Hudson's Bay Company are not satisfied with putting so insignificant value upon the furs, that the more active hunters only can gain a support, which necessarily leads to the death of the more aged and infirm by starvation and cannibalism, but they encourage the intemperate use of ardent spirits."

Says Mr. Alexander Simpson, one of the company's own chief traders: "That body has assumed much credit for the discontinuance of the sale of spirituous liquors at its trading establishments, but I apprehend that in this matter it has both claimed and received more praise than is its due. The issue of spirits has not been discontinued by it on principle, indeed it has not been discontinued at all when there is a possibility of diminution of trade through the Indians having the power to resent this deprivation of their accustomed and much-loved annual jollification, by carrying their furs to another market."

This means simply that Mr. Greenhow and all other admirers of the Hudson's Bay Company's manner of treating Indians have been humbugged by their professions of "*humanity and policy.*"

We are inclined to return Mr. Greenhow's compliment to the Rev. Samuel Parker in his own language, as found on the 361st page of his work. He says: "Mr. Samuel Parker, whose journal of his tour beyond the Rocky Mountains, though highly interesting and instructive, would have been much more so had he confined himself to the results of his own experience, and not wandered into the region of history, diplomacy, and cosmogony, in all of which he is evidently a stranger." So with Mr. Greenhow, when he attempts to reconcile the conduct of the Hudson's Bay Company with "*humanity*," and admires their policy, and gives them credit for honorable treatment of "Indians, missionaries, and settlers," he leaves his legitimate subject of history and diplomacy, and goes into the subject of the Hudson's Bay Company's moral *policy*, to which he appears quite as much a "stranger" as Mr. Samuel Parker does to those subjects in which Mr. Greenhow found him deficient.

But, notwithstanding we are inclined to return Mr. Greenhow's compliment in his own language, his historical researches and facts are invaluable, as developing a deep scheme of a foreign national grasping disposition, to hold, by a low, mean, underhanded, and, as Mr. Greenhow says, "false and malicious course of misrepresentation, the country west of the Rocky Mountains." There are a few pages in Mr. Greenhow's history that,—as ours is now fully written, and we see no reason to change a statement we have made,—for the information of our readers, and to correct what we conceive to be an erroneous impression of his relative to our early settlements upon this coast, we will quote, and request our readers to observe our corrections in the history or narration of events we have given them.

"Schools for the instruction of their children, and hospitals for their sick, were established at all their principal trading-posts; each of which, moreover, afforded the means of employment and support to Indians disposed to work in the intervals between the hunting seasons."

Says the Rev. Mr. Barnley, a Wesleyan missionary at Moose Factory, whose labors commenced in June, 1840, and continued till September, 1847: "A plan which I had devised for educating and turning to some acquaintance with agriculture, native children, was disallowed, * * * it being very distinctly stated by Sir George Simpson, that the company would not give them even a spade toward commencing their new mode of life."

Says Mr. Greenhow: "*Missionaries of various sects were encouraged to undertake to convert these people to Christianity, and to induce them to adopt the usages of civilized life*, so far as might be consistent with the nature of the labors in which they are engaged; care being at the same time taken to instill into their minds due respect for the company, and for the sovereign of Great Britain; and attempts were made, at great expense, though with little success, to collect them into villages, or tracts where the soil and climate are favorable to agriculture."

Mr. Barnley says: "At Moose Factory, where the resources were most ample, and where was the seat of authority in the southern department of Rupert's Land, the *hostility* of the company (and not merely their inability to aid me, whether with convenience or inconvenience to themselves) was most manifest."

Another of the English missionaries writes in this manner: "When at York Factory last fall (1848), a young gentleman boasted that he had succeeded in starting the Christian Indians of Rossville off with the boats on a Sunday. Thus every effort we make for their moral and spiritual improvement is frustrated, and those who were, and still are, desirous of becoming Christians, are kept away; the pagan Indians desiring to become Christians, but being made drunk on their arrival at the fort, 'their good desires vanish.' The Indians professing Christianity had actually exchanged one keg of rum for tea and sugar, at one post, but the successive offers of liquor betrayed them into intoxication at another."

The Rev. Mr. Beaver, chaplain of the company at Fort Vancouver, in 1836, writes thus to the Aborigines Protection Society, London, tract 8, page 19:—

"For a time I reported to the governor and committee of the company in England, and to the governor and the council of the company abroad, the result of my observations, with a view to a gradual amelioration of the wretched degradation with which I was surrounded, by an immediate attempt at the introduction of civilization and Christianity, among one or more of the aboriginal tribes; but my earnest representations were neither attended to nor acted upon; no means were placed at my disposal for carrying out the plan which I suggested."

Mr. Greenhow says, page 389: "Particular care was also extended to the education of the half-breed children, the offspring of the marriage or the concubinage of the traders with the Indian women, who were retained and bred as much as possible among the white people, and were taken into the service of the company, whenever they were found capable. There being few white women in those countries, it is evident that these half-breeds must, in time, form a large, if not an important portion of the inhabitants; and there is nothing to prevent their being adopted and recognized as British subjects.

"The conduct of the Hudson's Bay Company, in these respects, is worthy of *commendation;* and may be contrasted most favorably with that pursued at the present day by civilized people toward the aborigines of all other new countries."

It is a most singular fact, that while Mr. Greenhow was writing the above high commendation of the conduct and policy of the Hudson's Bay Company, in relation to their treatment of Indians and missionaries under their absolute control, that that company were driving from their posts at Moose Factory and Vancouver, their own Wesleyan and Episcopal missionaries, and doing all they could to prevent the settlement or civilization of the Indians, or allowing any missionary intercourse with them, except by foreign Roman Jesuits, and were actually combining the Indians in Oregon to destroy and defeat civil and Christian efforts among the Indians and American settlements then being established in the country. Page 390, Mr. Greenhow further says: "The course pursued by the Hudson's Bay Company, with regard to American citizens in the territory west of the Rocky Mountains, was equally *unexceptionable* and *politic.* The missionaries and immigrants from the United States, or from whatever country they might come, were received at the establishments of the company with the utmost kindness, and were aided in the prosecution of their respective objects, *so far and so long as those objects were not commercial;* but no sooner did any person, unconnected with the company, attempt to hunt, or trap, or trade with the Indians, than all the force of the body was turned against him."

The statement in the last part of the foregoing paragraph can be attested by more than one hundred American hunters and traders, who have felt the full force of that company's influence against them; as also by missionaries and settlers on first arriving in the country. But Mr. Greenhow says: "There is no evidence or reason to believe that violent measures were ever employed, either directly or indirectly, for this purpose; nor would such means have been needed while the company enjoyed advantages over all competitors, such as are afforded by its wealth, its organization, and the skill and knowledge of the country, and of the natives, possessed by its agents." This is simply an assertion of Mr. Greenhow, which our future pages will correct in the mind of any who have received it as truth. It is unnecessary to pursue Mr. Greenhow's history of the Hudson's Bay Company respecting their treatment of American or English missionaries or American settlers; the statements we have quoted show fully his want of a correct knowledge of the practices of that company in dealing with savage and civilized men. We only claim for ourselves close observation and deeply interested participation in all that relates to Oregon since 1832, having been permitted to be present at the forming of its early civil settlement and political history. This work of Mr. Greenhow's appears to be peculiarly political as well as strongly national, and in the passages we have quoted, with many other similar ones, he seems to us to have written to catch the patronage of this foreign English corporation, which, according to his own showing, has been an incubus upon the English, and, so far as possible, the Americans also. While he shows his utter ignorance of their internal policy and history, his researches in the history of the early discoveries on this western coast are ample and most useful as vindicating our American claim to the country. But as to its settlement and civilization, or its early moral or political history, as he says of Mr. Samuel Parker, "in all of which he is evidently a stranger."

Our reasons for giving the extracts from Mr. Greenhow's work are—

1st. That the reader may the better understand what follows as our own.

2d. To avoid a future collision or controversy respecting statements that may be quoted from him to contradict or controvert our own, respecting the policy and practices of the Hudson's Bay Company, which, Mr. Greenhow says, page 391, "did no more than they were entitled to do. If the Americans neglected or were unable to avail themselves of the benefits secured to both nations by the convention, the fault or the misfortune was their own, and they had no right to complain." If this is true, as against the American, what right has the Hudson's Bay Company to complain and ask pay for what had been rendered worthless to them by the American settlement of the country?

"The hospitable treatment extended to them [American citizens] by the agents of the Hudson's Bay Company was doubtless approved by the directors of that body; and all who know Messrs. McLaughlin and Douglas, the principal managers of the affairs of that body on the Columbia, unite in testifying that the humanity and generosity of those gentlemen have been always carried as far as their duties would permit. That their conduct does not, however, meet with universal approbation among the servants of the company in that quarter, sufficient evidence may be cited to prove." He quotes John Dunn's book, chap. 12.

Mr. Greenhow wrote his history with the light then existing, *i. e.*, in 1844. About that time Dr. McLaughlin was called to an account by the directors of the Hudson's Bay Company, in London. He explained to them his position, and the condition of the Americans, who came to this country both naked and hungry, and that, as a man of common humanity, he could do no less than he did. The directors insisted upon the enforcement of their stringent rule, which was, to starve and drive every American from the country. He then told them: "*If such is your order, gentlemen, I will serve you no longer.*" As to Mr. Douglas, we have no such noble sentiment to record in his behalf; he belonged to that English party called by Mr. Greenhow "*Patriots.*" He says: "There were two parties among the British in Oregon, the *Patriots* and the *Liberals*, who, while they agreed in holding all Americans in utter detestation, as *knaves* and *ruffians*, yet differed as to the propriety of the course pursued with regard to them by the company. The *Patriots* maintained, that kindness showed to the people of the United States was thrown away, and would be badly requited; that it was merely nurturing a race of men, who would soon rise from their weak and humble position, as grateful acknowledgers of favors, to the bold attitude of questioners of the authority of Great Britain, and her right, even to Vancouver itself; that if any attempts were made for the conversion of the natives to Christianity, and to the adoption of more humanized institutions (which they limited to British institutions), a solid and permanent foundation should be laid; and for that purpose, if missionaries were to be introduced, they should come within the direct control of the dominant power, that is, the British power, and should be the countrymen of those who actually occupied Oregon, etc. The *Liberals*, while admitting all that was said on the other side, of the character of the Americans, nevertheless charitably opined that those people should not be excluded, as they possessed some claim, 'feeble, but yet existing,' to the country, and until 'these were quashed or confirmed, it would be unjust and impolite' to prevent them from all possession; *that these missionaries, though bad*, were better than none; and that good would grow out of evil in the end, for the Americans, by their intercourse with the British, *would become more humanized, tolerant, and honest.*"

As most of the above sentiment relative to the two English parties in the country appears to be quoted by Mr. Greenhow from some author, it would be interesting to know who he is; still, the fact is all that is essential to know, and we have reason to believe and know that the sentiments expressed were entertained by the controlling authority of the company in London and in Oregon; and that Messrs. Douglas and Ogden, and the Roman priests under their patronage, acted fully up to them as Roman and British Jesuits, there is no question; and under such circumstances, it is not surprising that the immigration from the United States in 1843, '44, and '45, should increase that feeling of hostility and hatred of the American settlement and civilization in the country.

We do not propose at present to speak of the action of the American Congress relative to Oregon, but, as will be seen, to connect and bring into our own history such allusions of Mr. Greenhow as serve to illustrate and prove the several propositions we have stated respecting the early history of its settlement, and also to prepare the reader to understand in a manner the combined influences that were ready to contest any claim or effort any American company or citizen might make for the future occupation of the country.

It will be seen that no company of settlers or traders could have succeeded, having arrived in advance of the American missionaries. They were unquestionably the only nucleus around which a permanent settlement could have been formed, eleven different American fur companies having commenced and failed, as will be shown; and although Mr. Greenhow seems to regard and treat the American missionary effort with contempt, yet impartial history will place them in the foreground, and award to them an honorable place in counteracting foreign influences and saving the country to its rightful owners.

It will be seen by the preliminary and following remarks and narrative of events, and by a careful study of all the histories and journals to which we have had occasion to refer, or from which we have quoted a statement, that the forming, civilizing, and political period in our Oregon history is all a blank, except that the Hudson's Bay Company were the patron saints, the noble and generous preservers of the "*knaves*" and "*ruffians*" that came to this country to rob them of their pious and humane labors to civilize their accomplished native "concubines." That, according to their ideas, the missionaries, such as came from the United States, "*though bad*," could become "*humanized*, *tolerant*," and even "*honest*," by associating with such noble, generous, tolerant, virtuous, and pure-minded traders as controlled the affairs of that company, under the faithfully-executed and stringent rules of the honorable directors in London.

At the present time there is an additional important reason for a better understanding and a more thorough knowledge of the influences and operations of this British monopoly than formerly. Notwithstanding they have been driven from Oregon by its American settlement, they have retired to British Columbia, and, like barnacles upon a ship's bottom, have fastened themselves all along the Russian and American territories, to repeat just what they did in Oregon; and, with the savage hordes with whom they have always freely mingled, they will repeat their depredations upon our American settlements, and defeat every effort to civilize or Christianize the natives over whom they have any influence.

Six generations of natives have passed away under their system of trade and civilization. The French, English, and Indians before our American revolution and independence could not harmonize. The French were driven from their American possessions and control over the Indians, and peace followed. The Indians, English, and Americans can not harmonize; they never have, and they never will; hence, it becomes a question of vast moment, not only to the Indian race, but to the American people, as to the propriety and expediency of allowing the English nation or British or foreign subjects to further exercise any influence among our American Indians.

Mr. A. H. Jackson estimates the expense of our Indian wars, since 1831 to the present time, at one thousand millions of dollars and thirty-seven thousand lives of our citizens, not counting the lives of Indians destroyed by our American wars with them. If the reader will carefully read and candidly judge of the historical facts presented in the following pages, we have no fears but they will join us in our conclusions, that the Monroe doctrine is irrevocably and of necessity fixed in our American existence as a nation at peace with all, which we can not have so long as any foreign sectarian or political organizations are permitted to have a controlling influence over savage minds. A Frenchman, an Englishman, a Mormon, a Roman priest, any one, or all of them, fraternizing as they do with the Indian, can work upon his prejudices and superstitions and involve our country in an Indian war —which secures the Indian trade to the British fur company. This is the great object sought to be accomplished in nearly all the wars our government has had with them.

One other remarkable fact is noted in all our Indian wars, the American or Protestant missionaries have been invariably driven from among those tribes, while the Roman Jesuit missionaries have been protected and continued among the Indians, aiding and counseling them in the continuance of those wars. It is no new thing that ignorance, superstition, and sectarian hate has produced such results upon the savage mind, and our Oregon history shows that a shrewd British fur company can duly appreciate and make use of just such influences to promote and perpetuate their trade on the American continent.

CHAPTER XIII.

Occupants of the country.—Danger to outsiders.—Description of missionaries.

In 1832, this entire country, from the Russian settlement on the north to the gulf of California on the south, the Rocky Mountains on the east to the Pacific Ocean on the west, was under the absolute and undisputed control of the Honorable Hudson's Bay Company; and the said company claimed and exercised exclusive civil, religious, political, and commercial jurisdiction over all this vast country, leaving a narrow strip of neutral territory between the United States and their assumed possessions, lying between the Rocky Mountains and the western borders of Missouri. Its inhabitants were gentlemen of the Hudson's Bay Company,—their clerks, traders, and servants,—consisting mostly of Canadian-French, half-breeds, and natives.

Occasionally, when a venturesome Yankee ship or fur trader entered any of the ports of the aforesaid country for trade, exploration, or settlement, this honorable company asserted its licensed and exclusive right to drive said vessel, trader, explorer, or settler from it. Should he be so bold as to venture to pass the trained bands of the wild savages of the mountains, or, even by accident, reach the sacred trading-ground of this company, he was helped to a passage out of it, or allowed to perish by the hand of any savage who saw fit to punish him for his temerity.

While this exclusive jurisdiction was claimed and exercised by the company, four wild, untutored Indians of the Flathead tribe learned from an American trapper, who had strayed into their country, that there was a Supreme Being, worthy of worship, and that, by going to his country, they could learn all about him. Four of these sons of the wilderness found their way to St. Louis, Missouri, in 1832. Mr. Catlin, a celebrated naturalist and artist, I believe not a member of any religious sect, learned the object that had brought these red men from the mountains of Oregon, and gave the fact to the religious public.

This little incident, though small in itself, resulted in the organization, in 1833, of the Missionary Board of the Methodist Episcopal Church, the appointment of Rev. Jason Lee and associates, to the establishment of the Methodist Mission in the Wallamet Valley in 1834, the appointment of Rev. Samuel Parker and Dr. Marcus Whitman, by the American Board of Commissioners for Foreign Missions, to explore the country in 1835, and the establishment of a mission by said Board in 1836.

Rev. Jason Lee, of Stansted, Canada East, a man of light hair, blue eyes, fair complexion, spare habit, above ordinary height, a little stoop-shouldered, with strong nerve and indomitable will, yet a meek, warm-hearted, and humble Christian, gaining by his affable and easy manners the esteem of all who became acquainted with him, was the first to volunteer.

Rev. Daniel Lee, a nephew of Jason, was the second;—the opposite of the former in every particular—of medium height. The general impression of outsiders was, that his moral qualities were not of the highest order, yet it is not known that any specific charges were ever brought against him.

Cyrus Shepard, a lay member, was a devoted Christian, and a faithful laborer for the advancement of the objects of the mission and the general welfare of all in the country. We have never learned that he had an enemy or a slanderer while he lived in it. On his first arrival he taught the Hudson's Bay Company's school at Vancouver, consisting of children belonging to persons in the employ of the company, till the mission buildings were ready, when he gathered a large school of Indian and French half-breed children, and was quite successful in teaching the rudiments of an English education. Rev. D. Lee and Mr. Shepard were from New England.

Mr. P. L. Edwards, of Missouri, also a lay member, was of the company. But little is known of him; the inducements to become a permanent settler in the country do not appear in his case.

Rev. Samuel Parker, of Ithaca, New York, a man of good education and refinement, and exceedingly set in his opinions and conclusions of men and things, came to explore the country, and report to the American Board as to the feasibility of establishing missions among the Indians, one of the missionaries of the American Board, from the Sandwich Islands, having visited the coast in an American ship, several years previous, and made an unfavorable report on account of the fur-trade influence against American traders, giving the impression that American missionaries would not be tolerated in the country.

Mr. Parker was inclined to self-applause, requiring his full share of ministerial approbation or respect, though not fully qualified to draw it cheerfully from an audience or his listeners; was rather fastidious.

Dr. Marcus Whitman, of Rushville, New York, sent in company with Mr. Parker to explore the country. A man of easy, *don't-care* habits, that could become all things to all men, and yet a sincere and earnest man, speaking his mind before he thought the second time, giving his views on all subjects without much consideration, correcting and changing them when good reasons were presented, yet, when fixed in the pursuit of an object, adhering to it with unflinching tenacity. A stranger would consider him fickle and stubborn, yet he was sincere and kind, and generous to a fault, devoting every energy of his mind and body to the welfare of the Indians, and objects of the mission; seldom manifesting fears of any danger that might surround him, at times he would become animated and earnest in his argument or conversation. In his profession he was a bold practitioner, and generally successful. He was above medium height; of spare habit; peculiar hair, a portion of each being white and a dark brown, so that it might be called iron-gray; deep blue eyes, and large mouth.

The peculiarities of Messrs. Parker and Whitman were such, that, when they had reached the rendezvous on Green River, in the Rocky Mountains, they agreed to separate; not because Dr. Whitman was not willing and anxious to continue the exploring expedition, in company with Mr. Parker, but because Mr. P. could not "put up" with the offhand, careless, and, as he thought, slovenly manner in which Dr. Whitman was inclined to travel. Dr. W. was a man that could accommodate himself to circumstances; such as dipping the water from the running stream with his hand, to drink; having but a hunter's knife (without a fork) to cut and eat his food; in short, could *rough it* without qualms of stomach.

Rev. Mr. Parker had left a refined family circle, and his habits had become somewhat delicate from age and long usage in comfortable and agreeable society; hence his peculiar habits were not adapted to Rocky Mountain travel in those early days. Still, the great object on which they were sent must not be lost sight of. Their sense of moral obligation was such, that a reason must be given why Dr. Whitman returns to the States, and Mr. Parker proceeds alone on his perilous journey to this then unknown country. Here again the wild Indian comes in, by instinct, order, or providence (as the unbeliever may choose to call it), and offers to take charge of this delicate old gentleman, and carries him in triumph through the Rocky Mountains, and all through his country, and, in Indian pomp and splendor, delivers this rev. "*black coat*" to P. C. Pambrun, Esq., chief clerk of the Honorable Hudson's Bay Company, at old Fort Wallawalla, supplying his every want on the journey, caring for his horses and baggage, not asking or receiving any thing, except such presents as Mr. Parker chose to give them on the way and at parting.

Dr. Whitman, it will be remembered, was associated with Mr.

Parker, under the direction of the American Board. They had arrived at the rendezvous in the Rocky Mountains; most of the Nez Percés were at the American rendezvous. Ish-hol-hol-hoats-hoats, a young Nez Percé Indian (named by the American trappers, *Lawyer*, on account of his shrewdness in argument, and his unflinching defense of American against British and foreign influences), having learned of their arrival, came to them and settled matters quite satisfactorily to both, by requesting Mr. Parker to go with them to their country, they having heard of Rev. Mr. Lee and party going to settle near the *husus-hai-hai* (White Head), as the natives called Dr. John McLaughlin, in the Wallamet Valley. They consented to let the Doctor take two of their boys. To Ites he gave the name of John; Tuetakas he called Richard. Dr. Whitman was to go to the States, report to the American Board, and procure associates and the material to establish a mission in the Nez Percé country.

The Nez Percés were to take charge of Mr. Parker, and carry him forward in his explorations, and meet Dr. W., on his return next year, at the place of rendezvous in the mountains, to conduct him and his party to the place Mr. Parker might select for a mission establishment. Rev. S. Parker, in company with the Indians, went on, and Dr. Whitman, with his two Indian boys, with the American Fur Company, Capts. Fitzpatrick, Bridger, and others, started on their way to the States, or "home from the Rocky Mountains." Dr. Whitman, by his off-hand, easy manner of accommodating himself to circumstances, and by his kind-heartedness and promptness to relieve all who needed his professional skill, had won the esteem of all with whom he traveled, so that the gentlemen of the American Fur Company cheerfully supplied his wants on his return trip to the States, where he arrived in due time, made his report to the American Board, who decided to establish the mission, as per arrangement with Parker and Whitman, on separating in the Rocky Mountains.

Mrs. Whitman, formerly Miss Narcissa Prentiss, of Prattsburg, Steuben County, New York, was a lady of refined feelings and commanding appearance. She had very light hair, light, fresh complexion, and light blue eyes. Her features were large, her form full and round. At the time she arrived in the country, in the prime of life, she was considered a fine, noble-looking woman, affable and free to converse with all she met. Her conversation was animated and cheerful. Firmness in her was natural, and to some, especially the Indians, it was repulsive. She had been brought up in comparative comfort, and moved in the best of religious society in the place of her residence. She was a good singer, and one of her amusements, as well as that of her traveling companions, was to teach the Doctor to sing, which she did with considerable success,—that is, he could sing the native songs without much difficulty.

The American Board appointed Rev. H. H. Spalding and wife to accompany Dr. Whitman and wife, to aid in establishing the Nez Percé mission. Mr. Spalding and wife had just completed their preparatory course of education in Lane Seminary, near Cincinnati, Ohio.

The first impression of the stranger on seeing H. H. Spalding is, that he has before him an unusual countenance. He begins to examine, and finds a man with sharp features, large, brown eyes, dark hair, high, projecting forehead, with many wrinkles, and a head nearly bald. He is of medium size, stoop-shouldered, with a voice that can assume a mild, sharp, or boisterous key, at the will of its owner; quite impulsive, and bitter in his denunciations of a real, or supposed enemy; inclined in the early part of his missionary labors to accumulate property for the especial benefit of his family, though the practice was disapproved of and forbidden by the regulations of the American Board. In his professional character he was below mediocrity. As a writer or correspondent he was bold, and rather eloquent, giving overdrawn life-sketches of passing events. His moral influence was injured by strong symptoms of passion, when provoked or excited. In his labors for the Indians, he was zealous and persevering, in his preaching or talking to them, plain and severe, and in his instructions wholly practical. For instance, to induce the natives to work and cultivate their lands, he had Mrs. Spalding paint a representation of Adam and Eve, as being driven from the garden of Eden by an angel,—Adam with a hoe on his shoulder, and Eve with her spinning-wheel. He taught the natives that God commanded them to work, as well as pray. Had he been allowed to continue his labors with the tribe, undisturbed by sectarian and anti-religious influences, he would have effected great good, and the tribe been now admitted as citizens of the United States. As a citizen and neighbor he was kind and obliging; to his family he was kind, yet severe in his religious observances. He was unquestionably a sincere, though not always humble, Christian. The loss of his wife, and the exciting and savage massacre of his associates, produced their effect upon him. Charity will find a substantial excuse for most of his faults, while virtue and truth, civilization and religion, will award him a place as a faithful, zealous, and comparatively successful missionary.

Mrs. Spalding was the daughter of a plain, substantial farmer, by the name of Hart, of Oneida County, New York. She was above the medium height, slender in form, with coarse features, dark brown hair, blue eyes, rather dark complexion, coarse voice, of a serious turn of mind, and quick in understanding language. In fact she was remarkable in acquiring the Nez Percé language, so as to understand and converse with the natives quite easily by the time they reached their station at Lapwai. She could paint indifferently in water-colors, and had been taught, while young, all the useful branches of domestic life; could spin, weave, and sew, etc.; could prepare an excellent meal at short notice; was generally sociable, but not forward in conversation with or in attentions to gentlemen. In this particular she was the opposite of Mrs. Whitman. With the native women Mrs. Spalding always appeared easy and cheerful, and had their unbounded confidence and respect. She was remarkable for her firmness and decision of character in whatever she or her husband undertook. She never appeared to be alarmed or excited at any difficulty, dispute, or alarms common to the Indian life around her. She was considered by the Indian men as a brave, fearless woman, and was respected and esteemed by all. Though she was frequently left for days alone, her husband being absent on business, but a single attempted insult was ever offered her. Understanding their language, her cool, quick perception of the design enabled her to give so complete and thorough a rebuff to the attempted insult, that, to hide his disgrace, the Indian offering it fled from the tribe, not venturing to remain among them. In fact, a majority of the tribe were in favor of hanging the Indian who offered the insult, but Mrs. Spalding requested that they would allow him to live, that he might repent of his evil designs and do better in future. In this short sketch of Mrs. Spalding the reader is carried through a series of years. We shall have occasion, as we progress in our sketches, to refer to these two ladies. They are not fictitious characters,—they lived; came over the Rocky Mountains in 1836; they are dead and buried, Mrs. Spalding near the Callapooya, in the Wallamet Valley. Mrs. Whitman's remains, such portions of them as could be found, are buried not far from the place of her labors among the Cayuses. The last time we passed the ground not even a common board marked the place. We noticed a hollow in the ground, said to be the place where the very Rev. Mr. Brouillet, vicar-general of Wallawalla, says "the bodies were all deposited in a common grave which had been dug the day previous by Joseph Stanfield, and, before leaving, I saw that they were covered with earth, but I have since learned that the graves, not having been soon enough inclosed, had been molested by the wolves, and that some of the corpses had been devoured by them." Bear this statement in mind, reader, as we proceed. We will tell you just how much he knows of the why and wherefore such things occurred in those early times. A part of the facts are already in history.

Messrs. Whitman and Spalding, with their wives, and a reinforcement for the Pawnee mission, made their way to Liberty Landing, on the Missouri River. At that place they were joined by a young man by the name of W. H. Gray, from Utica, New York, who was solicited by the agents of the American Board to join this expedition as its secular agent.

CHAPTER XIV.

Missionary outfit.—On the way.—No roads.—An English nobleman.—A wagon taken along.—Health of Mrs. Spalding.—Meeting mountain men and Indians.—A feast to the Indians.

THE mission party had brought with them a full supply of all the supposed *et cœteras* for a life and residence two thousand miles from any possible chance to renew those supplies when exhausted, having the material for a blacksmith shop, a plow, and all sorts of seeds, clothing, etc., to last for two years. Gray found his hands full in making calculations for the transportation of this large amount of baggage, or goods, as the trader would say. In a few days wagons, teams, pack-mules, horses, and cows, were all purchased in the county of Liberty, Missouri, the goods all overhauled, repacked, loaded into the two mission wagons, and an extra team hired to go as far as Fort Leavenworth. Spalding and Gray started with the train, three wagons, eight mules, twelve horses, and sixteen cows, two men, two Indian boys, and the man with the extra team. Dr. Whitman, having the ladies in charge, was to come up the Missouri River in the first boat, and await the arrival of the train having the greater portion of the goods with it. Boats on the Missouri River not being so numerous as at the present time, the Doctor and party did not reach Leavenworth till the train had arrived. They rearranged their goods, discharged the extra team, held a consultation, and concluded that the Doctor and ladies would keep the boat to Council Bluffs, the point from which the American Fur Company's caravan was to start that year. Learning that the company was to start in six days, the conclusion was that the cattle and goods had better proceed as fast as possible.

The third day, in the morning, some forty miles from Fort Leavenworth, as we were about starting, a white boy, about sixteen years old, came into camp, having on an old torn straw hat, an old ragged fustian coat, scarcely half a shirt, with buckskin pants, badly worn, but one moccasin, a powder-horn with no powder in it, and an old rifle. He had light flaxen hair, light blue eyes, was thin and spare, yet appeared in good health and spirits. He said he had started for the Rocky Mountains; he was from some place in Iowa; he had been without food for two days; he asked for some ammunition; thought he could kill some game to get along; the rain the night previous had wet him quite effectually; he was really cold, wet, nearly naked, and hungry. He was soon supplied from our stores with all he wanted, and advised to return to his friends in Iowa. To this he objected, and said if we would allow him he would go with us to Council Bluffs, and then go with the fur company to the mountains. He agreed to assist all he could in getting along. He was furnished a horse, and made an excellent hand while he remained with the party, which he did till he reached Fort Hall, on Snake River. There he joined a party that went with the Bannock Indians, and became a member of that tribe, and, as near as we can learn, married a native woman (some say three), and is using his influence to keep the tribe at war with the United States. Of this we have no positive knowledge, though if such is the fact he may have been a deserter from Fort Leavenworth. His name was Miles Goodyear.

Within thirty miles of Council Bluffs a messenger overtook the missionary caravan, and stated that Mrs. Satterley, of the Pawnee mission, was dead; that Dr. Whitman and ladies were left at Fort Leavenworth; that they were coming on as fast as possible, with extra teams, to overtake us. Our party went into camp at once; the two wagons with horse teams started back to meet and bring up the balance of the party; wait two days at Omaha; fix one of the wagon boxes for a ferry-boat; Doctor and party arrive; cross all safe; get to camp late in the night. There was a slight jar in the feelings of some on account of haste, and slowness of movement, in others. However, as the fur company, with whom the mission party was to travel, was to start on a certain day, haste was absolutely necessary, and no time to be lost. Useless baggage overhauled and thrown away, cows started, mules and wagons loaded; Gray in charge of mules and cows, Spalding driver for a two-horse light wagon, Whitman the four-horse farm wagon. On goes the caravan; in two hours a message goes forward to Gray that Spalding has driven his wagon into a mud stream and broken his axletree; Gray goes back; soon repairs axletree by a new one; on Platte River; rains as it only can on that river, cold and almost sleet; nothing but a skin boat, that could carry but two trunks and one lady at a time; all day swimming by the side of the boat to get goods over; swim cattle, mules, and horses all over safe to north side.

Overhaul and lighten our baggage; Rev. Mr. Dunbar for pilot, three men, and two Indian boys, we hasten on to overtake fur company's caravan. Second day, met one hundred Pawnee warriors on their way to Council Bluff agency. Mr. Dunbar being the missionary of the

Pawnees, and understanding their language, we had no difficulty with them. Traveling early and late, we came up to the fur company at the Pawnee village, some two hours after their caravan had arrived and camped.

At this point the missionary menagerie was first exhibited, not that they attempted to make any display, or posted any handbills, or charged any fee for exhibiting, but the strange appearance of two white ladies in a caravan consisting of rough American hunters, Canadian packers with Indian women, with all the paraphernalia of a wild mountain expedition, drew the attention of all. The mission party had with them some fine cows, good horses and mules, and were tolerably well fitted out for their expedition, except a superabundance of useless things, causing much perplexity and hard labor to transport over the rough plains in 1836.

It will be borne in mind that at that early time there was no road,—not even a trail or track, except that of the buffalo; and those made by them were invariably from the river, or watering-places, into the hills or bluffs. Their trails being generally deep, from long use by the animal, made it quite severe and straining upon our teams, wagons, and the nineteen carts the fur company carried their goods in that year. The caravan altogether consisted of nineteen carts, with two mules to each, one in the shafts and one ahead, one light Dearborn wagon, two mules and two wagons belonging to an English nobleman, his titles all on, Sir William Drummond, K. B., who had come to the United States to allow his fortune to recuperate during his absence. He had been spending his winters in New Orleans with the Southern bloods, and his bankers in England complained that his income was not sufficient to meet his large expenditures; he was advised to take a trip to the Rocky Mountains, which would occupy him during the summer and sickly season, during which time he could only spend what he had with him, and could have a fine hunting excursion. This English nobleman with his party consisted of himself and a young English blood. I did not learn whether he was of the first, second, third, or fourth grade in the scale of English nobility; be that as it may, Sir William D., K. B., messed and slept in the same tent with this traveling companion of his, who, between them, had three servants, two dogs, and four extra fine horses, to run and hunt the buffalo. Occasionally, they would give chase to that swiftest of mountain animals, the antelope, which, in most instances, would, especially where the grass was short, leave them in the distance, when Sir William and his companion would come charging back to the train, swearing the antelope could outrun a streak of lightning, and offering to bet a thousand pounds that if he had one of his English 'orses he could catch 'em. The English nobleman, as a matter of course, was treated with great respect by all in the caravan; while in the presence of the ladies he assumed quite a dignified carriage, being a man (excuse me, your honor), a lord of the British realm, on a hunting excursion in North America, in the Rocky Mountains, in the year A. D. 1836. He was about five feet nine inches high. His face had become thin from the free use of New Orleans brandy, rendering his nose rather prominent, showing indications of internal heat in bright red spots, and inclining a little to the rum blossom, that would make its appearance from the sting of a mosquito or sand-fly, which to his lordship was quite annoying. Though his lordship was somewhat advanced in years, and, according to his own account, had traveled extensively in the oriental countries, he did not show in his conversation extensive mental improvement; his general conversation and appearance was that of a man with strong prejudices, and equally strong appetites, which he had freely indulged, with only pecuniary restraint. His two wagons, one with two horses, the other with four mules, with drivers, and a servant for cook and waiter, constituted his train—as large as his means would permit on that trip. All of the carts and wagons were covered with canvas to protect the goods from storms. Sir William traveled under the *alias* of Captain Stewart.

The order of march was as follows: Cattle and loose animals in advance in the morning, coming up in rear at night; fur company and Captain Stewart's teams in advance; mission party in rear till we reached Fort Laramie. All went smoothly and in order. At the Pawnee village the fur company was short of meat or bacon. Arrangements were made to slaughter one of the mission cows, and replace it at Laramie. Two days from Pawnee village the hunters brought into camp some bull buffalo meat; next day cow buffalo meat in abundance. Not far from Scott's Bluff, passed some hunters on their way down Platte River in boats; arrive at Fort Laramie, just above the mouth of that river; cross the Platte in two dug-outs, lashed together with sticks and poles, so as to carry the goods and carts all over to the fort. At that establishment the company and Captain Stewart leave all their wagons and carts except one, deeming it impracticable to proceed further with them.

On account of the ladies, Dr. Whitman insisted on taking one of the mission wagons along. The fur company concluded to try the experiment with him, and took one of their carts along. Overhaul all the baggage, select out all, that, with the knowledge any one had of the future wants of the mission party, could be dispensed with; put the balance up in packages of one hundred pounds each; for the top packs, fifty pounds; for mules, two hundred and fifty pounds; for horses, in proportion to strength. About the first of June, 1836, the caravan started from Laramie. All the goods on pack animals, wagon and cart light, Gray in charge of mission pack-train, with two men and one boy, two pack animals each; Spalding of cows, loose animals, and ladies, with the two Indian boys to assist in driving; Dr. Whitman in charge of the wagon train, consisting of the fur company's cart and mission wagon; but one man in the cart and one in the wagon. On we go; the first day from Laramie had some difficulty in getting through a cotton-wood bottom on the river, on account of fallen timber in the trail. Whitman came into the camp puffing and blowing, in good spirits, all right side up, with only one turn over with the wagon and two with the cart. The fur company being interested in exploring a wagon route to Green River, next day gave the Doctor two additional men to assist in exploring and locating the road, and getting the wagon and cart over difficult places. Second day all right; train moves on; hunters in advance; cattle usually traveling slower than the train, were started in the morning in advance of the train, which usually passed them about one hour before reaching camp at night; at noon they usually all stop together. At the crossing of Platte below Red Buttes, in the Black Hills, kill buffalo, took hides, made willow frames for boats, sewed the hides together to cover the frames, used tallow for pitch, dried the skin boats over a fire, the rain having poured down all the time we were getting ready to cross. However, as fortune always favors the brave, as the saying is, it did us this time, for in the morning, when our boats were ready, it cleared up, the sun came out bright and clear, so that we had a fine time getting all things over. Next day on we moved, over the hills, through the valleys, around and among the salt pits to a willow grove to camp.

With the company was a gentleman from St. Louis, a Major Pilcher. He usually rode a fine white mule, and was dressed in the top of hunting or mountain style, such as a fine buckskin coat trimmed with red cloth and porcupine quills, fine red shirt, nice buckskin pants, and moccasins tinged and nicely trimmed; he was, in fact, very much of a gentleman in all his conversation and deportment. The major was also considerable of a gallant (as I believe most titled gentlemen are). He was proceeding around one of those clay salt pits, and explaining to the ladies their nature and danger, when suddenly mule, major and all dropped out of sight, except the mule's ears and the fringe on the major's coat. Instantly several men were on hand with ropes, and assisted the major and mule out of the pit. *Such a sight!* you may imagine what you please, I will not attempt to describe it. However, no particular harm was done the major, only the thorough saturation of his fine suit of buckskin, and mule, with that indescribably adhesive mud. He took it all in good part, and joined in the jokes on the occasion. No other remarkable incident occurred till we arrived at Rock Independence. On the south end of that rock nearly all the prominent persons of the party placed their names, and date of being there.

Later wagon trains and travelers have complained, and justly, of sage brush and the difficulties of this route. Whitman and his four men opened it as far as they could with a light wagon and a cart. To him must be given the credit of the first practical experiment, though Ashtley, Bonneville, and Bridger had taken wagons into the Rocky Mountains and left them, and pronounced the experiment a failure, and a wagon road impracticable. Whitman's perseverance demonstrated a great fact—the practicability of a wagon road over the Rocky Mountains. You that have rolled over those vast plains and slept in your Concord coaches or Pullman palace cars, have never once imagined the toil and labor of that old off-hand pioneer, as he mounted his horse in the morning and rode all day in the cold and heat of the mountains and plains, to prove that a wagon road was practicable to the waters of the Columbia River. Even Fremont, seven years after, claims to be the discoverer of the passes through which Whitman took his cart and wagon, and kept up with the pack-train from day to day.

From Rock Independence the health of Mrs. Spalding seemed gradually to decline. She was placed in the wagon as much as would relieve her, and changed from wagon to saddle as she could bear, to the American rendezvous on Green River.

From Rock Independence information was sent forward into the mountains of the arrival of the caravan, and about the time and place they expected to reach the rendezvous. This information reached not only the American trapper and hunter in the mountains, but the Snake, Bannock, Nez Percé, and Flathead tribes, and the traders of the Hudson's Bay Company. Two days before we arrived at our rendezvous, some two hours before we reached camp, the whole caravan was alarmed by the arrival of some ten Indians and four or five white men, whose dress and appearance could scarcely be distinguished from that of the Indians. As they came in sight over the hills, they all gave a yell, such as hunters and Indians only can give; whiz, whiz, came their balls over our heads, and on they came, in less time than it will take you to read this account. The alarm was but for a moment; our guide had seen a white cloth on one of their guns, and said, "Don't be alarmed, they are friends," and sure enough, in a moment here they were. It was difficult to tell which was the most crazy, the horse or the rider;

such hopping, hooting, running, jumping, yelling, jumping sage brush, whirling around, for they could not stop to reload their guns, but all of us as they came on gave them a salute from ours, as they passed to the rear of our line and back again, hardly stopping to give the hand to any one. On to camp we went.

At night, who should we find but old Takkensuitas and Ish-hol-hol-hoats-hoats (Lawyer), with a letter from Mr. Parker, which informed the party that he had arrived safely at Wallawalla, and that the Indians had been kind to him, and from what he had seen and could learn of them, they were well disposed toward all white men. Mr. Parker, as his journal of that trip and observations will show, was a man of intelligence, and a close observer of men and things.

He soon learned, on arriving at Wallawalla, that there was a bitter anti-American feeling in the country, and that, notwithstanding he had arrived in it uninvited, and without the aid of the *Honorable* Hudson's Bay Company, he was in it, nevertheless, as the guest of the Nez Percé Indians. They had found him in the Rocky Mountains; they brought him to Wallawalla; they had received him, treated him kindly, and proved to him that they were not only friendly, but anxious to have the American influence and civilization come among them. Rev. Jason Lee and party were in the country. Abundance of unasked advice was given to him by Hudson's Bay Company's men; his caution prevailed; he was to let Dr. Whitman, or the mission party that might be sent across the mountains, hear from him by the Indians. Feeling certain that any advice or information he might attempt to communicate to his missionary friends would in all probability be made use of to their detriment, and perhaps destroy the mission itself, he did not deem it prudent to write or to give any advice. Should any party come on before he could reach them, his note was sufficient to inform them of the fact of his safe arrival and the friendly treatment he had received of the Indians; further than this he did not feel safe to communicate—not for want of confidence in the Indians, but from what he saw and learned of the feelings of the Hudson's Bay Company. Yet he felt that, notwithstanding they were showing him outwardly every attention, yet they evidently did not wish to see the American influence increase in any shape in the country.

Rev. Mr. Parker's letter, short and unsatisfactory as it was, caused considerable expression of unpleasant feeling on the part of those who considered they had a right to a more full and extended communication. But Mr. Parker was at Vancouver, or somewhere else; they might and they might not meet him; he may and he may not have written more fully.

At supper time old Takkensuitas (Rotten Belly) and Ish-hol-hol-hoats-hoats were honored with a place at the missionary board. With your permission, ladies and gentlemen, I will give you the bill of fare on this memorable occasion. Place—by the side of a muddy stream called Sandy, about thirty miles south of Wind River Mountain. This mountain, you will remember, is about as near the highest point of the North American continent as can be. This fact is established, not from geographical or barometrical observations, but from the simple fact that water runs from it by way of the Missouri, Colorado, and Columbia rivers into the eastern, southern, and western oceans, and but a short distance to the north of this mountain commences the waters of the Saskatchewan River, running into Hudson's Bay and the northern ocean. There are doubtless many other mountains whose peaks ascend higher into the clouds, but none of them supply water to so vast an extent of country, and none of them are so decidedly on top of the continent as this one. Of course our little party is in a high altitude, and in sight of this mountain, which may or may not have been ten thousand feet higher to its snow-capped peaks. Date—about the 20th day of July, 1836. Our table was the grass beside this muddy stream; cloth—an old broken oil-cloth badly used up; plates—when the company started were called tin, but from hard usage were iron in all shapes; cups—ditto; knives—the common short-bladed wooden-handled butcher knife; forks—a stick each cut to suit himself, or, if he preferred the primitive mode of conveying his food to its proper destination, he was at liberty to practice it; food extra on this occasion—a nice piece of venison, which the Indians had presented to the ladies, a piece of broiled and roast buffalo meat, roasted upon a stick before the fire, seasoned with a little salt, with a full proportion of sand and dirt. Dr. Whitman was inclined to discard the use of salt entirely; as to dirt and sand it was a matter upon which he and Mr. Parker differed on the trip the year previous, though Mrs. Whitman took sides with Mr. Parker against the Doctor, and with the assistance of Mrs. Spalding, the Doctor was kept in most cases within reasonable distance of comfortable cleanliness. On this occasion tea, with sugar, was used; the supply of bread was limited; we will not trouble the reader with an extra list of the dessert. Of this feast these sons of the wilderness partook with expressions of great satisfaction. The Lawyer, twenty-seven years after, spoke of it as the time when his heart became one with the *Suapies* (Americans).

CHAPTER XV.

Arrival at American rendezvous.—An Indian procession.—Indian curiosity to see white women.—Captain N. Wyeth.—McCleod and T. McKay.—Description of mountain men.—Their opinion of the missionaries.

In two days' easy travel we arrived at the great American rendezvous, held in an extensive valley in the forks formed by Horse Creek and Green River, on account of the abundance of wood, grass, and water all through the valley. Each party selected their own camp grounds, guarding their own animals and goods, as each felt or anticipated the danger he might be exposed to at the time. We will pass through this city of about fifteen hundred inhabitants—composed of all classes and conditions of men, and on this occasion two classes of women,—starting from a square log pen 18 by 18, with no doors, except two logs that had been cut so as to leave a space about four feet from the ground two feet wide and six feet long, designed for an entrance, as also a place to hand out goods and take in furs. It was covered with poles, brush on top of the poles; in case of rain, which we had twice during our stay at the rendezvous, the goods were covered with canvas, or tents thrown over them. Lumber being scarce in that vicinity, floors, doors, as well as sash and glass, were dispensed with. The spaces between the logs were sufficient to admit all the light requisite to do business in this primitive store. At a little distance from the store were the camps of the fur company, in which might be seen the pack-saddles and equipage of the mules, in piles to suit the taste and disposition of the men having them in charge. The trading-hut was a little distance from the main branch of Green River, so situated that the company's mules and horses could all be driven between the store and the river, the tents and men on either side, the store in front, forming a camp that could be defended against an attack of the Indians, in case they should attempt any thing of the kind. Green River, at the point where our city in the mountains is situated, is running from the west due east. West of the fur company's camp or store were most of the camps of the hunters and trappers; east of it, close to the river, was the missionary camp, while to the south, from one to three miles distant along Horse Creek, from its junction with Green River, where the Snake and Bannock Indians were camped, to six miles up that stream, were the camps of the Flatheads and Nez Percés. All these tribes were at peace that year, and met at the American rendezvous. The Indian camps were so arranged in the bends of the creek that they could defend themselves and their horses in case of any attack from the neighboring tribes, and also guard their horses while feeding in the day-time. The whole city was a military camp; every little camp had its own guards to protect its occupants and property from being stolen by its neighbor. The arrow or the ball decided any dispute that might occur. The only law known for horse-stealing was death to the thief, if the owner or the guard could kill him in the act. If he succeeded in escaping, the only remedy for the man who lost his horse was to buy, or steal another and take his chances in escaping the arrow or ball of the owner, or guard. It was quite fashionable in this city for all to go well armed, as the best and quickest shot gained the case in dispute. Of the number assembled, there must have been not far from one hundred Americans,—hunters and trappers; about fifty French, belonging principally to the caravan; some five traders; about twenty citizens, or outsiders, including the mission party. The Snakes and Bannocks mustered about one hundred and fifty warriors; the Nez Percés and Flatheads, about two hundred. By arrangement among themselves they got up a grand display for the benefit of their white visitors, which came off some six days after our American caravan had arrived at the rendezvous.

The procession commenced at the east or lower end of the plain in the vicinity of the Snake and Bannock camps. The Nez Percés and Flatheads, passing from their camps down the Horse Creek, joined the Snake and Bannock warriors, all dressed and painted in their gayest uniforms, each having a company of warriors in war garb, that is, naked, except a single cloth, and painted, carrying their war weapons, bearing their war emblems and Indian implements of music, such as skins drawn over hoops with rattles and trinkets to make a noise. From the fact that no scalps were borne in the procession, I concluded this must be entirely a peace performance, and gotten up for the occasion. When the cavalcade, amounting to full five (some said six) hundred Indian warriors (though I noticed quite a number of native belles covered with beads), commenced coming up through the plain in sight of our camps, those of us who were not informed as to the object or design of this demonstration began to look at our weapons and calculate on a desperate fight. Captain Stewart, our English nobleman, and Major Pilcher waited on the mission ladies and politely informed them of the object of the display; they assured them there would be no danger or harm, and remained at their tents while the cavalcade passed. Mrs. Whitman's health was such that she could witness most of the display. Mrs. Spalding was quite feeble, and kept her tent most of the time. All passed off quietly, excepting the hooting and yelling of the Indians appropriate to the occasion.

The display over, the mission camp around the tent was thronged. On first hearing the war-whoop, the savage yell, and the sound of the Indian war drum, all parties not in the secret of this surprise party, or native reception for their missionaries, at once drove in their animals, and prepared for the worst; hence the mission cows, horses, and camp, were all together. Major Pilcher and Captain Stewart enjoyed the surprise of the party, and were equally delighted with the effect and surprise manifested by the Indians, as they approached the mission camp. The wagon, and every thing about their camp, was examined. The Indians would pass and repass the tent, to get a sight of the two women belonging to the white men. Mrs. Spalding, feeble as she was, seemed to be the favorite with the Indian women; possibly from that fact alone she may have gained their sympathy to some extent. The Lawyer and Takkensuitas were constant visitors at the tent. Their Indian wives were with them, and showed a disposition to do all in their power to assist the missionaries. Mrs. Spalding's rest from the fatigues of the journey soon enabled her to commence a vocabulary of the Indian language. Mrs. Whitman also commenced one with her, but she was often interrupted by the attentions thought necessary to be paid to gentlemen callers. Excuse me, whoever believes that thirty-three years since there were no gentlemen on top of the Rocky Mountains. I can assure you that there were, and that all the refined education and manners of the daughter of Judge Prentiss, of Prattsburg, Steuben County, N. Y., found abundant opportunity to exhibit the cardinal ornaments of a religious and civilized country. No one, except an eye-witness, can appreciate or fully understand the charm there was in those early days in the sight of the form and white features of his mother. The rough veteran mountain hunter would touch his hat in a manner absolutely ridiculous, and often fail to express a designed compliment, which the mischief or good-humor of Mrs. Whitman sometimes enjoyed as a good joke. In consequence of these attentions or interruptions, she did not acquire the native language as fast as Mrs. Spalding, who showed but little attention to any one except the natives and their wives.

The Indian curiosity had not fully subsided before the company were introduced to, and cordially greeted by, Captain Wyeth, who had been to the lower Columbia on a trading expedition. He had conducted

Rev. Jason Lee and party to Fort Hall, where he had established a trading-post; thence he had gone to the lower country, received his goods from the brig *May Dacre*, made arrangements with the Hudson's Bay Company, sold his goods and establishment at Fort Hall to the Hudson's Bay Company, and was then on his way back to the States. Captain Wyeth, in all his motions and features, showed the shrewd Yankee and the man of business. He politely introduced the mission party to Messrs. John McLeod and Thomas McKay, of the Hudson's Bay Company. After the usual etiquette of introduction and common inquiries, Messrs. McLeod and McKay having retired to their camps, Captain W. entered into a full explanation of the whys and wherefores of Rev. Mr. Parker's short note, confirming the observations and suspicions of Mr. Parker, in reference to the treatment the missionaries might expect, giving a full statement of the feelings and efforts of the Hudson's Bay Company to get rid of all American influence, and especially traders. Turning, with a smile, upon the ladies, but addressing the gentlemen, he said, "You gentlemen have your wives along; if I do not greatly mistake the feelings of the gentlemen of the Hudson's Bay Company, they will be anxious to have their influence in teaching their own wives and children, and you will meet with a different reception from any other American party that has gone into the country." It would be useless to add in this sketch that the advice of Captain W. was of incalculable value in shaping the policy and conduct of the mission of the American Board in their necessary transactions and intercourse with the Hudson's Bay Company. Captain W. had fallen in with Rev. S. Parker, but could give no definite information about him or his plans, except that he was on his return to the United States, by way of the Sandwich Islands.

As we have never seen a description of these semi-civilized men, that in youth had left their native countries, and found themselves thousands of miles away, in the midst of the Rocky Mountains, surrounded on all sides by wild, roving bands of savages, cut off from communication with civilization, except by the annual return of the fur company's traders, or occasional wandering to some distant trading-post, a thousand or five hundred miles from the borders of any State or settlement, we will at this time introduce to the reader several men as we found them at this American rendezvous, most of them finding their way eventually into the settlement of Oregon, and becoming active and prominent men in the organization of the provisional government, as also good citizens. Among these veteran Rocky Mountain hunters was a tall man, with long black hair, smooth face, dark eyes (inclining to turn his head a little to one side, as much as to say, "I can tell you all about it"), a harum-scarum, don't-care sort of a man, full of "life and fun in the mountains," as he expressed it. He came and paid his respects to the ladies, and said he had been in the mountains several years; he had not seen a white woman for so long he had almost forgotten how they looked. He appeared quite fond of telling "yarns." In the conversation, Mrs. Whitman asked him if he ever had any difficulty or fights with the Indians. "That we did," said he. "One .time I was with Bridger's camp; we were traveling along that day, and the Blackfeet came upon us. I was riding an old mule. The Indians were discovered some distance off, so all the party put whip to their horses and started to get to a place where we could defend ourselves. My old mule was determined not to move, with all the beating I could give her, so I sung out to the boys to stop and fight the Indians where we were; they kept on, however. Soon, my old mule got sight of the Blackfeet coming; she pricked up her ears, and on she went like a streak, passed the boys, and away we went. I sung out to the boys, as I passed, 'Come on, boys, there is no use to stop and fight the Indians here.'" Fun and firmness were the two prominent characteristics of this young mountain hunter. He expressed a wish and a determination to visit and settle in lower Oregon (as the Wallamet Valley was then called). He had a native wife, and one son, just beginning to speak a few words. The father seemed, on my first noticing him, to be teaching this son of his to say "God d——n you," doubtless considering this prayer the most important one to teach his son to repeat, in the midst of the wild scenes with which he was surrounded. Though, to his credit be it said, this same wild, youthful mountaineer has become a good supporter of religious society, and has a respectable family, in an interesting neighborhood, near Forest Grove, in Oregon.

We will call these mountain hunters by numbers, for convenience, as we shall refer to them in our future political sketches, in which they participated.

No. 2. A man of medium height, black hair, black whiskers, dark-brown eyes, and very dark complexion; he was formerly from Kentucky. (I am not positive.) He was quite fond of telling yarns; still, as he was not considered very truthful, we will only give the story as we have it of the manner in which he and the one we will give as No. 3 obtained their titles. 2 and 3 were traveling together; 3 was from Cincinnati, Ohio. They had reached Independence, Mo.; says 3 to 2, "Titles are very necessary here in Missouri, what titles shall we take?" "Well," says 2, "I will take *Major.*" 3 says, "I will take *Doctor.*" Very good. They rode up to the best hotel in the place and called for lodgings.

2. "Well, Doctor, what shall we have for supper?"

3. "I don't care, Major, so as we get something to eat."

The Major and the Doctor enjoyed their supper and have borne their titles to the present time. The Major has never been, from all I could learn of him, a very truthful man or reliable citizen. He spent several years in Oregon and in the mountains, and found his way back to Missouri. The Doctor is now a resident of Idaho. The most remarkable trait in his composition is story-telling, or yarns, and a disposition to make friends of all political parties, or join all religious sects—something of a good lord and good devil order. He appeared in those early times to belong to that party that paid him the best. He was first in the employ of the American Fur Company, but appeared to lend his influence to the Hudson's Bay Company. He also had a native wife of the Nez Percé tribe, and was considered by the Hudson's Bay Company a useful man to divide the American influence in trade with the Indians in the mountains, and equally useful to distract and divide the political influence of the early settlers. By his connection with the natives in marriage, the Hudson's Bay Company in trade, and good lord and good devil principles, he could adapt himself to the Protestant or Catholic religion, and in this manner become a kind of representative man, something like *strong lye and aquafortis mixed*, and just about as useful as such a mixture would be. He succeeded, by political maneuvering, or as the sailors say, "boxing the compass," to fill a place and draw a salary from Uncle Sam; carrying out the principles he has acted upon in his whole life, his efforts have been to neutralize what good others might do.

No. 4. A young man from Ohio, of a serious turn of mind; at least I concluded this to be the case, from the fact that he asked of the ladies if they had any books to sell, or that they could spare. A nice pocket-bible was given him, for which he politely expressed his thanks, after offering to pay for it. The pay, of course, was declined, as a few bibles were brought along for distribution. This young man, in a few years, followed the mission party and became a settler and a prominent man in the provisional government.

No. 5. A wild, reckless, don't-care sort of a youth, with a Nez Percé wife, so thoroughly attached to Indian ideas and customs that he has felt it beneath his dignity to turn from the ancient habits of the Indian to a "more recent invention" of religion and civilization. His curiosity was a little excited, which induced him to pay his respects to the missionaries, on account of their wives. He called on them, and spoke of some day finding his way somewhere down about where the missionaries might be located; as he had bought him a Nez Percé wife, she might want to go and see her people, and he might make up his mind to go and settle. This man, from his utter disregard for all moral and civilized social relations, has coiled himself up in the tribe he adopted, and spit out his venomous influence against all moral and civil improvement, training his children so that the better portion of the natives treat them with contempt. For a time he had considerable influence in shaping government policy toward the tribe and securing his own personal Indian position, to the injury of all other interests. I am unable to say how he obtained his title of colonel, unless it was from the influence he once pretended to have with the Indians, and a disposition on the part of those of his countrymen to title those who aspire to such honors.

No. 6. What the miners nowadays would call a "plain, honest farmer," with a native wife and one child. He called on the party, took a look at their cattle, and some four years afterward, after going into Mexico and Taos, found his way to the Wallamet as a settler, with a few head of cattle, which he managed to get through. This man is a quiet and good citizen, and has a respectable family of half-native children. The accursed influence of slavery in his neighborhood has borne heavily upon his children. Whether they will be able to rise above it and stand as examples of good citizens remains for them to demonstrate.

No. 7. A short, thick-set man, with a Nez Percé wife; a good honest farmer; has done credit to himself and family in giving them every possible advantage for education and society, though the aquafortis mixture has been strong in his neighborhood; his family are respected; his Indian wife he considers as good as some of his neighbors', that don't like her or her children. In this opinion all who are not saturated with our *cultus* mixture agree with him. His title in the mountains was Squire, but I think it has been improved since he came to the settlements by adding the E to it, he having been duly elected to fill the office under the provisional, territorial, and State government. I have learned, with much regret, that the Squire of the Rocky Mountains, who had courage and strength to meet and overcome all the dangers and trials of early times, has not the courage to resist the approaches of false friends and bad whisky, which will ultimately bring himself and his family to that certain destruction that follows the debasing habit of using liquor in any shape.

No. 8. A fair, light-haired, light-complexioned, blue-eyed man, rather above the medium height, with a Nez Percé wife, came about the camp, had little or nothing to say. I am not quite certain that he had his native wife at that time, still he had one when he came into the settlement. He has a good farm, and if he avoids his false friends and the fatal habits of his neighbors, he may have a good name, which will be of more value to his children than his present social and vicious habits.

Doctor Marcus Whitman, they considered, on the whole, was a good sort of a fellow; he was not so hide-bound but what he could talk with a common man and get along easily if his wife did not succeed in "*stiffening*," starching him up; he would do first-rate, though there appeared considerable doubt in their minds, whether, from her stern, commanding manner, she would not eventually succeed in stiffening up the Doctor so that he would be less agreeable. Mrs. Whitman, they thought, was a woman of too much education and refinement to be thrown away on the Indians. "She must have had considerable romance in her disposition to have undertaken such an expedition with such a common, kind, good-hearted fellow as the Doctor. As to Spalding, he is so green he will do to spread out on a frog-pond; he may do to preach to Indians, but mountain men would have to be fly-blown before he could come near them. Mrs. Spalding is a first-rate woman; she has not got any starch in her; it is strange she ever picked up such a greenhorn as she has for a husband; she will do first-rate to teach the Indians, or anybody else; she has got good common sense, and doesn't put on any frills. As to Gray, he is young yet, is not quite so green as Spalding; he seems inclined to learn a little; by the time he goes to the Columbia River and travels about more, he will know a good deal more than he does now. He may do well in his department if he 'keeps his eye skinned.'"

I supppose by this expression was meant a sharp look out for swindlers, rogues, and thieves, to see that they do not lie, cheat, and steal, every opportunity they may have, or at least that you do not allow them to take your property under false pretenses. Be that as it may, the general conclusion was, that, as this mission party had succeeded in getting thus far on their journey, they might get still further, and perhaps (most were certain) make a failure, either by being sent out of the country by the Hudson's Bay Company, or destroyed by the Indians. Good wishes and hopes that they might succeed were abundant from all, as was plainly expressed, and a disposition, in case the mission succeeded in establishing themselves, to find their way down into the Columbia River Valley with their native families, and become settlers about the mission stations. Lightly as these frank, open expressions of good wishes and future ideas of the mountain hunter may appear, the missionaries saw at once there was the germ of a future people to be gathered in the Columbia River Valley, probably of a mixed race.

These men had all abandoned civilization and home for the wild hunter life in the midst of the mountains. They had enjoyed its wild sports, felt its fearful dangers and sufferings, and become, most of them, connected with native women—a large proportion of them with the Nez Percé and Flathead tribes. Their family, at least, could be benefited by education, and taught the benefits of civilization and Christianity. The men had expressed kind wishes, good feelings, and treated them kindly; why should they not include this class of men and their families in their efforts to benefit the Indians in the valleys of the Columbia River.

As before stated, the mission party had been introduced by Captain Wyeth to Mr. John McLeod, a gentleman holding the rank of chief trader in the Hudson's Bay Company. He had frequent interviews and conversations with the mission party while at rendezvous, and as often as any of these mountain men met him at the mission camp, he would leave without ceremony. There appeared a mutual dislike, a sort of hatred between them. This chief trader of the Hudson's Bay Company, in the conversations had with him, informed the mission party that it was not the wish of the company to encourage any of these mountain hunters and trappers to go to the Columbia River to settle, or to have any thing to do with them, assigning as a reason that they would cause trouble and difficulties with the Indians. He also gave them to understand that should they need manual labor, or men to assist them in putting up their houses and making their improvements, the company would prefer to furnish it, to encouraging these men in going into the country. This intimation was distinctly conveyed to the party, with the advice and intimations received from Captain Wyeth, who had seen and understood all the policy of the Hudson's Bay Company, and had been compelled to sell his improvements at Fort Hall to this same McLeod, and his goods designed for the trade to Dr. McLaughlin, soon after their arrival in the country. These facts and statements, with the decided manner of Mr. McLeod, compelled the mission party to defer any effort for these mountain men, but subsequently they advised the sending of a man to travel with their camps.

CHAPTER XVI.

Missionaries travel in company with Hudson's Bay Company's party.—The Lawyer's kindness.—Arrival at Fort Hall.—Description of the country.—The Salmon Indians.—The Hudson's Bay Company's tariff.

LETTERS all written to friends, and everybody supposed to have any particular interest in the person or individual who wrote them; the letters placed in the hands of Captain Wyeth; mission camp overhauled and assorted; all goods supposed unnecessary, or that could be replaced, such as irons for plows, blacksmith's tools, useless kettles, etc., etc., disposed of. (All articles left, the party were careful to learn, could be had at Vancouver of the Hudson's Bay Company, or Methodist Mission, at reasonable prices.) Tents struck; good-byes said; over the party goes to Horse Creek, not far from the Nez Percé camp, where we found that of McLeod and McKay. Soon after we reached camp, along comes Dr. Whitman with his wagon, notwithstanding all parties and persons, except the Indians, advised him to leave it. He was literally alone in his determination to get his old wagon through on to the waters of the Columbia, and to the mission station that might be established no one knew where. The man that says Dr. Whitman is fickle-minded, knows nothing of his character and less of his moral worth.

Next day, all camps, including those of the Flathead and Nez Percé Indians, were "raised," as the expression is, and on we went; the Hudson's Bay Company and mission camp, or caravan, together, Dr. Whitman in charge of his wagon, with some Indians to help him. They seemed rather to get the Doctor's ideas of this *chick-chick-shauile-kai-kash* (iron rolling carriage), and hunted a road around the bad places, and helped him along when he required their assistance. Our route was nearly the same as the great overland route to Bear River and Soda Springs.

Two days before we reached Soda Springs one of the mission party became quite unwell, and unable to sit upon his horse. He was left, at his own request, on a little stream, while the caravan passed on some six miles further to camp. After remaining alone and resting some two hours, The Lawyer and an Indian companion of his came along, picked up the sick man, put him upon a strong horse, got on behind him, and held him on till they reached camp. Dr. Whitman gave him a prescription, which relieved him, so that next day he was able to continue the journey with the camp. This transaction has always been a mystery to the writer. The place where the sick man was left was a beautiful stream, and a good place for a camp for the whole caravan. The sick man was wholly unable to proceed; did not ask the caravan to stop and bury him, but simply informed them he could proceed no further; his strength was gone; they could leave him to die alone if they chose. A word from McLeod would have stopped the caravan. Should the mission party remain with him? He said: "No; go on with the caravan and leave me; you will be compelled to seek your own safety in continuing with the caravan; I am but an individual; leave me to my fate." He requested a cup that he might get some water from the stream, close to the side of which he wished them to place him. Dr. Whitman remained with him as long as was deemed safe for him, and passed on to overtake the caravan. The Lawyer and his companion came along two or three hours afterward, picked up the dying or dead man (for aught the caravan knew), and brought him into camp. My impression of this transaction has always been that McLeod wished to get rid of this young American, who was then in the service of the mission party.

"That d——d Indian, Lawyer," as the Hudson's Bay Company's men called him, by his kindness of heart and determination not to let an American die if he could help it, defeated the implied wish of these Hudson's Bay Company's men in this case. The Lawyer says the sick man vomited all the way into camp, and called for water, which his young man got for him.

From the Soda Springs the Indian camps went north into the mountains for buffalo.

The Hudson's Bay Company and mission party continued their journey through the spurs of the mountains over on to the waters of the Portneuf to Fort Hall. It is due to Dr. Whitman to say that notwithstanding this was the most difficult route we had to travel, yet he persevered with his old wagon, without any particular assistance; from Soda Springs to Fort Hall his labor was immense, yet he overcame every difficulty and brought it safe through. I have thrice since traveled the same route, and confess I can not see how he did it, notwithstanding I was with him, and know he brought the wagon through.

Fort Hall, in 1836, was a stockade, made of cotton-wood logs, about twelve feet long, set some two feet in the ground, with a piece of timber pinned near the top, running entirely around the stockade, which was about sixty feet square. The stores and quarters for the men were built inside with poles, brush, grass, and dirt for covering, stamped down so as to partially shed rain, and permit the guards to be upon the tops of the quarters and see over the top of the stockade. It is situated on an extensive level plain or flat, with spurs of the Rocky Mountains on the east, at the distance of thirty miles, high ranges of barren sage hills on the south, some eight miles distant. As you leave the flat level bottom formed by the Snake and Portneuf rivers, all along its banks it is skirted with a fine growth of cotton-wood, relieving the landscape and forming a beautiful contrast to the high barren plains beyond. To the west is the valley of the Snake River, from thirty to sixty miles wide, a high, sandy, and barren sage plain. This valley is bounded on the south by a low range of hills, running from northwest to southeast. On the north side of Fort Hall is an extensive high plain; this plain is, from Fort Hall, across it, full forty miles. The only objects that meet the eye on this extensive plain are three high basaltic buttes or mountains thrown up near its center. At the foot of the one a little to the south and west of the two rounder and equally prominent ones, is a fine spring of water. In 1837, the writer, in his explorations of the country, was anxious to learn more than was then known of the character of this great basin in the mountains, having the year previous entered it by way of Soda Springs and Portneuf. This time he came into it from the north by Codie's Defile, and concluded he would take a straight course and pass between the two northeastern buttes, and reach Snake River near Fort Hall. His Indian guide objected; still, as we had good horses, and were traveling light, we took the precaution to water our animals before entering this plain. We were twenty-six hours on horseback, having stopped but six hours to rest; we tied our horses to the sage brush, to prevent them from leaving us to hunt for water. Not a drop did we find on our route till we reached Snake River, thirty-two hours from the time we left running water on the north and west sides of this plain. In our course we found nothing but barren, basaltic rock, sand, and sage. It is possible, had we turned to the right or left, we might have found water, but I saw nothing that gave indications that water was near; on the contrary, I noticed that the fine stream at which we watered our animals sank into the rocks, leaving no marks of a channel to any great distance. In fact, my impression was, after twelve hours' ride, that it was useless to spend our time and strength to hunt for water, and kept our course. Jaded and fatigued as our animals were, as we approached Snake River every nerve seemed strung to the utmost; our animals became frantic and unmanageable; they rushed forward at full speed and plunged into the first water they saw. Fortunately for them and the riders, the water was only about three feet deep; water appeared to be preferred to air; they plunged their heads deep in and held their breaths till their thirst was relieved.

This plain is bounded on the north and east by spurs of the Rocky and Bear River mountains; on the south and west by the high plains of Portneuf and Snake River valleys. There is a range of mountains commencing on the northwest of this plain, extending west and north along Snake River, dividing the waters of the Snake and La Rivière aux Bois (the wooded river.) This whole plain has the appearance of having been one vast lake of lava, spread over the whole surrounding country, appearing to have issued from the three basaltic mountains in the midst of it. I noticed, as we passed between the two, which were probably not more than ten miles apart, that we appeared to be on higher rock than in any direction around us. From this fact I concluded that the three must have been pouring out their volcanic lava at the same time and ceased together, leaving the country comparatively level. The small amount of soil found upon the surface, as well as the barrenness of the rock, indicated no distant period of time when this volcanic plain had been formed.

At Fort Hall we had another overhauling and lightening of baggage. The Doctor was advised to take his wagon apart and pack it, if he calculated to get it through the terrible cañons and deep, bottomless creeks we must pass in going down Snake Plains. Miles Goodyear, the boy we picked up two days from Fort Leavenworth, who had been assigned to assist the Doctor, was determined, if the Doctor took his wagon any further, to leave the company. He was the only one that could be spared to assist in this wild, and, as all considered, crazy undertaking. Miles was furnished a couple of horses, and the best outfit the mission party could give him for his services, and allowed to remain or go where he might choose. In his conclusions, he was influenced by the stories he heard about the treatment he might expect should he reach the lower Columbia. His idea of liberty was unlimited. Restraint and obedience to others was what he did not like at home; he would try his fortune in the mountains; he did not care for missionaries, Hudson's Bay men, nor Indians; he was determined to be his own man, and was allowed to remain at Fort Hall. This loss of manual strength to the mission party compelled the Doctor to curtail his wagon, so he made a cart on two of the wheels, placed the axletree and the other two wheels on his cart, and about the 1st of August, 1836, our camp was again in motion. As we reached camp on Portneuf the first night, in passing a bunch of willows, Mrs. Spalding's horse, a kind and perfectly gentle animal, was stung by a wasp, causing him to spring to one side. Mrs. S. lost her balance; her foot hung fast in the stirrup; the horse made but a single bound from the sting of the wasp, and stopped still till Mrs. S. was relieved from what appeared almost instant death. Next day we continued on down the river till we reached Salmon Falls, on Snake River.

We found a large number of the Salmon and Digger Indians at their fishing stations. Their curiosity was excited, and overcame all the fears that had been attributed to them by former travelers. All of them came about the camp, and appeared quite friendly, furnishing to the party all the fresh and dried salmon they wanted, at the most reasonable rates, say a fine fresh salmon for two fish-hooks; four for a common butcher-knife; ten dried ones for a shirt; in fact, receiving only such pay or presents for their fish and roots, as the Hudson's Bay Company's traders saw fit, or would *allow* the missionary party to give them. It will be remembered that, in the conversation with Captain Wyeth, the party had been cautioned as to dealing with the Indians, or in any way interfering with the Indian trade, or tariff, as the Hudson's Bay Company gentlemen call the prices they were in the habit of giving to the Indians, for any article of property they might have to dispose of, or that the company might want. If the Indian would part with it at all, he must receive the price or the article they chose to give him, not as an equivalent for his article, but as a condescension on the part of the trader, in allowing him the honor of making the exchange. The Indian's property or article, whatever it might be, was of no consequence to the trader, but the article he gave or furnished to him was of great value. The Indian knew no other system of trade; it was that or nothing; hence the wealth of this arrogant and overgrown company, claiming exclusive trading privileges, as also the right to occupy the country in such a manner, and for such purposes as they chose. As a matter of course, the mission party were not in a condition to vary or change this system of trade; neither were they allowed to encourage the Indians in the expectation of any future change, except as to the religious instructions they were at liberty to impart to them.

The gentlemen of the Hudson's Bay Company were frank with the mission in giving them their tariff: For a salmon at Salmon Falls, two awls or two small fish-hooks; one large hook for two salmon; for a knife, four salmon; for one load of powder and a charge of shot, or a single ball, one salmon. At Wallawalla the tariff was nearly double, say two balls and powder for one large-sized salmon; a three-point blanket, a check shirt, a knife, five or ten balls and powder, from half a foot to three feet of trail-rope tobacco, the price of a good horse. In short, there was but one single object the Indian could live for; that was to contribute his little mite of productive labor to enrich the Honorable Hudson's Bay Company, and to assist them, when required, to relieve the country of intruders. That they were in a state of absolute subjection to the control of the company no one that traveled in it at that early day can doubt for a moment. Speak of improving the condition of the Indians to gentlemen of the company, they would insist that it only made them more insolent, demand higher prices for their produce, and be less inclined to hunt for the furs necessary to supply the goods furnished for their use. The idea of improving the condition of the Indian, and raising him in the scale of civilization, and by that means increase his natural wants, and encourage him with a fair compensation for his labor, was no part of their chartered privileges. They found the Indian as he was; they would leave him no better. The country and all in it was theirs; they could not allow any interference with their trade. "If you missionaries wish to teach them your religion, we have no particular objection, so long as you confine yourselves to such religious instruction; as to trade, gentlemen, we will not object to your receiving from the Indians what you may require for your own personal use and subsistence, provided you do not pay them more for the article you buy of them than the company does. We will give you our tariff, that you may be governed by it in your dealings with the Indians. You will readily perceive, gentlemen, that it is necessary for us to insist on these conditions, in order to protect our own interests, and secure our accustomed profits."

CHAPTER XVII.

An explanation.—Instructions of company.—Their tyranny.—Continuation of journey.—Fording rivers.—Arrival at Boise.—Dr. Whitman compelled to leave his wagon.

It may be asked why the writer gives this explanation of trade and intercourse with the Indians and missionaries before they have reached the field of their future labors? For the simple reason that the party, and the writer in particular, commenced their education in the Rocky Mountains. They learned that in the country to which they were going there was an overgrown, unscrupulous, and exacting monopoly that would prevent any interference in their trade, or intercourse with the Indians. This information was received through the American fur traders, and from Captain Wyeth, who was leaving the country; and from Mr. John McLeod, then in charge of our traveling caravan. It is true, we had only reached Salmon Falls, on Snake River, and we only wished to buy of the miserable, naked, filthy objects before us, a few fresh salmon, which they were catching in apparent abundance; and as is the case with most American travelers, we had many articles that would be valuable to the Indian, and beneficial to us to get rid of. But this overgrown company's interest comes in. "You must not be liberal, or even just, to these miserable human or savage beings; if you are, it will spoil our trade with them; we can not control them if they learn the value of our goods."

This supreme selfishness, this spirit of oppression, was applied not only to the Digger Indians on the barren Snake plains and the salmon fisheries of the Columbia River, but to the miserable discharged, and, in most cases, disabled, Canadian-French. This policy the Hudson's Bay Company practiced upon their own servants, and, as far as was possible, upon all the early settlers of the country. In proof of this, hear what Messrs. Ewing Young and Carmichael say of them on the thirteenth day of January, 1837, just three months after our mission party had arrived, and had written to their friends and patrons in the United States glowing accounts of the kind treatment they had received from this same Hudson's Bay Company. How far the Methodist Mission joined in the attempt to coerce Mr. Young and compel him to place himself under their control, I am unable to say. The Hudson's Bay Company, I know, from the statement of Dr. McLaughlin himself, had an abundance of liquors. I also know they were in the habit of furnishing them freely to the Indians, as they thought the interest of their trade required. Mr. Young's letter is in answer to a request of the Methodist Mission, signed by J. and D. Lee, C. Shepard, and P. L. Edwards, not to erect a distillery on his land claim in Yamhill County (Nealem Valley). The Methodist Mission was made use of on this occasion, under the threat of the Hudson's Bay Company, that in case Mr. Young put up his distillery the Hudson's Bay Company would freely distribute their liquors, and at once destroy all moral restraint, and more than probable the mission itself. Lee and party offered to indemnify Mr. Young for his loss in stopping his distillery project. The Hudson's Bay Company held by this means the exclusive liquor trade, while the mission were compelled to use their influence and means to prevent and buy off any enterprise that conflicted with their interests. Mr. Young says, in his reply:—

"Gentlemen, having taken into consideration your request to relinquish our enterprise in manufacturing ardent spirits, we therefore do agree to stop our proceedings for the present; but, gentlemen, the reasons for first beginning such an enterprise were the *innumerable difficulties* placed in our way by, and the *tyrannizing oppression* of, the Hudson's Bay Company, here under the absolute authority of Dr. McLaughlin, who has treated us with more disdain than any American's feelings could support; but, gentlemen, it is not consistent with our feelings to receive any recompense whatever for our expenditures, but we are thankful to the society for their offer."

The writer of the above short paragraph has long since closed his labors, which, with his little property, have done more substantial benefit to Oregon than the Hudson's Bay Company, that attempted to drive him from the country, which I will prove to the satisfaction of any unprejudiced mind as we proceed. I am fully aware of the great number of pensioned satellites that have fawned for Hudson's Bay Company pap, and would swear no injustice was ever done to a single American, giving this hypocritical, double-dealing, smooth-swindling, called honorable, Hudson's Bay Company credit for what they never did, and really for stealing credit for good deeds done by others. The company insisted that the mission party should, as a condition of being permitted to remain in the country, comply with their ideas of Indian trade and justice in dealing with the natives. The utmost care and attention was given to impress this all-important fact upon the minds of these first missionaries. They were told: "Gentlemen, your own pecuniary interests require it; the good—*yes, the good*—of the natives you came to teach, requires that you should observe our rules in trade."

And here, I have no doubt, lies the great secret of the partial failure of all the Protestant missions. But, thank God, the country is relieved of a curse, like that of slavery in the Southern States. An overgrown monopoly, in using its influence with Catholicism to destroy Protestantism in Oregon and the American settlements, has destroyed itself. Priestcraft and Romanism, combined with ignorance and savagism, under the direction of the Honorable Hudson's Bay Company traders, is a kind of mixture which Mr. Ewing Young says "is more than any American citizen's feelings could support;" yet for six years it was submitted to, and the country increased, not so much in wealth, but in stout-hearted men and women, who had dared every thing, and endured many living deaths, to secure homes, and save a vast and rich country to the American Republic. Was the government too liberal in giving these pioneers three hundred and twenty acres of land, when, by their toil and patient endurance they had suffered every thing this arrogant, unscrupulous, overgrown monopoly could inflict, by calling to its aid superstition and priestcraft, in the worst possible form, to subdue and drive them from the country?

Is there an American on this coast who doubts the fact of the tyrannical course of the company? Listen to what is said of them in 1857, '58, in their absolute government of Vancouver Island and British Columbia, by a resident. He says:—

"In my unsophisticated ignorance, I foolishly imagined I was entering a colony governed by British institutions; but I was quickly undeceived. It was far worse than a Venetian oligarchy; a squawtocracy of skin traders, ruled by men whose lives have been spent in the wilderness in social communion with Indian savages, their present daily occupation being the sale of tea, sugar, whisky, and the usual *et cæteras* of a grocery, which (taking advantage of an increased population) they sold at the small advance of five hundred per cent.; by men, who, to keep up the *entente cordiale* with the red-skins, scrupled not (and the iniquitous practice is still continued) to supply them with arms and ammunition, well knowing that the same would be used in murderous warfare. I found these 'small fry' claiming, under some antediluvian grant, not only Vancouver Island, but a tract of country extending from the Pacific to the Atlantic Ocean, from British Columbia to Hudson's Bay—a territory of larger area than all Europe. The onward march of civilization was checked; all avenues to the mineral regions were closed by excessive, unauthorized, and illegal taxation; and a country abounding with a fair share of Nature's richest productions, and which might now be teeming with a hardy and industrious population, was crushed and blasted by a set of unprincipled autocrats, whose selfish interests, idle caprices, and unscrupulous conduct, sought to gratify their petty ambition by trampling on the dearest rights of their fellow-men. In Victoria and British Columbia the town lots, the suburban farms, and the water frontage were theirs,—the rocks in the bay, and the rocks on the earth; the trees in the streets, which served as ornaments to the town, were cut down by their orders and sold for fire-wood; with equal right (presumption or unscrupulousness is the appropriate term) they claimed the trees and dead timber of the forests, the waters of the bay, and the fresh water on the shores; all, all was theirs;—nay, I have seen the water running from the mountain springs denied to allay the parched thirst of the poor wretches whom the *auri sacra fames* had allured to these inhospitable shores. They viewed with a jealous eye all intruders into their unknown kingdom, and every impediment was thrown in the way of improving or developing the resources of the colony. The coal mines were theirs, and this necessary article of fuel in a northern climate was held by them at thirty dollars per ton. The sole and exclusive right to trade was theirs, and the claim rigidly enforced. The gold fields were theirs likewise, and a tax of five dollars on every man, and eight dollars on every canoe or boat, was levied and collected at the mouth of the cañon before either were allowed to enter the sacred portals of British Columbia. This amount had to be paid hundreds of miles from the place where gold was said to exist, whether the party ever dug an ounce or not. They looked upon all new arrivals with ill-subdued jealousy and suspicion, and distrusted them as a prætorian band of robbers coming to despoil them of their ill-gotten wealth."

Was this the case in 1858? Show me the man who denies it, and I will show you a man devoid of moral perception, destitute of the principle of right dealing between man and man; yet this same Hudson's Bay Company claim credit for saving the thousands of men they had robbed of their hard cash, in not allowing a few sacks of old flour and a quantity of damaged bacon to be sold to exceed one hundred per cent. above prime cost. "Their goods were very reasonable," says the apologist; "their trade was honorable." Has any one ever before attempted to claim honorable dealing for companies pursuing invariably the same selfish and avaricious course? This company is not satisfied with the privilege they have had of robbing the natives of this coast, their French and half-native servants, the American settlers, and their own countrymen, while dependent upon them; but now, when they can no longer rob and steal from half a continent, they come to our government at Washington and make a demand for five millions of dollars for giving up this barefaced open robbery of a whole country they never had the shadow of a right to. It is possible the honorable commissioners may admit this arrogant and unjust claim. If they do,—one single farthing of it,—they deserve the curses due to the company who have robbed the native inhabitants of all their labor, their own servants they brought to it, the country of all they could get from it that was of any value to them, and the nation upon whom they call for any amount, be it great or small.

I have not time, and it would be out of place, to say more upon this subject, at this time, in the historical sketches we propose to give. Be assured we do not write without knowing what we say, and being prepared to prove our statements with facts that have come under our own observation while in the country. We will leave the Hudson's Bay Company and return to our mission party.

After getting a full supply of salmon for a tin whistle, or its equivalent, a smell of trail-rope tobacco, we came to the ford at the three islands in Snake River, crossed all safe, except a short swim for Dr. Whitman and his cart on coming out on the north side or right bank of the river. As nothing serious occurred, we passed on to camp. The next day, in passing along the foot hills of the range of mountains separating the waters of the Snake River and La Rivière aux Bois, we came to the warm springs, in which we boiled a piece of salmon. Then we struck the main Boise River, as it comes out of the mountain, not far below the present location of Boise City; thence, about ten miles down the river, and into the bend, where we found a miserable pen of a place, at that time called Fort Boise. It consisted of cottonwood poles and crooked sticks set in a trench, and pretended to be fastened near the top. The houses or quarters were also of poles, open; in fact, the whole concern could hardly be called a passable corral, or pen for horses and cattle. I think, from appearances, the fort had been used to corral or catch horses in. We were informed that it was established in opposition to Fort Hall, to prevent the Indians, as much as possible, from giving their trade to Captain Wyeth, and that the company expected, if they kept it up, to remove it near the mouth of Boise River.

At this place, McLeod and McKay, and all the Johnny Crapauds of the company, united in the opinion that it was impossible to get the Doctor's cart any further without taking it all apart and bending the iron tires on the wheels, and packing it in par-fleshes (the dried hide of the buffalo, used as an outside covering for packs), and in that way we might get it through, if the animals we packed it upon did not fall with it from the precipices over which we must pass. *Impossible* to get it through any other way. After several consultations, and some very decided expressions against any further attempt to take the wagon further, a compromise was made, that, after the party had reached their permanent location, the Doctor or Mr. Gray would return with the Hudson's Bay Company's caravan and get the wagon and bring it through. To this proposition the Doctor consented. The wagon was left, to the great advantage of the Hudson's Bay Company, in removing their timber and material to build their new fort, as was contemplated, that and the following seasons.

All our goods were placed upon the tallest horses we had, and led across. Mrs. Spalding and Mrs. Whitman were ferried over on a bulrush raft, made by the Indians for crossing. The tops of the rushes were tied with grass ropes, and spread and so arranged that, by lying quite flat upon the rushes and sticks they were conveyed over in safety. Portions of our clothing and goods, as was expected, came in contact with the water, and some delay caused to dry and repack. This attended to, the party proceeded on the present wagon trail till they reached the Grand Ronde; thence they ascended the mountain on the west side of the main river, passed over into a deep cañon, through thick timber, ascended the mountain, and came out on to the Umatilla, not far from the present wagon route.

As the party began to descend from the western slope of the Blue Mountains, the view was surpassingly grand. Before us lay the great valley of the Columbia; on the west, and in full view, Mount Hood rose amid the lofty range of the Cascade Mountains, ninety miles distant. To the south of Mount Hood stood Mount Adams, and to the north, Mount Rainier; while, with the assistance of Mr. McKay, we could trace the course of the Columbia, and determine the location of Wallawalla. It was quite late in the evening before we reached camp on the Umatilla, being delayed by our cattle, their feet having become worn and tender in passing over the sharp rocks, there being but little signs of a trail where we passed over the Blue Mountains in 1836.

CHAPTER XVIII.

Arrival at Fort Wallawalla.—Reception.—The fort in 1836.—Voyage down the Columbia River.—Portage at Celilo.—At Dalles.—A storm.—The Flatheads.—Portage at the Cascades.

NEXT day Mr. McLeod left the train in charge of Mr. McKay, and started for the fort, having obtained a fresh horse from the Cayuse Indians. The party, with Hudson's Bay Company's furs and mission cattle, traveled slowly, and in two days and a half reached old Fort Wallawalla, on the Columbia River,—on the second day of September, 1836, a little over four months from the time they left Missouri. Traveling by time from two to three miles per hour, making it two thousand two hundred and fifty miles.

Their reception must have been witnessed to be fully realized. The gates of the fort were thrown open, the ladies assisted from their horses, and every demonstration of joy and respect manifested. The party were soon led into an apartment, the best the establishment had to offer. Their horses and mules were unloaded and cared for; the cattle were not neglected. It appeared we had arrived among the best of friends instead of total strangers, and were being welcomed home in the most cordial manner. We found the gentleman in charge, Mr. P. C. Pambrun, a French-Canadian by birth, all that we could wish, and more than we expected.

Mr. J. K. Townsend, the naturalist, we found at Wallawalla. He had been sent across the Rocky Mountains, in company with Dr. Nutall, a geologist, by a society in Philadelphia, in 1834, in company with Captain Wyeth. He had remained in the country to complete his collection of specimens of plants and birds, and was awaiting the return of the Hudson's Bay Company's ship, to reach the Sandwich Islands, on his homeward course, having failed to get an escort to connect with Captain Wyeth, and return by way of the Rocky Mountains. From Mr. Townsend the mission party received much useful information relating to the course they should pursue in their intercourse with the Hudson's Bay Company and the Indians. He appeared to take a deep interest in the objects of the mission, confirming, from his own observation, the information already received, cautioning the party not to do any thing with the Indians that would interfere with the Hudson's

Bay Company's trade. Repeating almost *verbatim* Captain Wyeth's words, "The company will be glad to have you in the country, and your influence to improve their servants, and their native wives and children. As to the Indians you have come to teach, they do not want them to be any more enlightened. The company now have absolute control over them, and that is all they require. As to Mr. Pambrun, at this place, he is a kind, good-hearted gentleman, and will do any thing he can for you. He has already received his orders in anticipation of your arrival, and will obey them implicitly; should the company learn from him, or any other source, that you are here and do not comply with their regulations and treatment of the Indians, they will cut off your supplies, and leave you to perish among the Indians you are here to benefit. The company have made arrangements, and expect you to visit Vancouver, their principal depot in the country, before you select your location."

Mr. Townsend had gathered from the gentlemen of the Hudson's Bay Company, during the year he had been in the country, a good knowledge of their policy, and of their manner of treatment and trade with the Indians. He had also learned from conversations with Rev. Samuel Parker and the various members of the company, their views and feelings, not only toward American traders, but of the missionary occupation of the country by the Americans. The mission party of 1836 learned from Mr. McLeod that the Hudson's Bay Company had sent for a chaplain, to be located at Vancouver, and from Mr. Townsend that he had arrived.

It will be borne in mind that this honorable company, on the arrival of Rev. J. Lee and party to look after the civil and religious welfare of the Indians, examined their old charter, and found that one of its requirements was to *Christianize* as well as trade with the natives of this vast country. They found that the English church service must be read at their posts on the Sabbath. To conform to this regulation, a chaplain was sent for. He came, with his wife; and not receiving the submission and attention from the chivalry of the country he demanded, became thoroughly disgusted, and returned to England (I think) on the same ship he came in. As we proceed, we will develop whys and wherefores.

Old Fort Wallawalla, in 1836, when the mission party arrived, was a tolerably substantial stockade, built of drift-wood taken from the Columbia River, of an oblong form, with two log bastions raised, one on the southwest corner, commanding the river-front and southern space beyond the stockade; the other bastion was on the northeast corner, commanding the north end, and east side of the fort. In each of these bastions were kept two small cannon, with a good supply of small-arms. These bastions were always well guarded when any danger was suspected from the Indians. The sage brush, willow, and grease-wood had been cut and cleared away for a considerable distance around, to prevent any Indians getting near the fort without being discovered. Inside the stockade were the houses, store, and quarters for the men, with a space sufficiently large to corral about one hundred horses. The houses and quarters were built by laying down sills, placing posts at from eight to twelve feet apart, with tenons on the top, and the bottom grooved in the sides, and for corner-posts, so as to slip each piece of timber, having also a tenon upon each end, into the grooves of the posts, forming a solid wall of from four to six inches thick, usually about seven feet high from floor to ceiling, or timbers overhead. The roofs were of split cedar, flattened and placed upon the ridge pole and plate-like rafters, close together; then grass or straw was put on the split pieces, covered with mud and dirt, and packed to keep the straw from blowing off. The roofs were less than one-fourth pitch, and of course subject to leakage when it rained. For floors, split puncheons or planks were used in the chief trader's quarters. In the corner of the room was a comfortable fireplace, made of mud in place of brick. The room was lighted with six panes of glass, seven inches by nine, set in strips of wood, split with a common knife, and shaped so as to hold the glass in place of a sash.

The doors were also of split lumber, rough hewn, wrought-iron hinges, and wooden latches; the furniture consisted of three benches, two stools, and one chair (something like a barber's chair, without the scrolls and cushions); a bed in one corner of the room upon some split boards for bottom; a rough table of the same material roughly planed. This, with a few old cutlasses, shot-pouches, and tobacco sacks (such as were manufactured by the Indians about the post), constituted the room and furniture occupied by P. C. Pambrun, Esq., of the Honorable Hudson's Bay Company. Into this room the mission party were invited, and introduced to Mrs. Pambrun and two young children-misses. The kind and cordial reception of Mr. Pambrun was such that all felt cheerful and relieved in this rude specimen of half-native, half-French dwelling. The cloth was soon spread upon the table, and the cook brought in the choice game of the prairies well cooked, with a small supply of Irish potatoes and small Canadian yellow corn. This was a feast, as well as a great change from dried and pounded buffalo meat "straight," as the miners say, upon which we had subsisted since we left the rendezvous, except the occasional fresh bits we could get along the route. Dinner being disposed of, some fine melons were served, which Mr. Pambrun had succeeded in raising in his little melon patch, in the bends of the Wallawalla River, about two miles from the fort. The supply of melons was quite limited, a single one of each kind for the party. Mr. Townsend on this occasion yielded his share to the ladies, and insisted, as he had been at the fort and partaken of them on previous occasions, they should have his share. Dinner over, melons disposed of, fort, stores, and quarters examined, arrangements were made for sleeping in the various sheds and bastions of the fort. Most of the gentlemen preferred the open air and tent to the accommodations of the fort. Rooms were provided for the two ladies and their husbands, Dr. Whitman and Mr. Spalding.

Next morning early, Messrs. McLeod and Townsend started for Vancouver in a light boat, with the understanding that Mr. Pambrun, with the company's furs, and the mission party, were to follow in a few days. Mr. McKay was to remain in charge of the fort. All things were arranged to Mr. Pambrun's satisfaction; two boats or barges were made ready, the furs and party all aboard, with seven men to each barge, six to row and one to steer, with a big paddle instead of a helm, or an oar; we glided swiftly down the Columbia River, the scenery of which is not surpassed in grandeur by any river in the world. Fire, earth, and water have combined to make one grand display with melted lava, turning it out in all imaginable and unimaginable shapes and forms on a most gigantic scale. In other countries, these hills thrown up would be called mountains, but here we call them high rolling plains, interspersed with a few snow-capped peaks, some fifteen and some seventeen thousand feet high. The river is running through these plains, wandering around among the rocks with its gentle current of from four to eight knots per hour; at the rapids increasing its velocity and gyrations around and among the rocks in a manner interesting and exciting to the traveler, who at one moment finds his boat head on at full speed making for a big rock; anon he comes along, and by an extra exertion with his pole shoves off his boat to receive a full supply of water from the rolling swell, as the water rushes over the rock he has but just escaped being dashed to pieces against. As to danger in such places, it is all folly to think of any; so on we go to repeat the same performance over and over till we reach the falls, at what is now called Celilo, where we find about twenty-five feet perpendicular fall.

Our boats were discharged of all their contents, about one-fourth of a mile above the main fall, on the right bank of the river. Then the cargo was packed upon the Indians' backs to the landing below the falls, the Indian performing this part of the labor for from two to six inches of trail-rope tobacco. A few were paid from two to ten charges of powder and ball, or shot, depending upon the number of trips they made and the amount they carried. The boats were let down with lines as near the fall as was considered safe, hauled out of the water, turned bottom up, and as many Indians as could get under them, say some twenty-five to each boat, lifted them upon their shoulders and carried them to the water below. For this service they each received two dried leaves of tobacco, which would make about six common pipefuls. The Indian, however, with other dried leaves, would make his two leaves of tobacco last some time.

This portage over, and all on board, we again glided swiftly along, ran through what is called the Little Dalles, and soon reached the narrowest place in the Columbia, where the water rushes through sharp projecting rocks, causing it to turn and whirl and rush in every conceivable shape for about three-fourths of a mile, till it finds a large circular basin below, into which it runs and makes one grand turn round and passes smoothly out at right angles and down in a deep smooth current, widening as it enters the lofty range of the Cascade Mountains. The river was deemed a little too high, by our Iroquois pilot, to run the Big Dalles at that time, although, in January following, the writer, in company with another party, did run them with no more apparent danger than we experienced on the same trip at what is called John Day's Rapids. At the Dalles our party made another portage, paying our Indians as at Celilo Falls.

The Indians' curiosity to look at the white women caused us a little delay at the falls, and also at the Dalles; in fact, numbers of them followed our boats in their canoes to the Dalles, to look at these two strange beings who had nothing to carry but their own persons, and were dressed so differently from the men.

We proceeded down the river for a few miles and met the Hudson's Bay Company's express canoe, in charge of Mr. Hovey, on its way to Lachine, going across the continent; stopped and exchanged greetings for a few minutes and passed on to camp just above Dog River. Next morning made an early start to reach La Cascade to make the portage there before night. We had proceeded but about one hour, with a gentle breeze from the east, sails all set, and in fine spirits, admiring the sublimely grand scenery, when, looking down the river, the ladies inquired what made the water look so white. In a moment our boatmen took in sail, and laid to their oars with all their might to reach land and get under shelter, which we did, but not till we had received considerable wetting, and experienced the first shock of a severe wind-storm, such as can be gotten up on the shortest possible notice in the midst of the Cascade Mountains. Our camp was just below White Salmon River. The storm was so severe that all our baggage, furs, and even boats had to be taken out of the water to prevent them from being dashed to pieces on the shore. For three days and nights we lay in this miserable camp watching the storm as it howled on the waves and through this mountain range. Stormy as it was, a few Indians found our camp and crawled over the points of rocks to get sight of our party.

Among the Indians of the coast and lower Columbia none but such as are of noble birth are allowed to flatten their skulls. This is accomplished by taking an infant and placing it upon a board corresponding in length and breadth to the size of the child, which is placed upon it and lashed fast in a sort of a sack, to hold its limbs and body in one position. The head is also confined with strings and lashing, allowing scarcely any motion for the head. From the head of the board, upon which the infant is made fast, is a small piece of board lashed to the back piece, extending down nearly over the eyes, with strings attached so as to prevent the forehead from extending beyond the eyes, giving the head and face a broad and flat shape. The native infants of the blood royal were kept in these presses from three to four months, or longer, as the infant could bear, or as the aspirations of the parent prompted. For the last fifteen years I have not seen a native infant promoted to these royal honors. My impression is that the example of the white mother in the treatment of her infant has had more influence in removing this cruel practice than any other cause. As a general thing, the tribes that have followed the practice of flattening the skull are inferior in intellect, less stirring and enterprising in their habits, and far more degraded in their morals than other tribes. To this cause probably more than any other may be traced the effect of vice among them. The tribes below the Cascade Mountains were the first that had any intercourse with the whites. The diseases never feared or shunned by the abandoned and profligate youth and sailor were introduced among them. The certain and legitimate effect soon showed itself all along the coast. So prevalent was vice and immorality among the natives, that not one escaped. Their blood became tainted, their bodies loathsome and foul, their communication corrupt continually. The flattened head of the royal families, and the round head of the slave, was no protection from vice and immoral intercourse among the sexes; hence, when diseases of a different nature, and such as among the more civilized white race are easily treated and cured, came among them, they fell like rotten sheep. If a remnant is left, I have often felt that the reacting curse of vice will pursue our advanced civilization for the certain destruction that has befallen the miserable tribes that but a few years since peopled this whole coast. It is true that the missionaries came to the country before many white settlers came. It is also true that they soon learned the causes that would sweep the Indians from the land, and in their feeble efforts to check and remove the causes, they were met by the unlimited and unbridled passions of all in the country, and all who came to it for a number of years subsequent, with a combined influence to destroy that of the missionaries in correcting or checking this evil. Like alcohol and its friends, it had no virtue or conscience, hence the little moral influence brought by the first missionaries was like pouring water upon glass: it only washed the sediment from the surface while the heart remained untouched. Most of the missionaries could only be witnesses of facts that they had little or no power to correct or prevent; many of them lacked the moral courage necessary to combat successfully the influences with which they were surrounded, and every action, word, or expression was canvassed and turned against them or the cause they represented.

The reader will excuse this little digression into moral facts, as he will bear in mind that we were in a most disagreeable camp on the Columbia River, between the Cascades and the Dalles, and for the first time were introduced to real live Flatheads and the process of making them such. The men, also, or boatmen, amused themselves in getting the members of the royal family who visited our camp drunk as Chinamen (on opium), by filling their pipes with pure trail-rope tobacco.

On the fourth morning after the storm stopped us, we were again on our way. Arrived at the Cascades and made a portage of the goods over, around, and among the rocks, till we reached the basin below the main shoot or rapids. The boats were let down by lines and hauled out to repair leakage from bruises received on the rocks in their descent. Damage repaired, all embarked again, and ran down to Cape Horn and camped; next day we reached the saw-mill and camped early. All hands must wash up and get ready to reach the fort in the morning. From the saw-mill an Indian was sent on ahead to give notice at the fort of the arrival of the party. Our captain, as the Americans would call Mr. Pambrun, who had charge of the boats, was slow in getting ready to start. Breakfast over, all dressed in their best clothes, the party proceeded on down the river. In coming round a bend of the upper end of the plain upon which the fort stands, we came in full view of two fine ships dressed in complete regalia from stem to stern, with the St. George cross waving gracefully from the staff in the fort. Our party inquired innocently enough the cause of this display. Captain Pambrun evaded a direct answer. In a short time, as the boats neared the shore, two tall, well-formed, neatly-dressed gentlemen waved a welcome, and in a moment all were on shore. Rev. Mr. Spalding and lady were introduced, followed by Dr. Whitman and lady, to the two gentlemen. One, whose hair was then nearly white, stepped forward and gave his arm to Mrs. Whitman. The other, a tall, black-haired, black-eyed man, with rather slim body, a light sallow complexion and smooth face, gave his arm to Mrs. Spalding. By this time Mr. McLeod had made his appearance, and bade the party a hearty welcome and accompanied them into the fort. We began to suspect the cause of so much display. All safely arrived in the fort, we were led up-stairs, in front of the big square hewed-timber house, and into a room on the right of the hall, where the ladies were seated, as also some six gentlemen, besides the tall white-headed one. The writer, standing in the hall, was noticed by Mr. McLeod, who came out and invited him into the quarters of the clerks. We will leave our ladies in conversation with the two fine-looking gentlemen that received them on arriving at the water's edge, while we take a look at the fort, as it appeared on September 12, 1836.

CHAPTER XIX.

Fort Vancouver in 1836.—An extra table.—Conditions on which cattle were supplied to settlers.—Official papers.—Three organizations.

FORT VANCOUVER was a stockade, built with fir-logs about ten inches in diameter, set some four feet in the ground, and about twenty feet above, secured by pieces of timber pinned on the inside, running diagonally around the entire stockade, which at that time covered or inclosed about two acres of ground. The old fort, as it was called, was so much decayed that the new one was then being built, and portions of the old one replaced. The storehouses were all built of hewn timber, about six inches thick, and covered with sawed boards one foot wide and one inch thick, with grooves in the edges of the boards, placed up and down upon the roof, in place of shingles; of course, in case of a knot-hole or a crack, it was a leaky concern. All the houses were covered with boards in a similar manner in the new quarters. The partitions were all upright boards planed, and the cracks battened; floors were mostly rough boards, except the office and the governor's house, which were planed. The parsonage was what might be called of the balloon order, covered like the rest, with a big mud and stone chimney in the center. The partitions and floors were rough boards. There were but two rooms, the one used for dining-room and kitchen, the other for bedroom and parlor. The doors and gates of the fort, or stockade, were all locked from the inside, and a guard stationed over the gate. In front of the governor's house was a half semicircle double stairway, leading to the main hall up a flight of some ten steps. In the center of the semicircle was one large 24-pound cannon, mounted on a ship's carriage, and on either side was a small cannon, or mortar gun, with balls piled in order about them, all pointing to the main gate entrance; latterly, to protect the fort from the savages that had commenced coming over the Rocky Mountains, a bastion was built, said to be for saluting her Majesty's ships when they might arrive, or depart from the country.

At 12 M. the fort bell rang; clerks and gentlemen all met at the common dinner-table, which was well supplied with potatoes, salmon, wild fowl, and usually with venison and bread. Dinner over, most of the gentlemen passed a compliment in a glass of wine, or brandy, if preferred; all then retired to the social hall, a room in the clerks' quarters, where they indulged in a stiff pipe of tobacco, sometimes filling the room as full as it could hold with smoke. At 1 P. M. the bell rang again, when all went to business.

The party had no sooner arrived than the carpenter was ordered to make an extra table, which was located in the governor's office, in the room where we left them on first bringing them into the house. This extra table was presided over by the governor, or the next highest officers of the fort; usually one or two of the head clerks or gentlemen traders were, by special invitation, invited to dine with the ladies, or, rather, at the ladies' table. The governor's wife was not sufficiently accomplished, at first, to take a seat at the ladies' table. I never saw her in the common dining-hall; neither was the mother of the chief clerk's children permitted this honor at first. However, as Mrs. Whitman and Mrs. Spalding soon learned the fort regulations, as also the family connection there was in the establishment, they very soon introduced themselves to the two principal mothers they found in the governor's house, one belonging to the governor, and the other to the chief clerk, and made themselves acquainted with the young misses; and, in a short time, in opposition to the wish of the governor and his chief clerk, brought them both to the ladies' table. They also brought the youngest daughter of the governor to the table, and took considerable pains to teach the young misses, and make themselves generally useful; so that, at the end of two weeks, when arrangements had been made for the party to return to Wallawalla to commence their missionary labors, the governor and chief clerk would not allow the ladies to depart, till the gentlemen had gone up and selected their stations and built their houses, so that they could be comfortable for winter. Captain Wyeth and Mr. Townsend were correct in their ideas of the reception of this party. The utmost cordiality was manifested, the kindest attention paid, and such articles as could be made about the establishment, that the party wanted, were supplied. The goods were all to be furnished at *one hundred per cent. on London prices*, drafts to be drawn on the American Board, payable in London at sight. They were cashed by the Board at thirty-seven cents premium on London drafts, costing the mission two dollars and seventy-four cents for every dollar's worth of goods they received; freight and charges from Fort Vancouver to Wallawalla were added. These goods were received and paid for, not as a business transaction with the Hudson's Bay Company, by any means, but as a *gracious gift;* or, to quote the governor and chief clerk, "You gentlemen *must* consider yourselves under great obligation to the Hudson's Bay Company, as we are only here to trade with the natives. In your future transactions you will make out your orders, and we will forward them to London to be filled at their rates, and with this understanding."

While at Vancouver, Dr. Whitman concluded that some more cattle than the mission had were necessary to facilitate the labor in breaking up the prairie for a spring crop; and a few cows might be useful to assist in getting a start in cattle. The proposition was made to the Hudson's Bay Company, to know upon what terms they could get them. "Certainly," said Dr. McLaughlin, "you can have what cattle you want on the conditions we furnish them to the company's servants and the settlers in the Wallamet." "What are those conditions?" said Dr. Whitman. "Why, in case of work cattle, you can take them from our band; we can not, of course, spare you those we are working, but the cattle you take, you break in, and when the company requires them you return them to the company." "And what are your terms in letting your cows?" said Dr. Whitman. "Why, we let them have the cows for the use of the milk; they return the cow and its increase to the company." "And how is it in case the animal is lost or gets killed?" "You gentlemen will have no difficulty on that account; you have some cattle; you can replace them from your own band."

Dr. Whitman seemed a little incredulous as to the conditions upon which cattle could be had of the company, and inquired if such were the conditions they furnished them to their servants and the settlers. Dr. McLaughlin replied emphatically, it was. We learned in this connection that there was not a cow in the country, except those of the American Board, that was not owned by the Hudson's Bay Company. The same was the case with all the beeves and work cattle. The mission party concluded they would not mortgage their own cattle for the use of the Hudson's Bay Company's; hence dropped the cattle question for the time being.

While at Vancouver, it was deemed necessary for a copy of the official papers of the mission party to be made out, and forwarded to the Sandwich Islands, to the American and British consuls, and one to the commercial agent of the Hudson's Bay Company, with an order from Dr. McLaughlin, to the agent of the Hudson's Bay Company, to forward any supplies or goods designed for the mission of the American Board. These documents were made out, and duly signed, by Rev. Mr. Spalding and Dr. Whitman. The question arose whether the name of the secular agent of the mission ought not also to be attached to the documents, and was decided in the affirmative. Gray was sent for; he entered the office with his hat under his arm, as per custom in entering the audience chamber where official business was transacted, examined hastily the documents, attached his name, and retired. The incident was noticed by Dr. McLaughlin, and while the mission party were absent, locating and building their stations, Dr. McLaughlin inquired of Mrs. Whitman who the young man was that Mr. Spalding and her husband had to sign a copy of the public documents sent to the Sandwich Islands. Mrs. Whitman replied, "Why, that is Mr. Gray, our associate, and secular agent of the mission." The inquiries about Mr. Gray were dropped till the ladies reached their stations, and Mr. Gray was advised, when he visited Vancouver again, to present his credentials, and show the Hudson's Bay Company his connection with the mission. Accordingly, when Mr. Gray visited Vancouver, in January, 1837, he presented his credentials, and was received in a manner contrasting very strongly with that of his former reception; still, the lesson he had learned was not a useless one. He saw plainly the condition of all the settlers, or any one in the country that had no official position or title; he was looked upon as a vagabond, and entitled to no place or encouragement, only as he submitted to the absolute control of the Hudson's Bay Company, or one of the missions. There was nothing but master and servant in the country, and this honorable company were determined that no other class should be permitted to be in it. To the disgrace of most of the missionaries, this state of absolute dependence and submission to the Hudson's Bay Company, or themselves, was submitted to, and encouraged. At least, no one but Rev. Jason Lee, of the Methodist Mission, fully comprehended the precise condition of an outsider. This will be shown as we proceed. We were made a party to a special contract, in 1837, touching this question.

Then we had three distinct organizations in the country: The first, and the most important in wealth and influence, was the Hudson's Bay Company's traders; the second, the Methodist Mission, with their ideas and efforts to Christianize the savages, and to do what they could to convert the gentlemen of the Hudson's Bay Company from the error of their ways; third, the mission of the American Board, to accomplish the same object. The fact of these two missions being in the country, both having the same object to accomplish, elicited a discussion as to the proper location for both to operate in. It was not deemed advisable to locate in the same tribe, as the field was large enough for both. The Cowlitz and Puget Sound district was proposed, but not favored by the Hudson's Bay Company; Mr. Pambrun kept the claims of the Nez Percés and Cayuses before the party. His interests and arguments prevailed.

CHAPTER XX.

Settlers in 1836.—Wallamet Cattle Company.—What good have the missionaries done? —Rev. J. Lee and party.—The Hudson's Bay Company recommend the Wallamet.—Missionaries not dependent on the company.—Rev. S. Parker arrives at Vancouver.

THERE were in the country, in the winter of 1836, besides those connected with the Hudson's Bay Company and the missions, about fifteen men, all told. The two missions numbered seven men and two women, making the American population about twenty-five persons. To bring the outsiders from the Hudson's Bay Company and the two missions into subjection, and to keep them under proper control, it was necessary to use all the influence the Methodist Mission had. They, as a matter of interest and policy, furnished to such as showed a meek and humble disposition, labor, and such means as they could spare from their stores, and encouraged them to marry the native women they might have, or be disposed to take, and become settlers about the mission. Such as were not disposed to submit to the government of the mission, or the Hudson's Bay Company, like Mr. E. Young, Carmichael, and Killmer, were "*left out in the cold.*" They could get no supplies, and no employment. They were literally outcasts from society, and considered as outlaws and intruders in the country. All seemed anxious to get rid of them.

McCarty, the companion of Mr. Young from California to Oregon, had fallen out with him on the way, as Young was bringing to the country a band of California horses (brood mares). McCarty, it seems, to be avenged on Young, reported to Dr. McLaughlin and the mission that Young had stolen his band of horses (though it has since been stated upon good authority that such was not the case); still McCarty was (I understand) a member of the class-meeting, on probation. His statements were received as truth, and Young suffered. Young was a stirring, ambitious man; he had spent some time in the Rocky Mountains, and in Santa Fé and California, and the little property he could get he had invested in horses, and brought them to Oregon. This fact, with the malicious reports circulated about him, made him an object of suspicion and contempt on the part of the Hudson's Bay Company and the mission. We find that Mr. Lee treated Mr. Young as an honest man, and, consequently, fell under the displeasure of Dr. McLaughlin and the Hudson's Bay Company. *With Mr. Young, Mr. Lee succeeded* in getting up the first cattle company, and gave the first blow toward breaking up the despotism and power of the company. Mr. Young, as Mr. Lee informed us, was the only man in the country he could rely upon, in carrying out his plan to supply the settlement with cattle. He was aware of the stories in circulation about him, and of the want of confidence in him in the mission and among the French-Canadians and Hudson's Bay Company. To obviate this difficulty, he suggested that Mr. P. L. Edwards, a member of the mission, should go as treasurer of the company, and Mr. Young as captain. This brought harmony into the arrangement, and a ready subscription to the stock of the Wallamet Cattle Company, all being anxious to obtain cattle. But few of the settlers had any means at command. Many of the discharged servants of the Hudson's Bay Company had credit on their books. There were outside men enough in the country willing to volunteer to go for the cattle, and receive their pay in cattle when they arrived with the band in Oregon. This brought the matter directly to the Hudson's Bay Company, and to Dr. McLaughlin. Rev. Jason Lee received the orders of the company's servants, went to Vancouver, and learned from the clerks in the office the amounts due the drawers, then went to the Doctor, and insisted that certain amounts should be paid on those orders.

The Doctor very reluctantly consented to allow the money or drafts to be paid. This amount, with all the mission and settlers could raise, would still have been too small to justify the party in starting, but W. A. Slacum, Esq., of the United States navy, being on a visit to the country, Mr. Lee stated the condition of matters to him. Mr. Slacum at once subscribed the requisite stock, and advanced all the money the mission wished on their stock, taking mission drafts on their Board, and gave a free passage to California for the whole party. (As the missionaries would say, "Bless God for brother Slacum's providential arrival among us.") Uncle Sam had the right man in the right place that time. It was but a little that he did; yet that little, what mighty results have grown out of it!

On the 19th of January, 1837, six days after Mr. Young had given up his projected distillery, he is on board Mr. Slacum's brig *Lariat*, lying off the mouth of the Wallamet River, and on his way to California with a company of stout-hearted men, eight (I think) in all, not to steal horses or cheat the miserable savages, and equally miserable settlers, out of their little productive labor, but to bring a band of cattle to benefit the whole country. In this connection, I could not do justice to all without quoting a paragraph which I find in Rev. G. Hines' history of the Oregon missions. He says:—

"Mr. Slacum's vessel left the Columbia River about the first of February, and arrived safely in the bay of San Francisco, on the coast of California. The cattle company proceeded immediately to purchase a large band of cattle and a number of horses, with which they started for Oregon. In crossing a range of mountains (Rogue River Mountains), they were attacked by the rascally Indians, and a number of their cattle were killed, but they at length succeeded in driving back their foe and saving the remainder. *Contrary to the predictions and wishes of the members of the Hudson's Bay Company*, who INDIRECTLY OPPOSED them at the outset, they arrived in safety in the Wallamet Valley with six hundred head of cattle, and distributed them among the settlers, according to the provisions of the compact. This successful enterprise, which laid the foundation for a rapid accumulation of wealth by the settlers, was mainly accomplished through the energy and perseverance of Rev. Jason Lee."

WHAT GOOD HAVE THE MISSIONARIES DONE IN THE COUNTRY? I do not know how Mr. Hines arrived at the conclusion that the Hudson's Bay Company "*indirectly opposed*" this cattle expedition. I know they did it *directly*, and it was only through the influence of Rev. J. Lee, and Mr. Slacum, of the United States navy, that they could have succeeded at all. Mr. Lee, in his conversation with Dr. McLaughlin, told that gentleman directly that it was of no use for the company to *oppose* the *expedition* any more; the party was made up, and the men were on the way, and the cattle would come as per engagement, unless the men were lost at sea. The Hudson's Bay Company yielded the point only on the failure of the Rogue River Indians to destroy the expedition. Mr. Slacum placed it beyond their control to stop it. The courage of the men was superior to the company's Indian allies. The cattle came, and no thanks to any of the Hudson's Bay Company's generosity, patronage, or power. They did all they dared to do, openly and secretly, to prevent the bringing of that band of cattle into the country; and, determining to monopolize the country as far as possible, they at once entered upon the PUGET SOUND AGRICULTURAL COMPANY, under the auspices of the Hudson's Bay Company and the English government.

Do you ask me how I know these things? Simply by being at Vancouver the day the brig dropped down the Columbia River, and listening to the discussion excited on the subject, and to the proposition and plan of the Puget Sound Company among the gentlemen concerned in getting it up.

The mission of the American Board had no stock in the cattle company of the Wallamet, not venturing to incur the displeasure of the Hudson's Bay Company by expressing an opinion any way upon it. The writer was picking up items and preparing for a trip to New York overland, with one of the Hudson Bay Company's traders, Mr. Francis (or Frank) Ermatinger. While in New York, Cincinnati, and other places, he stated the fact that the Methodist missionaries had fallen under the displeasure of the Hudson's Bay Company in entering too freely into trade and speculation in cattle in the country. Truth and justice to them require that I enter fully into their transactions as men and missionaries.

Rev. J. Lee, it will be remembered, was the first man to answer the call of the Indian to come to his country. The Methodist Board had been formed, and J. Lee accepted their invitation and patronage. In this expedition he gathered his associates, and at the same time made arrangements for future supplies to arrive by sea, coming around Cape Horn. Captain Wyeth was in Boston, getting up a trading expedition, and chartering a vessel for the mouth of the Columbia River, the *May Dacre.* On board Captain Lambert's brig Captain Wyeth and the Methodist Board shipped their goods for the two expeditions. The goods on the way, it became necessary for the future objects of the mission to have a few horses to carry on the improvements necessary to a civilized life. Lee and associates start across the continent. Missouri is the most western limit of civilization. They reach it, purchase their outfit, and, in company with Captain Wyeth, reach Fort Hall; here they fall in with Thomas McKay and our English nobleman, Captain Stewart. Captain Wyeth stopped to build his fort, while McKay, Stewart, Lee, Dr. Nutall, Townsend, and parties all made their way to Wallawalla, on the Columbia River. The supreme selfishness of the Hudson's Bay Company seems here to begin to develop itself. Lee and party were made to believe that the Flathead tribe, who had sent their messengers for teachers, were not only a small, but a very distant tribe, and very disadvantageously situated for the establishment and support of a missionary among them. These statements determined them to proceed to the lower Columbia, to find a better location to commence operations. Leaving their horses at Wallawalla, in charge of one of their party, they proceeded down the Columbia in one of the Hudson's Bay Company's boats, being eleven days in reaching the fort, and one hundred and fifty-two days on the way from Missouri. They were kindly received by the gentlemen of the fort, and in two days were on the hunt for a location.

The party that arrived just two years later, with two ladies, were not allowed to leave the fort to look for locations till they had remained twelve days, and been invited to ride all over the farm, and visit the ships, and eat melons and apples (being always cautioned to save all the seeds for planting).

Lee and party were frank to make known to the company their object, and plans of future operations. Questions of trade and morality were comparatively new with the company. As religious teachers and Christian men they had no suspicions of any interference in trade. Mr. Lee hailed from Canada, and so did Dr. McLaughlin and a large number of the servants of the company.

"Mr. Lee is the man we want to instruct our retired servants in religious matters. Mr. Shepard will be an excellent man to take charge of our little private school; we have commenced with a Mr. S. H. Smith, who has found his way into the country, in company with Captain Wyeth, an opposition fur trader and salmon catcher. We do not know much about him, but if you will allow Mr. Shepard to take charge of our school till you can make other arrangements, and you require his services, we will make it all right."

This arrangement placed the labor of selecting locations and the necessary explorations upon our friend Jason Lee. All being smooth and cordial with the company, Lee proceeds to French Prairie and up the river till he reaches a point ten miles below Salem, about two miles above Jarvie's old place, and makes his first location. From all the information he could gather, this was the most central point to reach the greatest number of Indians and allow the largest number of French and half-native population to collect around the station. In this expedition he occupied about ten days. The whole country was before them—a wilderness two thousand six hundred miles broad, extending from the gulf of California on the south, to the Russian settlements on the north, with a few scattering stations among the border Indians along the western territories of Missouri, and the great unknown, unexplored west, which the American Board, in a book published in 1862, page 380, says, "brought to light no field for a great and successful mission," showing that, for twenty-five years, they have neglected to give this country the attention its present position and importance demanded, and also a total neglect on their part to select and sustain proper men in this vast missionary field. They are willing now to plead ignorance, by saying, "Rev. Samuel Parker's exploring tour beyond the Rocky Mountains in 1836 and 1837 (but two years after the Rev. J. Lee came to it) brought to light *no field for a great and successful mission*," and console themselves by asserting a popular idea as having originated from Mr. Parker's exploration, "a practicable route for a *railroad* from the Mississippi to the Pacific." Mr. Parker never originated or thought of the practicability of the route till after Dr. Whitman had left his wagon at Fort Boise, and demonstrated the fact of a practicable wagon route. Then Mr. Parker, to give his work or journal a wider circulation, talked about a railroad. The American Board, I am sorry to feel and think, are good at attempting to catch at straws when important missionary objects have been faithfully placed before them.

Let us return to Mr. Lee. On Saturday, September 27, 1834, he was in council with Dr. McLaughlin, at Vancouver. The result of his observations were fully canvassed; the condition and prospects of the Indians and half-natives, Canadian-French, straggling sailors and hunters that might find their way into the country, were all called before this council. The call from the Flathead Indians and the Nez Percés was not forgotten. The Wallamet Valley had the best advocate in Dr. John McLaughlin. He "strongly recommended it, as did the other gentlemen of Vancouver, as the most eligible place for the establishment of the center of their operations." This located that mission under the direct supervision and inspection of the Hudson's Bay Company, and, at the same time, placed the American settlement south of the Columbia River.

Mr. Lee, the next day, was invited to preach in the fort. All shades of colors and sects attended this first preaching in the wilderness of Oregon. The effect in three months was the baptizing of four adults and seventeen children.

The Protestant missions were not dependent on the Hudson's Bay Company for supplies any more than the Sandwich Islands were, or the American Fur Company. If such were the fact, that they were dependent upon the Hudson's Bay Company, the missionaries themselves and the Boards that sent them to Oregon must have been a set of foolish men, not competent to conduct the commonest affairs of life. The idea that seven men and two women should be sent to a distant wilderness and savage country, and no provisions made for their subsistence and future supplies, is one originated without a soul, a lie to produce effect, a slander upon common honesty and common-sense Christianity. Whitman's party left in the Rocky Mountains a better set of tools than could be found in Vancouver. They brought seeds of all kinds. They had no occasion to ask of the Hudson's Bay Company a single seed for farming purposes, a single thing in establishing their mission,—only as they had disposed of things at the suggestion of McLeod and McKay as unnecessary to pack them further. Arrangements were made to forward around Cape Horn, as soon as was deemed necessary, such articles and supplies as might be required. Rev. Jason Lee and party did not arrive in the country (as those who have all along attempted to insinuate and make a stranger to the facts believe, and in 1865 claim the sum of $3,822,036.67 for stealing credit due to others, and preventing the good others might have done to the natives in advancing them in the scale of civilization) destitute and dependent upon the Hudson's Bay Company for supplies. On the contrary, by the time they had selected their station, the goods on the brig *May Dacre* had arrived, and were ready to be landed at the lower mouth of the Wallamet River. These goods, whether suitable or not, were all received and conveyed to the station selected by Mr. Lee by the 6th of October. The rainy season soon commenced; they had no shelter for themselves or their goods. All old Oregonians who have not been seduced and brought up by the Hudson's Bay Company can comprehend the condition they were in. Rev. Jason Lee, like Dr. Whitman with his old wagon, had undertaken a work he meant to accomplish. His religion was practical. Work, labor, preach, and practice his own precepts, and demonstrate the truth of his own doctrines. Religion and labor were synonymous with him, and well did the noble Shepard, though but a lay member of the mission and the church, labor and sustain him. These two men were really the soul and life of the mission, as Dr. Whitman and Mrs. Spalding were of the American Board. During the first winter, 1834–5, they were wholly occupied in building their houses and preparing for the cultivation of the land for their own subsistence. There was no alternative; it was work or starve. Rev. Jason Lee set the example. He held the plow, with an Indian boy to drive, in commencing his farming operations. The first year they produced enough for home consumption in wheat, peas, oats, and barley, and abundance of potatoes, with a few barrels of salt salmon. The superintendent of the mission put up at the Wallamet Falls late in the season of 1834. They had a supply of their own for the first year. It is true they did not have superfine flour to eat, but they had plenty of pounded and boiled wheat, and a change to pea and barley soup, with oats for the chickens they had received from the vessel.

Daniel Lee soon falls sick, and Edwards becomes dissatisfied. They both arrange to leave the country on the *May Dacre*. Rev. D. Lee is advised to go to the Sandwich Islands, and Edwards is induced to undertake an independent school at Champoeg.

Shepard toils on with his Indian and half-native school. Mr. Lee preaches and labors at the mission among the French, and at Vancouver.

In October, 1835, Rev. S. Parker arrived at Vancouver. In November he made a flying visit to Mr. Lee's mission. His Presbyterian spectacles were not adapted to correct observations on Methodist Episcopal missions. He was inclined to pronounce their efforts a failure. This impression of Mr. Parker's arose from the fact, that no female influence, except that of the natives of the country, was seen or felt about the mission. His impressions were also quite unfavorable to the Hudson's Bay Company from the same cause. These impressions were, at the suggestion of the writer, omitted in his first published journal. Four months after Mr. Parker's visit to Mr. Lee's mission, we find the gentlemen of the Hudson's Bay Company making a handsome donation to Mr. Lee's mission of $130, including a handsome prayer for a blessing upon their labors, in the following words: "And they pray our heavenly Father, without whose assistance we can do nothing, that of his infinite mercy he may vouchsafe to bless and prosper your pious endeavors." This is signed in behalf of the donors by John McLaughlin.

CHAPTER XXI.

Arrival of Rev. Mr. Beaver and wife.—His opinion of the company.—A double-wedding.—Mrs. Spalding and Mrs. Whitman at Vancouver.—Men explore the country and locate stations.—Their opinion of the country.—Indian labor.—A winter trip down Snake River.

NOTHING of note occurred till about the middle of August, 1836. The bark *Nereus* arrived from England, bringing back Rev. Daniel Lee, recovered from his sickness while in the Sandwich Islands, and Rev. Mr. Beaver and lady, an English Episcopal clergyman, as chaplain to the Hudson's Bay Company at Fort Vancouver. Mr. Beaver was a man below the medium height, light brown hair, gray eyes, light complexion, a feminine voice, with large pretensions to oratory, a poor delivery, and no energy. His ideas of clerical dignity were such, that he felt himself defiled and polluted in descending to the "common herd of savages" he found on arriving at Vancouver. "The governor was uncivil, the clerks were boors, the women were savages. There was not an individual about the establishment he felt he could associate with." This feeling was shared largely by Mrs. Beaver, who, from the little I saw of her at a double-wedding party at her own house, I concluded, felt she was condescending greatly in permitting her husband to perform the services.

She appeared totally indifferent to the whole performance, so far as giving it an approving smile, look, or word. The occasion was the marriage of the youngest daughter of Dr. McLaughlin to Mr. Ray; and of Miss Nelia Comilly to Mr. James Douglas, since governor of Vancouver Island and British Columbia.

While at Vancouver, I met Mr. Beaver once outside the fort, with his dog and gun. From what I could learn of him, he was fond of hunting and fishing;—much more so than of preaching to the "ignorant savages in the fort," as he called the gentlemen and servants of the company. "They were not sufficiently enlightened to appreciate good sermons, and to conform to the English church service. However, as he was the chaplain in charge, by virtue of his appointment received from the executive committee and governor in London, he had rights superior to any half-savage, pretended gentlemen at this establishment, and he would let them know what they were, before they were done with him; he did not come to this wilderness to be ordered and dictated to by a set of half-savages, who did not know the difference between a prayer-book and an otter skin, and yet they presumed to teach him morals and religion." This tirade, as near as I could learn, was elicited from his reverence soon after he arrived, on account of some supposed neglect or slight offered by Dr. McLaughlin, in not furnishing his quarters in the style he had expected. On reaching the post, in place of a splendid parsonage, well fitted up, and servants to do his bidding, he found what in early California times would be called an ordinary balloon house, made of rough boards, the floors (I think) not planed, and no carpets upon them, and none in the country to put upon them, except the common flag mats the Indians manufacture; and these the Rev. Mrs. Beaver considered "too filthy to step upon, or be about the house." In addition to these very important matters (judging from the fuss they made about them), "the doctor and all the pretended gentlemen of the company were living in *adultery*. This was a horrible crime he could not, and would not, put up with; he could scarcely bring himself to perform the church service in so polluted an audience." We had never been confirmed in the English church, and, consequently, did not feel at liberty to offer any advice after listening to this long tirade of abuse of the members of the Hudson's Bay Company by his reverence. A short time after, Mr. Beaver met Dr. McLaughlin in front of the house, and commenced urging him to comply with the regulations of the English church. The doctor had been educated in the Roman Catholic faith; he did not acknowledge Mr. Beaver's right to dictate a religious creed to him, hence he was not prepared to conform wholly to the English church service. Among other subjects, that of marriage was mentioned, Rev. Mr. Beaver insisting that the doctor should be married in accordance with the church service. The doctor claimed the right to be married by whom he pleased, and that Mr. Beaver was interfering and meddling with other than his parochial duties. This led his reverence to boil over and spill out a portion of the contemptuous feelings he had cherished from the moment he landed at the place. The doctor, not being in the habit from his youth of calmly listening to vulgar and abusive language, especially when addressed to his face, laid aside his reverence for the cloth, as also the respect due to his position and age, and gave Rev. Mr. Beaver a caning, some say kicking, causing his reverence to retreat, and abruptly suspend enforcing moral lessons in conformity to church usage. Rev. Mrs. Beaver very naturally sympathized with her husband, and they soon made arrangements and left the country, to report their case at head-quarters in London. Dr. McLaughlin chose to comply with civil usage, and as James Douglas had received a commission from her Majesty as civil magistrate under the English law, acting as justice of the peace, he united Dr. John McLaughlin in marriage to Mrs. Margaret McKay, whose first husband had been lost in the destruction of the bark *Tonquin* some years previous. This wedding occurred at Vancouver, about the end of January, 1837. The doctor was married privately, by Esquire Douglas, either a short time before, or a few days after, I have not yet learned which.

Rev. Mr. Beaver and lady arrived at Vancouver about four weeks before Mrs. Spalding and Mrs. Whitman. The gentlemen of the company, like the rough mountaineers who paid their respect to Mrs. Whitman and Mrs. Spalding at the American rendezvous, attempted to be polite and kind to Mr. and Mrs. Beaver. They most emphatically failed. The parsonage was a terror to them. They had become objects of *contempt*, *scorn*, and *derision* in the estimation of their religious guide and moral patron. Their wives and children were looked upon as filthy savages, not fit to associate with decent people. This feeling was so strong in the chaplain and his wife that it leaked out in very injudicious and indiscreet expressions of disapproval of actions and conduct, that, in a refined and polished society, would be considered offensive; yet these traders and Indian merchants, not having been in refined society for many years, did not understand or comprehend their own awkwardness and want of more refinement. They had forgotten that, in the progress of society, six hundred years had passed since their great great grandmothers were like the women they saw about them every day. They forgot that Mrs. Beaver was an English clergyman's wife, and claimed to belong to the best English society. They thought there was but little difference in womankind; in short, they were much better qualified to deal with Indians than with civilians. Under such circumstances, and with such feelings existing in Fort Vancouver, the reader will not be astonished at the reception of two ladies who could interest and command the esteem and respect of the savage, the mountain hunter, and the Hudson's Bay Company fur trader. They came among them expecting nothing but rough treatment; any little mistakes were overlooked or treated as a jest. They knew no distinction in classes; they were polite to the servant and the master; their society was agreeable and refining; not the least insult in word, or look, or act, was ever given them by any white man; their courage had been tested in the trip they had performed; their conversation and accomplishments surprised and delighted those permitted to enjoy their acquaintance, and, as Mr. Hines, in his history of the Oregon mission, says, "these were the first American women that ever crossed the Rocky Mountains, and *their arrival formed an epoch in the history of Oregon.*"

Our mission party, with Captain Pambrun, his two boats loaded, two-thirds of the goods for the mission, on their way up the Columbia River, arrived all safe at the Dalles. Gray took a decided stand in favor of the first location at that point, on account of its accessibility, and the general inclination of all the Indians in the country to gather at those salmon fisheries; Spalding and Pambrun opposed; Whitman was undecided; Pambrun would not wait to give time to explore, nor assist in getting horses for the Doctor and Gray to look at the country in view of a location. On we go; make the portages at La Chute; reach John Day's River; Pambrun leaves boats in charge of Whitman and Gray, and goes to Wallawalla on horseback. In four days' hard pulling, towing, and sailing, we reach Wallawalla all safe; find cattle and horses all improving, and every thing in order, that is, as good order as could be expected; boats discharged, goods all carefully stored. Next morning, early, a fine band of Cayuse horses came into the fort; four fine ones were selected and saddled, an extra pack animal with traveling case and kitchen furniture, tent for camping, and provisions all ready, a servant with two Indians, all mounted, off we go up the Wallawalla River about twenty-five miles. Most of the land we passed over we pronounced barren, and good for nothing except grazing cattle, sheep, and horses. In the bends of the river, saw a few acres of land that might be cultivated if arrangements could be made to irrigate. Passed the Tuchet, but did not consider its appearance justified much delay to examine it closely, though the whole bottom was covered with a heavy coat of tall rye grass; went on into the forks of the Wallawalla and Mill Creek (as it is now called), pitched our tent at the place where Whitman's station was afterward built, got our suppers. Whitman and Gray took a look around the place, went into the bends in the river, looked at the cotton-wood trees, the little streams of water, and all about till dark; came back to camp; not much said. Mr. Pambrun explained the quality of the soil, and what would produce corn, what potatoes, and what would produce (as he thought) wheat, though he had not tried it thoroughly; or, rather, he had tried it on a small scale and failed. A few Cayuses came about camp at night. Next morning up early; breakfast over, some fine fresh Cayuse horses were brought up, ready to mount. We proceeded through the valley in several directions; rode all day and returned to camp at night, stopping occasionally to pull up a weed or a bush, to examine the quality of the soil.

At night, if an artist could have been present and taken a picture of the group and the expressions of countenance, it certainly would have been interesting: Spalding, Whitman, Pambrun, and Gray discussing the quality of the soil, the future prospects of a mission, and of the natives it was contemplated to gather around. No white settlement was then thought of. They unanimously concluded that there was but a limited amount of land susceptible of cultivation, estimated at the place for the station at about ten acres. Along all the streams and at the foot of the Blue Mountains, there might be found little patches of from half an acre to six acres of land suitable to cultivate for the use of the natives. This, to say the least, was not an overestimate of the qualities of the soil that has proved, by twenty-five years' cultivation without manure, to be richer to-day than soils of a different character with all the manuring they have received. The great objection and most discouraging indication to the party was the unlimited amount of caustic alkali found all over those plains and all through the valley. This fact alone proves the soil inexhaustible. All it requires is sufficient water to wash from the surface the superabundant alkali that forms upon it. Any cereals adapted to alkaline soil may be cultivated to any extent in those valleys.

A stake was set to mark the place. Next day all returned to the fort, and soon the mission tents, horses, goods, and cattle were upon the ground and work commenced. The Indians, what few had not gone for buffalo, came to our camp and rendered all the assistance they were capable of in getting a house up and covered.

In a few days Spalding and Whitman started with the Nez Percés to look at their country, in view of a location among them, leaving Gray alone in charge of the building and goods, while they examined the country up the Clearwater River, and selected a location in a beautiful valley about two miles up the Lapwai Creek, and about twelve miles from Lewiston. Whitman returned to assist in erecting buildings at his station. Spalding started for Vancouver, to bring up the ladies. About the middle of November, Mrs. Whitman's quarters were ready, and she came to occupy them. Spalding and Gray, with Mrs. Spalding, started for the Lapwai station; arrived about the 1st of December, 1836, and, with the assistance of the Indians, in about twenty days a house was up, and Mrs. Spalding occupied it.

It is due to those Indians to say that they labored freely and faithfully, and showed the best of feelings toward Mr. and Mrs. Spalding, paying good attention to instructions given them, and appeared quite anxious to learn all they could of their teachers. It is also due to truth to state that Mr. Spalding paid them liberally for their services when compared with the amount paid them by the Hudson's Bay Company for the same service: say, for bringing a pine-log ten feet long and one foot in diameter from the Clearwater River to the station, it usually took about twelve Indians; for this service Mr. Spalding paid them about six inches of trail-rope tobacco each. This was about four times as much as the Hudson's Bay Company paid. This fact soon created a little feeling of unfriendliness toward Mr. Spalding. Dr. Whitman managed to get along with less Indian labor, and was able, from his location, to procure stragglers or casual men to work for him for a time, to get supplies and clothing to help them on their way down to the Wallamet settlement.

Mr. Spalding and Dr. Whitman were located in their little cabins making arrangements to get in their gardens and spring crops, teaching the Indians by example, and on the Sabbath interpreting portions of the Bible to them, and giving them such religious instruction as they were capable of communicating with their imperfect knowledge of their language; Mrs. Whitman and Mrs. Spalding teaching the children at their respective stations as much as was possible for them with their domestic duties to perform.

All things going on smoothly at the stations and all over the Indian country, it was thought advisable for Gray to visit Vancouver, procure the requisite spring supplies, and a suitable outfit for himself to explore the country, having in view further missionary locations, and return to the United States and procure assistance for the mission. Gray's expedition, as contemplated then, would not be considered with present facilities a very light one. He started from Spalding's station about the 22d of December, 1836. There had been about twenty inches of snow upon the ground, but it was concluded from the fine weather at the station that most of it had melted off. On reaching the forks of Clearwater (Lewiston), he learned from the Indians that the snow was too deep to go by land, sent his horses back to Spalding, got an Indian dug-out, started from Lewiston for Wallawalla with two Indians to pilot and paddle the canoe; reached the Paluce all safe; camped with the Indians; found them all friendly; that night came on bitter cold;—river full of floating ice; Indians concluded not safe to proceed further in canoe; procure horses and start down on the right bank of the river; travel all day; toward night, in passing over a high point, snow-storm came on, lost our trail; struck a cañon, followed it down, found the river and camped in the snow, turned our horses into the tall grass and made the best of a snow-camp for the night. Next day start early; wallow through the snow and drifts and reach an Indian camp near the mouth of Snake River at night; leave horses; next morning get canoe, leave one Paluce Indian; Paluce chief and chief of band at Snake River in canoe; two Indians to paddle; pull down the river into the Columbia in the floating ice, and reach Wallawalla, December 26, 1836; Pambrun pays Indians what he thinks right:

Paluce chief, for horses and services, one three-point Hudson's Bay blanket, one check shirt, one knife, half a brace (three feet) trail-rope tobacco. Gray thought the price paid was very reasonable,—quite little enough for the labor, to say nothing of the risk and suffering from cold on the trip. The river all closed up; Indians did not reach their homes for eight days; no communication in any direction for ten days. About the tenth day Whitman sends orders down for goods to be shipped from Vancouver. About the 10th of January, 1837, Mr. Ermatinger arrived from Colville by boat, having made several portages over ice in reaching Wallawalla. Next day we start down the river; pass through and over several fields of ice; reach Vancouver about the 12th of January. Rev. J. Lee and Mr. Slacum had just left the fort as our party arrived. We have previously given an account of the subjects of special interest, and also of the weddings that occurred about this time at the fort.

CHAPTER XXII.

The French and American settlers.—Hudson's Bay Company's traveling traders.—The Flatheads.—Their manner of traveling.—Marriage.—Their honesty.—Indian fight and scalp dance.—Making peace.—Fight with the Sioux.—At Council Bluffs.

THE reader is already acquainted with all of the first missionaries, and with the governing power and policy of the Hudson's Bay Company, and of the different parties and organizations as they existed. We will now introduce parties of men as we find them in the Wallamet settlement.

There were at this time about fifty Canadian-Frenchmen in the Wallamet settlement, all of them retired servants of the Hudson's Bay Company. These men, who had spent the most active part of their lives in the service of the company, had become connected with native women, and nearly all of them had their families of half-native children. This class of servants were found by the experience of the company not as profitable for their purposes as the enlisted men from the Orkney Isles, or even the Sandwich Islanders.

They were induced to allow those that had families of half-native children to retire from the service and settle in the Wallamet. In this manner they expected to hold a controlling influence in the settlement, and secure a population dependent upon them for supplies. It was upon this half-breed population that they relied to rally the Indian warriors of the country to prevent an American settlement. As was plainly stated by one of the Hudson's Bay Company, Mr. F. Ermatinger, in the fall of 1838, in case any effort should be made to remove them from the country, they had but to arm the eight hundred half-breeds the company had, and, with the Indians they could control, they could hold the country against any American force that could be sent into it. The Hudson's Bay Company knew very well the power and influence they had secured over the Indians. There was then too small a number of outside Americans to make any effort to remove them, other than to afford them facilities to leave the country. With all the facilities they furnished, and encouragement they gave to go to the Sandwich Islands and to California, there was a gradual increase of the population the company did not wish to see;—sailors from vessels, and hunters from the mountains. These sailors and hunters naturally gathered around the

American mission; many of them had, or soon took, native women for wives; the missionaries themselves encouraged them to marry these women. This soon commenced an influence exactly like that held by the Hudson's Bay Company through their Canadian-French settlement. The moral and religious influence of the English church had not been favorably received at Vancouver.

Gray procures his outfit at Vancouver, in January, 1837, and starts in company with Ermatinger on his return. First night camp at a saw-mill; meet a young man who had crossed the mountains with Captain Wyeth, and had remained as clerk at Fort Hall, under the Hudson's Bay Company. This young man has never risen very high in the community where he resides. For a time he considered he was an important member of the Hudson's Bay Company. His self-approbation was superior to the profits he brought to the company, and they found it convenient to drop him from their employ. He attempted a settlement out of the limits prescribed for Americans, and was soon compelled to locate himself under the influence of the Methodist Mission.

There was also in the settlement another young man, who about that time had taken a native wife and wished to locate at the mouth of the Columbia River. This privilege was denied him, unless he could procure some others to go with him. He had joined the Methodist class, and was considered a reliable man; he came to the country with Captain Wyeth, and had opened and taught the first school ever commenced in the country.

Ermatinger and company were detained fourteen days under the lee of a big rock just opposite Cape Horn, waiting for the east wind to subside and allow them to pass up the river. Ermatinger was a traveling trader of the Hudson's Bay Company. That year he was with the Flathead tribe. Gray continued with him, having his own tent and traveling equipage. The route traveled was nearly that since explored and located as Mullan's military road. We struck the Cœur d'Alêne Lake and took boats, passed through the lake and up the Flathead River, making two portages with our boats and goods before we reached Flathead House, as it was called, a common log hut, covered with poles and dirt, about 16 by 20. At this point our horses came up. Their packs and equipage were all put on board the boats, while the horses came light through the woods and along the rough river trail. At the place where we found our boats, we found a number of friendly Indians, also at the head of the lake, and a few at the Flathead House or hut. Here we found an old Frenchman in charge, with a small supply of goods, and about two packs of beaver which he had collected during the winter.

We were joined by a part of the Flathead tribe. In a few days all were ready. The tribe and trader started over the mountains on to the waters of the Missouri, to hunt the buffalo and fight the Blackfeet. Our route was along the main branch of Clark's fork of the Columbia, till we reached the Culas Patlum (Bitter Root). A halt was made to allow the natives to dig and prepare the root for the season. The root is quite nutritious, answering the Indian in place of bread; it is somewhat bitter in taste, and to a person not accustomed to its use, is not a very agreeable diet. This root secured for the season, the camp continued over the dividing ridge into the Big Hole, or Jefferson fork of the Missouri. In this place we were joined by the balance of the buffalo Indians. All parties, persons, and property were carried upon horses. The camps usually traveled from ten to fifteen miles per day. It is due to this tribe to say that truth, honesty, and virtue were cardinal principles in all their transactions. An article of property found during the day was carried to an old chief's lodge; if it were so light that he could hold it in his hand and walk through the camp, he would pass around and inquire whose it was. Sometimes several articles would be lost and picked up; in such cases the old chief would go through the camp on horseback and deliver them to the owner.

Their system of courtship and marriage was equally interesting. A youth wishing to marry a young miss was required to present a horse at the lodge of his intended, ready for her to mount as the camp should move. In case all were suited, her ladyship would mount the horse and ride it during the day; at night a feast was had at the lodge of the bride, the old chief announced the ceremony complete, and the parties proceeded to their own home or lodge. In case the suit was rejected the horse was not suitable; he was left for the owner to receive at his pleasure; the maid mounted her own horse and proceeded about her business.

In case of any visitors from other tribes, which they frequently had in going to buffalo, they would caution a stranger, and inform him of the propensity to steal which they had learned was the habit of the Indian visitor. This tribe claim to have never shed the blood of a white man. I believe it is the only tribe on the continent truly entitled to that honor; yet they are far more brave as a tribe than any other Indians. They never fear a foe, no matter how numerous.

Our sketches perhaps would not lose in interest by giving a short account of a fight which our Flathead Indians had at this place with a war party of the Blackfeet. It occurred near the present location of Helena, in Montana. As was the custom with the Flathead Indians in traveling in the buffalo country, their hunters and warriors were in advance of the main camp. A party of twenty-five Blackfeet warriors was discovered by some twelve of our Flatheads. To see each other was to fight, especially parties prowling about in this manner, and at it they went. The first fire of the Flatheads brought five of the Blackfeet to the ground and wounded some five more. This was more than they expected, and the Blackfeet made but little effort to recover their dead, which were duly scalped, and the bodies left for food for the wolves, and the scalps borne in triumph into the camp. There were but two of the Flatheads wounded: one had a flesh-wound in the thigh, and the other had his right arm broken by a Blackfoot ball.

The victory was complete, and the rejoicing in camp corresponded to the number of scalps taken. Five days and nights the usual scalp-dance was performed. At the appointed time the big war-drum was sounded, when the warriors and braves made their appearance at the appointed place in the open air, painted as warriors. Those who had taken the scalps from the heads of their enemies bore them in their hands upon the ramrods of their guns.

They entered the circle, and the war-song, drums, rattles, and noises all commenced. The scalp-bearers stood for a moment (as if to catch the time), and then commenced hopping, jumping, and yelling in concert with the music. This continued for a time, when some old painted women took the scalps and continued the dance. The performance was gone through with as many nights as there were scalps taken.

Seven days after the scalps were taken, a messenger arrived bearing a white flag, and a proposition to make peace for the purposes of trade. After the preliminaries had all been completed, in which the Hudson's Bay Company trader had the principal part to perform, the time was fixed for the meeting of the two tribes. The Flatheads, however, were all careful to dig their war-pits, make their corrals and breastworks, and, in short, fortify their camp as much as if they expected a fight instead of peace. Ermatinger, the company's trader, remarked that he would sooner take his chances for a fight off-hand than endure the anxiety and suspense of the two days we waited for the Blackfeet to arrive. Our scouts and warriors were all ready, and all on the watch for peace or war, the latter of which, from the recent fight they had had, was expected most. At length the Blackfeet arrived, bearing a red flag with H. B. C. in white letters upon it, and advancing to within a short distance of the camp, were met by Ermatinger and a few Flathead chiefs, shook hands, and were conducted to the trader's lodge,—the largest one in the camp,—and the principal chiefs of both tribes, seated upon buffalo and bear skins, all went through with the ceremony of smoking a big pipe, having a long handle or stem trimmed with horse-hair and porcupine quills. The pipe was filled with the trader's tobacco and the Indians killikinick. The war-chiefs of each tribe took a puff each of the pipe, passed it to his right-hand man, and so around till all the circle had smoked of the big medicine pipe, or pipe of peace, which on this occasion was made by the Indians from a soft stone which they find in abundance in their country, having no extra ornamental work upon it. The principal chief in command, or great medicine man, went through the ceremony, puffed four times, blowing his smoke in four directions. This was considered a sign of peace to all around him, which doubtless included all he knew any thing about. The Blackfeet, as a tribe, are a tall, well-formed, slim-built, and active people. They travel principally on foot, and are considered very treacherous.

The peace made with so much formality was broken two days afterward by killing two of the Flatheads when caught not far from the main camp.

It was from this Flathead tribe that the first Indian delegation was sent to ask for teachers. Three of their number volunteered to go with Gray to the States in 1837 to urge their claims for teachers to come among them. The party reached Ash Hollow, where they were attacked by about three hundred Sioux warriors, and, after fighting for three hours, killed some fifteen of them, when the Sioux, by means of a French trader then among them, obtained a parley with Gray and his traveling companions,—two young men that had started to go to the States with him. While the Frenchman was in conversation with Gray, the treacherous Sioux made a rush upon the three Flatheads; one Snake, and one Iroquois Indian belonging to the party, and killed them. The Frenchman then turned to Gray and told him and his companions they were prisoners, and must go to the Sioux camp, first attempting to get possession of their guns. Gray informed them at once: "You have killed our Indians in a cowardly manner, and you shall not have our guns," at the same time telling the young men to watch the first motion of the Indians to take their lives, and if we must die, to take as many Indians with us as we could. The Sioux had found in the contest thus far, that, notwithstanding they had conquered and killed five, they had lost fifteen, among them one of their war-chiefs, besides several severely wounded. The party were not further molested till they reached the camp, containing between one and two hundred lodges. A full explanation was had of the whole affair. Gray had two horses killed under him and two balls passed through his hat, both inflicting slight wounds. The party were feasted, and smoked the pipe of peace over the dead body of the chief's son; next day they were allowed to proceed with nine of their horses; the balance, with the property of the Indians, the Sioux claimed as part pay for their losses, doubtless calculating to waylay and take the balance of the horses. Be that as it may, Gray and his young men reached Council Bluffs in twenty-one days, traveling nights and during storms to avoid the Indians on the plains.

At Council Bluffs they found an Indian trader speaking the French language, meaner than the Sioux Indian, by the name of Papeon. The party had been twenty-one days on rations that ordinarily would have been consumed in four days; they had killed and eaten parts of two of the nine worn-out horses; they had with them six. The party entered the trading establishment and requested some food and the privilege of washing, not as beggars, but expecting to pay for what they required. They waited an hour or more; no food was forthcoming; Gray went to Papeon, the trader, and inquired the reason they could get no food. The old French imp inquired, in his broken French, "*Have you got any ting to pa for de tings you vant?*" He was asked if gold would pay him, or a draft on his company. "Oh, yes," he said, and in a short time food and what was required was produced.

This is only a specimen of most Indian traders of the Catholic stamp. There are honorable exceptions.

CHAPTER XXIII.

Re-enforcement to the Methodist Mission.—Re-enforcement to the mission of the American Board.

WE will leave Gray and party on their way down the Missouri River, and return to Oregon to introduce to the reader a re-enforcement to the Methodist Mission, consisting of Dr. Elijah White, a man that few who have dealt with can speak well of, utterly destitute of all morality and genuine piety, assuming the garb of religion to cover his baseness of heart and meanness of life. He arrived at the Columbia River in May, 1837. He entered upon his professional duties, and in a few months boasted of the liberties he had taken with most of the ladies of the mission who were so unfortunate as to receive his medical attention. It was easy to see the influence of such a man. His words were smooth and brotherly, his acts were poison and infamy. He never had a friend but he betrayed or swindled him in some deal. He would tell a lie when the truth would answer his purposes better. This man for a time had considerable influence; his calling as a physician was necessary and indispensable to the mission. Rev. Jason Lee soon found out the character of this wolf in sheep's clothing, and presented charges against him for his immorality, and expelled him from the mission. Previous to leaving the country, he called a public meeting and made his statements, and attempted to mob Mr. Jason Lee and get the settlers to give him a character, in both of which he failed, and left the country to impose upon the government at Washington, as he had done upon the mission and the early settlers of Oregon. We will leave Dr. White for the present, and give him all the credit due to his bad deeds and exhibitions of folly in his capacity as sub-Indian agent.

Mr. Alanson Beers, a blacksmith by trade, was a good honest man, a devoted Christian, a man whose moral worth was above price. True as steel, and honest as he was faithful, he was slow to believe others to be less true than himself. He was a pattern of honesty and piety, as well as industry and economy; the opposite of White in every respect, as was his wife when compared to Mrs. White. Though Mrs. Beers never claimed or aspired to shine or display more than she really was, yet her goodness of heart was manifested in her kind and generous treatment of all. If this man and his wife did not leave a handsome competency for their children it was no fault of theirs. Others may have felt it their duty to appropriate the orphan's portion and receive the miser's paradise. Mr. Beers came to the country full-handed, with a handsome competency to commence any business he might choose, independent of missionary patronage. He was more faithful in his department than most of his brethren.

He was considered by the early settlers an honest and sincere man; by the ruling spirits of the Methodist Mission, a faithful servant of their cause.

With this company came W. H. Wilson, an assistant missionary, of whose early life we have but little knowledge. From his own statements we learn that he had been connected with a whale ship as cooper. On arriving in Oregon as an assistant missionary, he was licensed as a preacher, and commenced the study of medicine with Dr. White, and, in later years, received the title of doctor instead of reverend. The doctor was a cheerful, whole-souled, good-sort of a fellow, with a greater abundance of interesting and funny yarns than profound medical skill, which always made him agreeable, and served to gain friends and popularity in a community that, as a general thing, would prefer a tincture of humbuggery.

The Misses Ann Maria Pitman, Susan Downing, and Elvira Johnson were also of this party. The first became the wife of Rev. Jason Lee, the second of Cyrus Shepard, the third of Rev. H. K. W. Perkins, who came to the country with the second re-enforcement to the mission, consisting of Rev. David Leslie, wife, and three daugters; H. K. W. Perkins; and Miss Margaret Smith, who afterward became the wife of an Englishman called Dr. Bailey. This gave to the Methodist Mission, on the 21st of November, 1837, Rev. Jason Lee (superintendent of the mission) and wife, Mr. C. Shepard and wife, Rev. Daniel Lee, Mr. P. L. Edwards, Rev. David Leslie and wife, Dr. Elijah White and wife, Rev. H. K. W. Perkins and wife, Mr. A. Beers and wife, Mr. W. H. Wilson, and Miss Margaret Smith,—nine men and seven women,—with three daughters of Rev. D. Leslie. From causes already mentioned, the moral strength of these early missionaries was neutralized. The larger portion of them had no knowledge of the influences that were sapping the foundation of their Christian effort, and tending to destroy the confidence of such as were considered ungodly outsiders. Instead of meeting sin, and vice, and lust which could not be hid, and condemning and banishing it, the attempt was made to excuse and cover up a fault in a professed brother, and reprove others for less faults,—*the mote and the beam*. The legitimate result followed,—though slow, yet certain.

Here was a noble field, had all the men sent to occupy it been of the right stamp! Still they toiled on, or rather continued to occupy a place in the country, to form a nucleus for a settlement. In this position they are entitled to much credit. The roving sailor and the wild mountain hunter looked to this wilderness for a home. The shrewdness of these men soon detected the assailable points in the mission's character, and adapted themselves to circumstances, and found it easy to profess compliance and receive the benefits of the association. There were few or none among this early set of missionaries that displayed much knowledge of human nature. They were totally ignorant of savage life, manners, and customs; hence were easily made the dupes of all.

In the winter of 1837–8, Gray is in the States giving an account of his trip across the Rocky Mountains in company with Messrs. Spalding and Whitman, and of his explorations of the country; the present and future prospects of the missionary efforts; the influence of the Hudson's Bay Company and of the missions; the fact that a wagon had been taken by Dr. Whitman and his party to Fort Boise, and that it could be taken to the Wallamet settlement. Said one man in the audience at Utica, New York: "How do you get through the timber on the route?" "My dear sir, the traveler is compelled to use the buffalo chips to cook his food for a large part of the route, for want of wood; there is not twenty-five miles of timber on the route from the Missouri to the Columbia." Of course a description of the vast plains and mountains had to be given, and the manner of travel and subsistence.

The American Board of Commissioners for Foreign Missions sent with Gray and wife, Rev. E. Walker and wife, C. Eells and wife, and A. B. Smith and wife, to re-enforce their mission. There was with this company a young man from Cincinnati, Ohio,—Cornelius Rogers,—active and useful in every department, respected and beloved by all who knew him. After remaining with the mission a few years, he received an appointment from the Board, but he had made up his mind to become a settler in the Wallamet, and made his arrangements accordingly. Captain Sutter came with this party to Wallawalla.

They reached Whitman's station the first of September, 1838, bring- with them to Fort Hall some fourteen cows. A majority of the party were made to believe that these could be replaced at Fort Colville with a better stock of cows, and thus be saved the trouble of driving them further, and accordingly made an even exchange of the choicest and best stock that could be found in Missouri for such California stock as the Hudson's Bay Company might have at Colville. This was considered by the *greenhorns* that made the bargain a good trade, till they came to receive the wild, furious, untamable California stock at Fort Colville, that required a Spaniard with his lasso to catch and hold, to get the milk for family use.

Rev. E. Walker was a tall, rather spare, stoop-shouldered, black-haired, brown-eyed, rather light-complexioned man, diffident and unassuming, always afraid to say *amen* at the end of his prayers, and requiring considerable effort to speak with confidence or decision upon any subject. This might arise from habit, or want of decision of character, or fear of offending. He had no positive traits of mind, yet he was studious, and kind as a friend and neighbor; faithful as a Christian, inefficient as a preacher. His efforts among the Indians were of the negative cast. The Indians respected him for his kindness, and feared him for his commanding appearance. Not at all adapted to fill the position he undertook,—as an Indian missionary in Oregon,—yet, as a citizen and settler, one of the best.

Rev. C. Eells, a short, slim, brown-haired, light-brown eyed, fair-complexioned man, with a superabundance of self-esteem, great pretensions to precision and accurateness of statement and strictness of conduct; very precise in all his actions, and about all his labors and property; with no soul to laud and admire nature, no ambition to lift his thoughts beyond the sphere of his own ideas of right, he was made to move in a small circle; his soul would be lost outside of it. There were but two instances on the trip from Boston to Oregon in which he ventured outside of himself. The first was at Soda Springs. The day the party arrived, notwithstanding they had made a long day's drive to reach that camp, the four ladies—Walker, Eells, Smith, and Gray—wished to go round and see the springs and drink of the water, and look at the Steamboat Spring, a place where water and gas issue at intervals of about a minute, like the blowing of steam. These places the ladies, tired as they were, must look at and admire. Rev. Mr. Eells puts up his saddles, buckles, and tents, and takes his Testament and reads his chapter, as usual, and after prayers retires to rest. Next morning all were up and admiring the grand display of nature around, drinking of the water, and enjoying its exhilarating influence. Camp all ready, on they move. Nothing would satisfy the ladies but another look at the Steamboat. All mounted their horses and rode down to it. Eells mounts his horse as usual, and comes along down where all stood watching and admiring the phenomenon, dismounts from his horse, and in utter astonishment exclaims: "*Well, this is really worth coming to see!*" The other instance in which he lost himself was in admiring the grandeur of the great fall on Snake River. He had no poetry or romance in his soul, yet by dint of perseverance he was a good artificial singer. He lacked all the qualities requisite for a successful Indian missionary and a preacher of the gospel in a new country. As citizens and neighbors, Mr. Eells and his family were highly respected; as a teacher, he was unreasonably strict.

Rev. A. B. Smith, a man whose prejudices were so strong that he could not be reasonable with himself. He attempted to make himself useful as a missionary, but failed for want of Christian forbearance and confidence in his associates. As to literary ability, he was superior to his associates, and probably excited their jealousy; so much so, that his connection in the mission became unpleasant, and he found an excuse to leave the country in 1841; not, however, till he and Mr. Rogers had, with the assistance of the Lawyer, completed a vocabulary and a grammar of the Nez Percé language, which was the cause of Ellis's jealousy of the Lawyer and Mr. Smith, and also of an extra effort through the Jesuits and the company to get rid of him.

CHAPTER XXIV.

Arrival of Jesuit missionaries.—Toupin's statement about Rev. A. B. Smith.—Death of Mrs. Jason Lee.—First express.—Jesuits at work.—The first printing-press.—The Catholic tree.

A SHORT time after the arrival of the re-enforcement to the mission of the American Board, Rev. F. N. Blanchet and Rev. Demerse arrived at Wallawalla by the annual overland boats of the Hudson's Bay Company. While at Wallawalla, they induced a Cayuse, Young Chief, to have one of his children baptized, Mr. Pambrun being sponsor, or godfather. This was the first Indian child ever baptized in the country. It caused considerable excitement among the Indians, as also a discussion as to who was teaching the true religion. The interpreters of Wallawalla being of the Catholic faith, made free to inform the Indians that theirs was the true religion. The Indians soon came to the station of Dr. Whitman and informed him of what had been done, and that they had been told by the priest that his was the true religion; that what he and Mr. Spalding had been teaching them for two years past was all false, and that it was not right for the Indians to listen to the Doctor and Mr. Spalding. The instructions given, and the baptizing of the Indian child, were, unquestionably, designed to create a diversion in the minds of the Indians, and ultimately bring about the abandonment or destruction of the mission. I have never been able to learn, from any source, that any other Indian child was baptized by these priests on that trip from Canada to Vancouver. In fact, I see from their published works that they claim this as their first station or place of instruction.

The Rev. Mr. Blanchet was a black-haired, brown-eyed, smooth-faced, medium-sized Frenchman.

The Rev. Mr. Demerse had dark-brown hair, full, round eye, fair complexion, rather full habit, something of the bull-neck, inclining to corpulency. He was fond of good cheer and good living; of the Jesuit order of the Roman church; he seemed to have no scruples of conscience; so long as he could secure subjects for "*mother church*," it mattered not as to intelligence or character.

During the year 1838, three clergymen arrived across the Rocky Mountains: Revs. Walker, Eells, and Smith, with their wives, and

Mr. Cornelius Rogers. Mr. Gray, with his wife, had also returned. These new arrivals gave an addition of nine to the mission of the American Board, making their number thirteen in all. The Methodist Mission had sixteen, and the Roman Catholic, two. The total number of missionaries in the country, in December, 1838, was thirty-one, twenty-nine of the Protestant religion from the United States, and two of the Roman Jesuitical order. The latter were located at Vancouver as their head-quarters. The Methodists were in the Wallamet Valley, with one out-station at the Dalles, Wascopum. The American Board had three stations, one at Wailatpu, one at Lapwai, and one at Cimakain, near Spokan.

This array of missionary strength looked like a strong effort on the part of the Christian world to convert the tribes upon our western coast. Had all the men been chosen with proper care, and all acted with a single eye to the cause which they professed to espouse, each in his distinct department; had they closed their ears to the suggestions of hypocritical fur traders, and met their vices with a spotless life and an earnest determination to maintain their integrity as representatives of religion and a Christian people, the fruits of their labor would, undoubtedly, have been far greater. As the matter now stands, they can claim the influence they reluctantly yielded to the provisional government of the early settlers of the country.

It will be seen at once that the Hudson's Bay Company was acting a double part with all the American missionary efforts in the country. On the arrival of Rev. J. Lee and party they sent for Mr. Beaver, an Episcopal clergyman. On the arrival of Dr. Whitman and party they sent for Blanchet and Demerse, and established their head-quarters at Vancouver. Blanchet took charge of the field occupied by the Methodists, and Demerse of that occupied by the American Board. A combination of Hudson's Bay Company Indian traders, Roman priests, Protestant missionaries, and American settlers, each having a distinct object in view. Unfortunately for the American missionaries and settlers, there was no one bold enough to attempt to act against these combinations. Cornelius Rogers and Robert Shortess were the first to show signs of rebellion against the policy of the Hudson's Bay Company; Spalding, Whitman, and Smith chafed under the Jesuits' proceedings in the interior.

"About the year 1839, in the fall, Mr. Smith, belonging to the same society as Dr. Whitman and Mr. Spalding, asked permission of Ellis to build upon his lands for the purpose of teaching the Indians as the other missionaries were doing, and of keeping a school. Ellis allowed him to build, but forbade him to cultivate the land, and warned him that if he did the piece of ground which he would till should serve to bury him in. In the following spring, however, Mr. Smith prepared his plow to till the ground; and Ellis, seeing him ready to begin, went to him and said to him: 'Do you not recollect what I told you? I do not wish you to cultivate the land.' Mr. Smith, however, persisted in his determination; but, as he was beginning to plow, the Indians took hold of him and said to him: 'Do you not know what has been told you, that you would be digging a hole in which you should be buried?' Mr. Smith then did not persist any longer, but said to them: 'Let me go, I will leave the place;' and he started off immediately. This circumstance had been related to me by the Indians, and soon after I saw Mr. Smith myself at Fort Wallawalla; he was on his way down to Fort Vancouver, where he embarked for the Sandwich Islands, whence he did not come back any more." This is the statement of old John Toupin, Pambrun's Roman Catholic interpreter, by Brouillet.

It will be borne in mind that Rev. Jason Lee started with P. L. Edwards and F. Y. Euing, across the Rocky Mountains, for the United States, in May, 1838. He met Gray, and party, at the American rendezvous that year, on the north fork of the Yellowstone River. Gray and party, on arriving at Fort Hall, received the news of the death of Mrs. Jason Lee, sent by Spalding and Whitman, and not by Dr. McLaughlin, as stated by Rev. G. Hines. Dr. McLaughlin may have allowed a messenger to go as far as Whitman's station, but made no arrangements for going any further. Spalding's Indian messenger delivered the packages to Gray, at Fort Hall. Gray employed Richardson (a young man he had engaged as guide and hunter for the party, on starting from Westport, Missouri), to take these letters, and deliver them to Lee, for which he was to receive $150.

This express was carried from the Wallamet Valley to Westport, Missouri, in *sixty days*, forming the first data for the overland express and mail routes. The sixty days included two days' detention at Wailatpu, and two at Fort Hall. It seems that Richardson, the messenger from Fort Hall, met Lee, and delivered his packages to him at the Shawnee mission, and received from Lee the price agreed upon. I am thus particular in these little facts, that those who claim so much credit for Hudson's Bay Company patronage may understand what influences were in those early times bringing about results for which a combination of British fur traders now claim pay, and are awarded $650,000, in gold coin.

I have said that in December, 1838, there were twenty-nine persons connected with the Protestant missions in the country. This is not strictly true. Rev. Jason Lee and Mr. P. L. Edwards had gone to the

States; Mr. C. Shepard and Mrs. J. Lee had gone to their reward. The devil had entered the field with his emissaries, and was exceedingly busy sowing tares among the wheat, through fear that the natives would be benefited, and the country become civilized. The Hudson's Bay Company and its servants, Indians and all, are about to become converted to Christianity. Strange as this statement may appear, it is literally true. The clerks, traders, and servants of the Hudson's Bay Company became *catechists*, to teach the Indians to repeat the catechism presented to them by their Reverences Blanchet and Demerse. Dr. McLaughlin and Esquire Douglas were both zealous supporters of the Christian reformation in progress in the country. During the year 1839, "Rev. Mr. Demerse (Jesuit priest) spent three weeks at Wallawalla, *in teaching the Indians and baptizing their children*," employing Mr. P. C. Pambrun as his catechist, and godfather to the native children. (See page 87 of Rev. J. B. A. Brouillet's "Protestantism in Oregon.") While the Protestant missions were struggling to improve the condition of the Indians, to teach them to cultivate their lands and become permanent settlers in their own country, and to give the Indian children a knowledge of books, the Hudson's Bay Company and Jesuit priests were equally busy in attempting to persuade them that the instructions given by these American or *Boston missionaries* were only to cover up a secret design they had to take their lands and property from them, and eventually to occupy the country themselves. To a certain extent Dr. Whitman's statement to them would confirm this idea. As soon as these priests arrived and commenced their instructions, under the patronage of the Hudson's Bay Company (for it will be remembered that their head-quarters were at Vancouver), their entire transportation was provided or furnished by the company. Doubtless it is to the assistance rendered these Roman missions to occupy the country, that the counsel for the Hudson's Bay Company, Mr. Charles D. Day, alludes, in speaking of the "*substantial benefits to the people and government of the United States.*" Dr. Whitman repeatedly told the Indians about his station that he did not come among them to buy their land, but he came to teach them how to cultivate and live from what they produced from their own lands, and at some future time, if the American government wished any of their country, then the President would send men to buy and pay them for it. The difficulty about land had no existence in the minds or thoughts of the Indians till the fall of 1839, and after the renewal of the Hudson's Bay Company's license for twenty-one years. From that time forward a marked change was manifest in the feelings of most of the gentlemen of the company.

The first printing-press in Oregon was received as a donation from the mission of the American Board of Foreign Missions in the Sandwich Islands, to the mission of the Board in Oregon. It reached its destination at Lapwai, and was put in operation by Mr. E. O. Hall, of the Sandwich Islands Mission, and commenced printing books in the Nez Percé language. Both Mr. Rogers and Mr. Spalding soon learned to set type, and print the small books required for the Indian schools that had been kept at the stations. The books and instructions were furnished gratuitously to all the Indians that wished to receive them. This caused special efforts on the part of the priests to counteract the influence of the books printed by Spalding. To illustrate their ideas, and show the evil of heretical books and teachings, they had a representation of a large tree, with a cross on top, representing all religious sects as going up the tree, and out upon the different branches, and falling from the end of the branch into a fire under the tree, with a priest by the side of the fire throwing the heretical books into it. This was an interesting picture, and caused much discussion and violent denunciations among the Indians. Mr. Spalding, to counteract the influences of the Roman Catholic tree among the Indians, had Mrs. Spalding paint a number of sheets of cap-paper, commencing with Adam and Eve in the garden of Eden, representing the shrubbery, and all kinds of fruits, and the serpent, and the angel (after the fall) as guarding the garden; giving the pictures of most of the prominent patriarchs; Noah and the ark, and the prophets, down to Christ and the twelve apostles; showing the crucifixion of Christ by the Roman soldiers, and on down to the time when they adopted the cross as a form of worship, and the priests as kneeling to images. Spalding's pictures were in such form, and contained so much Bible history and information, that his Indian preachers, to whom he gave them, could attract larger crowds of Indians, to listen to the instructions given by Spalding, than those who had the Catholic tree. This exasperated, or stirred up, as the Indians expressed it, all their bad feelings toward each other, and caused quarrels between those that were friends before,—a repetition of sectarian quarrels in all ages, and among every people not understanding the true principles of a genuine Christianity.

The main object of the priests was to destroy all interest in books, and thereby check the growing influence of the American missionaries in the country, substituting pictures and beads in place of knowledge.

CHAPTER XXV.

Independent missionaries arrive.—Their troubles.—Conversion of Indians at the Dalles.—Their motives.—Emigrants of 1839.—Blubber-Mouth Smith.—Re-enforcement of the Methodist Mission in 1840.—Father De Smet.—Rev. Harvey Clark and associates.—Ewing Young.—Names of missionaries and settlers.

In the fall of 1839, the Rev. J. S. Griffin and wife arrived at Dr. Whitman's station. Mr. Griffin had undertaken an independent mission, in company with a Mr. Munger and wife. They had received an outfit from some warm-hearted Christians of the Litchfield North Association, of Connecticut. Mr. Griffin reached St. Louis a single man, fell in love and married on sight, I do not know whether it was first or second. At all events, Rev. Mr. Griffin and Mr. Munger and their wives consented to travel together till they reached Fort Hall, at which place Mr. Griffin, being the getter-up of the mission and claiming ecclesiastical jurisdiction, took it upon himself to leave Mr. Munger and his wife at Fort Hall, to take care of themselves as best they could. Frank Ermatinger, of the Hudson's Bay Company, at once furnished Mr. Munger and his wife the means of transportation, and brought them to Dr. Whitman's station, where he knew Mr. Munger could find a place for himself and wife. This transaction of Mr. Griffin injured his usefulness as a minister, and left him in the country but little respected by any who knew of his conduct to a fellow-traveler and an intelligent Christian woman. The fact that Mr. Munger afterward became deranged, or even that he was partially deranged at Fort Hall, or before they reached that place, is no excuse for his treating a man in that condition and his wife as he did. Mr. Griffin claims that Mr. Ermatinger stole three of his horses, or had them hid, when at Fort Hall, to get Mr. Munger and wife to travel with him, and, by so doing, give the impression that he had abandoned them. From a careful review of Mr. Griffin's lengthy defense in this case, we can not conceive that any further change or correction is required, as the facts stated are by him admitted. From Mr. Griffin's statement we are satisfied that improper and undue influences were used to break up and defeat his Indian missionary plans and settlement by Mr. Ermatinger and the Hudson's Bay Company, and also to destroy his clerical influence in the country. Unfortunately, Mr. Griffin gave too much cause for his enemies to do as they did.

In the winter of 1839, Mr. Griffin made an attempt to pass the Salmon River Mountains to Payette River, to establish a mission among the Snake Indians, in which he failed, and found his way into the Wallamet as a settler, where he still remains.

There were with Mr. Griffin's party some four men, one by the name of Ben Wright, who had been a Methodist preacher in the States, but whose religion failed him on his way over the mountains. He reached the Dalles, where he renewed his religion under Rev. Mr. Perkins and D. Lee.

While at the Dalles, the three clergymen succeeded in converting, as they supposed, a large number of the Indians. While this Indian revival was in progress the writer had occasion to visit Vancouver. On his way, he called on the missionaries at the Dalles, and, in speaking of the revival among the Indians, we remarked that, in our opinion, most of the religious professions of the natives were from *selfish motives.* Mr. Perkins thought not; he named one Indian that, he felt certain, was really converted, if there was a true conversion. In a short time Daniel Lee, his associate, came in, and remarked: "What kind of a proposition do you think —— (naming Mr. Perkins' truly converted Indian) has made to me?" Perkins replied: "Perhaps he will perform the work we wished him to do." "No," says Lee; "he says he *will pray a whole year if I will give him a shirt and a capote.*" This fact shows that the natives who were supposed to be converted to Christianity were making these professions to gain presents from the missionaries. We have witnessed similar professions among the Nez Percé and Cayuse Indians. The giving of a few presents of any description to them induces them to make professions corresponding to the wish of the donor.

With Messrs. Griffin, Munger, and Wright, came Messrs. Lawson, Keiser, and Geiger, late in the fall of 1839; also a man by the name of Farnam, who seemed to be an explorer or tourist. I met him at Vancouver, where he was receiving the hospitality of the Hudson's Bay Company, and collecting material for a journal, or history of Oregon. It is said of him that, on starting from the States, he succeeded in getting himself appointed captain of a company consisting of some fourteen men. He soon attempted to exercise absolute control of the company, which caused a division. The party voted to suspend his official functions, and finally suspended him and expelled him from the train. On returning to the States he published a book, which, as was to be expected, was favorable to himself and friends (if he had any), and severe on his opposers or enemies. The professed object of the party was to form a settlement in Oregon. In consequence of the course pursued by Farnam, it all broke up. A man called Blubber-Mouth Smith, Blair, a millwright, and Robert Shortess were of the party. These all found their way into Oregon, while the balance of the party went south and wintered in the mountains. Mr. Farnam was furnished a free passage to the Sandwich Islands by the Hudson's Bay Company, for which his traveling companions and those best acquainted with him have given the company credit, as one good act.

Sydney Smith—called "Blubber-Mouth," from the fact that he was a great talker and fond of telling *big yarns*, which he, no doubt, had repeated so often that he believed them to be true, and would appear somewhat offended if his statements were not believed by others—had a tolerably fair education, and appeared to understand the lottery business, as conducted in some of the States. He was a man who had read considerable in his early days, and had he been less boisterous and persistent in statements that appeared improbable to others, would have been far more reliable and useful. As it was, in those early times, his knowledge and free-speaking became quite useful, when combined with the hearty action he gave to the objects in contemplation. He was ambitious and extremely selfish, and, when opposed in his plans, quite unreasonable.

Robert Shortess possessed a combination of qualities such as should have formed one of the best and noblest of men; with a good memory, extensive reading, inflexible purpose, strong hate, affectionate and kind, skeptical and religious, honest and liberal to a fault, above medium height, light-brown hair, blue eyes, and thin and spare features. His whole life is a mystery, his combinations a riddle. He early entered with heart and soul into the situation and condition of the settlements, and stood for their rights in opposition to all the combined influences in the country. As a politician he acts on the principle of right, without any regard to expediency. As a religious man he has no faith; as a skeptic he is severe on all alike. The country owes much to him for his labor and influence in combating slavery and shaping the organic policy of the settlements.

At the close of 1839, there were ten Protestant ministers and two Roman priests, two physicians, six laymen, and thirteen American women in the country—twenty-nine in all—connected with the Protestant missions, or under their immediate control, and twenty settlers, besides about ten men that were under the control of the Hudson's Bay Company, yet having strong American feelings. There were also ten American children, five of them born in the country. Mrs. Whitman gave birth to the first white child, a daughter, born on this coast, who was drowned in the Wallawalla River at about two years of age;

Mrs. Spalding the second, a daughter, still living; Mrs. Elkanah Walker the first boy, and Mrs. W. H. Gray, the second. These boys are both making good names for themselves. It is to be hoped that every act and effort of their lives will be alike honorable to their parents, themselves, and their native country. As to the first daughter of Oregon, I regret to say, she disobeyed the wish of her parents and friends, and married a man whose early education was neglected, but who has natural ability and energy to rise above his present position, obtain an education, and become an ornament to his adopted country, and an honor to Oregon's eldest daughter.

On the first of June of this year, the *Lausanne*, Captain Spalding, arrived in the Columbia River with a re-enforcement for the Methodist Mission of eight clergymen, five laymen, and one physician, all with wives, five single ladies, and fifteen children, belonging to the different families, with a full supply of goods, such as were needed and appropriate for the settlement, the various missions, and for Indian trade. September following, Rev. Harvey Clark and wife, A. T. Smith and wife, and P. B. Littlejohn and wife, arrived across the Rocky Mountains. With this company came eleven mountain men, eight of them with native wives. We now had twenty-one Protestant ministers, three Roman priests, fifteen lay members of the Protestant Church, thirty-four white women, thirty-five American settlers, and thirty-two white children—one hundred and eight persons immediately under control of the missions. Thirty-six settlers, twenty-five of them with native wives. These thirty-six settlers are counted as outside the missions and Hudson's Bay Company. There were about fifty Canadian-French under the control of the company.

Thus we can begin to see the development of the three influences or parties. The Hudson's Bay Company had in their religious element three Romish priests, assisted actively by all the Canadian-French Catholics and such clerks as Pambrun, Guinea, Grant, and McBean, with such interpreters as old Toupin, of whom Mr. Parker, in his journal, says: "The interpreter I had been expecting did not arrive, and consequently much of what I wished to say to these hundreds of Indians could not be communicated for want of a medium." On the preceding page, Mr. Parker remarks: "But as I have little prospect of the arrival of my interpreter, I shall probably be left to commiserate their anxiety, while it will be out of my power to do them good."

Old John Toupin, under the sanctity of a Roman Catholic oath, says, at St. Louis, of Wallamet, on September 24, 1848: "I have been seventeen years employed as interpreter at Fort Wallawalla. I was there when Mr. Parker, in 1835, came to select places for Presbyterian missions among the Cayuses and Nez Percés, and to ask lands for those missions. He employed *me as interpreter* in his negotiations with the Indians on that occasion." Mr. Parker has just said "*the interpreter I had been expecting did not arrive.*" Toupin says: "Mr. Pambrun, the gentleman then in charge of the fort, accompanied me to the Cayuses and Nez Percés. Mr. Parker, in company with Mr. Pambrun, an American, and myself, went first to the Cayuses, upon the lands called Wailatpu, that belonged to three chiefs,—Splitted Lip, or Yomtip; Red Cloak, or Waptachtakamal; and Feather Cap, or Tilokaikt." Having met them at that place, he told them that he was coming to select a place to build a preaching-house, to teach them how to live, and to teach school to their children, and that he would not come himself to establish the mission, but a *doctor, or medicine man*, would come in his place; that the doctor would be the chief of the mission, and would come in the following spring. "I came to select a place for a mission," said he, "*but I do not intend to take your lands for nothing.* After the doctor is come, there will come every year a *big ship loaded with goods* to be divided among the Indians. These goods will not be *sold*, but *given* to you. The mission will bring you plows and hoes to learn you how to cultivate the land, and they will not sell, but give them to you." From the Cayuses Mr. Parker went to the Nez Percés, and there he made the same promises to the Indians as at Wailatpu. "Next spring there will come a missionary to establish himself here and take a piece of land; *but he will not take it for nothing, you shall be paid every year; this is the American fashion.*" This statement is made by authority of Rev. J. B. A. Brouillet, vicar-general of Wallawalla.

Rev. Mr. Parker, as before remarked, and as his journal shows, soon understood all the maneuverings of this Hudson's Bay Company. He had no confidence in their friendship or their interpreters. As a matter of policy they could do no less than treat him kindly, or, more properly, *civilly*, and allow him to leave the country, as he did. But mark the strictness and care of the company to impress the necessity of compliance with their arrangements upon the minds of those that followed Mr. Parker. Keep the *massacre* to which Vicar-General Brouillet refers before your mind. *Life and blood and treasure have been expended.* The fair land we inhabit was not secured without a struggle. The early Protestant missions were not defeated and broken up without outside influences. The Indians were not abandoned till they had dipped their hands in the blood of their best and truest friend, and "become sevenfold more the children of the devil than they were in their native state," by the teachings they had received from *malicious* and *interested parties* to make them so.

Father P. J. De Smet, from Brouillet's statements, was among the Flatheads and at Wallawalla in 1840. This priest boasted of his belonging to the Jesuit order of the Romish Church. He usually wore a black frock-coat, was of full habit, arrogant and bigoted in his opinions, and spoke with considerable sarcasm and contempt of all Americans, and especially of the missionaries, as an ignorant set of men to represent the American churches. He would be considered, in his church, a zealous and faithful priest of the order of Jesus. His religious instructions to the Indians were simple and easy to be understood: "*Count your beads, hate or kill the Suapies* (Americans), *and kiss the cross.*"

Rev. Harvey Clark was a man whose religion was practical, whose labors were without ceasing, of slender frame, black hair, deep, mellow voice, kind and obliging to all. He organized the first Congregational Church in Tualatin Plains, and one in Oregon City, and was the getter-up of the Pacific University at Forest Grove; a warm friend to general education and all objects calculated to do good to any and all of his fellow-creatures. But few who knew him did not respect and esteem him for his sincere piety and Christian conduct. He came to the country as a missionary sent out by some of the northwestern churches in the United States, without any definite organization further than sufficient to furnish the means for outfit for himself and associates,—Smith and Littlejohn and their wives,—trusting Providence and their own strong arms and willing hearts to labor and do all they could for a subsistence. Mr. Clark was perhaps the best man that could have been sent with the early settlers. He early gained their confidence and esteem, and was always a welcome visitor among them. He had not that stern commanding manner which is usual to egotists of the clerical order, but was of the mild, persuasive kind, that wins the rough heart and calms the stormy passions. The country is blessed by his having lived in it.

A. T. Smith, the associate of Rev. H. Clark, was an honest and substantial farmer, a sincere and devout Christian, a man not forward in forming society, yet firm and stable in his convictions of right; liberal and generous to all objects of real worth; not easily excited, or ambitious of political preferment. His wife seemed, in all her life and actions, to be a suitable helpmeet for him. They came early to this country, and have ever been substantial and useful citizens, and supporters of morality and religion. They were among the earliest settlers at Forest Grove, and the first members of Rev. H. Clark's church.

P. B. Littlejohn was the opposite of Smith, a confirmed hypochondriac; yet, under excitement that was agreeable to his ideas, a useful man. Owing to his peculiar temperament, or the disease with which he was afflicted, his usefulness, and that of an interesting and Christian wife, were cramped and destroyed. He returned to the States with his family in 1845.

At this point, perhaps a statement of all the names of persons I have been able to collect and recollect, and the year they arrived in the country, will not be uninteresting to the reader. A short history of most of them has already been given.

In the year 1834, Rev. Jason Lee, Rev. Daniel Lee, Cyrus Shepard, and P. L. Edwards, connected with the Methodist Mission; Captain N. Wyeth, American fur trader, and of his party in 1832, S. H. Smith, Burdet, Greeley, Sergeant, Bull, St. Clair, and Whittier (who was helped to or given a passage to the Sandwich Islands by the Hudson's Bay Company); Brock, a gunsmith; Tibbets, a stone-cutter; Moore, killed by the Blackfeet Indians; Turnbull, who killed himself by over-eating at Vancouver. There was also in the country a man by the name of Felix Hathaway, saved from the wreck of the *William and Ann*. Of this number, Smith, Sergeant, Tibbets, and Hathaway remained. Of the party in 1834, James A. O'Neil, T. J. Hubbard, and Courtney M. Walker remained in the country, making six of Wyeth's men and one sailor. C. M. Walker came with Lee's company. With Ewing Young, from California, came, in this year, John McCarty, Carmichael, John Hauxhurst, Joseph Gale, John Howard, Kilborn, Brandywine, and George Winslow, a colored man. By the brig *Maryland*, Captain J. H. Couch, G. W. Le Breton, John McCaddan, and William Johnson. An English sailor, by the name of Richard or Dick McCary, found his way into the settlement from the Rocky Mountains.

In the year 1835 it does not appear that any settlers arrived in the country. Rev. Samuel Parker visited and explored it under the direction of the American Board of Foreign Missions.

In 1836, Rev. H. Spalding, Dr. M. Whitman, W. H. Gray, Mrs. Eliza Spalding, and Mrs. Narcissa Whitman, missionaries of the American Board, and Rev. Mr. Beaver, Episcopal chaplain at Vancouver, and Mrs. Beaver. There appear to have been no settlers this year; at least, none known to us.

In 1837, Mrs. A. M. Lee, Mrs. S. Shepard, Dr. E. White, Mrs. M. White, A. Beers, Mrs. R. Beers, Miss E. Johnson, W. H. Wilson, Mr. J. Whitcomb, members of the Methodist Episcopal Mission. Second re-enforcement this year: Rev. H. K. W. Perkins, Rev. David Leslie, Mrs. Leslie, Misses Satira, Mary, and Sarah Leslie, Miss Margaret Smith, Dr. J. Bailey, an Englishman, George Gay, and John Turner.

In 1838, Rev. Elkanah Walker, Mrs. Mary Walker, Rev. Cushing Eells, Mrs. Elvira Eells, Rev. A. B. Smith, Mrs. E. Smith, and Mrs.

Mary A. Gray, missionaries of the American Board. As laborers under special contract not to trade in furs or interfere with Hudson's Bay Company's trade, James Conner, native wife, and one child, and Richard Williams, both from Rocky Mountains. Jesuit priests: Rev. F. N. Blanchet, Rev. Demerse, located at Vancouver and French Prairie.

In 1839, Rev. J. S. Griffin, Mrs. Griffin, Asael Munger, Mrs. Mary Munger, Independent Protestant Mission; Robert Shortess, J. Farnam, Sydney Smith, Mr. Lawson, Rev. Ben. Wright (Independent Methodist), Wm. Geiger, Mr. Keizer, John Edmund Pickernel, a sailor.

In 1840, Mrs. Lee, second wife of Rev. Jason Lee; Rev. J. H. Frost and wife; Rev. A. F. Waller, wife, and two children; Rev. W. W. Kone and wife; Rev. G. Hines, wife, and sister; Rev. L. H. Judson, wife, and two children; Rev. J. L. Parish, wife, and three children; Rev. G. P. Richards, wife, and three children; Rev. A. P. Olley and wife. Laymen: Mr. George Abernethy, wife, and two children; Mr. H. Campbell, wife, and one child; Mr. W. W. Raymond and wife; Mr. H. B. Brewer and wife; Dr. J. L. Babcock, wife, and one child; Rev. Mrs. Daniel Lee; Mrs. David Carter; Mrs. Joseph Holman; Miss E. Phillips. Methodist Episcopal Protestant Mission: Rev. Harvey Clark and wife; P. B. Littlejohn and wife. Independent Protestant Mission: Robert Moore, James Cooke, and James Fletcher, settlers. Jesuit priest: P. G. De Smet, Flathead Mission.

Rocky Mountain men with native wives: William Craig, Robert or Dr. Newell, J. L. Meek, James Ebbets, William M. Dougherty, John Larison, George Wilkinson, a Mr. Nicholson, and Mr. Algear, and William Johnson, author of the novel, "Leni Leoti; or, the Prairie Flower." The subject was first written and read before the Lyceum, at Oregon City, in 1843.

In the above list I have given the names of all the American settlers, as near as I can remember them, the list of names I once collected having been lost. I never was fully informed as to the different occupations of all these men. It will be seen that we had in the country in the fall of 1840 thirty-six American settlers, twenty-five of them with native wives; thirty-three American women, thirty-two children, thirteen lay members of the Protestant missions, nineteen ministers (thirteen Methodist, six Congregational), four physicians (three American and one English), three Jesuit priests, and sixty Canadian-French,—making, outside of the Hudson's Bay Company, one hundred and thirty-seven Americans and sixty-three Canadians, counting the three priests as Canadians.

CHAPTER XXVI.

1840.—Petition to Congress of United States.—British subjects amenable to the laws of Canada.—Esquire Douglas as justice of the peace.—Mr. Leslie as judge.

EIGHTEEN hundred and forty finds Oregon with her little population all active and busy, laboring and toiling to provide the necessaries of life—food and raiment. And if a man did not wear the finest of broadcloth, his intelligence and good conduct secured him a cordial welcome to every house or shanty in the country among the American or French settlers and missions. This was an innovation upon Hudson's Bay Company customs, and a violation of aristocratic rules sought to be enforced by foreign influences and sustained by the missionaries then in the country.

Mr. Hines, in his 21st chapter on Oregon, says: "The number of people in the colony was so small, the business transactions so limited, and the difficulties so few, that the necessity of organizing the community into a body politic did not appear to be very great, though for two years persons had been chosen to officiate as judges and magistrates."

The fact that the judges and magistrates officiating were chosen by the Methodist Mission, in opposition to the wish of the settlers, and from whose decisions there was no appeal, and that there was no statute or law book in the country, and nothing to guide the decisions of the judge or magistrate but his own opinions, caprice, or preferences, Mr. Hines leaves out of sight. This state of things was submitted to from the combined organized influence of the Methodist Mission and the unorganized condition of the settlers. A petition was gotten up and sent to Congress. This petition is too important a document to be omitted. The writer has no means at present to give the names attached to it. The petition speaks for itself. As settlers, we saw and knew the objects of the Hudson's Bay Company and the English government, by their actions and oft-repeated insolent assertions that they meant to "*hold the country*" *by fair or by foul means*, which, as men understanding the unscrupulous and avaricious disposition of the entire English occupants of this country, we fully understood and duly appreciated, as will be readily demonstrated upon a perusal of the following:—

Petition of 1840.

To the Honorable the Senate and House of Representatives of the United States of America in Congress assembled:

Your petitioners represent unto your honorable bodies, that they are residents in the Oregon Territory, and citizens of the United States, or persons desirous of becoming such.

They further represent to your honorable bodies, that they have settled themselves in said Territory, under the belief that it was a portion of the public domain of said States, and that they might rely upon the government thereof for the blessings of free institutions, and the protection of its arms.

But your petitioners further represent, that they are uninformed of any acts of said government by which its institutions and protection are extended to them; in consequence whereof, themselves and families are exposed to be destroyed by the savages around them, and OTHERS THAT WOULD DO THEM HARM.

And your petitioners would further represent, that they have no means of protecting their own and the lives of their families, other than self-constituted tribunals, originated and sustained by the power of an ill-instructed public opinion, and the resort to force and arms.

And your petitioners represent these means of safety to be an insufficient safeguard of life and property, and that the crimes of *theft*, *murder*, *infanticide*, *etc.*, are increasing among them to an alarming extent; and your petitioners declare themselves unable to arrest this progress of crime, and its terrible consequences, without the aid of the law, and tribunals to administer it.

Your petitioners therefore pray the Congress of the United States of America to establish, as soon as may be, a Territorial government in the Oregon Territory.

And if reasons other than those above presented were needed to induce your honorable bodies to grant the prayer of the undersigned, your petitioners, they would be found in the value of this Territory to the nation, and the alarming circumstances that portend its loss.

Your petitioners, in view of these last considerations, would represent, that the English government has had a surveying squadron on the Oregon coast for the last two years, employed in making accurate surveys of all its rivers, bays, and harbors; and that, recently, the said government is said to have made a grant to the Hudson's Bay Company, of all lands lying between the Columbia River and Puget Sound; and that said company is actually exercising unequivocal acts of ownership over said lands thus granted, and opening extensive farms upon the same.

And your petitioners represent, that these circumstances, connected with other acts of said company to the same effect, and *their declarations that the English government own and will hold, as its own soil*, that portion of Oregon Territory situated north of the Columbia River, together with the important fact that the said company are cutting and sawing into lumber, and shipping to foreign ports, vast quantities of the finest pine-trees upon the navigable waters of the Columbia, have led your petitioners to apprehend that the English government do intend, at all events, to hold that portion of this Territory lying north of the Columbia River.

And your petitioners represent, that the said Territory, north of the Columbia, is an invaluable possession to the American Union; that in and about Puget Sound are the only harbors of easy access, and commodious and safe, upon the whole coast of the Territory; and that a great part of this said northern portion of the Oregon Territory is rich in timber, water-power, and *valuable minerals.* For these and other reasons, your petitioners pray that Congress will establish its sovereignty over said Territory.

Your petitioners would further represent, that the country south of the Columbia River, and north of the Mexican line, and extending from the Pacific Ocean one hundred and twenty miles into the interior, is of unequaled beauty and fertility. Its mountains, covered with perpetual snow, pouring into the prairies around their bases transparent streams of the purest water; the white and black oak, pine, cedar, and fir forests that divide the prairies into sections convenient for farming purposes; the rich mines of coal in its hills, and salt springs in its valleys; its quarries of limestone, sandstone, chalk, and marble; the salmon of its rivers, and the various blessings of the delightful and healthy climate, are known to us, and impress your petitioners with the belief that this is one of the most favored portions of the globe.

Indeed, the deserts of the interior have their wealth of pasturage; and their lakes, evaporating in summer, leave in their basins hundreds of bushels of the purest soda. Many other circumstances could be named, showing the importance of this Territory in a national, commercial, and agricultural point of view. And, although your petitioners would not undervalue considerations of this kind, yet they beg leave especially to call the attention of Congress to their own condition as an infant colony, without military force or civil institutions to protect their lives and property and children, sanctuaries and tombs, from the hands of uncivilized and merciless savages around them. We respectfully ask for the civil institutions of the American Republic. We pray for the high privileges of American citizenship; the peaceful enjoyment of life; the right of acquiring, possessing, and using property; and the unrestrained pursuit of rational happiness. And for this your petitioners will ever pray.

DAVID LESLIE, [*and others.*]*

We have before alluded to the fact that the English government, by act of Parliament, had extended the colonial jurisdiction and civil laws of Canada over all her subjects on this coast, and had commissioned James Douglas, Angus McDonald, and, I think, Mr. Wark, as justices of the peace, having jurisdiction in civil cases not exceeding two hundred pounds sterling. In criminal cases, if the magistrate found, on examination, sufficient cause, the accused was to be sent to Canada for final trial. In all minor matters the Hudson's Bay Company were absolute. Their men, by the articles of enlistment, were bound to obey all orders of a superior officer, as much so as a soldier in the army. Flogging was a common punishment inflicted by all grades of officers, from a petty clerk of a trading-post up to the governor of the company. All British subjects, or any that had been subjects to the British crown, were considered as amenable to the laws of Canada, which were delivered from the brain of the magistrate or judge, who perchance may have passed through some parts of Canada on his way to this coast, no one knew when. Of course he knew all about the laws he was to enforce upon her Majesty's subjects, the same as our American judge, I. L. Babcock, did of the laws he was called upon to administer among the American settlers. Although the following incident is not exactly in the order of time in which we are writing, yet it illustrates the legal knowledge of Esquire Douglas so well that the reader will excuse me for giving it just here. The case occurred in the summer of 1846, I think in August. The Hudson's Bay Company and the British subjects in the country had changed from the open opposition policy to that of union with the provisional government, and some of the members of the company had been elected to office. Mr. Douglas had received a commission as justice of the peace and county judge from Governor Abernethy. A man by the name of McLame had taken it into his head to jump a claim belonging to one of the company's servants, near Fort Vancouver. The fact was duly stated to Esquire Douglas, who issued his warrant commanding the sheriff, a servant of the company, to arrest McLame. The sheriff proceeded with his warrant and posse, took McLame, brought him to the fort, and put him in irons to keep him

* Senate Document, Twenty-sixth Congress, first session. No. 514.

secure until he could be tried. The day following, the writer arrived at the fort, and as he was an old acquaintance of Esquire Douglas, and also holding a commission of justice of the peace and judge of the county court, Esquire Douglas stated the case to him, and asked his advice how to conduct it. I inquired what it was McLame had done.

"Why, he went upon the land of one of our people and set up a claim to it, and made some threats."

"Did he use any weapons, or injure any one?"

"No; but he was very insulting, as the men tell me; used abusive language and frightened the men, and attempted to get them off the claim, is the most he did."

"Well, Esquire, I think if you do not manage this case carefully you will have a devil of a muss among these fellows."

"What do you think I had better do?" says the Esquire.

"If it was my case, as it is yours, I would call the court as soon as possible, and call the parties. McLame claims to know something of law, and he will plead his own case, or get some one that don't know any more about law than he does, and they will call for a nonsuit on account of some illegality in the warrant or pleadings, and the first show you have, give them a nonsuit, and decide against your own people. This will satisfy McLame and his party, and the matter will end there. The suit is a civil one, and should have been by notice and summons, for 'forcible entry and detainer,' instead of an arrest and confinement as a criminal. They may attempt to make false imprisonment out of it. If they do, I would settle it the best way I could."

I never learned the exact manner in which this case was settled. I think McLame received some compensation and the matter was settled. But the Esquire never fully recovered from the effect of this legal attempt at provisional American wisdom, as he came as near involving the two governments in a national war in the San Juan boundary question, in 1849, as he did the country, in attempting to protect the unreasonable claims of the company's servants in 1846. As to law books or legal knowledge, the country in those early times could not boast of having an extensive law library or profound lawyers, and, as was to be expected, some new and strange lawsuits occurred.

Of the following case we have no personal knowledge, and can only give it as related to us by parties present. T. J. Hubbard, of Champoeg, had a native wife. She was claimed and coveted by a neighbor of his, who threatened to take her from him. Hubbard was armed, and prepared to defend his own supposed or real right of possession from his covetous neighbor, who attempted to enter his cabin window, or space where a window might be put (in case the owner had one to go there). Hubbard shot him while attempting to enter, and submitted to a trial. Rev. Mr. Leslie presided as judge. A jury was called, and the statements of all parties that pretended to know any thing about the case made. The verdict was, "Justifiable homicide." The petition which was gotten up about this time, says that "theft, murder, and infanticide, are increasing among them to an alarming extent." A fact was unquestionably stated in the petition, that justice and virtue were comparative strangers in the country. Despotism and oppression, with false notions of individual rights and personal liberty, were strongly at variance. The leading men, or such as one would naturally suppose to be guides of the erring, seemed to have fixed a personal standard for virtue, justice, and right, not difficult for the most abandoned to comply with.

CHAPTER XXVII.

Death of Ewing Young.—First public attempt to organize a provisional government.—Origin of the provisional government.—First Oregon schooner.

In the early part of this year, about the 15th of February, 1841, Mr. Ewing Young, having been sick but a short time, died. He left a large band of cattle and horses and no will, and seems to have had no heirs in the country. On the 17th we find most of the settlers present at the funeral. After burying Mr. Young, a meeting was called, over which Rev. Jason Lee presided. After some discussion it was thought best to adjourn to meet at the Methodist Mission.

On thè next day, the 18th, short as the notice was, nearly all the settlers were present,—Canadians, French, English, Americans, and Protestant missionaries and Jesuit priests.

Rev. Jason Lee, for some cause not stated, was excused from acting as chairman, and Rev. David Leslie elected to fill his place. Rev. Gustavus Hines and Sydney Smith were chosen as secretaries. "The doings of the previous day were presented to the assembly and adopted in part." Why does not Mr. Hines give us all the proceedings of the previous day? Was there any thing in them that reflected upon the disposition of the reverend gentleman to control the property of the deceased Mr. Young, and apply it to the use of the mission, or distribute it among its members?

We are well aware of the fact that, on the death of a person in any way connected with, or in the service of, the Hudson's Bay Company, they at once administer upon his estate, to the setting aside of the will of the deceased, as in the case of Mr. P. C. Pambrun, which occurred the summer before Mr. Young's decease; and, more recently, of Mr. Ray, who died at San Francisco. Mr. Ray was an active, energetic young man, had won the heart and hand of Miss McLaughlin, youngest daughter of Governor McLaughlin, and by this marriage had three interesting children, a son and two daughters. By his trading and speculations with his private funds, he had acquired a handsome fortune for his young family. At his death the Hudson's Bay Company sent an agent to take charge of the property. He claimed that as Mr. Ray was a servant of the company, and in their employ, he had no right to acquire property outside of their business; hence, the property belonged to the company. The books were canceled, and left his estate in debt to the company, and his family destitute. His widow was obliged to take in washing, which was given her by some American officers then at that place. By this means she supported herself and young family till she could obtain help from her father, who had withdrawn from the company, and was then residing in Oregon City.

This is as good an illustration of the Hudson's Bay Company's generosity as can be given. They pursued Dr. McLaughlin and his children to the death. Their influence and statements have led the American people to mistake the doctor's unbounded generosity to them as wholly due to the company, and changed the friendly feeling and rewards due to Dr. McLaughlin for needed supplies in the hour of greatest peril to their own account, at the same time holding the doctor's estate responsible for every dollar, as they did Mr. Ray's.

As to Messrs. Shepard's and Olley's estates, they were both administered by the Methodist Mission, or some one or more of its members. I have never been able to learn the results, but have been informed that, as they were members of the mission, the little property they had was disposed of as per mission usage. In the case of Mr. Young, the settlers found themselves somewhat interested. As to any Frenchman or Roman Catholic, it was taken for granted, if he was not the servant of the Hudson's Bay Company, his property went to the priest.

The settlers were united in the opinion that some understanding or laws should be adopted to govern the settlement of estates, other than the custom adopted by the Hudson's Bay Company or the missions; hence they all turned out, and were completely defeated by the operations of the Jesuit and Methodist missions. A resolution was ready, prepared for the occasion:—

"*Resolved*, That a committee be chosen to form a constitution, and draft a code of laws, and that the following persons compose that committee: Rev. F. N. Blanchet, Rev. Jason Lee, Rev. Gustavus Hines, Rev. Josiah L. Parish; Mr. D. Donpierre, Mr. M. Charlevo, Mr. Robert Moore, Mr. E. Lucia, Mr. Wm. Johnson."

The committee first named in the resolution contained the names of the three first-named clergymen. This was clerical law and constitution a little too strong. It was then moved to put upon the committee some that were not clergymen. The committee was finally made up of nine. Now comes the test of all,—the governor. Revs. Leslie and Hines, and Drs. Babcock and Bailey were prominent candidates. The prospects were that the three Protestant missionary candidates would divide that influence so that Dr. Bailey would be elected.

It will be borne in mind that Dr. Bailey was a man of strong English prejudices, and opposed to religious societies and religion generally. He could secure the French Catholic vote, and the majority of the settlers. He was present at the meeting, with his Canadian, French, and Hudson's Bay servant voters, all trained to vote for him for governor. He nominated himself, and so disgusted the American settlers that they joined in the effort to defeat him.

Mr. Hines was the prominent candidate to enter the field, and secure the leading influence in the government. That office was the leading question,—Bailey could not be trusted, and Hines could not be elected; hence the office of governor was discarded, and the committee instructed to prepare a constitution and laws, to be executed without an executive. This was a shrewd and cunning device, to say the least of it, one calculated to make the judicial and executive office one, in the same person; which seemed by common consent to be Dr. I. L. Babcock, a man equally as ambitious and aspiring as Dr. Bailey, but in good standing in the mission, and a stranger to the settlers. This point gained, George W. Le Breton, a young adventurer, who came to the country in the employ of Captain Couch, on the brig *Maryland*, having a fair education, and generally intelligent and agreeable in conversation, who had been brought up in good society, and was inclined to, or educated in, the Roman faith. This young man was elected to fill the offices of clerk of the court and public recorder, as a compromise with the Jesuits. To harmonize the English element, Wm. Johnson was elected high sheriff. Zavia Ladaroot, Pierre Billique, and Wm. McCarty were chosen constables. Messrs. Gervais, Cannon, Robert Moore, and Rev. L. H. Judson were chosen justices of the peace. Here comes the climax of all wisdom:—

"It was then resolved, that, until a code of laws be drafted by the Legislative Committee and adopted by the people, Ira L. Babcock, the supreme judge, be instructed to act"—*just as he pleased.* Mr. Hines says in his book, 419th page—"according to the laws of the State of New York."

I query whether there was a single copy of the laws of that State in the country for ten years after the last resolution was passed. I know there was none at the time, and only a single copy of the laws of Iowa two years after; hence, Ira L. Babcock was law-maker, judge, and executive to the settlement, just as much so as John McLaughlin was to the Hudson's Bay Company.

To keep up the farce (for the whole proceeding deserves no other name), "it was then resolved to adjourn, to meet the first Thursday in June, at the new building near the Roman Catholic church." The record proceeds: "Thursday, June 11, 1841. The inhabitants of the Wallamet Valley met according to adjournment, and the meeting was called to order by the chairman, Rev. David Leslie. On motion, the doings of the former meeting were read, on which the committee for drafting a constitution and code of laws was called for, and information was communicated to the meeting by the chairman of the committee, that, in consequence of his not having called the committee together, no report had been prepared." *His Jesuitical Reverence*, F. N. Blanchet, was excused from serving on the committee, at his own request. The settlers and uninitiated were informed by his reverence that he was unaccustomed to make laws for the people, and did not understand how to proceed, while *divide and conquer*, the policy adopted by the Hudson's Bay Company, was entered into with heart and soul by this *Reverend Father* Blanchet and his associates. "On motion, it was then resolved, that a person be chosen to fill the place thus vacated in the committee for drafting a constitution and code of laws, and Dr. Wm. J. Bailey was chosen."

The motion that follows shows that the settlers were suspicious of influences operating against them to deprive them of a voice in their own government, for they then, "on motion, resolved that this committee be instructed to meet for the transaction of their business on the first Monday of August next." They further instructed this committee to report at a subsequent meeting, "to be held the first Thursday in October next. On motion, resolved, that the committee be advised to confer with the commander of the American exploring squadron now in the Columbia River, concerning the propriety of forming a provisional government in Oregon."

"*Resolved*, That the motion to adopt the report of the nominating committee presented at a previous meeting be rescinded." Were the settlers really in favor of an organization adapted to their wants, and contrary to the wishes of the Hudson's Bay Company and clerical government then existing? The above resolution shows the fact. They have handsomely relieved the Jesuits of their responsibility, and left them to work with their associates and co-laborers,—the Hudson's Bay Company and Indians. They, to soften matters, allowed the committee to consider the nature of the government about to be formed, and the officers necessary, and—

"*Resolved*, That the committee to draft a constitution be instructed to take into consideration the number and kind of officers it will be necessary to create, in accordance with their constitution and code of laws, and to report the same at the next meeting." It was also resolved that the report of the nominating committee be referred to the Legislative Committee.

Mr. Secretary Hines does not give us the names of the nominating committee and the officers they first reported.

The meeting held at or near the Roman Catholic church on the 11th of June was adjourned to meet at the Methodist Mission at eleven o'clock on the first Thursday in October following. Duly signed, David Leslie, chairman; Gustavus Hines, Sydney Smith, secretaries. The whole humbug had been completed; the Methodist Mission party was safe; the Hudson's Bay Company and Jesuits only wanted time to carry out their arrangements and drive the whole concern from the country, or make a grand sacrifice for the benefit of the Hudson's Bay Company's trade and mother church.

The idea of resisting the American influence was no new one; it was announced as early as 1838. The combinations were ready to be made that, at the proper time, every Hudson's Bay Company's man felt certain, would accomplish the object they desired. They were ready and did invest their money upon the issue? It is true other parties came in and formed combinations that they supposed themselves capable of destroying by a single word. They failed; and in 1865 we find them, the petitioners, with a host of those they sought to rob, crying against their injustice. They ask for compensation for attempting to prevent the rightful owners of the country from occupying it. This is in keeping with their whole course. Their impudence may carry them through and win their case, which justice and truth should deny them.

Mr. Hines says, page 240: "I have previously stated that the origin of the attempt to form a kind of provisional government was the removal by death of the late Ewing Young, leaving, as he did, a large and unsettled estate, with no one to administer it, and no law to control its administration. The exigency of this case having been met by the appointment of a judge with probate powers, who entered immediately upon his duties" (giving no bonds to any body), "and disposed of the estate of Ewing Young to the entire satisfaction of the community, and the fact that some of the *most influential citizens* of the country, and especially some of the *Legislative Committee*, were adverse to the idea of establishing a permanent organization so long as the peace and harmony of the community could possibly be preserved without it, the subject was permitted to die away and the committee for drafting a constitution and code of laws did not meet according to their instructions, nor did the meeting at which they were expected to report ever take place."

Mr. Hines, in his account of this affair, is not quite satisfied himself with the reasons he has given, so he goes on to state many facts as connected with the arrival of the exploring squadron of the United

States, under command of Captain Wilkes, and says, page 421: "In addition to this, the officers of the squadron were consulted on the subject of organizing the country into a civil compact, and were found to be decidedly opposed to the scheme, and recommended that the subject be allowed to rest. They encouraged the people in the belief that the United States government would probably soon extend jurisdiction over the country."

To the disgrace of the leader of that squadron, the general impression of all the early settlers of this country is, to the present day, that he understood and tasted the qualities of Dr. McLaughlin's liquors, and received the polite attentions of the gentlemen of the Hudson's Bay Company with far more pleasure than he looked into or regarded the wants of this infant settlement of his countrymen. Mr. Hines says "the *officers* of the squadron decidedly opposed the scheme." And why did they do it? Simply because the parties named above were opposed. They had absolute control of the persons and property of all in the country, and they scrupled not to keep and use their power to the last.

The unconquerable energy of the Americans was this year manifested in the building of a schooner, of about forty tons burden, on a little island some four miles above the present city of Portland. R. L. Kilborn, of the party of Ewing Young, Charley Matts, P. Armstrong, who was afterward killed in the Indian war on Rogue River, H. Woods, John Green, and George Davis engaged in this enterprise. They employed Felix Hathaway, who was saved from the wreck of the *William and Ann*, as head carpenter, and commenced their work. To obtain spikes and such irons as were required, they had it reported that they were going to build a ferry-boat to cross the Wallamet River. To obtain rigging, they induced the French farmers to go to Fort Vancouver and get ropes to use in the old Dutch harness for plowing, Dr. McLaughlin having informed them in the start, that he did not approve of their scheme, and would furnish them no supplies. They, however, were not to be deterred in their undertaking. Procuring a whip-saw of the mission, and such tools as they could spare, these men commenced their work; and when Captain Wilkes visited them, and found they had a substantial and sea-worthy craft well under way, he furnished them such articles from his stores as he could spare, and spoke favorably of their enterprise to Dr. McLaughlin, who became more liberal; so that, with the assistance of Captain Wilkes, the mission, and such as they received from Dr. McLaughlin, the vessel was launched and made trips to California, under the command of Captain Joseph Gale, who returned to Oregon in 1843, and was elected one of our Executive Committee, with David Hill and Alanson Beers.

CHAPTER XXVIII.

Lee and Hines explore the Umpqua River.—Mr. Hines tells a story.—Massacre and plunder of Smith's party by the Indians.—Sympathy of the Hudson's Bay Company.—Extract from the San Francisco *Bulletin.*

THE reader is requested to note the statements that follow, as they show influences operating that tell how active the enemies of the Protestant missions had been. Mr. Hines admits that he owed his own and Mr. Lee's life to the wife of Guinea. (See his journal, page 109.) He says: "During the evening Mr. Guinea came to us considerably excited, and warmly congratulated us on the safe guardianship his wife had exercised over us in our absence. He said that in all probability we should have been robbed of all we had, if we had not lost our lives, had it not been for the faithfulness of his wife and her brother. He told us that one of the chiefs of the clan we had visited was at the fort. Learning that we designed to visit his people on the coast, *excited with the utmost fear*, he hastened down the river and reported many evil things about us, intending thereby to instigate the Indians to prevent us from going among them."

Mr. Hines, can you vouch for the truth of this statement? I believe sincerely you have told the truth, for you even attempt to excuse the Indian for his fears, and have not the least suspicion of the sources from which the Indian received his instruction and is made to believe that you and Mr. Jason Lee had come with your *medicine bag* to destroy them. Let us hear Mr. Hines' excuse for the Indian's fears, in his own words. He says: "Mr. Lee had brought a fowling-piece with him, and had in his possession a patent shot-pouch. This was the thing that had alarmed the chief. One story he told was, that we had brought *medicine in a bag* that Mr. Lee wore on his neck, for the purpose of killing them all off; and that if we were permitted to come among them the fatal bag would be opened and they would all be destroyed."

How did these Indians learn about the missionary medicine bag? Our good friend, Guinea, Mr. Hines tells us, is from Montreal, and of a good family,—a Frenchman. This trip, it seems, was made in 1840, about the 26th day of October. Dr. Whitman had not yet gone to the States, but the medicine-bag story is tried with the Indians on the

Umpqua. Guinea has a little too much sense of moral responsibility to allow his Indians to commence the slaughter of Lee and Hines, as Dr. White had come with them and seen them safe at the fort, and had returned to the settlement. The medicine man of the Methodist Mission had escaped, and it was not best to commence on these preachers. Madam *Siwash* Guinea must accompany them, to watch and explain matters and protect them.

Mr. Hines says, page 100: "We had been informed by Mr. Guinea that there would be *great danger* in our going among them alone, and indeed he appeared to stand in the utmost fear of them, of their hostility to the whites, and especially to the *Americans*."

Can a reasonable man read this simple narrative with the light of history, and facts piled on facts, with the stains of the blood of our countrymen all over the country, and not trace the cause of these foul murders to their true source? While none but American traders and hunters were in the country, it was an easy matter to dispose of them, but when the American missionary comes among the natives, another element of opposition must be introduced; moral teachings must be met by religious superstitions, to secure the victim, to advance the interests of an unscrupulous trade. Let us take another statement from Mr. Hines before we proceed with his political history. On page 106, in speaking of the closing remarks of the chief at the mouth of the Umpqua, he tells us, the chief "said he was very glad we had come to see them; that their hearts toward us were like our hearts toward them; that he wanted us to continue with them another day and tell them about God; that they had heard about us, and had been told that we were a bad people." *Who told these wild Indians this?* Was it an American that had been living among them and teaching them that his countrymen were a bad people? "That they were glad to see us for themselves, and were convinced that what they had heard was a lie; that they now believe us to be good, and that they meant to be good also."

Mr. Hines tells a story, as he received it from the Hudson's Bay Company gentlemen, to show that these Indians are very treacherous and not to be relied upon, especially those on the coast. It relates to a company of fur hunters composed of Smith, Sublet, and Jackson. At page 110 of his book, he says: "In this division Smith was to take the country extending from the Platte River by the way of Santa Fé to California; then turn north along the Pacific Ocean as far as the Columbia River, and thence back into the interior to join the other partners of the company. The country was in the wildest state, but few white men having ever passed through it. But, nothing daunted, Smith and his companions marched through to California, and thence along the coast north as far as the Umpqua River, collecting in their course all the valuable furs they could procure, until they had loaded several pack animals with the precious burden [forty packs of furs]. On arriving here, they encamped on the borders of the river near the place where they intended to cross, but, on examination, found it would be dangerous, if not impossible, to effect the passage of the river at that place. Accordingly, Smith took one of his men [he had two] and proceeded up the river on foot, for the purpose of finding a better place to cross. In his absence, the Indians, instigated by one of the savage-looking chiefs whom we saw at the mouth of the river, rushed upon the party with their muskets [the same furnished by the Hudson's Bay Company for that purpose], bows and arrows, tomahawks, and scalping-knives, and commenced the work of death." Just as they were expected to do with all intruders in this fur traders' empire. "From the apparent kindness of the Indians previously, the party had been thrown entirely off their guard, and consequently were immediately overpowered by their ferocious enemies, and but one of the twelve in camp escaped from the cruel massacre. Scarcely knowing which way he fled, this one fell in with Smith, who was on his return to the camp, and who received from the survivor the shocking account of the murder of eleven of his comrades. Smith seeing all was lost, resolved upon attempting nothing further than to do his best to secure his own personal safety, with that of his surviving companions. The Indians had secured all the furs, horses, mules, baggage, and every thing the company had. The three immediately crossed the river and made the best of their way through a savage and inhospitable country toward Vancouver, where, after traveling between two and three hundred miles, and suffering the greatest deprivations, they finally arrived in safety."

Rev. Mr. Hines' savage-looking chief was no less a personage than a slave of a Frenchman by the name of Michel, or rather belonging to Michel's Umpqua wife. This slave had learned, from the statements and talk he had heard at Vancouver, that in case the Indians killed and robbed the Boston men, there would be no harm to them; that neither the Hudson's Bay Company nor the English or French would take any notice of it. Hence, the Indians were taught to regard the killing of a Boston man (American) as doing something that pleased the Hudson's Bay Company. Under this instruction it is said this slave ran away from Vancouver, and went back to his people, and was the cause of the massacre of Smith's party. He is again present, doing all he can to induce his people to rob and take the lives of Lee and Hines. Mr. Guinea, then in charge of the fort, is aware of his instructions and his object. He dare not tell Lee and Hines of their full danger, yet he knows all about it.

They were determined to visit the Indians and see for themselves. Guinea's Indian wife and her brother must go with them. This is considered sufficient protection. The story of the Indian slave's part in the massacre of Smith's party is related to us by Mrs. Smith, the wife of S. H. Smith, an intelligent and much respected native woman, a neighbor of ours for near twenty years, and by one of the men that accompanied McKay to recover the property; corresponding exactly to another event of the same kind that occurred in 1847, which will be given in detail as stated by eye-witnesses under the solemnity of an oath.

Mr. Hines, of course, believes the following statement, because the *gentlemen* of the company told it to him; just as I did the first time I heard it from them. It is said, Smith and companions, "rehearsing the story of their wonderful escape and subsequent sufferings to the members of the Hudson's Bay Company, the utmost *sympathy* was excited in their behalf, and a strong party was fitted out to go and rescue the *property* from the savage robbers, and restore it to its surviving owners. The vigor and perseverance of this party were equal to the promptitude with which it was fitted out. They proceeded to the scene of blood, and after committing the mangled bodies of Smith's murdered companions to the grave, compelled the Indians to relinquish the property they had taken," by giving them presents of blankets and powder, and such things as the Indians wished, as stated to us by a Frenchman, a servant of the company, who was one of McKay's party that went to get the furs. They found no bodies to bury, and had no fight with the Indians about the property, as stated by Mr. Smith also. But, as the Hudson's Bay Company tells the story through Mr. Hines, they "*spread terror through the tribes.*" Was this the case in the Whitman massacre in 1847? the Samilkamean massacre in 1857? the Frazer River murder of American citizens in 1858? No: Governor Douglas told the committee that asked him for protection, or for arms, to protect themselves; that "*if they* [the Americans] *molested her Majesty's subjects he would send a force to punish them.*" Mr. Hines says his Umpqua party "*returned in triumph to Vancouver.*" And well they might, for they had made the best season's hunt they ever made, in getting those furs and the property of Smith, which paid them well for the expedition, as there was no market for Smith, except London, through the hypocritical kindness of Mr. Simpson. By this time, Mr. Smith had learned all he wished to of this company. He preferred giving them his furs at their own price to being under any further obligations to them. Mr. Sublet, Mr. Smith's partner, did not speak as though he felt under much obligation to Mr. Simpson or the Hudson's Bay Company in 1836, which was not long after the transaction referred to.

I do not know how the company regard these statements of Mr. Hines, yet I regard them as true so far as Mr. Hines is concerned, but utterly false as regards the company. As old Toupin says Mr. Parker told the Indians, "It is their fashion" of taking credit to themselves for doing all they could against the Americans occupying the country in any way.

According to the testimony given in the case of The Hudson's Bay Company *v.* United States, the amount of furs seized by the company at that time was forty packs, worth at the time $1,000 each, besides the animals and equipments belonging to the party, a large portion of which was given to the Indians, to compensate them for their services rendered to the company, in destroying Smith's expedition and killing his men, corresponding with transactions of recent date, as stated in an article found in the San Francisco *Bulletin*:—

"HUDSON'S BAY COMPANY AND THE INDIANS.—A gentleman from Victoria gives us the following facts concerning the Indian outrages on the northern coast, and their allies, the Hudson's Bay Company: Captain D. Warren said to M. A. Foster and William McCurdy, that, on returning to Victoria and reporting the circumstances of the attack of the Indians upon his sloop, *Thornton*, to the first lieutenant of the ship *Zealous*, he was the next day arrested and put under $2,000 bonds. The *Sparrowhawk* was to leave last Wednesday, but had not yet gone to inquire into the matter. It is known that the same Indians murdered Captain Jack Knight and partner but a short time before. The same crowd or band of Indians robbed the *Nanaimo* packet. Since thus attacked, Captain Warren, the captain of the *Ocean Queen*, informed them that a friendly Indian chief told him to leave; the Indians were hostile; they were preparing for war with the neighboring tribes.

"From a statement found in the *Chronicle*, of the 27th of June, we learn that Captain Mowatt, of the Hudson's Bay Company, is in charge of Fort Rupert. We also learn that Captain Mowatt's prejudices and feelings are peculiarly hostile to all American fur traders, and not any too friendly to those claiming to be English. The facts indicate a strong Hudson's Bay Company Indian war influence against American or other traders in behalf of that company. It is evident from the statement of the two gentlemen above named that her Majesty's naval officers are inclined, and more than probably instructed, to protect the Hudson's Bay Company's people in encouraging the Indian hostility and murder of all outside venturers upon their trading localities, as they are prompt to insinuate and affirm that the whites are the aggressors, and to arrest them for punishment."

It is difficult to understand why our American government is so tolerant and generous to a foregn monopoly that has invariably sought and accomplished the destruction of its fur trade on its western borders, and used its entire influence against American institutions and citizens; not hesitating to incite the Indians to the most inhuman and brutal murders.

CHAPTER XXIX.

Missionaries leaving.—Hudson's Bay Company's Gold Exchange.—Population in 1842.—Whitman and Lovejoy start for the States.—The Red River emigration.—American merchants.—Settlers not dependent on the Hudson's Bay Company.—Milling Company.—The Oregon Institute.—Dr. Elijah White.—Proceedings and resolutions of a public meeting at Wallamet.—Correspondence with the War Department.

Rev. A. B. Smith and wife, Cornelius Rogers, and W. H. Gray and wife had left the mission of the American Board, on account of difficulties they had become fully satisfied would ultimately destroy the mission or drive it from the country. Mr. Spalding, it will be remembered, was a man of peculiar temperament, ambitious and selfish. He could not endure an associate of superior talent, or admit himself to be inferior in understanding the native language. From the time the Jesuits arrived (in 1838), some of his own pet Indians had turned Catholics and commenced a quarrel with him. These facts seemed to annoy and lead him to adopt a course opposed by Smith, Gray, and Rogers. Still he found it pleased the Indians as a whole, and was assented to by the balance of the mission. Smith and wife left for the Sandwich Islands; Rogers for the Wallamet in 1841; Gray and wife in 1842.

During the exploration of the country by Commodore Wilkes' exploring squadron, Mr. Cornelius Rogers was found a very useful man. His knowledge of Indian languages (which he was remarkably quick to acquire) and of Indian character generally enabled him to become a reliable and useful interpreter. The officers soon became aware of the fact, and employed him at once to assist and interpret for them. He was paid for his services in gold coin, which amounted to something over five hundred dollars. Not wishing to carry his coin about, he offered to deposit it with the Hudson's Bay Company. "Certainly, Mr. Rogers, we will receive your coin, and credit you upon our books twenty per cent. less, as the coin is not so valuable to us as our goods, at beaver prices." Mr. R. allowed them to take his coin and credit him with four hundred dollars in beaver currency. In a short time a party of the squadron were to go by land to California. Mr. R. concluded he would go with them, and that his coin would be more convenient than beaver orders on the company. He therefore requested them to return to him the coin. "Certainly, Mr. Rogers," and handed him back four hundred dollars less twenty per cent.,—three hundred and twenty dollars. "How is this?" says Mr. R.; "I supposed from the statement you made on depositing this money with you, that that money was a drug to you, and now you wish me to pay you twenty per cent. for money I have left in your care, after deducting twenty per cent. for leaving it with you. You may consider this a fair and an honorable transaction; I do not." He was told, "*Such is our manner of doing business*," and that was all the satisfaction he could get. He finally left his money and drew his goods, at what was called beaver prices, of the company.

Nothing further of note occurred in 1841, except the loss of the *Peacock*, in which no lives were lost, and the extra efforts of the company to show to the officers of the expedition their good deeds and kind treatment to all Americans, and to prove to them that the whole country was of little value to any one. "It would scarcely support the few Indians, much less a large population of settlers."

1842.—Our population, all told, in the beginning of this year, is twenty-one Protestant ministers, three Roman or Jesuit priests, fifteen lay members of churches, thirty-four white women, thirty-two white children, and thirty-five American settlers—twenty-five of them with native wives. Total, one hundred and thirty-seven Americans. At the close of the year we had an emigration from the States of one hundred and eleven persons,—some forty-two families,—with two lawyers, A. L. Lovejoy and A. M. Hastings. The latter became the lawyer of Dr. McLaughlin, and relieved the settlement in the spring of 1843 of a number of not very valuable settlers, by assisting them to get credit of the Hudson's Bay Company in procuring their outfits, giving their notes, payable in California; while settlers who remained could get no credit or supplies of the company, especially such as had asked protection of the American government. A. L. Lovejoy started from Whitman's station to return to the States with Dr. Whitman. He reached Bent's Fort with him, but stopped for the winter, while Whitman proceeded on to Washington in time to save the country from being given up to British rule. For an account of that trip, which we give in another chapter, we are indebted to the Honorable A. L. Lovejoy.

The Red River emigration, consisting of some forty families of English, Scotch, and Canadian-French half-breeds, had been ordered from the Red River, or Selkirk settlement, to locate in the Puget Sound district, by the Hudson's Bay Company's governor, Simpson. This company started across the plains with most of their property and families in carts, in the spring of 1842, directed, protected, and guided by the company, and expected to become settlers, subject to it, in Puget

Sound. This was in fact a part of the original plan of the Puget Sound Agricultural Company, and these families were brought on to aid in securing and holding the country for the British government and the use of the company,—a plan and arrangement exactly similar to that adopted by the Hudson's Bay Company in 1811–12, to cut off the trade of the French Northwest Fur Company, by establishing the Selkirk settlement directly in the line of their trade.

This Red River colony was a part of the company's scheme to control and outnumber the American settlement of Oregon; it being connected with the Puget Sound concern, and under the control of the Hudson's Bay Company,—which, by the decision of the commissioners, has won the company $200,000 from our national treasury. A more infamous claim could not well be trumped up, and the men who awarded it should be held responsible, and handed down to posterity as unjust rewarders of unscrupulous monopolies. Not for this alone, but for paying to the parent monopoly the sum of $450,000, for their malicious misrepresentations of the country, their murders, and their perjury respecting their claims to it.

As soon as the Red River colony reached the country, they found that the Hudson's Bay Company on the west side of the Rocky Mountains was a different institution from that of the Selkirk settlement; consequently a large number of the more intelligent among them refused to remain in the Puget Sound district, and found their way into the Wallamet and Tualatin districts, and were received and treated as Oregonians, or citizens of the provisional government. This had the effect to embitter the feelings of the ruling spirits of the company, and caused them to change their policy. They commenced fortifying Fort Vancouver, and had a war-ship, the *Modeste*, stationed in the Columbia River, while the fort was being prepared for defensive or offensive measures. This only increased the anxiety and hastened the effort to organize for self-defense on the part of the American settlers.

In the mean time, Hon. Caleb Cushing, of Newburyport, Massachusetts, had sent to the country a ship with supplies. A. E. Wilson had established himself, or was about to, at Wallamet Falls as a trader, and some families were on their way by water from the States,—F. W. Pettygrove, Peter Foster, and Peter H. Hatch. Pettygrove arrived with a small stock of goods. The same ship brought a supply for the Methodist Mission.

The settlers were not dependent upon the Hudson's Bay Company for supplies as much as has been asserted. I am certain that many of them never received a dollar's worth of the company's goods, except it might have been through the stores of Pettygrove, Wilson, or Abernethy. I know many of them were willing and did pay higher prices to their American merchants than they could get the same article for from the company's store, which was about this time established at Oregon City. Soon after, a trading-post and warehouse were established at Champoeg, and Mr. Roberts sent up with orders to *kick, change, and beat the half-bushel with a club* in order to get more wheat at sixty cents per imperial bushel in payment for all debts due the company for the goods furnished to them at one hundred per cent. or more on London prices.

During this year the Wallamet Milling Company was formed, and commenced to build a saw-mill on the island above the falls. Dr. McLaughlin also commenced active opposition to American enterprise.

The Oregon Institute was commenced this year, under the direction of the Methodist missionaries. They carefully guarded against all outside patronage or influence getting control of their institution, by requiring a certain number of trustees to be members of their church in good standing. It was during the discussions in the organizing of that institution that the disposition on the part of that mission to control not only the religious, but literary and political interests of the settlement, was manifested. The leading members took strong ground, yet hesitated when it was found they would be compelled to ask for outside patronage. However, they were able to commence operations with the Institute, and succeeded in getting up a building deemed suitable by the building committee.

Dr. Elijah White returned to the country, as he supposed and frequently asserted, with unlimited discretionary powers from the President of the United States to arrange all matters between the Hudson's Bay Company, Indians, and settlers, and "although his commission did not specify in so many words, yet, in short, he was the governing power of the United States west of the Rocky Mountains." He entered at once upon the duties of his office, and such a muss as he kicked up all over the country it would require the pens of a Squibob and a Junius combined to describe. Rev. Mr. Hines has given to the world many useful notices of this notorious blockhead, and from his descriptions of his proceedings one would infer that he was a most important character in promoting the peace and harmony of the settlement and keeping the Indians quiet. I have always been at a loss to understand Mr. Hines, whether he is speaking of Dr. White's proceedings in sober earnest or serious burlesque. Either he was woefully ignorant of the character of Dr. White, or he was cajoled and flattered and made to believe the doctor possessed power and influence at Washington that no document he could show gave any evidence of. Be that as it may, Dr. White arrived in the fall of 1842, in advance of the emigration. He pretended to have all power necessary for all cases, civil and criminal. He appointed temporary magistrates to try all cases as they might occur; and such as related to Indians and whites, or half-breeds and whites, he tried himself, and gave decisions to suit his own ideas of justice. Usually, in the case of two settlers, where he had appointed a justice to try the case, he would argue the case for one of the parties, and generally win it for his client or favorite. We attended two of the doctor's trials, one in Tualatin Plains, the other at the saw-mill near Salem. In both of these cases the conclusion of those not interested was, that if such was the justice to which we as settlers were reduced, our own energy and arms must protect us.

At the meeting called to receive him, a committee, being appointed, retired, and, after a short absence, reported the following resolutions:—

Resolved, That we, the citizens of the Wallamet Valley, are exceedingly happy in the consideration that the government of the United States have manifested their intentions through their agent, Dr. E. White, of extending their jurisdiction and protection over this country.

Resolved, That, in view of the claims which the aborigines of this country have upon the sympathies of the white man, we are gratified at the appointment of an agent by the United States government to regulate and guard their interests.

Resolved, That we highly approve of the appointment of Dr. E. White to the above office, and that we will cordially co-operate with him in carrying out the measures of government in reference to this country.

Resolved, That we feel grateful to the United States government for their intended liberality toward the settlers of this country, and for their intention to support education and literature among us.

Resolved, That it will give us the highest pleasure to be brought, so soon as it may be practicable, under the jurisdiction of our mother country.

On motion, it was

Resolved, That the report of the committee be adopted.

Resolved unanimously, That the doings of this meeting be transmitted to the government of the United States by Dr. E. White, in order that our views and wishes in relation to this country may be known.

The following communication shows the shrewdness of Dr. White, and the influence he was enabled to hold over Mr. Hines, who seems to have ignored all the doctor's conduct while a missionary, and considers him a suitable person to deal with the complicated relations then culminating on our western coast. It is given entire, to place Mr. Hines in his true character in the history of the country, though Dr. White does not deign to mention his name in his report to the department. We also give an extract from the report of the Commissioners of Indian Affairs, November 28, 1843, as found on fifth and sixth pages of Dr. White's report. Mr. Hines' letter is as follows:—

WALLAMET, April 3, 1843.

To the Honorable Secretary of War:

SIR,—I have the honor of addressing you a brief communication expressive of my views of the course pursued by Dr. E. White, sub-agent of Indian Affairs west of the Rocky Mountains.

I am not extensively acquainted with what properly belongs to the business of an Indian agent, but so far as I understand the subject, this agency requires the performance of duties which are of an *onerous* and *complicated* character.

The country is quite extensive, and an intercourse is carried on between the whites and Indians in almost every part of it. The principal settlements are on the Wallamet River and Tualatine Plains, but there are whites at the mouth of the Columbia River, the Falls, and among the Wallawalla, Cayuse, Nez Percé, and Snake Indians. Immediately after the arrival of your agent in this country, he received the most urgent calls from several of these places, if possible to come immediately and enter into such measures as would secure both the safety of the whites and welfare of the Indians.

He entered upon his business with diffidence, though with great energy and decision, and his indefatigable efforts to promote the interests of this country, with his untiring industry in the performance of his duties, entitle him to the warmest respect of the members of this infant and helpless colony, and to the confidence of the honorable department which has committed to him so important a trust. Although he has been with us but a short time in his official capacity, yet it is generally believed that the measures he has adopted to regulate the intercourse between the whites and Indians, particularly in the Cayuse, Nez Percé, and Wallawalla tribes, are wisely calculated to secure the protection of the former against the aggressions of the savages, and to secure to the latter the blessings of harmony, peace, and civilization.

Some time in November last news reached us from these formidable tribes that they were laying a plot for the destruction of this colony, upon which your agent, with characteristic decision, determined to proceed at once to the scene of this conspiracy, and, if possible, not only to frustrate the present designs of the Indians, but to prevent any future attempts of the same character.

This laborious journey was undertaken, and, accordingly, he set out on this perilous enterprise in the dead of winter, being accompanied by six men, and though the distance to be traveled by land and water was little less than one thousand miles, and the whole journey was one of excessive labor and much suffering, yet perseverance surmounted every difficulty, and the undertaking was brought to a most happy issue. In the fitting out and execution of such an expedition much expense must necessarily be incurred, but I am fully of the opinion the funds appropriated by your agent, for the purpose of accomplishing the object of his appointment, have been judiciously applied.

Not knowing the views I entertained in reference to the propriety of his course, Dr. White requested me to write to the honorable Secretary of War, definitely expressing my opinion. Considering this a sufficient apology for intruding myself upon your patience in this communication, allow me, dear sir, to subscribe myself most respectfully,

Your humble servant,

GUSTAVUS HINES,

Missionary to the Wallamet Settlement.

DEPARTMENT OF WAR,
OFFICE OF INDIAN AFFAIRS, Nov. 28, 1843.

I submit a report from the sub-agent west of the Rocky Mountains, received on the 9th of August last. It furnishes some deeply-interesting and curious details respecting certain of the Indian tribes in that remote part of our Territories. The Nez Percés are represented to be "more noble, industrious, sensible, and better disposed toward the whites," than the others. Their conduct on the occasion of an important meeting between Dr. White and their leading men impresses one most agreeably. The school established for their benefit is very numerously attended, while it is gratifying to learn that this is not the only establishment for Indian instruction which has been made and conducted with success.

There will also be found in this paper some particulars as to the soil, water-courses, etc., of the Territory of Oregon, which may be interesting at this time, when public attention is so much directed to the region beyond the Rocky Mountains.

Respectfully submitted,

T. HARTLEY CRAWFORD.

Hon. J. M. PORTER, Secretary of War.

CHAPTER XXX.

Dispatch of Dr. White to the Commissioner of Indian Affairs.—He praises the Hudson's Bay Company.—His account of the Indians.—Indian outrages.—Dr. White's expedition to the Nez Percés.—Indian council.—Speeches.—Electing a chief.—Laws of the Nez Percés.—Visit to the Cayuses.—Doings of the missionaries.—Drowning of Mr. Rogers and family.—George Geere.—Volcanoes.—Petition against Governor McLaughlin.

OREGON, April 1, 1843.

SIR,—On my arrival, I had the honor and happiness of addressing you a brief communication, giving information of my safe arrival, and that of our numerous party, to these distant shores.

At that time it was confidently expected that a more direct, certain, and expeditious method would be presented to address you in a few weeks; but that failing, none has offered till now.

I think I mentioned the kind and hospitable manner we were received and entertained on the way by the gentlemen of the Hudson's Bay Company, and the cordial and most handsome reception I met with at Fort Vancouver from Governor McLaughlin and his worthy associate chief factor, James Douglas, Esq.; my appointment giving pleasure rather than pain,—a satisfactory assurance that these worthy gentlemen intend eventually to settle in this country, and prefer American to English jurisdiction.

On my arrival in the colony, sixty miles south of Vancouver, being in advance of the party, and coming unexpectedly to the citizens, bearing the intelligence of the arrival of so large a re-enforcement, and giving assurance of the good intentions of our government, the excitement was general, and two days after we had the largest and happiest public meeting ever convened in this infant colony.

I found the colony in peace and health, and rapidly increasing in numbers, having more than doubled in population during the last two years. English, French, and half-breeds seem, equally with our own people, attached to the American cause; hence the bill of Mr. Linn, proffering a section of land to every white man of the Territory, has the double advantage of being popular and useful, increasing such attachment, and manifestly acting as a strong incentive to all, of whatever nation or party, to settle in this country.

My arrival was in good time, and probably saved much evil. I had but a short season of rest after so long, tedious, and toilsome a journey, before information reached me of the very improper conduct of the upper country Indians toward the missionaries sent by the American Board of Commissioners, accompanied with a passport, and a desire for my interposition in their behalf at once.

I allude to the only three tribes from which much is to be hoped, or any thing to be feared, in this part of Oregon. These are the Wallawallas, Cayuses, and Nez Percés, inhabiting a district of country on the Columbia and its tributaries, commencing two hundred and forty miles from its mouth, and stretching four hundred and eighty miles into the interior. The Wallawallas, most contiguous to the colony, number some three thousand, including the entire population. They are in general poor, indolent, and sordid, but avaricious; and what few have property, in horses and herds, are proud, haughty, and insolent. The Cayuses, next easterly, are less numerous, but more formidable, being brave, active, tempestuous, and warlike. Their country is well watered, gently undulating, extremely healthy, and admirably adapted to grazing, as Dr. Marcus Whitman, who resides in their midst, may have informed you. They are comparatively rich in herds, independent in manner, and not unfrequently boisterous, saucy, and troublesome in language and behavior. The Nez Percés, still further in the interior, number something less than three thousand; they inhabit a beautiful grazing district not surpassed by any I have seen for verdure, water privileges, climate, or health. The tribe forms, to some extent, an honorable exception to the general Indian character, being more noble, industrious, sensible, and better disposed toward the whites and their improvements in the arts and sciences; and, though as brave as Cæsar, the whites have nothing to dread at their hands, in case of their dealing out to them what they conceive to be right and equitable. Of late, these three tribes have become strongly united by reason of much intermarriage. For the last twenty years they have been generally well disposed toward the whites; but at the time Captain Bonneville visited this district of country, he dealt more profusely in presents and paid a higher price for furs than Mr. Pambrun, one of the traders of the Hudson's Bay Company, established at Wallawalla, who had long dealt with them, and was previously a general favorite. On Mr. Bonneville's leaving, the chiefs assembled at the fort, and insisted on a change of the tariff in their favor. Pambrun refusing, they seized him, stamped violently upon his breast, beat him severely, and retained him prisoner, in rather unenviable circumstances, till they gained, to a considerable extent, their object. Since that time, they have been more consequential in feeling, and shown less deference and respect to the whites. On the arrival of missionaries among them they have never failed to make, at first, a most favorable impression, which has, in most instances, unfortunately, led to too near an approach to familiarity, operating alike prejudicial to both parties. The Rev. Messrs. Lee and Parker, who made each but a short stay among them, left with like favorable impressions. Their successors, Spalding, Whitman, Gray, and ladies, with others who remained among them, were at last driven to the conclusion that Indians as much resembled each other in character as complexion. These worthy people, not well versed in Indian character, and anxious to accomplish a great deal in a short time, resorted to various expedients to induce them to leave off their wandering migratory habits, and settle down contiguous to them in herding and agricultural pursuits, so as to be able to send their numerous and healthy children to school. In these efforts they were zealous and persevering, holding out various inducements as so many stimulants to action, most of which would have operated well in civilized life, but generally failed with these Indians; and whatever was promised conditionally, whether the condition was met or otherwise, there was no reprieve—the promised articles must come; and sometimes, under circumstances sufficiently trying, had these missionaries been less devoted, they would have driven them from their post forever.

The Indians, having gained one and another victory, became more and more insolent, till at last, some time previous to my arrival, they were not only obtrusive and exceedingly annoying about and in the missionaries' houses, but seized one of the clergymen in his own house,* without a shadow of provocation, further than that of treating a better neighboring chief with more respect than they, and insulted him most shamefully, there being no other white person within fifty miles, save his sick and delicate lady. Soon after, they commenced on Dr. Whitman; pulled his ears and hair, and threw off his hat three times in the mud at his feet. A short time after, the chiefs assembled, broke into the house, violently assailed his person with war clubs, and, with an ax, broke down the door leading to his own private apartment. It is generally thought, and possibly with truth, that, on this occasion, Dr. Whitman would have been killed, had not a party of white men arrived in sight just at this moment.† Never was such an outrage and insult more

* Rev. A. B. Smith, who employed the Lawyer as his teacher in the Nez Percé language. Ellis was the chief who claimed the land, and had been at the Red River school. He was jealous of the Lawyer's influence with the American missionaries, and used his influence with the Hudson's Bay Company to drive Mr. Smith away.

† We were present at Dr. Whitman's at the time here referred to, and know that this difficulty originated from Jesuitical teachings.

undeserving. He had built, for the express purpose of Indian accommodation, a house of the same materials, and finished in like manner with his own, of respectable size, and joined to his, and at all times, night and day, accessible. In addition to this, they were admitted to every room in his house but one. This being closed, had like to have cost him his life. He had hardly left for the States last fall, when, shocking to relate, at the hour of midnight, a large Indian chief managed to get into the house, came to the door of Mrs. Whitman's bed-chamber, and had succeeded in getting it partly open before she reached it. A white man, sleeping in an adjoining apartment, saved her from violence and ruin. The villain escaped. There was but one thing wrong in this matter on the part of Dr. Whitman, and that was a great error,—leaving his excellent lady unprotected in the midst of savages.* A few days after this they burned down the mission mill on his premises, with all its appendages and considerable grain, damaging them not less than twelve or fifteen hundred dollars. About the same time, Mrs. Spalding was grossly insulted in her own house, and ordered out of it, in the absence of her husband. Information reached him of an Indian having stolen his horse near the same time; he hastened to the spot to secure the animal; the rogue had crossed the river; but, immediately returning, he presented his loaded gun, cocked, at the breast of Mr. Spalding, and abused and menaced as far as possible without shooting him.†

In addition to this, some of our own party were robbed openly of considerable property, and some twelve horses were stolen by night. All this information, coming near the same time, was embarrassing, especially as my instructions would not allow me to exceed, for office, interpreter, and every purpose, $1,250 per annum. On the other hand, their passport, signed by the Secretary of War, made it my imperative duty to protect them, in their persons, at least, from outrage. I did not long hesitate, but called upon Thomas McKay, long in the employment of the Hudson's Bay Company as explorer and leader of parties, who, from his frank, generous disposition, together with his universal success in Indian warfare, has obtained an extensive influence among the aborigines of the country, and, placing the facts before him, he at once consented to accompany me to this scene of discord and contention. We took but six men with us, armed in the best manner, a sufficent number to command respect and secure the object of our undertaking,—McKay

* There were good men left at the station; besides, the influence of Mr. McKinley was thought to be sufficient protection from any violence from the Indians.

† This transaction is represented by Rev. Mr. Brouillet as being that Mr. Spalding threatened the Indian with a gun,—being a mistake on the part of Rev. Mr. Brouillet.

assuring me, from his familiar acquaintance with these Indians, and their thorough knowledge of the use of arms, that if hostile intentions were entertained, it would require a larger party than we could raise in this country to subdue them. Obtaining Cornelius Rogers as interpreter, we set out on the 15th of November on our voyage of misery (as McKay justly denominated it), having a journey, by water and land, of not less than nine hundred and fifty miles, principally over open plains, covered with snow, and several times under the necessity of spending the night without wood or fire, other than what was made by a small growth of wild sage, hardly sufficient to boil the tea-kettle. The gentlemen, as we called at Vancouver, did every thing in their power to make the journey comfortable, but evidently felt anxious concerning our safety. We reached the Dalles, some two hundred and twenty miles from the Pacific, on the 24th, having been detained by wind, spent several days with the Methodist Mission families, who welcomed us joyfully, and made our stay agreeable and refreshing. Mrs. Dr. Whitman was here, having found it improper and unsafe to remain where she had been so lately grossly insulted. Her noble and intellectual mind and spirit were much depressed, and her health suffering; but still entertaining for the people or Indians of her charge the feelings of a mother toward ungrateful children. Our visit encouraged her. We procured horses and traveled by land to Wallawalla, 140 miles above, reaching the Hudson's Bay establishment on the 30th. Mr. McKinley, the gentleman in charge, to whom the missionaries are indebted for many kind offices in this isolated portion of earth, resolved to make it a common cause, and stand or fall with us. We reached Wailatpu, the station of Dr. Whitman, the day following, and were shocked and pained at beholding the sad work of savage destruction upon this hitherto neat and commodious little establishment. The Indians in the vicinity were few and shy. I thought best to treat them with reserve, but made an appointment to meet the chiefs and tribe on my return. Left the day following for the station of Mr. Spalding among the Nez Percés, some 120 or 130 miles from Wailatpu; reached it on the 3d of December, after a rather pleasant journey over a most verdant and delightful grazing district, well watered, but badly timbered. Having sent a private dispatch in advance, they had conveyed the intelligence to the Indians, many of whom were collected. The chiefs met us with civility, gravity, and dignified reserve, but the missionaries with joyful countenances and glad hearts.

Seldom was a visit of an Indian agent more desired, nor could one be more necessary and proper. As they were collecting, we had no meeting for eight and forty hours; in the mean time, through my able interpreter and McKay, I managed to secure confidence and prepare the way to a good understanding; visited and prescribed for their sick, made a short call at each of the chiefs' lodges, spent a season in school, hearing them read, spell, and sing; at the same time examined their printing and writing, and can hardly avoid here saying I was happily surprised and greatly interested at seeing such numbers so far advanced and so eagerly pursuing after knowledge. The next day I visited their little plantations, rude, to be sure, but successfully carried on, so far as raising the necessaries of life were concerned; and it was most gratifying to witness their fondness and care for their little herds, pigs, poultry, etc.

The hour arriving for the public interview, I was ushered into the presence of the assembled chiefs, to the number of twenty-two, with some lesser dignitaries, and a large number of the common people. The gravity, fixed attention, and decorum of these sons of the forest was calculated to make for them a most favorable impression. I stated explicitly, but briefly as possible, the design of our great chief in sending me to this country, and the present object of my visit; assured them of the kind intentions of our government, and of the sad consequences that would ensue to any white man, from this time, who should invade their rights, by stealing, murder, selling them damaged for good articles, or alcohol, of which they are not fond. Without threatening, I gave them to understand how highly Mr. and Mrs. Spalding were prized by the numerous whites, and with what pleasure the great chief gave them a paper to encourage them to come here to teach them what they were now so diligently employed in obtaining, in order that they and their children might become good, wise, and happy.

After me, Mr. McKinley, the gentleman in charge of the Hudson's Bay establishment at Wallawalla, spoke concisely, but very properly; alluded to his residence of some years, and of the good understanding that had generally existed between them, and of the happiness he felt that one of his brothers had come to stand and judge impartially between him, them, and whites and Indians in general; declared openly and frankly, that Boston, King George, and French, were all of one heart in this matter, as they, the Cayuses and Wallawallas should be; flattered them delicately in view of their (to him) unexpected advancement in the arts and sciences, and resumed his seat, having made a most favorable impression.

Next followed Mr. Rogers, the interpreter, who, years before, had been employed successfully as linguist in this section of the country by the American Board of Commissioners, and was ever a general favorite with this people. He adverted, sensibly and touchingly, to past difficulties between whites and Indians east of the mountains, and the sad consequences to every tribe who had resisted honorable measures proposed by the more numerous whites; and having, as he hoped, secured their confidence in my favor, exhorted them feelingly to adopt such measures as should be thought proper for their benefit.

Next, and lastly, arose Mr. McKay, and remarked, with a manner peculiar to himself, and evidently with some emotion: "I appear among you as one arisen from the long sleep of death. You know of the violent death of my father on board the ship *Tonquin*, who was one of the partners of the Astor company; I was but a youth; since which time, till the last five years, I have been a wanderer through these wilds, none of you, or any Indians of this country, having traveled so constantly or extensively as I have, and yet I saw you or your fathers once or more annually. I have mingled with you in bloody wars and profound peace; I have stood in your midst, surrounded by plenty, and suffered with you in seasons of scarcity; we have had our days of wild and joyous sports, and nights of watching and deep concern, till I vanished from among men, left the Hudson's Bay Company, silently retired to my plantation, and there confined myself. There I was still, silent, and as one dead; the voice of my brother, at last, aroused me; I spoke and looked; I mounted my horse—am here. I am glad it is so. I came at the call of the great chief, the chief of all the whites in the country, as well as all the Indians—the son of the mighty chief whose children are more numerous than the stars in the heavens or the leaves in the forest. Will you hear, and be advised? You will. Your wonderful improvement in the arts and sciences prove you are no fools. Surely you will hear; but if disposed to close your ears and stop them, they will be torn open wide, and you will be made to hear." This speech from Mr. McKay, whose mother is part Indian, though the wife of Governor McLaughlin, had a singularly happy influence, and opened the way for expressions on the other side, from which there had not hitherto been a sentence uttered.

First arose Five Crows, a wealthy chief of forty-five, neatly attired in English costume. He stepped gravely but modestly forward to the table, remarking: "It does not become me to speak first; I am but a youth, as yet, when compared with many of these, my fathers; but my feelings urge me to arise and say what I am about to utter in a very few words. I am glad the chief has come; I have listened to what has been said; have great hopes that brighter days are before us, because I see all the whites united in this matter; we have much wanted something; hardly knew what; been groping and feeling for it in confusion and darkness. Here it is. Do we see it, and shall we accept it?"

Soon the Bloody Chief (not less than ninety years old) arose, and said: "I speak to-day; perhaps to-morrow I die. I am the oldest chief of the tribe; was the high chief when your great brothers, Lewis and Clarke, visited this country; they visited me, and honored me with their friendship and counsel. I showed them my numerous wounds received in bloody battle with the Snakes; they told me it was not good, it was better to be at peace; gave me a flag of truce; I held it up high; we met and talked, but never fought again. Clarke pointed to this day, to you, and this occasion; we have long waited in expectation; sent three of our sons to Red River school to prepare for it; two of them sleep with their fathers; the other is here, and can be ears, mouth, and pen for us. I can say no more; I am quickly tired; my voice and limbs tremble. I am glad I live to see you and this day, but I shall soon be still and quiet in death."

The speech was affecting. Six more spoke, and the meeting adjourned three hours. Met at the hour appointed. All the chiefs and principal men being present, stated delicately the embarrassed relation existing between whites and Indians in this upper country, by reason of a want of proper organization, or the chiefs' authority not being properly regarded; alluding to some cases of improprieties of young men, not sanctioned by the chiefs and old men; and where the chiefs had been in the wrong, hoped it had principally arisen from imperfectly understanding each other's language, or some other excusable cause, especially so far as they were concerned. Advised them, as they were now to some extent prepared, to choose one high chief of the tribe, and acknowledge him as such by universal consent; all the other subordinate chiefs being of equal power, and so many helps to carry out all his lawful requirements, which they were at once to have in writing, in their own language, to regulate their intercourse with whites, and, in most cases, with themselves. I advised that each chief have five men as a body-guard, to execute all their lawful commands. They desired to hear the laws. I proposed them clause by clause, leaving them as free to reject as to accept. They were greatly pleased with all proposed, but wished a heavier penalty to some, and suggested the dog law, which was annexed. We then left them to choose the high chief, assuring them if they did this unanimously by the following day at ten, we would all dine together with the chief, on a fat ox, at three, himself and myself at the head of the table; this pleased them well, and they set about it in good cheer and high hopes; but this was a new and delicate task, and they soon saw and felt it; however, all agreed that I must make the selection, and so reported two hours after we left the council. Assuring them this would not answer, that they must select their own chief, they seemed somewhat puzzled, and wished to know if it would be proper to counsel with Messrs. McKay and Rogers. On telling them that it was not improper, they left, a little relieved, and worked poor Rogers and McKay severely for many hours; but altogether at length figured it out, and in great good humor, so reported at ten, appointing Ellis high chief.* He is the one alluded to by the Bloody Chief, a sensible man of thirty-two, reading, speaking, and writing the English language tolerably well; has a fine small plantation, a few sheep, some neat stock, and no less than eleven hundred head of horses. Then came on the feasting; our ox was fat, and cooked and served up in a manner reminding me of the days of yore; we ate beef, corn, and peas, to our fill, and in good cheer took the pipe, when Rev. Mr. Spalding, Messrs. McKinley, Rogers, and McKay, wished a song from our boatmen; it was no sooner given than returned by the Indians, and repeated again, again, and again, in high cheer. I thought it a good time, and required all having any claim to bring, or grievances to allege, against Mr. Spalding, to meet me and the high chief at evening, in the council-room, and requested Mr. Spalding to do the same on the part of the Indians. We met at six, and ended at eleven, having accomplished, in the happiest manner, much anxious business. Being too well fed to be irritable or disposed to quarrel, both parties were frank and open, seeming anxious only to learn our opinion upon plain undisguised matters of fact, many of the difficulties having arisen from an honest difference of sentiment respecting certain measures.

Ellis, the chief, having conducted himself throughout in a manner creditable to his head and heart, was quite as correct in his conclusions and firm in his decisions as could have been expected. The next day we had our last meeting, and one full of interest, in which they proposed to me many grave and proper questions; and, as it was manifestly desired, I advised in many matters, especially in reference to begging, or even receiving presents without, in some way, returning an equivalent; pointed out in strong language who beggars are among the whites, and how regarded; and commended them for not once troubling me, during my stay, with this disgusting practice; and as a token of respect, now, at the close of our long and happy meeting, they would please accept, in the name of my great chief, a present of fifty

* He had been educated by the Hudson's Bay Company at Red River, and was strongly attached to it.

garden hoes, not for those in authority, or such as had no need of them, but for the chiefs and Mr. Spalding to distribute among their industrious poor. I likewise, as they were very needy, proposed and ordered them some medicines, to be distributed as they should from time to time be required. This being done, I exhorted them to be in obedience to their chiefs, highly approving the choice they had made, assuring them, as he and the other chiefs were responsible to me for their good behavior, I should feel it my duty to see them sustained in all lawful measures to promote peace and order. I then turned, and with good effect desired all the chiefs to look upon the congregation as their own children, and then pointed to Mr. Spalding and lady, and told the chiefs, and all present, to look upon them as their father and mother, and treat them in all respects as such; and should they happen to differ in sentiment respecting any matter during my absence, be cautious not to differ in feeling, but leave it till I should again return, when the chief and myself would rectify it. Thus closed this mutually happy and interesting meeting, and mounting our horses for home, Mr. Spalding and the chiefs accompanied us for some four or five miles, when we took leave of them in the pleasantest manner, not a single circumstance having occurred to mar our peace or shake each other's confidence.

I shall here introduce a note, previously prepared, giving some further information respecting this tribe, and appending a copy of their laws. The Nez Percés have one governor or principal chief, twelve subordinate chiefs of equal power, being the heads of the different villages or clans, with their five officers to execute all their lawful orders, which law they have printed in their own language, and read understandingly. The chiefs are held responsible to the whites for the good behavior of the tribe. They are a happy and orderly people, forming an honorable exception to the general Indian character, being more industrious, cleanly, sensible, dignified, and virtuous.

This organization was effected last fall, and operates well, and with them, it is to be hoped, will succeed. A few days since Governor McLaughlin favored me with a note addressed to him from the Rev. H. H. Spalding, missionary to this tribe, stating as follows:—

"The Indians in this vicinity are remarkably quiet this winter, and are highly pleased with the laws recommended by Dr. White, which were unanimously adopted by the chiefs and people in council assembled. The visit of Dr. White and assistants to this upper country will evidently prove an incalculable blessing to this people. The school now numbers two hundred and twenty-four in daily attendance, embracing most of the chiefs and principal men of the nation."

Laws of the Nez Percés.

ARTICLE 1. Whoever willfully takes life shall be hung.

ART. 2. Whoever burns a dwelling-house shall be hung.

ART. 3. Whoever burns an out-building shall be imprisoned six months, receive fifty lashes, and pay all damages.

ART. 4. Whoever carelessly burns a house, or any property, shall pay damages.

ART. 5. If any one enter a dwelling, without permission of the occupant, the chiefs shall punish him as they think proper. Public rooms are excepted.

ART. 6. If any one steal he shall pay back twofold; and if it be the value of a beaver skin or less, he shall receive twenty-five lashes; and if the value is over a beaver skin he shall pay back twofold, and receive fifty lashes.

ART. 7. If any one take a horse and ride it, without permission, or take any article and use it, without liberty, he shall pay for the use of it, and receive from twenty to fifty lashes, as the chief shall direct.

ART. 8. If any one enter a field, and injure the crops, or throw down the fence, so that cattle or horses go in and do damage, he shall pay all damages, and receive twenty-five lashes for every offense.

ART. 9. Those only may keep dogs who travel or live among the game; if a dog kill a lamb, calf, or any domestic animal, the owner shall pay the damages and kill the dog.

ART. 10. If an Indian raise a gun or other weapon against a white man, it shall be reported to the chiefs, and they shall punish it. If a white do the same to an Indian, it shall be reported to Dr. White, and he shall punish or redress it.

ART. 11. If an Indian break these laws, he shall be punished by his chiefs; if a white man break them, he shall be reported to the agent, and punished at his instance.

After a severe journey of some four days, through the inclemency of the weather, we reached Wailatpu, Dr. Whitman's station, where we had many most unpleasant matters to settle with the Cayuse tribe,—such as personal abuse to Dr. Whitman and lady, burning the mill, etc. Several, but not all, of the chiefs were present. Learning what the Nez Percés had done gave them great concern and anxiety. Tawatowe, the high chief, and Feather Cap were there, with some few more dignitaries, but manifestly uneasy, being shy and cautious. I thought best under the circumstances to be quiet, distant, and reserved, and let them commence the conversation with my worthy and faithful friends, Rogers and McKay, who conducted it with characteristic firmness and candor. They had not proceeded far before Feather Cap, for the first time in his life, so far as we know, commenced weeping, and wished to see me; said his heart was sick, and he could not live long as he now felt. Tawatowe, who was no way implicated personally in the difficulties, and a correct man, continued for some time firm and steady to his purpose; said the whites were much more to blame than the Indians; that three-fourths of them, though they taught the purest doctrines, practiced the greatest abominations,—alluding to the base conduct of many in the Rocky Mountains, where they meet them on their buffalo hunts during the summer season, and witness the greatest extravagances. They were shown the inapplicability of such instances to the present cases of difficulty. He, too, at last, was much subdued; wished to see me; was admitted; made a sensible speech in his own favor; said he was constituted, eight years before, high chief; entered upon its duties with spirit and courage, determined to reduce his people to order. He flogged the young men and reproved the middle-aged, till, having none to sustain him, his popularity had so declined, that, except in seasons of difficulty brought about by their improprieties, "I am left alone to say my prayers and go to bed, to weep over the follies and wickedness of my people." Here his voice trembled, and he wept freely; acknowledged it as his opinion that the mill was burnt purposely by some disaffected persons toward Dr. Whitman. I spoke kindly and somewhat encouragingly to these chiefs; assured them the guilty only were to be regarded as such; and that candor was commendable, and would be honored by all the good; assured them I credited all they said, and deplored the state of their nation, which was in perfect anarchy and confusion; told them I could say but little to them now, as their chiefs were mostly abroad; but must say the shocking conduct of one of the chiefs toward Mrs. Whitman greatly afflicted me; and that, with the destruction of the mill, and their abominable conduct toward Dr. Whitman, if not speedily settled, would lead to the worst of consequences to their tribe. I made an engagement to meet them and all the tribe on the 10th of the ensuing April, to adjust differences and come to a better understanding, they earnestly wishing to adopt such laws as the Nez Percés had done. We should probably have accomplished a satisfactory settlement, had not several of the influential chiefs been too far away to get information of the meeting. We reached Wascopum on December 25, the Indians being in great excitement, having different views and impressions respecting the nature of the approaching visit. We spent four days with them, holding meetings daily, instructing them in the nature of government, civil relations, domestic duties, etc. Succeeded, in like happy manner, with them as with the Nez Percés, they unanimously adopting the same code of laws.

Late information from one of their missionaries you will see in the following note from Mr. H. B. Brewer:—

"The Indians of this place intend to carry out the regulations you left them to the letter. They have been quite engaged in cutting logs for houses, and live in expectation of better dwellings by and by. For the least transgression of the laws, they are punished by their chiefs immediately. The clean faces of some, and the tidy dresses of others, show the good effects of your visit."

And here allow me to say, except at Wascopum, the missionaries of this upper country are too few in number at their respective stations, and in too defenseless a state for their own safety, or the best good of the Indians, the latter taking advantage of these circumstances, to the no small annoyance, and, in some instances, greatly endangering the personal safety, of the former. You will see its bearings upon this infant colony, and doubtless give such information or instructions to the American Board of Commissioners, or myself, as will cause a correction of this evil. It has already occasioned some difficulty and much cost. I have insisted upon an increase of numbers at Mr. Spalding's mission, which has accordingly been re-enforced by Mr. Littlejohn and lady, rendering that station measurably secure; but not so at Wailatpu, or some of the Catholic missions, where some of them lost a considerable amount in herds during last winter, and, I am told, were obliged to abandon their posts, their lives being endangered. This was in the interior, near the Blackfoot country. You will observe, from the reports of the different missions, which, so far as I am otherwise informed, are correct, that they are doing some positive good in the country, not only by diffusing the light of science abroad among us, but also by giving employment to many, and, by their drafts upon the different Boards and others, creating a circulating medium in this country; but, though they make comparatively slow progress in the way of reform among the aborigines of this country, their pious and correct example has a most restraining influence upon both whites and Indians, and in this way they prevent much evil.

They have in successful operation six schools. Rev. Mr. and Mrs. Spalding (whose zeal and untiring industry for the benefit of the people of their charge entitle them to our best considerations) have a school of some two hundred and twenty-four, in constant attendance, most successfully carried forward, which promises to be of great usefulness to both sexes and all ages. Rev. Messrs. Walker and Eells I have not been at leisure to visit, but learn they have two small schools in operation; the one at Wailatpu, Dr. Whitman's station, is now recommenced with promise of usefulness.

The Rev. Mr. Blanchet and associates, though zealous Catholics, are peaceable, industrious, indefatigable, and successful in promoting religious knowledge among the Canadian population and aborigines of this country. Their enterprise in the erection of mills and other public works is very commendable, and the general industry, good order, and correct habits of that portion of the population under their charge is sufficient proof that their influence over their people has been exerted for good.* The Rev. Mr. Lee and associates, from their well-conducted operations at the Dalles, upon the Columbia, and a school of some thirty scholars successfully carried forward upon the Wallamet, are doing but little for the Indians; nor could great efforts produce much good among the scattered remnants of the broken tribes of this lower district, who are fast disappearing before the ravages of the most loathsome diseases. Their principal hopes of success in this country are among the whites, where they are endeavoring to lay deep and broad the foundations of science. The literary institution referred to by Mr. Lee is situated upon a beautiful rising ground, a healthy and eligible location. Could a donation of five thousand dollars be bestowed upon the institution, it would greatly encourage its friends. The donations made by individuals of this country have been most liberal, several giving one-third of all they possessed. There is a small school established at Tualatine Plains by Rev. Mr. Clark and lady. There is also a school at the Catholic Mission, upon the Wallamet, and also one upon their station at Cowlitz. For further information I will refer you to the reports made, at my request, by the several missions, and accompanying these dispatches.

* * * * * * * *

I must close by praying that measures may be speedily entered into to take possession of this country, if such steps have not already been taken. I left home before the close of the session of Congress, and by reason do not know what disposition was made of Hon. Mr. Linn's bill. As a reason for this praying, I would here say, the time was when the gentlemen of the Hudson's Bay Company and the missions wielded the

* This statement about Rev. Mr. Blanchet and associates, "their enterprise in erecting mills and other public works," shows how easy it was for the agent to belittle his own countrymen's labors, and attribute to others what they never attempted to do, and in the next paragraph say they "are doing but little for the Indians;" while the truth is, and was at the time, that Mr. Lee and his mission were the only persons in the Wallamet Valley doing any thing to improve the condition of the Indians, of which their Indian school, now Wallamet University, is a permanent monument, which Dr. White ignores in this report.

entire influence over this small population; but as they have been re-enforced latterly from whale ships, the Rocky Mountains, and the Southwestern States, these hitherto salutary restraints and influences are giving way, and being measurably lost.

At present I have considerable influence, but can not long expect to retain it, especially in the faithful discharge of my duty. As a reason for coming to such a conclusion, I had but just arrived from the interior, when I received an urgent call to visit the mouth of the Columbia. I left at once, in company with Nathaniel Crocker, Esq., Mr. Rogers (my interpreter), his lady, and her young sister (the females going only to the falls), with a crew of Indians, on our ill-fated expedition. We reached the falls at sunset, February 1, and, by reason of the water being higher than usual, in passing around a jutting or projecting rock, the canoe came up suddenly against a log constituting the landing, at which instant I stepped off, and in a moment the canoe was swept away, with all its precious cargo, over the falls of thirty-eight feet, three rods below. The shock was dreadful to this infant colony, and the loss was dreadful and irreparable to me, Mr. Rogers being more important to me than any one in the country; nor was there a more respectable or useful man in the colony. Nathaniel Crocker came in with me last fall from Tompkins County; he was much pleased with the country and its prospects, and the citizens were rejoiced at the arrival of such a man in this country; he was every way capacitated for usefulness. None of the bodies of the four whites or two Indians have been as yet found.

* * * * * * * *

On arriving at the mouth of the Columbia, I found a sailor by the name of George Geere, who had most evidently and maliciously labored to instigate the Indians to take the life of one of the mission gentlemen, by the offer of five blankets. Complaint being made, and having no better means, I prevailed upon Governor McLaughlin to allow him to accompany their express across the mountains to the States. I would here say, as the scamp was nearly a fool as well as villain, I allowed him to go without sending evidence against him, on condition of his going voluntarily, and never returning.

I here likewise found a rash, venturesome character, about starting off on a trapping and trading excursion among a somewhat numerous band of Indians, and nowise well disposed toward the whites. As he saw and felt no danger, arguments were of no avail, and threats only prevented.

Sir, shall men be allowed to go wherever they may please, however remote from the colony, and settle, under circumstances that endanger not only their own personal safety, but the peace and safety of the whole white population? Please give me specific instructions respecting this matter.

* * * * * * * *

I have eight prisoners on hand at present, for various crimes, principally stealing horses, grain, etc.; and crimes are multiplying with numbers among the whites, and with scarcity of game among the Indians.

* * * * * * * *

No intelligence from abroad has reached us this winter. Mount St. Helen, one of these snow-capped volcanic mountains, some 16,000 feet above the level of the sea, and eighty miles northwest of Vancouver, broke out upon the 20th of November last, presenting a scene the most awful and sublime imaginable, scattering smoke and ashes several hundred miles distance.

A petition started from this country to-day, making bitter complaints against the Hudson's Bay Company and Governor McLaughlin. On reference to it (as a copy was denied), I shall only say, had any gentleman disconnected with the Hudson's Bay Company been at half the pains and expense to establish a claim on the Wallamet Falls, very few would have raised an opposition. His half-bushel measure I know to be exact, according to the English imperial standard. The gentlemen of this company have been fathers and fosterers of the colony, ever encouraging peace, industry, and good order, and have sustained a character for hospitality and integrity too well established to be easily shaken.

I am, sir, sincerely and most respectfully, your humble and obedient servant,

ELIJAH WHITE,
Sub-Agent Indian Affairs, W. R. M.

T. HARTLEY CRAWFORD, Esq.,
Commissioner Indian Affairs.

CHAPTER XXXI.

Letter of H. H. Spalding to Dr. White.—Account of his mission among the Nez Percés.—Schools.—Cultivation.—Industrial arts.—Moral character.—Arable land. —Letter of Commissioner of Indian Affairs to the Secretary of War.

My Dear Brother,—The kind letter which our mission had the honor of receiving from yourself, making inquiries relative to its numbers, the character of the Indian tribes among whom its several stations are located, the country, etc., is now before me.

The questions referring to Indian character are very important, and to answer them demands a more extended knowledge of character and habits, from personal daily observation, than the short residence of six years can afford, and more time and attention than I can possibly command, amidst the numerous cares and labors of the station. I less regret this, as the latter will receive the attention of my better-informed and worthy associates of the other stations.

Concerning many of the questions, I can only give my own half-formed opinions, from limited observations which have not extended far beyond the people of my immediate charge.

Our mission is under the patronage of the American Board, and was commenced in the fall of 1836, by Marcus Whitman, M. D., and myself, with our wives and Mr. Gray. Dr. Whitman was located at Wailatpu, among the Cayuse Indians, twenty-five miles east of Fort Wallawalla, a trading-post of the Hudson's Bay Company, which stands nine miles below the junction of Lewis and Clarke rivers, three hundred from the Pacific, and about two hundred from Fort Vancouver. I was located at this place, on the Clearwater, or Koos-koos-ky River, twelve miles from its junction with the Lewis River, one hundred and twenty miles east of Wailatpu. Mr. Gray left the same winter, and returned to the States. In the fall of 1838, Mr. Gray returned to this country, accompanied by Mrs. Gray, Messrs. Walker, Eells, and Smith, and their wives, and Mr. Rogers. The next season, two new stations were commenced, one by Messrs. Walker and Eells at Cimakain, near Spokan River, among the Spokan Indians, one hundred and thirty-five miles northwest of this station, and sixty-five miles south of Fort Colville, on the Columbia River, three hundred miles above Fort Wallawalla; the second by Mr. Smith, among the Nez Percés, sixty miles above this station.

There are now connected with this mission the Rev. Messrs. Walker and Eells, Mrs. Walker and Mrs. Eells; at Cimakain, myself, and Mrs. Spalding at this station. Dr. Whitman is now on a visit to the States, and Mrs. Whitman on a visit to the Dalles; a station of our Methodist brethren. But two natives have as yet been admitted into the church. Some ten or twelve others give pleasing evidence of having been born again.

Concerning the schools and congregations on the Sabbath, I will speak only of this station. The congregation on the Sabbath varies at different seasons of the year, and must continue to do so until the people find a substitute in the fruits of the earth and herds for their roots, game, and fish, which necessarily require much wandering. I am happy to say that this people are very generally turning their attention, with much apparent eagerness, to cultivating the soil, and raising hogs, cattle, and sheep, and find a much more abundant and agreeable source of subsistence in the hoe than in their bows and sticks for digging roots.

For a few weeks in the fall, after the people return from their buffalo hunt, and then again, in the spring, the congregation numbers from one to two thousand. Through the winter it numbers from two to eight hundred. From July to the 1st of October, it varies from two to five hundred. The congregation, as also the school, increases every winter, as the quantity of provision raised in this vicinity is increased.

Preparatory to schools and a permanent congregation, my earliest attention, on arriving in this country, was turned toward schools, as promising the most permanent good to the nation, in connection with the written word of God and the preached gospel. But to speak of schools then was like speaking of the church bell, when as yet the helve is not put in the first ax by which the timber is to be felled, or the first stone laid in the dam which is to collect the water from whence the lumber in the edifice in which the bell is to give forth its sounds. Suffice it to say, through the blessing of God, we have had an increasingly large school, for two winters past, with comparatively favorable means of instruction.

But the steps by which we have been brought to the present elevation, if I may so speak, though we are yet exceedingly low, begin far, far back among the days of nothing, and little to do with.

Besides eating my own bread by the sweat of my brow, there were the wandering children of a necessarily wandering people to collect and bring permanently within the reach of the school. Over this department of labor hung the darkest cloud, as the Indian is noted for despising manual labor; but I would acknowledge, with humble gratitude, the interposition of that hand which holds the hearts of all men. The hoe soon brought hope, light, and satisfaction, the fruits of which are yearly becoming much more than a substitute for their former precarious game and roots, and are much preferred by the people, who are coming in from the mountains and plains, and calling for hoes, plows, and seeds, much faster than they can be furnished, and collecting around the station in increasing numbers, to cultivate their little farms; so furnishing a permanent school and congregation on the Sabbath, from four to eight months, and, as the farms are enlarged, giving food and employment for the year. I trust the school and congregation will be permanent through the year. It was no small tax on my time to give the first lessons on agriculture. That the men of the nation (the first chiefs not excepted) rose up to labor when a few hoes and seeds were offered them, I can attribute to nothing but the unseen hand of the God of missions. That their habits are really changed is acknowledged by themselves. The men say, whereas they once did not labor with their hands, now they do; and often tell me in jesting that I have converted them into a nation of women. They are a very industrious people, and, from very small beginnings, they now cultivate their lands with much skill, and to good advantage. Doubtless many more would cultivate, but for the want of means. Your kind donation of fifty hoes, in behalf of the government, will be most timely; and should you be able to send up the plows you kindly proposed, they will, without doubt, be purchased immediately, and put to the best use.

But to return to the school. It now numbers two hundred and twenty-five in daily attendance, half of which are adults. Nearly all the principal men and chiefs in this vicinity, with one chief from a neighboring tribe, are members of the school. A new impulse was given to the school by the warm interest yourself and Mr. McKay took in it while you were here. They are as industrious in school as they are on their farms. Their improvement is astonishing, considering their crowded condition, and only Mrs. Spalding, with her delicate constitution and her family cares, for their teacher.

About one hundred are printing their own books with a pen. This keeps up a deep interest, as they daily have new lessons to print, and what they print must be committed to memory as soon as possible.

A good number are now so far advanced in reading and printing as to render much assistance in teaching. Their books are taken home at nights, and every lodge becomes a schoolroom.

Their lessons are scripture lessons; no others (except the laws) seem to interest them. I send you a specimen of the books they print in school. It was printed by ten select adults, yet it is a fair specimen of a great number in the school.

The laws which you so happily prepared, and which were unanimously adopted by the people, I have printed in the form of a small school-book. A great number of the school now read them fluently. I send you a few copies of the laws, with no apologies for the imperfect manner in which they are executed. Without doubt, a school of nearly the same number could be collected at Kimiah, the station above this, vacated by Mr. Smith, the present residence of Ellis, the principal chief.

Number who cultivate.—Last season about one hundred and forty cultivated from one-fourth of an acre to four or five acres each. About half this number cultivate in the valley. One chief raised one hundred and seventy-six bushels of peas last season, one hundred of corn, and four hundred of potatoes. Another, one hundred and fifty of peas, one hundred and sixty of corn, a large quantity of potatoes, vegetables, etc. Ellis, I believe, raised more than either of the above-mentioned. Some forty other individuals raised from twenty to one hundred bushels of grain. Eight individuals are now furnished with plows. Thirty-two head of cattle are possessed by thirteen individuals; ten sheep by four; some forty hogs.

Arts and sciences.—Mrs. Spalding has instructed ten females in knitting, a majority of the female department in the schools in sewing, six in carding and spinning, and three in weaving. Should our worthy brother and sister, Mr. and Mrs. Littlejohn, join us soon, as is now expected, I trust, by the blessing of God, we shall see greater things than we have yet seen. From what I have seen in the field, the school, the spinning and weaving room, in the prayer-room, and Sabbath congregation, I am fully of the opinion that this people are susceptible of high moral and civil improvement.

Moral character of the people.—On this point there is a great diversity of opinion. One writer styles them more a nation of saints than of savages; and if their refusing to move camp for game, at his suggestion, on a certain day, reminded him that the Sabbath extended as far west as the Rocky Mountains, he might well consider them such. Another styles them supremely selfish, which is nearer the truth; for, without doubt, they are the descendants of Adam. What I have above stated is evidently a part of the bright side of their character. But there is also a dark side, in which I have sometimes taken a part. I must, however, confess that when I attempt to name it, and hold it up as a marked exception to a nation in similar circumstances, without the restraint of wholesome laws, and strangers to the heaven-born fruits of enlightened and well-regulated society, I am not able to do it. Faults they have, and very great ones, yet few of them seemed disposed to break the Sabbath by traveling and other secular business. A very few indulge in something like profane swearing. Very few are superstitiously attached to their medicine men, who are, without doubt, sorcerers, and are supposed to be leagued with a supernatural being (Waikin), who shows himself sometimes in the gray bear, the wolf, the swan, goose, wind, clouds, etc.

Lying is very common; thieving comparatively rare; polygamy formerly common, but now rare; much gambling among the young men; quarreling and fighting quite rare; habit of taking back property after it is sold is a practice quite common, and very evil in its tendency. All these evils, I conceive, can be traced to the want of wholesome laws and well-regulated society. There are two traits in the character of this people I wish to notice. One I think I can account for; the other I can not. It is often said the Indian is a noble-minded being, never forgetting a kindness. So far as my experience has gone with this people, the above is most emphatically true, but in quite a different sense from the idea there conveyed. It is true they never forget a kindness, but after make it an occasion to ask another; and if refused, return insults according to the favors received. My experience has taught me that, if I would keep the friendship of an Indian, and do him good, I must show him no more favor in the way of property than what he returns some kind of an equivalent for; most of our trials have arisen from this source. I am, however, happy to feel that there is a manifest improvement as the people become more instructed, and we become more acquainted with their habits. This offensive trait in the Indian character I believe, in part, should be charged to the white man. It has been the universal practice of all white men to give tobacco, to name no other article, to Indians when they ask for it. Hence two very natural ideas: one is, that the white man is in debt to them; the other is, that in proportion as a white man is a good man he will discharge this debt by giving bountifully of his provisions and goods. This trait in Indian character is capable of being turned to the disadvantage of traders, travelers, and missionaries, by prejudiced white men.

The last trait, which I can not account for, is an apparent disregard for the rights of white men. Although their eagerness to receive instruction in school on the Sabbath and on the farm is without a parallel in my knowledge, still, should a reckless fellow from their own number, or even a stranger, make an attack on my life or property, I have no evidence to suppose but a vast majority of them would look on with indifference and see our dwelling burnt to the ground and our heads severed from our bodies. I can not reconcile this seeming want of gratitude with their many encouraging characteristics. But to conclude this subject, should our unprofitable lives, through a kind Providence, be spared a few years, by the blessing of the God of missions, we expect to see this people Christianized to a great extent, civilized, and happy, with much of science and the word of God, and many of the comforts of life; but not without many days of hard labor, and sore trials of disappointed hopes, and nameless perplexities.

The number of this people is variously estimated from two thousand to four thousand. I can not give a correct estimate.

At this station there is a dwelling-house, a schoolhouse, storehouse, flour and saw mills (all of a rough kind), fifteen acres of land under improvement, twenty-four head of cattle, thirty-six horses, sixty-seven sheep. Rev. Messrs. Walker and Eells, I hope, will report of Wailatpu; but should they fail, I will say, as near as I can recollect, about fifty acres of land are cultivated by some seventy individuals; a much greater number of cattle and hogs than among this people. Belonging to the station are thirty-four head of cattle, eleven horses, some forty hogs; one dwelling-house of adobes (well finished), a blacksmith's shop, flour-mill (lately destroyed by fire), and some forty acres of land cultivated.

Arable land.—The arable land in this upper country is confined almost entirely to the small streams, although further observation may prove that many of the extensive rolling prairies are capable of producing wheat. They can become inhabited only by cultivating timber; but the rich growth of buffalo grass upon them will ever furnish an inexhaustible supply for innumerable herds of cattle and sheep. I know of no country in the world so well adapted to the herding system. Cattle, sheep, and horses are invariably healthy, and produce rapidly; sheep usually twice a year. The herding system adopted, the country at first put under regulations adapted to the scarcity of habitable places (say that no settlers shall be allowed to take up over twenty acres of land on the streams), and the country without doubt will sustain a great population. I am happy to feel assured that the United States government have no other thoughts than to regard the rights and wants of the Indian tribes in this country.

And while the agency of Indian affairs in this country remains in the hands of the present agent, I have the fullest confidence to believe that the reasonable expectations in reference to the intercourse between whites and Indians will be fully realized by every philanthropist and every Christian. But as the Indian population is sparse, after they are abundantly supplied, there will be remaining country sufficient for an extensive white population.

The thought of removing these tribes, that the country may come wholly in possession of the whites, can never for a moment enter the mind of a friend of the red man, for two reasons, to name no other: First, there are but two countries to which they can be removed, the grave and the Blackfoot, between which there is no choice; second, the countless millions of salmon which swarm the Columbia and its tributaries, and furnish a very great proportion of the sustenance of the tribes who dwell upon these numerous waters, and a substitute for which can nowhere be found east or west of the Rocky Mountains, but in herds or cultivating their own land. * * *

Your humble servant,

Dr. WHITE, H. H. SPALDING.

Agent for Indian Affairs west of the Rocky Mountains.

DEPARTMENT OF WAR,
OFFICE OF INDIAN AFFAIRS, Nov. 25, 1844.

Communications have been received from Dr. Elijah White, sub-agent for the Indians in Oregon Territory, dated, severally, November 15, 1843, and March 18, 1844. * * * They contain much of interest in considerable detail. The establishment of white settlements from the United States, in that remote region, seems to be attended with the circumstances that have always arisen out of the conversion of an American wilderness into a cultivated and improved region, modified by the great advance of the present time in morals, and benevolent and religious institutions. It is very remarkable that there should be so soon several well-supported, well-attended, and well-conducted schools in Oregon. The Nez Percé tribe of Indians have adopted a few simple and plain laws of their code, which will teach them self-restraint, and is the beginning of government on their part.

It is painful, however, to know that a distillery for the manufacture of whisky was erected and in operation west of the Rocky Mountains, which, however, the sub-agent, sustained by the resident whites, broke up and destroyed. There was, in February last, an affray between a very boisterous and desperate Indian and his party and a portion of the settlers, which ended in the death of several of the combatants. This unfortunate affair was adjusted, as it is hoped, satisfactorily and permanently, by the sub-agent, though he seems to apprehend an early outbreak. I trust he is mistaken.

Respectfully submitted,

T. HARTLEY CRAWFORD.

Hon. WILLIAM WILKINS,
Secretary of War.

CHAPTER XXXII.

Dr. E. White's letter to the Secretary of War.—Excitement among the Indians.—Visit to Nez Percés, Cayuses, and Wallawallas.—Destitution and degradation of the Coast Indians.—Dr. White eulogizes Governor McLaughlin and the Hudson's Bay Company.—Schools and missions.—Mr. Jesse Applegate.—Dr. White's second letter.—Letters of Peter H. Hatch and W. H. Wilson.—Seizure of a distillery.—Search for liquor.—Letter of James D. Saules.—Fight with Indians.—Death of Cockstock.—Description and character of him.—The Molallos and Klamaths.—Agreement with the Dalles Indians.—Presents to Cockstock's widow.—Dr. White's third letter.—Letter of Rev. G. Hines to Dr. White.—Letter of W. Medill.

WALLAMET VALLEY, OREGON,
November 15, 1843.

HONORED SIR,—Since my arrival, I have had the honor of addressing you some three or four communications, the last of which left early in April, conveyed by the Hudson's Bay Company's express over the Rocky Mountains, *via* Canada, which I hope and judge was duly received.

Immediately after this, I received several communications from missionaries of the interior, some from the Methodists and others from those sent out by the American Board, representing the Indians of the interior as in a state of great excitement, and under much apprehension from the circumstance that such numbers of whites were coming in, as they were informed, to take possession of their lands and country. The excitement soon became general, both among whites and Indians, in this lower as well upper district; and such were the constantly floating groundless reports, that much uneasiness was felt, and some of our citizens were under such a state of apprehension as to abandon their houses, and place themselves more immediately within the precincts of the colony. As in all such cases, a variety of opinions was entertained and expressed,—some pleading for me, at the expense of the general government, to throw up a strong fortification in the center of the colony, and furnish the settlers with guns and ammunition, so that we might be prepared for extremities. Others thought it more advisable for me to go at once with an armed force of considerable strength to the heart and center of the conspiracy, as it was represented, and if words would not answer, make powder and balls do it. A third party entertained other views, and few were really agreed on any one measure.

As may be imagined, I felt the awkwardness of my position; but, without stopping to consult an agitated populace, selected a sensible clergyman and a single attendant, with my interpreter, and so managed as to throw myself immediately into their midst unobserved. The measure had the desired effect,—though, as in my report I will more fully inform you, it had like to have cost me my life.

The Indians flocked around me, and inquired after my party, and could not be persuaded for some time, but that I had a large party concealed somewhere near, and only waited to get them convened, to open a fire upon and cut them all off at a blow. On convincing them of my defenseless condition and pacific intentions, they were quite astounded and much affected, assuring me they had been under strong apprehensions, having learned I was soon to visit them with a large armed party, with hostile intentions, and I actually found them suffering more from fears of war from the whites, than the whites from the Indians; each party resolving, however, to remain at home, and there fight to the last, though, fortunately, some three or four hundred miles apart.*

The day following, we left these Wallawallas and Cayuses, to pay a visit to the Nez Percés, promising to call on our return, and enter into a treaty of amity, if we could agree on the terms, and wished them to give general notice to all concerned of both tribes.

In two days we were at Mr. Spalding's station. The Nez Percés came together in greater numbers than on any former occasion for years, and all the circumstances combining to favor it, received us most cordially. Their improvement during the winter in reading, writing, etc., was considerable, and the enlargement of their plantations, with the increased variety and quantities of the various kinds of grains and products now vigorously shooting forth, connected with the better state of cultivation and their universally good fences, were certainly most encouraging.

Spending some three days with this interesting tribe, and their missionaries, in the pleasantest manner, they accepted my invitation to visit with me the Cayuses and Wallawallas, and assist by their influence to bring them into the same regulation they had previously adopted, and with which all were so well pleased.

Mr. Spalding, and Ellis, the high chief, with every other chief and brave of importance, and some four or five hundred of the men and their women, accompanied us to Wailatpu, Doctor Whitman's station, a distance of a hundred and twenty miles, where we met the Cayuses and Wallawallas in mass, and spent some five or six days in getting

* Who were the instigators of these alarms among the Indians?

matters adjusted and principles settled, so as to receive the Cayuses into the civil compact; which being done, and the high chief elected, much to the satisfaction of both whites and Indians, I ordered two fat oxen to be killed, and wheat, salt, etc., distributed accordingly. * * *

This was the first feast at which the Indian women of this country were ever permitted to be present, but probably will not be the last; for, after some explanation of my reasons, the chiefs were highly pleased with it; and I believe more was done at that feast to elevate and bring forward their poor oppressed women than could have been done in years by private instruction.

The feast broke up in the happiest manner, after Five Crows, the Cayuse chief, Ellis, and the old war chief of whom I made particular mention in my last report as being so well acquainted with Clarke and a few others, had made their speeches, and we had smoked the pipe of peace, which was done by all in great good humor.

From this we proceeded to the Dalles on the Columbia River, where I spent two months in instructing the Indians of different tribes, who either came in mass, or sent embassadors to treat with me, or, as they denominate it, take my laws, which are thus far found to operate well, giving them greater security among themselves, and helping much to regulate their intercourse with the whites. Being exceedingly anxious to bring about an improvement and reformation among this people, I begged money and procured articles of clothing to the amount of a few hundred dollars, not to be given, but to be sold out to the industrious women, for mats, baskets, and their various articles of manufacture, in order to get them clothed comfortably to appear at church; enlisted the cheerful co-operation of the mission ladies in instructing them how to sew and make up their dresses; and had the happiness to see some twenty of these neatly clad at divine service, and a somewhat large number out in the happiest mood to a feast I ordered them, at which the mission ladies and gentlemen were present.

During these two months I labored hard, visiting many of their sick daily; and by the most prompt and kind attention, and sympathizing with them in their affliction, encouraging the industrious and virtuous, and frowning in language and looks upon the vicious, I am satisfied good was done. They gave evidence of attachment; and my influence was manifestly increased, as well as the laws more thoroughly understood, by reason of my remaining so long among them.

During my up-country excursion, the whites of the colony convened, and formed a code of laws to regulate intercourse between themselves during the absence of law from our mother country, adopting in almost all respects the Iowa code. In this I was consulted, and encouraged the measure, as it was so manifestly necessary for the collection of debts, securing rights in claims, and the regulation of general intercourse among the whites.

Thus far, these laws have been of some force and importance, answering well in cases of trespass and the collection of debts; but it is doubtful how they would succeed in criminal affairs, especially if there should happen to be a division of sentiment in the public mind.

The Indians of this lower country, as was to be expected, give considerable trouble, and are most vexatious subjects to deal with. In mind, the weakest and most depraved of their race, and physically, thoroughly contaminated with the scrofula and a still more loathsome disease entailed by the whites; robbed of their game and former means of covering; lost to the use of the bow and arrow; laughed at, scoffed, and contemned by the whites, and a hiss and by-word to the surrounding tribes, they are too dejected and depressed to feel the least pleasure in their former amusements, and wander about seeking generally a scanty pittance by begging and pilfering, but the more ambitious and desperate among them stealing, and in some instances plundering on a large scale. Were it not that greater forbearance is exercised toward them than whites generally exercise, bloodshed, anarchy, and confusion would reign predominant among us. But thus far, it is but just to say, the Indians have been, in almost every instance, the aggressors; and though none of us now apprehend an Indian war or invasion, it appears to me morally impossible that general quiet can long be secure, unless government takes almost immediate measures to relieve the anxieties and better the condition of these poor savages and other Indians of this country. I am doing what I can, and by reason of my profession, with lending them all the assistance possible in sickness, and sympathizing with them in their numerous afflictions, and occasionally feeding, feasting, and giving them little tokens of kind regard, have as yet considerable influence over them, but have to punish some, and occasion the chiefs to punish more, which creates me enemies, and must eventuate in lessening my influence among them, unless the means are put in my hands to sustain and encourage the chiefs and well-disposed among them. *Good words*, *kind looks*, and *medicine* have some *power;* but, honored and very dear sir, *you* and *I* know they do not tell with Indians like blankets and present articles, to meet their tastes, wants, and necessities. Sir, I know how deeply anxious you are to benefit and save what can be of the withering Indian tribes, in which God knows how fully and heartily I am with you, and earnestly pray you, and through you our general government, to take immediate measures to satisfy the minds, and, so far as possible, render to these Indians an equivalent for their once numerous herds of deer, elk, buffalo, beaver, and otter, nearly as tame as our domestic animals, previously to the whites and their fire-arms coming among them, and of which they are now stripped, and for which they suffer. But, if nothing can be done for them upon this score, pray save them from being forcibly ejected from the lands and graves of their fathers, of which they begin to entertain serious fears. Many are becoming considerably enlightened on the subject of the white man's policy, and begin to quake in view of their future doom; and come to me from time to time, anxiously inquiring what they are to receive for such a one coming and cutting off all their most valuable timber, and floating it to the falls of the Wallamet, and getting large sums for it; some praying the removal of licentious whites from among them; others requiring pay for their old homestead, or a removal of the intruders. So, sir, you see already I have my hands, head, and heart full; and if as yet I have succeeded in giving satisfaction,—as many hundreds that neither know nor care for me, nor regard in the least the rights of the Indians, are now flocking in,—something more must be done, and that speedily, or a storm ensues.

I remove all licentious offenders from among them, especially if located at a distance from the colony, and encourage the community to keep within reasonable bounds, and settle as compactly as the general interest and duty to themselves will admit.

The large immigrating party have now arrived, most of them with *their herds*, having left the wagons at Wallawalla and the Dalles, which they intend to bring by land or water to the Wallamet in the spring. Whether they succeed in getting them through by land the last sixty miles is doubtful, the road not having been as yet well explored. They are greatly pleased with the country and its prospects. Mr. Applegate, who has been so much in government employ, and surveyed such portions of Missouri, says of this valley, it is a country of the greatest beauty and the finest soil he has seen.

The settlers are actively and vigorously employed, and the colony in a most prosperous state, crops of every kind having been unusually good this season. The little unhappy difference between the American settlers and the Hudson's Bay Company, arising from the last spring's petition to our government, has been healed, and we have general quiet,—both parties conducting themselves very properly toward each other at present. And here allow me to say, the seasonable services in which hundreds of dollars were gratuitously expended in assisting such numbers of our poor emigrant citizens down the Columbia to the Wallamet, entitle Governor McLaughlin, saying nothing of his previous fatherly and fostering care of this colony, to the honorable consideration of the members of our government. And I hope, as he is desirous to settle with his family in this country, and has made a claim at the falls of the Wallamet, his claim will be honored in such a manner as to make him conscious that we, as a nation, are not insensible to his numerous acts of benevolence and hospitality toward our countrymen. Sir, in the midst of slander, envy, jealousy, and, in too many instances, of the blackest ingratitude, his unceasing, never-tiring hospitality affects me, and makes him appear in a widely different light than too many would have him and his worthy associates appear before the world.

The last year's report, in which was incorporated Mr. Linn's Oregon speech and Captain Spalding's statements of hundreds of unoffending Indians being shot down annually by men under his control, afflicts the gentlemen of the Hudson's Bay Company, and is utterly without foundation,—no company or gentlemen ever having conducted themselves more judiciously among Indians than they uniformly have done in this country; and I am of the governor's opinion, who declares, openly, there have not been ten Indians killed by whites in this whole region west of Fort Hall, for the last twenty years, nor do I know of that number, and two of those were killed by our citizens. What were destroyed by the Hudson's Bay Company sufferered for willful murder, none pretending a doubt of the propriety of the course adopted.*

There are now four schools kept in the colony, of which I shall speak more fully in my annual report: one at the Tualatin Plains, under the direction and auspices of the Rev. Mr. Clark, a self-supporting missionary; a second (French and English) school is in successful operation by Mr. Blanchet, Roman Catholic missionary to this colony; a third is well sustained by the citizens, and kept at the falls of the Wallamet; a fourth (boarding and manual labor) sustained by the Methodist Board of Missions, for the benefit of Indian youth, of which Mr. Lee will speak particularly. The location is healthy, eligible, and beautiful, and the noble edifice does honor to the benevolent cause and agents that founded it. And while here, allow me to say, Mr. Jesse Applegate, from Missouri, is now surveying the mission claim, a plat of which will be presented to the consideration of the members of our government, for acceptance or otherwise, of which I have but little to say, as I entertain no doubt but Mr. Lee's representation will be most faithful. Should the ground of his claim be predicated upon the much effected for the benefit of the Indians, I am not with him; for, with all that has been

* This statement of Dr. White's shows his disposition to misrepresent his own countrymen, to favor the Hudson's Bay Company and the foreign subjects who were disposed to flatter his vanity.

expended, without doubting the correctness of the intention, it is most manifest to every observer that the Indians of this lower country, as a whole, have been very little benefited. They were too far gone with scrofula and venereal. But should he insist, as a reason of his claim, the benefit arising to the colony and country, I am with him heartily; and notwithstanding the claim is a valuable one, this country has been increased more by the mission operations than twice its amount in finance; besides, much has been done in advancing civilization, temperance, literature, and good morals, saying nothing of the evils that must have arisen in this lawless country in the absence of all moral restraint. Mr. Lee was among the first pioneers to this distant land, has struggled in its cares, toils, and trials, has risen with its rise; and it is but just to say, he and his associates are exerting a considerable and most salutary influence all abroad among us. I hope his reception will be such that he will return from Washington cheered and encouraged to pursue his benevolent operations in this country. The Catholic and the different Protestant missions have been prosperous during the last year, and are as generally acceptable to the whites as could, from their different pursuits, have been expected. * * *

Great expectations are entertained, from the fact that Mr. Linn's bill has passed the Senate; and as it has been so long before the public, and favorably entertained at Washington, should it at last fail of passing the Lower House, suffer me to predict, in view of what so many have been induced to undergo, in person and property, to get to this distant country, it will create a disaffection so strong as to end only in open rebellion; whereas, should it pass into a law, it will be regarded as most liberal and handsome, and will be appreciated by most, if not all, in Oregon.

As to the claim for the Oregon Institute, I need say nothing, having said enough in my last report; but, as that may have failed in reaching, I would just remark, that the location is a healthy one, and the site fine, with prospect charmingly varied, extensive, and beautiful.

I leave this subject with Mr. Lee and the members of our liberal government, not doubting but that all will be done for this Institute, and otherwise, that can be, and as soon as practicable, to lay deep and broad the foundation of science and literature in this country. * * *

Respectfully yours,

ELIJAH WHITE,

Sub-Agent Indian Affairs, W. R. M.

Hon. J. M. PORTER,

Secretary of War.

WALLAMET, March 18, 1844.

SIR,—On the evening of the 1st February, the two following letters came to me, finding me in the upper settlement of the Wallamet, distance forty miles:—

"WALLAMET FALLS, January 29, 1844.

"DEAR SIR,—The undersigned would take this occasion to inform you that there have been of late in this place some few cases of intoxication from the effects of ardent spirits. It is currently reported that it is distilled in this place, and the undersigned have good reason to credit such reports. While, therefore, the undersigned will not trouble you, sir, with a detailed exposition of the facts, they must be permitted to express their deliberate conviction that that which has inflicted so much injury upon the morals, the peace, and the happiness of the world, ought not to be permitted to be manufactured in this country under any circumstances. And your attention is respectfully invited to this subject. "We have the honor to be, dear sir,

"PETER H. HATCH, President.
"A. L. LOVEJOY, Vice-President.
"A. F. WALLER, Secretary.

"Dr. E. WHITE,
"Sub-Agent for Indian Affairs, Oregon Territory."

"WALLAMET FALLS, January 26, 1844.

"DEAR SIR,—I do not know but you have been written to already on the subject which is the cause of no inconsiderable excitement at this place, viz., the manufacture and use of that most degrading, withering, and damning of all the curses that have ever visited our race since the fall of Adam. As much as we regret it, deplore it, and anathematize the men who make it, it is nevertheless made, and men, or rather biped brutes, get drunk. Now, we believe if there is any thing that calls your attention in your official capacity, or any thing in which you would be most cordially supported by the good sense and prompt action of the better part of the community, it is the present case. We do not wish to dictate, but hope for the best, begging pardon for intrusions. "I am, dear sir, yours truly,

"ELIJAH WHITE, Esq., "W. H. WILSON.
"Sub-Agent Oregon Territory."

I accordingly left at sunrise on the following morning, and reached the falls at sunset. Without delay, I secured the criminal and his distillery, broke his apparatus, and buried it in the Wallamet River. I put the aggressor under bonds, in the strongest penalty the nature of the case would admit,—$300,—few being willing to be his bondsmen even for this amount.

Mr. Pettygrove, a merchant, of good habits and character, being accused of keeping and selling wine and brandy, I searched, and found, as he had acknowledged, half a gallon of brandy and part of a barrel of port wine, which has been used, and occasionally parted with, only for medicinal purposes; and, to avoid all appearance of partiality, I required the delivery of the brandy and wine on the delivery of the inclosed bond, which was most cheerfully and cordially given,—amount $1,000. I searched every suspicious place thoroughly, aided by the citizens, but found no ardent spirits or wine in the colony. Since this period, no attempts have been made to make, introduce, or vend liquors; and the great majority of the colonists come warmly to my support in this matter, proffering their aid to keep this bane from our community.

On the evening of February 20, I received the following communication, accompanied by corroboratory statements from Mr. Foster, of Oregon City:—

"WALLAMET FALLS, February 16, 1844.

"SIR,—I beg leave to inform you that there is an Indian about this place, of the name of Cockstock, who is in the habit of making continual threats against the settlers in this neighborhood, and who has also murdered several Indians lately. He has conducted himself lately in so outrageous a manner, that Mr. Winslow Anderson has considered himself in personal danger, and on that account has left his place, and come to reside at the falls of the Wallamet; and were I in circumstances that I could possibly remove from my place, I would certainly remove also, but am so situated that it is not possible for me to do so. I beg, therefore, that you, sir, will take into consideration the propriety of ridding the country of a villain, against the depredations of whom none can be safe, as it is impossible to guard against the lurking attacks of the midnight murderer. I have, therefore, taken the liberty of informing you that I shall be in expectation of a decided answer from you on or before the 10th of March next; after that date, I shall consider myself justified in acting as I shall see fit, on any repetition of of the threats made by the before-mentioned Indian or his party.

"I am, etc., with respect,

"JAMES D. SAULES.

"Dr. E. WHITE, Superintendent, etc."

As I well knew all the individuals concerned, I resolved to repair immediately to the spot, and, if possible, secure the Indian without bloodshed, as he was connected with some of the most formidable tribes in this part of the Territory, though a very dangerous and violent character. Accordingly I started, and reaching the falls on the following evening, collected a party to repair to the spot and secure him while asleep, knowing that he would not submit to be taken a prisoner without resistance. The evening was stormy, and the distance some eight miles, through thick wood and fallen timber, with two bad streams to cross. Being on foot, my party declined the attempt till morning,—a circumstance I much regretted; yet, having no military force, I was compelled to yield. In the morning I headed the party of ten men to take this Indian, who had only five adherents, in hopes to surprise and secure him without fighting,—enjoining my men, from many considerations, not to fire unless ordered to do so in self-defense. Unfortunately, two horses had just been stolen and a house plundered, and the Indians absconded, leaving no doubt on our minds of their being the thieves, as, after tracking them two or three miles into the forest, they had split off in such a manner as to elude pursuit, and we were forced to return to town unsuccessful, as further pursuit was little more rational than chasing an eagle amidst the mountains. Cockstock had sworn vengeance against several of my party, and they thirsted for his blood. Having no other means of securing him, I offered $100 reward to any who would deliver him safely into my hands, as I wished to convey him for trial to the authorities constituted among the Nez Percés and Cayuses, not doubting that they would feel honored in inflicting a just sentence upon him, and the colony thereby be saved from an Indian war, so much to be dreaded in our present weak and defenseless condition.

Some six days subsequent, Cockstock and his party, six in all, came into town at midday, rode from house to house, showing his loaded pistols, and not allowing any one, by artifice or flattery, to get them out of his bosom or hand. He and his party were horridly painted, and rode about the town, setting, as the citizens, and especially his enemies, construed it, the whole town at defiance. The citizens endured it for several hours, but with great impatience, when at length he crossed the river, and entered the Indian village opposite, and, as the chief states, labored for some time to induce them to join him and burn down the town that night, destroying as many of the whites as possible. Failing in this (if serious or correct in statement, which is much doubted by some, as the chief and whole Indian village were inimical to him, and doubtless wished, as he was a "brave," to make the whites the instrument of his destruction), he obtained an interpreter, and recrossed the river, as other Indians state, for the purpose of calling the whites to an explanation for pursuing him with hostile intentions. By this time, the excitement had become intense with all classes and both sexes among the whites, and, as was to be expected, they ran in confusion and disorder toward the point where the Indians were landing,—some to take him alive and get the reward; others to shoot him at any risk to themselves, the wealthiest men in town promising to stand by them to the amount of $1,000 each. With these different views, and no concert of action, and many running merely to witness the affray, the Indians were met at the landing, and a firing commenced simultaneously on both sides, each party accusing the other of firing first. In the midst of a hot firing on both sides, Mr. George W. Le Breton, a respectable young man, rushed unarmed upon Cockstock, after the discharge of one or more of his pistols, and received a heavy discharge in the palm of his right hand, lodging one ball in his elbow and another in his arm, two inches above the elbow-joint. A scuffle ensued, in which he fell with the Indian, crying out instantly, "He is killing me with his knife." At this moment a mulatto man ran up, named Winslow Anderson, and dispatched Cockstock, by mashing his skull with the barrel of his rifle, using it as a soldier would a bayonet. In the mean time the other Indians were firing among the whites in every direction, with guns, pistols, and poisoned arrows, yelling fearfully, and many narrowly escaped. Two men, who were quietly at work near by, were wounded with arrows (Mr. Wilson slightly in the hip, and Mr. Rogers in the muscle of the arm), but neither, as was supposed, dangerously. The five Indians having shot their guns and arrows, retired toward the bluff east of the town, lodged themselves in the rocks, and again commenced firing upon the citizens indiscriminately. Attention was soon directed that way, and fire-arms having been brought, the Indians were soon routed, killing one of their horses, and wounding one of them, thus ending the affray.

Mr. Le Breton (the surgeon being absent from town) was removed immediately to Vancouver, where he received every attention; but the canoe having been ten hours on the passage, the poison had diffused itself all abroad into his system, and proved mortal in less than three days from the moment of the horrid disaster. Mr. Rogers lived but one day longer, though but slightly wounded with an arrow in the muscles of his arm. Mr. Wilson has suffered comparatively little, but is not considered in a safe condition.

This unhappy affray has created a general sensation throughout the colony, and all abroad among the Indians of this lower district. Now, while I am penning these lines, I am completely surrounded by at least seventy armed Indians, just down from the Dalles of the Columbia, many of them the professed relatives of the deceased, on the way to the falls of the Wallamet, to demand an explanation, or, in other words, to extort a present for the loss of their brother.

They appear well affected toward me; remarkably so, though armed to the teeth, and painted horridly. I am every moment expecting my interpreter, when I shall probably learn particulars respecting their intentions. In the mean time, I will give a few particulars respecting this deceased Indian's previous course, which led to the disaster, showing how much we need authorities and discipline in this country.

As it is said, a negro hired Cockstock for a given time, to be paid in a certain horse. Before the time expired, the negro sold the horse and land claim to another negro, the Indian finishing his time with the purchaser, according to agreement. Learning, however, to his chagrin and mortification, that the horse had changed owners, and believing it a conspiracy against his rights, he resolved to take the horse forcibly; did so, and this led to a year's contention, many threats, some wounds, and at last to the three deaths, and may possibly lead to all the horrors of savage warfare in our hitherto quiet neighborhood. It was this identical Cockstock that occasioned much of the excitement last spring among the whites of the colony, actually driving several from their homes to the more central parts of the settlement for protection.

I saw and had an interview with the Indians in June following, and settled all differences, to appearances, satisfactorily; but, four months subsequently, having occasioned the authorities constituted among the Indians to flog one of his connections for violently entering the house of the Rev. H. K. W. Perkins, seizing his person, and attempting to tie, with a view to flog him, he took fire afresh, and in November last came with a slave to my house, with the avowed object of shooting me down at once; but finding me absent, after a close search in every part of the house, he commenced smashing the windows, lights, sash, and all, of my house and office, with the breech of his gun; and it is but just to say he did his work most effectually, not leaving a sound window in either. He next started hotly in pursuit of my steward, who was most actively retreating, but was soon overtaken and seized by the shoulder; his garment giving way saved the frightened young man from further violence.

I returned late in the evening,—this having occurred at three P. M.,—when the villains were too far away to be overtaken, though I pursued them with the best men of the colony during the whole night, and as long after as we could trace them. This was regarded as a great outrage, and created a strong sensation throughout the community: especially as none knew where to trace it until within a few weeks past. Some four weeks subsequently, fifteen Indians came riding into the neighborhood in open day, painted and well armed. I was the first, with one exception, that observed them, and learned that they were Molallas and Klamaths, and felt confident they were on an errand of mischief, being well informed of their marauding and desperate habits. As this is quite out of their province, the proper homes of the Klamaths being at least three hundred miles to the south, and the Molallas, with whom they intermarry, having their lodges in the Cascade Mountains, a distance of from forty to eighty miles, I resolved at once to turn their visit to account; sent my steward to Chief Caleb's lodge, where all had arrived, he being a Callapooya, and with his band having previously entered with me into the civil compact, and gave him a cordial invitation to call on me, with the chiefs of his district, in the morning, as I wished to see them and had some interesting and pleasing news to convey to them. The chiefs called in the morning, none, however, appearing so pleased and happy as Caleb. Of this I took no notice, but entered into cheerful conversation with Caleb for a few moments, and then rose up and invited them to walk out and see my plantation and herds.

When we reached the cattle, I, as by accident, or incidentally, asked Caleb if he was prepared to give a feast to his distant friends who had so lately and unexpectedly called upon him. Answering in the negative, I told him to shoot down at once a fat young ox that was passing before us, and, while some were dressing it, others to come to the house and get some flour, peas, salt, etc., and go immediately back and feast his friends, lest they form a very unfavorable opinion of us here. I need not say that the summons was promptly obeyed, and Caleb the happiest man in the world. Now the rigid muscles of the stranger chiefs began to relax; in short, all distrust was soon lost, and, as they were about leaving for Caleb's camp, they found themselves constrained to inform me that they came over with very different feelings from what they were now leaving us with, and were very glad they had listened to Caleb's advice, and called upon me. Professing to be very much engaged at the moment, I told them to go and dine, and at evening, or early the following morning, I would come with my friend, Mr. Applegate, and make them a call.

They feasted to the full, and I found them in fine humor, and in a better condition to smoke than fight. After some casual conversation I asked them how they would like to enter into the civil compact; and, while they were discussing the subject, this Indian (Cockstock) came first into my presence, well armed, and appeared cold and distant, though I had no suspicion of his being the character who had so lately broken to pieces the windows in my house and office.

They had no scruples in saying they were entirely willing, and should be pleased on their part to enter upon the same terms, but did not know how it might be regarded by the residue of their respective tribes. They engaged to meet me on the 15th March, with the residue of their people, and use their influence to bring about so desirable an object. The party left the same day, apparently in a cheerful mood, passed over the prairie singing, talking, and laughing merrily. As a part, however, were passing their horses over a difficult stream, the other part fell upon and massacred them in a most shocking manner, this villainous Cockstock acting a conspicuous part in the bloody affray.

I repaired to the spot without delay, as the whites were much excited, and wished to pursue and hang every one of them. I learned there had been unsettled feuds of long standing, and that in like manner, ten months previously, these unfortunate wretches had shot down a fellow-traveler. On conveying this information to the citizens, all I believe were satisfied to stay at home, and remain quiet for the present.

Thus much for this Indian affair, which, my interpreter having arrived, I have settled to-day with the Dalles Indians most satisfactorily. As was to be expected, they wished presents for the death of their brother. I prevailed on all to be seated, and then explained the whole case slowly and clearly to their understanding. I told them we had lost two valuable innocent men, and they but one; and should our people learn that I had given them presents, without their giving me two blankets for one, they must expect nothing but the hottest displeasure from the whites. After much deliberation among themselves, they, with one voice, concluded to leave the whole matter to my discretion.

I at once decided to give the poor Indian widow two blankets, a dress, and handkerchief, believing the moral influence to be better than to make presents to the chief or tribe, and to receive nothing at their hands. To this proposition they most cheerfully consented, and have now left, having asked for and obtained from me a written certificate, stating that the matter had been amicably adjusted. It is to be hoped that it will here end, though that is by no means certain, as at present there are so many sources of uneasiness and discontent between the parties.

As I said before, I believe it morally impossible for us to remain at peace in Oregon, for any considerable time, without the protection of vigorous civil or military law. For myself, I am most awkwardly situated; so much so, indeed, that I had seriously anticipated leaving this spring; but the late successful contest against the introduction of ardent spirits, in connection with the excitement by reason of the unhappy disaster at the falls of the Wallamet, together with the fact of too many of our people being so extremely excitable on Indian and other affairs relating to the peace and interest of the colony and country, I have concluded to remain for the present, in hopes of being soon in some way relieved. I hope the draft that I have this day drawn in favor of John McLaughlin will be honored, as otherwise I may be thrown at once into the greatest difficulties, having no other house in this country where I can draw such articles as I require for necessary presents to Indians, to defray traveling expenses, etc.

I have the honor to remain, with highest respect, your obedient humble servant,

E. White,
Sub-Agent Indian Affairs.

Hon. J. M. Porter,
Secretary of War.

Wallamet, March 22, 1844.

Honored Sir,—The within accounts, as per voucher No. 1, drawn on the Hudson's Bay House at Vancouver, are in part pay for interpreters and necessary assistants in guarding and conducting me from point to point, in my late unavoidable excursions during the excitement of the fall of 1842 and spring of 1843, and other necessary voyages since, together with the presents in hoes, medicines, and clothes, to enable me to secure and hold a sufficient influence over the aborigines to prevent threatened invasions and serious evils to the colony and country.

Those upon Mr. Abernethy and Mr. A. E. Wilson are for like purposes; drafts upon these houses being my principal means of paying expenses in this country.

As I hire only when requisite, and dismiss at once when no longer necessary, my interpreter's bills, including clerks and all assistants for the different tribes, do not exceed $300 per annum up to the present time; notwithstanding, at one time, for sixty days, I was under the necessity of hiring two men at the rate of three dollars per day each.

Traveling expenses in 1842, three hundred and eighty dollars ($380). In 1843, three hundred and ninety-six dollars and fifty cents ($396.50). In presents for the two years and two months, two hundred and ninety dollars and seventy-five cents ($290.75); in medicines, hoes, and sundry useful articles, to encourage them and strengthen my influence among them, this being my only way to succeed to any considerable extent. Presents become the more indispensable from the fact of the long-continued and constant liberality of the Hudson's Bay Company toward the Indians of this country.

Had all remained in as quiet a state as when the colony was small, and no jealousies awakened, most of those small expenses might have been avoided, but, unless a military post be at once established, or more means put into my hands to meet their increasing wants, my expense will be increased, and trouble multiply; but at this moment, were one thousand dollars placed in my hands to lay out judiciously in medicines, hoes, plows, blankets, and men, women, and children's clothes, to distribute annually, more security would be effected, and good done to the aborigines, than in ten times that amount expended in establishing and keeping up a military post,—such is their desire and thirst after the means to promote civilization.

As this voyaging is most destructive to my wardrobe, saying nothing of the perils and hardships to which it exposes me, shall I be allowed the sum usually allowed military officers, which Esquire Gilpin informs me is ten dollars per each hundred miles? I will place it down and leave it to your honorable consideration, not doubting, sir, but you will do what is proper and right in the premises. I shall charge only for such traveling as was unavoidable in the execution of my official business. With highest respect, I am, dear sir,

Your humble and obedient servant,

ELIJAH WHITE,

Sub-Agent Indian Affairs, W. R. M.

Hon. J. M. PORTER,

Secretary of War, Washington, D. C.

WALLAMET, Nov. 23, 1843.

MY DEAR SIR,—As, in the order of Divine Providence, it appears to be my duty to leave this country in a few days to return to the United States, and, as I have had the pleasure of an acquaintance with all the important transactions in which you have been engaged, in your official capacity, since your arrival in this country in the fall of 1842, I consider it a duty which I owe to yourself, to bear my unequivocal testimony in favor of the course which you have generally pursued. Not pretending to understand what properly belongs to the office of an Indian agent, I flatter myself that I am capable of judging in reference to those matters which are calculated to effect the elevation and prosperity of the Indians, and the peace and security of those whites who settle in the Indian country. As I can not speak particularly concerning all your official acts in the country, permit me to refer to one expedition, which I consider to have been the most important of any in which you have been engaged, and in which I had the pleasure of being associated with you. I mean that long and excessively toilsome journey which you performed into the interior of this country early last spring. The causes which prompted you to engage in the enterprise, in my humble opinion, were the most justifiable. The whites in the country had been thrown into a panic by information received from the missionaries in the interior, that the Indians were forming a plan to effect the destruction of the white population. It was everywhere observed that our Indian agent should immediately repair to the infected region, and endeavor to quell the tumult, "for (it was repeatedly remarked) it was better for one man to expose his life than for the whole settlement to suffer." Without delay the exposure was made. And though life was not taken, yet, in accomplishing the object, you were compelled to pass through much difficulty, excessive labor, and great danger. The plans proposed to quiet the Indians, whom you found in a state of great excitement, were doubtless conceived in wisdom, and produced the desired effect. The expenses incurred were no more than were absolutely necessary. And I doubt not, if the results of the expedition are correctly represented, that our enlightened government will make an appropriation to cover all the expenses which accrued in consequence of the undertaking.

With my most hearty and best wishes for your continued peace and prosperity, permit me to subscribe myself, yours, with feelings of unaltered friendship.

GUSTAVUS HINES,
Missionary of the M. E. Church.

DR. ELIJAH WHITE,
Sub-Agent of Indian Affairs west of Rocky Mountains.

DEPARTMENT OF WAR,
OFFICE OF INDIAN AFFAIRS, Nov. 24, 1845.

* * * * * * * *

Two interesting and very instructive reports have been received from the sub-agent west of the Rocky Mountains. They present that country in a new and important light to the consideration of the public.

The advancement in civilization by the numerous tribes of Indians in that remote and hitherto neglected portion of our territory, with so few advantages, is a matter of surprise. Indeed, the red men of that region would almost seem to be of a different order from those with whom we have been in more familiar intercourse. A few years since the face of a white man was almost unknown to them; now, through the benevolent policy of the various Christian churches, and the indefatigable exertions of the missionaries in their employ, they have prescribed and well adapted rules for their government, which are observed and respected to a degree worthy the most intelligent whites.

Numerous schools have grown up in their midst, at which their children are acquiring the most important and useful information. They have already advanced to a degree of civilization that promises the most beneficial results to them and their brethren on this side of the mountains, with whom they may, and no doubt will at some future period, be brought into intercourse. They are turning their attention to agricultural pursuits, and with but few of the necessary utensils in their possession, already produce sufficient in some places to meet their every want.

Among some of the tribes, hunting has been almost entirely abandoned, many individuals looking wholly to the soil for support. The lands are represented as extremely fertile, and the climate healthy, agreeable, and uniform.

Under these circumstances, so promising in their consequences, and grateful to the feelings of the philanthropist, it would seem to be the duty of the government of the United States to encourage their advancement, and still further aid their progress in the path of civilization. I therefore respectfully recommend the establishment among them of a full agency, with power to the President to make it an acting superintendency; and to appoint one or more sub-agents, whenever, in his judgment, the same may become necessary and proper.

All which is respectfully submitted.

W. Medill.

Hon. Wm. L. Marcy,
Secretary of War.

The reader will observe the clear statement of the United States Indian policy in the above communication. That schools, farming, and civilization are prominent. That the Indians, as the whole of this report indicates, are rapidly improving under the instructions of the missionaries in the interior,—Spalding and Whitman in particular. That Dr. White, in this report, as contained in the previous chapter, attempts to include Blanchet and associates as erecting mills, etc., for the benefit of the Indians, while Spalding's and Whitman's stations were the only places where mills had been erected.

These facts brought so prominently before the British and foreign mind their sectarian and commercial jealousies; and national pride was so excited that it knew no bounds and could not be satisfied short of the effort that was made in 1847–8. Subsequent Indian wars were but the spasmodic and dying action of the spirit that instigated the first.

It will also be observed that this report brings out the bold efforts of our foreign emissaries to excite the Indians in the settlement, and to disturb and divide the American population on the question of an organization.

CHAPTER XXXIII.

First council to organize a provisional government.—Library founded.—Origin of the Wolf Association.—The Methodist Mission influence.—Dr. White exhibits his credentials.—First "wolf meeting."—Proceedings of the second "wolf meeting."—Officers.—Resolutions.—Bounties to be paid.—Resolution to appoint a committee of twelve for the civil and military protection of the settlement.—Names of the members of the committee.

A CONSULTATION was held at the house of Gray to consider the expediency of organizing a provisional government. In it the whole condition of the settlement, the missions, and Hudson's Bay Company, were carefully looked at, and all the influences combined against the organization of a settlers' government were fully canvassed. The conclusion was that no direct effort could succeed, as it had already been tried and failed, from the combined influence of the Hudson's Bay Company and the Roman Catholic and Methodist missions. To the writer, who up to this time had not fully understood all the causes of the failure, it was doubtful. Two plans were suggested; one, at least, might succeed. The first was to get up a circulating library, and by that means draw attention and discussion to subjects of interest to the settlement, and secure the influence of the Methodist Mission, as education was a subject they had commenced. We found no difficulty in the library movement from them, only they seemed anxious to keep from the library a certain class of light reading, which they appeared tenacious about. This was not a vital point with the original movers, so they yielded it. The library prospered finely; one hundred shares were taken at five dollars a share; three hundred volumes of old books collected and placed in this institution, which was called the "Multnomah Circulating Library;" one hundred dollars were sent to New York for new books which arrived the following year. Now for the main effort to secure another position.

It will be remembered that in the winter of 1836–7 the Wallamet Cattle Company was formed. All the settlers that could raise the funds entered heartily into the project, and such as had no means to advance money for stock at the time had succeeded in buying from those that would sell. Besides, part of the estate of Ewing Young had been sold and distributed, and the Hudson's Bay Company had also organized the Puget Sound Company, and had begun to distribute cattle; hence almost every settler, the missions, the Hudson's Bay Company, and some Indians were owning cattle.

The wolves, bears, and panthers were very destructive to the cattle of all alike. Here was an object of sufficient interest to all, to bring a united action, and collect a large number of the settlers. Accordingly, a notice was given, requesting all interested in adopting some united action to get rid of the wild beasts, that were destroying our domestic animals, to meet at the house of W. H. Gray, on the 2d of February, 1843. This was the first move to the provisional government. While this was being done in the valley, at Wallamet Falls, since Oregon City, the question of a provisional government was up before a lyceum held at that place and debated warmly for several evenings, and finally voted down. Dr. John McLaughlin took the side of an independent government. Mr. Abernethy, afterward governor, moved that, in case our government did not extend its jurisdiction over the country in four years, that then the meeting would be in favor of an independent government. This idea was favored by Dr. White, upon condition that the settlers would vote generally to elect him as their governor, as from the fact that he held the office of sub-Indian agent by the appointment of the President, he could officiate as governor, and it would be no additional expense to the settlers. This was a plausible argument, and had Dr. White been a man of moral principle and capable of understanding his duties in the office he held, the settlers would without a doubt have adopted his suggestions; but, unfortunately for him, they had lost all confidence in his executive and judicial ability, as also in his ability to deal with Indians. Besides, the leading members of the Methodist Mission were opposed to him on account of his shameful course while one of their number, though Mr. Hines seems to have held to his skirts during the greater portion of the time he was creating all the disturbance he was capable of among the Indians, and being the dupe of the Hudson's Bay Company.

These facts were all known to the getters-up of the "Wolf Organization," as it was called. In fact, Le Breton had participated in the discussions at the Wallamet Falls, and reported them to those of us in the valley. Our idea was, to get an object before the people upon which all could unite, and as we advanced, secure the main object,—*self-preservation, both for property and person.*

The "wolf meeting" was fully attended, and all took a lively interest in it, for there was not a man in the settlement that had not been a loser from wild animals. There was a little suspicion in this first meeting that more than protection for animals was meant.

Dr. Ira L. Babcock, who was elected our chairman, and who, we supposed, would be the first to suspect the main object, seemed to discard the idea as foolish and ridiculous, as he thought "we had all the protection for our persons that we needed in the arrangements already entered into, and the object for which the meeting was called was a good and laudable one; we were all interested in it; we had all lost more or less from the ravages of wild animals, and it became necessary to have a united effort to get rid of them and protect our property." This was the very point we wished to hold the doctor to. He had expressed the idea exactly, and placed it in a clear light. As settlers, we had nothing to do but submit to the rule of the Hudson's Bay Company, the missions, and Dr. White, and do all we could to protect their cattle and herds.

The Oregon archives show that there were persons present who were prepared for the occasion. The remarks of our chairman were appropriate, for it was self-evident that our domestic animals needed protection; we could not spend all our time to guard them, hence a united effort would accomplish in a short time, and at comparatively little expense to all, what would otherwise be impossible, scattered as our settlements were, with our domestic animals exposed to the ravages of wild animals known to be numerous all over the country. It was moved that a committee of six be appointed to notify a general meeting, and prepare a plan, and report the matter for the action of the settlers.

The chairman was called upon to appoint a committee to call a public meeting. Gray, Beers, and Wilson, already known to the reader, and Gervais and Lucie, Canadian-Frenchmen, who came to the country with Wilson G. Hunt's party, and Barnaby, a French Rocky Mountain hunter, were appointed.

These three men were the most intelligent and influential French settlers that were then in the country, having considerable influence with the Canadian-French settlers, and generally favored American settlement and enterprise.

The preparation for the general meeting, which was moved by Alanson Beers to be called at the house of Mr. Joseph Gervais on the first Monday in March next, at ten o'clock A. M., devolved on Gray, Beers, and Wilson. The giving of the notices, which Le Breton with his ready pen soon prepared, devolved on Gervais, Barnaby, and Lucie. Up to this time, no intimation of the proposed civil government had been given to any member of the missions, or the Hudson's Bay Company. All was moving on harmoniously, and all were interested in caring for and protecting our domestic animals. The "wolf meeting," and what was to be done, was the subject of general interest. Le Breton and Smith were busy in finding out the men who could be relied upon, and the men that would oppose the *one great object* we had determined to accomplish, so that on the first Monday in March, 1843, the settlement, *except the clergy*, were all present. If my memory serves me, there was not in that meeting a single reverend gentleman of any denomination. James A. O'Neil, who came to the country with Captain Wyeth in 1834, and had remained in it, presided at this meeting. He was informed of the main object, and requested to hurry through the "wolf meeting" business as soon as possible.

It will be seen that we had placed before the settlement, the Hudson's Bay Company, and both missions, an object they were deeply interested in. The clergy were just then all asleep, and so were the company, for while they were all willing that we should pay our money, spend our time, and hunt wild animals to protect their by far the largest portion of property exposed, they did not suspect we were looking to a far more important object—our *personal liberty ;* hence the settlers' "wolf meeting" did not call for their attention, but they all gave it an encouraging word, and promised to contribute to its funds, which they did, till they saw the real object, when they dropped it without ceremony, or at least saw too late that their power was gone.

The Methodist Mission influence was the most difficult to deal with. We were fully aware of their large pretensions to land, and of the consummate duplicity of White, in dealing with all parties. White, to secure the approval of the Methodist Mission, encouraged their large pretensions to mission lands, and also spoke favorably of the Jesuit influence among the Indians ; while, if he had had two grains of common sense and common honesty, he could have seen their influence was tending to destroy all of his, as well as all American influence in the country. Still his supremely selfish ideas of self-honor and official dignity led him to pursue a course disgusting to all parties.

During the time between the first and second "wolf meetings," White was called upon in a public manner to exhibit his authority from the President, which he was foolish enough to do. It was seen at once that he was in the country *only as a spy upon the actions of the Hudson's Bay Company*, while he assumed to make treaties with Indians, and govern the country, and make pledges and promises, which no one believed the government would ever attempt to fulfill.

As a matter of history and curiosity, the proceedings of the "wolf meetings" are copied from the Oregon archives, which Mr. Hines, it seems, did not even know had an existence, showing, by his own statements, that he was so completely mixed up in his ideas of the origin of the provisional government, that though he is generally correct in his statements, yet he failed to distinguish the point of conception and birth of the *oldest State on the Pacific*, for I contend that justice to our effort and a proper understanding of our rights should have admitted us as a State instead of subjecting us to a Territorial *annoyance*, under such *demagogues* as were sent among us up to the time we became a State.

Proceedings of a Meeting held at the Oregon Institute, February 2, 1843.

A public meeting of a number of the citizens of this colony was called at the house of W. H. Gray, in order to take into consideration the propriety of adopting some measures for the protection of our herds, etc., in this country.

On motion, Dr. I. L. Babcock was called to the chair, who proceeded to state the objects of the meeting, and the necessity of acting.

Mr. W. H. Gray moved, and Mr. Torn seconded the motion, "that a committee of six be appointed to notify a general meeting, and report business, etc.," which motion was carried, and Messrs. Gray, Beers, Gervais, Wilson, Barnaby, and Lucie, were appointed said committee.

Mr. Beers moved "that a general meeting be called at the house of Mr. Joseph Gervais, on the first Monday in March next, at ten o'clock, A. M.," which motion was carried.

W. H. WILSON, Secretary. I. L. BABCOCK, Chairman.

Journal of a Meeting at the house of J. Gervais, first Monday in March, 1843.

In pursuance of a resolution of a previous meeting, the citizens of Wallamet Valley met, and, the meeting being called to order, Mr. James O'Neil was chosen chairman. Mr. Martin was chosen as secretary, but declining to serve, Mr. Le Breton was chosen.

The minutes of the former meeting were read.

The committee appointed to notify a general meeting and report business, made the following report, to wit:—

"Your committee beg leave to report as follows: It being admitted by all that bears, wolves, panthers, etc., are destructive to the useful animals owned by the settlers of this colony, your committee would submit the following resolutions, as the sense of this meeting, by which the community may be governed in carrying on a defensive and destructive war against all such animals.

"*Resolved*, 1st. That we deem it expedient for this community to take immediate measures for the destruction of all wolves, panthers, and bears, and such other animals as are known to be destructive to cattle, horses, sheep, and hogs.

"2d. That a treasurer be appointed, who shall receive all funds, and dispense the same, in accordance with drafts drawn on him by the committee appointed to receive the evidences of the destruction of the above-named animals; and that he report the state of the treasury, by posting up public notices, once in three months, in the vicinity of each of the committee.

"3d. That a standing committee of eight be appointed, whose duty it shall be, together with the treasurer, to receive the proofs, or evidences, of the animals for which a bounty is claimed having been killed in the Wallamet Valley.

"4th. That a bounty of fifty cents be paid for the destruction of a small wolf; three dollars for a large wolf; one dollar and fifty cents for a lynx; two dollars for a bear; and five dollars for a panther.

"5th. That no bounty be paid unless the individual claiming said bounty give satisfactory evidence, or present the skin of the head with the ears of all animals for which he claims a bounty.

"6th. That the committee and treasurer form a Board of advice to call public meetings, whenever they may deem it expedient, to promote and encourage all persons to use their vigilance in destroying all the animals named in the fourth resolution.

"7th. That the bounties specified in the fourth resolution be limited to whites and their descendants.

"8th. That the proceedings of this meeting be signed by the chairman and secretary, and a copy thereof be presented to the recorder of this colony."

On motion, the report was accepted.

It was then moved and seconded that the report be laid on the table, which was carried.

It was moved and seconded that the first resolution in the report of the committee be adopted, which was carried.

It was moved and seconded that a sum be raised by contribution for the protection of our animals, which was carried.

It was moved and seconded that the third resolution, as amended, be adopted, which was carried.

It was moved and seconded that two collectors be appointed to receive all subscriptions, retaining five per cent. for collecting the same, and pay the amount over to the treasurer, taking his receipt for the same, which was carried.

On motion, the fifth resolution was adopted.

On motion, it was resolved "that no one receive a bounty (except Indians) unless he pay a subscription of five dollars."

On motion, the seventh resolution was adopted.

On motion, the eighth and ninth resolutions were adopted.

It was moved and seconded that the Indians receive one-half as much as the whites.

It was moved and seconded that all claims for bounties be presented within ten days from the time of becoming entitled to said bounties, and, if there should be any doubts, the individual claiming a bounty shall give his oath to the various circumstances; which was carried.

On motion, W. H. Gray was chosen treasurer.

It was moved that Messrs. McRoy, Gervais, Martin, S. Smith, Dougherty, O'Neil, Shortess, and Lucie be the standing committee; which motion was carried.

It was moved that G. W. Le Breton and Mr. Bridgers be the collectors. Carried.

On motion, the following resolutions were adopted:—

"*Resolved*, That no money be paid to any white, or his descendants, previous to the time of his subscription.

"*Resolved*, That the bounty of a minor child be paid to a parent or guardian.

"*Resolved*, That the draft for receiving subscriptions be drawn by Mr. Gray and Mr. Le Breton.

"*Resolved*, That drafts on Fort Vancouver, the Mission, and the Milling Company be received on subscriptions, as payment."

As a kind Providence would have it, the "wolf meeting" at Mr. Gervais' house on the Wallamet River was one of the most harmonious meetings I ever attended. Every one seemed to feel that a unanimous war had been declared against the despoilers of our domestic animals that were dependent upon us for protection.

It was stated by one speaker "that no one would question for a moment that this was right. This was just and natural protection for our property in animals liable to be destroyed by wolves, bears, and panthers. How is it, fellow-citizens, with you and me, and our children and wives? Have we any organization upon which we can rely for mutual protection? Is there any power or influence in the country sufficient to protect us and all we hold dear on earth from the worse than wild beasts that threaten and occasionally destroy our cattle? Who in our midst is authorized at this moment to call us together to protect our own, and the lives of our families? True, the alarm may be given, as in a recent case, and we may run who feel alarmed, and shoot off our guns, while our enemy may be robbing our property, ravishing our wives, and burning the houses over our defenseless families. Common sense, prudence, and justice to ourselves demand that we act consistent with the principles we have commenced. We have mutually and unitedly agreed to defend and protect our *cattle and domestic animals;* now, fellow-citizens, I submit and move the adoption of the two following resolutions, that we may have protection for our persons and lives as well as our cattle and herds:—

"*Resolved*, That a committee be appointed to take into consideration the propriety of taking measures for the civil and military protection of this colony.

"*Resolved*, That said committee consist of twelve persons."

There was not a dissenting vote in that meeting. Drs. Babcock and White were not present, but prudence and policy gave them both a place upon the proposed committee of twelve, while we knew the feelings of the balance of the committee.

Messrs. Dr. Babcock, Dr. White, O'Neil, Shortess, Newell, Lucie, Gervais, Hubbard, McRoy, Gray, Smith, and Gay were appointed said committee.

CHAPTER XXXIV.

First meeting of the committee of twelve.—All invited to participate.—The Rev. J. Lee and Mr. Abernethy ridicule the organization.—Mr. Lee tells a story.—Letter from Governor Abernethy.—The main question at issue.—Drowning of Cornelius Rogers and party.—Conduct of Dr. White.—Methodist Mission.—Catholic boasts of conversions.

By mutual understanding the committee of twelve first met at Walamet Falls, about the middle of March, 1843. My impression is that Dr. Babcock was not present with the committee, and that Dr. White was chosen temporary chairman. G. W. Le Breton was secretary of the committee. A motion was made and carried to invite the citizens of the village to participate in the deliberations of the committee. Rev. Jason Lee, Rev. Mr. Waller, Mr. Abernethy, R. Moore, in fact, nearly all the prominent men of the place, were present, and participated in the discussions.

We found Rev. Jason Lee and Mr. Abernethy disposed to ridicule the proposed organization as foolish and unnecessary. Rev. Jason Lee in his argument illustrated the folly of the effort, by telling us of a company of militia gotten up somewhere in Canada. He said "the requisite notice had been given, and all the people liable to military duty were present on the day to elect the officers required for the company. When they had elected all their officers, there was one private soldier left. 'Well,' says the soldier, 'you may march me, you may drill me, you may face me to the right, or to the left, or about face, just as much as you please, but for mercy's sake don't divide me up into platoons.'"

Mr. Abernethy made a little attempt to ridicule the proposed organization, in moving to amend the resolution recommending three justices of the peace and three constables. We are now in receipt of an explanation from the governor in reference to the question of an independent government, as debated at the Lyceum, which we give *verbatim*, as it places the governor with his own explanation on that question, and I think gives us the correct statement of the case, and shows his policy, which was, to defeat not only the proposition for an independent government, but any effort for a provisional one, for at least four years,—which were not only the views of Mr. Abernethy, but those of Messrs. Lee, Leslie, Babcock, and Hines:—

PORTLAND, March 11, 1866.

DEAR SIR,—Allow me to correct one statement in your History of Oregon in the *Gazette* of 5th March. You speak of a debate in a Lyceum, and say: "Mr. Abernethy moved that in case our government did not extend its jurisdiction over the country in four years, that then the meeting would be in favor of an independent government." The facts are these: We had weekly meetings for discussion. Mr. Hastings, Dr. McLaughlin's lawyer, offered a resolution, "That it is expedient for the settlers on this coast to establish an independent government." This subject was warmly discussed, Mr. Abernethy being, with a few others, opposed to it. At the close of the discussion the vote was taken and decided in favor of an independent government. Mr. Abernethy then offered the following: "*Resolved*, That if the United States extends its jurisdiction over this country within four years, it will not be expedient to form an independent government," as the subject for the next discussion. This was warmly discussed, many who voted for the first resolution saying if the United States government is extended over us, it is all we want, and voted in the affirmative. The resolution was carried, and destroyed the effect of the first resolution.

You will see by this you have the thing all wrong.

Yours truly, GEO. ABERNETHY.

P. S.—Dr. White, I think, was present; am not certain. This independent government move was a prominent scheme of Dr. McLaughlin.

The main question at issue before the committee at the Falls meeting was the office of governor. Dr. Bailey was in the Sandwich Islands; nothing was to be feared from him; but Dr. White was, to say the least, an impudent candidate. I have been informed that Dr. Bailey, an Englishman, came to that meeting February 18, 1841, with all his French voters trained to vote for himself for governor, and that he nominated himself, in opposition to Mr. Hines and Dr. Babcock, for that office, and conducted himself in such a manner that it disgusted some, and was the means of breaking up the proposed civil government, as what Americans there were then in the country found they would be outnumbered by the French and English (which was unquestionably the fact), and thus they would be completely at the disposal of English rule.

Such being the case, much credit is due to the men who defeated that effort, and I see no reason why Mr. Hines, in his account, and as an actor in those meetings, should attempt to give a different impression, and say that "the officers of the squadron were consulted, and were found to be decidedly opposed to the scheme."

(Page 421 of his book.) This fact alone, and I have it from an actor and an eye-witness in the meeting referred to, is, to say the least, strange and unaccountable on the part of Mr. Hines. He either feared the influence of Bailey, or the truth, which he withheld in the case, and leaves a wrong impression upon the minds of his readers.

From the sickening, fawning, and contemptible course of Dr. White, the committee at the Falls meeting were induced to yield the point of an organization without an executive head, and by that means got a unanimous vote to call a public meeting to organize a provisional government at Champoeg, on the 2d of May, 1843. This was effort number one of February and June, 1841, over again. Those of us who commenced this move did not feel that we had gained much, still we hoped for the best and prepared for the worst as well as the meeting at Champoeg on the 2d of May, 1843.

We will let the provisional government rest till the 2d of May, 1843, while we take a look over the whole country, and at the actors in it, first stopping to drop a tear at the grave of our friends as we proceed. On the 2d of February our best and most esteemed friend, Cornelius Rogers, with whom we had spent years of the kindest confidence and friendship, left our house for Oregon City, as his future residence and home, with his young wife, the eldest daughter of Rev. David Leslie, and her youngest sister. They took passage down the river with W. W. Raymond, a man who came to the country with the re-enforcement of the mission of 1839–40. He was at that time a member of the Methodist Mission, in good standing. Dr. Elijah White and Esquire Crocker, of Lansingville, Tompkins County, New York, were also in the canoe, one of the largest of Chinook manufacturing. They arrived all safe at Canemah. It was let down stern first by a line, around a point of rocks just above the falls on the Oregon City side, since blasted away for a canal and boat channel. In the eddy formed by the point of rock a large tree had lodged, forming a convenient landing, and occupying a large portion of the eddy water, so that it was necessary for the canoe to remain close to the log for safety from the swift current. There were two Indians to guide the canoe into this landing, one in the bow and one in the stern. The one in the stern escaped by jumping from the canoe and catching upon a piece of drift-wood on a rock just above the fall. White, as the canoe came alongside of the log upon which all were to land, being near the bow of the canoe, and not thinking, or perhaps caring, for any one but himself, jumped upon the side of the canoe, and with a spring, upon the log, before there was time for any one to secure the bow of the canoe, to prevent it from swinging into the current. The force of White's spring upon the canoe to reach the log threw it into the current, which was too strong for Raymond and his Indians to hold, and in a moment it darted into the middle of the channel, and the next moment was plunged broadside over the falls, some twenty-five feet perpendicular. The force of the current threw the canoe to the bottom of the fall, right side up, but the under-swell threw it back to the sheet of falling water, which filled and upset the canoe in an instant. All that went over were lost. Raymond, who had attempted to hold the canoe, came over the point of rocks (a difficult place) and found White upon the log, and that he had made no effort to relieve the drowning party.

Mr. Hines, I see, gives a more favorable account of this transaction for White. I think this the nearest correct, as Raymond gave the alarm, and a boat was launched, and reached within ten feet of Mr. Rogers before he sank to rise no more. His and Esquire Crocker's bodies were found and interred. Those of Mrs. Rogers and her sister were never found. Rev. G. Hines, W. H. Gray, and Robert Shortess, were appointed by Judge Babcock to appraise the estate of Mr. Rogers, which was found to be worth about $800, clear of all liabilities. His heirs at law resided in Utica, New York. Rev. Harvey Clark was appointed administrator, discharging that duty faithfully, and I think without compensation. None of the appraisers received a dime for their services. There followed this affliction a severe storm, and an unusually high flood in the Wallamet River. The appraisers were detained several days on account of it, but finally reached their homes in safety.

The Methodist Mission had extended their stations to Fort Nasqualla on Puget Sound and Clatsop Plains, and made an effort to establish a mission station on the Umpqua River. At this last-named place the Indians had been prepared by the instructions they had received through the Hudson's Bay Company and the Jesuit priests to destroy Lee and Hines, and commence the slaughter of the settlement. (See Hines' account of the trip, pages 100 to 110 inclusive, made in 1842.)

Messrs. Frost and Cowan had become disgusted with their missionary calling, and Rev. Dr. Richmond had also found his Nasqualla location not a suitable one, or at least, he by some means had become convinced that he could not benefit the Indians about the fort, and made up his mind to leave.

It will be remembered that Vicar-General Brouillet, of Wallawalla, in his attempt to prove that the "Catholic stations and stationary priests" were early in the country, says "almost every Indian tribe possessed some Catholic members" as early as 1840, and that Mr. Demerse's labors among the Cayuses in 1840 "had made there a mission so fruitful that the Protestant missionaries had got alarmed and feared that all their disciples would abandon them if he continued his mission among them." (Page 87 of "Protestantism in Oregon," by Brouillet.) Neither Hines, Richmond, nor Smith could understand why it was that the Indians upon this coast and throughout the country were so different from the accounts they had heard and read of them up to 1840. In June, 1853, had either of those gentlemen picked up the New York *Freeman's Journal*, they would have seen the statement that, as early as 1840, "almost every Indian tribe [on this coast] possessed some Catholic members." A little further along they would have been startled with the announcement, that these Jesuit missions had become "so fruitful that the Protestant missionaries had got alarmed and feared that all their disciples would abandon them." This was but the work of two years,—from 1838, late in the fall, to 1840. This was, without doubt, a great triumph, and well does this Jesuit blow his trumpet; and well he may, for he had the active aid of an unscrupulous monopoly who are said to be attempting the same thing with just such implements upon their own countrymen in British Columbia. Why, I ask, have states and countries in Europe found it necessary to suppress that order of the Roman Church? And why is England, to-day, hesitating to give this church in particular the same confidence she does to all others?

CHAPTER XXXV.

Meetings to oppose organization.—Address of the French-Canadians.—Criticisms on it by the author.—The Jesuits.—Jesuit oath.—Article from the Cincinnati *Beacon*.

BETWEEN the meeting of the committee of twelve at Wallamet Falls, about the 16th of March, and the called meeting by that committee on the 2d of May, the priests and the Hudson's Bay Company were not idle. They held two distinct meetings, one at the falls and one at Vancouver, and two in the French Prairie at the Catholic church. At all of these meetings the course to be pursued by the company and the Catholic and French settlers was discussed and decided. The result of these meetings and discussions can be found on the 12th and 13th pages of the Oregon archives. The names of the signers should have been given. This document seems to be dated the 4th of March, 1843. The meeting at Gervais' was on the first Monday of March. So this document seems to have been prepared by our Jesuit Blanchet, just about the time the "wolf meeting" was convening, and in anticipation of the move for a provisional government. I am certain it was not before any public meeting of the settlers, and that it was handed in to the committee of three appointed by the Legislative Committee to revise and arrange the laws for the meeting on the 5th of July, 1843.

G. W. Le Breton, clerk of the Legislative Committee, handed it in, when it was examined by the committee of three, and handed back to him with the remark "it was well enough to keep it with the public papers, as it would show the influences operating, and who were opposed to our organization, and the reasons they had for their opposition. At the meeting of May 2, all the signers of that document were present with their priests at their head, and voted to a man against the proposed organization.

"Address of the Canadian citizens of Oregon to the meeting at Champoeg, March 4, 1843." It will be seen it should have been dated May 2. This mistake simply shows that it was prepared March 4, 1843, in anticipation of the action of the meeting to be held May 2, 1843.

The address above referred to is here submitted as a matter of history, and is as follows:—

"We, the Canadian citizens of Wallamet, considering with interest and reflection the subject which unites the people at the present meeting, present to the American citizens, and particularly to the gentlemen who called said meeting, the unanimous expression of our sentiments of cordiality, and desire of union and inexhaustible peace between all the people, in view of our duty and the interest of the new colony, and declare—

"1st. That we wish for laws, or regulations, for the welfare of our persons, and the security of our property and labors.

"2d. That we do not intend to rebel against the measures of that kind taken last year, by a party of the people; although we do not approve of certain regulations, nor certain modes of laws, let those magistrates finish their time.

"3d. That we will not address a new petition to the government of the United States, because we have our reasons, till the line be decided, and the frontiers of the States fixed.

"4th. That we are opposed to the regulations anticipated, and exposed to consequences for the quantity, direction, etc., of lands, and whatsoever expense for the same lands, because we have no direct guaranty from the government to come, and, perhaps, to-morrow, all those measures may be broken.

"5th. That we do not wish a provisional mode of government, too self-interested, and full of degrees, useless to our power, and overloading the colony instead of improving it; besides, men of laws and science are too scarce, and have too much to do in such a new country.

"6th. That we wish either the mode of senate or council to judge the difficulties, punish the crimes (except capital penalties), and make the regulations suitable for the people.

"7th. That the same council be elected and composed of members from all parts of the country, and should act in body, on the plan of civilized countries in parliament, or as a jury, and to be represented, for example, by the president of said council, and another member, as a judge of peace, in each county, allowing the principle of recalling to the whole senate.

"8th. That the members should be influenced to interest themselves to their own welfare, and that of the public, by the love of doing good, rather than by the hope of gain, in order to take off from the esteem of the people all suspicions of interest in the persons of their representatives.

"9th. That they must avoid every law loading and inexpedient to the people, especially to the new arrivals. Unnecessary taxes, and whatever records are of that kind, we do not want them.

"10th. That the militia is useless at present, and rather a danger of bad suspicion to the Indians and a delay for the necessary labors; at the same time, it is a load; we do not want it, either, at present.

"11th. That we consider the country free, at present, to all nations, till government shall have decided; open to every individual wishing to settle, without any distinction of origin, and without asking him any thing, either to become an English, Spanish, or American citizen.

"12th. So we, English subjects, proclaim to be free, as well as those who came from France, California, United States, or even natives of this country; and we desire unison with all the respectable citizens who wish to settle in this country; or we ask to be recognized as free among ourselves, to make such regulations as appear suitable to our wants, save the general interest of having justice from all strangers who might injure us, and that our reasonable customs and pretensions be respected.

"13th. That we are willing to submit to any lawful government when it comes.

"14th. That we do not forget that we must make laws only for necessary circumstances. The more laws there are, the more opportunities for roguery for those who make a practice of it; and, perhaps, the more alterations there will be some day.

"15th. That we do not forget in a trial that before all fraud on fulfilling of some points of the law, the ordinary proofs of the certainty of the fact ought to be duly weighed, so that justice may be done, and no shame given for fraud.

"16th. In a new country the more men employed and paid by the public, the less remains of industry.

"17th. That no one can be more desirous than we are for the prosperity, ameliorations, and general peace of the country, and especially for the guaranty of our rights and liberties; and such is the wish we make for all those who are, or may become, our fellow-countrymen, etc., for long years of peace."

Then follow our names and persons.

Which, if our memory is correct, were not given or signed to the original document, for, if they had been, the document would have been noticed in the legislative proceedings, and some action taken upon it. It was considered by the revising committee, as an expression of the feelings of the subjects named in the twelfth paragraph, and that while they were opposed to the proposed organization they would act as per thirteenth paragraph. The second paragraph indicates an approval of previous political action. The third, their opposition to a connection with the United States. The fourth, their decided opposition to the proposed government. The fifth is a reason, and shows that they had no confidence in the ability of the people to make laws for themselves.

The sixth indicates a preference for the Hudson's Bay Company's mode of government. The seventh shows a leaning to republican ideas of government. The eighth to the government of the country by the clergymen in it. The ninth, opposition to taxes which the French, or the class represented in that protest, continually manifested in refusing to pay until compelled by legal or superior force. The tenth shows that they considered themselves safe from Indian hostility, and were only anxious to expose the weakness of the settlement by avoiding a show of military strength. The eleventh affirms the freedom of the country to all, and their right to occupy it without interference. The fourteenth, a childish reason against restraint. The fifteenth is considerably mixed; it is advisory. We admit that the object of it is beyond our comprehension. The sixteenth looks to one man, or clerical rule. The seventeenth shows the ecclesiastical origin of the document, and a suspicion that in the future their conduct may be such that they may require a "guaranty" of their rights and liberties.

We have an article, published in the Cincinnati *Beacon*, August, 1843, giving the oath taken by the Jesuits, and a short account of their objects and proceedings, which, as they had been introduced into Oregon by the Hudson's Bay Company in 1838, and commenced their operations as in the above document, we will copy the article entire, as we shall have occasion to speak of the part taken by them in the settlement of this country:—

"The order of Jesuits was established by Loyola in 1535, having for its object the re-establishment of the pope's sway over the civil powers of the earth.

"At that time it was found that a mighty effort was needed to regain to the pope what he had just lost by the Reformation, and this order was established for that object. Members of that society may be of any profession or of no profession, as they choose, and as best suits the object. They may prosecute their own business as merchants in foreign countries, or serve in the meanest capacity, provided they can by stealth exercise some destructive influence on any or every form of government except that under the 'sacred confirmation of the pope.'

"A dispensation is granted them, *i. e.*, permission to lay aside all professions of regard to the Papal cause, and make outward professions to any religion or government they choose, if by so doing they can better 'do their utmost to EXTIRPATE *the heretical Protestant doctrine, and destroy all its pretended powers*, REGAL *or otherwise*.'

"Of course they were soon found in all the political intrigues which so long distracted Europe. This is a prominent fact on the page of history. One after another of the European powers became aware of this, and each, especially of the Protestant powers, when their intrigues could no longer be endured, banished the Jesuits as seen above. We may add Oregon as another spècial field of their operations since 1838.

"The Jesuits are the most active and efficient agents of Popery in propagating the Catholic religion in foreign countries. In the following oath we notice:—

"1. An acknowledgment that Protestant governments are illegal, without the 'sacred confirmation' of the pope, and may safely be destroyed.

"2. A renunciation of 'any allegiance as due to any heretical' state, named Protestants.

"3. A solemn pledge to do their utmost to 'destroy all their pretended powers, regal or otherwise.'

"Comment on the relations which these agents of the pope sustain to our Protestant government is needless.

"*The Oath of Secrecy of the Jesuits.*

"'I, A. B., now in the presence of Almighty God, the blessed Virgin Mary, the blessed Michael the Archangel, the blessed St. John Baptist, the holy apostles St. Peter and St. Paul, and the saints and sacred hosts of heaven, and of you my ghostly father, do declare from my heart, *without mental reservation*, that his holiness the Pope Urban is Christ's vicar-general, and is the true and only head of the Catholic or Universal Church throughout the earth; and that, by the virtue of the keys of binding and loosing given to his holiness by my Saviour Jesus Christ, he hath power to depose heretical kings, princes, states, commonwealths, and governments, all being illegal without his sacred confirm ation, and thatthey may safely be destroyed; therefore, to th eutmost of my power, I shall and will defend this doctrine, and his holiness' rights and customs, against all usurpers of the heretical (or Protestant) authority whatsoever; especially against the now pretended authority and Church of England, and all adherents, in regard that they and she be usurpal and heretical, opposing the sacred mother church of Rome. I do renounce and disown any allegiance as due to any heretical king, prince, or *state*, named Protestant, or *obedience to any of their inferior magistrates or officers.* I do further declare, that the doctrine of the Church of England, of the Calvinists, Huguenots, and of others of the name of Protestant, to be damnable, and they themselves are damned, and to be damned, that will not forsake the same; I do further declare, that I will help, assist, and advise all or any of his holiness' agents in any place wherever I shall be, in England, Scotland, and Ireland, or in any other territory or kingdom I shall come to, and do my utmost to extirpate the heretical Protestant doctrine, *and to destroy all its pretended powers, regal or otherwise.* I do further promise and declare, that notwithstanding I am dispensed with, to assume any religion heretical, for the propagating of the mother church's interests, to keep secret and private all her agents' counsels from time to time, as they intrust me, and not to divulge, directly or indirectly, by word, writing, or circumstance whatsoever; but to execute all that shall be proposed, given in charge, or discovered unto me, by you, my ghostly father, or any of this sacred convent. All which I, A. B., do swear, by the blessed Trinity, and blessed Sacrament, which I am now to receive, to perform, and on my part to keep inviolably: and do call all the heavenly and glorious host of heaven to witness these my real intentions, to keep this my oath. In testimony hereof, I take this most holy and blessed sacrament of the Eucharist; and witness the same further with my hand and seal, in the face of this holy convent, this day of Anno Domini, etc.'

"The Jesuits were banished from England in 1606. They were expelled from France, A. D. 1764; from Spain and Sicily, A. D. 1767; from Portugal, A. D. 1789; and totally suppressed by Pope Clement XIV., A. D. 1773. Everywhere they were prosecuted and repelled as injurious to youth, and dangerous to all existing forms of government. The present pope has revived the order, and now we find the Jesuits secretly and openly engaged again in their pernicious and wicked devices to re-establish his power in the United States, and in the Canadas."

CHAPTER XXXVI.

The meeting at Champoeg.—Tactics of the Jesuit party.—Counter-tactics of the Americans.—A division and its result.—Public record.—Opposition to clergymen as legislators.—Mr. Hines as an historian.—His errors.—Importance of Mr. Hines' history.—Extract.—Difficulty among the Indians.—Cause of the difficulty.

THE 2d of May, the day fixed by the committee of twelve to organize a settlers' government, was close at hand. The Indians had all learned that the "Bostons" were going to have a big meeting, and they also knew that the English and French were going to meet with them, to oppose what the "Bostons" were going to do. The Hudson's Bay Company had drilled and trained their voters for the occasion, under the Rev. F. N. Blanchet and his priests, and they were promptly on the ground in the open field near a small house, and, to the amusement of every American present, trained to vote "No" to every motion put; no matter, if to carry their point they should have voted "Yes," it was "No." Le Breton had informed the committee, and the Americans generally, that this would be the course pursued, according to instructions, hence our motions were made to test their knowledge of what they were doing, and we found just what we expected was the case. The priest was not prepared for our manner of meeting them, and, as the record shows, "considerable confusion was existing in consequence." By this time we had counted votes. Says Le Breton, "We can risk it; let us divide and count." "I second that motion," says Gray. "Who's for a divide?" sang out old Joe Meek, as he stepped out; "all for the report of the committee and an organization, follow me." This was so sudden and unexpected that the priest and his voters did not know what to do, but every American was soon in line. Le Breton and Gray passed the line and counted fifty-two Americans, and but fifty French and Hudson's Bay Company men. They announced the count —"fifty-two for, and fifty against." "Three cheers for our side," sang out old Joe Meek. Not one of those old veteran mountain voices were lacking in that shout for *liberty*. They were given with a will, and in a few seconds the chairman, Judge I. L. Babcock, called the meeting to order, when the priest and his band slunk away into the corners of the fences, and in a short time mounted their horses and left.

The minutes of the meeting are as follows:—

"At a public meeting of the inhabitants of the Wallamet settlements, held in accordance with the call of the committee, chosen at a former meeting, for the purpose of taking steps to organize themselves into a civil community, and provide themselves with the protection secured by the enforcement of law and order, Dr. I. L. Babcock was chosen chairman, and Messrs. Gray, Le Breton, and Wilson, secretaries.

"The committee made their report, which was read, and a motion was made that it be accepted, which was lost.

"Considerable confusion existing in consequence, it was moved by Mr. Le Breton, and seconded by Mr. Gray, that the meeting divide, preparatory to being counted; those in favor of the objects of this meeting taking the right, and those of a contrary mind taking the left, which being carried by acclamation, and a majority being found in favor of organization, the greater part of the dissenters withdrew.

"It was then moved and carried, that the report of the committee be taken up and disposed of article by article.

"A motion was made and carried, that a supreme judge, with probate powers, be chosen to officiate in this community.

"Moved and carried, that a clerk of the court, or recorder, be chosen.

"Moved and carried, that a sheriff be chosen.

"Moved and carried, that three magistrates be chosen.

"Moved and carried, that three constables be chosen.

"Moved and carried, that a committee of nine persons be chosen, for the purpose of drafting a code of laws for the government of this community, to be presented to a public meeting to be hereafter called by them, for their acceptance.

"A motion was made and carried, that a treasurer be chosen.

"Moved and carried, that a major and three captains be chosen.

"Moved and carried, that we now proceed to choose the persons to fill the various offices by ballot.

"A. E. Wilson was chosen to act as supreme judge, with probate powers; G. W. Le Breton was chosen to act as clerk of court, and recorder; J. L. Meek was chosen to fill the office of sheriff; W. H. Wilson was chosen treasurer.

"Moved and carried, that the remainder of the officers be chosen by hand ballot, and nomination from the floor.

"Messrs. Hill, Shortess, Newell, Beers, Hubbard, Gray, O'Neil, Moore, and Dougherty, were chosen to act as Legislative Committee; Messrs. Burns, Judson, and A. B. Smith were chosen to act as magistrates; Messrs. Ebbets, Bridgers, and Lewis, were chosen to act as constables; Mr. John Howard was chosen major; Messrs. Wm. McCarty, C. McRoy, and S. Smith were chosen captains.

"Moved and carried, that the Legislative Committee make their report on the 5th day of July next, at Champoeg.

"Moved and carried, that the services of the Legislative Committee be paid for at $1.25 per day, and that the money be raised by subscription.

"Moved and carried, that the major and captains be instructed to enlist men to form companies of mounted riflemen.

"Moved and carried, that an additional constable and magistrate be chosen.

"Mr. Compo was chosen as an additional magistrate. Mr. Matthew was chosen as an additional constable.

"Moved and carried, that the Legislative Committee shall not sit over six days.

"The meeting was then adjourned.

"The question having arisen with regard to what time the newly-appointed officers should commence their duties, the meeting was again called to order, when it was moved and carried, that the old officers act till the laws are made and accepted, or until the next public meeting.

"Attest,
"G. W. Le Breton."

It will be remembered by those present, that in the appointment of the members of the Legislative Committee, Rev. J. S. Griffin was named as one of the committee. I am not positive that Mr. Griffin was present, but I remember that his nomination was opposed, or any clergyman of any denomination having any thing to do with making laws for the settlers. It was stated as a reason, that their duties and calling were not such as qualified them to enact laws adapted to a promiscuous community; they, as a matter of conscience and duty to what they, as a general thing, considered higher laws, disqualified themselves to enter the halls of legislation as law-makers. Besides, the settlers had once placed it in their hands and requested them to aid in the enactment of suitable laws for the government and protection of the settlement. This request they had neglected and refused to comply with, and we had before us the example and influence of one who had openly opposed our effort. In placing upon this committee a reverend gentleman from one denomination, we, as a matter of courtesy, must do the same to another, and, as in the former case, we would be liable to be defeated. Mr. Griffin did not receive a single vote, without it was that of the Rev. Mr. Kone, from Clatsop, who, I think, was present.

We will now leave the Legislative Committee to do their business, as per instructions, and see what our very officious Indian agent and his friend, Rev. Mr. Hines, are about.

During the fall of 1842 and winter and spring of 1843, "our plot thickens." We must go back a little, and notice, among other things, that as soon as Uncle Samuel's exploring squadron had looked at Oregon a little and Dr. McLaughlin's good liquors more (when the infirmities of the stomach required something stronger than water), and had found occasion to express great praise of the kind treatment and generosity of the Hudson's Bay Company, they also found it convenient to sanction the opposition to a temporary government for the settlement,—at least, Mr. Hines tells us they opposed it,—and leave the company to continue their kicking and changing the bushel, calling in their cattle and pay for all lost, and enter vigorously upon a settled system of opposition to all American settlements in the country. Their Jesuit missions were doing them good service in the interior. Their clerks and interpreters were ready to do their part. The puff-ball of folly and ignorance, in the shape of a sub-Indian agent, had been among the Indians, who were made to believe from his foolish statements,—confirmed or made worse by such old liars as Toupin, as in the case of Parker,—that the great parent was going to make them wise and rich, and give them all they wanted, if they would adopt his advice, and do as he wished them. All things combined, aroused Mr. Hines to the solemn conclusion that it was his duty to volunteer and go with our sub-Indian agent, and assist him in pacifying the Indians. I suppose he must have gone in the capacity of prime minister or secretary of state. He says, page 146: "In the evening of the 17th, Dr. White arrived at my house, bringing intelligence from the falls." Le Breton returned the next day, and reported that Anderson's horse was stolen by an Indian,—the same that had stolen one from Mr. Hines two years before. Hines had the courage to go and get his horse, but Anderson, who was a Swede, had not. This transaction, it will be remembered, was on April 17, a month after the organizing committee of twelve had been appointed at Gervais'. White and Hines are in council at Hines' house. The visit to the interior tribes is before the council. White had been up among the Nez Percés and Cayuses in the fall of 1842, and with the aid of McKay (who was the most reliable half-native servant the company ever had), the Indians were induced to form a combination, exactly such a one as Frank Ermatinger, in 1838, told the writer the company would form, with the aid of their half-breed servants, to resist the occupancy of the country by the American government. Mr. Hines' stupidity led him to believe this was the policy of White, and not that of the company. He says, at the bottom of page 142:

"It had been the policy of the Hudson's Bay Company to destroy the chieftainship, cut the different tribes into small clans, and divide their interests as far as possible, so as to weaken them, and render them incapable of injuring the whites, thus preventing them from acting in concert." At the time this policy was adopted by the company there were no whites in the country but themselves. Mr. Hines believes that the American settlement was to be benefited by this shrewd policy of the company, and attributes to Dr. White the opposite policy. He says, page 143, that "the sub-agent adopted a different policy."

How natural and how easy for his reverence to fall into this error, and to say, on page 142, "Thomas McKay contributed much to allay the excitement among them, and, in connection with the sub-agent, induced the natives to adopt a code of laws and appoint a head chief, and inferior chiefs, sufficient to carry the laws into execution." Not the least suspicion of McKay's instructions and the Hudson's Bay Company's arrangements and consent in the matter, and that the sub-agent was the very man the company was making use of to get their own trained and educated Indian (Ellis) at the head of the Nez Percé tribe, to accomplish the object they had in view. Mr. Hines has given us a good history, for which we thank him in behalf of truth, and also for the assistance it has given us in showing to the world the damning policy, the accursed influences brought to bear against the little band of patriots that had the courage to contend against such fearful combinations of avarice, stupidity, superstition, and savagism; and here allow me to say, is the reason that Whitman, Harvey Clark, Shortess, Smith, Cornelius Rogers, J. L. Meek, Couch, and fifty others, had no confidence in White or his advisers and friends.

Le Breton acted well his part; the company knew him better than Mr. Hines did; his death was a victory, as they supposed, to them, but the effort moved on. The act of a few Indians, in going to St. Louis in 1832, for religious knowledge, brought Mr. Hines to the country with others more capable of meeting the combined influences of avarice, stupidity, bigotry, and superstition.

And although many things have combined to keep them from any pecuniary reward, still facts, and the history of the country they have saved as the golden gem of our great Republic, will seek to know who it was whose efforts could successfully contend with such influences as were then held by the company, the Jesuit priests, Dr. White, and the Methodist Mission. We now know why our little settlement wept and mourned the death of Rogers, Le Breton, and Whitman, as they were substantial pillars in our temple of liberty on this coast. Does a simple slab mark the place of their rest? Their surviving associates are not able to answer in the affirmative.

It will be borne in mind that while Dr. Whitman was on his way to Washington, Dr. White and Thomas McKay visited the Indians in the interior, in October, 1842,—about one month after Dr. Whitman had left for the States. Mr. Spalding was really more stupid than Mr. Hines in all matters of policy and deep-laid plans to accomplish any object. His courage was strong in ignorance of danger. Mr. Hines had personal courage, but his self-esteem was unbounded. Dr. White was shrewd enough to make use of both. Mr. Spalding was taken with Dr. White's smooth milk-and-water false statements about his office, powers, and duties. He was led to believe that White had all the powers he professed to have, and lent his influence to McKay to organize and combine the Indian tribes, supposing all the while he was doing it for Dr. White and the American cause.

Messrs. Hines and Spalding were alike in this particular. The reader will not forget that I am speaking of men and their actions, and the influence they had at a certain time, and the effect of those actions upon the Indians and the religious, political, and general interests of the country. Personally, I have no malice against a single man of whom I write; many of them I know are dead, and at the proper time I will give you as faithful an account of their good deeds as I now do of their errors. Besides, I hope the children and friends of all of whom I write, will see and feel the virtue there is in doing right at all times, and, as we are told, "try the spirits," or persons, "to know whether they are good or evil."

A large portion of the ninth chapter of Mr. Hines' book is too important in illustrating truth to be omitted in a history such as we are giving. The reader will understand the observations we have to make, bearing in mind that all these facts have an important bearing on a transaction that occurred four years later. He says:—

"April 14. This settlement has been thrown into a panic by intelligence which has just been received from the upper country, concerning the hostile intentions of the Cayuse, Nez Percé, and Wallawalla Indians. It appears that they have again threatened the destruction of the whites. Some time in October last, Indian report said that these tribes were coming down to kill off the 'Boston' people, meaning those from the United States. This intelligence produced considerable excitement at the time, and induced the sub-agent of Indian affairs to go directly to the upper country and ascertain the truth of the report, and, if possible, settle all matters of difficulty. On arriving among the Indians, he ascertained that the report was not without foundation, but entered into such arrangements with them as appeared to give satisfaction. Thomas McKay contributed much to allay the excitement among them, and, in connection with the sub-agent, induced the Nez Percés to adopt a code of laws, and appoint a head chief and inferior chiefs, sufficient to carry the laws into execution.

"It had been the policy of the Hudson's Bay Company to destroy the chieftainship, cut the different tribes into smaller clans, and divide their interests as far as possible, so as to weaken them, and render them incapable of injuring the whites, by preventing them from acting in concert. BUT THE SUB-AGENT ADOPTED A DIFFERENT POLICY. *The individual appointed to the high chieftainship over the Nez Percés was one Ellis, as he was called by the English, who, having spent several years in the settlement on Red River, east of the mountains, had, with a smattering of the English language, acquired a high sense of his own importance; and, consequently, after he was appointed chief, pursued a very haughty and overbearing course.* The fulfillment of the laws which the agent recommended for their adoption was required by Ellis with the utmost rigor. Individuals were severely punished for crimes which, from time immemorial, had been committed by the people with impunity. This occasioned suspicions in the minds of the Indians generally that the whites designed the ultimate subjugation of their tribes. They saw in the laws they had adopted, a deep-laid scheme of the whites to destroy them, and take possession of their country. The arrival of a large party of emigrants about this time, and the sudden departure of Dr. Whitman to the United States, with the avowed intention of bringing back with him as many as he could enlist for Oregon, served to hasten them to the above conclusion. That a great excitement existed among the Indians in the interior, and that they designed to make war upon the settlement, was only known to the whites through the medium of vague report, until a letter was received from H. K. W. Perkins, at the Dalles, in which he informed us that the Wascopum and Wallawalla Indians had communicated to him in substance the following information: That the Indians are very much exasperated against the whites, in consequence of so many of the latter coming into the country, to destroy their game and take away their lands; that the Nez Percés dispatched one of their chiefs last winter on snow-shoes, to visit the Indians in the buffalo country east of Fort Hall, for the purpose of exciting them to cut off the party that it is expected Dr. Whitman will bring back with him to settle the Nez Percé country; that the Indians are endeavoring to form a general coalition for the purpose of destroying all the 'Boston' people; that it is not good to kill a part of them, and leave the rest, but that *every one* of them must be destroyed. This information produced a great excitement throughout the community, and almost every man had a plan of his own by which to avert the impending storm. In the estimation of some, the Indians were to be upon us immediately, and it was unsafe to retire at night, for fear the settlement would be attacked before morning. The plan of the agent was to induce men to pledge themselves, under the forfeiture of one hundred dollars in case of delinquency, to keep constantly on hand and ready for use either a good musket or rifle, and one hundred charges of ammunition, and to hold themselves in readiness to go at the call of the agent to any part of the country, not to exceed two days' travel, for the purpose of defending the settlement, and repelling any savage invaders. This plan pleased some of the people, and they put down their names; but many were much dissatisfied with it; and as we had no authority, no law, no order, for the time being, in the country, it was impossible to tell what would be the result, if the Indians should attempt to carry their threats into execution."

We have before us, in these quotations, the facts of the change of policy of the Hudson's Bay Company, the combining of the Nez Percé tribe, the supposed ground of complaint against the Americans, and the failure of the sub-Indian agent to get the settlers to adopt his plan for protecting the settlement against the Indians. We will now give the reasons the company had for adopting the dividing and cutting-up policy among the Indians.

The reader is requested to observe Mr. Hines' description of Ellis, Dr. White's Indian chief. It was this same Indian that drove the Rev. A. B. Smith in 1840 from his land, as stated by old Toupin on 15th page of Brouillet's history of the Whitman massacre. Up to this time he was not considered an important character by the company, on account of his self-importance and insolence. In this respect he resembled Tawatowe, of the Cayuses, who, when he had been promoted to the head chieftainship of that tribe, became insolent, and going so far as to get possession of Fort Wallawalla, had tied Mr. P. C. Pambrun, and kept him tied till he agreed to give the Indians better prices for their horses and furs. As soon as they had liberated him, Mr. Pambrun made a few trades with them and treated them kindly, and induced them to leave the fort. He sent at once to Vancouver and increased the number of his men, and told the chiefs that had had him tied, that he no longer regarded them as chiefs, and at once commenced to destroy their influence by refusing to give them the accustomed presents, and gave them to lesser chiefs, and in that way divided them up and broke their power as principal chiefs.

While the American fur trader, Captain Wyeth, was in the country, the company had increased their tariff, and paid the Indians more for their horses and furs, but as soon as he had been driven from the country, they reduced it to their own prices. The Indians did not understand why the company gave them so much less than the Americans, or Bostons, did for the same things.

The principal chiefs of the Nez Percés and Cayuses were together in the attempt to get better pay for the property they sold to the company, whose policy was to keep all the principal men down, and divide their power and influence, and prevent any large combinations among the tribes,—thus making it easy to control them. This statement of facts and policy I had from Mr. Pambrun and Mr. Ermatinger, both of the Hudson's Bay Company.

Mr. Hines, on page 143, in speaking about the laws adopted by the Indians, seems altogether to ignore the fact that a desperate effort was then being made by the Hudson's Bay Company, as the conduct of the Indians plainly indicated, to drive all Americans from the country. The unreasonable punishments inflicted, and all other odious inferences, were the legitimate instruments to accomplish a specific object. The same was the case in the inferences drawn about Dr. Whitman's visit to the States. While Governor Simpson sends on his Red River settlers, and goes to Washington to secure the country to the British crown, Dr. Whitman and his mission become the special objects of misrepresentation and hate among the Indians. His mill and all his grain are burned, while a large immigration of British subjects and the Jesuit missionaries are received with open arms. Dr. Whitman and the American settlement must be stopped at all hazards. "An Indian is sent on snow-shoes to the Buffalo Indians east of Fort Hall, for the purpose of exciting them to cut off the party that is expected with Dr. Whitman.

The American government, according to Dr. White, is about to take possession of the country, and had sent him out as its first governor. He, to conciliate the Indians, adopts all the suggestions of the Hudson's Bay Company, and succeeds to his entire satisfaction, with the aid of Mr. McKay. While he can do nothing to unite the settlers for their own defense, the divide-and-weaken policy of the company is changed from Indians to the American settlers. White and Hines are equally useful to the company in doing the one, as they had been successful in the other. That the transaction related by Mr. Hines on his 145th page, under date of April 17, may be better understood, we will, in the next chapter, give a copy of the petition referred to. This document is mostly the work of Robert Shortess, and was signed by nearly every American in the country who had an opportunity.

CHAPTER XXXVII.

Whitman's visit to Washington.—A priest's boast.—A taunt, and Whitman's reply.—Arrival in Washington.—Interview with Secretary Webster.—With President Tyler.—His return.—Successful passage of the Rocky Mountains with two hundred wagons.—His mill burned during his absence.

In September, 1842, Dr. Whitman was called to visit a patient at old Fort Wallawalla. While there, a number of boats of the Hudson's Bay Company, with several chief traders and Jesuit priests, on their way to the interior of the country, arrived. While at dinner, the overland express from Canada arrived, bringing news that the emigration from the Red River settlement was at Colville. This news excited unusual joy among the guests. One of them—a young priest—sang out: "Hurrah for Oregon, America is too late; we have got the country." "Now the Americans may whistle; the country is ours!" said another.

Whitman learned that the company had arranged for these Red River English settlers to come on to settle in Oregon, and at the same time Governor Simpson was to go to Washington and secure the settlement of the question as to the boundaries, on the ground of the most numerous and permanent settlement in the country.

The Doctor was taunted with the idea that no power could prevent this result, as no information could reach Washington in time to prevent it. "It shall be prevented," said the Doctor, "if I have to go to Washington myself." "But you can not go there to do it," was the taunting reply of the Briton. "I will see," was the Doctor's reply. The reader is sufficiently acquainted with the history of this man's toil and labor in bringing his first wagon through to Fort Boise, to understand what he meant when he said, "*I will see.*" Two hours after this conversation at the fort, he dismounted from his horse at his door at Wailatpu. I saw in a moment that he was fixed on some important object or errand. He soon explained that a special effort must be made to save the country from becoming British territory.

Every thing was in the best of order about the station, and there seemed to be no important reason why he should not go. A. L. Lovejoy, Esq., had a few days before arrived with the immigration. It was proposed that he should accompany the Doctor, which he consented to do, and in twenty-four hours' time they were well mounted and on their way to the States. They reached Fort Hall all safe; kept south into Taos, and thence to Bent's Fort, on the Arkansas River, when Mr. Lovejoy became exhausted from toil and exposure, and stopped for the winter, while the Doctor continued on and reached Washington.

Thus far in this narrative I give Dr. Whitman's, Mr. Lovejoy's, and my own knowledge. I find an article in the *Pacific* of November 9, from Mr. Spalding, which gives us the result:—

"On reaching the settlements, Dr. Whitman found that many of the now old Oregonians—Waldo, Applegate, Hamtree, Keizer, and others—who had once made calculations to come to Oregon, had abandoned the idea because of the representations from Washington that every attempt to take wagons and ox-teams through the Rocky and Blue Mountains to the Columbia had failed. Dr. Whitman saw at once what the stopping of wagons at Fort Hall every year meant. The representations purported to come from Secretary Webster, but were from Governor Simpson, who, magnifying the statements of his chief trader, Grant, at Fort Hall, declared the Americans must be going mad, from their repeated fruitless attempts to take wagons and teams through the impassable regions to the Columbia, and that the women and children of those wild fanatics had been saved from a terrible death only by the repeated and philanthropic labors of Mr. Grant, at Fort Hall, in furnishing them with horses. The Doctor told these men, as he met them, that his only object in crossing the mountains in the dead of winter, at the risk of his life, and through untold sufferings, was to take back an American emigration that summer through the mountains to the Columbia, with their wagons and their teams. The route was practicable. We had taken our wagon, our cattle, and our families through, seven years before. They had nothing to fear; but to be ready on his return. The stopping of wagons at Fort Hall was a Hudson's Bay Company scheme to prevent the settling of the country by the Americans, till they could settle it with their own subjects from the Selkirk settlement. This news spread like wildfire through Missouri. The Doctor pushed on to Washington and immediately sought an interview with Secretary Webster,—both being from the same State,—and stated to him the object of his crossing the mountains, and laid before him the great importance of Oregon to the United States. But Mr. Webster lived too near Cape Cod to see things in the same light with his fellow-Statesman who had transferred his worldly interests to the Pacific coast. He awarded sincerity to the missionary, but could not admit for a moment that the short residence of six years could give the Doctor the knowledge of the country possessed by Governor Simpson, who had almost grown up in the country, and had traveled every part of it, and represents it as one unbroken waste of sand deserts and impassable mountains, fit only for the beaver, the gray bear, and the savage. Besides, he had about traded it off with Governor Simpson, to go into the Ashburton treaty, for a cod-fishery on Newfoundland.

"The Doctor next sought an interview with President Tyler, who at once appreciated his solicitude and his timely representations of Oregon, and especially his disinterested though hazardous undertaking to cross the Rocky Mountains in the winter to take back a caravan of wagons. He said that, although the Doctor's representations of the character of the country, and the possibility of reaching it by a wagon route, were in direct contradiction to those of Governor Simpson, his frozen limbs were sufficient proof of his sincerity, and his missionary character was sufficient guaranty for his honesty, and he would therefore, as President, rest upon these and act accordingly; would detail Fremont with a military force to escort the Doctor's caravan through the mountains; and no more action should be had toward trading off Oregon till he could hear the result of the expedition. If the Doctor could establish a wagon route through the mountains to the Columbia River, pronounced impossible by Governors Simpson and Ashburton, he would use his influence to hold on to Oregon. The great desire of the Doctor's American soul, and Christian withal, that is, the pledge of the President that the swapping of Oregon with England for a cod-fishery should stop for the present, was attained, although at the risk of life, and through great sufferings, and unsolicited, and without the promise or expectation of a dollar's reward from any source. And now, God giving him life and strength, he would do the rest; that is, connect the Missouri and Columbia rivers with a wagon-track so deep and plain that neither national envy nor sectional fanaticism would ever blot it out*. And when the 5th of September, 1843, saw the rear of the Doctor's caravan of nearly two hundred wagons, with which he started from Missouri last of April, emerge from the western shades of the Blue Mountains upon the plains of the Columbia, the greatest work ever accomplished by one man for Oregon was finished. And through that great emigration during that whole summer, the Doctor was their everywhere-present angel of mercy, ministering to the sick, helping the

* They reached Fort Hall in safety, but there, in the absence of Dr. Whitman from their camp, they were told by Captain Grant, in the interest of the Hudson's Bay Company, as others had been told before, that it was idle for wagons to attempt to reach the Columbia. For a time there was a heaviness of spirit among those families, which, like the Israelites of old, had penetrated the depths of the "great and terrible wilderness." But Dr. Whitman, on ascertaining what had happened, reassured them by his bold and manly words, saying to them, "My countrymen! you have trusted me thus far; believe me now, and I will take your wagons to Columbia River;" and he did so, and Oregon was saved by his patriotism to the Union.

weary, encouraging the wavering, cheering the mothers, mending wagons, setting broken bones, hunting stray oxen, climbing precipices; now in the rear, now at the front; in the rivers, looking out fords through the quicksands; in the deserts, looking out for water; in the dark mountains, looking out passes; at noontide or midnight, as though those thousands were his own children, and those wagons and flocks were his own property. Although he asked not, nor expected, a dollar as a reward from any source, he felt himself abundantly rewarded when he saw the desire of his heart accomplished, the great wagon route over the mountains established, and Oregon in a fair way to be occupied with American settlements and American commerce. And especially he felt himself doubly paid, when, at the end of his successful expedition, and standing alive at his home again on the banks of the Wallawalla, these hundreds of his fellow summer pilgrims, wayworn and sunbrowned, took him by the hand and thanked him with tears for what he had done.

"During the Doctor's absence, his flour mill, with a quantity of grain, had been burned, and, consequently, he found but a small supply at his station on his return, raised by Mr. Geiger, a young man. But what he had in the way of grain, garden vegetables, and cattle, he gladly furnished the needy immigrants at the very low figure of the Wallamet prices, which was six hundred per cent. lower than what they had been compelled to pay at Forts Hall and Boise, and one half lower than they are to-day in the same country. And this was his practice every year till himself and wife and fourteen immigrants were murdered in the fall of 1847, because, as Vicar-General Brouillet says, 'they were American citizens', and not, as I am bold to say and can prove, because he was a physician. Shame on the American that will intimate such a thing! This vicar-general of the Papal hosts on this coast does not thank you for such an excuse. He tells you plainly it was to break up the American settlements on this coast.

"Often the good Doctor would let every bushel of his grain go to the passing immigrants in the fall, and then would have to depend upon me for breadstuffs for the winter and the whole year till next harvest, for his own large family and the scores of immigrants who every year were obliged to stop at his station on account of sickness or give-out teams. Although the Doctor had done so much for his country, it seems his blood was necessary to arouse the government to take formal possession of this coast, as it was his death by savages that sent the devoted J. L. Meek over the mountains to Washington, in the spring of 1848, to beg the government, in behalf of the citizens of this coast, to send us help, and to extend its jurisdiction over us."

CHAPTER XXXVIII.

Petition of the citizens of Oregon in 1843.—Complaints against the Hudson's Bay Company.—The Milling Company.—Kicking the half-bushel.—Land claims of Dr. McLaughlin.—Names of the signers.—Reasons for not signing.—Notice, deed, and bond of John McLaughlin.—Claim of Alvin F. Waller.

Petition of Citizens of Oregon in 1843.

To the Honorable the Senate and House of Representatives of the United States of America in Congress assembled :—

We, the undersigned, settlers south of the Columbia River, beg leave respectfully to represent to your honorable body :

As has been before represented to your honorable body, we consider ourselves citizens of the United States, and acknowledge the right of the United States to extend its jurisdiction over us; and the object of the present memorial is to ask that the protection of the United States may be extended to us as soon as possible. Hitherto, our numbers have been small, and the few difficulties that arose in the settlement were speedily and satisfactorily settled. But, as our settlement increases in numbers, so our difficulties increase in number and importance; and, unless we can have laws to govern us that will be respected and obeyed, our situation will be a deplorable one. Where the highest court of appeal is the rifle, safety in life and property can not be depended on.

The state of the country, its climate, resources, soil, productions, etc., has already been laid before your honorable body, in Captain Wyeth's memoir, and in former memorials from the inhabitants of this place.

Laws are made to protect the weak against the mighty, and we feel the necessity of them in the steps that are constantly taken by the Honorable Hudson's Bay Company, in their opposition to the improvement and enterprise of American citizens. You have been apprised already of their opposition to Captain Wyeth, Bonneville, and others; and we find that the same spirit dwells with them at the present day. Some years ago, when the Hudson's Bay Company owned all the cattle in Oregon, they would not sell on any conditions; but they would lend their cows to the settler—he returning to the company the cows loaned, with all the increase; and in case of the death of a cow, he then had the privilege of paying for it. But after the settlers, at great risk and expense, went to California and purchased for themselves, and there was a fair prospect of the settlement being supplied, then the Hudson's Bay Company were willing to sell, and at lower rates than the settlers could sell.

In the year 1842, feeling the necessity of having mills erected that could supply the settlement with flour and lumber, a number of the inhabitants formed themselves into a joint-stock company, for the purpose of supplying the growing wants of the community. Many of the farmers were obliged to leave their farms on the Wallamet, and go six miles above Vancouver, on the Columbia River, making the whole distance about sixty miles, to get their wheat ground, at a great loss of time and expense. The company was formed and proceeded to select a site. They selected an island at the falls of the Wallamet, and concluded to commence their operations. After commencing, they were informed by Dr. McLaughlin, who is at the head of the Hudson's Bay Company's affairs west of the Rocky Mountains, that the land was his, and that he (although a chief factor of the Hudson's Bay Company) claimed all the land on the east side of the Wallamet, embracing the falls down to the Clackamas River, a distance of about two miles. He had no idea, we presume, that the company would succeed. However, he erected a shed on the island, after the stuff was on the island to build a house, and then gave them permission to build under certain restrictions. They took the paper he wrote them, containing his conditions, but did not obligate themselves to comply with the conditions, as they did not think his claim just or reasonable.

Many projects had been started by the inhabitants, but, for want of means and encouragement, failed. This fate was predicted for the Milling Company. But, after much labor and difficulty, they succeeded in getting a saw-mill erected, and ready to run, and entered into a contract to have a grist-mill erected forthwith. And now, as they have succeeded, where is the Hudson's Bay Company? Dr. McLaughlin employs hands to get out a frame for a saw-mill, and erect it at Wallamet Falls; and we find, as soon as the frame is up, the gearing, which has been made at Vancouver, is brought up in boats; and that which cost a feeble company of American citizens months of toil and embarrassment is accomplished by the chief factor of the Hudson's Bay Company in a few weeks. He has men and means, and it is said by him that in two weeks his mill will be sawing. And what will be the consequence? Why, if the Milling Company sell for $15 per thousand, he can sell for $12; if they reduce the price to $10, he can come to $8, or $5, or $2 per thousand. He says he will have a grist-mill started as soon as he gets the saw-mill in operation.

All the wheat in Oregon they are anxious to get, as they ship it to the Russians on the northwest coast. In the first place they measured the wheat in a half-bushel, called by them imperial measure, much larger than the standard measure of the United States; this not answering, they next proceeded *to kick the half-bushel with the foot to settle the wheat;* then they brought up a measure larger than the former one; and now they fill this measure, then strike it *three times with a stout club*, and then fill up, and call it fair measure. Against such proceedings we need law that will be respected and obeyed.

About twelve or fourteen years ago, the Hudson's Bay Company blasted a canal a few feet to conduct water to a mill they were going to build, the timber for which is now lying at the falls rotting. They, however, abandoned the thing altogether, and built their mills on the Columbia, about six miles above Vancouver, on the north side of the river.

In the year 1837, agreeably to orders left by Mr. Slacum, a house was erected at the falls, to secure the claim for him.

In 1840, the Methodist Mission erected buildings at the falls, and stationed two families there, and made a claim to sufficient land for their buildings, not interfering with any others who might wish to build. A short time previous to this, Dr. McLaughlin had a storehouse erected for the company, not occupied, however, further than to store wheat and other articles in, and as a trading-house during the salmon season.

After this, in 1841, a shanty was erected, and a man kept at the falls, whose business it was to trade with the Indians for furs and salmon, and look out for the doctor's claim, he said, and to forbid persons building at the falls, as some had built, and others were about building. This man was, and still is, a servant of the Hudson's Bay Company.

During the years 1841 and 1842, several families settled at the falls, when Dr. McLaughlin, who still resides at Fort Vancouver, comes on the ground, and says the land is his, and any person building without his permission is held as a trespasser. Without reference to any person's right or claim, he employs a surveyor to run out the plat; and as a bill was before the Senate of the United States to grant to every white male inhabitant a mile square, he has a mile run out to suit his views, and lays out a town plat at the falls, and calls it Oregon City. Although some, for peace' sake, asked him for the lots they had already in possession, and which he appeared very willing to grant, the doctor now felt himself secure, and posted up the annexed paper (marked A), which is the original; and all who had lots were required to pay Mr. Hastings five dollars for a deed of land which they knew very well the grantor did not own, but that Congress will pass a special act granting to each man his lot and improvements. Those that applied received (if they had a house on the lot) a deed, a copy of which is annexed (marked B); if they had no house, a bond was given for five dollars, a copy of which is annexed (marked C). To those that applied and paid their five dollars all was right with the doctor; while those who considered his title to the land not good, and that therefore he had no right to direct who should build and who should not, had their lots sold to others. In one case the purchaser came to the original claimant and ordered him to stop digging the ground which he was preparing for a garden, and commanded him to remove his fences, as he had Dr. McLaughlin's bond in his pocket for the lots; and if he did not move the fence he would, and take forcible possession. Those who desired to have no difficulty, and did not apply for a deed, have lost their lots, the doctor's promise, and all. And Mr. Hastings (the doctor's agent) is now offering for sale the lots on which part of the mission buildings stand; and if he succeeds in finding a purchaser, they must either contend or lose their buildings.

Dr. McLaughlin has held claims in other places south of the Columbia River: at the Tualatin Plains and Clackamas Plains he had huts erected, to prevent others from building; and such is the power of Dr. McLaughlin, that many persons are actually afraid to make their situation known, thinking, if he hears of it, he will stop their supplies. Letters were received here from Messrs. Ladd & Co., of the Sandwich Islands, in answer to a letter written by the late Mr. Ewing Young, for a few supplies, that orders were received forbidding the company's vessels carrying any goods for the settlers of Oregon. Every means will be made use of by them to break down every thing that will draw trade to this country, or enable persons to get goods at any other place than their store.

One other item, and we are done. When the United States government officers of distinction arrive, Vancouver is thrown open, and every facility afforded them. They were even more condescending to the settlers during the time the exploring squadron was in the Columbia; nothing was left undone to give the officers a high opinion of the Honorable Hudson's Bay Company. Our Indian agent is entirely dependent on them for supplies and funds to carry on his operations.

And now your memorialists pray your honorable body that immediate action of Congress be taken in regard to this country, and good and wholesome laws be enacted for our Territory, as may, in your wisdom, be thought best for the good of the American citizens residing here.

And your memorialists will ever pray.

Robert Shortess, A. E. Wilson,* W. C. Remick,* Jeffrey Brown, E. N. Coombs, Reuben Lewis, George Davis, V. Bennett, J. Rekener, T. J. Hubbard, James A. O'Neil, Jer. Horregon, William McCarty, Charles Compo, John Howard,* R. Williams, G. Brown, John Turner,* Theodore Pancott, A. F. Waller, J. R. Robb, J. L. Morrison, M. Crawford, John Anderson, James M. Bates, L. H. Judson, Joel Turnham,* Richard H. Ekin, H. Campbell,* James Force, W. H. Wilson,* Felix Hathaway,* J. Lawson, Thomas J. Shadden,* Joseph Gibbs, S. Lewis, Jr., Charles Roy, William Brown, S. Davis, Joseph Yatten, John Hopstatter,* G. W. Bellomy,* William Brown, A. Beers, J. L. Parish, William H. Gray, A. D. Smith,* J. C. Bridgers,* Aaron Cook, A. Copeland, S. W. Moss, Gustavus Hines, George W. Le Breton,* Daniel Girtman, C. T. Arrendrill, A. Touner, David Carter,* J. J. Campbell,* W. Johnson,* John Edmunds, W. Hauxhurst, W. A. Pfieffer, J. Holman, H. B. Brewer, William C. Sutton. Sixty-five in all.

The foregoing are all the names which appear to the petition printed as Senate document 105, and presented to the Senate at the first session of the twenty-eighth Congress.

W. J. McDonald,
Principal Clerk of Sec'y Senate.

Washington, D. C., Jan. 5, 1866.

Mr. George Abernethy declined to sign this petition through fear of injuring the Methodist Mission in its secular or business relations with the Hudson's Bay Company.

Hugh Burns would not sign it because he did not wish Congress to be asked to confirm his title to lots and improvements.

Jason Lee, though he thought it right to petition Congress for protection, yet on account of his position as superintendent of the Methodist Mission, and the influence of the company against them should he sign it, thought it best not to give his name.

Dr. I. L. Babcock refused, because, by signing, he would lose his influence with the company.

Walter Pomeroy, ditto.

Dr. Bailey *did not wish any protection from the Congress of the United States.*

* It is understood that the persons whose names are marked with an asterisk (*) are now dead; the balance are supposed to be still living.

Rev. H. K. W. Perkins was *ashamed* of the petition. "What does Congress care about measuring wheat? or a contest between two milling companies?"

George Gay did not care any thing about it. Congress might do as it pleased; he did not want its protection.

The people in Tualatin Plains did not have an opportunity to sign or refuse for want of time to circulate it in that section. The bearer of it, William C. Sutton, was on his way to the States across the Rocky Mountains. Through the influence of Dr. White, who had clandestinely procured a copy of the petition and the names attached, and had made an effort to prevent its reaching Mr. Sutton, it had been delayed, but through the perseverance and promptness of Robert Shortess and A. E. Wilson, it was sent by Davis and Johnson and some Indians in an express canoe, and reached Mr. Sutton before he left the Cascades. For this service to his country and the persevering efforts of Mr. Shortess to maintain the rights of American citizens in it, he was early placed under the ban of the Hudson's Bay Company, and, it may be added, the Methodist Mission; and reports prejudicial to him have been freely and persistently kept before the public mind, as also against any others that have taken an active part against the infamous and despotic course of that company. This is to weaken their testimony, and to render them powerless to prevent the present proposed robbing of our national treasury. Instead of paying one dime to that company for doing all they dared to do to prevent the settlement of Oregon by Americans, a pension should be paid to Robert Shortess and many others who dared to maintain the rights of the American people to this western coast. Whitman periled every thing and lost his life to save the country. Shortess has periled all, and worn himself out in struggling under an influence that took the life of Dr. Whitman and many others, for which this Hudson's Bay Company are now to receive pay.

It is unnecessary for me to make a single remark in reference to this petition. It is a history in itself of the times and events then occurring. Mr. Hines refers to it as of little moment, and on page 150 says: "Not being one of the authors, but merely a signer of the petition, I did not come under the ban of the company; consequently, I obtained my outfit for the expedition, though at first there were strong indications that I would be refused."

We would infer from this, that the Hudson's Bay Company did not regard it as a serious matter, but in the next line he tells us: "We remained at the fort over night and a part of the next day, and, after a *close conversation with the gentlemen in command*, were treated with great courtesy."

This lets us into the whole mystery of the affair. The gentlemen in charge of the fort had become satisfied that Mr. Hines in his visit among the Indians would not interfere with their arrangements already made with McKay and White; in fact, that Mr. Hines approved of Dr. White's policy of uniting the tribes in the interior to accomplish the one great object of the company. The documents that follow are given to show the fact stated in the petition, as also the high-handed measures of the company and Dr. McLaughlin.

A.

Notice is hereby given to all whom it may concern, that those who have obtained grants of lots in Oregon City, will be expected to call upon L. W. Hastings, my authorized agent at Oregon City, and obtain a bond for a deed or deeds, as the case may be. Those who hold claims to any lot, and who comply with the above requisite, on or before the first day of February next, will be entitled to their lot or lots; otherwise, the lots upon which they hold a claim will thereafter be subject to any disposition which the undersigned may think proper to make of them.

JOHN MCLAUGHLIN.

January 18, 1843.

OREGON CITY, March 27, 1843.

We, the undersigned, do hereby certify that the above notice of John McLaughlin was posted up in the most public places in this town.

R. SHORTESS.
A. E. WILSON.

B.

Deed—John McLaughlin to Walter Pomeroy.

Know all men by these presents, that I, John McLaughlin, of Fort Vancouver, in the Territory of Oregon, for and in consideration of the sum of one dollar, to me in hand paid by Walter Pomeroy, of Oregon City, of the Territory aforesaid, the receipt whereof is hereby acknowledged, have this day, and do, by these presents, remit, release, and forever quit claim unto the said Pomeroy, his heirs and assigns, all and singular, the following piece, parcel, and lot of land, bounded and described as follows, to wit: Commencing at the northeast corner, running thence southerly sixty-six feet to a stake, thence easterly one hundred feet to a stake at the place of beginning, being lot number four, in block number three, in the town of Oregon City, in the Territory of

Oregon, which will more fully appear from a reference to the map and plan of said town:

To have and to hold the same, together with all and singular the privileges and appurtenances thereunto in any wise appertaining or belonging unto the said Pomeroy, his heirs, executors, administrators, or assigns, forever.

And I, the said McLaughlin, for myself, do vouch and declare that I am the true and proper claimant of and to the said premises and lot of land, and that I have in myself full power, good right, and sufficient authority to remit, release, and quit my claim in and to said lot and premises, in manner and form aforesaid.

And I, the said McLaughlin, do hereby covenant and agree to warrant and defend the said premises, together with the privileges and appurtenances thereunto appertaining or belonging, to the said Pomeroy, his heirs and assigns, against all lawful claims of all persons whomsoever, *the claims of the government only excepted.*

In testimony whereof, I, the said McLaughlin, have hereunto set my hand and affixed my seal, this the 2d of March, A. D. 1843.

JOHN MCLAUGHLIN. [L. S.]

Per L. W. HASTINGS, his agent.

We, the undersigned, do hereby acknowledge that the above is a true and correct copy of the original.

R. SHORTESS.
A. E. WILSON.

C.

Bond—John McLaughlin to Albert E. Wilson.

Know all men by these presents, that I, John McLaughlin, of Fort Vancouver, in the Territory of Oregon, am held and firmly bound unto Albert E. Wilson, of Oregon City, in the Territory aforesaid, in the full sum of five hundred dollars, federal money; for the punctual payment of which, well and truly to be made, I bind myself, my heirs, executors or administrators, firmly by these presents.

In testimony whereof, I have hereunto below set my hand and affixed my seal, this the 26th day of December, A. D. 1842.

Now, know ye, that the condition of the above obligation is such, that whereas the said Wilson hath this day, and doth by these presents, purchase of the said McLaughlin all and singular the following pieces, parcels, tracts, and lots of land, namely: Lots Nos. four and five, in block No. two, in the town of Oregon City, in the Territory of Oregon, as is more fully shown by the map and plan of said town, and hath, and by these presents doth agree to build upon and improve each of the lots within the term of one year from the date of these presents. In consideration of which, the said McLaughlin hath, and doth by these presents covenant and agree to make the said Wilson a good and sufficient quit-claim deed for and to all and singular the above-mentioned pieces, parcels, tracts, and lots of land, whenever he, the said Wilson, shall have complied with the above conditions on his part. Now, if the said McLaughlin shall well and truly make, or cause to be made, the said deed to the said Wilson, upon the said Wilson's complying on his part with the above condition, then, and in such case, the within obligation shall become entirely void and of no effect; otherwise to be and remain of full force and virtue.

JOHN MCLAUGHLIN. [L. S.]

Per L. W. HASTINGS, his agent.

We, the undersigned, do hereby acknowledge the above to be a true and correct copy of the original.

R. SHORTESS.
A. E. WILSON.

Our history would not be complete without these documents. It will be noticed in Mr. Pomeroy's deed, as also all the other deeds given by Dr. McLaughlin, that he "warrants and defends" against all lawful claims of all persons whomsoever, *the claims of the government only excepted.* He would not insert *United States government*, for he expected the English would get the country. He asserts in his deeds, "And I, the said McLaughlin, *for myself*, do vouch and declare that I am the true and proper claimant of, and to the said premises and lot of land, and that I have in myself full power and good right."

Any one questioning his power and authority was made to feel it in a manner more severe than that of any governor of a State or of the President of the United States.

It was unfortunate that, at the time Dr. McLaughlin was making his claim to the land and his improvements at Oregon City, it was not known that he had, or would, sever his connection with the Hudson's Bay Company, and become an American citizen, as he afterward did. It was his connection with, and apparent control over, the affairs of the company, that created the strong American prejudice against him, and deceived many as to his intentions, besides giving occasion for a strong feeling in favor of Rev. Mr. Waller, who employed a Mr. John Ricord to prepare a declaration setting forth his claim to that location, as follows:—

"*To the People of Oregon:*

"FELLOW-CITIZENS,—Having been retained professionally to establish the claim of Mr. Alvin F. Waller to the tract of land on the east side of the Wallamet River, sometimes called the Wallamet Falls settlement, and sometimes Oregon City, I consider it a duty to my client and to the public to state, briefly and concisely, the several circumstances of his case, as they really exist, in order that his motives may not be impugned, nor his intentions misunderstood and misrepresented.

"The public are already aware that my client commenced the occupancy of this farm in the spring of A. D. 1840, when no one resided at the falls, and that, in the course of that summer, he built his house, moved his family into it, and cleared and fenced a good portion of the land; from which, in the ensuing years A. D. 1841 and 1842, he raised successive crops of corn, potatoes, and other vegetables usually cultivated by farmers. That he remained thus occupying undisturbed, until the month of December, A. D. 1842, about two years and six months, when Dr. John McLaughlin caused his farm to be surveyed, for the purpose of selling it in subdivisions to American citizens. It has since been currently reported and quite generally believed that my client had renounced his right in favor of Dr. McLaughlin. This I am authorized to contradict, having perused the letter written by Mr. Waller, which not only contains no renunciation, but, on the contrary, is replete with modest and firm assertions of his rights in the premises; offering at the same time to relinquish his claim if the doctor would comply with certain very reasonable and just conditions. Upon this offer the parties had come to no final conclusion until my arrival in the colony, when Dr. McLaughlin attempted to employ me to establish his claim, disregarding the rights of all other persons, which I declined doing. Mr. Waller thereupon engaged me to submit the conditions a second time to the doctor for his acceptance or rejection, which I did in the following words:—

"'1st. That your pre-emptive line be so run as to exclude the island upon which a private company of citizens have already erected a grist-mill, conceding to them as much water as may be necessary for the use of said mills.

"'2d. That Mr. Waller be secured in the ultimate title to the two city lots now in his possession and other lots not exceeding in superficial area five acres, to be chosen by him from among the unsold lots of your present survey.

"'3d. That the Rev. Mr. Lee, on behalf of the Methodist Episcopal Mission, be, in like manner, secured in the lots claimed for the use of said mission.' They consist of church and parsonage lots, and are well known to the public.

"I received a letter from Dr. McLaughlin, dated November 10, 1843, in answer to mine, in which he declines complying with the above conditions, and thus puts an end to the offer of my client to relinquish his right of pre-emption. Under these circumstances Mr. Waller has now applied to the Supreme Court of the United States, which, under the Constitution, has original jurisdiction of 'all cases in law and equity, arising under treaties,' to grant him a commission for perpetuating the testimony of the facts in his case, *de bene esse*, in order that whenever Congress shall hereafter see fit to prescribe, by law, the conditions and considerations, he may be enabled to demand of the United States a patent; also praying the court to grant him such other relief in the premises as may be consonant with equity and good conscience.

"The legality of Mr. A. F. Waller's claim rests upon the following grounds:—

"1st. He was a citizen of the United States, of full age, and possessed of a family when he came to reside on the premises; 2d. He built a house upon them and moved his family into it, thus becoming in fact and in law a householder on the land; 3d. He cleared, fenced, and cultivated a portion of it during two years and six months before he was disturbed in his actual possession; and 4th. That he is not at this moment continuing to cultivate his farm is not his fault, since it was wrested from him.

"The illegality of Dr. McLaughlin's claim rests upon the following grounds:—

"1st. He was a British subject owing allegiance to a foreign power, and has so continued to be ever since the spring of A. D. 1840. For this reason alone he could not acquire pre-emption to lands in the United States.

"2d. He is chief officer of a foreign corporative monopoly. For this reason alone he could not acquire pre-emption to lands in the United States.

"3d. He does not now, and never did, reside on the land in question; but, on the contrary, he resides, and has always continued to reside, on the north bank of the Columbia River, the section of country actually in dispute between the two governments, about twenty miles from the land claimed by Mr. Waller, and there he is obliged to remain so long as he continues to be chief factor.

"4th. He is not in fact the claimant. The Hudson's Bay Company, a foreign corporation, is in fact the claimant, while Dr. McLaughlin only lends his name; well knowing that a corporation, even though it be an American one, can not acquire a pre-emption. This is evinced by the employment of men to be his agents, and to sell lots for him, who are at the same time partners in, and receiving dividends and salaries from, the company.

5th. The pretensions of Dr. McLaughlin arose, if at all, two years and six months after the actual settlement of Mr. Waller; and therefore they are in direct violation of the treaty of A. D. 1827, converting the mutual and joint occupation into an exclusive occupancy by British subjects.

"6th. The treaty of joint occupation (1827) does not, and was never intended, on the part of the United States, to confer any rights of citizenship upon foreigners. The power to confer such rights is, by the Constitution, reserved to Congress. And the right to acquire title by pre-emption is peculiar to citizens.

"These, fellow-citizens, are the facts and some of the points of law in my client's case. Upon the same principle contended for by Dr. McLaughlin, any of you may incur the risk of being ousted from your farms in this colony, by the next rich foreigner who chooses to take a fancy so to do, unless in the first instance you come unanimously forward and resist these usurpations. It is not my client's intention to wrong any who have purchased lots of the doctor; and to guard against the injury which might result to individuals in this respect, I have carefully drawn up the form of a bond for a warrantee deed, which Mr. Waller is at all times ready, without any further consideration, to execute to any person who has, in good faith, bought of the doctor, prior to the date of this notice, by being applied to at his residence. Mr. Waller does not require one cent of money to be paid to him as a consideration for his bonds—the trouble, expense, and outlays they have already incurred, with a desire to save all such persons harmless from pecuniary loss, is a good and sufficient consideration in law to bind him in the proposed penalty of one thousand dollars. (See Cowan's Digest—Assumpsit, B).

"I am of opinion that Mr. Waller has rights in the premises, which neither Dr. McLaughlin, nor even Congress, by any retrospective legislation, can take away from him,—and therefore, fellow-citizens, in sincere friendship, I would counsel you to lose no time in applying to him for your new bonds.

"JOHN RICORD,
"Counselor in the Supreme Court of the United States,
and attorney for Alvin F. Waller.

"Dated December 20, 1843."

CHAPTER XXXIX.

Extracts from Mr. Hines' history.—Attempt to capture an Indian horse-thief.—Dr. McLaughlin refuses to sell supplies to the signers of the petition.—Excitement in the settlement.—Interview with Dr. McLaughlin at Vancouver.

"April 14.—Information was brought to the settlement from the Clackamas tribe of Indians, who live three miles below the falls of the Wallamet, which served to increase the excitement occasioned by the reports from the interior. It appears that an Indian of the Molalla tribe, connected with the Clackamas Indians by marriage, stole a horse from a man by the name of Anderson, and when asked by the latter if he had stolen his horse and rode him off, answered, 'Yes, I stole your horse, and when I want another one I shall steal him also.' To this Anderson replied, 'If you stole my horse you must pay me for him.' 'Yes,' said the Indian, 'I will pay you for him, take that horse,' pointing to a very poor horse which stood near by, with one eye out, and a very sore back. Anderson replied, 'That is a very poor horse, and mine is a good one; I shall not take him, and if you don't bring him back I will report you to Dr. White.' 'I am not afraid of Dr. White,' said the Indian; 'let him come if he wants to, and bring the Boston people with him; he will find me prepared for him.'

"Anderson not being able to effect a settlement with the Indian, immediately reported him to the agent, whereupon the latter wrote to a man at the falls, by the name of Campbell, to take a sufficient number of men armed with muskets, and go very early in the morning to the Indian camp, and take the horse-thief a prisoner, and bring him to the falls.

"Accordingly, Campbell procured five men, and went to the camp as commanded, but found thirty or forty Indians painted in the most hideous manner, and armed with muskets, bows and arrows, tomahawks and scalping-knives, and determined at all events to protect the horse-thief, and drive back those that should come to take him. Campbell rushed on to take the rogue, but met with much resistance from superiority of numbers; and finding that the enterprise, if urged forward, would terminate in bloodshed, if not in the loss of all their lives, sounded a retreat, and extricating himself from the Indians, returned to the falls. He communicated the result of his attempt to Dr. White, and the doctor started off immediately in company with G. W. Le Breton, resolved to capture the thief and bring the tribe to terms."

This day's proceedings are given as a specimen of the foolish conduct of Dr. White and his friends.

"April 17.—The excitement still continues, former reports having been confirmed, and all were engaged in repairing guns, and securing ammunition. A report was in circulation that Dr. McLaughlin refused to grant supplies for any consideration, to all those persons who subscribed the memorial praying the Congress of the United States to extend jurisdiction over Oregon. If this be so, the American population (as nearly all signed the memorial) will not be able to obtain ammunition, however necessary it may be, as there is none in the country except what may be found within the stockades of Vancouver. I think, however, that the report is false. Report says, furthermore, that the Klikitat Indians are collecting together back of the Tualatin plains, but for what purpose is not known. The people on the plains, consisting of about thirty families, are quite alarmed. There is also a move among the Calapooyas. Shoefon, one of the principal men of the tribe, left this place a few days ago, and crossed the Wallamet River, declaring that he would never return until he came with a band of men to drive off the Boston people. He was very much offended because some of his people were seized and flogged, through the influence of Dr. White, for having stolen a horse from some of the missionaries, and flour from the mission mill. His influence is not very extensive among the Indians, or we might have much to fear.

"The colony is indeed in a most defenseless condition; two hundred Indians, divided into four bands, might destroy the whole settlement in one night.

"In the evening of the 17th, Dr. White arrived at my house, bringing intelligence from the falls. He and Mr. Le Breton attempted to go to the falls on horseback, but in trying to ford Haunchauke River, they found the water so deep they were obliged to swim, and the doctor turned his horse's head and came out the side he went in; but Le Breton, being the better mounted of the two, succeeded in gaining the opposite shore; and having the doctor's letters in his possession, continued on to the falls. The doctor returned to the settlement. Le Breton returned the following day, and brought information from the five men who had attempted to take the Indian who had stolen Anderson's horse, that soon after their retreat the Indians became alarmed and broke up in great haste; but, before they left, they informed Anderson that the horse they had stolen from him was worn out and good for nothing, and tying a good horse to a tree near Anderson's house, they told him that he must take that and be satisfied. They then hurried away, saying that they should not be seen in that region again. It was ascertained that the Clackamas Indians had nothing to do with the stolen horse; that it was a band of the Molallas, the very same rascals that stole a horse from me two years before, and after having him in their possession several weeks, brought him down within a few miles of my house, where they encamped, and where I went with one man and took him from the midst of more than fifty grim-looking savages."

This shows at least that Mr. Hines had personal courage.

"On the 20th of April a letter was received in the settlement, written by H. B. Brewer, at the Dalles, which brings the latest intelligence from the infected region. This letter states that the Indians in the interior talk much of war, and Mr. Brewer urges Dr. White to come up without delay, and endeavor to allay the excitement. He does not inform us that the Indians design any evil toward the whites, but says that the war is to be between themselves, but that the Boston people have much to fear. As the doctor, in his visit to the interior last October, left an appointment to meet the Wallawalla Indians and the Cayuses, in their own country, on the 10th of May, and believing that a great share of the excitement originated in a misunderstanding of the Indians, he came to the conclusion at all hazards to go among them. At the solicitation of the agent, I determined to accompany him on the expedition.

"The great complaint of the Indians was that the Boston people designed to take away their lands, and reduce them to slavery. This they had inferred from what Dr. White had told them in his previous visit; and this misunderstanding of the Indians had not only produced a great excitement among them, but had occasioned considerable trouble betwixt them and the missionaries and other whites in the upper country, as well as influencing them to threaten the destruction of all the American people. Individuals had come down from Fort Wallawalla to Vancouver, bringing information of the excited state of things among the Indians, and giving out that it would be extremely dangerous for Dr. White to go up to meet his engagements. Their opinion was, that in all probability he and the party which he might think proper to take with him would be cut off. But it was the opinion of many judicious persons in the settlement, that the welfare of the Indians, and the peace and security of the whites, demanded that some persons qualified to negotiate with the Indians should proceed immediately to the scene of disaffection, and if possible remove the cause of the excitement by correcting the error under which the Indians labored. Accordingly Dr. White engaged twelve men besides myself, mostly French-Canadians who had had much experience with Indians, to go with him; but a few days before the time fixed upon to start had arrived, they all sent him word that they had decided not to go. They were doubtless induced to pursue this course through the influence of Dr. McLaughlin and the Catholic priests."

Most likely, Mr. Hines, but you seem to be afraid to express a decided opinion, even after they have accomplished their object.

"When the day arrived for starting, we found ourselves abandoned by every person who had engaged to go, except Mr. G. W. Le Breton, an American, one Indian boy, and one Kanaka. With the two latter the doctor and myself left the Wallamet settlement on the 25th of April, 1843, and proceeded on horseback to the Butte, where we found Le Breton in waiting for us. He had provided a canoe and a few pieces of pork and beef for our use on the voyage.

"Here we met a letter from Dr. John McLaughlin, at Vancouver, discouraging us from our undertaking in view of the difficulties and dangers attending such an expedition; but we had counted the cost, and were not to be diverted from our purpose, though danger stared us in the face. We supposed that if the Indians entertained any hostile intentions against the whites in general, there could be no better way to defeat their purposes than to go among them; convince them that they had no grounds of fear; and that the whites, instead of designing to bring them into subjection, were desirous of doing them good. Prevented by one thing and another from setting sail, on the night of the 27th we slept on a bank of sand at the Butte, and next day proceeded in our little canoe down to Wallamet Falls, where we continued until the 29th. Here we received another package from Dr. McLaughlin, giving us information that Rev. Mr. Demerse, a Catholic priest, had just come down from the upper country, bringing intelligence that the Indians are only incensed against the Boston people; that they have nothing against the French and King George people; they are not mad at them, but are determined that the Boston people shall not have their lands, and take away their liberties.

"On receiving this intelligence from Mr. Demerse, Dr. McLaughlin advised the Frenchmen, who had engaged to go with Dr. White, to have nothing to do with the quarrel, to remain quiet at home, and let the Americans take care of themselves. He also expressed, in his letter, the opinion that all the people should remain quiet, and in all probability the excitement among the Indians would soon subside.

"Not seeing sufficient reason to change our course, on the morning of the 28th we left our hospitable friends at the falls and continued our course down the Wallamet toward Vancouver. At noon we had sailed twenty miles, and stopped for dinner within five miles of the mouth of the Wallamet, on a low piece of ground, overgrown with luxuriant grass, but which is always overflowed at the rise of the Columbia, or about the first of June. Weighed anchor after dinner, and at four o'clock, P. M., arrived at Vancouver. Called on Dr. McLaughlin for goods, provisions, powder, balls, etc., for our accommodation on our voyage up the Columbia, and, though he was greatly surprised that, under the circumstances, we should think of going among those excited Indians, yet he ordered his clerks to let us have whatever we wanted. However, we found it rather squally at the fort, not so much on account of our going among the Indians of the interior, as in consequence of a certain memorial having been sent to the United States Congress, implicating the conduct of Dr. McLaughlin and the Hudson's Bay Company, and bearing the signature of seventy Americans. I inquired of the doctor if he had refused to grant supplies to those Americans who had signed that document; he replied that he had not, but that the authors of the memorial need expect no more favors from him. *Not being one of the authors, but merely a signer of the petition, I did not come under the ban of the company;* consequently I obtained my outfit for the expedition, though at first there were strong indications that I would be refused.

"We remained at the fort over night and a part of the next day, and after a close conversation with the gentleman in command, were treated with great courtesy."

CHAPTER XL.

A combination of facts.—Settlers alive to their danger.—Mr. Hines' disparagement of the Methodist Mission.—Indians want pay for being whipped.—Indian honesty.—Mr. Hines' opinion of the Indians' religion.—Mr. Geiger's advice.—Dr. McLaughlin's answer to Yellow Serpent.—Baptiste Doreo.—Four conflicting influences.

We now have before us a combination of facts and statements that no one living at the time they occurred will attempt to deny. Shortess and others still live to vouch for the truth of what is written. If Mr. Hines has shown the least partiality in his writings, it is strongly in favor of influences that were operating against him and the cause he advocated; while such men as Rogers, Le Breton, Wilson, Whitman, and others still living, spoke and acted the American sentiment of the country. Mr. Hines and Dr. White had received two packages from Dr. McLaughlin advising them not to go to the interior, and the Jesuit priest, Demerse, had come down bringing word that the "quarrel" was not with the *French* and *English*, and that Dr. McLaughlin advised his Frenchmen to remain at home and let the Americans take care of themselves. Mr. Brewer is deceived as to the cause of the war rumors about him, and seems solicitous only about the Indians. With all these facts, as given by Mr. Hines, with his ability and experience, we are at a loss to understand how it is that he could take notes and publish, in 1851, statements as above quoted, and then proceed with the account that follows, rather excusing Dr. McLaughlin and the priests in the part they are taking in attempting to crush the American settlement, and actually aiding the Hudson's Bay Company in combining and marshaling the savages to weaken and destroy his countrymen!

The writer does not believe he intended to do any thing of the kind, yet the influences brought to bear upon him were such that he became an active instrument with Dr. White to accomplish the one great object of the Hudson's Bay Company and English government, and becomes the apologist for a premeditated and deliberate murder of his countrymen. The Whitman massacre he does not even mention.

The settlers were alive to their danger. They had no head, no organization, no one to look to for supplies or protection. They knew that the sub-agent of the United States government was the dupe of their worst enemy, and had betrayed them. They knew that it was the policy and disposition of the missions to keep them under their control.

We are fully aware of the fact that the leading clergymen of all the missions attempt to deny the position above stated. But in the covenant of Mr. Griffin with Mr. Munger, he admits that the articles of compact and arrangement of the various missionary societies all affirm the one principle, that laymen or members of their societies were subject to the orders and dictation of the clergymen, not only in religious, but all financial and secular matters,—hence the disposition and determination on the part of these clerical gentlemen to govern the early settlement of the country. The Hudson's Bay Company system of absolute government was favorable to this idea. The Jesuit priests, who combined their influence with the company, all contributed to oppress and keep down the settler. While the priests were active in combining and preparing the Indians in middle Oregon to rob and destroy the emigrant on his lonely, weary, toilsome way to this country, their agents and principal clerks were equally active in shaping matters in the various neighborhoods and settlements west of the Cascades.

On the 156th page of Mr. Hines' book he gives us a short summary of the labors of Revs. Daniel Lee, H. K. W. Perkins, and Mr. H. B. Brewer: "They are laboring to establish a permanent mission at this place [the Dalles] for the benefit of the Indians, but with doubtful success." That the Methodist Mission should be misled and become inefficient is not to be wondered at when such men as Mr. Hines, holding the position and assuming a controlling influence as he did, should express himself in the language quoted above. The "doubtful success" attending all the missionary labors of the Methodist Mission was unquestionably attributable to the opinions of just such men, privately and publicly expressed, with corresponding "doubtful" and divided labors, while the ignorance of the religious supporters of the Roman missions enabled them to deceive their neophytes and patrons, and keep up their own missions and destroy those of the Protestants.

Soon after Mr. Hines and party arrived at the Dalles, some twenty Indians assembled to have a talk with Dr. White, who had in his visit in the fall of 1842 prevailed upon this band to organize an Indian government by appointing one high chief and three subordinates to see that all violators of his rules were punished by being flogged for offenses that formerly were considered trifling and evidence of native cunning and smartness. As was to be expected, some of the Indians would resist and use their knives and weapons in their own defense.

There is an interesting incident related by Mr. Hines, in reference to Indian character, on his 157th page:—

"The Indians want pay for being whipped, in compliance with Dr. White's laws, the same as they did for praying to please the missionaries, during the great Indian revival of 1839. Those appointed by Dr. White were desirous that his regulations should continue, because they placed the people under their absolute control, and gave them the power to regulate all their intercourse with the whites, and with the other Indian tribes. But the other influential men who were not in office desired to know of Dr. White of what benefit this whipping system was going to be to them. They said they were willing it should continue, provided they were to receive shirts and pants and blankets as a reward for being whipped. They had been whipped a good many times and had got nothing for it, and it had done them no good. If this state of things was to continue, it was all *cultus*, good for nothing, and they would throw it away. The doctor wished them to understand that they need not expect pay for being flogged when they deserved it. They laughed at the idea, and separated."

Just here the writer will give one other incident, related of Yallop, an Indian belonging to the same tribe, as stated by Rev. Mr. Condon, of the Dalles:—

"Yallop was requested to remain at the house of Mr. Joslin during the absence of the family, one cold day, and see that nothing was disturbed, with the understanding that he was to go into the house and make himself comfortable till the family returned. On coming home they found the Indian outdoors under a tree, cold and nearly frozen. They inquired the reason of his strange conduct, and wanted to know why he did not stay in the house. Yallop said he went into the house and found every thing so nice and comfortable that by and by the old Indian came into him again and he wanted to steal all there was in the house, and the only way he could get over that feeling was to go out under the tree in the cold."

Mr. Hines, in speaking of this same band, says, 158th page: "As a matter of course, lying has much to do in their system of trade, and he is the best fellow who can tell the biggest lie, make men believe it, and practice the greatest deception. A few years ago a great religious excitement prevailed among these Indians, and nearly the whole tribe, consisting of a thousand, professed to be converted, were baptized, and received into the Christian church; but they have nearly all relapsed into their former state, with the exception that many of them still keep up the outward form of religion.

"Their religion appears to be more of the head than of the heart, and though they are exceedingly vicious, yet doubtless they would be much worse than they are, but for the "—(" doubtful success," as Mr. Hines affirms on his 156th page, while here he says)—"*restraining influences* exerted by the missionaries."

Mr. Hines has given us an interesting history of those early missionary labors, but the greater portion of his book relates to himself,—to his travels on shipboard, and at the Sandwich Islands, a trip to China and back to New York, and his trip to the interior of Oregon.

He says: "The Cayuse Indians, among whom this mission is established, had freely communicated to Mr. Geiger, whom they esteemed as their friend, all they knew concerning it. When the Indians were told that the Americans were designing to subjugate them and take away their land, the young chiefs of the Cayuse tribe were in favor of proceeding immediately to hostilities. They were for raising a large war party and rushing directly down to the Wallamet settlement and cutting off the inhabitants at a blow. They frequently remarked to Mr. Geiger that they did not wish to go to war, but if the Americans came to take away their lands and make slaves of them they would fight so long as they had a drop of blood to shed. They said they had received their information concerning the designs of the Americans from Baptiste Doreo, who is a half-breed son of Madame Doreo,—the heroine of Washington Irving's 'Astoria,'—understands the Nez Percé language well, and had given the Cayuses the information that had alarmed them. Mr. Geiger endeavored to induce them to prepare early in the spring to cultivate the ground as they did the year before, but they refused to do any thing, saying that Baptiste Doreo had told them that it would be of no consequence; that the Americans would come in the summer and kill them all off and destroy their plantations.

"After Doreo had told them this story, they sent a Wallawalla chief —Yellow Serpent—to Vancouver, to learn from Dr. McLaughlin the facts in the case.

"Yellow Serpent returned and told the Cayuses that Dr. McLaughlin said he had nothing to do in a war with the Indians; that he did not believe the Americans designed to attack them, and that if the *Americans did go to war with the Indians, the Hudson's Bay Company would not assist them.* After they got this information from the Emakus Myohut (big chief), the Indians became more calm. Many of them went to cultivating the ground as formerly, and a large number of little patches had been planted and sown before we arrived at the station."

Mr. Hines soon learned that the reports about war that had reached the lower country were not without foundation. That the Indians still had confidence in Mr. Geiger, and that they did not wish to go to war. The reader will observe the statement of the Indians after they had told Mr. Geiger they would fight if forced to do so. "They," the Indians, "said they had received their information concerning the designs of the Americans from Baptiste Doreo." This half-breed is also an interpreter of the Hudson's Bay Company, and an important leader among the half-breeds—next to Thomas McKay. After Doreo had told them his story, the Indians were still unwilling to commence a war against the Americans. They sent a messenger to Vancouver to consult Dr. McLaughlin, just as these same Indians in 1841 went to Mr. McKinley, then in charge of Fort Wallawalla, and wanted to know of him, if it was not good for them to drive Dr. Whitman and Mr. Gray away from that station because the Doctor refused to pay them for the land the mission occupied? Mr. McKinley understood their object, and was satisfied that there were outside influences that he did not approve of, and told the Indians, "Yes, you are braves; there is a number of you, and but two of them and two women and some little children; you can go and kill them or drive them away; you go just as quick as you can and do it; but if you do I will see that you are punished." The Indians understood Mr. McKinley. Whitman and Gray were not disturbed after this.

Dr. John McLaughlin we believe to have been one of the noblest of men while he lived, but, like Messrs. Hines, White, Burnett, Newell, Spalding, and many others, influences were brought to bear upon him that led him to adopt and pursue a doubtful if not a crooked course. It was evident to any one conversant with the times of which we are writing that there were at least four elements or influences operating in the country, viz., the unasserted or *quasi* rights of the American government; the coveted and actual occupancy of the country by the English Hudson's Bay Company and subjects, having the active civil organization of that government; the occupancy of the country by the American missions; and the coveted occupancy of the same by the Roman Jesuit missions.

These four influences could not harmonize; there was no such thing as a union and co-operation. The struggle was severe to hold and gain the controlling influence over the natives of the country, and shape the settlements to these conflicting views and national and sectarian feelings. The American settler, gaining courage and following the example and the track of the American missionaries with their wives, winds his way over the mountains and through the desert and barren plains down the Columbia River and through the Cascade Mountains,—weary, way-worn, naked, and hungry. In one instance, with his rifle upon his shoulder, and his wife and three children mounted upon the back of his last ox, he plods his weary way through Oregon City, and up the Wallamet, to find his future home; and there the warm heart of the early missionary and his family is ready to feed, clothe, and welcome the wanderer to this distant part of our great national domain, in order that he may aid in securing Oregon to its rightful inhabitants, and in forming a fifth power that shall supersede and drive away all foreign influences.

For a time the struggle with the four influences was severe and doubtful; but men who had crossed the Rocky and Cascade mountains with ox-teams, were not made to give up their country's cause in the hour of danger, though Britain and Rome, with their savage allies, joined to subdue and drive them from it. With the British Hudson's Bay Company, Roman Jesuit missions, savage Indians, American missions, and American settlers the struggle is continued.

CHAPTER XLI.

Governor Simpson and Dr. Whitman in Washington.—Interviews with Daniel Webster and President Tyler.—His cold reception in Boston by the American Board.—Conducts a large emigration safely across the Rocky Mountains into Oregon.—The "Memorial Half-Century Volume."—The Oregon mission ignored by the American Board.—Dr. McLaughlin.—His connection with the Hudson's Bay Company.—Catholic Cayuses' manner of praying.—Rev. C. Eells.—Letter from A. L. Lovejoy.—Description of Whitman's and Lovejoy's winter journey from Oregon to Bent's Fort on the Arkansas River.

Governor Simpson, of the Hudson's Bay Company, had reached Washington and been introduced to Mr. Webster, then Secretary of State, by the British Minister. All the influence a long-established and powerful monopoly, backed by the grasping disposition of the English government, can command, is brought to bear upon the question of the northwestern boundary. The executive of the American republic is about ready to give up the country, as of little value to the nation.

Just at this time, in the dead of winter, an awkward, tall, spare-visaged, vigorous, off-hand sort of a man, appeared at the Department in his mountain traveling garb, consisting of a dark-colored blanket coat and buckskin pants, showing that to keep himself from freezing to death he had been compelled to lie down close to his camp-fire while in the mountains, and on his way to Washington he had not stopped for a moment, but pushed on with a vigor and energy peculiarly his own. It is but justice to say of this man that his heart and soul were in the object of the errand for which he had traversed the vast frozen and desert regions of the Rocky Mountains, to accomplish which was to defeat the plans of the company, as shown by the taunting reply of the Briton, "*that no power could make known to his government the purposes of those who had laid their plans and were ready to grasp the prize they sought.*" While they were counting on wealth, power, influence, and the undisputed possession of a vast and rich country, this old pioneer missionary (layman though he was), having no thought of himself or of his ridiculous appearance before the great Daniel Webster and the President of a great nation, sought an interview with them and stated his object, and the plans and purposes of the Hudson's Bay Company and the British government: that their representations of this country were false in every respect as regards its agricultural, mineral, and commercial value to the nation; that it was only to secure the country to themselves, that the false reports about it had been put in circulation by their emissaries and agents; that a wagon road to the Pacific was practicable; that he had, in 1836, in opposition to all their false statements and influence to the contrary, taken a wagon to Boise; and that, in addition, wagons and teams had, in 1841, been taken to the Wallamet Valley, and that he expected, his life being spared, to pilot an emigration to the country that would forever settle the question beyond further dispute. He asserted that a road was practicable, and the country was invaluable to the American people. Mr. Webster coolly informed him that he had his mind made up; he was ready to part with what was to him an unknown and unimportant portion of our national domain, for the privilege of a small settlement in Maine and the fisheries on the banks of Newfoundland.

There was but one other hope in this case. This old off-hand Oregon missionary at once sought an interview with President Tyler. He repeated his arguments and reasons, and asked for delay in the final settlement of the boundary question, which, to those high in office, and, we may add, total ignorance of all that related to this vast country, was of small moment. But that Dr. Whitman (for the reader has already guessed the name of our missionary) stood before the President of the United States the only representative of Oregon and all her future interests and greatness, a self-constituted, self-appointed, and without a parallel self-periled representative, pleading simply for delay in the settlement of so vast and important a question to his country,—that he should be able to successfully contend with the combined influences brought against him,—can only be attributed to that over-ruling power which had decreed that the nation, whose interests he represented, should be sustained.

Mr. Tyler, after listening to the Doctor's statements with far more candor and interest than Mr. Webster was disposed to do, informed him that, notwithstanding they had received entirely different statements from gentlemen of the Hudson's Bay Company and the British minister, then in Washington, yet he would trust to his personal representation and estimate of the value of the country to the American people. He said: "Dr. Whitman, in accordance with your representations and agreeable to your request, this question shall be deferred. An escort shall be furnished for the protection of the emigration you propose to conduct to that distant country."

It is with deep regret, not to say shame, that truth and justice compel us to give in this connection any notice of this faithful and devoted missionary's reception and treatment, on his arrival in Boston, derogatory to the Board whom he had served so faithfully for seven years. Instead of being received and treated as his labors justly entitled him to be, he met the cold, calculating rebuke for unreasonable expenses, and for dangers incurred without order or instructions or permission from the mission to come to the States. Most of his reverend associates had, as the writer is credibly informed, disapproved of his visit to Washington, being ignorant of the true cause of his sudden determination to defeat, if possible, the British and Jesuitical designs upon the country; hence, for economical and prudential reasons, the Board received him coldly, and rebuked him for his presence before them, causing a chill in his warm and generous heart, and a sense of unmerited rebuke from those who should have been most willing to listen to all his statements, and most cordial and ready to sustain him in his herculean labors.

His request at Washington to save this richest jewel of our nation from British rule is granted, while the American Board of Commissioners for Foreign Missions is appealed to in vain for aid to save the Indians and the country from becoming the boast of the Italian Jesuit, and a prey to his degrading superstitions. The Doctor's mission, with all its accumulated influence, labors, and importance, is left to be swallowed up and destroyed by the same influence that had divided and destroyed that of the Methodist Mission.

Dr. Whitman disposed of his own little private property in the States, and, with the aid of his brother and brother's son, returned to Missouri, joined the emigration of 1843, and, as he had intimated to President Tyler, brought on an emigration outnumbering all the Hudson's Bay Company had brought to aid in securing the country to the British crown, proving to the American people and the world, what had long been asserted as impossible, that there was a practicable wagon road to the Pacific Ocean on American soil. His care, influence, aid, and attention to the emigration of 1843, I leave with those who can speak from personal observation. Their gratitude and deep sympathy for this self-devoted, faithful, and generous missionary led five hundred of them with uplifted hand to say they were ready with their own life-blood to avenge his death, and protect and defend the country. But influences, such as we have been speaking of, came in, justice was robbed of its right, and crime and murder permitted to go unpunished.

The cause in which Dr. Whitman enlisted, labored, and fell a victim, is allowed to suffer and fall, and in a Memorial Volume of the American Board, page 379, a false impression is given to the world, and a whole mission ignored. In this splendid, well-bound, and elegantly gotten up "Memorial Half-Century Volume," justly claiming much credit for the fifty past years of its labors, this Board has ignored all its errors and mistakes, and with one fell swoop of the pen consigned to oblivion, so far as its great standard record is concerned, one whole mission and a vast Indian population, as unworthy of a name or a notice in their record, further than as "Rev. Samuel Parker's exploring tour beyond the Rocky Mountains, under the direction of the Board, in 1835, 1836, and 1837, brought to light *no field for a great and successful mission*, but it added much to the science of geography, and is remarkable as having made known a practicable route for a *railroad* from the Mississippi to the Pacific." This shows a want of candor and also a disposition to ignore all influences and causes of failure of one of their own missions, and directs the attention of the reader to foreign objects, leaving their missions to become an easy prey to avarice, the Indian tribes to ignorance and superstition, and their missionaries to be despised and superseded by Jesuits; giving their enemies the benefit of that influence which they should have exerted to save their own missionary cause. Such being the case, we are not to wonder at the cold reception of Dr. Whitman, or the boundless influence and avarice of the men who compassed the early destruction of that mission; and, failing to destroy the American settlement, that they should now seek to rob our national treasury as they sought to rob the nation of its rightful domain. After being defeated by the American settlers in the organization of the provisional government in 1843, by the provisional army of 1847–8, they now come forward with the most barefaced effrontery and claim millions of dollars for a few old rotten forts. They have fallen to the lowest depths of crime to obtain compensation for improvements of no real value.

As we said when speaking of the "combination of influences and no harmony," we believe Dr. John McLaughlin to have been one of the best and noblest of men; yet the governing power of the Hudson's Bay Company would, if it were possible, have compelled him to starve the immigrants, and sacrifice all the early settlers of the country. Do you ask me how I know this? I answer, by the oaths of good and true American citizens, and by my own personal knowledge. These depositions or statements under oath but few of the readers of this history will ever see. In this connection we will give part of one deposition we listened to and penciled down from the mouth of the witness, who was the legal counselor and confidential friend of Dr. McLaughlin from the fall of 1846 till his death. This witness, in answer to the inquiry as to what Dr. McLaughlin told him about the Hudson's

Bay Company's encouraging the early settlement of Oregon, said Dr. McLaughlin *had not encouraged the American settlement of the country*, but from the fact that immigrants arrived poor and needy, they must have suffered had he not furnished supplies on a credit; that he could have wished that this had not been necessary, because he believed there were those above him who *strongly disapproved of his course in this respect, affirming that it would lead to the permanent settlement of the country by American citizens*, and thus give to the United States government an element of title to the country; the United States government could not have a title to the country without such settlement, and these persons, thus alluded to as being dissatisfied, would report him to the Hudson's Bay Company's house in London; that he ascertained finally that such complaints had been made, but that he still continued to furnish the supplies, because, *as a man of common humanity*, he could not do otherwise; and he resolved that he would continue thus to do and take whatever consequences might result from it; that the company's managing and controlling office in London did finally call him to an account for thus furnishing supplies as already stated, and for reasons indicated; that he represented to them the circumstances under which he had furnished these supplies, alleging that as a man of *common humanity it was not possible for him to do otherwise than as he did;* that he foresaw as clearly as they did that it aided in the American settlement of the country, but that this he could not help, and it was not for him but for God and government to look after and take care of the consequences; that the Bible told him, "If thine enemy hunger, feed him; if he is naked, clothe him;" that these settlers were not even enemies; that in thus finding fault with him they quarreled with heaven (the witness said, "I do not know as that was the exact expression or word") *for doing what any one truly worthy the name of a man could not hesitate to do*, and that he immediately concluded by indignantly saying, "*Gentlemen, if such is your order, I will serve you no longer*," and from that day Oregon secured a warm and faithful friend in that old white-headed man, and he a base and infamous enemy in those who claimed the title of the Honorable Hudson's Bay Company, who in 1866 are claiming all the credit and pay for this old man's generous and noble deeds.

The readers of our history will excuse this interruption in the order of events, or rather the introduction of this testimony at this time in our sketches, for we shall still have to speak of Dr. McLaughlin as the head of the Hudson's Bay Company, and continue him as a representative of that influence, as also connected with the Roman Catholic efforts in the country; for while we condemn and speak of base and infamous acts in all alike, we will not forget the good and the noble. We have other items of testimony that reveal to us the deep-laid plans, the vast influence used, and efforts made, *to prevent the American settlement of this country*, which shall be brought to light as we proceed.

One other item we will now give as developed by the testimony above referred to. Dr. McLaughlin informed his attorney "that he had proposed to the company's authority in London, that if they would allow him to retain the profits upon the supplies and advances made as above mentioned to the settlers, he would very cheerfully personally assume the payment to the company of all the sums thus advanced, but this the company declined to do." The witness said: "My memory is not very distinct, at least, not so much as it is as to the statement above made, but my recollection is that he also informed me that the company, although it refused to permit him to retain the profits above mentioned, did hold him responsible for every dollar of the advances he made, and I do know that he regarded and treated the debts thus owing by American citizens as debts owing not to the Hudson's Bay Company, but to himself individually."

Dr. McLaughlin charges ingratitude upon those who were able to, and did not pay him, and were guilty of denouncing him as an aristocrat. He was no aristocrat, but one of the kindest, most obliging, and familiar men; yet his tall, erect, and noble frame, a head covered with white hair, a long white beard, light complexion, rather spare but open countenance, with a full light blue or gray eye, made the coward and the mean man hate him, while the truly noble man would love him for his generous and unbounded benevolence. Like Dr. Whitman, the influences around him weighed heavily upon his soul; he keenly felt the pain of ingratitude in others; he felt it from the Hudson's Bay Company, whom he had faithfully served, and from the persons he had befriended. An attempt was made by a member of the company, who had previously sworn to the justness of their infamous claims, to excite the sectarian prejudice of the witness against Dr. McLaughlin on his cross-examination, by handing to the company's attorney the following questions to be asked the witness:—

Ques.—"Do you not recollect that Dr. McLaughlin told you that Sir George Simpson's complaint against him was his allowing a credit of ten thousand pounds sterling to Bishop Blanchet, of the Catholic mission, without any security?"

Ans.—"This is the first time I have heard of that transaction."

Ques.—"Do you not know from what Dr. McLaughlin told you, that he gave large credits to the Catholic Mission while in charge of the company's business?"

Ans.—" I do not."

In reference to the last two questions and answers, in looking over the items of account against our government, something over this amount is stated as an item of claim for improvements and a Catholic church building and two schoolhouses at Vancouver, as having been made by the Hudson's Bay Company for the Catholic missions and the benefit of the company's business, which are still standing and in possession of the priests and nuns of that order. This matter should be closely investigated. We have abundance of other evidence to show the intimate and continued connection of the Jesuit missions with the company, and we look upon this attempt to change the responsibility of that connection from the company to Dr. McLaughlin's individual account, as among the basest of their transactions. The Jesuitical Catholic concern was a child of their own, and one they are still nursing in all their vast dominions. They made use of Dr. McLauglin as long as they could, and when they found he was inclined to favor the American settlement of the country, he fell under the displeasure of his superiors and was called to an account.

These facts explain the careful and repeated injunctions, and positive directions given to the early missionaries not to interfere with the Hudson's Bay Company's trade, *and by no means to encourage the settlement of white men about their stations, compelling those white men to become subject to, and connected with, the missions.* They also explain the reasons for the extreme caution exercised by the company over the supplies granted to the American missions. They invariably limited them to the smallest possible necessity, and by this means sought to prevent the settlement of the country. It also explains fully the complaint of Rev. Mr. Griffin in his effort for an independent mission, and shows conclusively the continued effort of the company to check as much as possible the progress of the settlement, as also the desperate effort they made in 1847 to destroy the missions and all American settlements; and more than this, it explains the continued wars with all the Indians who have ever been under the influence of the company, or their *pet child, the Jesuit missions.*

The Hudson's Bay Company had no fault to find with Dr. McLaughlin, except in his refusing to carry out their base designs upon the American settlers and for the assistance he rendered upon his own responsibility to the naked and starving immigrants that Grant, at Fort Hall, with the Indians along the route, had combined to deceive and rob, while on the way to the country. This old, white-headed man, who had served them for forty years, *was compelled,* in maintaining his honor as a man possessing one noble feeling of humanity, to leave their service.

What think you, kind reader, of the Hudson's Bay Company's kindness and generosity to the American settler, when this same company held this old faithful servant of theirs individually responsible for every dollar, principal and profits, of the supplies his generous heart, claiming to be humane, was induced to advance to the early settler in the hour of his greatest need?

Will you vote and pay a tax to pay claims of such a company, when one of the managing partners is still base enough to say, "It was a neglect of the company's agent, after Dr. McLaughlin's decease, that they did not present their accounts for payment to the doctor's heirs or administrator before the year's notice was up. It was now too late, and it was lost to the company unless they could get it allowed by the United States government?"

We justly deprecate piracy, slavery, highway robbery, and Indian massacres. In what light shall we hold a company and government, who have pursued a course directly and indirectly calculated to produce all these, and with the uplifted hand say they are entitled to pay for such conduct?

But we must still refer to Dr. McLaughlin as representing the Hudson's Bay Company, as we proceed with our history of events, agencies, men, and things occurring in 1843.

Dr. Whitman is on his way back to Oregon with eight hundred and seventy-five persons, with all their equipments and cattle. Simpson is foiled and disappointed at Washington. Hines and Dr. White are among the Upper Columbia Indians. Dr. McLaughlin and the French-Canadians and priests are in commotion about the effort to organize the settlement into a provisional government, and the influence the Americans appear to be gaining over the Indians. Piopiomoxmox (Yellow Serpent) has returned and reported to the Cayuses the result of his visit to Dr. McLaughlin, and the determination of the company that, in case of a war with the Americans, "*they would not aid the Americans*, but let them take care of themselves." The old Indian chiefs had advised the young men to wait and see what the future designs of the Americans were; while the Jesuits had been careful to impress upon the savage mind their peculiar sectarian notions and prejudices, as illustrated by the religious instructions given by the priests to the Cayuses.

The Rev. H. K. W. Perkins called at Young Chief's (Tawatowe) lodge, and was informed on entering, that they had not yet had their morning prayer. The chief caused a bell to be rung, at the sound of which all his band came together for devotion. Tawatowe then said to Mr. Perkins: "We are Catholics, and our worship is different from yours." He then fell upon his knees, all the rest kneeling and facing him. The chief had a long string of beads on his neck to which was attached a brass cross. After all were knelt, they devoutly crossed themselves, and commenced their prayer as follows: "We are poor, we are poor," repeating it ten times, and then closing with "Good Father, good Son, good Spirit," and then the chief would slip a bead on the string. This was continued until all the beads were removed from one part of the string to the other. When this mock devotion closed, Tawatowe said: "This is the way in which the priest taught us to worship God;" but Elijah (a boy that had been educated at the Methodist Indian school) said that "Tawatowe and his band prayed from the head, but we [meaning his own Wallawalla tribe] pray from the heart."

Since writing the above, we have found in the *Missionary Herald* of December, 1866, page 371, a letter from Rev. C. Eells, formerly of the Spokan Mission. In speaking of Dr. Whitman's visit to the States, he says: "Mr. Walker and myself were decidedly opposed, and we yielded only when it became evident that he would go, even if he became disconnected with the mission in order to do so. According to the understanding of the members of the mission, the single object of Dr. Whitman in attempting to cross the continent in the winter of 1842–43, amid mighty perils and sufferings, was to make a desperate effort to save this country to the United States."

We are not much surprised at Mr. Eells' ignorance of influences operating in this country. His fears and caution have made him unreasonably timid. He is always so fearful that he will do or say something wrong, that the saving of this country to our government, and an attempt on the part of his associates to counteract Roman Catholic superstitions and maintain the influence of the Protestant religion on our western coast, are opposed by him and his equally timid associate. He has not the frankness or courage to state the whole truth in the case, as developed in Mr. Treat's remarks, who, after giving Mr. Eells' letter, says: "*It was not simply an American question, however;* it was at the same time a Protestant question. He [Dr. Whitman] was fully alive to the efforts which the Roman Catholics were making to gain the mastery on the Pacific coast, and he was firmly persuaded that they were working in the interests of the Hudson's Bay Company, with a view to this very end. The danger from this quarter [which Messrs. Eells and and Walker could never see, or, if they did, were too timid to speak or act] had made a profound impression upon his mind. Under date of April 1, 1847, he said: "In the autumn of 1842, I pointed out to our mission the arrangements of the Papists to settle in our vicinity, and that it only required that those arrangements should be completed to close our operations."

It is in reference to the facts above quoted from Dr. Whitman's letter—made in our presence to those timid associates—that we say they were cowards in not speaking and acting as they should have done at that time, and since his death.

The following letter from General A. L. Lovejoy gives further proof of Dr. Whitman's efforts to save Oregon to his country:—

PORTLAND, OREGON, November 6, 1869.

William H. Gray, Esq.:

MY DEAR SIR,—Your note of the 27th ult., making inquiries touching the journey of the late Dr. Marcus Whitman to the United States from this coast in the winter of 1842 and '43, and his reception at Washington, and by the American Board of Commissioners for Foreign Missions, etc., has but just come to hand, owing to my being absent from home.

True, I was the traveling companion of the Doctor in that arduous and trying journey, but at this late hour it will be almost impossible for me to give many of the thrilling scenes and hairbreadth escapes that we went through, traveling as we did, almost the entire route, through a hostile Indian country, as well as suffering much from the intense cold and snows that we had to encounter in passing over the Rocky Mountains in midwinter.

Previous to our leaving Wailatpu, I often had conversations with the Doctor touching the prospects of this coast. The Doctor was alive to its interests, and manifested a very warm desire to have this country properly represented at Washington, and, after some arrangements, we left Wailatpu, October 3, 1842, overland, for the Eastern States.

We traveled rapidly, and reached Fort Hall in eleven days, and remained only a day or two and made some few purchases; took a guide and left for Fort Wintee, as the Doctor changed from a direct route to one more southern through the Spanish country, *via* Taos and Santa Fé. On our way from Fort Hall to Fort Wintee we met with terribly severe weather; the snows greatly retarded our progress, and blinded the trail, so much so that we lost much time. After reaching Fort Wintee and making some suitable purchases for our trip, we took a new guide and started on our journey for Fort Macumpagra, situate on the waters of Grand River, in the Spanish country.

Here again our stay was very short. We simply made some few purchases, took a new guide, and left for Taos. After being out some four or five days, as we were passing over high table-lands, we encountered a most terrific snow-storm, which forced us to seek shelter at once. A deep ravine being near by, we rapidly made for it, but the snow fell so rapidly, and the wind blew with such violence, that it was almost impossible to reach it. After reaching the ravine, and cutting some cotton-wood trees for our animals, we attempted some arrangements for camp as best we could under the circumstances, and remained snowed in for some three or four days, when the storm subsided, and it cleared off intensely cold. It was with much difficulty that we made our way up upon the high lands; the snow was so deep and the wind so piercing and cold, that we felt compelled to return to camp and wait a few days for a change of weather.

Our next effort was more successful, and after spending several days wandering round in the snow, without making much headway, and greatly fatiguing our animals, to little or no purpose, our guide informed us that the deep snows had so changed the face of the country, that he was completely lost, and could take us no further.

This was a terrible blow to the Doctor. He was determined not to give it up without another effort. And we at once agreed that the Doctor should take the guide and make his way back to the fort, and procure a new guide, and that I should remain in camp with the animals until his return, which was on the seventh day, with a new guide.

We were soon under way, on our route, traveling through the snows at rather a snail's pace. Nothing occurred of much importance, other than hard and slow traveling until we reached, as our guide informed us, the Grand River, which was frozen, on either side, about one-third across. The current was so very rapid, that the center of the stream remained open, although the weather was intensely cold.

This stream was some one hundred and fifty, or two hundred yards wide, and looked upon by our guide as very dangerous to cross in its present condition. But the Doctor, nothing daunted, was the first to take the water. He mounted his horse, and the guide and myself pushed them off the ice into the boiling, foaming stream. Away they went completely under water—horse and all; but directly came up, and after buffeting the waves and foaming current, he made to the ice on the opposite side, a long way down the stream—leaped from his horse upon the ice, and soon had his noble animal by his side. The guide and myself forced in the pack animals; followed the doctor's example, and were soon drying our frozen clothes by a comfortable fire.

With our new guide, traveling slowly on, we reached Taos in about thirty days. We suffered considerably from cold and scarcity of provisions, and for food were compelled to use the flesh of mules, dogs, and such other animals as came in our reach.

We remained at Taos some twelve or fifteen days, when we changed off our animals, and made such purchases as our journey required, and left for Bent's Fort, on the headwaters of the Arkansas River, where we arrived about the third day of January, 1843.

The Doctor left here on the 7th, at which time we parted, and I did not meet him again until some time in the month of July, above Fort Laramie, on his way to Oregon with a train of emigrants.

The Doctor often expressed himself to me about the remainder of his journey, and the manner in which he was received at Washington and by the Board of Missions at Boston.

The Doctor had several interviews with President Tyler, Secretary Webster, and many members of Congress, touching the interests of Oregon. He urged the immediate termination of the treaty with Great Britain relative to this country, and the extension of the laws of the United States, and to provide liberal inducements to emigrants to come to this coast.

He felt much chagrined at the lack of interest, and the great want of knowledge concerning Oregon, and the wants of this country, though he was very cordially and kindly received, and many seemed anxious to obtain every information which he could give them; and I have no doubt, the Doctor's interviews resulted greatly to the benefit of Oregon and the entire coast.

But his reception at Boston was not so cordial. The Board censured him for leaving his post, for the waste of time and the great expense attending so long a journey across the continent at that season of the year.

The Doctor returned to the frontier settlements, urging the citizens to emigrate to the Pacific coast. After his exertions in this behalf, he left for Independence, Missouri, and started for Oregon with a large emigrant train some time in the month of May. With his energy and knowledge of the country, he rendered them very great assistance, and continued to do so, till he reached his home about the first of October (one year from the time he left), to find the home of his choice sadly neglected, and the flouring mill burned to the ground.

The Indians were very hostile about the Doctor's leaving at the time he did, and I have no doubt, that during his absence, the thistles of his destruction—the seeds of that awful massacre of himself, Mrs. Whitman, and many others—were then sown by those haughty and savage Cayuses, although it did not take place till four years afterward.

As to your fourth inquiry relative to the Cayuse war. It is a long time since these events took place; and most of them are on record, and have passed into the history of the country; so that I would not like to make many statements from memory, although I was an adjutant-general, and was also one of the commissioners to raise means to equip the first company, which was dispatched to the Dalles the day after the sad news of the massacre reached Oregon City.

There being no supplies at Oregon City suitable to fit out this company, the commissioners proceeded at once to Fort Vancouver to procure supplies for an outfit. The Hudson's Bay Company refused to let us have any thing on account of the government; but would on our joint and several note, to the amount of $1,000, which was cheerfully given, and the outfit was obtained, and the company was pushed on to its destination, and reached the Dalles in time to prevent further bloodshed at that place by the red devils.

Yours, with great respect,

A. L. LOVEJOY.

W. H. GRAY, Esq., Astoria, Oregon.

CHAPTER XLII.

Assembly of the Nez Percés, Cayuses, and Wallawallas.—Mock fight.—Council with the Indians.—Speeches by Yellow Serpent, Tilokaikt, the Prince, and Illutin.—The secret of the whole difficulty.—John, the Kanaka.—A cow for a horse.—Killing of a medicine woman.

We will return to Rev. Mr. Hines' narrative of his trip among the Cayuses, May 22, 1843.

"As the Indians refused to come together unless Ellis and his men came down to meet us, we informed them that we would go up and see Ellis in his own country; but being suspicious that we intended to prevent his coming down, they were much opposed to our going. Explaining to the chiefs the object of our visit, they seemed to be satisfied."

We have, in this short statement of Mr. Hines, an important fact. The Cayuse Indians had been instructed what to do; they were not to be diverted by any arrangements of the sub-agent. Notwithstanding, the agent and Mr. Hines had learned that Ellis was coming with several hundred warriors, they knew not for what purpose, some saying to make war upon the Cayuses, and they had determined to prevent the meeting of the two tribes if possible. During their absence the Cayuses all collected not far from Dr. Whitman's, and were waiting the arrival of the Nez Percés. On the 22d of May the Nez Percés, some six hundred strong, with a thousand horses, arrived on the plain. Some three hundred of the Cayuses and Wallawallas uniting formed a grand Indian cavalcade on the plain in front of Dr. Whitman's house, when a grand display of Indian horsemanship commenced, such as advancing in mock fantastic fight, with discharges of blank cartridges, wheeling and running in all directions, till the Indians had nearly worked themselves into a real fight and a great excitement. Ellis said that he thought the Cayuses were determined to have a fight in earnest.

Tawatowe, the *Catholic* chief, as he approached them appeared quite angry and disposed to quarrel. Seeing the excitement increasing, and fearing that it might end seriously unless the attention of the Indians could be drawn to some other subject, Mr. Spalding, who was present, gave notice that all would repair to Dr. Whitman's house for *tallapooso* (worship). But Tawatowe came forward in a very boisterous manner and inquired what we had made all this disturbance for. The

American party, followed by several hundred Indians, repaired to the station and engaged in religious exercises, when the excitement subsided for the night.

On May 23, the chiefs and principal men of the three tribes assembled at the station to hear what the self-constituted United States Indian commissioner and his secretary of state had to say.

"They were called to order by Tawatowe, who by this time had got over his excitement, and then was placed before them the object of our visit. They were told that much had been said about war, and we had come to assure them that they had nothing to fear from that quarter." If Dr. White was no more explicit in setting forth the object of this visit to the Indians than Mr. Hines is in giving the account of it, there certainly was room for a misunderstanding between him and the Indians. He said "the President of the United States had not sent him [Dr. White] to make war upon them, but to enter into arrangements with them to regulate their intercourse with the white people. We were not there to catch them in a trap, as a man would a beaver, but to do them good; and if they would lay aside their former practices and prejudices, stop their quarrels, cultivate their lands, and receive good laws, they might become a great and happy people; that in order to do this *they must all be united*." Exactly what the Hudson's Bay Company wished to have done to aid them in crushing the American settlement and preventing further American emigration to the country.

As a reason for their being united, Mr. Hines says, 178–9th pages: "They were told they were few in comparison to the whites, and if they were not all of one heart they would be able to accomplish nothing. The chiefs should set the example and love each other, and not get proud and haughty, but consider the people as their brothers and their children, and labor to do them good, that the people should be obedient, and in their morning and evening prayers they should remember their chiefs.

"Ellis remarked that it would not be proper for the Nez Percé chiefs to speak until the Cayuse people should receive the laws. The Cayuse chiefs replied: 'If you want us to receive the laws, bring them forward and let us see them, as we can not take them unless we know what they are.'

"A speech was then delivered to the young men to impress them favorably with regard to the laws. They were told that they would soon take the places of the old men, and they should be willing to act for the good of the people; that they should not go here and there and spread false reports about war; and that this had been the cause of all the difficulty and excitement that had prevailed among them during the past winter."

With the information which Mr. Hines has already given us in the first part of his ninth chapter, we would suppose he would avoid this apparently incorrect statement to the Indians of the cause of the difficulties then existing. He and Dr. White appear to have acted under the same influence with Dr. McLaughlin, and to have carried all their acts and counsels to the one object, which was to combine the Indians, and divide and destroy the settlement. He tells us, in continuation of the proceedings of this council, that "the laws were then read, first in English, and then in Nez Percé."

"Yellow Serpent then rose and said: 'I have a message to you. Where are these laws from? I would that you might say they were from God. But I think they are from the earth, because, from what I know of white men [a term claimed by Brouillet as belonging to the Hudson's Bay Company and Frenchmen], they do not honor these laws.' In answer to this, the people were informed that the laws were recognized by God, and imposed on men in all civilized countries. Yellow Serpent was pleased with the explanation, and said that it was according to the instructions he had received from others, and he was glad to learn that it was so, because many of his people had been angry with him when he had whipped them for crime, and had told him that God would send him to hell for it, and he was glad to know that it was pleasing to God.

"Tilokaikt, a Cayuse chief, rose and said: 'What do you read the laws for before we take them? We do not take the laws because Tawatowe says so. He is a *Catholic*, and as a people we do not follow his worship.' Dr. White replied that this did not make any difference about the law; that the people in the States had different modes of worship, yet all had one law.

"A chief, called the Prince, arose and said: 'I understand you gave us liberty to examine every law,—all the words and lines,—and as questions are asked about it, we should get a better understanding of it. The people of this country have but one mind about it. I have something to say, but perhaps the people will dispute me. As a body, we have not had an opportunity to consult, therefore you come to us as in a wind, and speak to us as to the air, as we have no point, and we can not speak because we have no point before us. The business before us is whole like a body; we have not dissected it. And perhaps you will say it is out of place for me to speak, because I am not a great chief. Once I had influence, but now I have but little.'"

This was one of the principal chiefs of the tribe that assisted in taking Fort Wallawalla and tying Mr. Pambrun to compel him to give more goods for horses and furs. "He was about to sit down, but was told to go on. He then said: 'When the whites first came among us, we had no cattle; they have given us none; what we have now got we have obtained by an exchange of property. A long time ago Lewis and Clarke came to this country, and I want to know what they said about us. Did they say they found friends or enemies here?' Being told that they spoke well of the Indians, the Prince said: 'That is a reason why the whites should unite with us, and all become one people. Those who have been here before you have left us no memorial of their kindness, by giving us presents. We speak by way of favor; if you have any benefit to bestow, we will then speak more freely. One thing that we can speak about is cattle, and the reason why we can not speak out now is because we have not the thing before us. My people are poor and blind, and we must have something tangible. Other chiefs have bewildered me since they came; yet I am from an honorable stock. Promises which have been made to me and my fathers have not been fulfilled, and I am made miserable; but it will not answer for me to speak out, for my people do not consider me as their chief.' [This was just what Mr. Pambrun, of the Hudson's Bay Company, had done to this Indian chief to break his power and destroy his influence with his tribe and his people. But let us hear him through.] 'One thing more; you have reminded me of what was promised me some time ago, and I am inclined to follow on and see, though I have been giving my beaver to the whites and have received many promises, and have always been disappointed; I want to know what you are going to do?'

"Illutin, or Big Belly, then arose and said that the old men were wearied with the wickedness of the young men; that if he was alone he could say 'Yes' at once to the laws, and that the reason why the young men did not feel as he felt, was because they had stolen property in their hands, and the laws condemned stealing. But he assured them that the laws were calculated to do them good and not evil.

"But this did not satisfy the Prince. He desired that the good which it was proposed to do them by adopting the laws might be put in a tangible form before them.

"He said that it had been a long time since the country had been discovered by whites, and that ever since that time people had been coming along promising to do them good; but they had all passed by and left no blessing behind them."

This chief said that "the Hudson's Bay Company had persuaded them to continue with them, and not go after the Americans; that if the Americans designed to do them good, why did they not bring goods with them to leave with the Indians? that they were fools to listen to what *Suapies* (Americans) had to say; that they would only talk, but the company would *both talk and give them presents.*"

This Indian, as his speech shows, was shrewd, and thought he was certain to obtain his object, either from the Hudson's Bay Company or the Americans. He had been humbled by the company, and an offer to buy him back had been made. He bid for a higher price with the Americans. In doing so, he naturally exposed the secret influence of the company, which is given in this book of Mr. Hines', as a matter of course, and he passes along without note or comment upon what he saw, and heard.

"In reply to the last Indian speech, Dr. White told the Indians that he did not come to them as a missionary or as a trader."

To Ellis and Lawyer, who called on them in the evening to have a talk, "they said they expected pay for being chiefs, and wanted to know how much salary Dr. White was going to give them. Ellis said he had counted the months he had been in office, and thought that enough was due him to make him rich. They left at a late hour without receiving any satisfaction. In the council, efforts were made to induce the Nez Percés to unite under one chief in the fall of 1842. Thomas McKay had promised these chiefs large salaries and many presents that Dr. White and his government would give them as an inducement to form a union, knowing that White had not the ability or means to make good his promises to them, and in this way any influence as an agent of the American government he might have would be lost in this tribe.

"Ellis was a Hudson's Bay Indian, educated at the Red River settlement. They left this private interview with White without any satisfaction, showing that the policy of the company was producing its legitimate effect upon Ellis's mind. The Lawyer, however, understood the matter in its true light. He explained to us the whole transaction, and the promises of McKay from the company. He thought Dr. White was foolish to let McKay talk so much for him and the American government.

"Some hundreds again assembled the next day (May 24) to renew the business relative to laws; but the first thing investigated was the shooting of John, the Kanaka, by the Indian. John had gone to a lodge the day before, and in a dispute in a trade he had dared the Indian to shoot him. The Indian had seized his gun and fired it at John's head, making considerable of a hole in the scalp, but none in the scull. The Indian fled, but was brought back and found guilty and kept till the laws were adopted for sentence and punishment, and finally punished with forty lashes on the bare back.

"The Indians continued to speak in reference to the laws. Their speeches were grave, energetic, mighty, and eloquent, and generally in favor of receiving the laws. After all had spoken it was signified that they were ready to vote whether they would take the laws or not, and the vote was unanimous in the affirmative. Having adopted the laws, it was now necessary to elect their chief, according to the provisions of the laws, and Tawatowe was nominated to the highest chieftainship. Some were opposed; a majority were in favor, and while the question was pending [this Indian had not consulted his priest, or he would have declined at once on this first proposition to elect him chief], Tawatowe arose and said, 'My friends, I rise to speak to you, and I want you all to listen.' He then adverted to his past history, and told them how much he had suffered in consequence of their divisions and quarrels. Tawatowe joined his influence with the Prince to get more pay from the Hudson's Bay Company for horses and furs, hence his tribe were encouraged to quarrel with and disrespect him. When we first arrived in the country he was seldom invited to the fort, and received no presents from the company. He inquired of his people if they would lay aside all their past difficulties and come up and support him if he would accept of the chieftainship.

"It was now time to close for the day, and the vote being put, Tawatowe was declared duly elected to the high chieftainship of the Cayuse tribe.

"Dr. White bought of Mrs. Whitman a fat ox and presented it to the Indians. Mrs. W. gave them a fat hog, which they butchered and feasted upon at night.

"May 25.—A number of the chiefs came early in the morning at Mr. Hines' request, to settle a difficulty concerning some horses which they gave to Rev. Jason Lee when he first came to Oregon in 1834, Mr. Lee having requested Mr. Hines to come to some arrangement with them if possible. After a long talk we succeeded in settling with them by proposing to give them a cow for each horse that they had given to Mr. Lee. We found that the Indians always expected to be well paid for a present."

The Jesuit missionaries and the Hudson's Bay Company had represented to the Indians that Mr. Lee's receiving their horses and not making them any presents was the same as stealing from them, and in this way the American missionary was regarded as having stolen the Indians' horses. In the conversations and talks the Indians had with Dr. Whitman about the land the mission occupied, the horses given to

Mr. Lee were generally mentioned. Dr. Whitman was anxious that some arrangement should be made to settle that matter as soon as he learned the facts in the case. The Indians, as per arrangement with Mr. Hines, did receive a cow for each horse given, and thus the matter was satisfactorily settled.

The Indians having again assembled, Tawatowe came forward and said that he had made up his mind that he could not accept of the chieftainship, in consequence of the *difference of his religion* from that of most of his people.

Here is Jesuitism and Hudson's Bay, combined with ignorance and religious bigotry, and shows the influence then operating upon the savage mind. This Indian declared a reason why he could not accept the chieftainship, which, four years later, would have fixed at once a crime upon that sect, without a shadow of doubt in their favor. As it was, the plan was deeper, and a Protestant Indian, or one that favored the Protestant cause and American missions, a younger brother of Tawatowe is selected. Tawatowe resigned, and his brother Five Crows is elected the American head chief of the Cayuse tribe, with the approval of the sub-agent of the United States. Bear these facts in mind as we proceed, that you may fully understand the deep-laid plots of the foreign influence then operating in the country to secure the whole or a large portion of it for themselves and their own government.

In connection with this we will give one other incident as related by Mr. Hines on his tour among the Indians, to show the shrewdness, as also the long premeditated baseness of the Hudson's Bay Company in their efforts to get rid of all American missionaries and settlers, and to bring on a war with the Indians. Mr. Hines and party returned to the Dalles, and from there Mr. Hines embarked on one of the Hudson's Bay Company's boats with Mr. Ogden for Vancouver. A short distance below the Dalles they were driven ashore by a wind storm. While there, Mr. Ogden told the following story of the killing of a medicine woman, or doctress:—

"Mr. Ogden related some of his wonderful adventures among the Indians, with whom he had resided more than thirty years. He was an eye-witness to a remarkable circumstance that transpired at the Dalles during one of his voyages up the Columbia.

"He arrived at the Dalles on the Sabbath day, and seeing a congregation of some three hundred Indians assembled not far from the river, he drew near to ascertain the cause, and found the Rev. H. K. W. Perkins dispensing to them the word of reconciliation through a crucified Redeemer. There was in the outskirts of the congregation an Indian woman who had been for many years a doctress in the tribe, and who had just expended all her skill upon a patient, the only son of a man whose wigwam was not far distant, and for whose recovery she had become responsible by consenting to become his physician. All her efforts to remove the disease were unavailing; the father was doomed to see his son expire. Believing that the doctress had the power of preserving life or inflicting death according to her will, and that instead of curing she had killed his boy, he resolved upon the most summary revenge. Leaving his dead son in the lodge, he broke into the congregation with a large butcher-knife in his hand, and, rushing upon the now terrified doctress, seized her by the hair, and with one blow across her throat laid her dead at his feet."

This story is a very plausible one, as much so as the one Mr. Hines tells us on the 110th page of his book, about Smith, Sublet, and Dripse's partner. There is an object in telling this story at this time to Mr. Hines, as much so as there was in a letter written by James Douglas, Esq., to S. N. Castle, Esq., and published in the March number of the *Friend*, at Honolulu, Sandwich Islands, which we will give in due time.

The reader will observe in these sketches that our effort has been to speak of all the principal events and prominent and prospective influences in our early history, as in the year in which they occurred. In attending to other duties we have not been able to keep as close to dates and chronological order as we could wish; still, with patience and perseverance we can restore the "lost history" of our early settlement upon this coast, so that the future historian can have the material before him for an interesting chapter in the history of our country.

We have, in addition to personal and public duties, to wade through an immense amount of what is called Oregon history, to gather up dates and events that have been given to the public at different times, without order, or apparent object, only to write a book on Oregon. We have no hesitancy in saying that Rev. G. Hines has given to the public the fullest and best book, and yet there is but a single chapter that is useful to the historian.

Rev. Samuel Parker has many scientific and useful statements and observations, but all come in before our civil history began to develop itself.

CHAPTER XLIII.

The Legislative Committee of nine.—Hon. Robert Moore, chairman.—Description of the members.—Minutes of their proceedings.—Dr. R. Newell, his character.—Two specimens of his speeches.—The dark clouds.

In 1843 the people of Oregon showed signs of life, and sprang into existence as an American Territory with their provisional government, which we have allowed to be silently forming in the Wallamet Valley, while we have traced the operations of the Hudson's Bay Company, and Dr. Whitman to Washington; and also Dr. White and Mr. Hines among the Indians, all over the country. This will enable the reader to understand the strong influences operating against the American settlement; and if he will go with us, we will introduce him to the first Legislative Committee of nine, and tell him just what we know of their proceedings all through their deliberations.

The record shows no instruction from the settlers, as to when or where the committee should meet to prepare the laws, to report at Champoeg, only, that they were limited to six days, and to be allowed $1.25 per day, and that the money be raised by subscription. Every member at once subscribed to the full amount of his own per diem pay, and in addition to this, Mr. Alanson Beers, Rev. J. L. Parish, and Dr. Babcock subscribed the full amount of the board of the whole nine, and the Methodist Mission furnished without charge the use of their granary at the old mission, as the first council chamber on this western coast. The building was a frame some sixteen by thirty feet, one and a half stories high, boards upright, with one square room in front, and the balance used for a granary, from which it derived its name; the upper part was for storing and sleeping use. The square room was used for schoolhouse and church, and now, for a legislative hall.

We will enter this hall and introduce you to an old gray-headed man with a fair complexion, bald head, light eye, full face, frequent spasmodic nodding forward of the head, and a large amount of self-importance, not very large intellectual developments, with a super-abundance of flesh, sitting by a square-legged table or stand, in a chair with square posts, and strips of rawhide for bottom; dressed in fustian pants, large blue vest, and striped shirt, and a common brown coat, who, on motion of Mr. Hill, was chosen Speaker of the House, and hereafter will be known in our history as Hon. Robert Moore, Esq.

The first difficulty the committee found was to organize a government without an executive. They could organize a legislative body, and appoint all the committees and officers and draft all the laws necessary, but the folly and absurdity of the effort without an executive, was so apparent, that the first thing decided upon, was, Shall we have an executive head, called a governor, or a committee with executive powers! This was a difficult question, under all the votings and the discussions that had taken place. The committee were fully aware of all the opposition they must contend with. The judgeship had passed by vote of the people at Champoeg from a member of the Methodist Mission to Mr. A. E. Wilson, an intelligent, unassuming, and excellent young man, who came to the country in the employ of Mr. Cushing, and had become a settler.

The committee were well assured that they could eventually secure the Methodist Mission influence, yet at this time it was extremely doubtful, and they feared that it would, as in the previous effort of 1841, go against them, with that of the Catholic Mission and the Hudson's Bay Company. An executive committee consisting of three men would form a council that could act in any emergency, and at the same time enable the Methodist Mission to be represented by one of their members in the Executive Council.

Alanson Beers was a good, honest, faithful, and intelligent Christian man, acting with heart and soul with the interests of the settlement and the American cause. The settlers could rely upon him.

David Hill was a resident of Hillsborough, Tualatin Plains, and was known to be decidedly opposed to the company, and not any too favorable to the Catholic and Methodist missions. He could be relied upon so far as the outside settlers were concerned, and Robert Newell could represent the Rocky Mountain men and such of the Canadian-French Hudson's Bay Company, and Roman Catholics as were disposed to join our organization. It was in consequence of his contending so strongly for the Hudson's Bay Company's rights, interests, and privileges, at Champoeg, on the 5th of July, that he was dropped, and Joseph Gale (who was one of the Ewing Young party to bring cattle from California to the Wallamet settlement) elected in his place.

With the understanding as above indicated, the Legislative Committee, consisting of Hon. Robert Moore, David Hill, Robert Shortess, Alanson Beers, W. H. Gray, Thomas J. Hubbard, James A. O'Neil, Robert Newell, and William Dougherty, with the uplifted hand solemnly declared before God that they would faithfully perform the duties assigned them by the people of this settlement, at Champoeg, on the 2d day of May, A. D. 1843, so far as they understood the duties thus assigned them. W. H. Gray then by request administered an oath to the Speaker elect, that he would faithfully and impartially discharge the duties of his office as presiding officer of the present appointed Legislative Committee of the people of Oregon, so help you God; to which Beers said, Amen. The question arose as to the appointment of a clerk for the committee, when the members agreed, if necessary, to pay his expenses per diem, if no other means were provided.

George W. Le Breton, a young man of active mind, ready with the pen, useful and agreeable, and practical in his conversation, having come to the country as an adventurer in a vessel with Captain Couch, was chosen secretary and duly qualified by the Speaker. The records of the proceedings, as published, seem to have left out the preliminary part of this Legislative Committee's proceedings. This is owing to the fact that the compiler had no personal knowledge of them, and perhaps sought information from those as ignorant of the facts as himself; hence the meager and unsatisfactory document given to the country. Most, or all of the proceedings thus far mentioned were with closed doors, as will be seen by the record published. It was not deemed important by Messrs. Newell, O'Neil, and Hubbard, to have any record of our daily proceedings, only the result or report. Messrs. Shortess, Beers, Gray, Dougherty, and Hill thought it best to keep a record, which was commenced.

"Wallamet, May 15, 1843.—The Legislative Committee met, and after the preliminary discussions above alluded to, came to order by electing Robert Moore, Esq., chairman, and G. W. Le Breton, secretary.

"On motion of W. H. Gray, a committee of three was appointed by the chairman to prepare rules and business for the house. This committee (Messrs. Gray, Shortess, and Newell), at once, in a hasty manner, prepared eight rules, and suggested the business proposed for the committee as a whole to perform. The rules were taken up and adopted with scarcely a single objection. Up to this time no one except members of the committee had been allowed a place in the house as spectators.

"On motion, it was decided that the committee sit with open doors. O'Neil, Hubbard, and Dougherty favored the closed-door sessions, as they did not want to expose their ignorance of making laws. Newell thought we had better make as little display as possible, for it would all be known, and we might be ashamed of what we had done.

"Shortess, Hill, Gray, and Beers were willing that all our efforts to make laws for ourselves should be fully known, and were ready to receive instructions and advice from any source. The deliberations of the committee, they were confident, would not prevent opposition or aid the opposers of our proposed organization.

"On motion, a judiciary committee was appointed by the Speaker or chairman, consisting of Messrs. Beers, Hubbard, and Shortess.

"On motion, a committee of ways and means was appointed, consisting of Messrs. Shortess, O'Neil, and Dougherty."

The minutes at this stage show that there was a doubt as to the disposition of the Speaker, Mr. Moore, to place the best men as chairmen of the several committees. Mr. Moore had peculiar notions of his own about land claims, and had placed upon the committee, I think, Robert Newell, as favoring his and Dr. McLaughlin's pretensions to the entire water privileges at Wallamet Falls, which resulted in the appointment as above stated. The record seems to convey the idea that the first appointment was conferred by vote. This was not the case. It was the final action that was repeated and entered.

"On motion, a committee, consisting of Hubbard, Newell, and Gray, was appointed on military affairs."

We have not the original documents to refer to, but are of the impression that considerable correction was made in the first day's journal, and that more should have been made at the time. There was a little feeling on the part of the Speaker and the writer as to the necessity of an extended minute, and a disposition on the part of Mr. Le Breton to do as little writing as possible, not for want of time and material, but, from the deep interest he took in the discussions, he seemed to forget his work. I am not prepared to think the compiler has abridged the minutes, yet such may be the fact.

"On motion, Messrs. Shortess, Dougherty, and Hill were appointed a committee on private land claims.

"On motion, Messrs. Gray, Dougherty, and Beers were appointed a committee on districting the Territory into not to exceed five districts."

This committee, it seems by the motion, was to be appointed by the chairman or Speaker.

"Adjourned to 8 o'clock, A. M., May 17, 1843.

"The house was called to order by the chairman, and Mr. Gray appointed secretary, *pro tem.* The session was then opened with prayer by A. Beers. The minutes of yesterday's session were then read, corrected, and accepted."

The house then adjourned for one hour and a half to prepare business, at the expiration of which time they were called to order by the chairman.

The judiciary committee reported progress. The military committee reported in part; also committee on districts.

"Reports accepted.

"It was moved that there be a standing committee on finance, which was lost, as the vote at Champoeg had directed that the finance of the government should be by subscription and voluntary contribution.

"Adjourned to 1.30 P. M.

"House called to order by Speaker.

"On motion, house went into committee of the whole upon reports of committees, Gray in the chair. It was soon found that the business before the committee of the whole was not in a shape to be properly acted upon, and that by an open and informal meeting of the members, it could be brought into shape for action, or rather that the several members of the different committees had not had a full expression upon the reports that were before them, and these expressions could be shortened by separate committee consultation and agreement among the members of the several committees; hence an adjournment of one hour was agreed upon.

"At the close of the hour the house met and agreed, went into committee of the whole as to the number of districts. The report of the committee accepted, as amended in committee of the whole."

The question arises here why did not this committee on districts, and the whole Legislative Committee, specify all north of the Columbia River?

It will be remembered that the Hudson's Bay Company, with all the influence and votes they, with the priests, could collect, had met the settlers at Champoeg on the 2d of May previous, and opposed the entire organization; and the French priest had sent to the Legislative Committee a protest against any organization; at least the districting committee was aware that such would be the case, as the protest already given was in the hands of Le Breton, the secretary of the committee, and of the whole house. In specifying the districts beyond the limits named, or north of the Columbia, the additional votes and personal influence of the company would be thrown against us. The district committee contended that that influence and vote would defeat us, and make us an English or Hudson's Bay Company settlement. We could, without the interference of the company, manage our own affairs with such of the French settlers as chose to remain and vote with us. Such as did not like our laws could have a place to which they could continue their allegiance. Besides, we were confident we should receive a large immigration in the fall, and in that case we could extend our settlements and districts and laws to that section of the country.

Another prominent, and perhaps the most prominent reason of all was, we were afraid to attempt to enforce any laws we might wish to adopt, or think necessary among ourselves, upon the servants of the company. We did not acknowledge their right to enforce any English laws over us, and we, as the writer thought then, and still thinks, wisely concluded if they would not openly interfere with us, we would not openly interfere with them, till we were strong enough to outnumber and control them, as will hereafter be clearly demonstrated.

The journal of the proceedings of that committee shows that there were frequent short adjournments. These moments were all occupied in discussing and agreeing upon some report that was soon to be acted upon, and in coming to a unanimous vote as to the final result; there was but one thought and but one object with the majority of the members of the Legislative Committee.

That thought and object was, to establish the provisional government they had undertaken to organize. They felt that union in their action was absolutely necessary, as the opposing elements were so strong, that without it we must fail, and subject ourselves and the settlement to the worst possible tyranny and humiliation from Dr. White and the Hudson's Bay Company.

After the second recess, during the second day, the report of the military committee was before the house and instructions asked. Newell was opposed to any military arrangements at all. Hubbard was undecided. Gray insisted on carrying out the instructions and ideas of the meeting of the 2d of May in regard to military officers that had been appointed at that meeting, and in preparing rules to govern them in organizing and drilling the men. He was unwilling to leave the military power without any responsibility to any one but themselves; hence instruction was asked, and given, to proceed as indicated in the meeting at Champoeg, and prepare a military law, to be included in the articles of organic compact.

"May 18, 1843.—House met pursuant to adjournment. Session was opened by prayer. Minutes of yesterday's session read, corrected, and accepted.

"Robert Newell moved, and was seconded, that a committee be appointed to prepare a paper for the signature of all persons wishing an organization."

The reader is already informed of the appearance of the French protest, and that it was in the possession of Le Breton. It is possible that Newell may have received it from the French priest. The writer has never been able to learn the exact facts in the case. At all events Newell's resolution shows, that however willing and ready he was to commence the organization of an American government with his *adopted* countrymen, he is now in doubt as to the propriety of the step he, with others, had undertaken.

He presents a resolution to get up a committee to prepare a paper to circulate among the people, to find out who were in favor of the organization we were then attempting to bring into shape, under the instructions already received.

Perhaps the reader will understand Mr. Newell better if he is more fully informed as to his real genealogy, as there has always been a little doubt whether he belonged to the American or British nation. From the best information we could get about him, he was formerly from Cincinnati, Ohio, and the Rocky Mountains. From the earliest history we have of him, he has claimed to be an American, and represented the interests of a foreign monopoly, under a religious belief that he was conscientiously right in so doing. By keeping himself talking strong American sentiments to Americans, and acting strongly anti-American while in the mountains and in the settlement, he succeeded in obtaining and holding positions to benefit the trade of the Hudson's Bay Company; also a place in the Legislative Committee, and in the settler's government, to shield and protect those who were seeking the destruction of all American trade and influence in the country. He was a man of quite ordinary ability, yet smooth and insinuating in his manners, with a great abundance of plausible stories, to make a stranger believe he was learned in a profession. His real sentiments could never be learned except by his vote; his thoughts only read by his acts, which always tended to complicate and confuse legislation. This probably arose from a disposition to seek popularity and places he was incompetent to fill; as, also, from the title he assumed in early life, it naturally made him a hypocrite in action as well as profession. He had not the moral principle requisite to make known the truth, and to assume his proper position and be regarded as a plain man without a title. As plain Bob Newell he could be respected for his natural and genial talent. As *Dr.* Newell he assumes an air to correspond with the title, and shows the hypocrisy of his life. He was at this time, and has continued to be, a faithful representative of the Hudson's Bay Company and Jesuit interests in the country, for which service they should enter his name upon their calendar of saints. As a public man, we are not aware that he ever originated a single act or law; but as representing a clique, or the interests of his masters, he has always been ready to do his utmost in every possible way. At the time we were called to vote upon Mr. Newell's first resolution, his position was fully known to but few, yet enough was understood of his duplicity to reject his proposition at once, and the house proceeded to amend its rules and add a ninth to those already adopted.

The report of the military committee was recommitted with instructions for further action. Mr. Hubbard was considerably under the influence of Newell, and in consequence of this fact the military rules or laws were remodeled in committee of the whole. Newell and Hubbard were disposed to defeat it altogether as unnecessary, as intimated in the tenth proposition in the French priest's address. In fact, Mr. Newell acted all through the proceedings of the Legislative Committee upon the ideas contained in that address, and opposed all measures looking beyond the suggestions contained in it.

At this point, the judiciary committee, consisting of Beers, Hubbard, and Shortess, reported in part on the executive power, and opened the eyes of Dr. Newell to the awful responsibility and to a full realization of the fact that a majority of the committee were in favor of an organization, and a real, actual American government. He took the floor and commenced: "Wall, reelly now, Mr. Chairman, this 'ere report is a stumper. I see from the report of this 'ere committee that you are going on a little too fast. I think you had better find out if we can carry this thing through before we go too far. We have a good many people that don't know what we are about, and I think we had better adjourn before we go too far."

In the midst of this speech, which was a repetition of the reasons for getting up the paper to find out who were favorable to our proposed government, the house was so uncourteous as to adjourn and leave the balance of Dr. Newell's speech unrepeated. Suffice it to say, that in those short adjournments as noted in the Oregon archives, nearly or quite all the little differences of opinion were quickly explained and understood by a majority of the members. The exact subjects that were before them at the several meetings we have no documents to indicate, and we can only be governed by such documents as we have, to wit, the record and our own memory.

Newell was the only prominent opposer of the report of the judiciary committee, which was prepared by Robert Shortess, to whose memory we are indebted for a remarkable speech of Hon. Mr. Robert Newell on that occasion. Mr. Shortess says the discussion was on the question of who should be deemed voters. Most of the committee were in favor of universal suffrage, and, as Dr. Newell had a native wife, naturally supposed he would be quite as liberal as those who had full white families; but the doctor gave us one of his "stumpers," or, as he calls it, "*big fir-tree speeches*," by saying: "Wall, now, Mr. Speaker, I think we have got quite high enough among the *dark clouds*; I do not believe we ought to go any higher. It is well enough to admit the English, the French, the Spanish, and the half-breeds, but the Indian and the negro is a little too dark for me. I think we had better stop at the half-breeds. I am in favor of limiting the right to vote to them, and going no further into the dark clouds to admit the negro."

We confess that till Mr. Shortess reminded us of this speech, and the manner of its delivery, it had escaped our memory, and that, without it, Mr. Newell could scarcely receive his proper position in the history of our early struggle for American liberty upon this coast. His position and the patronage he received from the Hudson's Bay Company were sufficient for him to work effectually in their interests through all our struggle.

"At the evening session of May 18, the committee on ways and means were instructed to prepare a subscription for presenting at the general meeting, to procure funds to defray the expenses of the government, after spending a short time in committee of the whole.

"Adjourned till next day.

"May 19, 1843.—House met pursuant to adjournment. Opened with prayer. Moved that the minutes of the 18th be accepted. Taking the whole subject of the organization into consideration, Gray presented the following resolution that a committee of three be appointed to prepare and arrange all the business that has been done, or may be done hereafter at this session, revising statutes of Iowa, etc., report at the next session of the committee, and request the clerk to copy the same.

"Resolution adopted.

"Messrs. Gray, Beers, and O'Neil were appointed; these three living within fifteen miles of each other, it was thought could meet and superintend and revise the whole proceedings, and get them in shape for the public meeting.

"Committee of ways and means reported a subscription, which was accepted, and the military committee reported in part, which was accepted.

"Adjourned to 2 P. M.

"At 2 P. M. house met. The judiciary committee reported in full. Report accepted."

On the 20th page of the archives, and in reference to the proviso in the fourth article of the organic law, the record does not give us the fact. The proviso referred to was pre› red but not included in the original act, as reported and read at Champoeg, but was adopted at Champoeg. The report was duly referred to the revising committee, and the proviso left in the hands of Le Breton to be withheld or presented, as the occasion might require, in the final action of the people. The large pretensions to lands by the Methodist and Catholic missions were fully understood by the entire committee. They wished to curtail them as much as possible, and were fully aware that any direct action to this end would bring the whole influence of both missions against them.

CHAPTER XLIV.

Fourth of July, 1843.—Oration by Mr. Hines.—Meeting of July 5.—Debate on the land law.—How the Jesuits and the Hudson's Bay Company secured their land claims.—Speech of the Rev. G. Hines against the proposed Executive Committee. —The committee supported by O'Neil, Shortess, and Lee.—W. H. Gray closes the debate.—The report of the committee adopted.—Committee appointed to report to Congress, another to make a Digest of Territorial laws, and a third to prepare and administer an oath of office

On the 4th of July our national anniversary was observed, and an oration was delivered by the Rev. G. Hines. The committee favored the selection of Mr. Hines as orator, that they might gain his views, and be ready to meet him on the main questions that would be brought up on the fifth. In this, however, we failed, as he dwelt principally upon the subjects of temperance, the glorious deeds of our forefathers on the other side of the Rocky Mountains, and the influences and blessings of the day. No Englishman, or foreigner, could have taken any exceptions to his sentiments or language. On the 5th, Dr. Babcock, chairman of the meeting of May 2, being absent, the meeting was called to order by G. W. Le Breton, one of the secretaries of the May meeting. On motion, the Rev. Gustavus Hines was elected president of the convention by acclamation. R. Moore, Esq., chairman of the Legislative Committee, presented his report, which was read by Secretary Le Breton, and on motion accepted. Rev. L. H. Judson moved that the report of the committee on ways and means be accepted. This motion brought the land law up for discussion. The Legislative Committee as a whole reported that law entire, to the proviso in the fourth article. Upon the first part of that article a discussion arose between Mr. Newell and the members of the Methodist Mission, as to the right of any single individual to hold a claim of 640 acres upon a city or town site, or extensive water privilege. Mr. Moore agreed with Mr. Newell on that question, as he claimed one side of the Wallamet River at the falls, and Dr. McLaughlin the other. The Methodist Mission also claimed a right to the east side of the Wallamet, and the Milling Company claimed the island, upon which they were erecting mills. Mr. Newell opposed the fourth article, to favor Dr. McLaughlin; the Methodist Mission and Milling Company favored the article on the ground that it secured them in their rights, and prevented a monopoly of that water-power by any single individual. Rev. Jason Lee was anxious to secure the rights and claims of the Methodist Mission. So far as the water privilege and town sites were concerned, there were no fears on the part of the committee, but in reference to the large claims of the Methodist Mission, there were fears that Mr. Lee and Mr. Hines would oppose our whole effort, and combine the influence of their mission against the organization. To satisfy Rev. Jason Lee, Le Breton presented the proviso as contained in the fourth article, which removed his objection. The committee were well assured that the Jesuit missions would claim the same right to land, and in this way, the one mission would be induced to give up to curtail the other. This occurred as anticipated, only the Methodist Mission held on to their claims, and attempted to maintain them publicly, while the Jesuits did the same thing silently, and by having their lands recorded in the supposed names of their members, or priests, the same as the Hudson's Bay Company recorded all their improvements and forts in the names of their different servants, so as to hold them for the company; the company and the Jesuits having, as they supposed, secured their own claims to land in the name of their respective servants, joined with the new immigrants, in condemning the large pretensions of the Methodist Mission, and in this way prejudiced the minds of the settlers against it for doing, openly, just what they had done in the names of their servants, secretly.

On the final vote there were but few dissenting voices, except upon the adoption of the proviso. It may be asked why the land law was brought up first. The minutes as recorded on the twenty-third and twenty-fourth pages of the Oregon archives, show that Mr. Judson moved the adoption of the report of the committee on ways and means. This was all the minute that was made, as the business and discussion progressed. The report on the land law was deemed, by the committee, to be of the first importance, as all were personally interested in the law about land claims; and upon the discussion of that report, they could learn the result of the whole effort, and the feelings of the people as to the permanence of the proposed government. The notice of the report of the committee on ways and means, on page 24, and of the proviso, is entered, to show that the amendments alluded to were made. We are of the opinion, that had Mr. Le Breton lived to copy those minutes, he would have so changed them. He says such amendment and proviso were adopted. To this fact we have affirmed under oath as being a part of the provisional law adopted at that meeting. This brings us to the first clause of the organic law, as adopted by the people in mass convention.

The preamble and first article were adopted on motion of Joseph McLaughlin, the second son of Dr. John McLaughlin, who took an active part in favoring the organization, against the wishes and influence of his family.

The second article was read, and, on motion of L. H. Judson, was adopted.

The third, on motion of C. McRoy, and the fourth, on motion of Joseph Holman, were also adopted.

On motion to adopt the fifth article, "on the executive power," it was plain to be seen that the Rev. Mr. Hines was swelling and becoming uneasy, in proportion as the Rev. Jason Lee appeared to be satisfied with the proceedings. He hesitated to put the motion, called Robert Moore, the chairman of the Legislative Committee, to the chair, and commenced:—

"Mr. President, gentlemen, and fellow-citizens,—The Legislative Committee which you appointed to prepare certain laws, and perform a certain duty, have assumed to present for your approval something they had no right, in all the instructions given them, to present. They have commenced a course which, if not checked, will lead to the worst possible form of despotism. Grant them the privilege which they now ask, of imposing upon this settlement, upon you and me and our families, this *hydra-headed monster* in the shape of an Executive Committee, and we have but the repetition of the Roman Triumvirate—the Cæsars upon the throne. We may be told by them, in excuse for the violation of plain and positive instructions, that they found it difficult to proceed with the organizing of a temporary government without an executive; and here they have brought before you this *monstrosity*—this *black bear*—this *hydra-headed monster*, in the shape of an Executive Committee; and ask you to adopt it, as necessary to preserve your civil liberties and rights.

"Gentlemen and fellow-citizens,—You have but to look to past history, to warn you of the dangers of so palpable a violation of instructions on the part of public servants. You instructed them to do a certain work, to prepare certain laws. If they could not do as instructed, let them resign and go home. So far as they performed the duties assigned them, we can approve of their acts; but when they attempt to force upon us what we have not asked of them, but said to them we do not want this monstrosity with three heads, yet they persist in saying we do; and have gone on and made their laws to correspond with this absurd and outrageous thing they call *Executive Committee.* Is it wise, is it reasonable, that we should submit to it? What assurance have we that the next Legislative Committee, or body we may appoint, following the example set by this one, will not give us a king or emperor, and tell us it is necessary to complete our organization?"

Many of the persons present at Champoeg on the 5th of July, 1843, will recollect this speech, and the strong and emphatic manner in which it was delivered. Why Mr. Hines did not move to strike out the executive clause has always been a mystery to us. When he had resumed his seat as president of the convention, Mr. O'Neil made a few remarks, explaining the position of the committee. Mr. Shortess followed, denying the assumption of power attributed to the committee, or a disposition to go beyond their instructions, and urged the necessity of a head or some controlling influence somewhere. Could we rely upon Captains McCarty, or McKay, or Smith to call out their companies; or Major Howard? Should the military control the civil power? "The thing is absurd," said Shortess. Rev. Jason Lee could not see the proposed executive head of the proposed provisional government in the light Mr. Hines did. If it was thought necessary to have a government at all, it was necessary to have a head, and an executive, or the laws were of no effect.

It was arranged with the Legislative Committee, that Gray should meet Hines on this question, and make the last speech in favor of the executive department. Hence O'Neil and Shortess both spoke in favor of it. Dr. Babcock was opposed, on account of its going beyond present necessities, and looking too much like a permanent and independent government; whereas we only wished to form a temporary one. He thought with Mr. Hines, that the committee had gone beyond their instructions in providing for this executive power, still he was willing to abide the decision of the people. There was a little uncertainty as to Mr. Lee's final vote. Dr. Babcock was clearly against us. Mr. Hines made but the one speech. From the course the debate had taken, Gray had no fears as to the final result, and waited until it was evident that no more opposing speeches would be made when he commenced:—

"Mr. President and fellow-citizens,—The speech which we have just listened to, from our presiding officer, is in the main correct. It is true that the Legislative Committee were not instructed to bring before you an executive department in the laws and government you proposed to form, when you appointed your committee to prepare those laws. It is also true, that when that committee met, they found that they could not advance one step in accomplishing the work you instructed them to perform, without some supervising influence, or power, somewhere; in short, without a head. Their instructions were against a governor. They have provided an Executive Committee, in place of a single man for governor. This executive head is to act in the place of senate, council, and governor. This provision is before you for your approval or rejection. With this Executive Committe our organization is complete; without it we have no head; no one to see that our laws are executed, and no one to grant a reprieve or pardon in case a law should be enforced against the life or property of any one, for the violation of any law, no matter what the circumstances connected with that real or supposed violation might be. The pardon and mercy part of our law is in that '*horrible hydra-headed monster*' that the gentleman spoke about, and warned us against; and instead of its being as black as his '*bear*,' it becomes light and mercy to the erring and the ignorant. As to the example set by your committee for future despots to rob us of our liberty, and place over us a king or an emperor, you and I have no fears so long as we elect our own legislative bodies.

"Now, fellow-citizens, let us look calmly at our true situation. We are two thousand five hundred miles from any point from which we can receive the least assistance by land; and seventeen thousand miles by water. A portion of our community are organized and ready to protect themselves, and to defend all their rights and interests. Another organization of a religious character is in our midst,—I should say, two. They each have a head—an executive. How is it with us? Who is our head in all that pertains to our civil liberty, rights, and property? It is possible the gentleman may wish us to remain as unprotected, as helpless and exposed to all the dangers that surround us on every hand, as we have heretofore been. If he does, you, fellow-citizens, I am sure, do not wish to add to his feebleness by destroying the organization you have commenced, because he is afraid of what some Cæsar did in Rome some centuries past. We are acting for ourselves and those immediately dependent upon us for protection. In union there is strength. I believe you are fully satisfied that your committee have acted honestly, and, as they thought, for the good of all they represented. If such is the case, you will approve of their acts, and our organization will be complete as they have prepared it for this meeting."

On the question being taken, there were but two or three votes against the executive, or fifth section. Mr. Lee informed the writer that he saw plainly enough that the meeting was determined to have a government of some kind, and that probably the Executive Committee was the best at first. This point gained, the remainder was soon disposed of.

The marriage fee was changed, in the seventeenth article, from three dollars to one dollar.

The resolution referred to as the nineteenth was: "*Resolved*, That a committee of three be appointed to draw up a digest of all the laws and proceedings of the people of this Territory, in relation to the present provisional government, and the reasons for forming the same; and forward said digest and report to the Congress of the United States for their information." Rev. Jason Lee, Rev. Gustavus Hines, and Mr. C. M. Walker were chosen that committee, and instructed to have access to all public documents, and to call upon any individual for any information they might deem necessary in carrying out their instructions.

That committee, so far as performing their duty and carrying out the wishes of the people were concerned, did the same as the reverend Legislative Committee did in 1841; they neglected the thing altogether, and paid no attention to the object of the resolution. Still, at the present day, when the same reverend gentlemen are charged with having done all they could against the early settlers' government, they attempt to repel the charge, and take great credit to themselves for the perseverance of others in securing permanent laws and protection for themselves and the settlements.

Messrs. Beers, Hill, and Gale, were chosen by ballot as the first Executive Committee.

Hugh Burns, who had been chosen at the May meeting as justice of the peace, had resigned, and Robert Moore was chosen to fill his place.

The committee had prepared a full list of the laws of Iowa, to recommend for the adoption of the people, which was presented and read, some slight amendments made, and the list adopted.

The report of the Legislative Committee was adopted as a whole; and on motion it was "*Resolved*, That the president of the convention assisted by the Rev. Messrs. Lee, Clark, and Leslie, be a committee to draft and administer an oath of office to the civil officers elected on the 2d of May, 1843, and that said officers be required to subscribe to the same; and administer the oath to the supreme judge, who shall hereafter qualify all civil and military officers to be elected by the people." At this point, a question arose in the mind of the last-named committee, whether they would proceed that night to administer the proposed oath, or defer it till some other time. There were some earnest and determined men in that convention, who were not to be defeated at the last moment by the disposition of these reverend gentlemen to delay the concluding ceremony of drafting and administering the oath of office to the persons the people had chosen. To relieve them of all doubt as to the wish of the convention (although it was then nearly dark), it was moved and carried, "that the committee to qualify officers proceed to the performance of their duty, as far as practicable, this evening." Judge Wilson was not present.

Rev. Jason Lee noticed that Mr. Beers received the smallest number of votes given for any member of the Executive Committee. This to him, and probably to Messrs. Leslie and Hines, was unaccountable; but not so to us, who understood the general feeling of opposition against the rule of the missionaries and their large claims to land; as also the secret prejudices excited against them by the Hudson's Bay Company and the Jesuits, who attributed the entire government movement to them, while the organization was that of the settlers unaided by any mission, except individual members of the Protestant missions. This was probably the reason for the proposition to delay qualifying the officers elected, and carrying out the decided wish of the convention. This fact simply shows a reluctant assent to the organization by the principal members of the missions. The French address showed the feelings of the French and Catholics, while the Hudson's Bay Company stood entirely aloof from it, and expected to defeat the whole movement by the influence of such men as the Rev. G. Hines, Dr. White, Robert Newell, and the Indians.

We have two copies of the organic laws adopted by the people at Champoeg; one published by Charles Saxton in 1846, and the other by the compiler of the Oregon archives in 1853. That published by Mr. Saxton corresponds nearer with our own recollections of the facts of the case; hence we will copy them as given by him.

CHAPTER XLV.

Organic laws.—Resolutions.—Districts.—Militia law.—Land claims.—Certificate.

THE Legislative Committee recommend that the following *organic laws* be adopted:—

WE, the people of Oregon Territory, for purposes of mutual protection, and to secure peace and prosperity among ourselves, agree to adopt the following laws and regulations, until such time as the United States of America extend their jurisdiction over us:—

SECTION I.

Be it enacted by the free citizens of Oregon Territory, That the said Territory, for the purposes of temporary government, be divided into not less than three, nor more than five, districts; subject to be extended to a greater number when an increase of population shall require.

For the purpose of fixing the principles of civil and religious liberty as the basis of all laws and constitutions of government that may hereafter be adopted, *Be it enacted*, That the following articles be considered articles of compact among the free citizens of this Territory.

ARTICLE 1. No person demeaning himself in a peaceable or orderly manner shall ever be molested on account of his mode of worship or religious sentiments.

ART. 2. The inhabitants of said Territory shall always be entitled to the benefit of the writ of *habeas corpus* and trial by jury, of a proportionate representation in the Legislature, and of judicial proceeding according to the course of common law. All persons shall be bailable, unless for capital offenses, where the proof shall be evident, or the presumption great. All fines shall be moderate, and no cruel or unnatural punishments inflicted. No man shall be deprived of his liberty but by the judgment of his peers, or the law of the land; and should the public exigences make it necessary, for the common preservation, to take any person's property, or to demand his particular services, full compensation shall be made for the same. And in the just preservation of rights and property, it is understood and declared that no law ought ever to be made, or have force in said Territory, that shall in any manner whatever interfere with, or affect, private contracts, or engagements *bona fide* made and without fraud previously formed.

23

ART. 3. Religion, morality, and knowledge, being necessary to good government and the happiness of mankind, *schools* and the means of education *shall forever be encouraged.*

ART. 4. The utmost good faith shall always be observed toward the Indians, their lands and property shall never be taken from them without their consent, and in their property, rights, and liberty, they shall never be invaded or disturbed, unless in just and lawful wars, authorized by the representatives of the people. But laws, founded in justice and humanity, shall, from time to time, be made, for preventing injustice being done to them, and for preserving peace and friendship.

ART. 5. There shall be *neither slavery nor involuntary servitude* in said Territory, otherwise than for the punishment of crimes, whereof the party shall have been duly convicted.

SECTION II.

ARTICLE 1. *Be it enacted* by the authority aforesaid, That the officers elected on the 2d of May instant shall continue in office until the second Tuesday of May, 1844, and until others are elected and qualified.

ART. 2. An election for civil and military officers shall be held annually upon the second Tuesday in May in the several districts, at such places as shall be designated by law.

ART. 3. Each officer heretofore elected, or that shall hereafter be elected, shall, before entering upon the duties of his office, take an oath or affirmation to support the laws of the Territory, and faithfully discharge the duties of his office.

ART. 4. *Every free male descendant of a white man*, inhabitant of this Territory, of the age of twenty-one years and upward, who shall have been an inhabitant of this Territory at the time of its organization, shall be entitled to vote at the election of officers, civil and military, *and be eligible to any office* in the Territory; *Provided*, That all persons of the description entitled to vote by the provision of this section, who shall emigrate to this Territory after the organization, shall be entitled to the rights of citizens after having resided six months in the Territory.

ART. 5. The executive power shall be vested in a committee of three persons, elected by the qualified voters at the annual election, who shall have power to grant pardons and reprieves for offenses against the laws of the Territory, to call out the military force of the Territory, to repel invasions or suppress insurrections, to take care that the laws are faithfully executed, and to recommend such laws as they may consider necessary to the representatives of the people for their action. Two members of the committee shall constitute a quorum for the transaction of business.

ART. 6. The legislative power shall be vested in a committee of nine persons, to be elected by the qualified electors at the annual election; giving to each district a representation in the ratio of its population, excluding Indians; and the said members shall reside in the district for which they shall be chosen.

ART. 7. The judicial power shall be vested in a Supreme Court, consisting of the supreme judge and two justices of the peace; a Probate Court and Justice Court. The jurisdiction of the Supreme Court shall be both appellate and original; that of the Probate Court and Justice Court as limited by law; *Provided*, That individual justices of the peace shall not have jurisdiction of any matter or controversy when the title or boundaries of land may be in dispute, or when the sum claimed exceeds fifty dollars.

ART. 8. There shall be a Recorder, elected by the qualified electors at the annual election, who shall keep a faithful record of the proceedings of the Legislative Committee, Supreme and Probate courts; also record all boundaries of land presented for that purpose, and brands used for marking live stock; procure and keep a record of the same; and also record wills, deeds, and other instruments of writing required by law to be recorded. The Recorder shall receive the following fees, viz.: For recording wills, deeds, and other instruments of writing, twelve cents for every hundred words; and for every weight or measure sealed, twenty-five cents. For granting other official papers and the seal, twenty-five cents; for services as clerk of the Legislature, the same daily pay as members of the Legislature; and for all other services required of him by this act, the same fees as allowed for similar services by the laws of Iowa.

ART. 9. There shall be a Treasurer, elected by the qualified electors of the Territory, who shall, before entering upon the duties of his office, give bonds to the Executive Committee in the sum of fifteen hundred dollars, with two or more sufficient sureties, to be approved by the Executive Committee of the Territory, conditioned for the faithful discharge of the duty of his office. The Treasurer shall receive all moneys belonging to the Territory that may be raised by contribution, or otherwise, and shall procure suitable books in which he shall enter an account of his receipts and disbursements.

ART. 10. The Treasurer shall in no case pay money out of the Treasury but according to law, and shall annually report to the Legislative Committee a true account of his receipts and disbursements, with necessary vouchers for the same, and shall deliver to his successor in office all books, moneys, accounts, or other property belonging to the Territory, as soon as his successor shall become qualified.

ART. 11. The Treasurer shall receive for his services the sum of five per cent. upon all moneys received and paid out according to law, and three per cent. upon all money in the Treasury when he goes out of office, and two per cent. upon the disbursement of money in the Treasury when he comes into office.

ART. 12. The laws of Iowa Territory shall be the laws of this Territory in military and criminal cases, *where not otherwise provided for;* and where no statute of Iowa Territory applies, the principle of common law and equity shall govern.

ART. 13. The law of Iowa regulating weights and measures shall be the law of this Territory; *Provided*, The Supreme Court shall perform the duties required of the commissioners, and the recorder shall perform the duties of the clerk of the county commissioners, as prescribed in said laws of Iowa; and proved, that sixty pounds avoirdupois shall be the standard weight of a bushel of wheat, whether the same be more or less than two thousand one hundred and fifty and two-fifths cubic inches.

ART. 14. The laws of Iowa respecting wills and administrators shall be the laws of this Territory in all cases not otherwise provided for.

ART. 15. The laws of Iowa respecting vagrants is hereby adopted as far as adapted to the circumstances of the citizens of Oregon.

ART. 16. The Supreme Court shall hold two sessions annually, upon the third Tuesdays of April and September, the first session to be held at Champoeg upon the third Tuesday of September, 1843, and the second session at Tualatin Plains, upon the third Tuesday of April, 1844. At the sessions of the Supreme Court the judge shall preside, assisted by two justices; *Provided*, That no justice of the peace shall assist in trying any case that has been brought before the court by appeal from his judgment. The Supreme Court shall have original jurisdiction in cases of treason and felony, or breach of the peace, and in civil cases where the sum claimed exceeds fifty dollars.

ART. 17. All male persons of the age of sixteen years and upward, and all females of the age of fourteen years and upward, shall have the right to marry. When either of the parties shall be under twenty-one years of age, the consent of the parents, or guardians of such minors, shall be necessary to the validity of such matrimonial engagement. Every ordained minister of the gospel, of any religious denomination, the supreme judge, and all justices of the peace, are hereby authorized to solemnize marriage according to law, to have the same recorded, and pay the recorder's fee. The legal fee for marriage shall be one dollar; and for recording, fifty cents.

ART. 18. All offices subsequently made shall be filled by election and ballot in the several districts upon the day appointed by law, and under such regulations as the laws of Iowa provide.

1. *Resolved*, That a committee of three be appointed to draw up a digest of the doings of this Territory with regard to an organization, and transmit the same to the United States government for their information.

2. *Resolved*, That the laws of Iowa—as laid down in the "Statute Laws of the Territory of Iowa, enacted at the first session of the Legislative Assembly of said Territory, held at Burlington, A. D. 1838–9, published by authority in Dubuque, Russell & Reeves, printers, 1839;" certified to be a "correct copy," by William B. Conway, secretary of Iowa Territory—be adopted as the laws of this Territory.

The Legislative Committee recommend that the Territory be divided into four districts, as follows:—

First District, to be called the *Tualatin District*, comprising all the country south of the northern boundary line of the United States, west of the Wallamet or Multnomah River, north of the Yamhill River, and east of the Pacific Ocean.

Second District, to be called the *Yamhill District*, embracing all the country west of the Wallamet or Multnomah River, and a supposed line running north and south from said river, south of the Yamhill River, to the parallel of forty-two degrees north latitude, or the boundary line of the United States and California, and east of the Pacific Ocean.

Third District, to be called the *Clackamas District*, comprehending all territory not included in the other three districts.

Fourth District, to be called the *Champoeg District*, and bounded on the north by a supposed line drawn from the mouth of the Haunchauke River, running due east to the Rocky Mountains, west by the Wallamet or Multnomah River, and a supposed line running due south from said river to the parallel of forty-two degrees north latitude, south by the boundary line of the United States and California, and east by the summit of the Rocky Mountains.

The Legislative Committee also recommend the above districts to be designated by the name of "Oregon Territory."

The Legislative Committee recommend that a subscription paper be put in circulation to collect funds for defraying the expenses of the government, as follows: We, the subscribers, hereby pledge ourselves to pay annually to the treasurer of Oregon Territory the sum affixed to our respective names, for defraying the expenses of government; *Provided*, That in all cases each individual subscriber may, at any time, withdraw his name from said subscription upon paying up all arrearages, and notifying the treasurer of the colony of such desire to withdraw.

Militia Law.

Article 1. The militia of this Territory shall be arranged into one battalion, consisting of three or more companies of mounted riflemen.

Art. 2. That in case of the vacancy of the office of major by death or otherwise, it shall be the duty of the Executive Committee to appoint another whose duty it shall be to serve in the place of such removed officer, until the annual election.

Art. 3. That when a portion of country is so distant, or so situated, that in the opinion of the Executive Committee it would be inconvenient for persons residing therein to belong to an organized company, they shall be organized as a separate company under the command of a captain appointed by themselves, and give due notice to the major of the battalion, and be subject to the same laws and regulations as the other companies of the battalion.

Art. 4. That all companies shall meet once in each year for company inspection upon the last Tuesday in September, well mounted, with a good rifle, or musket, and accouterments for company inspection and military exercise.

Art. 5. It shall be the duty of the major to notify each captain of a company to notify each member of his company of the day and place of each annual meeting of his battalion and company at least six days previous to such time of meeting.

Art. 6. It shall be the duty of each and every male inhabitant, over the age of sixteen years and under sixty, that wishes to be considered a citizen, to cause himself to be enrolled, by giving his name to the proper officers of the militia, and serve under the same, except such as are hereafter excepted.

Art. 7. That fines shall be laid upon all who fail to adhere to the commands of the Executive Committee, and the same shall be expended for ammunition and arms, without delay, and persons appointed to take charge of the magazine wherever the Executive Committee shall direct its location.

Art. 8. It shall be the duty of the Executive Committee to appoint a surgeon to the battalion, who shall serve in his profession when so ordered by the Executive Committee.

Art. 9. It shall be lawful for any commissioned officer in case of invasion, or insurrection, to order out the militia under his command, provided he has sufficient reason for so doing, and give immediate notice thereof to the Executive Committee.

Art. 10. The militia of this Territory shall, with the advice and consent of the Executive Committee, be subject to the call of the authorized agents of the United States government until she may send troops to support the same.

Land Claims.

Article 1. Any person how holding or hereafter wishing to establish a claim to land in this Territory, shall designate the extent of his claim by natural boundaries, or by marks at the corners and upon the lines of said claim, recorded in the office of the Territorial recorder, in a book to be kept by him for that purpose, within twenty days from the time of making said claim; *Provided*, That those who shall be already in possession of land shall be allowed one year from the passage of this act, to file a description of their claims in the recorder's office.

Art. 2. All claimants shall, within six months from the time of recording their claims, make permanent improvements upon the same, by building or inclosing, and also become occupant upon said claims within one year of the date of such record.

Art. 3. No individual shall be allowed to hold a claim of more than one square mile, or 640 acres, in a square or oblong form, according to the natural situation of the premises, nor shall any individual be able to hold more than one claim at the same time. Any person complying with the provisions of these ordinances shall be entitled to the same process against trespass as in other cases provided by law.

Art. 4. No person shall be entitled to hold such a claim upon city or town lots, extensive water privileges, or other situations necessary for the transaction of mercantile or manufacturing operations; *Provided*, That nothing in these laws shall be so construed as to affect any claim of any mission of a religious character made prior to this time, of extent not more than six miles square.

Approved by the people, as per minutes, Wallamet, July 5, 1843.

A true copy from original papers. Attest

George W. Le Breton,
Recorder.

Certificate.

This certifies that David Hill, Alanson Beers, and Joseph Gale were chosen the Executive Committee of the Territory of Oregon, by the people of said Territory, and have taken the oath for the faithful performance of the duties of their office as required by law.

George W. Le Breton,
Recorder.

Wallamet, Oregon Territory, July 5, 1843.

CHAPTER XLVI.

Description of the State House.—Conduct of the French settlers.—Arrival of Dr. Whitman's party of immigrants.—Prosperity of the settlers.—Change in the policy of the Hudson's Bay Company.—Their exorbitant claims.

A PRIMITIVE State House was built with posts set upright, one end in the ground, grooved on two sides, and filled in with poles and split timber, such as would be suitable for fence rails; with plates and poles across the top. Rafters and horizontal poles held the cedar bark, which was used instead of shingles for covering. It was twenty by forty feet. At one end, some puncheons were put up for a platform for the president; some poles and slabs were placed around for seats; three planks one foot wide and about twelve feet long, placed upon a sort of stake platform for a table, for the use of the Legislative Committee and the clerks.

Perfect order and decorum prevailed throughout the proceedings. The bolder and more independent portion of the French settlers participated in this convention, and expressed themselves pleased with the result. They looked to this organization to relieve them from British tyranny; while by far the greater number of them kept aloof and refused to have any thing to do with, or to submit to, the organization.

This arose from the advice they had received from the company, and the instructions of the priests who were among them, as in the case of Dr. White's effort to get a few of them to go with him to the interior, on the report of threatened Indian difficulties. The Hudson's Bay Company, as indicated in a communication to the Executive Committee, felt themselves abundantly able to defend themselves and their political rights.

This year, through the influence and representations by letters, reports, and the personal efforts of that devoted friend to Oregon, Dr. Marcus Whitman, an immigration of eight hundred and seventy-five persons arrived in the fall, notwithstanding that deceitful servant of the Hudson's Bay Company, Grant, at Fort Hall, did all he could, under the instructions of the company, to induce as many as possible to go to California, by telling them all the frightful stories he and his men could invent, of their danger, and the difficulties they must encounter in getting through to the settlement on the Wallamet. This company brought with them thirteen hundred head of cattle. The immigration of 1842 amounted to one hundred and thirty-seven men, women, and children, a limited supply of cattle, and a number of wagons to Fort Hall, where they were induced to abandon most of them, through the false statements of the man in charge.

The immigration of 1843, under the guidance of Dr. Whitman, brought most of their wagons, teams, and cattle through all safe. They opened the road to the Columbia, and the trail through the Cascade Mountains, which was only an obscure Indian trail quite difficult to pass in 1842, on account of brush, logs, and fallen timber.

Our population, all told, now amounted to not far from twelve hundred. Among the immigrants of 1842 and '43 there were many excellent families, and intelligent, industrious, noble-hearted young men; with a full proportion of miserable scoundrels. Most of the families soon found locations, and having some little means, with the assistance they could obtain from the Methodist Mission, and such as was brought by Captain Couch in the brig *Maryland*, and the barks *Lausanne* and *Toulon*, by Captain Crosby, sent by Mr. Cushing of Newburyport, soon commenced permanent improvements. The winter was mild and the larger portion of them were prosperous and happy in their new homes.

The provisional government was formed and put in operation in July previous to the arrival of the large immigration of 1843. Supplies of flour, sugar, and tea had been sent from the settlement to meet such as might be in want on their way into the Wallamet Valley.

From the time it was known that Dr. Whitman had safely arrived in Washington, and the boundary line was not settled, the whole policy of the Hudson's Bay Company changed. Advances of outfits were made to such men as Hastings and his party, Burnett, and other prominent men. Employment was given to a select few, and every encouragement and inducement held out to assist as many as could be prevailed upon to go to California; while those who contemplated making Oregon a permanent home were denied supplies or employment, especially those who had asked the protection of the American government. Those who proposed going to California could readily get all the supplies they required of the company by giving their notes payable in California.

It was well understood by most of them when they gave their notes that they never expected to pay them. Two of them informed us that they did not intend to pay if they went out of the country, as they understood it as equivalent to hiring, or giving them their outfit to induce them to leave.

This last remark applies particularly to the immigration of 1842, and the company that went to California with Mr. Hastings in the spring of 1843. This policy continued up to 1847–8, when the company found themselves, as they supposed, through the influence of their Jesuit missions and Indian allies, prepared to fully maintain their licensed mercantile privileges, but found themselves confronted by an army of five hundred brave and determined men, and an organization sufficiently strong and united to compel them to again change their policy, though not their secret hatred of what they termed American intrusion upon their imaginary rights in the country. In the seventeenth page of their memorial, they assert, "And they had therein and thereupon a right of trade which was virtually exclusive. * * * And such right of trade, and the control, possession, and use of said Territory, for the purposes thereof, independent of their foreign commerce and the sale of timber, exceeding in total value the sum of two hundred thousand pounds sterling ($973,333.33)." This statement is made in behalf of that company as their profits in trade before and up to 1846, which, together with the declaration of Dr. McLaughlin and Mr. Douglas, as found in chapter fifty-four, addressed to our Executive Committee under date March 11 and 12, 1845, is sufficient to indicate the true policy of the company, which will be more fully developed as we proceed.

CHAPTER XLVII.

Actions speak louder than words.—Efforts of the Hudson's Bay Company to discourage immigration.—Account of the two Jesuits, F. N. Blanchet and P. J. De Smet.—Protestant missionaries discouraged.—Important position of the Rev. G. Hines.—Recall of the Rev. Jason Lee.—Efforts of the Hudson's Bay Company to prevent emigration to the Territory.—Statement of General Palmer.—Indian combinations.—The Donner party.—Mr. McBean's character.—Extent of Oregon at this time.

REACHING thoughts by actions. This the historian of the times has a right to do; and by comparing the act and result, he can arrive with almost mathematical certainty as to what the thought was that originated the act, and produced the result. But we are not confined to this mode of reasoning. We have their own, and the statements of those favorable to them, to substantiate our conclusions.

1st. The inadvertent statement of F. Ermatinger, one of their chief traders, in 1838, that in case the American government attempted to take this country, the Hudson's Bay Company would arm their eight hundred half-breeds, and with the aid of the Indians, drive back any force that could be sent across the continent to take it. Their navy could defend the coast. The Jesuits could influence the Indians.

2d. The arrangements made to bring to the country the Red River immigrants in 1842.

3d. The stationing of a ship of war at Vancouver to protect the company.

4th. The building of bastions at Fort Vancouver, and strengthening that post in 1845–6.

5th. The refusal of Mr. Douglas to furnish supplies to the provisional troops, sent to punish the parties engaged in the Wailatpu massacre.

6th. The supplying of Indians, by Mr. Ogden, with a large amount of war material, and his avowal not to have any thing to do with American difficulties.

7th. The letters and correspondence of Sir James Douglas.

8th. The positive statements of William McBean.

9th. The statements of Vicar-General Brouillet.

10th. The correspondence and letters of Bishop Blanchet.

11th. The testimony they have produced in support of their claims.

12th. The designs of the British government as indicated by James Edward Fitzgerald.

13th. The sending of American immigrants from Fort Hall and Oregon to California.

14th. The attempt to supply the Indians in the interior, by the aid of Romish priests, with a large amount of ammunition.

15th. The implacable hatred implanted in the mind of the Indian against Americans, through the influence of the Hudson's Bay Company and the Jesuit missionaries brought to the country for that purpose.

16th. The strict rules of the company, and the continued effort to enforce those rules to the destruction of life and property.

We now come to the thoughts which originated and caused the foregoing acts.

These American missionaries have done more to defeat us, to settle the country, and defer the establishment of the boundary line, than all other efforts and causes combined. We must make another effort to destroy their influence, and drive them and their settlements from the country; and thus secure it to the British crown, for the use of the company, at the risk of a war between the two countries.

It will be remembered that Messrs. Lee, Parker, Whitman, Spalding, Gray, and other missionaries, had their passports from the Secretary of War of the United States, giving them permission to travel through, and settle as teachers in, the Indian country; and that all military officers and agents of the government were instructed to facilitate their efforts, and, if at any time it was necessary, afford them protection. These passports had been duly presented to the Hudson's Bay Company at Vancouver, and had the effect to prevent a direct effort to destroy or drive them from the country, as they had done to all who preceded them.

Hence, an extra effort must be made to get rid of this American missionary influence, and the settlements they were gathering around them.

We will now proceed to give historical facts as connected with results.

Two intelligent, jovial, yet bigoted priests had been brought to the country by the company. They had traveled all through it, and had actually discovered the pure silver and golden ores of the Rocky Mountains, and carried specimens to St. Louis and to Europe. These priests fully understood the licensed rights of the Hudson's Bay Company, and the efforts they were making to secure it to the British crown. They were also assured that, in case the American Protestant influence could be driven from it, the Papal would become the prevailing religion, as in California and Mexico. They knew that the English

Episcopal effort was an early and utter failure, and that no renewed effort would be made in their behalf by the company, and that they were then using their influence to drive the Wesleyan missionaries from Moose Factory. Hence, they and their associates entered upon their work with a zeal and energy only equaled by him who was their first victim.

F. N. Blanchet visited Canada, New York, and Rome, and was made Bishop of Oregon. His associate, P. J. De Smet, gathered his priests and nuns, returned to the country, and entered vigorously upon their missionary work, having the substantial aid of the Hudson's Bay Company, and the personal assistance of its members. Their churches, nunneries, and schools sprung up as if by magic in French Prairie, Oregon City, Vancouver, the Dalles, Umatilla, Pen d'Oreille, Colville, and St. Marie. The Protestant missions in the country were greatly annoyed by the unreasonable and threatening conduct of the Indians about their stations. They were demanding unreasonable pay for the lands upon which the stations were located, and paying but little or no attention to their American teachers. The American missionaries were becoming disheartened and discouraged, and were beginning to abandon their stations. Rev. A. B. Smith, of the Nez Percé mission, Dr. Richmond, from Nasqualla, Rev. Messrs. Kone and Frost, from Clatsop, and Mr. Edwards had left the country. Rev. Daniel Lee, Rev. H. K. W. Perkins, Mr. Brewer, and Dr. Babcock, had all become dissatisfied, and thought they had found a plausible excuse for leaving. A simple statement of a man in the employ of the Hudson's Bay Company had more influence with them than their missionary vows and obligations to the churches that sent them out.

They were not satisfied with leaving themselves, but made charges against the purest and best man of their number, simply because that, while he was absent from Oregon in 1838–9, influences were brought into the country by the company, with the intent to defeat them, and destroy all Protestant missions,—applying the same policy to destroy the harmony and usefulness of the American missions, that they had used to destroy the power and influence of the Indian tribes; which was to divide them up into factions, and get them to quarreling among themselves, as in the case of Rev. J. S. Griffin and party. This would destroy their influence, and help to break up their settlements.

The Rev. Mr. Hines, with all his wisdom, sound judgment, and experience, became, unwittingly, an important instrument and apologist in this deep-laid scheme to rid the country of Protestant missionaries and American settlements. He was led to join his influence against his truest and best friend, who is called home and superseded, and the mission stations abandoned and broken up.

Mr. Hines, on pages 236–7 of his book, says: "With regard to the objections against Mr. Lee, arising from his not furnishing the Board with the desirable report concerning the disbursement of the *large appropriations*, it should be observed that no such charge of delinquency appears against him, up to the time of the appointment of the great re-enforcement." Dr. White was known to be a bitter enemy of Rev. Jason Lee, and a willing tool of the Hudson's Bay Company. Mr. Hines, as his book, and the letters he wrote to Dr. White and the Indian Department at Washington, show, was favorable to the proceedings and policy of Dr. White and the Hudson's Bay Company.

We understand, through Rev. Mr. Geary, that Mr. Hines attributed to Mr. Lee's advice expenditures for buildings that were the pet objects of Mr. Hines himself; and thus Rev. J. Lee, to gratify the wish of others, yielded his own convictions of right, and in this way became an object of censure, which was the cause of his removal. The "changes inconceivably great with respect to the Indians of Oregon," which, Rev. Mr. Hines says "took place betwixt the time the great re-enforcement was called for, and the time of their arrival in the Columbia River," were brought to bear, and had their influence and effect, upon *him*, in his Umpqua missionary trip, in his trip to the interior, in his representations to his Missionary Board, in his opposition to the provisional government, and had their influence upon his missionary brethren. These men, Mr. Hines included, instead of studying the true interests of the country,—their obvious duty to the churches that sent them out, and the cause they represented,—were flattered and cajoled by the artful members of a foreign monopoly, and made to believe they had talents superior to the field in which they were placed by the influence and advice of the superintendent, Mr. Lee, forgetting the changes above intimated, and having no suspicions that a secret foreign influence was working to bring about the utter failure of their Indian missions; nor supposing that the brightest and best talents would secure the most attention, and the surest effort to render them dissatisfied.

The whole statement about Mr. Lee's recall, and the reasons assigned, appear to us to be unjust (though, perhaps, not intended) to the character of Mr. Lee. It was after the great re-enforcement spoken of, that the large expenditures referred to were made; hence, Mr. Hines' excuse confirms the charge, and he only attempts to change the responsibility to another; while Mr. Lee, like Dr. McLaughlin, is suffered to fall by the influence of his professed friends.

The Jesuit priests, co-laborers with the Hudson's Bay Company, did not hesitate to poison the minds of all who would listen to them against the Protestant missionaries and all their efforts; neither did they hesitate as to the means, so long as a certain object was to be accomplished. Le Breton, Lee, and Whitman must fall by their influence. The character of others must suffer by their malicious slanders and false statements. See Brouillet, pages 20 and 21, in which he attempts to show that Dr. Whitman and others were in the habit of poisoning melons to prevent the Indians from stealing them, while the fact is, the Doctor encouraged the Indians to come and get melons at freely, in order to induce them to cultivate for themselves; and we are certain that no one at the station at that time thought of putting poison into melons.

As we said, we are reading thoughts by words and acts, so as to arrive at a correct conclusion as to the thought that caused the act.

The American missionaries and settlements must be driven from the country. To do this, the Indians that have heretofore been kept at war among themselves, must now be united. Some changes must be made; Grant, of the Hudson's Bay Company, must occupy Fort Hall, and do all he can to turn immigrants to California, and rob such as persist in coming to Oregon.

General Palmer says in his journal, page 43: "While we remained at this place (Fort Hall) *great efforts* were made to induce the immigration to pursue the route to California. The most extravagant tales were related respecting the dangers awaiting a trip to Oregon, and the difficulties and trials to be surmounted. The perils of the way were so magnified as to make us suppose the journey to Oregon almost impossible. For instance, the two crossings of Snake River, and the crossings of the Columbia and other smaller streams, were represented as being attended with great danger. Also, that no company heretofore attempting the passage of these streams, succeeded but with the loss of men, from the violence and rapidity of the currents, as also that they had never succeeded in getting more than fifteen or twenty head of cattle into the Wallamet Valley.

"In addition to the above, it was asserted that three or four tribes of Indians in the middle regions *had combined for the purpose of preventing our passage through their country.* In case we escaped destruction at the hands of the savages, that a more fearful enemy—famine—would attend our march, as the distance was so great that winter would overtake us before making the Cascade Mountains. On the other hand, as an inducement to pursue the California route, we were informed of the shortness of the route when compared with that to Oregon, as also of the many other superior advantages it possessed."

It is not our intention to go into the history of California, but give what strictly relates to Oregon and her people in those early times. In the paragraph we have quoted from General Palmer's journal, the reader will see a fiendish, a damning policy; and if our language has any severer terms to express evil motives and intentions, let him use them, as belonging to the course pursued by that organization yclept Honorable Hudson's Bay Company, in attempting to prevent the settlement of Oregon, and sending whole families to starve and perish, and become cannibals in the mountains of California, rather than tell the truth, and aid them in getting to Oregon; as will be seen by the following extract from the *Gold Hill* (Nevada) *News*, concerning the horrible sufferings of "The Donner Party:"—

"The world perhaps never produced a sadder and a truer story, nor one which will be so long remembered by many whose fortunes were cast on the Pacific slope in the early days of its settlement by the Americans. We personally knew one of the families that perished among the Donner party, and on reading the interesting letter in the *Union* it awakened in our memory a little incident in connection with this sad calamity, which happened in the State of Illinois twenty years ago last April. At that time we were publisher of a newspaper in Putnam County, Illinois. Oregon and California were beginning to attract the attention of the Western people; and in the spring of 1846 a party of about fifty persons, farmers with their families, and young men, was made up in that county destined for Oregon. When the day of departure arrived, the whole party assembled in a village called Magnolia to agree upon camp regulations, appointment of officers, etc. As a journalist, we attended that meeting and published a full account of its proceedings. Among the party was "Uncle Billy Graves" and his family, consisting of father, mother, two daughters, and a son, the ages of the children ranging from fifteen to twenty years. Uncle Billy Graves was a well-to-do farmer, with every thing comfortable about him; and, having already reached the age of threescore, it was a matter of surprise to many that he should sell his farm and start off to make a new home in such a far-off and wild country as Oregon then was. But the country in Illinois was getting too thickly settled for the old man, and he longed for the wild adventures of the far west. He pleaded and persuaded us to go with him, and to bring our office along, as Oregon would some day be a great country, and we would have the credit of having been the first to publish a newspaper in it. But circumstances over which we had no control prevented us, although we certainly had the will and the wish just as Uncle Billy Graves advised. We remained in Illinois, and the Graves family joined with the overland party for Oregon. Letters written by the party during the summer were published in our paper. The last one written by any of the Graves family was dated at Fort Laramie, and this was the last heard of the old farmer. He joined the Donner party, which separated from the emigration to Oregon at Fort Hall, near the headwaters of the Columbia, and wending his way westward toward California, before its gold-fields were known in the world, he perished in the mountains, and his good old wife perished with him. The son and daughters of the Graves family were among the persons who were rescued by the relief party of sailors and others who were sent out by the benevolent Americans at Sutter's Fort and San Francisco. A long letter written by one of the Graves girls was published in our paper in the year 1847, and which contained a full and sad account of the awful sufferings of the party. We shall never forget the manuscript of the letter. It was blotted all over with the tears which the poor girl shed while describing the sufferings of her famishing parents, their death, and the flesh of their dead bodies furnishing food for their starving children! Horrible! horrible! Let the bleached bones and skulls of the Donner party be gathered together and decently buried, for they once belonged to good Christian people."

The Indians also have become deeply interested in their schemes to prevent the settlement of the country.

We are told by Mr. Hines, on page 143, that they sent one of their chiefs on snow-shoes, in the winter of 1842–3, to excite or induce the Buffalo Indians to join them to cut off the immigrants that were expected to come to the country with Dr. Whitman.

Mr. McKinley, a professedly warm friend of Dr. Whitman, was removed from having charge of Fort Nez Percés, and William McBean, who (Mr. Roberts, an old clerk of the Hudson's Bay Company, says) "is one of the d——dest scoundrels that ever lived," put in his place.

The reader will not forget that we are speaking of events and movements in a country where an Indian in a canoe or on horseback or snow-shoes was our swiftest messenger, and that its boundaries included what is now the State of Oregon, the Territories of Washington, Idaho, and Montana, besides Vancouver Island and British Columbia.

The Hudson's Bay Company was a powerful and unscrupulous monopoly, and the only representative of a vast empire on this western part of our continent. To possess the whole, or a valuable part of it, was an object worth using the influence they had spent years of labor and thousands (not millions, as they claim) of dollars to secure.

The time has now arrived when all is at stake. *The American missionary societies have accomplished what American commerce and fur traders have failed to do.* The trouble is now between a "*squawtocracy of British skin traders*" and Italian and Belgian Jesuits on one side, and American missionaries and settlements on the other. The traders and Jesuits have nearly overcome the American missionary influence. The settlements are organized. The old policy to get rid of all opposition fur traders, destroy Indian influence, and break up missions, must be tried, to prevent and destroy the settlements.

The thoughts expressed in this chapter have carried us in advance of the date of culminating events; hence, we must return, in order that we may bring them in the order of their occurrence.

CHAPTER XLVIII.

1844.—The settlements alarmed.—Indian attack.—Death of G. W. Le Breton.—Meeting at Mr. La Chapelle's.—Volunteer company formed.—The *Modeste* in the Columbia River.—The Legislative Assembly.—Names of the members.—Peter H. Burnett.—Mr. David Hill.—Oregon social standard.—M. M. McCarver.—"Old Brass Gun."—A. L. Lovejoy.—Daniel Waldo.—Thomas D. Keizer.—Black act.—Prohibitory liquor law.

1844.—March 9th of this year found our settlements alive and in great alarm. The Indians in the vicinity of Oregon City had made an attack upon the town on the 4th instant, and three white men had been wounded and one Indian killed. G. W. Le Breton was wounded while attempting to take the Indian that commenced the attack, by a ball entering and breaking his arm, from the effect of which he died some twelve days after, and was buried at Vancouver, where he had been taken for surgical treatment. The other two received slight flesh wounds, although one proved fatal—probably made by a poisoned arrow. The Indians commenced the fight in open day, and continued it till their leader was taken by Le Breton, after his arm was broken.

The Indian was placed under guard, and, on attempting to make his escape, was killed. Those who were with him, and took part in the fight, fled into the thick wood back of the town, and escaped.

This account, which we have received from other sources, will be seen to differ slightly from the one already given by Dr. White in his letter to the Secretary of War.

A proclamation was issued by the Executive Committee, calling for an organization of the military forces in the settlement. It appears, from the record of those times, that but one company was organized in Champoeg District. The proceedings of that meeting, as noted by the writer, and signed by the secretary, gives the fullest account we have, and properly belongs to the history of the times. The attempt to destroy the people and town at Wallamet Falls was made on the 4th of March; the news was conveyed to the old mission and Salem on the 5th; notices were immediately sent to the American population to meet on the 9th, with arms, to organize for defensive or offensive measures. In the mean time, each individual and family took such precautionary measures as were thought advisable, keeping guard over their separate and individual possessions. Most of the French or Hudson's Bay Company's servants showed no alarm on the occasion, and very few of them turned out, or paid any attention to the military call, though the meeting was at the house of a Frenchman.

The citizens of Champoeg having met on March 9, at the house of Mr. La Chapelle, in accordance with the proclamation issued, the meeting was called to order by one of the Executive Committee, and the proclamation read.

Upon the suggestion of the executive, W. H. Wilson was chosen chairman of this meeting, and T. D. Keizer, secretary.

The object of the meeting was briefly explained by one of the Executive Committee, Hon. A. Beers, and the chairman. Information was called for concerning the depredations committed at Wallamet Falls on the 4th instant.

Mr. Beers presented an official letter from Hon. D. Hill, one of the Executive Committee, which was read. Statements were made by Mr. Garrison respecting accounts received from other sources, and a letter was presented by the United States sub-Indian agent, from A. L. Lovejoy, Esq., respecting the affair of the 4th, which was read.

Statements were made by Hon. A. Beers concerning the steps they had taken, and the orders they had issued.

On motion, the United States sub-Indian agent was requested to give his views and advice on the subject. He accordingly related his proceeding in reference to the matter; said he was unprepared to give advice, or suggest what was best to be done in the present case. He was fully aware of the defenseless state of the colony and the dangers to which it was exposed. He knew the character of the Indian that was killed to be of the vilest kind, and that he had threatened and attempted the lives of citizens before. The agent said he had made an unsuccessful attempt to take him, and have him punished by the Cayuses, to avoid the danger that might result from the whites punishing him themselves. This renegade had attempted to induce the Indians at the falls to burn the town; and, failing in this object, he returned across the river. The citizens attempted peaceably to take him, but in the affray three whites were wounded, and one Indian killed. The agent thought a more efficient organization of the Territory necessary.

Some remarks were made by W. H. Gray, and a resolution offered as follows:—

Resolved, That in view of the facts presented, we deem it expedient to organize a volunteer company of mounted riflemen, to co-operate with other companies, to bring to justice all the Indians engaged in the affair of the 4th of March, and to protect our lives and property against any attempt at future depredations.

Carried unanimously. Whereupon W. H. Gray presented some articles of compact as the basis of an organization of a volunteer company, which, on motion, and with warm expressions of approbation from the United States sub-Indian agent, were adopted, and immediately subscribed to by nineteen volunteers.

The articles of compact allowed the company to elect a captain, lieutenant, and ensign, as soon as twelve men should be enlisted, so the company proceeded, by nomination, to elect their officers, to wit: For captain, T. D. Keizer; first lieutenant, J. L. Morrison; for ensign, Mr. Cason. The captain gave notice to the company of his acceptance of the appointment, requesting them to meet at the Oregon Institute, armed and equipped, on the 11th inst., for company drill.

On motion, the following resolution was adopted, viz.:—

Resolved, That this meeting recommend to our fellow-citizens of this Territory, to organize volunteer companies in their respective districts forthwith; and to rendezvous at the Oregon Institute, on Saturday, the 23d instant, at 12 M.

Moved, that the proceedings of this meeting be signed by the chairman and secretary, and as much of them as is deemed proper be transmitted to other districts. Carried.

On motion, adjourned.

W. H. Wilson, Chairman.
T. D. Keizer, Secretary.

It will be seen by Dr. White's statement, that the Indian killed was a renegade from the Cayuse or upper country Indians. He was doing all he could to excite the Indians and get them to join in a general combination to destroy the American settlements in the Wallamet Valley. Dr. White, as he stated to the meeting, had now reached the utmost limit of his authority and influence. He knew not what to do. He was too big a coward to propose any bold measure, and too mean to be trusted by the settlers; hence, if the reader will carefully study the proceedings of this meeting, he will find a firm and steady influence, on the part of the settlers, leading on through all the dangers and excitements of the occasion. The proposed company was at once organized and elected its officers. Gray accepted the office of first sergeant in the company, which was soon filled up and drilled, and all were mounted on good horses. This soon became known throughout the settlements, and had the effect to frighten the Indians and keep them quiet, so that no further disturbance was made in the settlements of the Wallamet. It also had the effect to secure in the Columbia River the presence of the *Modeste*, a war vessel of the English government, which became *absolutely necessary* (ironically speaking) to protect the property and interests of the Hudson's Bay Company from the threatened depredations of the Indians about their posts at Vancouver, as they were represented to be becoming far more hostile than formerly. The company had found that, since the Americans began to settle in the country, these Indians had become more dangerous and hostile to them; and as their people were scattered more extensively over the Indian country, it was absolutely necessary to have their principal depot more strongly fortified and protected, not against Indians, for they, by the course already pursued by that company, were fast melting away. Their country had been "hunted up" and made destitute of fur-producing animals by the advanced prices they had given in 1838–40, and now starvation was their their only portion, unless the American settlers would share with them what they produced from the soil. This Indian difficulty was only an attempt to bring on an Indian war in the Wallamet to see how strong the settlements were, what means of protection they possessed, and what their offensive measures were likely to be.

This opened the eyes of Sir James Douglas to the natural weakness of Fort Vancouver. The *Modeste* was ordered to the river, and other preparations were made to defend that establishment from an attack of the American settlers. They found from the results of what occurred on the 4th of March, that there *was a real substantial power in the country*, and an influence of combination that they did not dream of; hence they found themselves, with all their Indian combinations, the weaker power.

We will now leave the Honorable Hudson's Bay Company under the protection of the guns of her Majesty's ship *Modeste*, the fort being repaired, bastions built, and all other protective and defensive measures completed, while we look after the election and proceedings of the Legislative Assembly of 1844.

The members elected from Tualatin District (since divided into Washington, Multnomah, Columbia, Clatsop, and Tilamook counties) were Peter H. Burnett, David Hill, M. M. McCarver, and Mr. Gilmore.

Clackamas District, including all of Washington Territory, Idaho, Montana, and half of the eastern part of the State of Oregon, was represented by A. L. Lovejoy. Champoeg District, including Marion, Linn, Baker, Douglas, and Jackson counties, was represented by Daniel Waldo, from Missouri, Thomas D. Keizer, from Arkansas, and Robert Newell, from the Rocky Mountains.

Peter H. Burnett was a lawyer from Missouri, who came to Oregon to seek his fortune, as well as a religion that would pay the best, and give him the most influence; which in the Legislative Committee was sufficient to induce that body to pay no attention to any organic law or principle laid down for the government of the settlements. In fact, he asserted that there were no constitutional provisions laid down or adopted by the people in general convention at Champoeg the year previous. Mr. Burnett was unquestionably the most intelligent lawyer then in the country. He was a very ambitious man—smooth, deceitful, and insinuating in his manners.

On motion of Mr. Lovejoy (another lawyer), the several members were excused from producing their credentials, and on motion of the same gentleman, the house proceeded to elect a Speaker. M. M. McCarver was duly elected.

The journal of the proceedings of this Legislative Committee shows that no regard was paid to any previous laws, or constitutional provisions.

David Hill, of Tualatin District, was from Ohio. He was a tall, slim man, of sallow complexion, black hair, with strong prejudices, having no regard for religion or morality. He left an interesting wife and family in Ohio, and passed himself off in Oregon for a widower or bachelor. He was favorable to all applications for divorces, and married a second wife, as near as we could learn, before he obtained a divorce (if he ever did) from his first wife. He early took an active part in the provisional government, and was a decided opponent of the Hudson's Bay Company, as also of all missionary efforts in the country. This rendered him popular among the settlers, and secured his election as a representative for that district for several years, although his education was quite limited. As a citizen he was generally respected. Though intimately acquainted with two of his sons, we could never learn that he was any thing but kind and affectionate as a husband and father. The fact of his leaving a wife and young family in Ohio, coming to Oregon, and remaining for years without making any provision for them, is evidence of guilt in some one. The friends of his wife and family spoke of them as being highly esteemed by all who knew them. But it is of his public acts, as connected with the history of Oregon, that we wish particularly to speak.

The social standard adopted by the people of Oregon was peculiarly adapted to favor men of Mr. Hill's morality, and aid them in rising from the effect of any former misconduct they may have been guilty of in any other country. This standard was, to receive as fellow-citizens all who came among us; to ignore their former actions, and give them a chance to start anew, and make a name and character in the country.

There must be something noble and generous in a people occupying a new and wild country, as Oregon was in those days, that would lead them to adopt a standard for common action and citizenship, so peculiary republican and in accordance with the most liberal and enlightened Christianity. To this spirit of toleration and benevolence must be attributed, under an all-wise Providence, the complete success and stability of the first civil government formed on this coast. Hence, as we have before said, we shall deal with men, morals, and politics as they belonged to Oregon at the time of which we are writing.

M. M. McCarver, from having acted as commissary in the Black Hawk war, in Iowa, was called General. This title secured to him considerable influence, and many favors from the Hudson's Bay Company. General McCarver was a man of common education, making large pretension to political knowledge, without much judgment or understanding of political economy. He was an intolerable debater, and acquired, among the lobby members of the Legislature, the name of "*Old Brass Gun.*" In his political course, he strove hard for popularity, and attempted to secure places of honor for personal promotion. He was what would be considered a *Simon Pure* pro-slavery Democrat. Like the silly moth in the fable, he fluttered around the shadow of Dr. White, the sub-Indian agent, and assisted him in insulting the Legislative Committee of 1845, and attempted to get his name before the Congress of the United States as an important and influential man, which was divulged and defeated by another member of the same committee, though in a cowardly and dishonorable manner. We are not aware that General McCarver ever originated any important measure, or performed any extensive or important service in the country. His political schemes were generally so supremely selfish that they died still-born.

Mr. Gilmore, from the same district, was a substantial farmer. He neither said or did much, and but little is known of him.

A. Lawrence Lovejoy, formerly from Massachusetts, was a man of medium size, light complexion, light hair, rather impetuous and dogmatical in his conversation. He crossed the mountains with the immigration of 1842 to Dr. Whitman's station; from that place he attempted to return to the United States with Dr. Whitman. As near as we can learn, he became utterly exhausted by the time they reached Bent's Fort on the Arkansas River, and was left there by the Doctor. In the summer of 1843 he returned to Oregon and pursued his profession of law. In Oregon he has always acted with the radical Democratic party, rather doubtfully on the pro-slavery platform. He was the first regular nominee for governor of Oregon. George Abernethy, the secular agent of the Methodist Mission, was run as an independent candidate, and, with the assistance of Peter H. Burnett, Mr. Russell, and his friends, who bolted the general convention, was elected governor, though at the time he was on a visit to the Sandwich Islands. A large number of political friends still adhered to Mr. Lovejoy, and made a second attempt to elect him governor. Mr. Abernethy was again the opposing candidate. It appeared in the canvass of that year, that the Hudson's Bay Company generally voted for Mr. Lovejoy; but the personal kindness of Mr. Abernethy to a priest traveling up the Wallamet, induced him to tell his people to vote for Mr. Abernethy, and by this vote he was elected, although a fair majority of the votes of the American settlers was given for Mr. Lovejoy. Mr. Lovejoy, like many of us, leaves but little usefulness or philanthropy to record, that his talents and position should have led him to aspire to. As a citizen and neighbor, he is kind and obliging, as a lawyer not above mediocrity, and it is generally understood that he makes no pretensions to religion.

Daniel Waldo, formerly of Missouri, was a plain, substantial farmer, and the first man who ventured to experiment upon the hills, or upland portions of Oregon. He had owned extensive tracts of land on the banks of the Missouri, a large portion of which had been washed away by the floods, which cause continual changes along the banks of that river. In coming to Oregon, he had made up his mind to take the hills, if there were any in the country. He did so, and has proved by his experiment the value of a large portion of country that was before considered worthless for cultivation. From the time Mr. Waldo arrived in the country he became an enthusiastic admirer of Oregon. Soon after he had located in the hills bearing his name, an old acquaintance of his, and also of his brother in Missouri, came to Oregon on a visit, and was about to return to the States. He paid Mr. Waldo a visit, and after chatting awhile and looking over his farm, on which we could not see a single rail, except a few he had in a corral, his friend (Colonel Gilpin) said to him: "What shall I say for you, to your brother in Missouri?" "Tell him," said Waldo, "that I would not give the bare idea of owning a section of land in Oregon for all I own in Missouri [which was then two sections, 1,280 acres], and that I would not give a section of land here for the whole State of Missouri." Such men gave a good report of Oregon, and it is to such that the country is indebted for her stability and prosperity. Mr. Waldo's experiment has shown the capacity of the country for settlement to be more than double what it was previously considered, and while some of those who laughed at him and called him an enthusiast have had their farms, cattle, and houses swept away by floods, he has remained in the hills uninjured and secure.

Thomas D. Keizer, from Arkansas. Of this man's early history we have learned but little. It seems that, for some cause, he and his family were compelled to leave the State. Their story is that a gang of counterfeiters was exposed by them, and in consequence of their becoming informers they were surrounded by a mob and compelled to leave. On first arriving in the country they were not scrupulous as to the rights of their neighbors, or those of the Oregon Institute, or mission claims. They found themselves comfortably housed in the first buildings of the Oregon Institute, and occupied them till it suited their pleasure to leave, and to find other quarters upon land claimed by the mission. As was to be expected, Mr. Keizer was inclined to do all he could to curtail the mission and Institute claims, he being the gainer by curtailing the claims of others. As a politician, he considered all little dirty tricks and slanders against an opponent justifiable. In religion he professed to be a Methodist.

Robert Newell has been previously described.

Such being the composition of the Legislative Committee of Oregon in 1844, it is not surprising that interests of classes and cliques should find advocates, and that the absolute wants of the country should be neglected. The whole time of the session seems to have been taken up in the discussions of personal bills. The question of convention of the people was before this session and was lost.

There was one inhuman act passed by this Legislative Committee, which should stamp the names of its supporters with disgrace and infamy. We find its inception recorded on the 25th of July, the sixth day of the session.

On motion, the rules were suspended for the special purpose of allowing Hon. P. H. Burnett to introduce a bill for the prevention of *slavery in Oregon*, without giving previous notice; which was received and read first time. It was read a second time next day in the forenoon, and in the afternoon of the same day the bill to prevent slavery in Oregon, *and for other purposes*, was read a third time, and on the question, "Shall the bill pass?" the yeas and nays were demanded, when the vote stood: yeas, Burnett, Gilmore, Keizer, Waldo, Newell, and Mr. Speaker McCarver—6; nays, Lovejoy and Hill—2.

The principal provisions of this bill were, that in case a colored man was brought to the country by any master of a vessel, he must give bonds to take him away again or be fined, and in case the negro was found, or came here from any quarter, the sheriff was to catch him and flog him forty lashes at a time, till he left the country.

These six Solons, who got up and carried through this measure, did it for the good of the black man of course, as one of the first principles laid down by the people the year previous in the organic law, and unanimously carried, was: "That slavery, except for the punishment of crime, whereof the parties shall have been previously convicted, shall never be tolerated."

The principles of Burnett's bill made it a crime for a white man to bring a negro to the country, and a crime for a negro to come voluntarily; so that, in any case, if he were found in the country, he was guilty of a crime, and punishment or slavery was his doom.

Mr. Burnett claimed great credit for getting up a prohibitory liquor law, and made several speeches in favor of sustaining it, that being a popular measure among a majority of the citizens.

At the adjourned session in December, we find the executive urging the Legislative Committee to adopt measures to secure the permanent interests and prosperity of the country, also to amend their act relative to the corporal punishment of the blacks, and again urging the calling of a convention of the people.

CHAPTER XLIX.

Message of the Executive Committee.—Observations on the message.—Generosity of the Hudson's Bay Company.—The Methodist Mission.—The Oregon Printing-press Association.—George Abernethy, Esq.

To the Honorable the Legislative Committee of Oregon:

GENTLEMEN,—As the expectation of receiving some information from the United States relative to the adjustment of the claims of that government and of Great Britain upon this country, was the principal cause of the adjournment of this assembly from June last to this day, we feel it our duty to communicate such information as we have been able to collect on the subject, and likewise to recommend the adoption of further measures for the promotion and security of the interests of Oregon.

The lines defining the limits of the separate claims of the United States and Great Britain to this portion of the country had not been agreed upon when our latest advices left the United States, and as far as we can learn, the question now stands in the same position as before the convention in London, in 1818. At that time, the United States government proposed to draw the division line on the forty-ninth parallel of north latitude from the Lake of the Woods to the Pacific Ocean. To this Great Britain would only consent in part, that the line should run on the forty-ninth parallel from the Lake of the Woods to the dividing ridge of the Rocky Mountains; and it was finally agreed upon, between the parties, that all the country lying west of the Rocky Mountains, and on the Pacific Ocean, should, with its harbors, bays, and rivers, remain open for ten years to the vessels, subjects, or citizens of both countries. But it was at the same time expressly understood, that the said agreement was not to be construed to affect or prejudice the claims of either party, or any other power, to any portion of said country. Before this agreement expired, another convention was held in London, in 1827, by the two contracting powers, by which the former treaty was extended, with the provision, that when either of the parties thought fit, after the 20th of October, 1828, to abrogate the convention, they were at liberty to do so, by giving twelve months' notice to the other contracting party; but nothing in the treaty of 1827 was to be construed so as to affect, in any manner, the claims which either of the contracting parties, or any other power, might have to any of the country lying west of the Rocky Mountains.

The subject has again been called up for investigation by the two powers, and a negotiation was begun at Washington in the early part of the present year, but was for the time being suspended on account of a disagreement between the parties; and notice of the abrogation of the convention of 1827 had not been given by either party when our latest information left the United States. And we find that after all the negotiations that have been carried on between the United States and Great Britain relative to settling their claims to this country, from October, 1818, up to May, 1844, a period of nearly twenty-six years, the question remains in the following unsettled position, viz.:—

Neither of the parties in question claim exclusive right to the country lying west of the Rocky Mountains, between the parallels of forty-two degrees and fifty-four degrees forty minutes north latitude, and bordering on the Pacific Ocean; but one claims as much right as the other, and both claim the right of joint occupancy of the whole without prejudice to the claims of any other state or power to any part of said country.

We have submitted to you this information, gentlemen of the Assembly, for two reasons:—

1st. To correct an error that occurred in our last communication to this body relative to the claims of the United States and Great Britain to this country.

2d. That you may bear in mind, while legislating for the people of Oregon, the position in which this country stands with regard to those claims.

We would advise that provision be made by this body for the framing and adoption of a constitution for Oregon, previous to the next annual election, which may serve as a more thorough guide to her officers, and a more firm basis of her laws. It should be constructed in such a manner as would best suit the local situation of the country, and promote the general interests of the citizens, without interfering with the real or pretended rights of the United States or Great Britain, except when the protection of life and property actually require it.

We would suggest for your information that this government has now in its possession notes given by different individuals residing in the country, amounting to $3,734.26, most of which are already due. These notes are a balance in favor of Ewing Young, of Oregon, deceased, intestate, A. D. 1840, after all legal dues, debts, and damages are paid, that have come to the knowledge of the administrator or Probate Courts of Oregon up to this date. We would, therefore, advise that these claims should be collected and appropriated to the benefit of the country, the government being at all times responsible for the payment of them to those who may hereafter appear to have a legal right to the same.

We would again call your attention to a measure recommended in our last communication, to wit, the expediency of making provision for the erection of a public jail in this country. Although the community has suffered very little as yet for the want of such a building, and perhaps another year might pass without its being occupied, which it is hoped may be the case, yet we are assured that it is better policy to have the building standing without a tenant than a tenant without the building. And in order to promote industry and the peace and welfare of the citizens of Oregon, this government must be prepared to discountenance indolence, and check vice in the bud.

We would now recommend to your consideration the propriety of making provision for filling public offices which now are or may become vacant by resignation or otherwise, previous to the next annual election.

We would recommend that the act passed by this assembly in June last, relative to blacks and mulattoes, be so amended as to exclude corporal punishment, and require bonds for good behavior in its stead.

We consider it a highly important subject that the executive of this government should have laws which may direct them in settling matters relative to lands reserved by Indians, which have been, or may hereafter be, settled upon by whites.

We would also recommend that provisions be made for the support of lunatics and insane persons in Oregon.

With regard to the state of the treasury, we would refer you to the treasurer's report to this Assembly.

We are informed that the number of immigrants who have come to this country from the United States during the present year amounts to upward of seven hundred and fifty persons.

We would recommend that the act passed last June, defining the northern boundaries of Tualatin and Clatsop counties, be so explained as not to conflict with the act passed in this Assembly in June, 1843, extending the limits of Oregon to fifty-four degrees forty minutes north latitude.

And we would suggest, in conclusion, that to preserve the peace, good order, and kind feeling, which have hitherto existed among the inhabitants of this country, depends very much upon the calm and deliberate judgment of this Assembly, and we sincerely hope that Oregon, by the special aid of Divine Providence may set an unprecedented example to the world of industry, morality, and virtue.

And although we may now be unknown as a state or power, yet we have the advantages, by the united efforts of our increasing population, in a diligent attention to agriculture, arts, and literature, of attaining, at no distant day, to as conspicuous an elevation as any State or power on the continent of America.

But in order to carry this important measure, and arise to that distinguished station, it becomes the duty of every citizen of this country to take a deep interest in its present and future welfare.

As descendants of the United States and Great Britain, we should honor and respect the countries which gave us birth; and, as citizens of Oregon, we should, by a uniform course of proceeding, and a strict observance of the rules of justice, equity, and republican principles, without party distinction, use our best endeavors to cultivate the kind feeling, not only of our native countries, but of all the powers or states with whom we may have intercourse.

Signed, OSBORNE RUSSELL,
P. G. STEWART.
Executive Committee of Oregon.

Dated, WALLAMET FALLS, Dec. 16, 1844.

To the honor of the country, Peter H. Burnett's negro-whipping law was never enforced in a single instance, against a white or black man, as no officer of the provisional government felt it incumbent upon himself to attempt to enforce it.

The proposed constitutional revision was also strongly recommended by the Executive Committee, and the Legislative Committee went through the farce of calling a convention, and increased the number of representatives, and called it a Legislature. In fact, the whole proceedings seemed only to mix up and confuse the people; so much so, that some doubted the existence of any legal authority in the country, and the leading men of the immigration of 1843 denounced the organization as a missionary arrangement to secure the most valuable farming lands in the country.

The Hudson's Bay Company, under the guidance of James Douglas and P. S. Ogden, carried forward their plans and arrangements by placing men at their posts along the line of the immigrant route, who were doing all they could, by misrepresentation and falsehood, to deceive and rob those who were journeying to this country.

But, says the sycophant, the early settlers of Oregon are greatly indebted to the Hudson's Bay Company for supplies of goods and provisions sent to aid the starving immigrants. General Palmer tells us (page 42) that flour at Fort Hall, when he came along, was twenty dollars per one hundred pounds; cattle were from five to twelve dollars per head. They could not be prevailed upon to receive any thing in exchange for their goods or provisions, except cattle or money.

Two to four cows, or two yoke of oxen for a hundred pounds of flour is *great generosity*, and rēnders the man who gives his last cow or ox to the company, under great obligations; as much so as the early settlers and the company's servants were in taking care of their cattle for the little milk they could get from them, the company claiming the cow and increase, and pay for any animal lost. This was Hudson's Bay Company's generosity to the early settlers!

They found that through the influence of Burnett, Newell, Pomeroy, and a few other Americans, they could accomplish more than by direct opposition, and therefore began to change their course, and manifest approval of the provisional government; so much so, that Ermatinger, a member of the company, was elected treasurer in 1845, in opposition to P. Foster, who served in 1844.

During the summer of 1844, Rev. George Geary arrived in the country, "clothed with discretionary power," and had the destiny of missionaries, laymen, property, and all, put into his hands. He superseded Mr. Lee. Mr. Hines returned from the Sandwich Islands, and they proceeded at once to dispose of the missionaries and property of the Methodist Mission.

The stations at Clatsop, Nasqualla, and the Dalles were given up. That at the Dalles was sold to the American Board, that on Clatsop to Rev. J. L. Parish, while the station at Nasqualla was abandoned by Rev. J. P. Richmond, who, with Rev. Messrs. Kone and Frost, had become dissatisfied with their Indian missionary labors, and returned to the States. Rev. Messrs. D. Lee and H. K. W. Perkins, Dr. Babcock, and Mr. Brewer had all made up their minds to leave the country.

These missionaries, having enlisted in a cause surrounded, at the time of their engagements, with all the romance of early missionary life in the far west, as soon as they reached their field of labor, had found that romance and real life among the Indians did not accord with the feelings of their proud and supremely selfish hearts. They were not satisfied with silently withdrawing from the country, and encouraging others more capable and better adapted to the missionary work to come to it; but they joined with Dr. White, a bitter enemy of Rev. J. Lee, and succeeded in obtaining the latter gentleman's removal from the superintendency, and, through Rev. Messrs. Geary and Hines, the abandonment of their Indian mission.

As an outside eye-witness of these transactions, we will state frankly our impressions as to the general closing up of the Methodist missionary labors among the Indians. The special and general watchfulness of the Hudson's Bay Company, and their influence over the leading members of the mission, and the effort they made to counteract the moral and civil improvement of the Indians, was brought to bear both directly and indirectly upon the superior and subordinate members, the same as it had been upon the members of the missions of the American Board, and caused a division in sentiment as to the usefulness and results of missionary labor, and thus crippled their efforts, and caused many of them to join with Dr. White, and complain of Superintendent Lee, as an excuse to abandon the missionary work.

While these influences were working their intended results upon all the American missionaries, the Jesuits, having explored the country, under the patronage and by the assistance of the Hudson's Bay Company, were making extensive preparations to occupy it with their missionaries, who were then being collected, and sent from Belgium and Canada to Oregon, under the direction of that arch-Jesuit, P. J. De Smet, and Bishop Blanchet.

By the time they arrived, the Methodist Indian missions were all disposed of; thus enabling the Jesuits to fix their undivided attention and combine their united influence against the missions of the American Board, which all admitted were accomplishing a noble work among the tribes of their charge.

As Mr. Fitzgerald says: "But the company not only get rid of missionaries as soon as they can do so without dangerous unpopularity, but they obstruct them in the performance of their duties while in the country." (See page 189 of his work.)

This opposition to the missionaries was not caused by the Indians, but the personal opposition of the company, as proved by Sir J. Pelly's answer to the question, "Have you found a disposition on the part of the natives to receive moral and religious instruction." "Very great. There were a couple of young lads sent from the Columbia District, to whom the names of Pelly and Garry were given; these lads were revered by the natives, when they returned, for the religious instructions they were enabled to give." (See page 195, of the work above quoted.)

One Congregational and five Methodist ministers have left the country with their families. Five Jesuit priests and as many nuns are coming to it. Eight hundred emigrants are plodding their way over the mountains and plains with ox-teams, to find a home in this country. The sub-Indian agent has worked himself quiet. The Indians are waiting orders, watching the immigration, and getting ready to strike at the proper time.

Mr. Lease had brought a band of five hundred head of California cattle to the country and disposed of most of them to the Hudson's Bay Company.

The Oregon Printing-Press Association was formed, and about eighty shares, at $10 each, were subscribed, and the money sent to New York for press, type, and paper, by George Abernethy, Esq., who, after the provisional organization in 1843, became a valuable supporter of all the best interests of the country. His integrity of character, consistent piety, and unbounded generosity, but few will question. From his position, and connection with the Methodist Mission, he has suffered much pecuniary loss, from men who were ever ready to take undue advantage of a confiding and generous disposition.

As a public officer he always held a negative position, the tendency of which was to hold all in suspense, and wait for some future action, or to be carried forward by events that might occur. He could not be called a leader in any civil, religious, or political measure, yet he truly represented, in his public capacity, the organization of which he was a member. So far as he was capable, he held in abeyance all laws and measures, to what he considered would be the policy of the United States government at some future time. The natural result of this position was, to accomplish nothing definitely. Hence we find in all his public acts, this tender spirit, and want of decided action.

Mr. Hines started for the United States by way of China. The property of the Methodist Mission was distributed, and the settlers had increased; while the Hudson's Bay Company were busily preparing to defend their assumed rights by arming their forts and Indians in a manner so as not to excite suspicion, or alarm the American settlements

CHAPTER L.

Dr. White's report.—Seizure and destruction of a distillery.—Homicide of Joel Turnham—State of the Territory.—Trials of Dr. White.—The liquor law.—Revenue act.—Case of the negro Saul.—The Indians kill an ox.—Other Indian difficulties.—Indian expedition to California.—Death of the Indian Elijah.—State of the Territory.—Claim of the Hudson's Bay Company on the north bank of the Columbia.—Letter of Peter H. Burnett.—The Nez Percés and Cayuses.—Extract from the report of the United States Senate.

WE give the following extracts from Dr. White's Indian report and proceedings in Oregon, that the reader may be informed as to what he claimed to be his influence, and also the way he maneuvered with the Indians and settlers; with his full account of the killing of the young Indian Elijah in California.

The letters from the different missionaries show the condition of the American missions at the time. Mr. Lee and the Jesuit missionaries did not deem him the proper agent to report to. Notwithstanding, in his report, given in a previous chapter, he attributes to the Jesuit missionaries improvements wholly made by the Americans, not from ignorance of the fact, but from personal prejudice.

It will be seen that the committee in Congress, to whom his report and petition was referred, deemed it equitable and just on general principles, and allowed it.

WALLAMET, November 4, 1844.

SIR,—The Hudson's Bay ship *Columbia* sailing in a few days, *via* Sandwich Islands, for England, by the politeness of her owners I have the honor of again addressing you, and certainly under circumstances most favorable and gratifying.

Since my last, forwarded in March, aside from two or three incidents of an unpleasant nature, the colony and country have been in a state of unusual quietness, and the season has been one of great prosperity.

The legislative body, composed of nine members, met on the 24th of May, at the falls at Wallamet, and closed their short but effective session in nine days; having passed, in due form, twenty-five bills, most of which were of importance to us in the regulation of our intercourse. A few of these laws I transmit to you, and would here remark, the taxes were in general cheerfully paid. The liquor bill is popular, and the laws of Oregon are honored.

The Liquor act not coming in force under sixty days from its passage, a few individuals (having clandestinely prepared, before its passage) improved this favored moment to dispose of all they could with any hopes of safety. Of this I was immediately notified, and hastened in from the Tualatin Plains, all the mischief, "as heretofore," being done in and about the town at the falls of the Wallamet.

Liquor was in our midst, as was but too manifest from the noisy, vulgar, obscene, and even diabolical expressions of those who had previously ever conducted themselves in a quiet and orderly manner.

This was perplexing and exciting, as all professed ignorance; and many opinions prevailed regarding the amount manufactured, and the number interested, and especially regarding the seat of mischief or point where distilled.

I resolved, at whatever danger or cost, to nip this in the bud, procured the call of a public meeting at once, and had the happiness to receive the following expression from all but one convened:—

"*Resolved,* That it be the sense of this meeting, that Dr. White, in his official relation, take such assistance as he may require, and forthwith search out and destroy all intoxicating liquor that may be found in this vicinity or district of country.

"P. G. Stewart.
"Executive Chairman.

"John E. Long,
"Secretary."

I started with ten volunteers early the ensuing morning, and found the distillery in a deep, dense thicket, eleven miles from town, at three o'clock, P. M. The boiler was a large-size potash kettle, and all the apparatus well accorded. Two hogsheads and eight barrels of slush or beer were standing ready for distillation, with a part of one barrel of molasses. No liquor could be found, nor as yet had much been distilled.

Having resolved on my course, I left no time for reflection, but at once upset the nearest cask, when the noble volunteers immediately seconded my measures, making a river of beer in a moment; nor did we stop till the kettle was raised, and elevated in triumph at the prow of our boat, and every cask, with all the distilling apparatus, was broken to pieces and utterly destroyed. We then returned, in high cheer, to the town, where our presence and report gave general joy.

Two hours after my arrival, I received from James Connor, one of the owners, a written challenge for a bloody combat; which ended last week in his being indicted before the grand jury, fined $500, and disfranchised for life.

Six weeks since, an unhappy affray occurred between one Joel Turnham, late from Missouri, and Webley Hauxhurst, of Wallamet, and serious threats passing from the former, a warrant was issued, and Turnham, resisting with a deadly weapon, was shot down by the officer; for which he comes before the grand jury to-morrow. Turnham expired at once, being shot with three mortal wounds through the neck and head, but with singular desperation fought and resisted to the last.

So far as I understand the public expression, all unite in acquitting the officer, who has ever been a harmless, quiet, good citizen; while Turnham was regarded as a most desperate and dangerous character all abroad, having left Missouri under circumstances most unfavorable to his reputation and quiet here, where he has been particularly sour, irritable, and quarrelsome; and was the more obnoxious as he was reputed brave and generally too stout for his antagonist.

November 8.—Since penning the last, the grand jury have unanimously declared no bill; and here allow me to say, having accompanied Judge Babcock to four of the courts embraced in the circuit of five counties, I have not seen in any country such uniform decorum and quietness as has prevailed throughout at these courts. Much of this mildness, sobriety, and good order, is doubtless attributable to the absence of all intoxicating drinks.

The laws of this country, framed to meet present circumstances, are taking deeper and stronger root continually. And some are already suggesting, "notwithstanding our infancy," whether, if longer left without a mother's protection, it will not be well to undertake to run alone.

The resources of the country are rapidly developing, and the expectations of the people are generally high; the mildness of the climate and the strength of the soil greatly encourage the large immigration of last year. For the last twelve months, mercury has ranged from 96 to 30; four-fifths of the time from 80 to 55; making an agreeable summer and mild winter, grazing being good throughout; so much so that the jaded and worn-down animals of the poor immigrants fatted up greatly to their surprise, before spring, without feeding or the least attention.

Crops of all kinds usually good, even to Indian corn, and cheerfulness prevails throughout since harvesting. As statements have been made in the States derogatory to our soil, allow me to say, it is believed, with the same cultivation, no country produces better wheat, oats, peas, barley, potatoes, or any crop save Indian corn, for which the nights are generally too cool for a heavy growth. The wheat crops, being never injured by the frosts of winter or the rains of summer, as in the States, are remarkably sure; nor as yet have our crops been disturbed by flies or insects.

Wheat crops are heavy, as you will judge when I assure you, from simply turning over the prairie in June, scattering the seed in October, and then with no further trouble than passing the harrow over it, ten acres upon my plantation grew five hundred and forty-one bushels and a half. The river flats, containing much alluvial deposit, are very rich; the plains beautiful and verdant, being admirably watered, but generally sparsely timbered; the high lands well timbered and watered in many parts, the soil tolerable, producing herbage for an abundance of deer, elk, mountain sheep, etc. The entire Wallamet and Umpqua valleys, capable of sustaining a population of several millions, it is generally believed can not be excelled, as a whole, for richness of soil, variety, grandeur, or beauty of scenery; nor, considering the latitude, can be equaled in mildness, equability, and agreeableness of climate.

Since last writing, abundance of limestone has been found at the mouth of the Columbia, and likewise in this valley, conveniently obtained, and proves of an excellent quality. The Rev. Mr. De Smet arrived here in August last, bringing, as a part of his cargo, six priests and as many nuns, fine, hale-looking girls, very acceptable just now, particularly as the Methodist Mission is breaking up, and the half-breed Canadian daughters are rapidly multiplying.

Having no pilot or chart to depend upon, and his commander a stranger, he sailed in through the south channel, greatly to the surprise and alarm of all on shore, but without injury or difficulty, not once touching, and reporting abundance of water for the heaviest burden ships.

The sands are supposed to have changed and improved the channel; but of this I know nothing, and am not a little skeptical. I am induced to attribute their success more to the fine day and small vessel than change of the sands in their favor since Captain Wilkes left. Captain Couch, however, who has now been passing in and out here for the last five years in the service of Mr. Cushing, of Newburyport, pronounces it a better port to enter than theirs, and says, with pilots, there will be little difficulty or danger.

Our exports are wheat, beaver, salmon, and lumber, for which, in return, we obtain from the Sandwich Islands, sugar, molasses, tea, coffee, and other commodities brought there from China, England, and America.

We are much in want of a currency and market, American merchants being as yet a slender reliance; and in view of the large immigrating parties of each year, we should be greatly distressed for necessary articles of wearing apparel, but for the most commendable spirit of accommodation on the part of the Hudson's Bay Company.

Could some arrangement be entered into for us to supply the navy of the Pacific with bread, beef, pork, fish, etc., we would thereby be much improved in our condition. This might, and perhaps ought to be done, in view of the encouragements held out for our people to emigrate to this country. Should it not be convenient for our ships of war to come to the Columbia for such supplies, they could be shipped to the Sandwich Islands, if required. But more of this another time.

Having just taken the tour of the colony for the purpose of attending the courts and visiting the schools, it affords me pleasure to say I felt amply rewarded. I found throughout health, cheerfulness, and prosperity, and, certainly, most surprising improvements for the short time since the settlers commenced. The decorum of the courts I have spoken of, and now have only to speak of the schools and Indians, and I am done, fearing I have already wearied your patience. For the want of means, the Methodist manual labor Indian school has lately been broken up, and this is now occupied as a boarding-school for white children of both sexes. The school is yet small, but well conducted, and promises usefulness to the colony. The school at the falls of the Wallamet and Tualatin Plains, and likewise the one under the direction of Rev. Mr. Blanchet, Catholic clergyman, are all small,—numbering from fifteen to thirty only,—but are all well kept and doing good. I feel solicitous on this subject, and am saying and doing what I can to encourage education, but, like all other new countries, the people need and require their children much at home.

Since the unhappy affair last spring, the Indians have been unusually quiet, and the summer has been spent without alarm. I sent my interpreter, Mr. Lee, to the Wallawallas six weeks since, to make some presents to the chiefs, as a safe conduct to the immigrants down to this place, but having, as yet, nothing from him of interest, I addressed a line to Mr. J. B. Littlejohn, who is just down from there, and received the annexed reply; all other statements are corroborative:—

"WALLAMET, November 1, 1844.

"DEAR SIR,—It is with the utmost pleasure I undertake to give you what information I am able to do. I have resided with the missionaries of the American Board for two years past; I have known their hearts, and am well acquainted with all they have done. Their influence among the Indians is by no means small, or their efforts vain, as their condition is very much improved, both in a spiritual and temporal point of view. And, dear sir, your efforts among and for them have been much to their advantage, and at the same time not to the disadvantage of the missionaries, but greatly to increase their usefulness among them. I have no doubt you have labored with this motive in view. The Indians are becoming civilized as fast or faster than any tribes concerning whom I am informed. Their anxiety for cattle, hogs, and sheep is very great; leading them to make most commendable efforts to obtain them, and their efforts are by no means vain. They have purchased a good number from those who are emigrating to this country, by exchanging their horses for cattle. Thus, while their horses have been very useful to the immigrants, they have greatly benefited themselves. They are enlarging their farms yearly,—improving much in fencing, etc. Quite a number of families are enabled to live from what they raise on their farms, the milk of their cows, and their beef. There is perfect quietness existing between them, and I have no doubt this state of things will continue to exist. Many things that are interesting might be written, but time does not allow me to say more at present.

"I am, dear sir, yours with the greatest respect,

"J. B. LITTLEJOHN."

Thus far the Indians have kept their treaties of amity with me astonishingly well, and it is thought we have now as much to hope as fear from them, if we succeed in keeping out liquor, which, by the grace of God, not a few of us are resolved to do, though we do not pass unopposed, nor slightly opposed; and had it not been for that most salutary liquor law, and the hearty co-operation of some of the friends of temperance with your agent, liquor would have already made ruinous havoc among us.

The Methodist Mission, though we have not agreed on all subjects, has behaved very properly on this. And to it, in connection with the Honorable Hudson's Bay Company, will the colony be lastingly indebted for its commendable efforts.

Since my first arrival, I have not received a line from the department save my last year's report. As my condition is peculiar, and not a little embarrassing, I should feel greatly obliged for an expression and further instruction from the department. I have had, as may well be judged, much to contend with, in the midst of lawless Indians of so many different tribes, and lawless whites of so many nations,—some bred upon old whale-ships, others in the Rocky Mountains, and hundreds on the frontiers of Missouri. I have at times waded in deep perplexing difficulties, but am now greatly relieved by the colonial government, which as yet is well administered. By reason of this I now have less to do, and sail in smoother seas, meeting with less opposition than heretofore, my proper official relations toward the whites and Indians being better understood.

I have the honor to be, etc.,

E. WHITE,

Sub-Agent Indian Affairs, W. R. M.

Hon. J. M. PORTER,

Secretary of War, Washington

An Act to prohibit the Manufacture and Sale of Ardent Spirits.

Whereas the people of Oregon, now occupying one of the most beautiful and interesting portions of the globe, are placed in the most critical and responsible position ever filled by men, owing, as they do, important duties to themselves, to their country, to posterity, and to mankind, as the founders of a new government and a young nation; and whereas the introduction, distillation, or sale of ardent spirits, under the circumstances in which we are placed, would bring withering ruin upon the prosperity and prospects of this interesting and rising community, by involving us in idle and dissolute habits, inviting hither swarms of the dissipated inhabitants of other countries, checking immigration, destroying the industry of the country, bringing upon us the swarms of savages now in our midst, interrupting the orderly and peaceable administration of justice, and, in a word, producing and perpetuating increasing and untold miseries that no mind can rightly estimate; therefore,

Be it enacted by the Legislative Committee of Oregon as follows:—

SECTION 1. That if any person shall hereafter import or introduce any ardent spirits into Oregon, with intent to sell, barter, or trade the same, and shall offer the same for sale, barter, or trade, he shall be fined the sum of fifty dollars for each and every such offense, which may be recovered by indictment or by trial before a justice of the peace, without the form of pleading.

SEC. 2. That if any person shall hereafter sell, barter, or trade any ardent spirits of any kind whatever, directly or indirectly, to any person within Oregon, he shall forfeit and pay the sum of twenty dollars for each and every such sale, barter, or trade, to be recovered by indictment in the Circuit Court, or before a justice of the peace, without the form of pleading.

SEC. 3. That if any person shall hereafter establish or carry on any manufactory or distillery of ardent spirits in Oregon, he shall be subject to be indicted before the Circuit Court as for a nuisance; and if convicted, he shall be fined the sum of one hundred dollars, and the court shall issue an order to the sheriff, directing him to seize and destroy the distilling apparatus, which order the sheriff shall execute.

SEC. 4. That it shall be the duty of all sheriffs, judges, justices, constables, and other officers, when they have reason to believe that this act has been violated, to give notice thereof to some justice of the peace or judge of a court, who shall immediately issue his warrant and cause the offending party to be arrested, and, if such officer has jurisdiction to try such case, shall proceed to try such offender without delay, and give judgment accordingly; but, if such officer shall not have jurisdiction to try the case, he shall, if the party be guilty, bind him over to appear before the next Circuit Court of the proper county.

SEC. 5. That all sales, barters, or trades, made under color of gifts or otherwise, with intent to evade this act, shall be deemed a violation of the same, and all fines and penalties recovered under this act shall go into the general treasury, and all officers receiving the same shall pay over to the sheriff, whose duty it shall be to pay the same into the treasury.

SEC. 6. That this act shall not be so construed as to prevent any practicing physician from selling such liquors for medicine, not to exceed one gallon at one time.

SEC. 7. That the clerk shall make out a copy of this act and put the same up in Oregon City as early as practicable.

SEC. 8. That this act shall take effect within sixty days from and after its passage.

Passed 24th June, 1844. M. M. MCCARVER, Speaker.

Attest: J. E. LONG, Clerk.

An Act to provide for Ways and Means.

Be it enacted by the Legislative Committee of Oregon as follows:—

SECTION 1. That in order to raise a revenue for the purpose of defraying the expenses of the government, there shall be levied and collected a tax of one-eighth of one per cent. upon the following property, at a fair valuation, to wit: All merchandise brought into this country for sale; improvements in town lots; mills; pleasure-carriages; clocks; watches; horses; mules; cattle and hogs.

SEC. 2. Every male citizen over the age of twenty-one years, being a descendant of a white man, shall be subject to pay a poll-tax of fifty cents.

SEC. 3. That it shall be the duty of the collector of revenue to require of each and every merchant of Oregon to give him a statement of the amount of all merchandise on hand, in writing, to be stated upon oath or affirmation, which oath or affirmation the collector shall administer;

and said collector shall collect and receipt for the tax upon such merchandise, which receipt shall serve said merchant for a license for the next year, commencing from the time given; and that, when a merchant shall wish to renew his license, he shall give a similar statement of all merchandise received by him for sale in the preceding twelve months, and the collector shall only require him to pay tax upon the amount of said imports.

SEC. 4. That any person refusing to pay tax, as in this act required, shall have no benefit of the laws of Oregon, and shall be disqualified from voting at any election in this country.

SEC. 5. That the sheriff shall serve as *ex officio* collector of the revenue, for which he shall receive, as a compensation for his services, ten per cent. upon all moneys collected as revenue.

SEC. 6. That the sheriff, before entering upon the duties of his office as collector of the revenue, shall enter into bond, with two or more good and sufficient securities, in a sum not less than five nor more than ten thousand dollars, to be approved by the executive, which approval shall be written upon the back of said bond, and the said collector's bond shall be filed in the office of the clerk of the court.

SEC. 7. That the collector shall pay over to the treasury, on the first Monday in each and every month in the year, all moneys that may be in his hands, and get the treasurer's receipt therefor.

SEC. 8. That it shall be the duty of the tribunal transacting county business to require the collector to settle with said court at each and every regular term of the court in Clackamas County.

SEC. 9. The collector of the revenue shall make full payment into the treasury on or before the first Monday in December in each year.

SEC. 10. The revenue of Oregon shall be collected in specie or available orders on solvent merchants in Oregon.

SEC. 11. That all acts and parts of acts contrary to this act be, and the same are hereby, repealed.

SEC. 12. This act to take effect from and after its passage.

M. M. McCARVER, Speaker.

Attest: J. E. LONG, Secretary.

Oregon Territory, *Tualatin District*, *United States of America*, *May* 1, 1844.

Charles E. Pickett, plaintiff, in the name of Oregon Territory, threatening to incense the Indians, *against* Saul, a man of color.

Complainant's oath and warrant issued, directed to J. L. Meek, sheriff, and summons for three witnesses, viz.: James Conner, William Hill, and Mr. Bird.

May 3.—Sheriff made his return with defendant and witnesses, and jury of good and lawful men, viz., Philip Foster, W. C. Dement, J. W. Nesmith, John McCaddan, C. Spencer, and S. W. Moss, being duly sworn, returned a verdict of guilty of the charges alleged to him, and signed their names, viz.: Philip Foster, J. W. Nesmith, William C. Dement, John McCaddan, Chauncey Spencer, and S. W. Moss.

Two witnesses, viz., William Hill and Mr. Bird, of lawful age, being duly sworn, did depose and say: that the threats in the deposition of Charles E. Pickett were correct; and that the Indians had come in a menacing manner; and that Saul said he would stand for the Indians' rights; and that he (Saul) was armed and prepared to do so; and that the Indians would burn and destroy his house and property. The charges being of a higher character than the Oregon laws have cognizance of, judgment is, that the United States sub-Indian agent, Dr. Elijah White, is the proper officer to take cognizance of him; and he, Saul, a man of color, be forthwith delivered into said agent's hand; which was forthwith done.

ROBERT MOORE, Justice of the Peace.

The criminal was received and kept in custody for some weeks; but having no prison-house or jail to lodge him in, and the captain absolutely declining taking him on board his vessel, after the storm had blown over I suffered and encouraged him to leave this place, and stop with one of the mission families for the present, at the mouth of the Columbia.

Though unsuccessful in getting employment as I had hoped, he remains in that vicinity with his Indian wife and family, conducting, as yet, in a quiet manner, but doubtless ought to be transported, together with every other negro, being in our condition dangerous subjects.

Until we have some further means of protection, their immigration ought to be prohibited. Can this be done?

E. WHITE, Sub-Agent.

TERRITORY OF OREGON,
DISTRICT OF TUALATIN. } *ss.*

Charles E. Pickett, being duly sworn, says, that Saul (a man of color), of said Territory, has threatened to incense the Indians against his person and property, to destroy the same; and that he, the said Charles E. Pickett, verily believes that, unless measures are taken to prevent him, there are sufficient grounds to apprehend that he will carry those threats into execution.

Sworn to and subscribed this 1st day of May, 1844, before me,

ROBERT MOORE, J. P.

We, the jury, find the prisoner guilty of the charges alleged against him.

PHILIP FOSTER,
J. W. NESMITH,
WM. C. DEMENT,
JOHN MCCADDAN.
CHAUNCEY SPENCER.
S. W. MOSS.

OREGON, WALLAMET VALLEY,
April 4, 1845.

* * * Starting too late, and the winter rains setting in earlier than usual, subjected the immigrants to incredible suffering and hardships, especially from the Dalles of the Columbia down to the Wallamet Valley; but our early and delightful spring is exerting a cheering and most salutary influence upon their hitherto depressed spirits. They have, bee-like, been hived up in Oregon City during the winter, and are now swarming, to the entire satisfaction of the first occupants of the hive, it not being wide and large enough for such an unexpected increase. The last immigration, numbering about a thousand, are generally pleased with the country, and are setting about their spring work with becoming spirit and fortitude.

The Indians of this lower country, whose national honor and dignity are laid in the dust, are looking upon the rapid growth and increased strength of the whites with sorrowful countenances and sad hearts. The present state of things between us and them is peculiar, critical, unenviable, and dangerous, at least, so far as peace and property are concerned.

For instance, in proof: Soon after I sent my last dispatches, the chief of the Tualatin Plains, whose orderly conduct and that of his clan did honor to the Nez Percé laws, and the engagement we had mutually entered into, called on me, desiring my offices in procuring the mending of his gun. This being done, he invited me to come and see him and his people; said all was not right at his lodge; his tribe was divided, and all was not right; his influence was waning, and some of his people were becoming very bitter toward the Americans. Observing anxiety and mental reservation, I endeavored to draw out the secret, reminding him of the frequent communications he had brought me from the Rev. Messrs. Clark and Griffin, bearing such satisfactory testimony to their previous quiet, orderly, and proper conduct, etc.; but all I could learn was, "Things are not right with us, and we are miserable."

The *camass*, their principal dependence for food, was cut off last season by reason of drought; and the deer are hunted so much by the late hungry western immigrant riflemen, that they have become wild, poor, and few in number. The chief left.

A few days after, I learned they had killed an ox and ate it, belonging to a neighboring white man. The owner was excited, and applied to one of the executive; a proclamation was issued, the military was called out (if it be lawful to call it such), and ample preparations made to avenge this national insult, and seek redress for this astounding loss. The army collected upon the opposite bank of the river, about six miles from the position occupied by the enemy, talked bravely, long, and loud, but the river was a little too high to cross that day; appointed another, the river being lower; none of the warriors appeared; nor could the executive, or owner, simply for the want of a few gallons of alcohol, obtain the necessary assistance to avenge the horrid wrong, and perform a brilliant military exploit. The chief, in his embarrassment and distress, came to me as usual for sympathy and succor. My coldness and look of severity (for which Heaven forgive me!) keenly afflicted him. After a deep sigh and painful pause, peculiar to a wounded or injured Indian, he slowly rose, gently smiting his breast, and said, "Dr. White, I am a true man, and carry an honest heart. Do you remember my coming to get my gun mended last fall? Do you remember my words, that all was not right with our people, and my inviting you to come and see us? We had just before killed that old ox, and were then eating it." I inquired, "Had you any thing to do with it personally?" "Yes, I helped to kill it, and, with my family, took and ate one-half of the animal. You saw the condition of my gun;—our provisions were out; I and others had hunted for two days,—our hunger was great. We held a council; and, hoping for success, I promised, on condition nothing was caught till the setting of another sun, we would kill the first animal we met. I traveled far, and wearied myself till evening; shot often but killed nothing;—we met this poor old ox, which our people would scorn to kill or eat but in case of extreme hunger;—my word was passed to my people; I could not go back from my word; I helped to kill and butcher the ox, and joined in eating him; and now my peace is gone. I am ashamed to see a white man's face; they look cold on me and shake the head;—I can not bear it—I can not live so; I come to you to help me, for I am told they want to kill me. I do not want such feelings to exist; nor do I want to be hunted as a bear or wild beast, for slaughter. I stand here a wisher of peace, willing to have you dictate the terms; but wish to have it remembered that we were distressed with hunger." "Suppose," said I, "the owner should require your rifle and four horses?" "You stand to judge between us, and I shall abide your decision." "But you have broken your engagement and forfeited confidence, and I fear it can not be settled, and some think you have killed before." "Dr. White, I am a true man, and lie not. I, nor my people, can not be so accused justly; this is injurious; none can meet my face and say it." I wrote, through him, to the owner, praying, as it was the first offense so far as we had the least evidence, and especially in view of our critical situation and his general good behavior, that he would fully indemnify himself; and then, in view of what I knew of the condition of his gun, and the probability that it was induced by hunger, to settle it; and requested him to assure the chief that he was convinced from my letter and all the circumstances, in connection with his past good conduct, that it must have been brought about by hunger.

The advice was rejected, as the laws of the organization now had cognizance of the offense, and he wished to see them faithfully enforced. Public opinion became divided, and no judicial expression being made, and the poor chief becoming excessively tired of being held by public opinion in durance vile, came to see me a second time. I wrote again, and learned it was settled by the chief and his people paying his rifle and eight horses. If this be correct (as I fear it is), I abominate the act and dread its prejudicial influence.

Week before last a hungry and mischievous lodge killed a cow. They were pursued by a party of whites, overtaken, and, in attempting to take them, the Indians fired upon the whites, killing one horse, and wounded another. The fire was returned; one Indian killed, and a second wounded. Thus ended this affair, which creates very little excitement among whites or Indians.

The most painful circumstance that has occurred lately, transpired last fall at California. The Cayuses, Wallawallas, and some of the chiefs of the Spokans, entered upon the hazardous but grand and important enterprise of going directly through the Indian country to California, with a view of exchanging their beaver, deer, and elk skins, together with their surplus horses, for neat stock. As they had to travel through an extensive country inhabited by the savage and warlike Klamaths and Shastas, where Smith, Turner, and so many other white parties had been defeated, we are at a loss to conclude whether their valor is more to be commended than the rashness of their stupendous enterprise to be censured. They were well mounted and equipped; the chiefs clad in English costume, and the residue attired in dressed skins, molded according to their several tastes. The journey of seven or eight hundred miles, after some fighting, watching, and much fatigue, was accomplished, and their numbers not lessened.

Taking their own statement, their reception was cordial, and the impression made upon the whites by these distant and half-civilized people, upon an errand so commendable, was most favorable. The treating and salutations being over, the trade commenced in good faith, and to mutual satisfaction. All moved on well, till, on an excursion to procure elk and deer skins, they met a marauding band of mountain freebooters; fought them, and, being victorious, took a prize of twenty-two horses, all previously stolen from the whites.

On returning to the settlements, the Spaniards laid claim to the animals. The chiefs remonstrated, and said, agreeably to their customs, the horses were theirs. The Spaniards explained their laws, and showed the animals not to be vented, *i. e.*, bearing a transfer mark, and told the Indians they must give them to the rightful owners, as all Americans and others did. The Indians seemed grieved and rather incensed; said in their country six nations of people were on terms of amity, and that in case any one of these six nations stole a horse, the tribe was responsible for the safe delivery of that animal to the rightful owner; but in case the Blackfeet or other formidable enemy steal or capture, the property is supposed lost, without redemption; and as we have captured these horses at the hazard of our lives, from your long openly declared enemies, we think they ought in justice to be ours. The Spaniards condescended to offer ten cows for the redemption of the horses; the chief not replying, five more were added; he still remaining moody and without replying, the negotiation unhappily broke off. A day or two after, an American, seeing his mule among the number captured, told the Indians it was his mule, and have it he would. "Will you?" said a young chief by the name of Elijah Heading; and stepping into the lodge, he immediately loaded his rifle, came out and observed significantly, "Go now and take your mule." The American, much alarmed, remarked, "I hope you are not going to kill me." "No! I am going to shoot yonder eagle" (perched upon a neighboring oak). Not liking the appearances, the man left without attempting to obtain his mule. A day or two after, the Indians left their encampment and walked down to the fort of Captain Sutter to church; and from the best information we have obtained (all being *ex parte*), the following appears to be near the truth: After service Elijah was invited into another apartment, taking with him his uncle, a brave and sensible chief of the age of five and forty; while there, in an unarmed and defenseless condition, they commenced menacing him for things alleged against the river Indians of this upper country, in which none of them had any participation; called them indiscriminately dogs, thieves, etc. This American then observed: "Yesterday you were going to kill me;

now you must die"—drawing a pistol. Elijah, who had been five or six years at the Methodist Mission, and had learned to read, write, and speak English respectably, said, deliberately: "Let me pray a little, first;" and kneeling down, at once commenced; and while invoking the Divine mercy, was shot through the heart or vitals dead upon the spot. Every measure, as the Indians say, was taken to cut them all off by the Spaniards, who brought out the cannon, with other fire-arms, and hotly pursued them, and tried to prevent their escape by checking and interrupting their passage across the ferries, etc. But at length they all arrived safely, after manifest suffering, leaving the herds they had paid for in California.

They met three Americans on the way as they left the California settlements and had them in their power, but instead of revenging the death of Elijah, they mounted each on a horse of their own, and sent them on, telling them to go to the fort and acquaint the people that they could not kill innocent white people in their power and lodge.

Taking for truth an Indian report, this horrible affair creates considerable excitement, and there is some danger of its disturbing the friendly relation that has hitherto existed between us here, and all those formidable tribes in the region of Wallawalla and Snake River. They had no sooner arrived, than Ellis, my interpreter, the high chief of the Nez Percés, was deputed to come down and learn our opinions regarding the affair. They could not have sent a better agent, the whites all giving him a handsome and cordial reception. From Wallawalla, he accompanied Mr. Grant, the chief trader at Fort Hall, down to Vancouver. He called on Dr. McLaughlin, whose great experience and address were serviceable. He spoke touchingly of the violent death of his own son upon the northwest coast, and left the impression that he could not avoid sympathizing with the father and friends of the deceased young chief. Mr. Douglas, too, an early friend, patron, and favorite of Ellis, aided much in convincing him that all the good and virtuous could not avoid the most painful regrets at so melancholy a circumstance, which must have occurred by reason of the difference in their customs or laws, imperfectly understanding each other, or from some, as he would charitably hope, excusable circumstance.

Under the influence of this salutary language and interview, Ellis arrived at my residence, in Wallamet, about the 1st instant, having, a short time before, got a hasty communication, written in excitement, from Dr. Whitman, who was under serious apprehensions that it might be avenged upon some of the whites of the upper country. Be assured I was happy to see this my most faithful friend and interpreter. Sir, pardon me for saying—isolated as we are here, agitated as we have a thousand times been by faithless savages and still more faithless whites, responsible, yet powerless and defenseless, in our unsettled state of things—to meet with this honest man, this *real* friend, though an Indian, gave me hearty pleasure.

His thorough education at Red River molded him into more of the white man than Indian. His prudence and good management with his tribe sanctioned the choice that had been made, and all the whites spoke handsomely of his kind offices and obliging deportment, while immigrating through his country. Being satisfied of the safety and policy, I feasted him, and took at once unobserved measures to have him invited to every respectable place abroad, where the ladies and gentlemen received him so cordially, and feasted him so richly and delicately, that he almost forgot the object of his embassy, and, I verily believe, thought extremely highly of the whites of Wallamet, however ill he might have thought of the conduct of the Californians.

Being anxious to make this visit useful to him and his people, as well as pleasant, after spending a few days in visiting the schools, as well as the principal inhabitants and places of interest, I showed him my little library; told him to make himself at home; put on my farmer's garb and commenced working upon my plantation. He soon came out, accompanied by a wealthy cousin, and begged for tools to assist me. I loaned them, and found he was much at home in their use. He spent with me a sufficient length of time to convince me of the truth reported concerning his cheerfulness in labor, as well as his knowledge, application, and assiduity in business. He spoke sensibly of the advantages of industry, and the astonishing change that had been effected among his people by the cultivation of the soil; assured me that every family or lodge now raised an abundance for home consumption, besides having considerable quantities to barter with the whites. He says he raised, himself, the past season, six hundred bushels of peas, with a fine crop of wheat, potatoes, beans, etc.; spoke properly of its moral and social effects. Wars were no longer talked of, and the chase was nearly abandoned; the book and the Bible consumed their leisure moments. Polygamy, once so common, was now done away with, except in two solitary cases, and not a lodge of his people but observed the Sabbath, and regularly attended morning and evening devotion. This was only corroborative of what I had previously heard from other sources. He spent ten days with me in the most cheerful, agreeable, and profitable manner, and at the close I felt myself the happier and better for the visit; nor did I marvel that his influence was increasing and the prospects of his people brightening.

Pardon me, for, in thinking of his visit and dwelling upon his excellences, I had like to have forgotten his agency. Learning from Dr.

Whitman, who resides in their midst, how much they were all excited by reason of the treacherous and violent death of this educated and accomplished young chief, and perhaps more especially by the loss they had sustained; and then, after suffering so many hardships and encountering so many dangers, losing the whole,—I apprehended there might be much difficulty in adjusting it, particularly as they lay much stress upon the restless disaffected scamps late from Wallamet to California, loading them with the vile epithets of "dogs," "thieves," etc., from which they believed, or affected to, that the slanderous reports of our citizens caused all their loss and disasters, and therefore held us responsible. He assured me that the Cayuses, Wallawallas, Nez Percés, Spokans, Ponderays, and Snakes were all on terms of amity, and that a portion of the aggrieved party were for raising about two thousand warriors of these formidable tribes and marching to California at once, and, nobly revenging themselves on the inhabitants by capture and plunder, enrich themselves upon the spoils; others, not indisposed to the enterprise, wished first to learn how it would be regarded here, and whether we would remain neutral in the affair. A third party were for holding us responsible, as Elijah was killed by an American, and the Americans incensed the Spaniards. Ellis reminded me at the same time of the ill-success the chiefs met with in trading off their ten-dollar drafts for herds with the immigrants; which drafts I had sent up by Mr. Lee, my interpreter, to secure peace and safety while the immigrants were passing through their country, the year before so many having been pillaged and robbed of their effects, through the inattention of the chiefs.

Sir, how this affair will end is difficult to conjecture; the general impression is, that it will lead to the most disastrous consequences to the Californians themselves, or to the colony of the Wallamet Valley. My principal fear is, that it will result in so much jealousy, prejudice, and disaffection, as to divert their minds from the pursuit of knowledge, agriculture, and the means of civilization, which they have been for such a length of time so laudably engaged in obtaining.

Should this be the case with these numerous, brave, and formidable tribes, the results to them, and to us, would be indeed most calamitous. To prevent such a result, I wrote, through Ellis, a long, cordial, and rather sympathizing letter to the chiefs of these tribes, assuring them that I should at once write to the governor of California, to Captain Sutter, and to our great chiefs respecting this matter. With a view to divert attention, and promote good feeling, I invited all the chiefs to come down in the fall, before the arrival of the immigrants, in company with Dr. Whitman and Mr. Spalding, and confer with me upon this subject; at the same time, as they had been so unfortunate, to bring along their ten-dollar drafts, and exchange them with me for a cow and calf each, out of my own herds. I likewise wrote them, that on condition they would defer going to California till the spring of 1847, and each chief assist me to the amount of two beaver skins, to get a good manual labor literary institution established for the English education of their sons and daughters (a subject they feel the deepest interest in), I would use every measure to get the unhappy affair adjusted; and, as a token of my regard for them, would, from my private funds, give the chiefs five hundred dollars, to assist them in purchasing young cows in California. I likewise proffered, as they are so eager for it, to start the English school next fall, by giving them the services of Mr. Lee, my interpreter, for four months, commencing in November next.

Ellis more than properly appreciated my motives and proffers, and said he was of the full belief the chiefs would accede to my proposition; spoke of the importance of the English school, and of the strong and general desire to obtain it. He left in high hopes of a continuance of peace and onward prosperity to his people.

A few days later brought me into another excitement and difficulty at Vancouver. Two young men, named in McLaughlin's communication to this government (a copy of which, marked A, together with a reply, accompanies these dispatches), crossed the Columbia River, and, unobserved, in the midst of a little thicket something over half a mile from Fort Vancouver, felled some timber, threw up a few logs in the shape of a hut, intending soon to finish it, put up a paper upon a contiguous tree, stating that they had commenced and intended to establish a claim agreeably with ——; here the note ended. Some one about the establishment, observing the paper and commencement of the hut, reported it to the governor, who sent down at once and had all the timber removed from the vicinity, the tree felled, and that, with the paper likewise, removed. They had hardly cleared the ground when the claimants arrived with a surveyor, and commenced surveying off a section of land, embracing the post first commenced upon. They were inquired of, at the instance of Governor McLaughlin, as to their object and intentions. They at once laid down the chain, dropped all business, and walked up to the fort. Several respectable and influential American citizens happened to be present on business, who, with myself, were respectfully invited to hear the discussion.

Williamson, a modest and respectable young man, demeaned himself with propriety; but Alderman, his associate, a boisterous, hare-brained young fellow, caused me (as occasionally others do) to blush for American honor. His language was most severe, and, but for the sake of the country's quiet, could not have been endured; the governor and Mr. Douglas displaying their usual calmness and forbearance. I heard the discussion for two hours; and, becoming satisfied that no possible good could grow out of it, remarked that with the cheerful consent of both parties I would give my sense of the matter.

Each readily consenting, I thought best to come up on the blind side of Alderman; treated his measures with less severity, and himself with more consideration and respect, than he anticipated; then spoke of Greenough's construction of the treaty between the two governments (which I happened to have with me); of the immense district of country dependent upon this establishment for supplies in beef, pork, etc., and as evidence that they had no more land contiguous than was necessary for their purposes, spoke of the number of cattle and other stock that had died of starvation during the last winter; dwelt upon the importance of union and good feeling among all the whites, surrounded as we were by savages, in our weak and defenseless condition, and especially of the propriety of establishing correct precedents in our unsettled state, regarding land claims; and, without advising particularly either party, took my seat.

Williamson and Alderman soon manifested a desire for a private interview, which resulted in a suspension of hostilities for the present, and probably an abandonment of the claim.

Now, my dear sir, suffer me to write a few things concerning this country, which seemed to me strongly to demand the speedy attention of the members of our government. Take fifty men from the colony, of the most intelligence, firmness, and prudence, and anarchy and confusion follow. Suffer a free introduction of ardent spirits, and desolation, horror, dismay, and bloodshed ensue. Never were a people more illy prepared for self-government, nor more unfavorably circumstanced to succeed,—aside from the single fact of the absence of all intoxicating drinks.

Sir, too great a portion of our population comes from the western suburbs of civilization, for one moment's safety to us in our present condition. I know not but I have as much patience as most men, but am heartily tired of this state of things. Nor would I run the risk again, by land and water, from whites and savages, for the safety and quietness of the colony and country, for all the wealth of earth. I have not shrunk from toil, danger, nor hardships, and though alone-handed and unsustained, black-balled and traduced, astonishing to say, my measures have yet succeeded. I think of the past with a clear conscience, yet at present, at peace as we are, I look upon our critical condition with an anxious, aching heart, feeling that the members of our government err exceedingly toward their citizens in Oregon.

As I have so often said of this lower country, with its beauty, excellence of soil, and mildness of climate, it might be rendered the paradise of earth; but, sir, every thing is jeoparded by the tardiness of our government measures; not only the poor, injured natives, but the whites generally, have become wearied to impatience in waiting for an expression from our government, and disaffection, with a want of confidence, is taking the place of previous warm feeling and strong attachment.

I regret this exceedingly, but feel it my duty to speak out in truth and distinctness upon this important point. I have said and done what I could to keep up confidence and hope; but already demagogues are haranguing in favor of independence, and using the most disparaging language regarding the measures of our government as a reason for action. These are but the beginnings, and, though I am glad to say such sentiments do not generally obtain, yet they are more favorably listened to this year than last; their natural results and practical tendency you will readily perceive.

Your annual report of 1843 reached me only a few days since, having been broken open on the way, then put into the hands of Indians, and forwarded to me through that channel. And while I have to regret never having received any thing from your pen, be assured I am not insensible to the honor done me, in speaking as you did of my report, through yours of 1843 to the Secretary of War. I feel any kind expression from home the more sensibly, from the torrent of opposition I have been forced to meet and contend with here; but am happy to observe that my influence is increasing, and my measures are being better understood and appreciated.

Influence here is most important; I felt this strikingly a few weeks since. Three among the most correct and sensible men of the colony formed a co-partnership to enter largely upon the brewery business. They had already taken some steps; and as the business promised to be lucrative, the probabilities were against me in attempting to dissuade them from their purpose. I visited them, labored calmly, honestly, and faithfully, and felt the difference dealing or talking with men of sense and principle, over many with whom I have to do in Oregon.

The interview broke up most agreeably, not an unpleasant sentence having passed; the gentlemen engaging to give me their decision very soon. This was communicated to me two days after, in a delicate and handsome manner, which was entirely to my wishes, the business being altogether abandoned. This was most gratifying to me, as from such a quarter should beer be introduced, it would be impossible for us to prevent the introduction of stronger drink into the colony and country, which, of all others, is most illy prepared to receive it.

The colony, now numbering about four thousand, is in a most flourishing state, and I am doubtful if any like number are more pleased or better contented in our wide domain. The schools of the country during the last winter have been well sustained; I have contributed to each, as was necessary, from ten to fifteen dollars, to pay rents, etc., and to encourage them forward in their laudable struggle to educate their rising families.

I attended the examination of the Methodist Institute school a few weeks since, and was most agreeably impressed regarding the institution.

The pleasant deportment and improved manners of the young ladies and gentlemen of the school, saying nothing of their astonishing advancement in the different departments of literature, was a cause of the highest gratification. I have nowhere attended an examination, taking all things into the account, more creditable to the principal or institution. I have called for a report, but am sorry it has not yet come to hand.

The branches taught are rhetoric, grammar, geography, arithmetic, reading, writing, and spelling. The most enlightened and best disposed are using their influence to strengthen the organization, and perfect the laws of the colony. Many are favorable to the adoption of a constitution, by calling a convention for that purpose the present season. This being the most enlightened sense, and meeting with little opposition, I am of the opinion it will prevail. Should this be effected, the constitution, accompanied with a petition, will probably be forwarded by a delegate from this country to Washington City the coming winter. As the friends of the constitution generally wish best to the country, and desire to have every thing so conducted as not to embarrass, but to meet with acceptance at home, I am solicited to be said delegate, and represent the wants of Oregon. A circulating medium is greatly needed; however, the enterprise and onward march of this people can not easily be repressed. Through the auspices of the Hudson's Bay Company almost every man, requesting and needing it, is helped to sufficient means to commence upon his section of land; and, certainly, by far the greater number give evidence of well-placed confidence. The prairies are dotted over with houses, and the fruitful fields are spreading out widely all around us. Moral and religious influence, I regret to say, is waning; yet it is gratifying to observe an increasing interest upon the subject of schools and education; and I am happy to say we have now eleven schools this side the mountains, most of them small, to be sure, but they are exerting a salutary and beneficial influence.

Pardon the length and want of interest of my report. Did not duty hold me here, or had I funds appropriated to travel abroad to explore this delightful region of surrounding country, from what I learn of vague reports I have little doubt but much interesting, curious, and important information might be collected. But here I am, doomed to sit, watch, and sometimes almost *fight* for peace between whites and Indians—the question of right and wrong becoming more and more complicated continually; while here, allow me to say, the settling these difficulties necessarily costs me not a little. I believe most fully, in making a settlement with an Indian or tribe, to have it a happy, earnest, and hearty one; and, in order to effect this, they require a present as a seal. And, sir, this is my principal means of usefulness or influence over these poor, and, in many instances, injured natives. Their seeming confidence and regard makes one the more patient and cheerful in doing for them; nor can I complain, as so many east of the mountains have been obliged to, of violated faith on the part of the Indians. From all I can learn, on much of which little reliance is to be placed, there appear to be about forty-two thousand Indians in the Territory, allowing it to extend to 54° 40′ north latitude.

Mr. Lee's (my interpreter) report accompanying this you will observe. I would have accompanied him but for the season of the year, and the prevalence of the dysentery, which is sweeping off the poor natives of this lower country. This gave rise to Dr. Long's bill, which, I hope, will be honored, as it was a work of humanity as well as policy. I directed it, as I could not possibly attend to those and these at the same time, there being forty miles between us.

I hope, Providence permitting, to have the pleasure of seeing you and the other gentlemen of the departments, at Washington, in a few weeks, or months at longest, after this reaches, and of explaining my accounts and reasons for expenditures.

I had not expected to draft on the department this spring; but there were no other means of settling with Governor McLaughlin, for the want of a circulating medium through which to operate.

Inclosed is a letter from Peter H. Burnett, Esq., which I proposed forwarding in my last dispatches, but received too late for transmission.

With great respect, I am, dear sir, your most humble and obedient servant,

ELIJAH WHITE,
Sub-Agent Indian Affairs, W. R. M.

To the Citizens of Oregon:

GENTLEMEN,—We take the liberty of informing you that a person named "Henry Williamson," some time about the 15th of February, this year, took the liberty of erecting on the premises of the Hudson's Bay Company a few logs, in the form of a hut, and wrote a notice upon an adjoining tree that he had taken a section of land there. This was done without our knowledge or consent, within a few hundred yards of a house occupied by one of the Hudson's Bay Company's servants, and within the limits of their improvements. As soon as we were informed of that proceeding, we had the tree cut down and the logs removed, in order to prevent any future difficulty with a person who had, in a manner so unjustifiable, intruded on the Hudson's Bay Company's premises.

The Hudson's Bay Company made their settlement at Fort Vancouver under the authority of a license from the British government, in conformity with the provisions of the treaty between Great Britain and the United States of America, which gives them the right of occupying as much land as they require for the operations of their business.

On the faith of that treaty, they have made a settlement on the north bank of the Columbia River; they have opened roads and made other improvements at a great outlay of capital; they have held unmolested possession of their improvements for many years, unquestioned by the public officers of either government, who have, since the existence of their settlements, repeatedly visited it; they have carried on business with manifest advantage to the country; they have given the protection of their influence over the native tribes to every person who required it, without distinction of nation or party; and they have afforded every assistance in their power toward developing the resources of the country and promoting the industry of its inhabitants.

The tract of land they occupy, on the north bank of the Columbia River, is indispensable to them as a range for their flocks and herds, but otherwise of little value, being in part inundated every summer by the waters of the Columbia, and in part unimprovable forest land.

Occupying the said tract of land by the authority of law, and under the protection of the British government, they can not submit to the infringement of rights so acquired; and we, as their representatives, are bound to use every means sanctioned by the law which governs us against all trespassers on their premises, until otherwise directed by orders emanating from the Hudson's Bay Company.

Permit us to assure you, gentlemen, that it is our earnest wish to maintain a good understanding, and to live on friendly terms with every person in the country. We entertain the highest respect for the provisional organization; and knowing the good it has effected, as well as the evil it has prevented, we wish it every success, and hope, as we desire, to continue to live in the exercise and interchange of good offices with the framers of that useful institution.

The advantages of peace and harmony, of the support and maintenance of established rights, must be as evident to every member of the community as the evils flowing from a state of lawless misrule.

With these considerations before us, we feel confident that every person who desires the well-being of the country, who wishes to see it prosperous and flourishing, will unite in putting down every course which may have a tendency to disturb the public peace, and in promoting, by every means in his power, the cause of justice, obedience to the laws, and mutual accommodation.

With a fervent prayer to the Divine bestower of all good for the happiness and prosperity of every individual in the country, we have the honor to be, gentlemen, your obedient servants,

JOHN McLAUGHLIN.
JAMES DOUGLAS.

VANCOUVER, March 18, 1845.

GENTLEMEN,—I am sorry to inform you that Mr. Williamson is surveying a piece of land occupied by the Hudson's Bay Company, alongside of this establishment, with a view of taking it as a claim; and as he is an American citizen, I feel bound, as a matter of courtesy, to make the same known to you, trusting that you will feel justified in taking measures to have him removed from the Hudson's Bay Company's premises, in order that the unanimity now happily subsisting between the American citizens and British subjects residing in this country may not be disturbed or interrupted. I beg to inclose you a copy of an address to the citizens of Oregon, which will explain to you our situation and the course we are bound to pursue in the event of your declining to interfere.

I am, gentlemen, your obedient humble servant,

J. McLAUGHLIN.

WILLIAM BAILEY,
OSBORNE RUSSELL,
P. G. STEWART,
Executive Committee of Oregon.

[The above documents must be considered a full declaration of war by the Hudson's Bay Company, as all future operations of theirs were merely preparatory to the final consummation and attack that was made through the Cayuses. The answer of our Executive Committee acknowledged treaty rights that did not exist, as neither the sovereignty of the soil, nor the boundary line, were settled, hence the joint occupancy of both as per treaty was good.]

OREGON CITY, March 21, 1845.

SIR,—We beg to acknowledge the receipt of your letters,—one dated 11th of March, and the other 12th of March,—accompanied with an address to the citizens of Oregon.

We regret to hear that unwarranted liberties have been taken by an American citizen upon the Hudson's Bay Company's premises, and it affords us great pleasure to learn that the offender, after due reflection, desisted from the insolent and rash measure.

As American citizens, we beg leave to offer you and your much esteemed colleague our most grateful thanks for the kind and candid manner in which you have treated this matter, as we are aware that an infringement on the rights of the Hudson's Bay Company in this country, by an American citizen, is a breach of the laws of the United States, by setting at naught her most solemn treaties with Great Britain.

As representatives of the citizens of Oregon, we beg your acceptance of our sincere acknowledgments of the obligations we are under to yourself and your honorable associate for the high regard you have manifested for the authorities of our provisional government, and the special anxiety you have ever shown for our peace and prosperity; and we assure you that we consider ourselves in duty bound to use every exertion in our power to put down every cause of disturbance, as well as to promote the amicable intercourse and kind feelings hitherto existing between ourselves and the gentlemen of the Hudson's Bay Company, until the United States shall extend its jurisdiction over us, and our authority ceases to exist.

We have the honor to be, sir, your most obedient servants,

OSBORNE RUSSELL.
P. G. STEWART.

JOHN McLAUGHLIN, Esq.

TUALATIN PLAINS, November 2, 1844.

DEAR SIR,—Your communication of the 20th October, 1844, was duly received, and a press of business has delayed my reply till now.

In relation to the subject of inquiry contained in your letter (being the natural resources of Oregon), I can truly say that I entertain a very high opinion of the great and decided advantages bestowed by nature upon this most interesting and beautiful portion of our globe.

Our facilities for commercial enterprise are most decided, as the rapidly increasing commerce of the great Pacific lies at our very door. The climate of this country is more *equable*, subject to fewer extremes than any, perhaps, in the world. I have been here about one year, and have found it most delightful, and I can truly say that it is the most healthy country I have ever lived in. During the present year, I have scarcely heard of a case of fever in the whole country. The timber of Oregon is indeed most superior, and constitutes a large portion of its wealth; and we have not only the tallest, finest timber in the world, but we have everywhere water power to any desirable extent, suitable for propelling all kinds of machinery.

The soil of this country is most excellent, and can be prepared and cultivated with less labor than that of any other country. Wheat is the great staple of the world, and as a wheat-growing country, this ranks in the very first class. The crop is not only of the *best quality, but is always large, and there is no such occurrence as a failure of the wheat crop.* For potatoes, melons, turnips, and garden vegetables generally, our soil is superior. Indian corn does not succeed well, and in fact we have no use for it, as our cattle live all the year upon the natural pastures of the country. Since I have been here, I have been myself engaged in farming occupations, and I have been astonished at the very small amount of labor required to cultivate a farm. Potatoes are planted, and nothing more is done to them until they are ready for digging, when they are not dug, but generally turned up with the plow. Peas are sown broadcast, like wheat, and are neither staked nor cultivated, and produce in great abundance. Plowing is done here from the month of September until July, and wheat is sown from October to May, and potatoes are planted in March, April, and May. A team of two horses, with a very light, easy plow, can break prairie land, but a team of two yoke of oxen is most generally used. I am informed that timothy, clover, and blue grass all grow well in the soil of Oregon. For pasturage this country is pre-eminent. Horses, cattle, and sheep require neither feed nor shelter, and keep fat all the year round. Hogs are raised here with partial feeding, and pork is generally fattened upon wheat, and finer pork I never saw anywhere.

I omitted to mention in its appropriate place that our harvesting commences about the 20th of July, and continues throughout the month of August; and during the present year we had no rain from about the 1st of July to the 15th of October, so that we had the finest weather for saving our crops imaginable.

One thing that strikes the beholder of this conntry with greatest force, is the unsurpassable beauty of its scenery. We have snow-clad mountains, beautiful valleys, pure, rapid streams running over pebbly beds, with numerous cascades and waterfalls, and trees of superior grandeur and beauty.

The government of Oregon has grown up from necessity; and perhaps no new organization has been adopted and sustained with so much unanimity and good order. Every circumstance has tended to strengthen it. I attended the last term of the Circuit Courts in most of the counties, and I found great respect shown to judicial authority everywhere, and did not see a *solitary drunken juryman, or witness, or spectator.* So much industry, good order, and sobriety, I have never observed in any community. Our population seem to be exceedingly enterprising, and is making rapid progress to comfort and wealth. As yet, we have had no murders, no robberies, thefts, or felonies of any kind, except one assault with intent to kill. Our grand juries have exhibited very laudable assiduity in discharging their duties, and criminals here will meet with certain and prompt punishment.

Nature has displayed here her most magnificent powers, and our country has its full share of natural advantages. Our prospects are most brilliant. If we can keep out intoxication, *and we will do it,* half a century will not roll away before there will exist in Oregon one of the most industrious, virtuous, free, and commercial nations in the world.

I have already protracted this communication beyond its appropriate length, and will now close it by subscribing myself,

Yours, etc., PETER H. BURNETT.

DR. E. WHITE.

WALLAMET, OREGON, April 4, 1845.

SIR,—I have the honor and happiness of informing you, and through you, if it be your pleasure, the American public, that measures have been taken by myself and the citizens in this colony, to open a wagon route through from the upper part of this valley, the present season, directly to Fort Hall, or Green River; the pilot returning and escorting the immigrants through the much shorter, easier, and every way more advantageous route. The immigrants will thereby be enabled to bring with them their herds, wagons, and all their effects at once directly into the heart of the Wallamet Valley; saving thereby an immense amount of toil, hardship, and suffering, saying nothing of the necessary destruction and increased danger of the other route.

Your humble and obedient servant,

E. WHITE,

Sub-Agent Indian Affairs, W. R. M.

The messenger is leaving.

OREGON CITY, March 4, 1845.

Dr. E. White:

SIR,—In compliance with the request you made to me, that I should notice and communicate to you whatever I might deem of interest during my visit, in your employ, to the various Indian tribes east of the Cascade Mountains, bearing to them presents with admonitions and advice from you in order to secure the safety and peace of the immigrants in their passage through their country, the following is submitted :—

1. *The Nez Percés.*—Your acquaintance with this promising people renders it unnecessary for me to speak of their general character. I would simply remark, that their anxieties to become a civilized and literary nation have suffered no abatement since I left them in March last, after passing the winter with them most pleasantly, as teacher, in the employ of Rev. H. H. Spalding, missionary. Ellis, with most of the chiefs, was absent, having gone to meet the immigrants, then in the vicinity of Fort Boise, with a view to furnish them provisions, and trade them horses for cattle. You are aware of their eagerness to obtain domestic stock with all farming utensils, which I regard as one of the most interesting facts connected with Indian affairs west of the Rocky Mountains. Avarice is doubtless the ruling passion of most Indians, and forms a capital upon which those engaged in Indian affairs may operate for good or evil. With the Nez Percés, it has thus far been turned to good account, effecting results as beneficial to the whites and more salutary to the natives themselves, on this side the mountains, than has been effected on the other side by military force. Such is the prevalence of this "love of gain" among the Indians, that all efforts to control them by motives held out to any other passion, must prove ineffectual, at least, while we are unable to awe them by martial parade.

The individual difficulties existing between James, Timothy, and others, in relation to their claims on the valley, about the Clearwater Mission, are, for the time, put to rest, by the promise that you will visit them soon, and have the matter properly adjusted. Their crops this year have been abundant, and they have furnished the immigrants large supplies of provisions, which, I am happy to say, were bartered in good faith, and the trade conducted with much amity and good feeling on both sides, while I have to regret that Ellis and his people were unable to procure cattle to any extent worthy of notice. The presents were received, and the advice heard with a most respectful attention.

2. *The Cayuses* are also manifesting a spirit of enterprise, highly commendable. They too, have raised much grain and potatoes, and are

trading freely with the immigrants. A number of their chiefs and principal men were absent at the time, having gone, in company with a party of Wallawallas, to California, with horses to trade for cattle. They have since returned, and I sincerely regret to learn the failure of this, their first expedition of the kind. The Spaniards and other whites treated them badly; murdered one of the most promising young men of the Wallawallas, and the party returned without effecting the object of their trip. What influence this affair will have upon the conduct of these two tribes in reference to the next immigration passing through their countries, time alone must determine.

The lawless bands along the river, from Fort Wallawalla to the Dalles, are still troublesome to the immigrants; and the immigrants are still very imprudent in breaking off into small parties, just when they should remain united. The Indians are tempted by the unguarded and defenseless state of the immigrants, and avail themselves of the opportunity to gratify their cupidity. Here allow me to suggest a thought. These robbers furnish us a true miniature likeness of the whole Indian population, whenever they fail to obtain such things as they wish in exchange for such as they have to give. These are robbers now, because they have nothing to give; all others will be robbers when, with what they have to give, they can not procure what they wish. I am satisfied of the correctness of this conclusion, from all that I have witnessed of Indian character, even among the praiseworthy Nez Percés. And should the government of the United States withhold her protection from her subjects in Oregon, they will be under the necessity of entering into treaty stipulations with the Indians, in violation of the laws of the United States, as preferable to a resort to force of arms. Hitherto, the immigrants have had no serious difficulty in passing through the territory of these tribes; but that their passage is becoming more and more a subject of interest to the Indians, is abundantly manifest. They collect about the road from every part of the country, and have looked on with amazement; but the novelty of the scene is fast losing its power to hold in check their baser passions. The next immigration will, in all probability, call forth developments of Indian character, which have been almost denied an existence among these people. Indeed, sir, had you not taken the precaution to conciliate their good feelings and friendship toward the whites, just at the time they were meeting each other, it is to be doubted whether there had not been some serious difficulties. Individuals on both sides have been mutually provoked and exasperated during the passage of each immigration, and these cases are constantly multiplying. Much prudence is required on the part of the whites, and, unfortunately, they have very little by the time they reach the Columbia Valley. Some of the late immigrants, losing their horses, and very naturally supposing them stolen by the Indians, went to the bands of horses owned by the Indians and took as many as they wished.

You are too well acquainted with Indians to suppose that such a course can be persisted in without producing serious results. I am aware that this is looking at the dark side; but sir, perhaps it is wisdom to look at that side when it is more than half turned toward us, if, by looking, we can find some way to turn it back again. I look to Ellis, and the speedy action of the general government of the United States, as the brightest features in the prospect now before us. Your knowledge of my situation and circumstances render any apology unnecessary for this imperfect scroll.

I remain, your humble servant,

Dr. E. White, H. A. G. Lee.

Sub-Agent Indian affairs, W. R. M.

Oregon Territory, July 8, 1845.

To the Hon. the Secretary of the War Department:

Dear Sir,—I beg leave, most respectfully, to submit a few thoughts for your consideration, relative to the course pursued by Dr. E. White, our late Indian sub-agent, now on the eve of leaving us. I would not venture to intrude upon your time, but for the reason that I am aware that Dr. White leaves with an anxious and laboring mind, in view of the state of his finances, fearing, perhaps, a proper consideration might not be given to the situation and circumstances in which he has been placed in this isolated portion of our wide domain. I consider it but justice to Dr. White, to say, having crossed the mountains with him, that he exerted himself, and did much toward raising the first party that were of a sufficient number to travel independent of the trading companies to the mountains; thereby opening the way, and making the first track to Oregon; and since his arrival, by his promptness, decision, and firmness, we have been saved from the baneful influence and degradation of ardent spirits here, in our infant colony; and by his kind, conciliatory measures, active charity, and judicious conduct among the Indians, he has done much for them, and probably, in several instances, fended off the arrow of savage warfare.

The indefatigable perseverance, expense, and time Dr. White has been at in ferreting out a road across the Cascade Mountains,* which

* The Cascade ridge of mountains was found to be high and difficult to pass; and it is doubtful with me if the immigrants succeeded in crossing over with their wagons and effects, into the valley of the Wallamet.

will intersect the old wagon road in the vicinity of Fort Hall, cutting off some two or three hundred miles of the worst portion of the road, entirely avoiding the Columbia River, and the dangers incident to these waters, by an inexperienced, worn-out, and fatigued immigration. By this new route, the immigrants will find themselves greatly relieved, and saved from immense trouble, as they will as readily reach the head of the Wallamet settlement, as they would, by the old, reach Wallamet; avoiding the difficulties and dangers of the Snake and Columbia rivers.

In conclusion, allow me to observe that the sacrifice one is obliged to make in funds of this country, to render them specie, or available drafts, is immense; and it is almost impossible to do it at all, to any amount. Consequently, the doctor finds himself very much embarrassed in his financial concerns, being obliged to draft on his government for his entire expenditures in his official capacity.

Be pleased to accept, etc., my dear sir,

While I remain yours,

With due regard and great respect,

A. LAWRENCE LOVEJOY.

OREGON, August 14, 1845.

The following resolution was introduced and adopted in the House of Representatives of Oregon Territory, this day:—

Resolved, That this House recommend to the favorable consideration of the government of the United States, the just claims of Dr. Elijah White, sub-Indian agent, to remuneration for the heavy expense by him incurred, in attempting to discover a southern pass through the Cascade Mountains.

M. M. McCARVER, Speaker.

Attest: J. E. LONG, Clerk.

WASHINGTON CITY, Dec. 9, 1845.

Hon. W. Medill:

DEAR SIR,—Allow me to say a word in behalf of my friend, Dr. Elijah White, Indian agent in Oregon, who desires to arrange at the department the accounts of his four years' service in that Territory. Dr. White, with whom I passed the winter of 1844 upon the Wallamet, has had unnumbered difficulties surrounding him, and has performed his duties with great delicacy and happy success. My conviction is, that he has performed services in Oregon, both to whites and Indians, equal to those of several agencies combined, on our western frontier, at a very

27

inadequate compensation, and with very stinted means. All whom I heard comment upon the administration of his office have accorded to him great praise for ardor and industry; and those among whom he has officially acted will be gratified to hear that he has met a generous reception at the department.

Yours, with great respect,

WILLIAM GILPIN.

WAR DEPARTMENT,
OFFICE OF INDIAN AFFAIRS, Jan. 5, 1846.

SIR,—The Secretary of War is desirous that you should return to your agency as early as practicable, and has authorized me to say that the Department will allow to you the sum of three hundred dollars ($300) to defray your expenses there.

Instructions in relation to your duties will be given you when you reach this city, or will be forwarded to you at such place as you may designate. An immediate reply will be expected.

Very respectfully, your obedient servant,

W. MEDILL.

Dr. ELIJAH WHITE, Lansingville, Tompkins Co., N. Y.

Since the above requirement I have been detained here waiting the action of Congress upon the following bill, to release me from the responsibilities of my government protested drafts, which, from the rapid influx of white population to that distant Indian country, the necessities of my position have compelled me to incur.

I am now out of employment, and on heavy expenses, and under obligation, from important engagements, to leave for Oregon soon, in order to reach my destination this fall.

Should the following report of the Senate committee prove satisfactory, and all be persuaded that I have acted correctly, and expended no more than the honor of our government and the necessities of my position required, I will feel greatly obliged if Congress, "now so much relieved from heavy national and public affairs," will take up my bill and pass it through informally, as these protested drafts crowd and embarrass me much.

The Indian Department have reconsidered the case, and, as the report of the committee will show, done for me what they felt authorized to do; and I now most respectfully pray your honorable consideration to the payment of the residue, that I may go back to the land of my adoption unembarrassed, and happy in the consideration that our Congress will do right. And that any small presents, and other reasonable expenses to conciliate Indians where our citizens are settling on their unbought lands, will be cheerfully met.

Should any member desire an explanation, please drop me a note, and I will call at the moment required. Only pray act, and let me be off; for I thirst to be on the prairies of the far west, making my way to the valley of the Wallamet.

The documents from the Legislature of Oregon arrived and defeated the doctor.

The following extract is from the report of the Senate Committee on Indian Affairs on the petition of Dr. White:—

"Your committee finds this first charge to be the amount actually and necessarily expended by the petitioner, and believes it to be moderate and equitable, and that it ought to be allowed.

"The second charge appears equally just, and to have been made in compliance with the instructions of T. Hartley Crawford, superintendent of Indian affairs, of February 9, 1842, and enforced by the resolution of the Oregon Legislature, expressing the hope that Congress will reimburse the expenses of the petitioner thereby incurred.

"The third charge is for moneys actually paid under the specified heads by the petitioner, and for which drafts are now under protest, being disallowed by the department. These accounts, your committee finds, have been suspended by the department under a decision made to restrict the petitioner to the amount allowed by law to sub-agents, viz., $1,250 per annum in all. Your committee believes that these amounts are equitably and justly asked, and should be granted by Congress, although the committee approves of the decision of the department, and thinks, in cases like the present, that such extra allowances should be made only by Congress.

"Your committee has had a variety of testimony before it, showing that the affairs of his position have compelled the petitioner to transact and regulate Indian relations among ten large tribes, and many more smaller ones, speaking different languages, and for the most part warlike, excitable, and suspicious people. The Indian population, among whom he has been the only official organ, amounts to twenty-five thousand souls. The petitioner has been left to support himself by his solitary energies and exertions, without the aid of troops, annuities, or the awe which the power of the government exercises over Indians to whom it is known. The prices of all articles (especially provisions), and the wages of interpreters and assistants, and the means of traveling and transportation are very high, and difficult to be procured.

"Your committee believes that the petitioner would be left without any compensation for four years of arduous, harassing, and vexatious services, unless the relief for which he prays be extended to him by Congress.

"The committee, therefore, reports the accompanying bill, and recommends its passage, as sanctioned by the equity and justice of the case, and according with the uniform policy and practice of the Congress of the United States in similar cases."

We wish to state that the reason for quoting Dr. White's report so extensively is from the facts embodied in it, wholly independent of his self-lauding statement. Did we not know that Mr. Cornelius Rogers and Mr. H. A. G. Lee were his advisers and interpreters, we would not quote him as at all reliable in any of his Indian councils or proceedings.

CHAPTER LI.

1845.—Public meetings to elect delegates to convention.—Candidates for governor.—Members elected to the Legislative Committee.—Oath of office.—Mr. Applegate's announcement.—Dr. McLaughlin's amphibiousness.—Description of the members of the Legislative Committee.—Business of the session.—Ermatinger's election contested.—Mr. Garrison's resolutions.—Anti-slavery resolution.—Organic law revised.—Improvements and condition of the country.

1845.—Public meetings had been held in most of the districts, and nominations made for the Legislative Committee. Delegates were elected to meet at Champoeg in convention, to nominate candidates for governor, supreme judge, and Territorial recorder.

In this convention A. L. Lovejoy, George Abernethy, O. Russell, and Dr. Bailey were candidates for governor. After several ballotings, Mr. Lovejoy received a majority of the votes, and was declared the regularly nominated candidate. Mr. Russell's friends were dissatisfied, and in the final vote at the June election, joined with Mr. Abernethy's friends and elected him, although he was absent from the country. This left the old Executive Committee in power until after the meeting of the Legislative Committee, and revision of the organic laws, which was the first business the committee attended to, and submitted the amended organic compact to the people for their approval.

The members elected were:—

From Clackamas County: H. A. G. Lee, W. H. Gray, H. Straight.

From Champoeg County: R. Newell, J. M. Garrison, M. G. Foisy, and B. Lee.

From Yamhill County: Jesse Applegate and A. Hendricks.

From Tualatin County: M. M. McCarver, J. W. Smith, and David Hill.

From Clatsop County: John McClure.

The oath administered to this Legislative Committee shows the feelings of the mover (Mr. Applegate) toward the Hudson's Bay Company.

Oath of Office.—"I do solemnly swear that I will support the organic laws of the provisional government of Oregon, so far as the said organic laws are consistent with my duties as a citizen of the United States, or a subject of Great Britain, and faithfully demean myself in office. So help me God."

In starting from Missouri to come to this country in 1843, Mr. Applegate announced to his traveling companions, as we have been credibly informed, that he meant to drive the Hudson's Bay Company from the country. To reach the country independent of them, he had sold or mortgaged his cattle to get supplies at Wallawalla. On arriving at Vancouver, he found Dr. McLaughlin to be much of a gentleman, and disposed to aid him in every way he could. The doctor advised him to keep his cattle and gave him employment as a surveyor, and credit for all he required. This kind treatment closed Mr. Applegate's open statements of opposition to the company, and secured his friendship and his influence to keep his Missouri friends from doing violence to them. He carried this kind feeling for them into the Legislative Committee.

At this point the amphibious disposition of Dr. McLaughlin (a term applied to the doctor, by a member of the company, for his supposed friendship to the American cause) began to develop itself; and in proportion as he favored American interests he fell in the estimation of the company and the English government.

The oath of office presented by Mr. Applegate, and supported by Messrs. Newell, Foisy, McCarver, Garrison, Smith, and Hendricks, shows that these men were favorable to a union with the company or the English party in the country. This would have been right and honorable, had there been a corresponding honorable confidence on their part; but, as the sequel will show, this was not the case. They were willing to favor our organization and give it a *quasi* support while it served their purposes and afforded them an opportunity to work for its final overthrow.

As a citizen, Mr. Applegate has been one of our best; as a politician, he has acted on the old Whig platform, that, with him, has never been revised. Though half the American continent has been changed since he adopted it, yet his political creed is the same as that announced by Hamilton in the *Federalist*. My first impression of him was, that he was better versed in the principles of that party than in those of religion, or the general interests of a new country. The fact that the Hudson's Bay Company, or rather Dr. McLaughlin, early secured his personal friendship, was the cause of his losing caste among his Missouri friends, and also among the larger portion of the settlers that the company were not disposed to favor. In his legislative capacity he was invaluable. His mind was clear and distinct, and he was generally correct in his conclusions. Though not a good debater, yet his mathematical calculations, and straight lines, always came close to the mark. He was kind and obliging to a friend or favorite, but severe on his enemies.

Mr. Abijah Hendricks, from the same county, was a plain farmer, who followed the lead of Mr. Applegate, causing him to always count two in any vote.

Mr. J. H. Smith, of Tualatin County, was also a plain farmer, and generally voted with Mr. Hill.

Mr. M. G. Foisy, from Champoeg, a Frenchman, followed the lead of Mr. Newell.

Mr. Barton Lee was of the independent Democratic pro-slavery school, generally voting against mission interests, from personal prejudice, and was equally ignorant of and prejudiced against the Hudson's Bay Company; following the lead of H. A. G. Lee.

J. M. Garrison was a perfect weathercock, and none could tell from his speeches or actions what his vote would be.

H. Straight, of Clackamas County, was a man of strong prejudices and but little legislative ability, pro-slavery in sentiment, and strongly opposed to the company and mission influences. He generally voted with Mr. Hill, of Tualatin District.

John McClure, of Clatsop County, a man of fine appearance and generally respected for his age, but, as a politician, having no influence—merely occupying a place. He was of the pro-slavery school—extremely bitter and sarcastic in his conversation against all who fell under his displeasure, yet liberal to personal friends, and kind to strangers; but severe alike on the Hudson's Bay Company and religious societies. He was inclined in his own religious ideas to Romanism.

H. A. G. Lee was a young man of talent, firmness, and unimpeachable character. He acted with caution, and generally right. He was not a verbose, but a conclusive debater. In short, the words of a debate were uttered by McCarver, and the conclusions and final action followed Lee, who was always ready, with Applegate and Gray, to do his full share of writing and labor.

As we have before stated, the first business of this Legislative Committee was, to revise and prepare an organic law, which could be submitted for the adoption of the people. The whole number of voters was about eight hundred.

While this was being done by a special committee consisting of H. A. G. Lee, Newell, Applegate, Smith, and McClure,—one from each county represented,—another special committee, consisting of Gray, Applegate, H. A. G. Lee, McClure, and D. Hill, were appointed to draft a memorial and petition, to be forwarded to the Congress of the United States, setting forth the condition, situation, relations, and wants of this country. These two objects occupied the greater portion of the time of this Legislative Committee, during their session of eleven days.

On the third day of the session, the question as to the legality of allowing Francis Ermatinger to hold the office of treasurer came up, and it was finally decided that there were not sufficient grounds for contesting the election. Ermatinger was then a member of the Hudson's Bay Company, and so was Dr. McLaughlin. Hill and Straight were the only two who voted against Ermatinger's holding that office. I have no doubt, from the feeling and influence just then operating among the officers and servants of the company and English colonists (which subsequent events have proved), that they were laboring to divide the American influence, by coming in and appearing to act with us. Ermatinger was popular among the Americans, and received the entire French vote, and was declared duly elected by the Legislative Committee.

On the fifth day of the session, J. M. Garrison (I think he was called Rev. in those days) brought in a set of resolutions which speak for themselves.

"On motion of Mr. Garrison—

"*Resolved*, That whereas the people of Oregon, assembled *en masse*, did, on the 2d day of May, 1843, resolve that no tax should be levied upon this people, confirming the same by the adoption of the report of the committee of ways and means, adopted by the Legislative Committee and referred to the people *en masse*, and by them enacted on the 5th day of July, 1843; therefore,

"*Resolved*, That this house has no right to levy a tax of any kind, without the consent of the free voters of this Territory previously obtained.

"*Resolved*, That all acts and parts of acts on that subject passed by the Legislative Committee were contrary to the express resolution and action of the people."

These resolutions were referred to committee of the whole, where they found a silent grave.

Dr. White by this time is coming up for a big splurge. Our young friend H. A. G. Lee proposes to make him the bearer of our memorial to Congress, by introducing a resolution, "That the clerk be required to furnish to Dr. E. White a copy of the memorial to Congress, as soon as it shall be properly signed, as per resolution of yesterday."

This resolution elicited a little discussion, and a statement that Dr. White was not to be trusted with any public document to the government, as he would more than probably change, or so arrange those documents as to secure his own personal ends, whatever they might be. By those unacquainted with Dr. White this was considered strange and unreasonable prejudice against him; so that on the final question there were but Gray, Hill, and Straight who voted against placing the documents in his hands.

On the last day of this session Mr. Applegate introduced a test question on the subject of slavery, precisely the same as that introduced by Garrison four days previous.

"*Resolved*, That this government can recognize the right of one person to the services of another only upon *bona-fide* contract made and entered into, and equally binding on both parties."

Yeas—Applegate, Gray, Smith, McCarver, Garrison, Hill, H. A. G. Lee, Hendricks, and Foisy—10.

Nays—Straight, B. Lee, and McClure—3.

We must now adjourn our Legislative Committee a few days, and see what is going on outside.

The organic laws of the people first adopted at Champoeg, July 5, 1843, had been revised, and unanimously adopted by the Legislative Committee, and submitted for the vote of the people, July 26, 1845.

On page 431 of Mr. Hines' book, he says: "In the spring of 1844 a new Legislative Committee was elected, which embraced two or three lawyers, who arrived in the country the previous fall. This committee passed a vote recommending several important alterations in the organic laws, which were found to be, in their practical operations, somewhat defective. As the people had not yet surrendered their law-making power into the hands of the Legislative Committee, it was necessary to call an election to ascertain the will of the people in relation to the proposed alterations and amendments. This election took place, and resulted in the adoption of the organic laws, with the proposed alterations and amendments, by an overwhelming majority. The principal alterations thus effected relate to the three powers of government,—the legislative, executive, and judicial. Instead of a committee of nine, whose acts were to be confirmed or rejected by a subsequent vote of the people, the legislative power was vested in a House of Representatives, to consist of not less than thirteen nor more than sixty-one members, possessing all the powers usual to such bodies. Instead of a committee of three, the executive power was vested in one person, to be elected by the qualified voters at the annual election, and possessing the powers common to the governors of the different States."

We are unable to understand Mr. Hines when he says, "As the people had not yet surrendered their law-making power into the hands of the Legislative Committee, it was necessary to call an election to ascertain the will of the people." This statement shows the ignorance of Mr. Hines as regards the organic laws adopted by the people of Champoeg. Mr. Saxton, who was in the country at the time, and took copies of those laws attested by Mr. Le Breton (which have already been given), found an organic law with an executive, legislative, and judicial department, the same as the committee of 1845, and all that was requisite was to revise, select out, and define the powers and duties of the several departments.

As a matter of policy, and to harmonize and consolidate, as much as was possible, all the conflicting interests and influences in the country, the presence of British subjects was admitted, their treaty rights were acknowledged by our laws, aud they were admitted to a voice and representation in the provisional government.

The liberal course pursued by the Legislature of 1845 has fixed the deep stain of ingratitude and infamy upon the British subjects who participated in our organization, and received its benefits and protection, till they had completed their arrangements for its destruction, just as slavery grew under the fostering care of a liberal and generous government, and then attempted to crush and destroy its protector.

From a review of Mr. Hines' book, I find that he was on a tour from Oregon to New York by way of China during 1845 and 1846. This will account for his want of information regarding the political events that were taking place during that time; and also shows the views he entertained on leaving the country.

Dr. McLaughlin had completed his saw-mill and flour-mill at Oregon City. The Milling Company had also put up mills at that place which were now in successful operation, and the country generally was in a prosperous condition.

Dr. Whitman had much annoyance and difficulty with the Indians on account of interference and tales told them by old Toupin, Doreo, Gervais, the priests, and others who were jealous of his labors and success among them.

He had purchased the Dalles station of the Methodist Mission, and engaged Mr. Hinman to occupy it until other arrangements could be made.

Mr. Spalding was engaged in improving his farm, also printing books in the Nez Percé language on his small press, and translating and printing portions of the Bible, for the use of the natives. He had a saw-mill and grist-mill at his station; and about three hundred of his Indians, and one hundred at Dr. Whitman's, were cultivating patches of ground.

Messrs. Walker and Eells were staying at Cimakain, ready to depart any time, as stated by Mr. Brouillet. On page 9 of his narrative, he says: "A missionary of the Spokans, writing to Dr. Whitman, as early as 1839, has said: 'The failure of this mission is so strongly impressed upon my mind, that I feel it necessary to have cane in hand, and as much as one shoe on, ready for a move. I see nothing but the power of God that can save us.'" *Query.*—Where did Rev. Vicar-General Brouillet get this letter, and for what purpose did he preserve it? Did he find it among Dr. Whitman's papers, when he was hunting them over to find the vial of poison to show the Indians as per deposition in the case?

Brouillet continues: "These facts and statements prove clearly, I think, that there existed among the Indians, long before the arrival of the bishop of Wallawalla and his clergy, *strong causes of dissatisfaction against the Protestant missionaries and the Americans in general, and that they formed a leaven that had been fermenting several years.*" This statement of Vicar-General Brouillet is unquestionably true, but, unfortunately for him, he is standing on the outer line of the circle, and has no personal knowledge of inside influences; hence he reasons from effect and guesses at the cause. He is anxious to so arrange cause and effect, as to remove suspicion of crime from a sect, and thereby involves his friends and himself, and furnishes the strongest proof of the complicity and guilt of both in the crime alleged against them. The "leaven" that had been fermenting is just what we are bringing to light.

The Hudson's Bay Company were repairing and strengthening their forts, under the plea that they wished some bastions from which they could salute her Majesty's ships on their arrival and departure from the river; at the same time they were laboring to secure political influence in the settlements, through their American dupes and tools.

While combining the Indian tribes, they were encouraging Jesuitical religious teachers among them; and while preparing for self-defense, they were dividing the settlement into parties and factions.

The Methodist Mission influence was but little, and mission credit was worse than greenbacks in 1864. As to commerce, it was nearly or quite under the control of the Hudson's Bay Company, also the market value of all produce in the country.

CHAPTER LII.

1845.—Second session of the Legislative Committee.—Mr. McCarver removed from the office of Speaker.—Mr. Applegate's resolutions.—Protest of Gray, Foisy, and Straight.—A legislative incident.—Law against dueling.—Dr. White addresses the Legislature.—Resolutions.—Dr. White denies the right of the settlers to organize a provisional government.—McCarver signs documents without authority.—Resolutions by the house on the subject.—Impertinent letter from Dr. White to the house.—White cornered by President Polk.—Incidents in White's temperance movements.—Proposition to repeal all laws for the collection of debts.—The Currency act.—Adjournment of the Legislature in August.—Meets again in December. —Proposal to locate the capital.

The Legislative Committee, at their second session, August 5, 1845, met under the revised and amended organic law, which had been previously adopted by the people by a majority of two hundred and three. There were between two and three hundred votes against the revision or amendments. Many voted against it, on account of its allowing the Hudson's Bay Company's English and French followers an equal voice with the Americans and others, and on account of its allowing the Legislature the power to *regulate* the introduction, manufacture, and sale of liquors.

McCarver claimed that he was Speaker of the house, under the organic law as revised. This caused some discussion and voting, and the introduction of a resolution requesting him to resign his position as Speaker, which he declined to do. Gray moved that the vote electing him Speaker of the house be reconsidered. McCarver then proceeded to organize the house, to suit his views of matters, by appointing new committees, and went forward as if no previous committees had been appointed. When his appointments were all made, Gray inquired if, in the opinion of Mr. Speaker McCarver, the house was properly organized. He replied that it was. Gray then appealed to the house, and was sustained, McCarver having denied his own position by appointing new committees. On motion of Mr. Straight, Mr. McCarver was removed from his office as Speaker, and Robert Newell elected *pro tem.*

Applegate, for reasons never fully explained, introduced two resolutions, which show either a short-sighted view of matters, or a foolish policy on his part, to wit:—

"*Resolved*, That the people of Oregon are not, in the opinion of this house, morally or legally bound by any acts of the officers or agents of the people not expressly authorized or sanctioned by the instrument in virtue of which they had their official existence.

"*Resolved, further*, That this house can not assume, in behalf of the people, the payment of any debt, or the refunding of any funds borrowed, or otherwise unlawfully contracted or obtained, without first obtaining the consent of the people."

On motion, the vote referring said resolution to committee of the whole was reconsidered, when the rules were suspended, the resolution read a second time, and referred to committee of the whole.

On the fifth day of the session, the resolutions of Mr. Applegate were called up, and Messrs. Applegate, Garrison, Hendricks, Hill, H. Lee, B. Lee, McClure, and Smith voted for, and Foisy, Gray, Straight, and McCarver against. Newell asked to be excused. These resolutions had the effect, designed or not, to destroy the credit of the provisional government.

On the sixth day of the session, Gray, Foisy, and Straight presented, and, on motion, were allowed to enter, their protest against their adoption, as follows:—

"*Whereas*, A resolution, with a preamble, containing a direct and positive censure upon the proceedings of the Oregon government, was introduced into this house by Jesse Applegate, asserting that this house, and the people of Oregon, are not morally or legally bound for any act of said government, to the payment of any debts contracted, or unlawfully borrowed, except they had previously obtained the consent of the people.

"*And whereas*, From the wording of said resolution, two constructions may be placed upon it; the one amouuting to a repudiation of all debts heretofore contracted, or money borrowed; the other implying a want of confidence in the agents and officers of this government; therefore,

"We, the undersigned, decidedly and solemnly protest against the adoption of any such resolutions or expressions by this house, as they not only do no good, but tend to great evil, in destroying the confidence of the people in the agents and officers of this government, without sufficient cause.

"W. H. Gray.
"M. G. Foisy.
"H. Straight.

"Oregon City, Aug. 7, 1845."

The effect of these resolutions was at once manifest. Measures were taken to procure the launch of the *Peacock* (which had been left in the care of Dr. McLaughlin by Captain Wilkes), for a pilot-boat at the mouth of the Columbia. The doctor informed the committee that he was not authorized to give it in charge of any irresponsible parties, without an order from as high authority as that from which he had received it. Hence the launch was allowed to rot upon the beach at Astoria; Mr. McClure, from that place, being one who voted to repudiate responsibility on the part of the provisional government.

On the 11th of August, in the midst of business under the order of the day, Mr. Applegate came in, apparently under considerable excitement, and in quite an earnest manner asked that the rule be suspended, to allow him to present *a bill to prevent dueling.* No immediate or pressing reason was assigned, but from the earnest manner of Mr. Applegate, and from what a number of the members knew, or pretended to know, the rule was suspended, Mr. Applegate's bill to prevent dueling read first time; rule further suspended, his bill read by title second and third time and passed, and on his further motion, a special messenger, P. G. Stewart, Esq., was sent with it to the governor, for his approval and signature; and in half an hour's time from its introduction and reading in the house it became a law in this vast country, bounded by the Russian possessions on the north, the Rocky Mountains on the east, California on the south, and the Pacific on the west.

Not long after this *telegraphic* law on dueling was passed, it was discovered that a young man by the name of Holderness had considered himself insulted and slandered by some report said to have originated with Dr. White. Holderness was about to send him a challenge, or at least there was a prospect that they might fight, if either of them had the courage to do so. This law gave the doctor an honorable excuse to decline the challenge, and have Holderness indicted and punished for sending it. This matter was engineered through so handsomely by Mr. Applegate, that Dr. White expressed himself *highly gratified and pleased.*

On the next day, the 12th, Mr. Applegate was honored with an important dispatch from Dr. White, which he presented in due form, together with a resolution of thanks to Dr. White, and an order was entered on the journal to have the doctor's communication filed for publication. This was not exactly what the doctor wanted, as the sequel will show. He had found that Applegate had the talent and influence requisite to carry through the resolutions necessary to accomplish his purposes.

He, having spent a part of the summer in running about the Wallamet Valley, made a trip over to the coast, and one into the Cascade

Mountains; wrote a journal of these trips, and presented it to the house through Mr. Applegate. After White's journal was read, Applegate presented a resolution, that the thanks of this house are due to Dr. E. White and his party for their meritorious exertions to find a passage through the Cascade Mountains, and that his account be filed for publication. On motion, *White was allowed to address* the house, which he did in his usual self-lauding, plausible manner, insinuating the great labor and benefit he had done, in keeping the Indians quiet and in exploring the country. His chaff and bombast secured the co-operation of Robert Newell and Mr. Applegate. On the 14th, Mr. Applegate informed the house that he had in his possession several official documents, belonging to Dr. E. White, which he was requested to lay before the house. The report and documents were received.

On motion of Mr. Applegate—

"*Resolved*, That, whereas the adoption of the amended organic law by the people of Oregon was an act of necessity rather than choice, and was intended to give to the people the protection which, of right, should be extended to them by their government, and not as an act of defiance or disregard of the authority or laws of the United States; therefore,

"*It is further resolved*, 1st. That, in the opinion of this house, the Congress of the United States, in establishing a Territorial government, should legalize the acts of the people in this country, so far as they are in accordance with the Constitution of the United States. 2d. That Dr. Elijah White, sub-Indian agent of Oregon, be requested to furnish a copy of the amended organic law to the Congress of the United States. 3d. That these resolutions be indorsed on said copy, with the vote of this house adopting the same."

On the adoption of the above, the vote was unanimous, which vote was taken by yeas and nays; and, on motion, the house decided that the members should not sign their names to said resolutions.

It will be seen by the statement of Applegate in the first part of this resolution, or preamble, that he wished to deny an attempt to resist the government of the United States on the part of the people and provisional government; and the fact that Dr. White had allowed him to examine his official papers, and present them to the Legislative Committee, shows the manner he was working with Applegate to get documents, resolutions, and papers from the Legislature into his hands; also the desperate effort there was made to get a unanimous vote favoring White as the bearer of those documents.

Dr. White had from the first *denied the right* of the settlers to organize a provisional goverment unless they would elect him as their governor. Applegate is caught in his trap, as we shall see, and from that day he began to lose his influence, and soon found that he had committed an egregious mistake, notwithstanding he had obtained a unanimous vote, to place those documents in Dr. White's hands. In order to head off McCarver, the house had voted that the members should not sign their names to the resolutions. McCarver could not withstand the temptation to get his name as Speaker of the Oregon Legislature before the Congress of the United States; so, as soon as the documents came into White's hands, he went to the clerk and attached his name as Speaker of the house. Newell was not quite satisfied, or rather Dr. White was not; so he got Newell to present a resolution, as follows:—

"*Resolved*, That this house recommend to the favorable consideration of the Congress of the United States the just claims of Dr. E. White, sub-Indian agent, for a remuneration for the heavy expenses by him incurred, in attempting to discover a southern passage through the Cascade Mountains."

In the afternoon session the resolution of Mr. Newell was called up, and, on its final passage, the yeas and nays were demanded, and were as follows:—

Yeas—Messrs. Applegate, Foisy, Hendricks, H. Lee, McClure, Newell, Straight, and the Speaker—8.

Nays—Messrs. Gray, Garrison, Hill, B. Lee, and Smith—5.

So the resolution was passed.

Dr. White waited for the passage of this resolution (keeping quiet as to McCarver's signing the others in violation of the order of the house), and as soon as it was safely in his pocket, left for Vancouver, on his way to the States.

White had no sooner gone, than it leaked out that McCarver had signed the documents, and White *had broken the seals, and destroyed private letters intrusted to him* to convey to the States, and had made Garrison his confidant respecting breaking open and destroying the letters. Here was a muss on hand such as none but White and McCarver could "*kick up.*" Applegate was too much excited and insulted by these men to say any thing; but he presented through B. Lee a resolution as follows:—

"*Resolved*, That M. M. McCarver has been opposed to the organic law, as adopted by the people of Oregon; and, contrary to the voice of this house in regular session, clandestinely, and in a manner unworthy the confidence reposed in him, placed his name to a copy of those laws transmitted to the United States, thereby conveying a false impression; and did, also, sign his name to two resolutions, contrary to a direct vote of this house; therefore,

"*It is further resolved*, That we disapprove of the course he has pursued, and feel ourselves under the humiliating necessity of signifying the same to the United States government, by causing a copy of this resolution to accompany those documents."

Which was received, and referred to committee of the whole.

In the afternoon, Dr. J. E. Long, clerk of the house, A. L. Lovejoy, Smith, and Hill were called before the house, and put on oath, to state what they knew of the matter. Mr. Applegate was chairman. The committee rose and reported that they had been engaged in investigating the subject referred to in Mr. B. Lee's resolution, but had not adopted the resolution. McCarver had been allowed to explain his course.

On motion of Mr. Applegate—

"*Resolved*, That, whereas a copy of the organic laws of Oregon, together with some resolutions, intended to be sent to the United States, have not been attested and dispatched according to the directions of this house; therefore,

"*Resolved*, That the clerk dispatch for them a messenger, to Vancouver, with authority to bring said documents back, and that he deliver them to the secretary, and that the expenses incurred be paid by the members of this house who voted for the resolution."

On the adoption of which the yeas and nays were called, and were as follows:—

Yeas—Messrs. Applegate, Gray, B. Lee, McClure, and Newell—5.

Nays—Messrs. Hill, Smith, and Straight—3.

So the resolution was adopted. Messrs. Foisy, Garrison, Hendricks, and the Speaker were excused from voting.

On motion, the house went into committee of the whole, Mr. Applegate in the chair.

The committee rose, and reported, that the resolution of B. Lee having been under consideration, was laid upon the table.

It is but justice to state that the clerk of the house, J. E. Long, favored Dr. White's and Mr. McCarver's course, and allowed McCarver to sign the documents he well knew the house did not wish him to sign. A majority of the house were inclined to believe that White had been slandered; and had McCarver allowed the documents to go as per vote, White's designs, as stated by his opponents, would not have been revealed; so the messenger was sent for the documents on account of McCarver's course.

August 16, 1845.—The House met pursuant to adjournment.

The rules were suspended to allow the introduction of resolutions, when, on motion of Mr. McClure, it was

"*Resolved*, That, whereas the Speaker of this house has signed certain documents, ordered to be sent to the United States by a vote of this Legislature, from a mistaken sense of duty, and not from contumacy or contempt for this house; therefore,

"*Resolved*, That M. M. McCarver, said Speaker, have leave of absence, for the purpose of following Dr. E. White to Vancouver; and this house enjoins that said Speaker erase his name from said documents, to wit, the organic laws, and two resolutions in favor of Dr. E. White."

On motion of Mr. Applegate, it was

"*Resolved*, That it was not the intention of this house, in passing resolutions in favor of Dr. E. White, to recommend him to the government of the United States as a suitable person to fill any office in this Territory; and,

"*Be it further resolved*, That the clerk of this house forward, by some suitable person, an attested copy of this resolution, to the United States government."

The house appointed J. M. Garrison, Speaker, *pro tem.*

McCarver, being thus plainly invited, left the house, and found that the clerk's messenger had already gone for the documents. He returned in the afternoon and induced Mr. Smith, from Tualatin, to present the following resolution:—

"*Resolved*, That the vote requiring the Speaker to go in quest of Dr. E. White, for the purpose of erasing his name from certain documents in his possession to be by him conveyed to the United States, be reconsidered, and the Speaker restored to the chair."

On the 18th of August, the arrival of a letter from Dr. E. White was announced, which was read, as follows:—

August 17, 1845.

To the Hon., etc.:

Gentlemen,—Being on my way, and having but a moment to reflect, I have been at much of a loss which of your two resolutions most to respect, or which to obey; but at length have become satisfied that the first was taken most *soberly*, and, as it answers my purpose best, I pledge myself to adhere strictly to that. Sincerely wishing you good luck in legislating,

I am, dear sirs, very respectfully yours,

E. White.

On the 20th, on motion of Mr. Applegate, it was

"*Resolved*, That the secretary be requested to forward to the United States government, through the American consul at the Sandwich Islands, a copy of the articles of compact, as adopted by the people of

Oregon Territory, on the last Saturday of July, A. D. 1845; and that the same be signed by the governor, and attested by the secretary; also, all resolutions adopted by this house relative to sending said documents by E. White, late Indian agent of this Territory; also, a copy of the letter of E. White, directed to this house."

These documents and papers, with depositions respecting White's opening and destroying private letters, were prepared, duly signed, and sent on to the Sandwich Islands by Captain Couch, of the *Lausanne*, and reached Washington just in time for President Polk to refuse White an important commission in New Mexico. The President, on receiving the documents and learning of White's course, asked an explanation, which he at first declined to give, on account of an attempt, as he alleged, of *some low blackguards in Oregon to slander him.* The legislative documents were referred to, when he found he was cornered, and left the President's house without his appointment.

Thus ended, for a time, the official course of a base and unprincipled man, who seemed only to live and move for selfish ends. His influence as a missionary, and as an officer of the government, were alike vile and unprincipled. He sought friends and partisans only to deceive and betray them. Applegate, McCarver, Garrison, Lee, McClure, and Newell were compelled to acknowledge his deception. In fact, no one but the Hudson's Bay Company could make any use of him, and with them he was considered an irresponsible man, and only useful as a tool to combine the Indians, and divide and destroy the influence of the settlement, as he had done that of the Methodist Mission.

The history of Dr. White, as connected with Pacific City and Spiritualism, and his secret agency under President Lincoln's administration, are of small moment when compared with the moral blight he fixed on the cause of missions and religion, in his early relations in Oregon. All who have ever attempted to associate with him, or assist him, have been made to feel his immoral influence. He made great professions of sustaining the temperance cause, while acting as Indian agent, and still allowed the Hudson's Bay Company to do as they pleased with their liquors, without a single word of complaint or remonstrance to the American government, while he pursued a high-handed and injudicious course toward the American citizen in his efforts to prevent the introduction or manufacture of liquors in the country. In his zeal, he boarded a vessel of which Captain J. H. Couch was master, and asserted his right to search and seize all the liquors he had on board. Captain Couch, knowing his rights and duties better than the Indian agent did his, ordered his men to get ready a couple of swivels he had on board, ranging them fore and aft along the vessel. He then said to Mr. Indian

Agent: "If you are able to take my ship, you can search and seize her, and not otherwise." The doctor found he was dealing with the wrong person, and left, to visit Mrs. Cooper, who had recently arrived in the country from Sydney, New South Wales, with a supply of liquors. He succeeded in getting a dram from "Old Mother Cooper," as she was called, and inquired if she had any more like it. The old woman had by this time a suspicion of his object, and informed him that, if she had, he could have no more.

Soon after, he learned that Dick McCary had put up a teapot distillery somewhere near his own house. He then got a party of men and went down and destroyed the whole concern, except the kettle, which answered for a bell, upon which he beat and drummed on his way back to Oregon City, and then took an adz and stove a hole in it, thus destroying it. If this had been done on the ground, no exceptions would have been taken to it; but White's proceedings disgusted the friends of temperance so much, that a few days after, when Newell presented a communication from him to the Legislature, with a bill to prevent the sale of liquor, it was defeated—5 for and 8 against.

The governor, having confidence in the morality and honesty of the people, suggested in his message the repeal of all laws for the collection of debts. He seemed to be of the opinion, that as they had lived and prospered under the mission and Hudson's Bay Company's rule without any such laws, the same rule would apply to a more numerous and civilized community. He was sustained in his opinion by Applegate, Hendricks, H. Lee, B. Lee, and Newell—5; Foisy, Gray, Garrison, Hill, McCarver, McClure, Straight, and Smith—8, were of a different opinion.

This vote seemed to annoy Applegate, as he had taken an active part in shaping the governor's suggestions into a bill to prevent litigation, and he seemed to insist upon the experiment being tried in a more extensive manner in the government of Oregon. It is due to this legislative body and to the governor to state, that none of them had ever had any experience in law-making until they found themselves in a country where there were no laws, and where the representatives were without law-books (with the single exception of a copy of the statutes of Iowa) to guide them. They had to originate, revise, and do as the majority thought best, in all the laws presented. That they were adapted to the time and the people then in the country there can be no question. This shows the innate love of law and order in the American people, as also a disposition to abide by and sustain right principles, though not immediately in the presence of prisons and punishment.

Had there been no foreign influences in the country, it would, perhaps, have been safe to risk the governor's suggestion, and Applegate's experiment. I arrive at this conclusion from my experience in four times crossing the continent, and in visiting the early mining regions of California, British Columbia, and Oregon. In all American caravans and mines, the company and miners make their own laws. In British mines, the government makes the laws, and the revenue officers enforce them. So with the Hudson's Bay Company and Roman missions: the committee in London, and the pope in Rome, give their subjects certain laws by which to be governed; and whenever those laws come in conflict with the more liberal American idea of government, there is opposition; for the disposition to oppress and the desire to be free can never harmonize. With the one is organized wealth and superstition, backed by irons, flogging, and ignorance. With the other is liberty and the love of right, sustained by intelligence, honesty, and virtue. No one acquainted with the early history of the people of Oregon can fail to admire their virtue and stability, and the firmness they displayed in maintaining their natural rights. We have already explained the secret influences that were combined to hold them in a state of half-savage and half-religious or ecclesiastical vassalage, till some action should be taken by the United States government.

This state of things did not accord with the feelings of a great majority of the people. They had ruled their own individual actions too long to submit quietly to any religious or political power, in which they had no voice. Hence they were ready for any mutual organization, that was of their own choice and creation.

They adopted a system of currency suitable to the time and country. This system became necessary, from the known disposition of the Hudson's Bay Company to oppress and force payment, in what did not then exist in sufficient quantity to meet the wants of the settlement; besides, they held the commercial power; and here again protection was required. The two petitions to the Congress of the United States of 1840 and 1842 state their policy as to internal matters. The first section of this currency law is:—

"*Be it enacted by the House of Representatives of Oregon Territory:* 1st. That, in addition to gold and silver, treasury drafts, approved orders on solvent merchants, and good merchantable wheat at the market price, delivered at such place as it is customary for people to receive their wheat at, shall be a lawful tender for the payment of taxes and judgments rendered in the courts of Oregon Territory, and for the payment of all debts contracted in Oregon Territory, where no special contracts have been made to the contrary.

"2d. The personal estate of every individual, company, body politic or corporate, including his, her, or their goods or chattels, also town or city property, or improvements claimed and owned in virtue of occupancy, secured and allowed by the treaty between Great Britain and the United States, shall be subject to execution, to be taken and sold according to the provisions of this act; excepting, that wearing-apparel shall not be considered as any part of the estate of any defendant or defendants in execution; and no land claim or improvement upon a land claim, held according to the laws of this Territory, shall be subject to execution; and no stay upon execution shall be permitted or allowed, except by the consent of the party in whose favor the execution has been issued, nor for any time other than the time agreed upon by the parties.

"3d. Specifies that personal property shall be sold previous to town lots.

"4th. Exempts (if a family) one Bible, one cow and calf, one horse, or yoke of cattle, five sheep, five hogs, household and kitchen furniture not to exceed in value thirty dollars, one stove fixed up in the house, one bed for every two in the family, farming utensils not to exceed in value fifty dollars, one month's provisions for all the family, all mechanics' necessary tools, and all the books of private libraries not to exceed one hundred dollars' worth."

Who says we were not willing to give a poor family a good show to start with in Oregon in 1845?

"5th. Fifteen days' notice of any sale was to be given.

"6th. No property was to be sold for less than two-thirds its appraised value."

On the second section of this act, there was a long and animated discussion, Newell and Garrison claiming that we had no right to subject the property of the Hudson's Bay Company, and the Methodist and other missions, to our laws; McCarver and Hill, that we ought to exempt town sites and lots from execution. On its final passage, the vote was Applegate, Foisy, Gray, Hendricks, McClure, Smith, Straight, and H. Lee—8, for; Garrison, Hill, B. Lee, Newell, and McCarver—5, against.

This body adjourned *sine die* on the 20th of August, 1845, and in consequence of there being no provision made for a new election in the amended organic compact, they were again called to meet on Tuesday, December 2, 1845, in accordance with the organic law, to arrange and fill up any deficiencies in the offices and laws.

Applegate had resigned. There were present, Foisy, Garrison, Newell, and Barton Lee from Champoeg; Gray and Straight from Clackamas; Hill and McCarver from Tualatin; and McClure from Clatsop.

There were absent, from Yamhill, Hendricks; from Tualatin, J. M. Smith; and from Clackamas, H. A. G. Lee.

Newell, of Champoeg, was elected on the final vote as Speaker; Dr. J. E. Long, clerk.

Jefferson's Manual, which had for the first time strayed across the Rocky Mountains, was presented to the house, and used to govern its proceedings, so far as it was applicable. I think it must have come into the Multnomah Circulating Library, in part payment for a share in that institution. Gray moved its adoption to govern the proceedings of the house, which was considered organized by the election of Speaker, clerk, and sergeant-at-arms.

On the second day all the members were present except Applegate. The governor was called upon to issue his warrant to fill the vacancy, which he did. I think, however, that no election was held, as no representative appeared to claim the seat.

An effort was made to locate the seat of government, but failed, on account of Dr. McLaughlin not having put in his bid in time to have it considered by the house; and a remonstrance was got up by Ermatinger and the Hudson's Bay Company's influence, with sixty names attached, against locating it at all.

This was in accordance with the short-sighted policy of Dr. McLaughlin, aided by the influence secured over the people by such men as Ermatinger, Long, Newell, and McCarver, who had become a resident of Clackamas, while he represented Tualatin County.

CHAPTER LIII.

The liquor law.—Amended act of 1845.—Message of the governor on the same.—Repeal of the prohibitory and passage of the license law.—Letter of James Douglas.—Reply of Mr. Samuel Parker.—Dr. Tolmie's resolution on the judiciary.—The governor's veto of the license law.—Immigration for Oregon and California in 1846.—Arrival of the brig *Henry*.—The Oregon Printing Association.—The *Spectator*, the first newspaper in Oregon.—W. G. T. Vault, first editor.—H. A. G. Lee, second editor.—G. L. Curry, third editor.—Judge Wait, fourth editor.

The Liquor Law.—Peter H. Burnett framed a law on this subject, which was revised by Newell in the summer of 1845, and lost on the final vote. In December, 1845, Gray, from committee on ways and means, reported a bill on ardent spirits, expressing the views, and gaining the approval of a decided majority of the people. Governor Abernethy, in his annual message the next year, expressed an opinion that this law required some amendment, but, by combining the whole liquor influence in the country, the law was repealed, and a license law substituted, by a two-thirds vote over his veto ; while, at the same time, nearly two-thirds of the voters of the Territory voted to *prohibit* the sale of liquor, instead of to *regulate* it, as expressed in the organic law.

The law, as reported by the committee of ways and means, was passed December 6, 1845, by the following vote: Gray, Garrison, Hendricks, H. Lee, B. Lee, McClure, and McCarver—7, for; Foisy, Hill, Straight, and Newell—4, against.

On the 8th, the Monday following this vote (Hendricks and Barton Lee having been treated and tampered with), on motion of B. Lee—

"*Resolved*, That the house now reconsider the vote on the final passage of the bill on ardent spirits."

Yeas—Hendricks, Hill, B. Lee, Smith, Straight, and Newell—6.

Nays—Foisy, Gray, Garrison, H. Lee, McCarver, and McClure—6.

So the motion to reconsider was lost, and the bill published in the first newspaper ever published on this coast, as provided for in the bill itself, which is as follows:—

Amended Act of 1845.

Section 2. That if any person shall hereafter sell, barter, give, or trade any ardent spirits of any kind whatever, directly or indirectly, to any person within the Territory of Oregon, he shall forfeit and pay the sum of twenty dollars for each and every such sale, trade, barter, or gift, to be recovered by indictment in the County Court, or before a justice of the peace, without the form of pleading.

SEC. 3. That if any person shall hereafter establish or carry on any manufactory or distillery of ardent spirits in Oregon, he shall be subject to indictment before the County Court, as for a nuisance, and if convicted, he shall be fined the sum of one hundred dollars, and the court shall issue an order to the sheriff, directing him to seize and destroy the distilling apparatus, which order the sheriff shall execute.

SEC. 4. Whenever it shall come to the knowledge of any officer of this government, or any private citizen, that any kind of spirituous liquors are being distilled or manufactured in Oregon, they are hereby authorized and required to proceed to the place where such illicit manufacture is known to exist, and seize the distilling apparatus, and deliver the same to the nearest district judge or justice of the peace, whose duty it shall be immediately to issue his warrant and cause the house and premises of the person against whom such warrant shall be issued to be further searched, and in case any kind of spirituous liquors are found in or about said premises, or any implements or apparatus that have the appearance of having been used, or constructed for the purpose of manufacturing any kind of spirituous liquors, the officer who shall have been duly authorized to execute such warrant shall seize all such apparatus, implements, and spirituous liquors, and deliver the same to the judge or justice of the peace who issued the said warrant. Said officer shall also arrest the person or persons in or about whose premises such apparatus, implements, or spirituous liquors are found, and conduct him or them to said judge or justice of the peace, whose duty it shall be to proceed against such criminal or criminals, and dispose of the articles seized according to law.

SEC. 5. All the fines or penalties recovered under this act shall go, one-half to the informant and witnesses, and the other half to the officers engaged in arresting and trying the criminal or criminals, and it shall be the duty of all officers into whose hands such fines and penalties may come, to pay over as directed in this section.

SEC. 6. This act shall not be so construed as to prevent any practicing physician from selling such liquors for medicines, not to exceed half a pint at one time.

SEC. 7. That it shall be the duty of the secretary to publish this act in the first newspaper published in Oregon.

I, John E. Long, secretary of Oregon, do hereby certify that the foregoing act on ardent spirits is truly and correctly revised by me.

JOHN E. LONG, Secretary.

It will be seen in the final vote, that Foisy at first voted against this bill; but Hendricks and B. Lee changed their vote and Foisy changed his; thus the liquor law remained as it was, and was published February 5, 1846, and remained in force till Saturday, December 19, 1846. On December 4 of that year, the governor called the attention of the Legislature to this law, in the following language:—

"The act passed at the last session of the Legislature, entitled 'An Act to prevent the introduction, sale, and distillation of ardent spirits in Oregon,' is one I should recommend for revision; there are several points that are thought to be defective. The organic law provides that the Legislature shall have power to pass laws to regulate the introduction, manufacture, or sale of ardent spirits. It is held that the power to prohibit the introduction, manufacture, or sale is not granted by the organic law. Another objection is that the fines collected under the act shall go, one-half to the informant and witnesses, and the other half to the officers engaged in arresting and trying: in fact, making the witnesses and judges interested in the case. The fourth section makes it the duty of any officer, or any private citizen, to act whenever it shall come to their knowledge that any kind of spirituous liquors are being distilled or manufactured in Oregon. It would be much better if it were made the duty of the sheriff of each county to act, whenever he should be informed that any liquor was being made or sold in his county, and authorize him to raise a sufficient *posse* to aid and assist him in enforcing the law. We have, as a community, taken a high stand in the cause of temperance; among our earliest efforts may be found the abolishing of ardent spirits from our land, and to this, in a great measure, may be attributed our peace and prosperity. No new country can be pointed out where so much harmony prevailed in its first settlement as in this: laws, we had none, yet all things went on quietly and prosperously. I have no doubt if ardent spirits are kept within their proper bounds, we shall continue prosperous.

"It is said by some we have no right to say what a man shall make or what he shall not make; yet, we find, in all large cities, certain manufactories are forbidden to be carried on within the limits of the city, because they annoy the inhabitants, and hence are declared to be public nuisances, and by law are compelled to be removed; and, if the city increase and extend to the place where they are relocated, they are removed again. Intoxicating drink is an enormous public injury and private wrong; its effects, in every way, shape, and form, are evil, and therefore should be restrained within proper limits by law. It deprives the wife and children of the inebriate of the support and protection they have a right to expect from him; it deprives the community of the labor which constitutes a nation's wealth, for it is a well-known fact that a nation's wealth is made up of individual labor, and every day, therefore, lost by the laborer, caused by the effects of alcoholic drink, is a loss to the community at large. Persons who have become habitually addicted to ardent spirits, hearing that we had excluded the poison from our land, and, believing they never could be free if they remained near its influence, have left their homes and crossed the Rocky Mountains to escape the ruin that threatened them. Shall *they* be disappointed? During the last year, persons taking advantage of the defect in our law, have manufactured and sold ardent spirits. We have seen the effects (although the manufacture was on a small scale) in the midnight carousals among the Indians in our neighborhood, during their fishing season, and while they had property to dispose of; and, let me ask, what would be the consequences if the use of it should be general in the country and among the different tribes of Indians in the Territory? History may, hereafter, write the page in letters of blood! And what are the consequences, as presented to us in the history of older countries, of an indiscriminate use of ardent spirits? Almshouses, hospitals, prisons, and the gallows. I would, therefore, recommend that but one person, and that person a physician, be authorized to import or manufacture a sufficient quantity to supply the wants of the community for medicinal purposes; to dispose of no liquor except when he knows it to be necessary, or on an order from a regular physician, stating that the person applying stands in need of it for medicinal purposes; and to physicians to be used in their practice; the person so empowered to import, manufacture, and sell, to keep a record of the quantity manufactured or imported; also, a record of the quantity sold, or disposed of, and to whom, and name of physician on whose certificate given. This would be attended with but little trouble, and might be required to be given under oath. Many articles require alcohol to dissolve them; this could be done by taking the article to the person appointed and having the alcohol put into the ingredients in his presence. Section fifth I would recommend to be altered, so that the fines should go one-half to the informer, and the other half into the treasury. I would recommend that the penalties be increased. If the indiscriminate sale of liquor be admitted an evil, no good citizen can wish to be engaged in it. Why should the majority suffer to benefit a few individuals?

"I have said more on this subject than I should have done, did I not fear an attempt will be made to break down the barriers raised by the early settlers of this land. Much of our prosperity and happiness as a community depends upon your action in this matter."

I am inclined to think that the governor was misinformed or mistaken in the statement that liquor had been manufactured in the settlement otherwise than by drugs and a composition called *rot-gut*, which there were men in the country base enough to produce. Had the governor been more energetic and taken the matter in hand, no manufacturing of liquors would have been allowed. He seems to have thrown himself back upon the faults of the law as an excuse for not seeing that it was executed as it should have been, and as it was executed in other places. Some of this drugged liquor was brought to Astoria by one George Geere, of Dr. White notoriety, and the citizens of Clatsop Plains being notified of the fact, came over prepared for a fight, and found Geere, with his liquors, his pistols, and a seven-shooter rifle. They took him and his pistols and rifle, also his two kegs, and several bottles of liquor. The liquor they turned out on the ground,—took Geere before Esquire Tibbetts, and gave him a jury trial before six men of his own choice, who found him guilty. He was fined one hundred dollars and costs of suit, which was all given, by unanimous consent, to the county. When such a man as Governor Abernethy could excuse himself from acting and enforcing a law, because he thought the distribution of the fines imposed made the officers and witnesses interested persons, it is not surprising that men of no principle should engage in destroying their fellow-men. The fact is, that the men whom the people had honored and trusted with their legal and executive duties were destitute of the firmness requisite to the position they occupied, with some few honorable exceptions. The people generally were in advance of their leaders in sustaining good and wholesome laws, hence but few cases of lawsuits or quarrels occurred.

We will now give what we conceive to be the cause of the failure of the law.

By a reference to the organization of the house in December, 1845, it will be seen that the Hudson's Bay Company was represented by Messrs. Dr. W. F. Tolmie, Chamberlain, McDonald, Newell, and Peers. The liquor interest was represented by Messrs. Boon, Hall, Hembree, Looney, Meek, Summers, Straight, T. Vault, Williams, and the Speaker. Six of the last-named representatives should have been fined for violations of the law on a small scale, and all of the first on a large scale, as connected more or less with the Hudson's Bay Company, and selling and giving to their men and Indians.

While the Hudson's Bay Company yielded a *quasi* assent to the organization, and had their representatives in the Legislature, they were using their influence to curtail the privileges of American citizens. They were ready to vote against the manufacture and sale of liquors, while they were constantly bringing it to the country in their ships, and distributing it to suit their trade.

The composition of the house was peculiarly American and antagonistic to the Hudson's Bay Company. Any measure that gave to the company any advantage, such as it was urged the prohibitory law did, could not stand. Hence the friends of prohibition had to yield the point, on the ground of self-defense for national rights, and not from a disposition to consider the law unjust or improper. In other words, they licensed and sustained a great evil, to combat a privilege of equal evil, claimed and used by a foreign monopoly in our midst.

When we take into account the facts as stated by the governor in his message, the actual condition of the country, the temporary nature of our government, and all the combinations that were forming at the time the license law was passed, I think all will join with me in condemning the course of the men who cursed the country with such a law. It is asserted that the organic law provided that the Legislature should *regulate* this traffic. Very true; which they did by placing it in the hands of the practicing physician, where it belongs, and nowhere else. But these wise Solons of 1846 came to the conclusion that three, two, or one hundred dollars was ample pay to the country for the loss of any man in it. That for three hundred dollars the whole country might be filled with poisonous *rot-gut*, and for two hundred the wholesale business might go on, while for one hundred the miserable victims of the business could be turned loose to degrade themselves and blight the hopes of kindred and friends. I can count a hundred victims who have lost one hundred dollars' worth of property for every dollar received by the Territory, besides their own lives, in consequence of this traffic. I can count five hundred families that have suffered poverty and want, insult and abuse, purely chargeable to this *regulating* law of these men.

We read in histories of the church, that the pope of Rome sold indulgences to commit certain sins which by the common law would be considered crimes, such as adultery, theft, and even murder. The price of the indulgence was according to the crime to be committed. This law proceeds upon the principle of the amount of profits in the business, while its nature and effect upon the community is lost sight of. Or, in other words, the government sells the indulgence to commit the crime proposed by the manufacturer or wholesale and retail dealer. While the former law admitted that liquor as a medicine might be useful, and placed it in the hands of the practicing physician, the license law puts each seller under a one thousand dollar bond to keep a quiet house. They were ready to license *hells* all over the land, provided the keepers would bind themselves not to violate the sanctity of the Sabbath. The morality and political economy of the business is forced to be satisfied with the amount paid as per law provided.

This act, as a matter of course, opened all the liquor shops of the Hudson's Bay Company and of all the unprincipled men in the country. To give a better idea of this liquor question, a letter of James Douglas, found in No. 10, volume 1, of the *Oregon Spectator*, June 11, 1846, is given. Mr. Parker, in his stump speech, alluded to the liquor law, and asserted that it was daily violated by the Hudson's Bay Company. Mr. Douglas attempts to refute the charge and sustain the law. The italics in the following letter are the author's:—

"Mr. Editor,—In Mr. Parker's address to the electors of Clackamas County, delivered at the meeting lately held in Oregon City, as reported in the *Spectator* of the 28th of May, I observe that he is pleased to point out Mr. Douglas, a judge of the County Court, who, he understood, was in the habit of selling ardent spirits. This may have suited Mr. Parker's purpose, while attempting to establish a position which appears to be a favorite with him, "that the oath of office binds a man to do just as he pleases!" As it can not, however, be supposed that I admire the mode of illustration he has chosen, and as I also happen to entertain a *very different opinion* touching the force and propriety of that oath, I hope it will not be considered a breach of courtesy on my part, to offer, through the medium of your respectable paper, a direct and *unqualified denial of this charge of rum-selling*, in the only sense it is plainly meant to be received, and can be considered at all applicable to the subject in question. As a particular favor, I ask Mr. Parker to bring forward a single proof in support of the assertion he has so wantonly advanced. I refer him to all his fellow-citizens. I ask him to search the country from one extremity to another, and to put the question to each individual member of the community with the absolute certainty that not one person will be found who ever purchased ardent spirits from Mr. Douglas. A stranger in the country, evidently unacquainted with its early history, Mr. Parker may not have been informed that the members of the Hudson's Bay Company have for many years past uniformly discouraged intemperance" (by a regular daily allowance of liquor to their men, as we shall see Mr. Douglas says) "by every means in their power, and have also made great and repeated pecuniary sacrifices to prevent the sale of ardent spirits in the country: an article, moreover, which forms no part of their trade, either with the white man or the Indian." (See Mr. Dunn's book, in which it is asserted the company sells to Indians, and Fitzgerald, page 162). "Mr. Parker does not indeed pretend to speak from his own personal experience of the fact, but on the authority of others; and should any doubt still linger in his mind with respect to the correctness of what I have just said, he may perhaps have no objection to seek other means of arriving at the truth; suppose, for instance, he was to try the experiment of negotiating a purchase, I venture to predict he would soon be convinced that Mr. Douglas is not in the habit of selling ardent spirits.

"But let us inquire a little further into this matter. What could have induced a person of character to hazard an observation in public, which, he must know, would, if false, be as openly exposed. Mr. Parker must have had some grounds for his assertion; he may possibly have heard, or he may have supposed that her Majesty's ship *Modeste* was daily receiving supplies at Fort Vancouver. If, with reference to these supplies, he had told his hearers that her Majesty's ship *Modeste*, now stationed at Fort Vancouver, had, with other supplies for ship use from the stores of the Hudson's Bay Company, received several casks of rum; or if, referring to the company's own ships, he had stated that a *small allowance of spirits is daily served out to the crews* of the company's vessels; and that other classes of the company's servants, according to long-accustomed usage, receive, on certain *rare occasions*, a similar indulgence, he would have told the *plain and simple truth*, and his statement would not this day have been called in question by me.

"These acts, which I fully admit, and would on no account attempt to conceal, can not by the fair rules of construction be considered as infringing upon any law recognized by the *compact which we have agreed to support*, in common with the other inhabitants of Oregon. [The same argument is used to justify Mr. Ogden in furnishing powder and arms to the Indians at the commencement of the Cayuse war.]

"The framers of these laws, with a degree of wisdom and foresight which does them honor, never entertained the idea that a person, in becoming a member of the compact, thereby relinquished his *distinctive national character*.

"On the contrary, *British subjects* and citizens of the United States, casting aside every shadow of illiberal prejudice, extended to each other the right hand of good-fellowship, for the purpose of mutual protection, to secure the peace and promote the prosperity of the country, until protected by their respective governments. The compact was formed and perfected upon that principle, and can rest with security upon no other foundation.

"We are pledged, and do faithfully intend to support the organic laws. They do not bind us to violate pre-existing engagements with our servants, nor to withhold from the officers of our government supplies of whatsoever kind the company's stores can provide. *In the high character of the latter we enjoy the fullest security against abuse to the detriment of the country.* With all other parties we have most rigidly, and shall continue to enforce the prohibitory statutes of Oregon. My wish in addressing you, Mr. Editor, is to set Mr. Parker right in respect to this matter of rum-selling, and the people may rest assured that if my wishes could influence the community, there would never be a drunkard in Oregon.

"James Douglas."

Mr. Parker's answer, which, like the letter of Mr. Douglas, is addressed to the *Spectator*, says:—

"Mr. Editor,—Our friend Mr. Douglas, in the *Spectator* of the 11th instant, denies, in the most unqualified terms, the charge of rum-selling at Vancouver, and challenges me to the proof of the assertion, by calling individually on all of our fellow-citizens for testimony; and no other alternative is left me but to proceed in accordance with his request; he will, I am sure, pardon me if I seek this among the highest authorities, and I will produce one at least whose veracity will not, I am sure, be called in question by our friend.

"When I, in my speech, adverted to the fact that rum was sold at Vancouver, contrary to law, the statement was based on the thousand-tongued rumor, and I so qualified my remarks. But in Mr. Douglas's confession, found in the paper alluded to, the matter of doubt is settled, and we are now furnished with the authority of no less a personage than Mr. Douglas himself. Hear his testimony. 'If,' says he, 'with reference to these supplies, he had told his hearers that her Majesty's ship *Modeste*, now stationed at Fort Vancouver, had, with other supplies for ship use from the stores of the Hudson's Bay Company, received *several casks* of rum; or if, referring to the company's own ships, he had stated that a *small allowance of spirits is daily served out to the crews* of the company's vessels; and that other classes of the company's servants, according to long-accustomed usage, receive, on certain rare occasions, a similar indulgence, he would have told the plain and simple truth,' etc.

"These facts, Mr. Douglas, who has charge of the trading-post at Vancouver, fully admits, and upon his testimony in the matter I place the most implicit confidence. It was not my intention to charge our friend with having kept a tippling-shop at Vancouver, and I wish to correct such, if any there are, who may have come to such a conclusion;

but I confess, I had not supposed that the law in relation to ardent spirits (and which may be found in the first number of the *Spectator*) had been so wantonly disregarded. We know, from personal observation, that rum in considerable quantities had found its way among our citizens from some quarter, and the disclosure here made furnishes a key to the mystery, and we are now broadly told that *casks of this article* have been furnished to her Majesty's officers stationed in Oregon, but that *in their high character we enjoy the fullest security against its abuse, etc.*

"And now, my dear sir, having heard much of the hollow and ceremonious professions and hypocritical grimaces of courts, and men in high places, and disgusted with every thing that savors of aristocratical or monarchical parade, and smitten with the love of republican simplicity and honesty, I can not admit that rank or men in high places are guaranteed against our laws, nor are they so framed as to justify such a conclusion. Raised as I was under these simple institutions, which tend to bring all on an equality, I can not perceive those *high guaranties* or *pledges* which are said to emanate from rank or station in high places in society. With us, men give pledges of honor and character, alone from their moral conduct; and the bacchanalian carousals (one was a most disgraceful drunken row kept up for several days by the officers of the *Modeste*, in honor of the Queen's birthday) which came off in the Tualatin Plains on Vancouver rum, last winter and spring, at the expense of the good morals of our farming community, gave me abundant and additional evidence to admire our simple and republican usages, while it serves as a moral worthy the consideration of a prince, or the strongest appendage of nobility. Our laws make no distinction in favor of the officers on board of her Majesty's ship *Modeste*, nor of the Hudson's Bay Company's servants. If their ships visit our ports, our laws will protect them, and, according to the usages of all nations, we expect them to submit to their provisions; but should these officers, through the plenitude of their power, determine to disregard our laws, it certainly could find no justification with one filling the high judicial station which Mr. Douglas occupies. He has sanctioned our law-making authority by accepting one of the highest judicial offices under our organization. According to his own confession, he has disregarded the law, not only only by giving in small quantities, but by selling ardent spirits by the cask; nor can he find justification by dealing it out under pre-existing contracts to the servants of the company. To admit that principle, dealers in this article would only be required, when the prohibitory law was about being passed, to contract for the supply of all their old customers, and thus defeat the object and intention of the law by a pre-existing contract. And as for the argument of long-existing usages, that pays the poorest tribute of all. Why, the very toper may plead his long indulgence in the use of this article, with as much propriety. I should not have noticed the subject again, but for my anxious desire that the matter should be fairly placed before the public:

"SAMUEL PARKER."

These two laws, and the two communications we have given, place the temperance question fully before the reader. The communication of Mr. Douglas shows the position and feelings of the English and the Hudson's Bay Company in relation to our laws, as also the liberty they claimed to violate them whenever it suited their interest or their convenience. Mr. Douglas says, "*with all other parties we have most rigidly, and shall continue to enforce the prohibitory statutes of Oregon.*" It also shows another fact. "*The Modeste, now stationed at Fort Vancouver,*" *is our* (the company's) protection, and you must not attempt to enforce a law upon English subjects, or English ships that enter the rivers or ports of the conntry. To say that many of us did not feel keenly this *taunt*, and almost despair of securing this vast country from the rapacious mouth of the crouching lion, whose drunken, beastly representatives were distributing their rum to every family that would receive them, would not be true.

When their representatives entered our legislative councils, the most stupid of its members understood their object. They wished to make laws for Americans. Their own people needed no laws, and no other government than such as was provided for them by the Hudson's Bay Company. The reader is already informed how those laws were enforced.

Dr. Tolmie, who at the present time (1870) stands at the head of the company in Vancouver Island and British Columbia, presented the following resolution to the house on the sixth day of the session, showing the true position of the English element:—

"*Resolved,* That the judiciary committee be discharged from further duty, as the present Legislature deems it inexpedient to organize the judiciary at the present time, in any manner different from the present organization."

By a reference to the journal of the house, we find Dr. Tolmie to be a member of the judiciary committee. Four days after, we find this same gentleman presenting another resolution:—

"That the Legislature deems it inexpedient, at the present time, to legalize the manufacture and sale of ardent spirits."

Yeas—Chamberlain, *McDonald*, and *Tolmie*—3. *Nays*—Boon, HALL, Hembree, LOUNSDALE, LOONEY, Meek, *Newell*, *Peers*, Summers, Straight, T. Vault, Williams and the Speaker—13. Hudson's Bay Company men in *italics*; doubtful, in SMALL CAPITALS.

On the motion of Newell to lay the bill to regulate the manufacture and sale of ardent spirits on the table, it stood: *Yeas*—Chamberlain, Hall, Lounsdale, Looney, McDonald, Newell, and Tolmie—7. *Nays*—Boon, Hembree, Meek, Summers, Straight, T. Vault, Williams, and the Speaker—8. Peers absent.

On the final vote to carry this bill over the veto of the governor, we find Hall, Lounsdale, and Looney changing their votes in favor of passing the bill over the veto, which is as follows:—

OREGON CITY, Dec. 17, 1846.

GENTLEMEN,—I return to your honorable body the act entitled "An Act to regulate the manufacture and sale of wine and distilled spirituous liquors," with my objections to the same.

Previous to our organization as a provisional government, public sentiment kept liquor from being manufactured or sold in this Territory. Heretofore, every act of the Legislature has been, as far as ardent spirits were concerned, prohibitory in character. The act lying before me is the first act that has in any manner attempted to legalize the manufacture and sale of ardent spirits. At the session of the Legislature in June, 1844, an act was passed entitled "An Act to prevent the introduction, sale, and distillation of ardent spirits in Oregon," and, as far as my knowledge extends, the passage of that act gave satisfaction to the great majority of the people throughout the Territory. At the session of December, 1845, several amendments were proposed to the old law, and passed. The new features given to the bill by those amendments did not accord with the views of the people; the insertion of the words "give" and "gift," in the first and second sections of the bill, they thought was taking away their rights, as it was considered that a man had a right to give away his property if he chose. There were several other objections to the bill, which I set forth to your honorable body in my message. I would therefore recommend that the amendments passed at the December session of 1845 be repealed; and that the law passed on the 24th of June, 1844, with such alterations as will make it agree with the organic law, if it does not agree with it, be again made the law of the land. It is said by many that the Legislature has no right to prohibit the introduction or sale of liquor, and this is probably the strongest argument used in defense of your bill. But do you not as effectually prohibit every person who has not the sum of one, two, or three hundred dollars to pay for his license, as does the law now on the statute-book? Are not your proposed fines and penalties as great or greater than those of the old law? Where, then, is the benefit to the people? There is no doubt in my mind, but that the law will be evaded as easily, and as often, under the new law, as it was under the old, and, in addition to this, there will be the legal manufacturers, importers, and sellers, who will be able, under the sanction of law, to scatter all the evils attendant upon the use of alcoholic drinks. We are in an Indian country; men will be found who will supply them with liquor as long as they have beaver, blankets, and horses to pay for it. If a quantity should be introduced among the Wallawallas, and other tribes in the upper country, who can foretell the consequences; there we have families exposed out, off from the protection of the settlements, and perhaps, at the first drunken frolic of the Indians in that region, they may be cut off from the face of the earth. But we need not go so far; we are exposed in every part of our frontier, and when difficulties once commence, we can not tell where they will cease.

It has been proved before the House of Commons that one-half of the insanity, two-thirds of the pauperism, and three-fourths of the crimes of Great Britain may be directly traced to the use of alcoholic drink. The testimony of our most eminent judges in the United States shows that the same proportion of crime is attributable to ardent spirits in that country. Statistics might be produced, showing the enormous evil and expense of an indiscriminate use of liquor.

As to revenue, the small amount received for licenses, instead of being a revenue, would be swallowed up in the expenses attending trials for crimes, etc., caused by the crime of these licenses.

But, leaving all other countries out of view, let us consider our own state. Surrounded by Indians, no military force to aid the executive and other officers in the discharge of their duties, not a solitary prison in the land, in which to confine offenders against the laws, and consequently no way of enforcing the penalties of the law, I think these things should call for calm and serious reflection, before passing your final vote on this bill. My opinion is, the people are opposed to legalizing the introduction and sale of liquor in this land. I may be mistaken, and therefore should be in favor of the old law, or something similar should be adopted, of referring the whole matter to the polls at the next general election. If the people say "No liquor," continue to prohibit; if they say, through the ballot-box, "We wish liquor," then let it come free, the same as dry-goods, or any other article imported or manufactured; but, until the people say they want it, I hope you will use your influence to keep it out of the Territory.

It is with regret that I return any bill unsigned, but I feel that we both have duties to perform, and when we think duty points out the way, I trust we may always be found willing to follow it.

GEO. ABERNETHY.

To the Hon. the Legislature of Oregon Territory.

On motion of Mr. Hall, the communication was laid on the table.

AFTERNOON SESSION.—At two o'clock the house met. A call of the house was made, and the sergeant-at-arms dispatched for the absent members, who, after a short absence, returned, and reported that the absentees had been notified, and were now present. Thereupon, the further call of the house was dispensed with.

The house then reconsidered the bill to regulate the manufacture and sale of ardent spirits, and, after some deliberation, the question being put upon the passage of the bill, it was decided affirmatively, by the following vote:—

Yeas—Messrs. Boon, Hall, Hembree, Lounsdale, Looney, Meek, Summers, Straight, T. Vault, Williams, and the Speaker—11.

Nays—Messrs. Chamberlain, McDonald, Newell, Peers, and Dr. W. F. Tolmie—5.

At St. Josephs, Elizabethtown, Iowa Point, Council Bluffs, and the Nishnabatona, were 271 wagons for Oregon and California. Allowing five to the wagon gives us about 1,355 souls that crossed the Missouri at these points. The quantity of loose stock was estimated at 5,000 head. From Independence, Missouri, for Oregon, 141 men, 71 women, 109 children, and 128 wagons. From Independence, for California, 98 men, 40 women, 57 children, 320 oxen, and 46 wagons. Total, 1,841 souls, as stated in Mr. Saxton's pamphlet, 1846. The larger portion of this immigration found their way into Oregon, notwithstanding the Hudson's Bay Company and Mr. Hastings did all they could to turn them to California. A statement by Mr. S. K. Barlow shows that 141 wagons, 1,559 head of horses, mules, and horned cattle, and some 15 head of sheep passed on his road; seven more teams passed after this report was made. Besides the number that came over the Mount Hood or Barlow road, there were some persons, with wagons, who attempted to come in on the Applegate route, and a number came down the Columbia River.

This year, on the 21st of February, the brig *Henry*, Captain Kilborn, started from Newburyport for Oregon, with eight passengers, including women and children; also the *Angelo*, Captain Hastings, from Boston, made the attempt, but failed. The brig *Henry* arrived late in 1846.

On Thursday, February 5, 1846, the first newspaper published on the Pacific coast was issued from the press of the Oregon Printing Association, at Oregon City. The originators of the Printing-Press Association were the same that started the Multnomah Circulating Library, the Wolf Association, and the provisional government, in 1842–3.

Constitution of the Oregon Printing Association.

PREAMBLE.—In order to promote science, temperance, morality, and general intelligence,—to establish a printing-press to publish a monthly, semi-monthly, or weekly paper in Oregon,—the undersigned do hereby associate ourselves into a body, to be governed by such rules and regulations as shall from time to time be adopted by a majority of the stockholders of this compact, in a regularly called and properly notified meeting.

Articles of Compact.

ARTICLE 1. This association shall be known by the name of the "Oregon Printing Association," and shall hold an annual meeting at Oregon City, on the first Tuesday of December of each year.

ART. 2. Its officers shall be a president, vice-president, secretary, treasurer, and a Board of three directors, who shall be elected annually by ballot, and shall hold their offices until their successors are elected.

ART. 3. It shall be the duty of the president to preside at all the meetings of the association, to sign all certificates of stock, and drafts upon the treasurer for the payment of funds, and to preside at the meetings of the Board of Directors.

ART. 4. It shall be the duty of the vice-president to perform the duties of the president in case of his absence, by death, or by removal from office.

ART. 5. * * * The secretary to attend, and keep a record of all the meetings of the association, and of the Board of Directors, and to publish the proceedings of the annual and special meetings of the association, and such portions of the proceedings of the Board of Directors as the Board shall direct from time to time; to give one month's notice of all special meetings of the association.

ART. 6. It shall be the duty of the treasurer to take charge of the funds of the association, and keep an account of all moneys received and disbursed, and pay out the same in accordance with drafts drawn on him by the president, and signed as per third article of this compact; to give such security to the president as shall be deemed sufficient by the Board of Directors for the faithful performance of his trust; to report the state of the treasury to the Board of Directors quarterly, and to pay over to his successor in office all funds of the association.

ART. 7. * * * The officers and Board of Directors to manage and superintend, or procure a suitable person to do so, the entire printing and publishing association; to employ all persons required in the printing or editorial departments of the press; to publish a full statement of their proceedings semi-annually; to draft and adopt such by-laws as may be deemed proper for their government, provided no by-law contravenes the spirit of these articles of compact; to declare a dividend of any profits arising from the printing establishment as often as they shall deem it expedient; to fill any vacancy that may occur in their number; three of whom shall constitute a quorum, and be competent to transact business.

ART. 8. *The press owned by or in connection with this association shall never be used by any party for the purpose of propagating sectarian principles or doctrines*, nor for the discussion of exclusive party politics.

ART. 9. The stock of this association shall consist of shares, of ten dollars each, payable in cash or its equivalent.

ART. 10. For every ten dollars paid to the treasurer of the association, the payer thereof shall receive a certificate for the same, signed by the president and countersigned by the secretary; and for every such certificate, the holder thereof, or his agent, on presenting to the Board of Directors satisfactory evidence that he is such, shall be entitled to one vote in all the annual and special meetings of this association; shall receive *pro rata* of all moneys that may accrue from the profits of the printing establishment, and be allowed to transfer his stock to any one, by certifying and indorsing his name upon the back of his certificate.

ART. 11. These articles, *except the 8th*, may be altered or amended at any annual or special meeting of the association, provided that the proposed amendment shall have been published in at least two numbers of the paper published by order of the association.

Officers of the Association,

W. G. T. VAULT, President.
J. W. NESMITH, Vice-President.
JOHN P. BROOKS, Secretary.
GEORGE ABERNETHY, Treasurer.
JOHN H. COUCH,
JOHN E. LONG,
R. NEWELL, } Directors.

The first editor of this paper was W. G. T. Vault. A man more unfit for the position could scarcely have been found in the country. He professed to have been an editor of a paper in Arkansas, and blew and swelled like the toad in the fable, and whined like a puppy when he gave his valedictory, in the fifth number of the *Spectator*. He says: "We have among us a class of *mongrels*, neither American nor anti-American, a kind of foreign, hypocritical go-betweens,—as we would say in the States, *fence men*,—whose public declarations are, 'All for the good of the public, and not a cent for self.' The political sentiments of the conductors were at variance with his." Mr. T. Vault was led to believe that Mr. Newell was his only friend, from the fact that he was absent from the meeting of the Board when his successor was appointed; and complains of Dr. Long and J. W. Nesmith. Newell and Long acted together. H. A. G. Lee, who succeeded T. Vault as editor, was far better qualified for the position, though he did not suit this same Board of Directors, as Newell was the maneuvering spirit. Lee was too strongly American in his sentiments, and too intelligent to be a dupe of the influence of which T. Vault complained.

Mr. Douglas declares the position of the English element in the tenth number of the *Spectator*. Mr. S. Parker answers him in the eleventh number; and Mr. Lee, in the fourteenth number, tenders his thanks to the Board for relieving him. The fifteenth, sixteenth, and seventeenth numbers, each "run itself," as the expression is.

On the eighteenth number, G. L. Curry, Esq., took charge, to the twenty-sixth number, which completed the first volume of the paper. He continued his editorial position till the twenty-fourth number of the second volume, when he brought his duties to a close by publishing a set of resolutions calculated to injure J. Q. Thornton, who had gone on to Washington to have a history of the country published, and, as was supposed, to secure the best federal appointments for himself and his friends. One-half of the legislators believing that unfair and improper means had been used by Mr. Thornton and his friends, the other half not caring to vote against Mr. Thornton's proceedings, being, perhaps, his real friends, the resolutions were lost by a tie vote. Mr. Curry, as editor of the *Spectator*, took sides against Mr. Thornton, and in favor of the objectionable resolutions, and published them under an editorial article, notwithstanding he had been requested, as he admits, not to publish them.

Judge A. E. Wait succeeded Mr. Curry in the editorial department of the paper, and, by a foolish, vacillating course, continued to hold his position so as to please the Hudson's Bay Company and the Roman Catholic and Methodist influences in the country. The paper, by this means, became of little value to its patrons and the country, and soon getting involved in its financial affairs, it was sold and lost financially to the original proprietors.

CHAPTER LIV.

The Whitman massacre.—Narratives of, by J. B. A. Brouillet and J. Ross Browne.—Extract from the New York *Evangelist.*—Statements of Father Brouillet criticised.—Testimony of John Kimzey.—Dr. Whitman at Umatilla.—Returns home.

We have before us two works purporting to give a true and authentic account of the Whitman massacre,—the one prepared by a Jesuit priest, J. B. A. Brouillet; the other by one J. Ross Browne, special agent of the United States revenue department. As this part of our history was written before that of J. Ross Browne (purporting to be an official report to the 35th Congress, 1st session, House of Representatives, Executive Document No. 38) came into our hands, it is proper that we should give this report a passing notice.

Mr. Browne, upon the second page of his report, says: "In view of the fact, however, that objections might be made to any testimony coming from the citizens of the Territory, and believing also that it is the duty of a public agent to present, as far as practicable, *unprejudiced statements*, I did not permit myself to be governed by any representations unsupported by *reliable* historical data."

One would naturally conclude, from such a statement, that a candid, unprejudiced, and truthful report would be given; but, to our astonishment, we find that fifty-three of the sixty-six pages of this official document are an exact copy of the Rev. J. B. A. Brouillet's work, thus indorsing, and placing in an official document, one of the most maliciously false and unreliable accounts that a prejudiced and deeply implicated sectarian could give, claiming such to be "*reliable historical data*,"—thus showing both his prejudice and ignorance in the conclusion he arrived at as to the causes of the Indian wars.

Had J. Ross Browne been willing to lay aside his unreasonable sectarian prejudice, and listen to the positive testimony then in the country, he could easily have learned who were the prime cause of all the Indian wars in it; or, had he made himself familiar (as he flippantly claims to have done) with the history of the English and American people, the policy of the English political and sectarian powers, and the commercial policy of the Hudson's Bay Company, he would have escaped the folly of placing in an official document such palpable errors, and showing such willful ignorance of the subject he was commissioned to investigate.

He says, on page 2, "It was a war of *destiny*,--bound to take place whenever the causes reached their *culminating point*." The "*destiny*" and culminating point of that war was fixed by the Hudson's Bay Company and the Jesuit priests, as also the second and third wars with the Indians that followed, as we shall show by positive testimony of witnesses who are unimpeachable.

Had J. Ross Browne carefully examined the tissue of statements prepared by Father Brouillet, he could have found statements like this on page 53 (38 of J. R. B.), "*I knew that the Indians were angry with all Americans;*" page 54 (39 of J. R. B.), "*All that I know is that the Indians say the order to kill Americans* has been sent in all directions."

There was but one party in the country that could issue such an order, which Brouillet well knew, and the testimony we shall give will prove.

On his third page, he says: "The same primary causes existed in every case,—encroachments of a superior upon an inferior race." He then refers to the agitation of the Oregon question in the Senate in 1840–41; to Mr. Thurston's course as a delegate; the treaties with the Indians, etc.,—showing conclusively the sources of his information, and his ignorance of the causes he professed to give a truthful and impartial account of,—barely alluding to the unwarranted assumptions of the British Hudson's Bay Company of an exclusive right to trade with the Indians. In fact, the whole report appears to be a studied effort to cover the prime causes of the difficulty, and of the Indian wars he was commissioned to investigate and report upon.

It is not surprising that with the foreign emissaries then in the country, and the stupid ignorance or malicious bigotry of the United States agent, that such reports should be made; but that the government should adopt, and act upon, or publish them, is indeed surprising; unless, as the history of the late rebellion shows, it was the design of those agents to involve the whole nation in an ultimate dismemberment, and distinct, separate nationalities, under the auspices of African, Indian, and religious slavery. We regret the necessity of prefacing a chapter in this work with so severe a stricture upon a government official, yet his report is so manifestly false and malicious, and without the evidence of truth or candor toward the Protestant missionaries, to whom is due, more than to any other influence, the settlement of the country by the American people,—that, in justice to them, and the truth of history, we can say no less, while we proceed with the account of the murder of Dr. Whitman and those at his station.

The necessity and importance of an extended and particular account becomes still more important from the fact that the Roman Jesuits in the country have succeeded in placing through such an agent their false account of the massacre in a permanent government document,—thus slandering not only the dead, but the living, whose duty it becomes to refute such vile slanders by publishing the whole truth in the case. Besides, the very Rev. J. B. A. Brouillet, in a second edition of his false and absurd production, refers to this report of J. R. Browne, as additional official evidence of the truth of his own false statements, previously made through such agents, and such men as Sir James Douglas,—compelling us, in vindicating the truth of history, to place before the reader more of the statements of parties implicated than was our original design.

Since this work has been in press, we have an article in the New York *Evangelist* of 6th of January, 1870, from the pen of Rev. Mr. Treat, D. D., containing a brief statement of the Whitman massacre, and the following as the result of the investigations as had in several religious bodies in Oregon; the conclusion is as follows:—

"It so happens, however, that men who are more competent to adjudicate the case have not hesitated to do so. The Congregational Association of Oregon adopted a report in June last, which condemns the 'prominent and absolute falsehoods' of Father Brouillet's pamphlet, and expresses the belief, 'from evidence, clear and sufficient to them, that the Roman Catholic priests did themselves instigate violence to the missions, resulting in massacre.' Similar action was taken by the Old School Presbytery, the Cumberland Presbytery, and the U. P. Presbytery. The Methodist Conference, composed of more than seventy preachers, and under the presidency of Bishop Kingsley, adopted a comprehensive and able report, which was published at Portland, September 25, 1869, in which the massacre at Wailatpu is declared to have been 'wholly unprovoked by Dr. Whitman or any other member of the mission,' and to have arisen from the policy of the Hudson's Bay Company 'to exclude American settlers,' and the 'efforts of Roman priests directed against the establishment of Protestantism in the country.' It is believed that the other evangelical denominations in Oregon have spoken with the same distinctness and the same confidence.

"Valuable testimony is borne to the character of the missionaries who survived Dr. Whitman, and who have been residents of Oregon to this day, as also to the fidelity and success of their labors, but there is not space for it in the present article. Suffice it to say, that, while the motives of Hon. J. Ross Browne, in appending Father Brouillet's pamphlet to his 'Letter,' and the reasons of the House of Representatives for publishing the same, are open to grave suspicion, facts and opinions have been elicited, which throw additional light upon the manifold bearings and uses of the missionary enterprise."

On page 40 of Rev. J. B. A. Brouillet's "Protestantism in Oregon," and page 33 of J. Ross Browne's report, we find, under date of September 5, 1847, that "the Right Rev. Bishop Blanchet arrived at old Fort Wallawalla (now called Wallula), where he was cordially received by Mr. McBean, clerk in charge of said fort. He was accompanied by the superior of Oblates and two other clergymen. He had the intention of remaining but a few days at the fort, for he knew that Tawatowe (or Young Chief), one of the Cayuse chiefs, had a house which he had designed for the Catholic missionaries, and he intended to go and occupy it without delay; but the absence of the Young Chief, who was hunting buffalo, created a difficulty in regard to the occupation of the house, and in consequence of it he had to wait longer than he wished."

The house here spoken of was erected during the summer of 1837, before any Catholic missionaries were thought of, at least among the Indians, or by the American missionaries, and it was late in the fall of 1838 that Revs. Blanchet and Demerse passed down the Columbia River. These first missionaries of the Society of Jesus, wishing to do Mr. P. C. Pambrun, then clerk of the post, a special favor, baptized the infant son of the Young Chief, for whose benefit and occupation, Mr. Pambrun said, the company had ordered that house to be built. If it was designed for these priests, who was the designer?

Mr. Brouillet, in his narrative, says:—

"On the 23d of September, Dr. Whitman, on his way from the Dalles, stopped at Fort Wallawalla. His countenance bore sufficient testimony to the agitation of his heart. He soon showed by his words that he was deeply wounded by the arrival of the bishop. 'I know very well,' said he, 'for what purpose you have come.' 'All is known,' replied the bishop; 'I come to labor for the conversion of the Indians, and even of Americans, if they are willing to listen to me.' The doctor then continued, in the same tone, to speak of many things. He attributed the coming of the bishop to the Young Chief's influence! made a furious charge against the Catholics, accusing them of having persecuted Protestants and even of having shed their blood wherever they had prevailed. He said he did not like Catholics * * * that he should oppose the missionaries to the extent of his power. * * * He spoke against the *Catholic Ladder!* * and said that he would cover it with blood, to show the persecution of Protestants by Catholics. He refused

* A picture explaining the principal points of Catholic faith.

to sell provisions to the bishop, and protested he would not assist the missionaries unless he saw them in starvation."

It is barely possible that Dr. Whitman said all that this priest says he did. In that case, did he forfeit his own and the lives of all that fell with him? This narrative of *Protestantism* reveals a dark page in our history,—one that should be thoroughly investigated as well as understood by all.

On the 24th page, 33d of Ross Browne's report, this priest says:—

"After such a manifestation of sentiment toward Catholics in general and priests in particular, the bishop was not astonished in hearing some hours after that Dr. Whitman, on leaving the fort, went to the lodge of Piopiomoxmox (Yellow Serpent); that he had spoken a great deal against the priests; that he had wished to prevail upon this chief to co-operate with him, in order that by the aid of his influence with the Cayuses, Des Chutes, and Dalles Indians, he might be enabled to excite these nations against them, etc."

That Dr. Whitman did as he is represented to have done no one acquainted with him will believe for a moment. But Bishop Blanchet's letter to Governor Abernethy is evidence conclusive that he and his priests had done exactly what they here say Dr. Whitman attempted to do.

"During the months of October and November," Brouillet says "the Doctor came to the fort several times to render his professional services to Mrs. Maxwell and Mr. Thomas McKay; he was a little more reserved than at the first interview, but it was always visible enough that the sight of the bishop and his clergy was far from being agreeable to him."

It will be remembered that Mr. Brouillet is giving this narrative and speaking of a man whose blood had been shed in the cause of "*Protestantism in Oregon*," as he calls the title of his work, which he is writing to correct the impression that he and his associates were in some way concerned in bringing it about. In his allusions and statements, he seems to be anxious to prove that Dr. Whitman and all Protestants and Americans in the country are guilty of the crime laid to the influence of the priests, and by giving these statements expects everybody will believe *them* to be wholly innocent. J. Ross Browne, in his report, 3d page, agrees with this priest, and refers to supposed transactions (*that did not occur*) in 1835. At that time there was not a band or tribe of Indians west of the Rocky Mountains but was ready to give land to any white man that would come and live in their country. This land question, as stated by Brouillet and Ross Browne, or the "*encroachments of a superior upon an inferior race*," had no part in the matter. It was a foreign national question, as we have already shown, and we now propose to quote these statements from his narrative, to show the intimate connection there was between the Jesuit priests, the Hudson's Bay Company, the Indians, and the Whitman massacre.

According to Brouillet, the bishop and his priests remained at Fort Wallawalla from the 5th of September till the 26th of October (fifty days), enjoying the hospitality of Mr. McBean, and seeing Dr. Whitman occasionally, till, on the 26th, the Young Chief arrived. "The bishop wished to know of him if he wanted a priest for him and his young men, telling him that he could only give him one for the whole nation, and if the Cayuses wished to avail themselves of his services *they would do well to come to an understanding together concerning* the location of the mission. The chief told the bishop he wished a priest, and that he could have his house and as much land as he wanted." So far this statement bears the natural impress of truth, but mark the words here put into the chief's mouth, "*but as a means of reuniting the Cayuses* who had been heretofore divided, and in order to *facilitate their religious instruction*, he suggested the idea of establishing the mission near Dr. Whitman's, at the camp of Tilokaikt."

The previous history of this chief, as given by Revs. Hines, Perkins, and Dr. White, all goes to prove that he never made such a suggestion, and no one acquainted with Indian character will believe for a moment that he did. But the suggestion was without doubt made to him to impress upon his mind the importance of uniting with other bands of his tribe to get rid of Dr. Whitman, as shown by this priest in the council that was held on the 4th of November, by special request of the bishop sent to Tilokaikt on the 29th October, purporting to be by request of the Young Chief. The dates show, as per Brouillet, that the Young Chief was with the bishop on the 26th; on the 29th the bishop sent for Tilokaikt; and on the 4th of November the council was held, "at the bishop's request," who opened the meeting in the fort. At this meeting the proposition is said to have been made to the bishop to give him Dr. Whitman's station, first driving him away. Says T. McKay, in his statement to acquit these priests, speaking of this meeting on the 4th of November: "One of the chiefs told the bishop that they would send the Doctor off very soon; they would give him his house if he wished. The bishop answered that he would not take the Doctor's house, that he did not wish him to send the Doctor away, and that there was *room enough for two missions*." This was, as understood by the Indians, "The bishop intends to have a place near Dr. Whitman's, and he wishes us to dispose of the Doctor in some way so that he can have a place where all the Cayuses can be instructed together in his religion."

In accordance with the understanding had with the bishop and Cayuses in this council on the 4th, this priest says (see p. 44 of Brouillet, 34 of J. R. Browne): "On the 8th of November I went by order of the bishop to Wailatpu to look at the land which Tilokaikt had offered; but he had changed his mind, and refused to show it to me, saying that it was too small. He told me that he had no place to give me but that of Dr. Whitman, whom he intended to send away. I declared to him a second time the same as the bishop had done at the meeting, that I would not have the place of Dr. Whitman. I then went immediately to the camp of Young Chief, to notify him that I would take his house, since I was unable to procure a place from Tilokaikt." He further says he returned to the fort on the 10th, and on the 11th, an associate, Rev. Mr. Rousseau, left with his men to repair the house, which was ready by the 26th, and on the 27th of November the bishop and his party started for the house, said to have been designed for them (of which there is no doubt). On their first arrival at Wallawalla, it would have been the wiser course for them to have accepted of it, instead of attempting, through the influence of the company, to get possession of Dr. Whitman's station, or the consent of the Indians, as they say they did, to locate near the station. But we have positive proof of the design of Mr. McBean, the agent of the company, and the bishop, as given in the testimony of Mr. John Kimzey.

He says: "On my way to this country with my family last fall (1847), I called at Fort Wallawalla to exchange my team and wagon for horses. There were at the fort two Roman Catholic priests. During my stay of about two days, Mr. McBean, in the presence of my wife, said, '*The fathers have offered to purchase Dr. Whitman's station*, but Dr. Whitman has refused to sell.' He said they had requested the Doctor to fix his own price and they would meet it, but the Doctor had refused to sell on any conditions. I asked him who he meant by the fathers? He said '*The holy fathers, the Catholic priests.*' He said the *holy fathers* were about to commence a mission at the mouth of the Umatilla,—one in the upper part of the Umatilla, one near Dr. Whitman's station, *if they could not get hold of the station*, one in several other places which I can not name. They hired Mr. Marsh, whose tools I brought, to do off a room for the priests at the fort. He said, '*Dr. Whitman had better leave the country or the Indians would kill him; we are determined to have his station.*' He further said, 'Mr. Spalding will also have to leave this country soon.' As I was about leaving, Mr. McBean said: 'If you could pass as an Englishman, the Indians would not injure you; if they do disturb you, show them the horses and the marks, and they will know my horses; show them by signs that you are from the fort, and they will let you pass.' The Indians noticed the marks on the horses and did not disturb me.

"JOHN KIMZEY."

"Subscribed and sworn to before me, at my office in Tualatin Plains [now Washington County], this 28th day of August, 1848.

"DAVID T. LENOX, Justice of the Peace."

This is fully confirmed by the oath of R. S. Wilcox, as having heard the statement from Mr. Kimzey the night after he left the fort, in camp at the mouth of the Umatilla, before the same justice of the peace. Mr. Wilcox says Mr. Kimzey was much alarmed, and really believed that it was the design of the priests' party to kill Dr. Whitman and drive the American missionaries out of the country. His reply was, "The Catholics have not got that station yet."

Had we not the best English testimony, Fitzgerald's, and the statements of P. J. De Smet and Hoikin in their letters to their missionary society in Brussels, to show the connection of the Hudson's Bay Company with this transaction, the facts above stated would fasten the conviction of a strong and outspoken determination to overthrow the Protestant missions. It will be remembered that these threats and efforts to get rid of Dr. Whitman were made before the appearance of any sickness or measles among the Cayuses.

Mr. Brouillet, on the 84th page of his narrative, says "But I affirm that such a demand has never been made to Dr. Whitman by any one of us." We are not disposed to dispute Mr. Brouillet's affirmation, be it true or false. The truth is all we seek to know.

The reader will not be particularly interested in the long details of statements made by this priest to show that they had no part in bringing about the destruction of the Protestant missions and the Whitman massacre. Mr. McBean and Sir James Douglas have written extensively, together with P. H. Burnett, Esq., and this Rev. Vicar-General Brouillet, to show that nobody is responsible for that crime but the missionaries who were murdered and the Indians, while Rev. Messrs. Griffin and Spalding have attempted to fasten the whole crime upon the Roman priests alone. It appears from Mr. Spalding's account that he met Mr. Brouillet and the bishop at Wallawalla on the 26th of November, and had a sectarian discussion with them, which he thought was friendly, yet from the fact that this priest barely alludes to the visit, and not a word of the discussion is mentioned, we infer that Mr. Spalding had the best of the argument, and that he was entirely mistaken as to the friendly manner in which they could conduct their missions in the same section of country. We will not attempt to reconcile the conflicting statements of these missionary parties, but will collect the most reliable facts and particulars of the tragic events in which these parties and the whole country became so deeply involved,—a part of them so strongly implicated.

That the massacre was expected to take place in a short time, and that all the Americans at the station, and all in any way connected with, or favoring, the Protestant missions and American settlements in the country, were to be included in the ultimate overthrow of those upper, or middle Oregon missions, there can be no doubt; as shown in the quotations we have given from our English Hudson's Bay Company's historian and Sir Edward Belcher, and the efforts of the company to colonize the country with English subjects from Red River, instead of encouraging them to come direct from England.

It appears from the dates and accounts we have, that Dr. Whitman was sent for to visit Five Crow's lodge on the Umatilla, not far from the house to be occupied by the bishop and his priests; that Mr. Spalding accompanied the doctor to visit some of the Protestant Indians in that vicinity; that the same day (the 27th of November), the bishop and his priests started from Wallawalla to go to their station and occupy the house of Young Chief. They arrived at their places and learned that Dr. Whitman and Mr. Spalding were in the neighborhood. On the next day, Sunday, 28th, Dr. Whitman made a short call on them, and hastened home to attend on the sick about his place. While at the lodge of a French half-breed named Nicholas Finlay, the Indians were holding a council, to decide and arrange the preliminaries of the massacre, with Joe Lewis, a Canadian-Indian, and Joe Stanfield, a Frenchman. Of this last-named man, Mr. Brouillet says: "As to Joseph Stanfield, I admit that he was born and has been educated a Catholic." He lays great stress on the fact that this fellow had been tried and acquitted. He says: "Why should we pretend now to be more enlightened and wiser than the tribunals have been, and judge him more severely than they have done."

Dr. Whitman arrived at his station about twelve o'clock at night, attended upon the sick, and retired. That night an Indian had died. In the morning, the Doctor, as usual, had a coffin and a winding-sheet prepared, and assisted the friends in burying their dead. He observed, on returning to the house, that but two or three attended at the grave. As he returned, great numbers of Indians were seen gathering about the station; but an ox had been killed, and was being dressed, which was supposed to be the cause, as the Indians on such occasions always collected in great numbers, and often from a distance.

CHAPTER LV.

Occupations of the victims immediately before the massacre.—Description of the mission buildings.—The Doctor called into the kitchen to be murdered.—Joe Lewis, the leader in the massacre.—The scene outside.—The Doctor's house plundered.—Mrs. Whitman shot.—Brutalities to the dead and dying.—Escape of some and murder of others.—Safety of the French Papists and the servants of the Hudson's Bay Company.—Fate of Joe Lewis.

JOSEPH STANFIELD had brought in the ox from the plains, and it had been shot by Francis Sager. Messrs. Kimball, Canfield, and Hoffman were dressing it between the two houses; Mr. Sanders was in the school, which he had just called in for the afternoon; Mr. Marsh was grinding at the mill; Mr. Gillan was on his tailor's bench in the large adobe house, a short distance from the doctor's; Mr. Hall was at work laying a floor to a room adjoining the Doctor's house; Mr. Rogers was in the garden; Mr. Osborn and family were in the Indian room adjoining the Doctor's sitting-room; young Mr. Sales was lying sick in the family of Mr. Canfield, who was living in the blacksmith shop; young Mr. Bewley was sick in the Doctor's house; John Sager was sitting in the kitchen but partially recovered from the measles; the Doctor and Mrs. Whitman, with their three sick children, and Mrs. Osborn and her sick child, were in the dining or sitting room.

The mission buildings occupied a triangular space of ground fronting the north in a straight line, about four hundred feet in length. The Doctor's house, standing on the west end, and fronting west, was 18 × 62 feet, adobe walls; library and bedroom on south end; dining and sitting room in the middle, 18 × 24; Indian room on north end, 18 × 26; kitchen on the east side of the house, 18 × 26, fireplace in the middle, and bedroom in rear; schoolroom joining on the east of the kitchen, 18 × 30; blacksmith shop, 150 feet east; the house called the mansion on the east end of the angle, 32 × 40 feet, one and a half stories; the mill, made of wood, standing upon the old site, about four hundred feet from either house. The east and south space of ground was protected by the mill-pond and Wallawalla Creek—north front by a ditch that discharged the waste water from the mill, and served to irrigate the farm in front of the Doctor's house, which overlooked the whole. To the north and east is a high knoll, less than one-fourth of a mile distant; and directly to the north, three-fourths of a mile distant, is Mill

Creek. In a military or defensive question, the premises could be easily protected from small-arms or cavalry.

While the Doctor was sitting with his family as above stated, several Indians, who had come into the kitchen, came to the door leading to the dining-room, and requested him to come into the kitchen. He did so, taking his bible in his hand, in which he was reading, and shut the door after him. Edward Sager sat down by his side and asked for medicine. Tilokaikt commenced a conversation with him, when Tamsaky, an Indian, called the Murderer, and the one that told the bishop at Wallawalla he would give him the Doctor's station, came behind him, and, drawing a pipe tomahawk from under his blanket, struck the Doctor on the back of his head. The first blow stunned him and his head fell upon his breast, but the second blow followed instantly upon the top of his head, and brought him senseless but not lifeless to the floor.

John Sager, rising up, attempted to draw a pistol; the Indians before him rushed to the door by which they had entered, crying out, "He will shoot us;" but those behind seized his arms and threw him upon the floor; at the same time he received shots from several short Hudson's Bay muskets, which had been concealed under their blankets. He was cut and gashed terribly with knives, his throat was cut, and a woolen tippet stuffed into it,—still he lingered. In the struggle, two Indians were wounded, one in the foot, the other in the hand, by each other.

Mrs. Whitman, as soon as the tumult commenced, overhearing and judging the cause, began in agony to stamp upon the floor and wring her hands, crying out, "Oh, the Indians! the Indians! That Joe (referring to Joe Lewis) has done it all!" Mrs. Osborn stepped into the Indian room with her child, and in a short time Mr. Osborn and family were secreted under the floor.

Without coming into the other rooms, the Indians left the kitchen, to aid in the dreadful destruction without. At this moment Mrs. Hays ran in from the mansion-house, and, with her assistance, Mrs. Whitman drew her dying husband into the dining-room, and placed his mangled, bleeding head upon a pillow, and did all her frightful situation would allow to stay the blood and revive him, but to no purpose. The dreadful work was done. To every question that was put to him, he would simply reply, "No," in a low whisper. After receiving the first blow, he was probably insensible.

About this time, Mr. Kimball ran into the room through the kitchen, and rushed up-stairs with a broken arm hanging by his side. He was immediately followed by Mr. Rogers, who, in addition to a wounded arm, was tomahawked in the side of the head and covered with blood. He assisted Mrs. Whitman in making fast all the doors, and in removing the sick children up-stairs.

Joe Lewis, a Roman Catholic Indian, is asserted, by those who have traced his course, to have come from Canada with the party of priests and French that crossed the plains in 1847, and by whom it is affirmed the measles were brought into the immigrant trains that year. The priests' party brought him to Boise, and there left him to find his way to Dr. Whitman's. He attempted to make arrangements with an immigrant family to come to the Wallamet, but was afterward furnished with a horse and supplies, and traveled with a Cayuse Indian. While at Boise, making his arrangements with the immigrant family, he told them there was going to be a *great overturn at Dr. Whitman's and in the Wallamet.* How or what the overturn was to be, the party did not learn, but supposed it might be from immigration or some change in the government of the country. He arrived at Dr. Whitman's apparently destitute of clothes and shoes. He made himself at home at once, as he could speak English, French, and a little Nez Percé. He had been at the station but a few days, before the Doctor and the two Sager boys learned that he was making disturbance among the Indians. The Doctor finding some immigrant families who wanted a teamster, furnished him with shoes and a shirt, and got him to go with them. He was gone three days, and the second night ran away from the man he had agreed to go with, and returned about the station. He spent most of his time in the lodge of Nicholas Finlay, the common resort of Stanfield and the Indians engaged in the scenes we are relating; and was the leader in the whole affair. He was seen several times approaching the windows with a gun, but when Mrs. Whitman would ask, "Joe, what do you want?" he would run away.

The scene outside, by this time, had attained the summit of its fury. The screams of the fleeing women and children, the groans and struggles of the falling, dying victims, the roar of musketry, the whistling of balls, the blows of the war-club, the smoke of powder, the furious riding of naked, painted Indians, the unearthly yells of infuriated savages, self-maddened, like tigers, by the smell of human blood,—the legitimate fruits of Romish superstitions faithfully implanted in the savage mind.

Mrs. Whitman remained by the side of her husband, who was pale and gasping in death. Two Americans were overpowered and cut down by the crowd under her window, which drew her attention, and gave an opportunity for an Indian, that had always been treated kindly by her, to level his gun. His victim received the ball, through the window, in her right breast, and fell, uttering a single groan. In a few moments she revived, rose and went to the settee, and kneeling in prayer was heard to pray for their adopted children (the Sager family, who had lost father and mother in crossing the plains, now again to be left orphans), and for her aged father and mother in the States, that they might be sustained under this terrible shock (made a thousand-fold more so by the infamous account of it given by Sir James Douglas in his Sandwich Islands letter), which the news of her fate must occasion. Soon after this she was helped into the chamber, where were now collected Mrs. Whitman, Mrs. Hays, Miss Bewley, Catharine Sager, Messrs. Kimball and Rogers, and the three sick children.

They had scarcely gained this temporary retreat, when the crash of windows and doors, and the deafening war-whoop, tore the last hope from their fainting hearts. The rooms below were plundered of their property,—the furniture dashed to pieces and cast out. Joe Lewis was seen to be among the foremost to dash in the windows and bring out the goods. Here a deed was perpetrated similar to that of the refined and Christian Catholic people of Burgos, in Spain, when they murdered and cut up their governor for attempting to obey the law and take an invoice of church property.

The Cayuse Indian Tilokaikt went into the room where the Doctor lay yet breathing, and with his hatchet deliberately chopped his face terribly to pieces, but left him still alive. Some Indian, also, cut the face of John Sager while he was yet alive.

About this time, Joe Lewis went into the schoolroom and sought out the children, who were hid in the upper loft, and brought them into the kitchen to be shot. As Francis passed by his mangled, gasping brother, he stooped and took the woolen tippet from the gash in his throat, when John attempted to speak, but immediately expired. Upon this, Francis turned to his sister and said, "I shall soon follow my brother." The children were kept in this painful position for some time. Eliza Spalding was among them, and understood every word spoken by the Indians, who, having finished their terrible slaughter without, were filling the room and the doorways, with their guns pointed at the heads and hearts of the children, constantly yelling, "*Shall we shoot?*" Eliza says her blood became cold, and she could not stand, but leaned over upon the sink, covering her face with her apron, that she might not see them shoot her. From this place they were removed out of the door by the side of the Indian room, just before Mrs. Whitman was brought out to be shot.

Immediately after breaking into the house, the Indians called to Mrs. Whitman and Mr. Rogers to come down, and on receiving no answer, Tamsaky (the Indian who was the most anxious to have the bishop and his priests take the Doctor's place), started to go up-stairs, but discovering the end of an old gun (placed there by Miss Bewley), he desisted, and entered into conversation with those above. He urged them to come down, assuring them that no one should hurt them. Mrs. Whitman told him she was shot, and had not strength to come down, besides she feared they would kill her. Tamsaky expressed much sorrow on learning that Mrs. Whitman was wounded, and promised that no one should be hurt if they would come down. Mrs. Whitman replied, "If you are my friend, come up and see me." He objected, and said there were Americans hid in the chamber with arms to kill him. Mr. Rogers, standing at the head of the stairs, assured him there were none, and very soon he went up and remained some time, apparently sympathizing with the sufferers, assuring them that he was sorry for what had taken place, and urged Mrs. Whitman to come down and be taken over to the other house where the families were, intimating that the young men might destroy the house in the night. About this time the cry was heard from Joe Lewis, "We will now burn."

Mrs. Whitman was assisted down by Mr. Rogers and Mrs. Hays; on reaching the lower room, becoming faint, she was laid upon a settee, and taken through the kitchen over the dead body of young Sager, and through a crowd of Indians. As the settee passed out of the door, the word was given by the chief not to shoot the children. At this moment Mr. Rogers discovered their treachery, and had only time to drop the settee, raise his hands and exclaim, "O my God!" when a volley of guns was fired from within and without the house, part at Mrs. Whitman and part at himself. He fell upon his face, pierced with many balls.

An Indian seized Francis Sager from among the children, and Joe Lewis drew his pistol, and with the expression, "*You bad boy,*" shot him. All manner of Indian brutality and insult were offered to the mangled bodies while they lay groaning and dying, till night closed upon the scene, and the Indians retired to Finlay's and Tilokaikt's lodges to consult as to further outrage upon the still living and helpless victims.

The Canadian-Indian, Joe Lewis, was as active in abusing the helpless girls as he had been in selecting the children of the Hudson's Bay Company's servants to be protected and sent away from such as were to be abused and slaughtered.

Mr. Kimball, the three sick children, and Catharine Sager remained in the chamber all night. Mr. Osborn lay under the floor of the Indian room till the Indians retired. He then made his escape to the fort at Wallawalla, with his family. The three men at the beef found themselves surrounded, and in the midst of a volley of balls from pistols and guns pointed at them. All three were wounded, but neither fell. They fled as best they could: Mr. Kimball to the house; Mr. Canfield to the blacksmith shop, and thence to the mansion, where he hid himself, and remained till night; then fled and reached Lapwai before Mr. Spalding did. Mr. Hall wrenched a gun, which had missed fire, from an Indian's hand, and ran for the bushes; reached the fort next morning; was put across the Columbia River by Mr. McBean's order; and was lost,—starved to death, or murdered by the Indians, we know not which. Mr. Gillan was shot upon his bench. Mr. Marsh was shot at the mill; ran a short distance toward the Doctor's house and fell. Mr. Saunders, hearing the guns, rushed to the door of the schoolroom, where he was seized by several Indians, who threw him upon the ground amid a shower of balls and tomahawks. Being a strong and active man, he rose, though wounded, and ran some rods, but was overtaken, surrounded, and cut down. Mr. Hoffman was cut down, after fighting desperately with a knife, his body cut open, and his heart and liver torn out.

In the midst of all this fury and savage shedding of blood, *no children or servants of the Hudson's Bay Company, or Roman Catholics, or such as professed friendship for that faith*, were harmed in the least. Finlay, a half-breed of the company's, who had formerly kept its horses, was stopping close to the station, assisting and counseling with the Indians; Joe Lewis selected the two Manson boys and a half-breed Spanish boy the Doctor had raised, and arranged to send them to the fort. Whoever this Indian was, or wherever he was from, he seems to have understood and acted fully and faithfully his part in the "*great overturn*" that he said, while at Boise, was to take place at that station and in the lower country. How he came to know there was to be any change or overturn is yet a secret only to be guessed at. Mr. McBean says he returned to Boise and Fort Hall; and Mr. McDonald, that he killed the guide to a company of United States troops in the mountains, and was himself shot.

CHAPTER LVI.

Comments on Vicar-General Brouillet's arguments against the Whitman massacre being the act of Catholics.—Joe Stanfield: Brouillet's story in his favor.—Murders on the second day.—Deposition of Daniel Young.—More murders.

Vicar-General Brouillet, in his narrative of "Protestantism in Oregon," says: "I could admit that *Joseph Lewis*, *Joseph Stanfield*, and *Nicholas Finlay*, who may have been seen plundering" (as proved on the trial of Stanfield), "*were Catholics*, without injuring in the least the cause of Catholicism; because, as in good reasoning" (Roman Catholic, of course), "it is never allowed to conclude from one particularity to another particularity, nor to a generality; in like manner, from the guilt of three Catholics it can not be reasonably concluded that other Catholics are guilty, nor, *a fortiori*, that all Catholics are guilty and Catholicism favorable to the guilt."

No man, set of men, or sect, not interested in the result of a measure or a crime, will ever use an argument like the one we have quoted from this priest. Dr. Whitman and those about his station had been slaughtered in the most brutal and cowardly manner, by a band of Indians that this priest, his bishop, and associates, backed by the consent and influence of the Hudson's Bay Company, had brought about through the direct influence of these three men: all of whom knew, and consulted with the Indians as to the commission of the crime. And we have the strongest reason to believe that this priest and his party were, by their conversation, instructions, and direct teachings, adding their influence and approval to that horrid transaction. Besides, when the crime is committed, we find this same band of *fur traders and priests protecting*, *shielding*, *advising*, *and assisting the murderers* to the utmost of their power and influence, both in the country and in their foreign correspondence. If such facts do not implicate a party, we ask what will? The very book from which we are quoting, containing 108 pages, has not a single sentence condemning the course or crime of these men, but every page contains some statement condemning Spalding, Whitman, or some American supposed to belong to, or in favor of, the American settlements or missions.

But let us return to further particulars of this Whitman massacre. We have gathered up the statements and facts on both sides of this question, and with our own knowledge, previous to and since its occurrence, we write with assurance, if not with the best judgment in selecting the facts and evidence to place the truth before the public.

We were in the midst of describing that horrible scene of savage blood and carnage, when we stopped for a moment to inquire after the character of three of the prominent actors, in fact, the leaders in the tragedy.

Brouillet tells us (on page 89 of his narrative, page 56 of Ross Browne) in extenuation of the guilt of Stanfield, that "the following circumstance, if true, speaks very highly in his favor, and shows that if he has at any time forgotten the good principles he had received in his infancy, once, at least, those principles prompted him to an heroic action. It was on the morning of the day that followed the massacre. There were several Indians scattered in the neighborhood of the mission buildings, but especially a crowd of Indian women was standing near the door of the house in which all the white women and children were living. Stanfield, being then at a short distance from the house, Tilokaikt, the chief of the place, came up and asked him if he had something in the house. 'Yes,' said Stanfield, 'I have all my things there.' 'Take them away,' said the Indian to him. 'Why should I take them away? they are well there.' 'Take them off,' he insisted, a second time. 'But I have not only my things there; I have also my wife and children.' 'Yes,' replied Tilokaikt, who appeared a little surprised, 'you have a wife and children in the house! Will you take them off?' 'No,' replied Stanfield, 'I will not take them away, and I will go and stay myself in the house. I see that you have bad designs; you intend to kill the women and children; well, you will kill me with them. Are you not ashamed? Are you not satisfied with what you have done? Do you want still to kill poor innocent creatures that have never done you any harm?' 'I am ashamed,' replied Tilokaikt, after a moment's hesitation. 'It is true, those women and children do not deserve death; they did not harm us; they shall not die.' And, turning to the Indian women who were standing near the door of the house waiting with a visible impatience for the order to enter and slaughter the people inside, he ordered them to go off. The Indian women then became enraged, and, showing them the knives that they took from beneath their blankets, they insulted him in many different ways, calling him *a coward, a woman who would consent to be governed by a Frenchman;* and they retired, apparently in great anger for not having been allowed to imbrue their hands in the blood of new victims. The above circumstance was related at Fort Wallawalla to Mr. Ogden, by Stanfield himself, under great emotion, and in presence of the widows, none of whom contradicted him. An action of that nature, if it took place, would be, of itself, *sufficient to redeem a great many faults.*"

We do not wish to question any good act this Frenchman may have done; but the guilt of knowing that crime was to be committed, and that the Americans were to be killed around him like the ox he had brought to the slaughter, which he knew was to be the signal for its commencement; and the manner he and his two associates conducted themselves on the ground; *the influence he had* to stop the massacre at any time, and his *robbing the widows and orphans* in the midst of the slaughter;—these make up a complication of crime that none but the vilest will attempt to excuse.

On the 30th of November, Mr. Kimball and Mr. Young, a young man from the saw-mill, were killed. Mr. Kimball, in attempting to go from his concealment in the chamber for water for himself and the sick children, was shot by a young Indian, who claimed his eldest daughter for a wife as his lawful pay for killing her father.

We will now give an original deposition which explains the killing of Mr. Young, and also of two other young men, who escaped the first and second, and became victims of the third more brutal slaughter.

Deposition of Mr. Daniel Young relative to the Wailatpu Massacre.

QUESTION.—When, and in what manner, did you learn of the massacre?

ANSWER.—I was residing with my father's family at Dr. Whitman's saw-mill, about twenty miles from Wailatpu, where we had gone for the winter. My brother, a young man about twenty-four years of age, and about two years older than myself, had gone down to the station, the Tuesday before, with a load of lumber, and for provisions, and was expecting to return about the last of the week. Joseph Smith and family were also living at the saw-mill, except his oldest daughter, who was at the station. His family was out of flour and meat, and ours was now out of meat. On Saturday evening, he proposed to me to go down the next day for provisions. I did not wish to go down; told him if he wanted provisions he could go. He said if he had a horse he would go. We offered him a horse. He still urged me to go, as there was no one, he said, to stay with his family. I went down on horseback on the Sabbath, being the next Sabbath after the massacre. I did not go to the place till about an hour after dark, and learned nothing of the massacre till after I had got into the house. In the room where I expected to find my brother, I found them eating supper, with several Indians in the room. At the table was Mrs. Hays, and Joseph Stanfield, and Mrs. Hall, with the remnant of her family.

About a couple of minutes after I went in, Joseph Stanfield left the table and went out of the house (this was some time previous to the rest leaving the table), and was gone for about three hours, I knew not where; but after he returned, he said he had started to go to Nicholas Finlay's, a half-breed's lodge, but had got lost. Nicholas had come in about half an hour before Stanfield returned. In the mean time I had learned from the Indian Beardy, through Eliza Spalding (his interpreter), of the massacre. This was in short sentences and much confused. Beardy said, however, that the Doctor was his friend, and he did not know of it until a good many had been killed, and he was sorry for what had taken place; he said the Indians said the Doctor was poisoning them, and that was the reason they did it, *but he* (Beardy) *did not believe it.* That he was there to protect the women and children, and no more should be killed. During the evening I also learned of the number that had been killed, and of those who had escaped from the place; but it was not known what had become of them.

I was informed by Stanfield that my brother had met an Indian who had told him to go back and stay for a week, but another Indian told him he could safely go on for provisions, and that he would go with him. He went on to within half a mile of the mission. The Indians were said to have gone thus far with him. Stanfield said he there found him dead, shot through the head near one eye, and there he buried him. *Stanfield said* also that evening that the Doctor was poisoning the Indians, which had caused the massacre; that Joe Lewis had heard from an adjoining room one night the Doctor and Mrs. Whitman talking of poisoning them, and that the Doctor had said it was best to destroy them by degrees, but that Mrs. Whitman said it was best to do it at once, and they would be rid of them, and have all their land and horses as their own; and that he (Joe Lewis) had told the Indians this before the massacre.

Stanfield also asked me if I had heard of his being married. I told him I had heard from my brother that he was going to take Mrs. Hays for a wife. He said: "We are married, but have not yet slept together." I said: "Yes, I understand, you pretend to be married." He said: "We are married; that is enough." I thought it strange why he was saved unless he was a Catholic, and during the evening took an occasion, when I thought he would not suspect my object, to ask Stanfield whether he was a Catholic? He said, "*I pass for one.*"

I slept with Stanfield that night; did not retire till late. Next morning, Crockett Bewley, a young man about twenty-one or twenty-two, I should think, who was sick at the time of the first massacre, and whose clothes had been stolen (by Stanfield), came into the room wrapped in a blanket or a quilt. *Bewley seemed to speak of the Doctor's poisoning the Indians as something commonly reported among them* as the cause of the massacre, but said he did not believe any thing of it, *but he believed Joe Lewis was one of the leaders*, and *the Catholic priests were the cause of it.* Stanfield replied, "*You need not believe any such thing, and you had better not let the Indians hear you say that,*" and spoke in a voice as though *he was somewhat angry.* Soon after this, Bewley left the room; Stanfield turned to me and said: "*He had better be careful how he talks; if the Indians get hold of it the Catholics may hear of it.*" As soon as I could do it without being suspected, I sought an opportunity to caution Bewley about the danger I thought he was running in speaking thus in the presence of Stanfield, and asked him if he did not know of Stanfield being a Catholic? He said he did not. I told him he might have known it from the fact of most French being Catholics. He replied he did not know of the French being Catholics more than any other people. I told him to be cautious hereafter how he spoke, and he said he would.

Soon after the conversation with Bewley, I told Stanfield I must return home; he said I must not, the Indian chiefs would be there after a while and would tell me what I must do; said he did not think I could get off till the next day.

We now commenced making a coffin for one of the Sager children that had died the night before. Soon after, the chief Tilokaikt came. He told me I could not go back till the next day, that he would then send two Indians back with me. I told Stanfield, in the chief's presence, that I had told my folks I should be back on Monday if I came at all. Stanfield told me in reply, that the chief says, "Then you may go;" Stanfield also said, "The chief says tell them all to come down and bring every thing down that is up there; we want them to come down and take care of the families and tend the mill. Tell them, '*Don't undertake to run away; if you do, you will be sure to be killed;*' not be afraid, for they shall not be hurt."

The chief had now done talking. Stanfield now told me to caution them, our people, at the saw-mill, as to *what they should say;* if they said any thing on the subject, "say that the Doctor was a bad man, and was poisoning the Indians." He had also before that told me the same. I got a piece of meat and asked for some salt, but he said there was none about the house; afterward I found this was not the case. I then returned home, and informed our people as to what had taken place, and my father's first reply was, "*The Catholics are at the bottom of it.*" Mr. Smith admitted it, but said, immediately, we must all become Catholics for our safety, and before we left the saw-mill, and afterward, he said he believed the Doctor was poisoning, and believed it from what Joe Stanfield had told him before about the Doctor's misusing the half-breeds and children at his mission. The next day, Tuesday, we went down to the mission, and arrived after dark; found the young men, Bewley and Amos Sales, who were sick at the time of the first massacre, were both killed, and their bodies were lying outside of the door near the house where they lay during the night, and Stanfield said he could not bury them until he got the permission of the Indians. The next day we helped to bury them.

Here I would say that the two Indians the chief wished to send with me, as he said, to see us safe down, as Stanfield interpreted to me at the time, were the chief's sons, and he wished me to wait because Edward, Tilokaikt's son, had gone to the Umatilla to the *great chief*, to see what to do with the two young men who were sick. This, Stanfield told me, was the business which Edward Tilokaikt had gone for, and he would not get back so as to go with me that day. Three Indians, however, arrived within an hour after I got to the saw-mill, viz., Clark Tilokaikt, Stikas and one whose name I never knew, and came down a part of the way with us next day. I learned from Mrs. Canfield and her daughter, that this same Edward Tilokaikt, after he returned from the Umatilla, gave the first blow with his whip, and broke and run out of doors, when other Indians finished the slaughter of the sick men. While at the station, Joseph Smith threatened me with the Indians if I did not obey him. I felt our condition as bad and very dangerous from the Indians, and feared that Smith would join them. He sometimes talked of going on to the Umatilla to live with them. His daughter was taken by the chief's sons (first Clark, and in the second place, Edward) for a wife. I told Mr. Smith, were I a father, I would never suffer that, so long as I had power to use an arm; his reply was, "You don't know what you would do; I would not dare to say a word if they should take my own wife." I continued to regard our situation as exceedingly dangerous till we got out of the country.

After we had arrived at Wallawalla, I said, in the presence of Mr. McBean, that I supposed there were present some of the Indians who had killed my brother, and if I knew them I would kill them yet. Mr. McBean said, "*Take care what you say, the very walls have ears.*" He was very anxious to get us safe to the Wallamet.

Q.—Would you suppose one who was acquainted at that place liable to get lost in going that evening to Finlay's lodge?

A.—I would not. It was in sight and a plain path to it, and was not more than twenty-five yards off.

Q.—When did you learn from your brother that Stanfield was going to take Mrs. Hays as a wife?

A.—Some two or more weeks before the massacre, something was said as to Mr. Hoffman taking Mrs. Hays. My brother says, "No, I heard Joe Stanfield say that he was going to take her as a wife."

Q.—Did your brother appear to believe that this was about to take place?

A.—He did, and my brother talked about it,—made us believe it was going to take place.

Q.—What opportunity had your brother to know about this, more than yourself?

A.—He boarded at the station, and was some of the time teaming from the saw-mill, and Mrs. Hays cooked for him and several others of the Doctor's hands, among whom was Stanfield.

Q.—Why did you think Stanfield was a Catholic, as a reason for his being saved?

A.—Because I heard Dr. Whitman say at the mill, that the Catholics were evidently trying to set the Indians upon him, but he thought he could keep it down for another year, when he would be safe. I supposed he expected safety from the government being extended over the country.

Q.—How did Stanfield seem to know that the chief would be there after a while, and would tell you what you might do as to going back to the saw-mill?

A.—I did not know.

Q.—Why did you tell your people that you would be back on Monday, if at all?

A.—Because we were in an Indian country, and I remembered what I had heard the Doctor say at the Umatilla, and my brother had not returned as expected.

Q.—Had you any means of knowing what "*great chief*," at the Umatilla, Tilokaikt spoke of, where his son Edward had gone to learn what to do with the sick young men?

A.—I had not.

Q.—Did you know at that time that the bishop was said to be at Umatilla?

A.—Yes.

Q.—Did you form in your own mind, at that time, any opinion as to whom Edward had gone to consult?

A.—I thought the term "*great chief*" might have been put in to deceive me, as Stanfield had told me, the evening before, that the Catholics were going to establish a mission right away at that place, and that they would protect the women and children, and *I thought it might be the Catholics* he was consulting, or it might be some great Indian chief. This talk of establishing a station there continued for more than a week after we got down to the station. After I found Bewley and Sales were killed, I seemed to forget much until even after I had got down, and even to the plains, when the facts again came more clearly to my recollection, and I spoke of them freely to my parents and to others.

(Signed,) DANIEL YOUNG.

Sworn and subscribed to, before me, this 20th day of January, A. D. 1849, in Tualatin Plains, Oregon Territory.

G. W. COFFINBURY, Justice of the Peace.

CHAPTER LVII.

How the country was saved to the United States.—Article from the New York *Evening Post.*—Ingratitude of the American Board.—Deposition of Elam Young.—Young girls taken for Indian wives.—Statement of Miss Lorinda Bewley.—Sager, Bewley, and Sales killed.

In taking up our morning *Oregonian* of November 16, 1866, our eye lit upon the following article from the New York *Evening Post*, which we feel assured the reader will not regret to find upon these pages, and which will explain the desperate efforts made to secure this country to the United States by Dr. Whitman, the details of whose death we are now giving from the depositions of parties upon the ground, who were eye-witnesses and fellow-sufferers at the fall of that good and noble man whose labors and sacrifices his countrymen are at this late day only beginning to appreciate. We ask in astonishment: Has the American Board at last opened its ears, and allowed a statement of that noble martyr's efforts to save Oregon to his country to be made upon its record? It has! it has! and here it is:—

"We presume it is not generally known to our citizens on the Pacific coast, nor to many people in the Atlantic States, how near we came to losing, through executive incompetence, our just title to the whole immense region lying west of the Rocky Mountains. Neither has due honor been accorded to the brave and patriotic man through whose herculean exertions this great loss and sacrifice was prevented.

"The facts were briefly and freshly brought out during the recent meeting at Pittsburg of the 'American Board of Commissioners for Foreign Missions,' in the course of an elaborate paper read by Mr. Treat, one of the secretaries of the Board, on the 'Incidental Results of Missions.'

"In the year 1836 the American Board undertook to establish a mission among the Indians beyond the Rocky Mountains. Two missionaries, Rev. Mr. Spalding and Dr. Whitman, with their wives,—the first white women who had ever made that perilous journey,—passed over the mountains with incredible toil, to reach Oregon, the field of their labor. After remaining there for a few years, Dr. Whitman began to understand the object of the misrepresentations of the Hudson's Bay Company. He saw, contrary to the reiterated public statements of that company—

"1. That the land was rich in minerals.

"2. That emigrants could cross the Rocky Mountains in wagons, a feat which they had constantly asserted to be impossible.

"3. That the Hudson's Bay Company was planning to secure the sole occupancy of the whole of that country, by obtaining a surrender of the American title into the hands of the British government.

"Seeing these things, but not knowing how very near the British scheme was to its accomplishment, Dr. Whitman resolved, at every hazard, to prevent its consummation. He undertook, in 1842, to make a journey on horseback to Washington, to lay the whole matter clearly before our government by personal representations. Being a man of great physical strength and an iron constitution, he accomplished the long and perilous journey, and reached Washington in safety. The remainder of the story we will relate in the language of the Boston *Congregationalist:* Reaching Washington, he sought an interview with President Tyler and Daniel Webster, then Secretary of State, and unfolded to them distinctly what was going on. Here he learned that a treaty was almost ready to be signed, in which all this northwestern territory was to be given up to England, and we were to have in compensation greater facilities in catching fish. Dr. Whitman labored to convince Mr. Webster that he was the victim of false representations with regard to the character of the region, and told him that he intended to return to Oregon with a train of emigrants. Mr. Webster, looking him full in the eye, asked him if he would pledge himself to conduct a train of emigrants there in wagons. He promised that he would. Then, said Mr. Webster, this treaty shall be suppressed. Dr. Whitman, in coming on, had fixed upon certain rallying-points where emigrants might assemble to accompany him on his return. He found nearly one thousand ready for the journey. After long travel, they reached Fort Hall, a British military station, and the commandant undertook to frighten the emigrants by telling them that it was not possible for them to go through with wagons; but Dr. Whitman reassured them, and led them through to the Columbia, and the days of the supremacy of the Hudson's Bay Company over Oregon were numbered."

Twenty-four years after that noble, devoted, faithful servant and missionary of theirs had received a cold reproof, after enduring one of the severest and most trying journeys of several thousand miles, his Board at home, and unreasonably cautious associates in Oregon, have consented to acknowledge that they owe to him a debt of respect for doing, without their consent or approval at the time, a noble, patriotic, and unselfish act for his country.

And how shall we regard the cold indifference they have manifested to the present day, in regard to the infamous manner in which his life, and the lives of his wife and countrymen were taken, and the continued slanders heaped upon their names? Have they asked for, or even attempted an explanation, or a refutation of those slanders? Their half-century volume speaks a language not to be mistaken. Mr. Spalding, his first and most zealous associate, attempted to bring the facts before the world, but the caution of those who would whitewash his (Dr. Whitman's) sepulcher induced Mr. Spalding to give up in despair,—a poor broken-down wreck, caused by the frightful ending of his fellow-associates, and of his own missionary labors.

Is this severe, kind reader, upon the Board and a portion of Dr. Whitman's associates? We intend to tell the truth if it is, as we are endeavoring to get the truth, the whole truth, and as few mistakes as possible in these pages. Therefore we will copy another deposition relative to this massacre.

Deposition of Mr. Elam Young.

I met Dr. Whitman on the Umatilla, about the 1st of October, 1847. He engaged me to build a mill for him at his mission. As the lumber was not handy at the station, I moved up to the saw-mill to do a part of the work there.

Some time in November, my son James, who was teaming for the Doctor, went from the saw-mill with a load of lumber for the mission station, and was to return with provisions for us. This was on Tuesday after the murder. Shortly after he had gone away, Mr. Smith, who was also at the saw-mill, appeared to be very uneasy; stated repeatedly that he was sure something had happened to him; said he had a constant foreboding of some evil; stated that Dr. Whitman was abusing the children at the mission, as he had understood by Stanfield; frequently spoke against Dr. Whitman. The next Sunday, beginning to feel uneasy, I sent my second son Daniel down to the station, who returned on Monday and brought the news of the massacre. *It instantly struck my mind that the Catholic priests had been the cause of the whole of it.* This conviction was caused by repeated conversations with Dr. Whitman, together with my knowledge of the principles of the Jesuits. Mr. Smith observed at the same time that we must all be Jesuits for the time being. Soon after Daniel returned, three Indians came up and told us we must go down to the station, which we accordingly did the next day. When we got there it was after night; we found that Crockett Bewley and Amos Sales had both been killed that day. The women told us that they had told the Indians, before we came down, that we were English, and we must not contradict it. The Indians soon began to question whether I was English. I told them I was of English parents, but born in the United States.

A few days after we got there two young women were taken as wives for the Indians, which I opposed, *and was threatened by Mr. Smith*, who was very anxious that it should take place, and that other little girls should be given up for wives. Was employed while there in making coffins and grinding for the Indians.

While there, Miss Bewley was taken off to the Umatilla. Tried to comfort her as much as I could, believing she would be *safer there at the Catholic station than where we were.* First ten days we were constantly told that the Catholics were coming there to establish a mission. Heard that Mr. Ogden had come up to Wallawalla to rescue us from the Indians. Went to grinding and preparing provisions for our journey. Smith and Stanfield, who appeared to be very friendly with each other, had the management of the teams and loading, took the best teams and lightest loads, gave us the poorest teams and heaviest loads. On the way to Wallawalla they drove off and left us. The hindmost teams had to double in the bad places. Reached the fort perhaps half an hour after Smith and Stanfield had; met Smith at the gate, who says: "Well, you have got along?" "Yes." "It is well you did, for the Indians found out that *you were not an Englishman, and were determined to have your scalp.*" I asked him, "How do you know this?" to which he made no reply. Went into the fort and met Mr. McBean and the priest; supposed they would all rejoice at our escape, but their manner was very cold and distant. But Mr. Ogden greeted us cordially. The next day the Indians came into the fort in considerable numbers, and their actions were suspicious, and Mr. McBean seemed to interest himself very much in our belalf, and *told us to be very quiet and to keep in our own rooms*, and be careful what we said, as the very walls had ears. [If this does not show the sneaking dog, what does? Ogden is apparently all friendship, and McBean is all caution to the captives.]

We arrived on Monday, and Mr. Spalding on Saturday after, and the next day all took boat for the lower country.

Q.—Did your son give you any caution as to what to say when you reached the station.

A.—He said Stanfield said we must say the Doctor poisoned the Indians.

Q.—What did you learn about Mr. Rogers as having made a confession.

A.—*Stanfield said that Mr. Rogers had made a confession that the*

Doctor had poisoned the Indians. I replied, "Who knows this?" He said Mrs. Hays and Mrs. Hall heard it. I afterward asked Mrs. Hays if she did hear it. She replied, "*We must say so now.*" I afterward, at the station, told Stanfield he had better not mention that to Americans, for there was not one from Maine to Georgia that would believe it. He replied, "We must say so." I told him I never would.

Q.—What conversation with the Doctor led you to believe the Catholics were at the bottom of the whole of it?

A.—That some years before (1841) he had had difficulty with the Indians, and he had found out satisfactorily where it came from, by charging the Indians of having been made jealous of a certain man. I do not recollect the name, but I think he said he was from Canada, and the Indians acknowledged it. [The difficulty here spoken of was about the horses given as a present to Rev. Jason Lee, on his way to Wallamet. The Indians had been told by the company's interpreter, old Toupin, that he had as good as stolen their horses, as he made them no presents in return, and they were encouraged to make that a cause of difficulty with Dr. Whitman.] At that time they had knocked off his hat, etc., but other Indians would obey him and pick it up, and so long as they would obey, he was satisfied of his safety; but this had long since passed off. [The writer was present, and saw the whole performance here alluded to, the particulars of which are given elsewhere]. And they were never in a better state until of late, when a body of priests and Jesuits had come in, and were constantly saying in their ears that this sickness came on them by the Americans; that the Americans were a very bad people, that the Good Being had sent on them as a punishment.

Q.—Why did Mr. Smith appear anxious to have the young women given to the Indians?

A.—I do not know, unless to appease them, and get their affection.

Q.—Did the Doctor appear to wish to remain, against the wish of a majority of the Indians?

A.—I heard him say repeatedly, if the Indians wished him to leave he would, but a large majority said he must not, and he thought the times would soon change. I understood him to expect a change from the extension of government.

Q.—Did your son Daniel say any thing, before you moved from the saw-mill, of having cautioned C. Bewley for speaking unadvisedly before Joe Stanfield?

A.—Yes, he gave that; that amounts to the same as he has given in his statement.

Q.—Did you have any fears, while at the station, that Mr. Smith was liable, had the circumstances become more dangerous, to act with the Indians?

A.—Certainly I did.

Q.—Did you get any reason why Bewley and Sales were killed?

A.—Though I did not get it directly from them, the Indian account was, the *great chief at the Umatilla said their disease would spread; but I believe it was because Bewley had spoken before Stanfield unadvisedly.*

(Signed,) ELAM YOUNG.

Sworn and subscribed to before me, this 20th day of January, 1849.
G. W. COFFINBURY, Justice of the Peace.

What shall we say of these depositions, and the facts asserted under the solemnity of an oath, the witnesses still living, with many others confirming the one fact, *that Roman priests and Hudson's Bay men, English and Frenchmen, were all safe and unharmed* in an Indian—and that American—territory, *while American citizens were cut down by savage hands without mercy?* Can we regard the conduct of such men in any other light than as enemies in peace? Without the aid of religious bigotry and the appeal to God as sending judgments upon them, not one of those simple-minded natives would ever have lifted a hand to shed the blood of their teachers or of American citizens. We see how faithful and persevering Joe Lewis, Finlay, and Stanfield were in their part, while the bishop and his priests, and Sir James Douglas, at Vancouver, were watching at a distance to misrepresent the conduct of the dead, and excuse and justify their own instruments, as in Mr. Douglas's letters to Governor Abernethy and the Sandwich Islands; and Vicar-General Brouillet's narrative, with more recent proceedings, which are given in another chapter.

We intended to give in this connection the account of this tragedy as given by Vicar-General Brouillet, but it accords so nearly with that given by Sir James Douglas in his Sandwich Islands letter to Mr. Castle, that the impression is irresistibly forced upon the mind that the whole account is prepared by one and the same person; hence we will not encumber our pages with more than a liberal amount of extracts, sufficient to show the full knowledge of the bishop and his priests of what was expected to take place at the Whitman station, and the brutal and inhuman part they took in forcing Miss Bewley into the arms of Five Crows, after that Indian was humane enough to permit her to return to the house of those, that Mr. Young, and all others who were ignorant of their vileness, might naturally suppose would be a place of safety from such treatment. She that was Miss Bewley is now dead, but she has left on record the statement of her wrongs. We give it a permanent place in our history, not to persecute or slander the Jesuit fraternity (for truth is no slander), but to warn Americans against placing their daughters and sons under any such teachings or influences.

Statement of Miss Lorinda Bewley.

Q.—What time did the massacre commence?

A.—I think half-past one.

Q.—Who fled to the chamber?

A.—Mrs. Hall, Mrs. Hays, Mrs. Whitman, Mr. Kimball, Mr. Rogers,—the three last wounded,—myself, Catharine Sager, thirteen years of age, her sisters Elizabeth, Louisa, and Henrietta, the three half-breed girls,—Miss Bridger, Mary Ann, and Helen,—last four very sick. After we got into the chamber the Indians broke in the windows and doors, filled the house and broke down the stair-door. Mr. Kimball advised to attempt the appearance of defense at the stairway. Mrs. Whitman and Mr. Rogers said, let all prepare for death. I found an old gun, and it was held over the staircase by Mr. Rogers. They appeared cool and deliberate in ordering all to prepare for death, when they were breaking up the house. The appearance of the gun appeared to check the Indians from coming up-stairs. A few words passed between Mr. Rogers and one of the Indians. Mr. Rogers said, "The Indians wish me to come down." Mrs. Whitman objected at first; some words passed between Mrs. Whitman and Mr. Rogers about his going down which I do not recollect; finally Mrs. Whitman took his hand and said, "The Lord bless you; go!" and he went nearly to the bottom of the stairs, but his head was all the time above the stairs; he was not there longer than two or three minutes. A few words passed between them, but I did not understand the language. Mrs. Whitman said, "The Indians say you have guns and want to kill us." Mr. Rogers says, "No, you wish to get us down to kill us." This seemed to be all they talked about. Mr. Rogers says to Mrs. Whitman, "Shall we let them come up?" Mrs. Whitman says, "Let one, Tamsaky, come up." Tamsaky came up and shook hands with us all, and spoke and advised us all to go down and go over to the other house, for the young men would burn the house; he led the way down while the Indians were hallooing wildly in the room below, but when we had got down, the Indians had gone out and were very still. While we were up-stairs the Doctor's face had been cut awfully to pieces, but he was yet breathing. Mrs.

Whitman saw him and said she wanted air; they led her to the settee and she lay down. She appeared to think then, that we were going to be spared, and told us to get all the things from the press we needed. I put a blanket I had over her, and got a sheet for myself, and we put a good many clothes from the press on the settee; Mrs. Hall and Mrs. Hays got their arms full also. Mr. Rogers was going to take us over to the other house, and then come back for the sick children. This was Tamsaky's advice, as he said the Indians were going to burn the house. It was now getting dark. Mr. Rogers and Joe Lewis carried out the settee, over the bodies of the Doctor and John Sager, which were dreadfully mangled; they passed through the kitchen, and through the outside door toward the end of the house occupied as the Indian room. Here, to our surpise and terror, the Indians were collected, with their guns ready; the children from the school were huddled in the corner of the building. When the settee had gone about its length from the door, Joe Lewis dropped the end he was holding and the guns were immediately fired. Mr. Rogers had only time to raise his hands and say, "O my God, save me," and fell. I felt my fingers numb till next morning, from a ball that passed so near as to sting them. Mrs. Whitman received two balls when on the settee.

I could not see what was done at the same time on all sides of me. On turning round I saw Francis Sager down bleeding and groaning. The children said an Indian hauled him out from among them and Joe Lewis shot him with a pistol. Mr. Rogers fell down by my feet and groaned loud. All three appeared in great agony, and groaned very loud. The Indian women were carrying off things, and the Indians were shouting terribly; the Indians also started and cut Mrs. Whitman's face with their whips and rolled her into the mud. [This treatment of Mrs. Whitman will be explained in the statement of Stikas, as given from Mr. McLane's journal.] At this I attempted to escape to the other house. One of the Indians from Mrs. Whitman caught me,—I had run about two rods,—when I screamed and he shook his tomahawk over my head, and I kept screaming, not knowing that he wanted me to hush; then a great many others came round, and pointed their guns and shook their hatchets. I finally discovered they wanted me to be still, and when I was silent, one of them led me by the hand over to the mansion.

Q.—Was Mr. Rogers wounded when he started into the house?

A.—Yes; shot through the arm and tomahawked in the head.

Q.—Did Mr. Rogers have any interview with the Indians after he got in until the one on the stairs?

A.—No. As soon as he got in the house was locked, and none got in after that till we were all up-stairs, when they broke the doors and windows.

Q.—Did the Indians have an interview with Mr. Rogers after the one on the stairs, up to the time he was shot?

A.—No; the Indians were not in the room, except Tamsaky and Joe Lewis, and we were all very still and Mr. Rogers was all the time in my sight, except as I stepped to the bed for the sheet, and I was very quick.

Q.—Did you hear it reported that Mr. Rogers said he overheard Dr. and Mrs. Whitman and Mr. Spalding talking at night about poisoning the Indians?

A.—No; but after being taken to Umatilla, *one* of the two *Frenchmen said* that the Indians' talk was that an Indian who understood English overheard such conversation.

Q.—Did you consider Mr. Rogers and Mrs. Whitman were meeting their fate like devoted Christians?

A.—Yes.

Q.—When did the priest arrive?

A.—Wednesday, while the bodies were being prepared for the grave. The bodies were collected into the house on Tuesday evening.

Q.—Did the Indians bury a vial or bottle of the Doctor's medicine?

A.—They said they did. Joe Stanfield made the box to bury it in, and the Indians said they buried it.

Q.—Why did they bury it?

A.—They said *the priests said it was poison.* Stanfield and Nicholas were their interpreters to us.

Q.—How did they obtain this vial?

A.—The Indians said *the priests found it* among the Doctor's medicines, and showed it to them, and *told them if it broke it would poison the whole nation.*

Q.—Was there much stir among the Indians about this bottle?

A.—Yes, a great deal.

Q.—Why did the Indians kill your brother?

A.—Edward Tilokaikt returned from the Umatilla, and told us (after they had killed him) the *great chief told them their disease would spread.*

Q.—Did your brother make any effort to escape?

A.—He told me the night before he was killed that he was preparing to make an effort to escape. I told him he must not, he was not able to walk. He said he had that day agreed with Stanfield to get him a horse, and assist him away. I said, "What will become of me?" He said, "I know you have been greatly abused, and all I care for my life is to get away, and make an effort to save you; but I may be killed before to-morrow at this time, but, if it is the Lord's will, I am prepared to die." This was Monday, a week from the first massacre. About three o'clock the next day my brother and Mr. Sales were killed, and *I have always thought that Joe Stanfield betrayed them.*

Q.—Did the Indians threaten you all, and treat you with cruelty from the first?

A.—They did.

Q.—Did they on Tuesday assemble and threaten your lives?

A.—Yes, and frequently threatened our lives afterward. (See statement of Stanfield by Brouillet, in a previous chapter, confirming the fact of his unbounded influence over the Indians.)

Q.—When were the young women first dragged out and brutally treated?

A.—Saturday night after the first massacre, and continually after that.

Q.—When were you taken to the Umatilla?

(Miss Bewley will answer this question after we have given Vicar-General Brouillet an opportunity to state his part in this tragedy.)

CHAPTER LVIII.

Vicar-General Brouillet's statement.—Statement of Istacus.—The priest finds the poison —Statement of William Geiger, Jr.—Conduct of Mr. McBean.—Influence of the Jesuit missions.

WE left Vicar-General Brouillet and Bishop Blanchet and his priests on their way to their station on the Umatilla, where they arrived on November 27. On the 28th, Brouillet says, page 47: "The next day being Sunday, we were visited by Dr. Whitman, who remained but a few minutes at the house, and appeared to be much agitated. Being invited to dine, he refused, saying that he feared it would be too late, as he had twenty-five miles to go, and wished to reach home before night. On parting, he entreated me not to fail to visit him when I would pass by his mission, which I very cordially promised to do.

"On Monday, 29th, Mr. Spalding took supper with us, and appeared quite gay. During the conversation, he happened to say that the Doctor was unquiet; that the Indians were displeased with him on account of the sickness, and that even he had been informed that the Murderer (an Indian) intended to kill him; but he seemed not to believe this, and suspected as little as we did what was taking place at the mission of the Doctor."

The reader will note and remember the statement which follows: Brouillet says, on the 48th page of his narrative, the 36th of J. Ross Browne's report:—

"Before leaving Fort Wallawalla, it had been decided that, after visiting the sick people of my own mission on the Umatilla, I should visit those of Tilokaikt's camp, for the purpose of baptizing the infants and such dying adults as might desire this favor; and the Doctor and Mr. Spalding having informed me that there were still many sick persons at their mission, I was confirmed in this resolution, and made preparations to go as soon as possible.

"After having finished baptizing the infants and adults of my mission, I left on Tuesday, the 30th of November, late in the afternoon, for Tilokaikt's camp, where I arrived between seven and eight o'clock in the evening. It is impossible to conceive my surprise and consternation when, upon my arrival, I learned that the Indians the day before had massacred the Doctor and his wife, with the greater part of the Americans at the mission. I passed the night without scarcely closing my eyes. Early the next morning I baptized three sick children, two of whom died soon after, and then hastened to the scene of death, to offer to the widows and orphans all the assistance in my power. I found five or six women and over thirty children in a situation deplorable beyond description. Some had just lost their husbands, and others their fathers, whom they had seen massacred before their eyes, and were expecting every moment to share the same fate. The sight of those persons caused me to shed tears, which, however, I was obliged to conceal, for I was the greater part of the day in the presence of the murderers, and closely watched by them; and if I had shown too marked an interest in behalf of the sufferers, it would only have endangered their lives and mine; these, therefore, entreated me to be upon my guard."

The women that lived through that terrible scene inform us that this priest was as familiar and friendly with the Indians as though nothing serious had occurred. We have seen and conversed freely with four of those unfortunate victims, and all affirm the same thing. Their impression was, that there might be others he expected to be killed, and he did not wish to be present when it was done. According to the testimony in the case, Mr. Kimball and James Young were killed while he was at or near the station. Brouillet continues, on the 49th page:—

"After the first few words that could be exchanged under the circumstances, I inquired after the victims, and was told they were yet unburied. Joseph Stanfield, a Frenchman, who was in the employ of Dr. Whitman, and had been spared by the Indians, was engaged in washing the corpses, but being alone, he was unable to bury them. I resolved to go and assist him, so as to render to these unfortunate victims the last service in my power to offer them. What a sight did I then behold! Ten dead bodies lying here and there, covered with blood, and bearing the marks of the most atrocious cruelty,—some pierced with balls, others more or less gashed by the hatchet. Dr. Whitman had received three gashes on the face. Three others had their skulls crushed so that their brains were oozing out.

"I assure you, sir, that, during the time I was occupied in burying the victims of this disaster, I was far from feeling safe, being obliged to go here and there gathering up the dead bodies, in the midst of assassins, whose hands were still stained with blood, and who, by their manners, their countenances, and the arms which they still carried, sufficiently announced that their thirst for blood was yet unsatiated. Assuming as composed a manner as possible, I cast more than one glance aside and behind at the knives, pistols, and guns, in order to assure myself whether there were not some of them directed toward me."

The above extract is from a letter addressed to Colonel Gilliam. The cause of the priest's alarm is explained in a statement found in the journal of Mr. McLane, private secretary to Colonel Gilliam, while in the Cayuse country, taken from the Indians' statement in the winter of 1847–48. He was compelled to find the poison. Brouillet says:—

"The ravages which the sickness had made in their midst, together with the conviction which a half-breed, named Joseph Lewis, had succeeded in fixing upon their minds that Dr. Whitman had poisoned them, were the only motives I could discover which could have prompted them to this act of murder. This half-breed had imagined a conversation between Dr. Whitman, his wife, and Mr. Spalding, in which he made them say that it was necessary to hasten the death of the Indians in order to get possession of their horses and lands. 'If you do not kill the Doctor,' said he, 'you will be dead in the spring.'"

Statement of Istacus, or Stikas.

In the first place, Joe Lewis told the Indians that the Doctor was poisoning. Tamsaky went to Camaspelo and told him he wanted to kill the Doctor, and wished him to help. He replied, pointing to his child, that his child was sick, and that was as much as he could attend to. Tamsaky then went to Tilokaikt, and he said he would have nothing to do with it. But his son and young men wished to do it, and they contended so long that at last he said: "If you are determined to do so, go and kill him." Afterward, the Indians presented a gun two different times to Tamsaky, and told him to go and kill the Doctor. He said he would not kill him.

When the priests came, they got to quarreling; the Catholic priests told them that what the Doctor taught them would take them to the devil, and the Doctor told them what the priests taught them would take them to the devil. After the priests told them that, the Indians said they believed it, for the Doctor did not cure them.

After the Doctor was killed, *the priest told the Young Chief* that it was true that the Doctor had given them poison; before that, the Doctor had given them medicine and they died. After the massacre, all the Indians went to the priest's house (an Indian lodge near Dr. Whitman's station), and I said that I was going to ask the priest himself whether it was true or not, so that I could hear with my own ears. He (the priest) told them that the priests were sent of God. They did not know how to answer him. The Five Crows told me *that the priest told him the Doctor was poisoning them. I then believed it.*

They then went and killed the two sick men I asked the Indians, if he gave us poison, why did the Americans get sick?

[It is evident that this conversation took place at the camp of Tilokaikt, where Mr. Brouillet says he spent the night of the 30th of November.]

Afterward, they went to the Doctor's place, and *the priest was there too*, and they asked him where the poison was that the Doctor gave them. After searching some time among the medicines, he found *a vial with something white in it*, and told them, "*Here it is.*" I tell you what I heard.

The priest then told them that *Mrs. Whitman had a father in the States that gave poison to the people there*, and that he had given this to her, to poison them all; then they all believed. I told them that I did not believe that the Doctor was poisoning them; I said I expected they brought the sickness with them from California, for many of them died coming from that place. Joe Lewis told them to make a box, and Beardy buried the vial in the square box, stating, if they did not, the Americans would get it and poison them all.

The head man of the priests told them all these things, and the priest took all the best books to his house.

The above is a true extract from the journal of Mr. McLane, private secretary to Colonel Gilliam, the same as was read in my hearing to Mungo, the interpreter for Colonel Gilliam, when these statements were made, and he said it was true and correctly written.

(Signed,) L. H. Judson.

Sworn to and subscribed before me, this 25th day of November, 1848, Champoeg County, Oregon Territory.

Aaron Purdy, Justice of the Peace.

There are three important facts stated by this Indian which are confirmed by other testimony.

First. That the priest was upon the ground, or in at the death.

Second. He was ready to overhaul the Doctor's medicines and hunt out some vial, and tell the Indians, "*Here it is,—the medicine the Doctor has been killing you with.*"

Third. That he told them it was sent to the Doctor by Mrs. Whitman's father, who poisoned people in the States.

This explains the terrible and brutal treatment of Mrs. Whitman's body, even after death.

Brouillet says, "*Joseph Lewis had succeeded in fixing upon their minds that Dr. Whitman had poisoned them,*" but Istacus, one of the first and most truthful Indians we became acquainted with in the country, tells us that the Indians did not believe Joe Lewis till the priest confirmed his statements, and this priest was required to show them the poison.

It would not be strange, if, while he is compelled to hunt over the medicines of Dr. Whitman, to find any that he could call poison, and in exhibiting such evidence to the deluded murderers about him, that he should feel himself in danger, yet his whole conduct belies such a statement, for he well knew the ignorance of those about him as to any medicine he might select and call *poison.*

This Indian's statement also explains the killing of the two young men, Sales and Bewley, and that as these priests "were sent of God," the disease of these young men would spread; in other words, their testimony would convict the parties implicated.

We find in this same letter to Colonel Gilliam, other statements that are important in the history we are giving. He says: "*I knew that the Indians were angry with all Americans, and more enraged against Mr. Spalding than any other.*" If this was the case, why did they not kill him first? There is certainly some mistake in this statement of Mr. Brouillet, or else the Indians were too hasty, which is probably the case. The Indians were not quite as much "*enraged*" against Mr. Spalding as his reverence, who claimed to know their feelings so well.

Again, on the 54th page (39th of Ross Browne), in answer to Mr. Spalding's wild, despairing cry, "But where shall I go?" he answers: "I know not; you know the country better than I; all that I know is that the Indians say *the order to kill Americans has been sent in all directions.*"

How did this Rev. Father Brouillet know all this? We have yet to learn that he ever gave a single American, except Mr. Spalding, any information respecting their danger,—which he certainly could have done with perfect safety, by sending any one or all of them a written notice of the "order to kill Americans;" but instead of warning them of their danger, he was present to show to the Indians a vial of Dr. Whitman's medicine and tell them it was the *poison.*

The long list of statements collected and given to the world as reliable historical data, by this priest, and embodied in an official report by J. Ross Browne, do but show the active part he, with his associate priests and the Hudson's Bay Company, took to destroy the American influence and settlements then in the country.

Says the historian Bancroft: "It is the duty of faithful history to trace events not only to their cause, but to their authors."

We will direct our attention for a short time to the proceedings of Mr. McBean in charge of Fort Wallawalla (or Fort Nez Percés), in council with the Indians. From the statement of Mr. Wm. Geiger, Jr., who was at Dr. Whitman's station during the winter of 1846–7, teaching school, we learn that the Indians showed some dissatisfaction, and were called together by Dr. Whitman, to consult and decide what they would do. The Doctor proposed to them that a majority of the tribe should let him know definitely, and a vote was taken, and but two or three were found to favor his leaving. During this council Mr. Geiger and the Doctor learned that there had been conversation and a council with the Indians at the fort, by Mr. McBean. That he had informed them of the Mexican war between the United States and Mexico, and of the prospect of a war between the United States and England (King George men), and that he was anxious to know which side the Cayuses would take in the event of such a war. This question Mr. McBean kept constantly before the Indians whenever they went to the fort. They would return to the station and say that Mr. McBean had given them more news of the prospect of war between the King George people and Americans, and that he wished to know which side they would take. Tamsaky, Tilokaikt, and one other Indian said they had told Mr. McBean that they would join the King George. Some said they had told him their hearts favored the Americans; others professed to be on the "*back-bone*," *i. e.*, hesitating. All matters and causes of dissatisfaction between the Doctor's mission and the Indians were amicably settled. The Doctor and Mr. Geiger could not see why Mr. McBean should beset the Indians on that subject, unless it was to bring about what had been before, viz., to make allies of the Indians in case of war.

On account of this dissatisfaction, the Doctor thought of leaving. Mr. Geiger says, "I told them I thought it their duty to remain. I thought the Indians as quiet as communities in general; in old places there were more or less difficulties and excitements."

In the communication signed by Mr. Geiger, he is asked, "What was the cause of discouragement with the Doctor and Mr. Spalding at that time?"

A.—"The influence of the Roman priests, exercised in talking to the Indians, and though the French half-breed, Lehai, Tom Hill, a Delaware Indian, and others."

Q.—"What did the Indians mention was the instruction they received from Roman Catholics?"

A.—"That the Protestants were leading them in wrong roads, *i. e.*, even to hell. If they followed the *Suapies* (Americans) they would continue to die. If they followed the Catholics, it would be otherwise with them; only now and then one would die of age. That they would get presents,—would become rich in every thing."

We have a statement made by Brouillet as to their influence among the Indians on this coast, found on the 87th page of his narrative, "Protestantism in Oregon" (55th of Ross Browne). He says:—

"Messrs. Blanchet and Demerse, the first Catholic missionaries that came to Oregon, had passed Wallawalla in 1838, where they had stopped a few days, and had been visited by the Indians. In 1839, Mr. Demerse had spent three weeks in teaching the Indians and baptizing their children. In 1840, he had made there a mission so fruitful that the Protestant missionaries had got alarmed, and feared that all their disciples would abandon them if he continued his missions among them. Father De Smet, after visiting the Flatheads in 1840, had come and established a mission among them in 1841; and from that time down to the arrival of the bishop, the Indians of Wallawalla and of the Upper Columbia had never failed to be visited yearly, either by Mr. Demerse or by some of the Jesuits, and those annual excursions had procured every year new children to the church. Almost every Indian tribe possessed some Catholic member."

We can bear positive testimony as to the effect and influence of those teachings up to 1842 among the Upper Columbia Indians; and it is to illustrate the bearing and result of those teachings, continued for a series of years upon the savage mind, and the influence of a foreign monopoly in connection with such teachers, that we bring these statements before the reader.

The vast influence wielded by this foreign fur and sectarian monopoly was used to secure Oregon for their exclusive occupation. The testimony of Rev. Messrs. Beaver and Barnley, and Sir Edward Belcher, as given by Mr. Fitzgerald, and that of his Reverence Brouillet, as found on the 56th page of his narrative, all affirm the close connection of these two influences. Leaving out of the question the statement of many others, we have that of this priest. He says:—

"Some days after an express reached us from the fort, informing us that our lives were in danger from a portion of the Indians who could not pardon me for having deprived them of their victim; and this was the only reason which prevented me from fulfilling the promise which I had made to the widows and orphans of returning to see them, and obliged me to be contented with sending my interpreter" to the scene of the murder, to bring Miss Bewley to be treated as the evidence in the next chapter will show.

CHAPTER LIX.

Continuation of Miss Bewley's evidence.—The priests refuse her protection.—Forcibly taken from the bishop's house by Five Crows.—Brouillet advises her to remain with her Indian violator.—Indecent question by a priest.—Mr. Brouillet attempts to get a statement from her.—Two questions.—Note from Mrs. Bewley'.—Bishop Blanchet's letter to Governor Abernethy.—Comments on the Jesuits' proceedings.—Grand council at the bishop's.—Policy in forcing Miss Bewley to Five Crows' lodge.—Speeches by Camaspelo and Tilokaikt.—Killing of Elijah and the Nez Percé chief commented on.—The true story told.—Dr. White's report.—The grand council again.—Review of Brouillet's narrative.—Who were the real authors of the massacre.

Miss Bewley's Deposition Continued.

Q.—When were you taken to the Umatilla?

A.—Just at night, on Thursday the next week after the first massacre, having shaken with the ague that day; slept out that night in the snow-storm.

Q. Whose horses came after you ?

A.—Eliza Spalding said they belonged to her father; this led us to suppose Mr. Spalding was killed.

Q.—When did you leave Umatilla ?

A.—On Monday before the Wednesday on which we all went to Wallawalla.

Q.—When did you reach Wallawalla ?

A.—On Wednesday before the Saturday on which Mr. Spalding and company arrived, and we all started the next day for the lower country.

Q.—Where did you spend your time when at the Umatilla ?

A.—Most of the time at the house of the bishop; but the Five Crows (Brouillet's Achekaia) most of the nights compelled me to go to his lodge and be subject to him during the night. I obtained the privilege of going to the bishop's house before violation on the Umatilla, and *begged* and *cried to the bishop for protection* either at his house, or to be sent to Wallawalla. I told him I would do any work by night and day for him if he would protect me. *He said he would do all he could.* [The sequel shows that in this promise the bishop meant to implicate and involve the Five Crows; should a war with the American settlement grow out of the massacre.] Although I was taken to the lodge, I escaped violation the first four nights. There were the bishop, three priests, and two Frenchmen at the bishop's house. The first night the Five Crows came, I refused to go, and he went away, apparently mad, and *the bishop told me I had better go*, as he might do us all an injury, and *the bishop sent an Indian with me.* He took me to the Five Crows' lodge. The Five Crows showed me the door, and told me I might go back, and take my clothes, which I did.

Three nights after this, the Five Crows came for me again. *The bishop finally ordered me to go;* my answer was, I had rather die. After this, *he still insisted on my going* as the best thing I could do. I was then in the bishop's room; the three priests were there. I found I could get no help, *and had to go, as he told me, out of his room.* The Five Crows seized me by the arm and jerked me away to his lodge.

Q.—How long were you at the Umatilla?

A.—Two weeks, and from Friday till Monday. I would return early in the morning to the bishop's house, and be violently taken away at night. The bishop provided kindly for me while at his house. On my return one morning, one of the young priests asked me, in a good deal of glee, *how I liked my companion.* I felt that this would break my heart, and cried much during the day. When the two Nez Percés arrived with Mr. Spalding's letter, they held a council in the bishop's room, and the bishop said they were trying to have things settled. He said Mr. Spalding was trying to get the captives delivered up; I do not recollect what day this was, but it was some days before we heard that Mr. Ogden had arrived at Wallawalla. When the tall priest (Brouillet) that was at the Doctor's at the first was going to Wallawalla, after hearing of Mr. Ogden's arrival, he called me out of the door and told me if I went to the lodge any more I must not come back to his house. I asked him what I should do. He said I must insist or beg of the Indian to let me stop at his house; if he would not let me, then I must stay at his lodge. I did not feel well, and toward night I took advantage of this and went to bed, determined I would die there before I would be taken away. The Indian came, and, on my refusing to go, hauled me from my bed and threw my bonnet and shawl at me, and told me to go. I would not, and at a time when his eyes were off I threw them under the table and he could not find them. I sat down, determined not to go, and he pushed me nearly into the fire. The Frenchmen were in the room, and the bishop and priests were passing back and forth to their rooms. When the Indian was smoking, I went to bed again, and when he was through smoking he dragged me from my bed with more violence than the first time. I told the Frenchman to go into the bishop's room and ask him what I should do; he came out and told me that the *bishop said it was best for me to go.* I told him the tall priest said, if I went I must not come back again to this house; he said the priests dared not keep women about their house, but if the Five Crows sent me back again, why come. I still would not go. The Indian then pulled me away violently without bonnet or shawl. Next morning I came back and was in much anguish and cried much. *The bishop asked me if I was in much trouble?* I told him I was. He said it was not my fault, that I could not help myself. That I must pray to God and Mary. He asked me if I did not believe in God; I told him I did.

We will not stop to comment on the simple narrative of this young woman. No language of mine will more deeply impress the reader with the debasing character of these "holy fathers, the Catholic priests," that served the *Honorable* Hudson's Bay Company and mother church so faithfully.

It appears that Miss Bewley arrived at the bishop's on the 10th of December. On the 58th page of Brouillet's narrative (41st of Browne's) we find the following language:—

"On the 11th of December we had the affliction to *hear* that one of the captives had been carried off from the Doctor's house by the order of Five Crows, and brought to him; and we learned that two others had been violated at the Doctor's house."

How seriously these holy fathers were afflicted, Miss Bewley has told us in language not to be misunderstood. Her statement continues:—

Last summer, when I was teaching school near Mr. Bass, the tall priest, whose name I have learned was Brouillet, called on me, and told me that Mr. Spalding was trying to ruin my character and his, and said that Mr. Spalding had said that I had told him (Mr. S.) that the priests had treated me as bad as the Indians ever had. I told him I had not said so. He said he wanted to ask me some questions, and would send the Doctor, who could speak better English; he wished me to write it; I told him I would rather not do it. When at the Umatilla, the Frenchmen told me that they were making arrangements to locate the priests,—two at Mr. Spalding's as soon as Mr. S. got away, and two at the Dalles, and they were going to the Doctor's next week to build a house. This conversation was before Mr. Ogden arrived at Wallawalla.

Q.—Did Dr. Whitman wish to have Joe Lewis stop at his place?

A.—He let him stop at first only because he said he had no shoes nor clothes, and could not go on; but when a good many, on account of sickness, had no drivers, the Doctor furnished Joe with shoes and shirts, and got him to drive a team. He was gone three days, and came back, but the Doctor never liked it. I heard Mrs. Whitman and the Sager boys say that Joe Lewis was making disturbance among the Indians.

Q.—Did you ever hear the Doctor express any fears about the Catholics?

A.—Only once; the Doctor said at the table: "Now I shall have trouble; these priests are coming." Mrs. Whitman asked: "Have the Indians let them have land?" He said: "I think they have." Mrs. Whitman said: "It's a wonder they do not come and kill us." This land was out of sight of the Doctor's as you come this way (west of the station). When the Frenchman was talking, at Umatilla, of going to build a house there, he said it was a prettier station than the Doctor's.

(Signed,) LORINDA BEWLEY.

Sworn to and subscribed before me, this 12th day of December, 1848.

G. WALLING, Justice of the Peace,
Clackamas County, Oregon Territory.

We have another original statement of Miss Bewley's, as taken by Rev. J. S. Griffin, which we will give as a part properly belonging to the above statement.

OREGON CITY, February 7, 1849.

Questions to Miss Lorinda Bewley, in further examination touching the Wailatpu massacre:—

Q.—Did the Five Crows, when you were taken to his lodge from the bishop's house by an Indian, send you back with your things in apparent anger, or did he appear at that time to pity you?

A.—I thought at the time that I had good evidence, from his manner and behavior to me at the lodge in giving me up, that he was disposed to pity me, and not to abuse me.

Q.—Did you anticipate that evening that he would demand you afterward?

A.—No; I did not think he was disposed to.

Q.—What was this Five Crows' English name?

A.—Hezekiah (Brouillet's Achekaia).

Q.—Did you have evidence that it was necessary for Hezekiah to hold you as a wife to save you from a general abuse by the Indians?

A.—I was overwhelmed with such evidence at Wailatpu, but saw none of it at the Umatilla.

Q.—What was the order of conversation to you when the priest went to Wallawalla, after hearing of Mr. Ogden's arrival?

A.—I besought him to do all he could at the fort to obtain my delivery from bondage, and he said he would. A little after he called me to step out of the door from the rest, and told me if I went with the Indian I must not come back to his house any more, when I burst out crying, and asked him what to do; he said I must insist or beg the Indian to let me remain, or I must remain there. I begged him, as I was alone there, he would do every thing in his power to get Mr. Ogden to take me away, whether he could obtain all the prisoners or not.

Q.—Did you know of the priests having baptized any at the time of the burial at Wailatpu?

A.—I did not; but they were baptizing a great many at the Umatilla, principally children; two the same day after I went there, and very frequently afterward. On Christmas day they baptized many.

Q.—Was it understood among the Indians that the families at the mill were English?

A.—Yes, sir; and Mr. Smith was an Englishman.

Q.—Did the report reach the Indians at Wailatpu before you went to Umatilla, that the Indians were told at the Fort Wallawalla that they must not kill any more Americans?

A.—Yes, sir. This seemed to be generally understood.

Q.—Was it made known to you captives what Edward Tilokaikt was gone to the Umatilla for?

A.—It was made known to us, after a council, that Edward was to go to the big chief at the Umatilla and see what was to be done with us, and especially with the young women; and, after his return, he immediately commenced the massacre of the sick young men, and the next morning announced to us that the arrangement had been made for Hezekiah to come and take his choice among the young women, and that Edward and Clark Tilokaikt were then to take the other two. Hezekiah was a chief [the one appointed by Dr. White in 1843], and regarded by us, and I believe by others, as a single man. Edward and Clark were only the sons of a chief. Hezekiah did not come for me himself, but sent a man [Brouillet says, page 56 (Ross Browne, 40), the caution he received from Mr. McBean "obliged me to be content with sending my interpreter"] and a boy for the young woman that was a member of Mrs. Whitman's family. The contract between my mother and Mrs. Whitman was, that I was to continue my studies with Mrs. Whitman, and take part with her in the instruction and care of the children.

Q.—After Mr. Rogers entered the house wounded, and closed the doors, did he have any conversation with Nicholas or the Manson boys?

A.—No. Neither of them came into the house.

LORINDA BEWLEY.

Rev. J. S. Griffin says he is ready to testify to the fact that the above is a true statement, as made by Miss Bewley, and it was his own oversight at the time that her oath was not attached before a justice of the peace.

There was no other person living at the time that could positively state the facts as given by Miss Bewley; others have given their depositions, which confirm her statements, and show them to be the simple, unvarnished truth of the whole scene that passed before her, and her treatment by those "*holy fathers, the bishop and his priests.*"

We are forced to confess, that, after studying and copying these old documents and papers, we dare not trust ourselves to express an opinion, lest the reader should say our feelings have overcome our better judgment. Therefore we will simply ask a question or two, and let each reader answer for himself.

What think you, kind reader, of the Hudson's Bay Company and Roman Catholic Jesuits, and priests and bishop in Oregon in 1847–8?

Did not Dr. Whitman, his wife, and all at his mission suffer, and many of them die, to save Oregon as a part of the great American Republic?

We know that a few of the poor miserably deluded Indians belonging to his mission have suffered an ignominious death by being hung like dogs (a death, of all others, the most odious to them), and for what? Simply because they were deceived by those who knew at the time they were deceiving them; and who have since so managed as to deceive the Christian world, and bring falsehood to cover their participation in the transaction.

We would not have been so particular, nor copied documents so extensively, had we not before us a narrative of 108 pages, written by one of these "*holy fathers,*" Vicar-General Brouillet, purporting to give the causes both remote and immediate of this horrible massacre; giving it the title of "*Protestantism in Oregon,* account of the *murder of Dr. Whitman,* and the ungrateful calumnies of H. H. Spalding, Protestant missionary," in which he searches back even before the arrival of Dr. Whitman in the country, and cites Rev. Mr. Parker's first supposed or imaginary statements to the Indians as a cause of the massacre, which we know to be false and unfounded from the six years' early acquaintance we had with those Indians; and also from the personal allusions he makes to transactions with which we were intimately acquainted, and know to be false in fact and inference. These statements of this priest and his associates, McBean and Sir James Douglas, have induced us to extend the particulars of that massacre beyond our original design in giving the history of Oregon. As he claims great credit for himself and associates, Stanfield in particular, in burying the dead, and showing kindness to the widows and orphans, we will give another item to show the character of the *thief*, *liar*, and *accomplice* in that massacre, whom this priest is so ready in his narrative to claim as a saint.

Mrs. Catharine Bewley says: "Dr. Prettyman said to me that Joe Stanfield told him at his own house, when the sheriff had him in custody, that 'the morning of the day when young Bewley was killed, he had gone into the room and had hid every thing in the room back of the bed he was upon.' This, the doctor thought, showed that he was the cause of his being killed."

Under date of Umatilla, December 21, 1847, Father Blanchet, bishop of Wallawalla, writes to Governor Abernethy as follows:—

"As soon as I had been informed what had happened, I instantly told the two chiefs near my house that *I hoped the women* and children would be spared until they could be sent to the Wallamet. They answered: 'We pity them,—they shall not be harmed; they shall be taken care of, as before.' *I have since had the satisfaction to hear that they have been true to their word*, and that they have taken care of these poor people."

In Father Brouillet's narrative, page 57 (Ross Browne, page 41), he says: "On the 3d, the bishop called for the Young Chief and his brother Five Crows, in order to express to them how deeply he had been pained by the news of the horrible affair at Wailatpu, and *to recommend to their care the widows and orphans*, as well as the men who had survived the massacre. They protested to have given no consent to what had happened at Wailatpu, and promised to do all in their power for the survivors.

"On the 10th we received the painful intelligence that two other young men, who, being sick, had been spared by the Indians at the time of the first massacre, had since been torn from their beds and cruelly butchered."

The positive testimony in regard to these two young men is already before the reader. *If this bishop and priest do not act and narrate falsely, we ask, What is falsehood?*

After giving a description of the grand council held at the Catholic mission house by Tawatowe, Tilokaikt, Achekaia, and Camaspelo, Brouillet says, on page 67: "Before taking leave of the chiefs, the bishop said to them all publicly, as he had also done several times privately, that those who had taken American girls should give them up immediately. And then all entreated Five Crows repeatedly to give up the one whom he had taken, but to no purpose." How does this compare with Miss Bewley's testimony?

We must ask to be excused from at present commenting further upon the notes and extracts from the statements of these several parties. They are before you, reader, not as fiction or imagination; they are transactions connected with the history we are writing. The statements on the part of this bishop and his priests have been published and extensively circulated, and have been believed, and have had far too much influence in encouraging and sustaining them among their deluded victms; besides mystifying, and causing a public sentiment to be generally entertained derogatory to the Protestant and American missionary influence in Oregon.

We have given an account of this bishop and his priests on the first commencement of their missionary efforts among the Cayuse Indians, and have followed them through their *labors*, and their legitimate results, till we now come to the 16th of December, the day on which they received a wild, incoherent—not to say injudicious and foolish—letter from Rev. Mr. Spalding, which they gave, with a flourish of trumpets and shout of triumph, on their arrival in Wallamet, to be published as evidence of their extensive influence over the Indians, and to destroy the influence of Mr. Spalding as a missionary. In this they have succeeded but too well, and for which we should look closely into their proceedings with the Indians.

Brouillet, on the 58th and 61st pages (41st and 43d of Browne), in speaking of the Nez Percés who brought Mr. Spalding's letter, says:—

"We had reason to be astonished at that confidence of those Indians, as we had had as yet no opportunity of seeing any one of the Nez Percés since our arrival in the country.

"The two Nez Percé chiefs advised the Cayuses to take measures for avoiding a war with Americans. They requested the bishop to write to Governor Abernethy, begging him not to send up an army, but rather to come himself in the spring and make a treaty of peace with the Cayuses, who promised that they would then release the captives of Wailatpu,—promising besides to offer no injury to Americans until they heard the news from Wallamet. *The bishop told them that he was glad of their proceeding, and was disposed to assist them to the extent of his power*, but that he could not write without knowing the opinion of the Cayuses, and that as soon as he could learn this he would send an express below. He then encouraged them to see all the chiefs about it."

From the above and subsequent statements and transactions, we have no reason to doubt the truth of the bishop's remark, "*that he was glad of their proceeding.*" There can be no question that he did all he could to help the Indians, and to defeat the provisional troops and government, as is proved by the evidence already given, and will be seen as we proceed. He tells the Indians that he could not write, without knowing the opinion of the Cayuses; he must be satisfied that they are all united, and when he has learned that fact, he can write with more assurance and effect to the governor. He extends consolation and encouragement to Camaspelo on the 18th, and two days after convenes the council alluded to.

"Accordingly, on Monday, 20th December, 1847, at the Catholic Mission, the Cayuses assembled in grand council held by Tawatowe (or Young Chief), Tilokaikt, Achekaia (or Five Crows), and Camaspelo, all the great chiefs of the Cayuses, in presence of many other great men (second chiefs) of the nation." This council was held just three months and three days after. Brouillet says "that Bishop Blanchet met Dr. Whitman at Wallawalla, and said to him, "All is known, I come to labor for the conversion of Indians, and even of Americans, if they are willing to listen to me." And we say, to crush and drive the Protestant missions from the country, including their heretical settlements.

We wish to give these foreign *priests* the full benefit of their own statements, as we shall express fully our opinion of them; besides, we presume that not one in a thousand will be able to understand the wonderful workings of Jesuitism among the Indians and the people of our country, without extensive quotations from their books.

The narrative continues: "About ten o'clock in the morning they all entered the mission house. The bishop was present, together with Messrs. Rousseau, Leclaire, and myself [Vicar-General Brouillet, the writer of the narrative we are quoting from]. After a deep silence of some minutes, the bishop explained to them the object of the meeting. He began by expressing to them the pleasure he felt in seeing them thus assembled for the purpose of deliberating on a most important subject,—that of avoiding war, which is always a great evil. He told them that in matters of importance they should always hold a council and consult those who might be best able to give them good advice; that in giving their advice separately, they were liable to be misunderstood, and thereby expose themselves and their people to great misfortunes; that he was persuaded that if the chiefs had deliberated together they would not now have to deplore the horrible massacre of Wailatpu, nor to fear its probable consequences."

The reader can understand how sincere these "holy fathers" were in saying "horrible massacre at Wailatpu," when, instead of calling on Dr. Whitman, as Brouillet says he "cordially promised to do," he went to an Indian lodge, learned of the massacre, and remained all night, writing, the Indians say, this false and infamous account of the transaction, to slander the dead and clear the guilty; and the next morning baptized three of the Indian children before going to the assistance of the widows and orphans.

The bishop told them "that two Nez Percé chiefs had asked him to write to the great chief of Wallamet (Governor Abernethy) to obtain peace, but that he could not do so without the consent of the Cayuses."

It will be remembered that up to the arrival of Dr. White, in 1842, as an official spy upon the proceedings of the Hudson's Bay Company, drawing the pay of a sub-Indian agent, the company had not allowed any effort to combine the Indians; but on the arrival of Dr. White, they at once made use of him, and also of the bishop and his priests, to form just the combinations they wished to make use of, to strike at the settlements at the proper time.

Tawatowe, or Young Chief, was, up to the time of the taking of Fort Nez Percés, considered a head chief; but in consequence of the part he had taken in that affair his power had been broken. His brother, Five Crows, was advanced, and had become the favorite of Dr. Whitman, as well as of Dr. White, and was looked upon as friendly to the mission and the American cause. *Miss Bewley's being forced to become his wife was a part of the scheme to involve him in the war then in contemplation, and to bring about a union of the tribe under the very plausible reason given by this "holy father," and was one of the most important measures to implicate that humane and Protestant Indian in the war measure now in discussion before this grand Indian council at the house of the bishop.* The bishop says "that the propositions which those chiefs wished to send were these: 1st. That Americans should not come to make war; 2d. That they should send up two or three great men to make a treaty of peace; 3d. That when these great men should arrive, all the captives should be released; 4th. That they would offer no offense to Americans before knowing the news from below.

"The bishop then desired them to speak and to say what they thought of these propositions.

"Camaspelo spoke first. He said he was blind and ignorant, and had despaired of the life and salvation of his nation, but that the words of the bishop had opened his eyes, consoled and encouraged him; that he had confidence, and that he approved the propositions.

"The chief Tilokaikt then rose to say that he was not a great speaker, and that his talk would not be long. He then reviewed the history of the nation since the arrival of the whites (French people or Hudson's Bay Company) in the country down to the present time. He said that before they had been visited by white men the Indians were always at war; that at the place where Fort Wallawalla now stood nothing but blood was continually seen; that they had been taught by the *whites* that there was a God who forbids men to kill each other." "A jewel of gold in a swine's snout." This is the Indian that assisted in killing Dr. Whitman, and engaged his attention while his companion gave the first blow; and he afterward cut the Doctor's face horribly with a hatchet, while he was yet alive. But let us continue this "holy father's" lesson of peace and morality from the mouth of his converted Indian, for we have every reason to believe he is now fully converted to that faith, and has given us a specimen in the practice of the religion he has just commenced to learn. He says, "that since this time they had always lived in peace, and endeavored to persuade others to do the same. He eulogized Mr. Pambrun; spoke of a Nez Percé chief who had been killed when going to the States; afterward of the son of Yellow Serpent, who had been killed by Americans in California; said that that they had forgotten all this. He spoke also of Dr. Whitman and Mr. Spalding, and finished by saying that since they had forgotten all, he hoped that the Americans would also forget what had been recently done; that now they were even."

This priest is careful to make his converted Indian tell a plausible story, as also to eulogize Mr. Pambrun and the Hudson's Bay Company, and to state that two Indians had been killed while in company with, or by Americans.

As to the killing of the Nez Percé chief (so called), we know much more of it than this priest or his Indian. The Nez Percé was killed in open fight with the Sioux, at Ash Hollow, on the Platte River, after the party had fought three hours, and killed fifteen and wounded eight of the Sioux. He was no connection of this Cayuse tribe, and is only referred to for effect. The bishop makes Tilokaikt tell a falsehood to shield a crime in himself and associates.

The killing of Elijah, the son of Yellow Serpent, is equally false in the statement of the fact, and relation of the circumstances. Dr. White, sub-Indian agent, etc., was never known to tell the truth when a falsehood would suit his plans and purposes better; as is evident in this case, which is given that the reader may judge of its truth. Mr. Brouillet comments upon Dr. White's letter to the Department at Washington, April 4, 1845, as follows: "After speaking of some difficulties that occurred in California between the Cayuses and Wallawallas on one part, and the Spaniards and Americans on the other, on account of some stolen horses that the Cayuses and Wallawallas had taken from hostile Indians by fighting them [this is altogether a mistake, as the horses belonged to the Americans and Spaniards, and they had their Indians guarding them, and the party here referred to killed the guard and attempted the life of an American], Mr. White passes on to relate a murder there, committed coolly by an American the fall previous upon the person of Elijah, the son of Yellow Serpent, the chief of the Wallawallas, in the following way: 'The Indians had gone to the fort of Captain Sutter to church, and, after service, Elijah was invited into another apartment, taking with him his uncle, Young Chief, of the Umatilla River, a brave and sensible chief of the age of five and forty.'" This priest, on page 30 (J. Ross Browne, page 28), makes Mr. McKinley say that in the fall of 1844, the Indians, a short time after their return from California, met one day at Fort Wallawalla, seven hundred in number, all armed, and decided to walk down immediately upon the colony of the Wallamet, and that they could be stopped only by the Young Chief, who, by his entreaties, decided them to abandon their undertaking, and to go home. We are led to inquire, why did not these Indians, at this time, direct their attention to the American missions in their midst, and take their revenge then, instead of waiting three years, and then, as Brouillet says, making this murder a cause of the massacre? McBean, and Bishop Blanchet and his priests, were not then at the fort, nor among those Indians, to aid them in avenging themselves on the innocent.

But let us finish the account of this horrid transaction on the part of our countrymen, as repeated by Brouillet to excuse the Wailatpu massacre.

He says the Young Chief went into the room with Elijah, and "while there in an unarmed and defenseless condition, they commenced menacing him for things alleged against the River Indians of this upper country, in which none of them had any participation; called them indiscriminately dogs, thieves, etc." The truth is, that this party went from the Cayuse country to California expressly to steal horses and cattle. This same educated Indian boy was the leader of the party in going to the fort. He and the Young Chief were both arrested, and tried by a military court; the chief was acquitted, upon the evidence of the American referred to, as he saved his life, while Elijah was for killing him. Elijah was condemned, and shot, to prevent other similar parties from disturbing the settlements and killing peaceable Indians in California. This is the reason, as Mr. McKinley doubtless told Brouillet, why the Young Chief used his influence to prevent any attempt at retaliation.

The narrative continues: "This American then observed, 'Yesterday you were going to kill me; now you must die,' and drawing a pistol—Elijah, who had been five or six years at the Methodist Mission, and had learned to read, write, and speak English respectably, said deliberately, 'Let me pray a little first;' and kneeling down, at once commenced, and, when invoking the Divine mercy, was shot through the heart or vitals, dead upon the spot. Taking for truth an Indian report [which in this case suited this priest and Dr. White's purposes better than a true statement of the facts would], this horrible affair created considerable excitement [which, he tells us in another place, the Young Chief, who was present, was able to quell], and there is some danger of its disturbing the friendly relations that hitherto existed between us here and all those formidable tribes in the region of Wallawalla and Snake River."

This Indian story or tragedy is useful for three purposes. First, to show Dr. White's disposition to have his importance known to the department at Washington. Second, to show the disposition of this "*holy father, the Catholic priest*," to quote a case of the kind, to justify the Whitman massacre by the Indians, and deceive his readers and the world as to the real cause of that transaction; thus aiding us in bringing home the guilt of a crime where it belongs. Third, to show how capable he is of misrepresenting and falsifying historical facts, to excuse a foul murder of American citizens. He continues to quote Dr. White as follows:—

"Learning from Dr. Whitman, who resides in their midst, how much they were all excited by reason of the treacherous and violent death of this educated and accomplished young chief, and, perhaps, more especially by the loss they had sustained, and then, after suffering so many hardships and encountering so many dangers, losing the whole, I apprehended there might be much difficulty in adjusting it, particularly as they lay much stress upon the restless, disaffected scamps, late from Wallamet to California, loading them with the vile epithets of dogs, thieves, etc., from which they believed or affected to believe that the slanderous reports of our citizens caused all their loss and disasters, and therefore held us responsible. He, Ellis, the Nez Percé chief, assured me that the Cayuses, Wallawallas, Nez Percés, Spokans, Ponderays, and Snakes were all on terms of amity, and that a portion of the aggrieved party were for raising a party of about two thousand warriors of those formidable tribes, and march to California at once,* and, nobly revenging themselves on the inhabitants by capture and plunder, enrich themselves upon the spoils; while others, not indisposed to the enterprise, wished first to learn how it would be regarded here, and whether we would remain neutral in the affair. A third party

* Brouillet, in his haste to bring Dr. White to prove his statements of the causes of the Whitman massacre, has forgotten that he was assured by Mr. McKinley that they intended to go to the Wallamet, instead of California.

were for holding us responsible, as Elijah was killed by an American, and the Americans incensed the Spaniards."*

The above extract is quoted by Brouillet for so base a purpose, that it seems necessary, in order to correct the errors of Dr. White and this priest, to give it in full. We have given the statement of Mr. McKinley, as quoted by Brouillet, which shows the absurdity of this whole document. If the Young Chief went into the room and saw Elijah shot down in the brutal manner represented by Dr. White, he certainly must have been a very remarkable and forgiving Indian if he used his influence to prevent his tribe from seeking revenge; besides, we find in the subsequent history, that even Elijah's own father did not seek to avenge his death, as stated by this priest on page 30 of this narrative (28th of Ross Browne's report).

He says: "And in the spring of 1847, the Wallawalla chief himself, Yellow Serpent, started with a party of Wallawallas and Cayuses for the purpose of attacking the Americans in California, whom they thought unsuspicious. But having found them on their guard, and too strong to be attacked without danger, he took their part against the Spaniards, offered his services to them, and fought in their ranks."

This, with the statement of Mr. McBean, as will be given in his letter, shows that this very Rev. Father Brouillet knew nothing of the subject he was writing about, and was ready to pick up any statement that might be made, without any regard to its absurdity or plausibility. I query whether there is a living man well acquainted with Dr. White, who will state that he believes he would tell the truth, officially or otherwise, when a falsehood would suit his purposes better; and from a careful study of the statements and writings of this reverend priest, we are forced to the same conclusion.

Rev. Mr. Brouillet has filled four pages and a half of his narrative with the statements of William Craig, in answer to questions asked by Hon. P. H. Burnett, all of which show that Mr. Craig knew nothing of the massacre only as he was told, by two Indians, what some other Indian said that some other Indian had said. We are not surprised that Mr. Burnett gave up the contest with Mr. Spalding, after examining such a witness as Mr. Craig, and finding that he knew so little relative to the subject in question. Suppose Tom Hill and the Indian messenger that brought the news to Mr. Spalding's station told all they heard of the matter, did that make their statements true? Or did the repeating of these Indian statements by Mr. Craig make them true? Rev. Father Brouillet has showed, in these four pages, a weakness we

* See the whole of Dr. White's report, chapter 50, page 387 *et seq.*

did not expect to find in a man with so many sacred titles to his name. In fact, the greater part of his statements are from persons who make them as coming second-hand from the Indians. He makes Mr. Craig repeat from the mouth of the Indian messenger the statement first published in Sir James Douglas's letter to the Sandwich Islands; and then in conclusion says, on page 29:—

"Now I am satisfied that every impartial and unprejudiced person, after reading attentively the above documents, will come with me to the conclusion that the true causes, both remote and immediate, of the whole evil must have been the following: 1st. The promise made by Mr. Parker to the Cayuses and Nez Percés of paying for their lands every year, and the want of fulfillment of that promise."

Which promise Mr. Parker never made, and which the Hudson's Bay Company and these Roman priests made up to cause difficulty with the Indians and American missions and settlements.

"2d. The death of the Nez Percé chief, killed on his way to the United States, when he was in company with Mr. Gray, and in his service." This Mr. Gray knows to be false, both in statement and inference, as already explained.

This priest says: "The conclusion is evident, from the circumstances which preceded that death, and from the proceedings of the Nez Percés against Mr. Spalding and all the people of his establishment on account of it, and likewise from the general habit of the Indians in such cases."

We will here state that we were two years at Mr. Spalding's station, on returning from the States, and saw the whole Nez Percé tribe, and employed them for days and months, and worked with them, and explored their country to select farms for them, and know that the Nez Percés never, on any occasion, made the least disturbance about the station, or in any other place, on account of the death of that Indian; and we know that neither Mr. Spalding nor any of the people at his place were ever confined in their houses for an hour on account of it; and we further know that the statement made by Brouillet, as coming from old Toupin, is false and malicious, and only shows the ignorance and malice of this priest, who has made these false statements, as he has those about the killing of Elijah, to cover his own guilt in the infamous crime charged upon him and his associates.

"3d. The murder committed by an American in California on the person of Elijah, the son of the Wallawalla chief, in 1844." Answered already.

This priest says of Yellow Serpent: "On his way coming back from California he lost many of his people from sickness [to which Istacus alludes in his reasons for not believing that Dr. Whitman was the cause of the Indians dying by poison], so that he and his young men, when arrived at home in the fall, felt more ill-disposed than ever toward the Americans." This priest's fourth reason embraces the tales told by Tom Hill, Joe Lewis, Finlay, old Toupin, and Stanfield, which are all of the same class, and have all been learned from the same reverend teachers, and copied into Sir James Douglas's letter, for the benefit of the American Board, going by way of the Sandwich Islands.

His fifth reason, about the small-pox, as stated by Craig—the Doctor and Gray's poisoning melons—the Doctor being a physician, shows that he is terribly pressed for a plausible reason for the crime he attempts to excuse. His sixth reason—lack of sincerity. Here he quotes Mr. Spalding's letter, written soon after his return home, after being exposed six days and nights to extreme fatigue, hunger, and cold,—his mind racked with anxiety and fear in regard to himself and family, and tortured with thoughts of the scene at Wailatpu; being ignorant of any of the particulars of the massacre, and of the part the bishop and his priests were taking in it, he wrote as to friends whom he thought would feel for his situation. He also quotes a letter he received through P. H. Burnett, signed J. Magone, who says: "I recollect distinctly, however, that he (Mr. Spalding) was not in favor of killing all the Cayuses, for he gave me names of some four or five that he knew to be friendly, and another whom I marked as questionable." (Mr. S. had learned more of the particulars of the massacre.) Does this letter prove that he was in favor of killing all the Indians but the ones mentioned, or does it show his anxiety lest the innocent should perish with the guilty, which led him to give those names to Major Magone, an officer in the provisional army?

We have naturally left that deep, silent grand council of Indians, presided over by his reverence, Bishop Blanchet, and directed our attention to other important facts and statements relative to the subject of this chapter.

We now have the touching appeal of Edward Tilokaikt, with whom the reader has become acquainted in the depositions already given. He is now brought before us in this grand council at the bishop's house (page 66 of Brouillet; page 44 Ross Browne).

"Edward, the son of Tilokaikt, then came forward, bearing in his hand the *Catholic Ladder* stained with blood; he repeated the words which Dr. Whitman had used when he showed it to them, one or two weeks before he died: '*You see this blood! it is to show you that now, because you have the priests among you, the country is going to be covered with blood! You will have nothing now but blood!*' He then related what had passed, gave a touching picture of the afflicted families in seeing borne to the grave a father, a mother, a brother, or a sister; spoke of a single member of a family who had been left to weep alone over all the rest, who had disappeared. He stated how and for what the murder had been committed, entered into the most minute details, avoiding, however, *to give any knowledge of the guilty*, repeated the words which *Joseph Lewis* said had passed between Dr. Whitman, his wife, and Mr. Spalding, and finally spoke of the pretended declaration of Mr. Rogers at the moment of his death: 'that Dr. Whitman had been poisoning the Indians.'"

Reader, need I tell you that the language and sentiment above quoted as coming from Edward Tilokaikt, never entered his savage Indian brain; that this speech is the carefully combined and studied production of the author of the narrative we have quoted it from? It is given in connection, repeated and combined with a little variation, by every individual who makes a statement favorable to those priests; and in the whole list of statements this priest Brouillet and McBean are the only two that could write or translate the Indian ideas into French or English; so that at the time these Indian speeches were said to have been made, and purport to have been translated by Brouillet, it is plain to be seen that he tells his own story to suit the case in hand; and the letter of Sir James Douglas to the Sandwich Islands shows this priest to be the author of the statements contained therein. These Indian assemblies or councils were held to more closely unite the tribe, and give a coloring of truth to the malicious statements of Joe Lewis and Edward Tilokaikt.

All these false statements were written out and sent to the Sandwich Islands under date, Vancouver, 9th December, 1847, while Brouillet says this Edward Tilokaikt repeated them as a reason for the massacre on the 20th December, 1847, eleven days before they are said to have been repeated by the Indians.

Many important facts can only be reached by carefully studying the language of this priest, in connection with the evidence obtained from the survivors, and their subsequent conduct, and the foreign correspondence of the parties who were seeking the exclusive occupation of our country.

From the statement that follows, it will be seen how careful this Jesuit is to inform us that these propositions come from the Nez Percés.

He says, on page 65: "After having deliberated together, the chiefs concluded by adding something to the propositions of the Nez Percés, insisting principally upon the reasons which they pretended ought to excuse their action, and requested the bishop to send to the governor in their name the following manifesto."

Before copying this important document and the letter which accompanied it to the governor of Oregon, we will place before our readers the "preface" to the book in which we find it, that they may see the full object of the author of that narrative in publishing it :—

"NEW YORK, June, 1853.

"The following interesting narrative was prepared by the very Rev. Mr. Brouillet, vicar-general of Wallawalla, at the time of the excitement consequent on the murder of Dr. Whitman by the Indians, and in answer to Mr. Spalding, and other of Dr. Whitman's former associates. Although the immediate occasion has passed away, it is proper, still, to put the *facts of the case* on record; and these pages, which appeared recently in the columns of the New York *Freeman's Journal*, will form an interesting and authentic chapter in the history of Protestant missions. "J. A. McMASTERS."

We will now turn to the 65th page of this false and malicious narrative, and find a document carefully prepared, *as stated by its author*, in grand council assembled under the eye of Bishop Blanchet, then bishop of Wallawalla, by the very Rev. Mr. Brouillet, etc. By a cursory glance at this narrative and document, it will be seen that it is prepared as coming from the Indians for the express purpose of blackening the character of Dr. Whitman, his wife, Mr. Spalding, and Mr. Rogers, and of charging them with being the cause of their own murder, and the murder of all who fell at Wailatpu by the hands of their own Indians, the Cayuses. That it embodies all the foul slanders against those missions that have been collected for a series of years, and asserts them to be true, without a single deposition or statement having been made before any court or justice of peace, known to the laws then in the country. These statements, from *preface to finis*, go upon the presumption that the title and professions of the men whose names are attached are sufficient evidence of the truth of any statements they may make, however unreasonable or false they may be. The documents above referred to are as follows (J. R. Browne, page 45) :—

"The principal chiefs of the Cayuses, in council assembled, state: That a young Indian (Joseph Lewis) who understands English, and who slept in Dr. Witman's room, heard the Doctor, his wife, and Mr. Spalding express their desire of possessing the lands and animals of the Indians; that he stated also that Mr. Spalding said to the Doctor, 'Hurry giving medicines to the Indians, that they may soon die;' that the same Indian told the Cayuses, 'If you do not kill the Doctor soon, you will all be dead before spring;' that they buried six Cayuses on

Sunday, November 28, and three the next day; that Mr. Rogers, the schoolmaster, stated to them before he died that the Doctor, his wife, and Mr. Spalding poisoned the Indians; that for several years past they had to deplore the death of their children; and that, according to these reports, they were led to believe that the whites had undertaken to kill them all; and that these were the motives which led them to kill the Americans. The same chiefs ask at present—

"1st. That the Americans may not go to war with the Cayuses.

"2d. That they may forget the lately committed murders, as the Cayuses will forget the murder of the son of the great chief of Walla-walla, committed in California.

"3d. That two or three great men may come up to conclude peace.

"4th. That as soon as these great men have arrived and concluded peace, they may take with them all the women and children.

"5th. They give assurance that they will not harm the Americans before the arrival of these two or three great men.

"6th. They ask that Americans may not travel any more through their country, as their young men might do them harm.

"(Signed,) "TILOKAIKT.
"CAMASPELO.
"TAWATOWE.
"ACHEKAIA.

"PLACE OF TAWATOWE, UMATILLA, December 20, 1847."

"The bishop accompanied this manifesto with a letter addressed to the governor, which concluded in these terms: 'It is sufficient to state that all these speeches went to show, that since they had been instructed by the whites they abhorred war, and that the tragedy of the 29th had occurred from an anxious desire of self-preservation, and that it was the reports made against the Doctor and others which led them to commit this act. *They desire to have the past forgotten and to live in peace as before.* Your excellency has to judge of the value of the documents which I have been requested to forward to you. *Nevertheless, without having the least intention* to influence one way or the other, *I feel myself obliged to tell you,* that by going to war with the Cayuses, *you will likely have all the Indians of this country against you. Would it be for the interest of a young colony to expose herself?* That you will have to decide with your council.'"

Reader, you now have before you a full statement of the most important facts of the Whitman massacre, and of the part taken in it by "*the holy fathers, the Catholic priests,*" as they were styled by Mr. McBean, of Fort Nez Percés, to Mr. Kimzey and his wife.

The part taken by Mr. McBean, Mr. Ogden, and Sir James Douglas, will be given in another chapter.

The above manifesto is given as having been made on the 20th of December, 1847. On the 23d, three days after, when this very Rev. Mr. Brouillet mounted his horse to go to the fort, he told Miss Bewley that "if she went to Five Crows' lodge any more she must not come back to his house." Miss Bewley says: "*The bishop told me I had better go.* * * * The bishop sent an Indian with me; he took me to Five Crows' lodge. * * * *The bishop finally ordered me to go.* * * * *I found I could get no help.*"

These are the solemn affirmations of this intelligent young American lady, who was present at the bishop's house when this manifesto was prepared.

Were this Bishop Blanchet and his priests true and sincere in what they said, and in the advice they say they gave to the Indians?

We have now traced what may be termed the missionary account of this painful tragedy, as given by both parties. Our readers must judge for themselves as to the guilt or innocence of all the parties involved, and also of the application to our subject of the extensive extracts we have given. We will now turn our attention to those whom we conceive to be the prime movers, and, in consequence, the most deeply implicated in this tragedy.

We have had occasion to allude to the intimate connection existing between the Jesuit missions in Oregon and the Hudson's Bay Company. As early as 1836, that company brought a Protestant Episcopal chaplain to Vancouver for political reasons, whom they soon dismissed and attempted to disgrace, as unworthy of belief in any statement he might make. Soon after, in the fall of 1838, two Roman priests arrived at Vancouver and took charge of the religious and literary instructions of the members of the company,—of their children and servants, and, as far as possible, of all the Indians in the country; and while the company professed friendship for the American missionaries, they were active and vigilant to defeat all their efforts to enlighten and civilize the Indians, enlisting sufficient American influence to distract and divide the American people, so as to cover up their main object of securing the country for British Territory. This will be seen by evidence already quoted from our English authors, Mr. Fitzgerald and Sir Edward Belcher, and the refusal of Sir James Douglas to aid the provisional government, or furnish supplies for their troops, and the fact that they did embrace every opportunity to supply the Indians with guns, powder, and balls, and sought to combine the whole Indian power and prejudice against the settlements.

CHAPTER LX.

The Hudson's Bay Company's and the priests' part in the massacre.—McBean's messenger.—Plot divulged to Hinman, Ogden, and Douglas.—Douglas's remark to Hinman.—McBean's letter.—His perversion of facts.—Comments.—Sir James Douglas's letter to Governor Abernethy.—His Sandwich Islands letter.—Its falsehood and absurdity.—Mr. Hinman's letter to Governor Abernethy.—The dates.—Assertion of Robert Newell.—Hudson's Bay Company *v.* United States.

WE learn from Mr. McBean's letter, given below, that his horse guard and interpreter were at Dr. Whitman's mission and saw the dead bodies; and from Indians we learn that they were kept by the Rev. Mr. Brouillet, and took his account of the massacre (which he spent most of the night in preparing) to Mr. McBean. They also reported to him that three parties of Indians were preparing, and about to start, to destroy the remaining Protestant missions and American settlements in middle Oregon, including the station at the Dalles; that the women and children were to be held as hostages, or captives for future disposal; that letters and a statement were prepared by Mr. McBean, and instructions given to his messenger that he might inform the Indians on his way down to Vancouver of what had happened, but he must not give any information to any American on the way, or at the Dalles. We learn from the Hon. A. Hinman that this messenger went to him at the Dalles station, and told him that he was sent by Mr. McBean to Vancouver for men, to replace such as had died of sickness at Fort Nez Percés. The messenger took dinner with Mr. Hinman, who went with him to the Indian lodges, where the messenger told the Indians of the massacre. Mr. Hinman procured a canoe and started with him to go to Vancouver. They reached Cape Horn, some thirty miles above that place, and there, while windbound, he informed Mr. Hinman of what had occurred, making a full confession, that "the *priests*, Mr. *McBean*, and *he* were bad in trying to deceive him and have his family and people killed by the Indians;" told of his instructions, and of what was expected to be done with all the Americans in the country, and that he was the bearer of letters to Governor Ogden from Mr. McBean.

We will now go with this express to Vancouver. Says the Hon. A. Hinman, who is still alive, and has made oath to the truth of his statements: "We went first to Mr. Ogden's room and informed him of the massacre. He was shocked, and said: '*Mr. Hinman, you can now see what opposition in religion will do.'* We then went to Mr. Douglas's room and informed him, and when Mr. Ogden was pacing the room, he said: '*Mr. Douglas, you see now what opposition in religion does.'* After a moment's pause, Mr. Douglas replied, '*There may be other causes.*'"

Reader, will you turn back and read over the chapter on the English Hudson's Bay Company's effort to secure Oregon, and see if there has not been a desperate effort made, since Dr. McLaughlin left that company, to overcome his mistakes and his humane policy toward Americans. Look also at the chapter on the *English Hudson's Bay Company's policy* relative to Rupert's Land and Oregon, and learn fully what Mr. Ogden and Mr. (now Sir James) Douglas meant by these expressions made to Mr. Hinman, who says: "Mr. Douglas turned to me, and wished to know why I was not at home at so perilous a time. I told him I had received no letter from Wallawalla, and did not learn of the massacre till below the Cascades. At this he expressed surprise, and said, 'Mr. McBean ought by all means to have informed you of your danger.'

"After this the express was opened, and Mr. Douglas read, and I listened to the account as given by Mr. McBean, and also of his account of three parties, which, Mr. McBean's letter said, Indian report says are fitting out, one to the saw-mill to kill the Americans at that place, and one to Rev. Mr. Spalding's station to cut off the Americans at that place, and one also to the Dalles to cut off those at that station.

"I said to Mr. Douglas, 'How is it possible that Mr. McBean could have treated me in this way? How is it possible he did not inform me?' Mr. Douglas, after a little pause, said, '*Mr. Hinman, we must consider that the poor man was in circumstances of great perplexity, and might not know what to do.*'"

This was not the case, for Mr. McBean did give him positive instructions, as we learn from Mr. Hinman's statement. He says: "After hearing this dreadful account from the Canadian, I asked him why he did not inform me before I left my house. *He said Mr. McBean told him to say nothing about it to them at the Dalles!*"

Soon after the messenger and Mr. Hinman left the Dalles, the Indians went to the station and informed P. Whitman, the doctor's nephew, that his uncle and aunt, and all the Americans at that place, were killed. This Indian report was not credited; they could not believe that Mr. McBean would send a messenger, as he had done, and not inform them of what had actually taken place.

The reader will remember the deposition of Mr. Kimzey in relation to Mr. McBean's statements about the "holy fathers, the Catholic priests," and the subsequent instructions to him, to let the Indians know he was from the fort.

We will now direct our attention to the mutilated letter of William McBean, as furnished by Sir James Douglas to Governor Abernethy, and published in the Oregon *Spectator*, December 10, 1849:—

"FORT NEZ PERCÉS, NOV. 30, 1847.

"*To the Board of Managers:*

"GENTLEMEN,—It is my painful duty to make you acquainted with a horrible massacre which took place yesterday at Wailatpu, about which I was first apprised, early this morning, by an American who had escaped, of the name of Hall, and who reached this place half-naked and covered with blood, as he started at the outset; the information I received was not satisfactory. He, however, assured me that the Doctor and another man were killed, but could not tell us the persons who did it, and how it originated. I immediately determined on sending my interpreter and one man to Dr. Whitman to find out the truth, and, if possible, to rescue Mr. Manson's two sons and any of the survivors. It so happened that, before the interpreter had proceeded half-way, the two boys were met on their way hither, escorted by Nicholas Finlay, *it having been previously settled among the Indians* that these boys should not be killed [Mr. McBean should have added, as per my instructions]; as also the American women and children [as per Joseph Stanfield's direction, as he had taken Mrs. Hays for a wife, and several Indians were to have the young women at the station for wives]. Tilokaikt is the chief who recommended this measure. I presume that you are well acquainted that fever and dysentery have been raging here and in the vicinity, in consequence of which a great number of Indians have been swept away, but more especially at the Doctor's place, where he had attended upon the Indians. About thirty souls of the Cayuse tribe died, one after another, who evidently believed the Doctor poisoned them, and in which opinion they were, unfortunately, confirmed by one of the Doctor's party. As far as I have been able to learn, this has been the sole cause of the dreadful butchery. In order to satisfy any doubt on that point, it is reported that they requested the Doctor to administer medicine to three of their friends, two of whom were really sick, but the third feigned sickness, and that the three were corpses the next morning. After they were buried, and while the Doctor's men were employed slaughtering an ox, the Indians came one by one to his house, with their arms concealed under their blankets, and, being all assembled, commenced firing on those slaughtering the animal, and in a moment the Doctor's house was surrounded; the Doctor, and a young lad brought up by himself, were shot in the house. His lady, Mr. Rogers, and the children had taken refuge in the garret, but were dragged down and dispatched (excepting the children) outside, where their bodies were left exposed.

"It is reported that it was not their intention to kill Mr. Rogers, in consequence of an avowal to the following effect, which he is said to have made, and which nothing but a desire to save his life could have prompted him to do. He said, 'I was one evening lying down, and overheard the Doctor telling Rev. Mr. Spalding that it was best you should all be poisoned at once, but that the latter told him it was best to continue slowly and cautiously, and between this and spring not a soul would remain, when they would take possession of your lands, cattle, and horses.'

"These are only Indian reports, and no person can believe the Doctor capable of such an action without being as ignorant and brutish as the Indians themselves. One of the murderers, not having been made acquainted with the above understanding, shot Mr. Rogers."

This confession is made, as the reader will notice, and attributed to Mr. Rogers, in order to give the coloring of truth to Joe Lewis's statement. There appears, as will be seen by comparing the statements of Vicar-General Brouillet's Indian council and this of McBean's, a little doubt which to make the author of that story. Sir James Douglas has adopted McBean's statement, as the most plausible, in his report, as it is attributed to one of the *Doctor's own party.*

The whole thing, as will be seen by the testimony of Miss Bewley, is utterly false, and, as McBean has said, only Indian reports; and, we will add, told to them by *Stanfield*, *Joe Lewis*, and *Finlay*, a Frenchman, an Indian, and a half-breed, all under the influence, and probably in the service, of the Hudson's Bay Company and priests. And McBean, Sir James Douglas, and Brouillet are more brutish than the Indians, in putting such reports in circulation. If they had no confidence in them, why did they repeat them, giving them the color of truth? And why do they pretend to say "his life would have been spared," and it was only a mistake that he was shot? Bewley and Sales were brutally murdered the eighth day after Rogers was, for Bewley's saying he did not believe the stories about poisoning Indians, and that he believed the priests were the cause of it. If the Doctor, and Mr. Spalding, and Mrs. Whitman were the only ones they thought injuring them, why attempt to kill all the Americans at the station? Why make the arrangements as extensive as Vicar-General Brouillet tells Mr. Spalding they were (on page 51 of his narrative, 38 of Ross Browne's report): "*I knew that the Indians were angry with all Ameri-*

cans, and more enraged against Mr. Spalding than any other;"—on 54th page: "I know not; you know the country better than I do. All that I know is, that the Indians say *the order to kill Americans has been sent in all directions.*"

Without the history of the Hudson's Bay Company and the Northwest Fur Company before us, we would be quite incapable of comprehending the expressions and statements of this priest to Mr. Spalding. Were we ignorant of that history, and without a knowledge of the statements to which they have made oath in relation to their claims against our government, we could not understand these letters of McBean and Douglas.

We are also in possession of other facts, respecting the treatment of their own countrymen who have unfortunately fallen under their displeasure, which is here repeated upon Dr. Whitman and Mr. Rogers.

We would cut all these communications short, and make a general statement, but we would be charged (as we have already been) with "stringing together statements without facts;" besides, all these Hudson's Bay documents and statements have had a powerful influence to destroy the characters of good men who are dead, and shield the vile conduct of the guilty, who are still living.

So far as McBean was concerned, he obeyed orders as implicitly as Grant of the Hudson's Bay Company did, when *he sent forty families, in* 1846, *into the mountains of California, to perish in the snow with cold and hunger.* McBean must assist in blackening the character of Whitman, Rogers, and Spalding, to protect that of the "*holy fathers, the Catholic priests.*"

McBean in his letter further says: "It is well understood that eleven lives were lost and three wounded. It is also rumored that they are to make an attack upon the fort; let them come if they will not listen to reason; though I have only five men at the establishment, I am prepared to give them a warm reception; the gates are closed day and night, and bastions in readiness. In company with Mr. Manson's two sons was sent a young half-breed lad brought up by Dr. Whitman; they are all here, and have got over their fright."

This portion of the letter is supposed, by Mr. Hinman, to have been put in by Mr. Douglas in place of that which related to sending parties to destroy Americans at other places; and to show to the world that they were threatened by the Indians, as well as the Americans. The same as Brouillet is careful to tell us that "he was afraid the Indians would kill him," and that the priests were not safe among them.

"The ringleaders in this horrible butchery are Tilokaikt, his son, Big Belly, Tamsaky, Istacus [a true friend of the Americans, who was only a witness of the murders], Towmoulisk, etc. I understand from the interpreter that they were making one common grave for the dead. The houses were stripped of every thing in the shape of property; but when they came to divide the spoils, they all fell out among themselves, and all agreed to put back the property. *I am happy to state the Wallawalla chief* had no hand in the whole business."

If this is true, the killing of the Wallawalla chief's son in California could not have been one of the causes of the massacre, as alleged in the narrative of the very Rev. Mr. Brouillet.

"*They were all the Doctor's own people,—the Cayuses.*"

This we should expect, as it would enable those who wished to make their own guilt appear innocence. The Doctor's people alone were to commence killing the Americans. It is asserted by good authority, that a part of Mr. Spalding's, and the Indians at the Dalles, were ready to engage in the same business, from the same advice and orders.

"*One American shot another, and took the Indians' part to save his own life.*"

This statement by McBean is made, as will be seen, to give the impression that there was a quarrel among the Americans, and that they were ready to betray and shoot each other and take the part of the Indians. The reader will recollect that this shooting refers to the Indian Joe Lewis, in killing one of the Sager boys, and is explained particularly by Sir James Douglas in his Sandwich Islands letter, for the information of the American Board of Missions. This fact goes to show that Sir James had received a more particular and carefully prepared account than Mr. McBean had; while the one was a summary, the other was the particulars so arranged as to implicate Dr. Whitman, Mr. Spalding, Mr. Rogers, Mrs. Whitman, and another American, to show that they were not only ready to poison the Indians, but to kill and betray each other to save their own lives; thus showing the intimate connection and complicity of Sir James with the very rev. vicar-general, in giving countenance to this infamous slander, and publishing it to the world over his own signature, and using all his influence to shield and clear the instigators of the crime.

It can not be urged that Sir James received his particular information at some other time, for his letters to Governor Abernethy and the Sandwich Islands were dated, the one to the governor, December 7, 1847, in which he says, "A copy of Mr. McBean's letter herewith will give you *all the particulars known to us* of this indescribably painful event;" and the one to the Islands, December 9, 1847, in which he gives more particulars.

The impression is irresistibly fixed in the mind, that Mr. Brouillet spent most of the night, on arriving at Wailatpu (before the dead were buried), in Tilokaikt's lodge or camp, arranging and writing those statements and particulars, so that Sir James Douglas could give his approval, and that they would go to the American Board of Missions and the friends of the murdered dead, with the sanction of his name, implicating the dead as having brought about this horrible massacre.

Another reason for this impression is, that in all the public and private correspondence between any of these parties, there is, and always has been, the most intense anxiety shown to prevent the open discussion of that transaction, as will be seen in the next paragraph in McBean's letter, and by the promptness with which Mr. Ogden reported to Bishop Blanchet; Mr. Spalding's injudicious remarks to Major Magone on the trip down the river; the manner of Mr. Spalding's very unwise and imprudent letter to the bishop and his priests, was published and commented upon by them; the promptness of Mr. Douglas to demand an explanation of Colonel Gilliam's supposed statement; the refusal of the Hudson's Bay Company to furnish supplies to the provisional troops; and the fact, that the company did supply 1,080 pounds of powder, 1,800 pounds of balls and shot to the priests for the Indians, with three cases containing thirty-six guns, all of which were seized by Lieutenant Rogers at the Dalles, and should have been (but were not) confiscated. We will now ask the attention of the reader to the remainder of this (to the Hudson's Bay Company and Romanists in general) glorious news of the complete victory they had obtained over *Protestantism* and its missions in Oregon.

Mr. McBean, or Sir James Douglas, we do not know which, says: "Allow me to *draw a veil over this dreadful affair* which is too painful to dwell upon, and which I have explained conformable to information received and with sympathizing feelings.

"I remain, with much respect, gentlemen,

"Your most obedient humble servant,

"WILLIAM McBEAN."

We can scarcely retain the expressions of Whew! Horrible! etc., as we give the balance of this important letter, copied and given to the public of Oregon, under the eye of Sir James Douglas, with the—

"N. B.—I have just learned that the Cayuses are to be here to-morrow to kill Serpent Jaune, the Wallawalla chief. "W. McB."

"Names of those who were killed: Dr. Whitman, Mrs. Whitman, Mr. Rogers, Hoffman, Sanders, Osborn [not killed], Marsh, John and

Francis Sager, Canfield [not killed], and a sailor, besides three that were wounded more or less—Messrs. Hall, Kimball, and another whose name I can not learn. "W. McBEAN."

Could the reader look at the exact original copy of that letter, and of that as found in the *Spectator* of December 10, 1847, and hear the expressions of sentiment and feeling among a portion of the people at Oregon City; and listen to some of the private consultations, and hear the opinions there expressed, he would be able to understand the impression that this, with some other letters published at that time, made upon the public mind.

There was in one little council of a number of the then representatives of Oregon, a disposition to let that foul murder pass, without making an effort to avenge those deaths, or punish the Indians. One of that little council exclaimed with an oath, "Gentlemen, we must not allow that murder to pass, without an effort to punish those concerned in it; and for one, I know that Dr. Whitman did not bring it upon himself. Our own existence in this country is involved in the action we take in this matter. It becomes absolutely necessary that we take measures to protect ourselves and punish the murderers."

"FORT VANCOUVER, Dec. 7, 1847.

"*George Abernethy, Esq.:*

"SIR,—Having received intelligence last night (on the 4th), by special express from Wallawalla, of the *destruction* of the *missionary settlement* at Wailatpu *by the Cayuse Indians of that place*, we hasten to communicate the *particulars* of that dreadful event, one of the most atrocious which darkens the annals of Indian crime.

"Our lamented friend Dr. Whitman, his amiable and accomplished lady, with nine other persons, have fallen victims to the fury of those remorseless savages, who appear to have been instigated to the appalling crime by a horrible suspicion which had taken possession of their superstitious minds, in consequence of the number of deaths from dysentery and measles, that Dr. Whitman was silently working the destruction of their tribe, by administering poisonous drugs under the semblance of salutary medicines.

"With a goodness of heart and benevolence truly his own, Dr. Whitman had been laboring incessantly, since the appearance of the measles and dysentery among *his Indian converts*, to relieve their sufferings, and *such has been the reward of his generous labors.*

"*A copy of Mr. McBean's letter herewith will give you all the particulars known to us of this indescribably painful event.*

"Mr. Ogden, with a strong party, will leave this place as soon as possible for Wallawalla, to endeavor to prevent further evil, and we beg to suggest to you the propriety of taking instant measures for the protection of the Rev. Mr. Spalding, who, for the sake of his family, *ought to abandon* the Clearwater Mission *without delay*, and retire to a place of safety, as he can not remain at that isolated station without imminent risk in the present excited and irritated state of the Indian population.

"I have the honor to be, sir,
"Your most obedient servant,
"JAMES DOUGLAS."

We now give Sir James Douglas's letter to the Sandwich Islands, as found in the March number of the *Friend*:—

"FORT VANCOUVER, Dec. 9, 1847.

"*S. N. Castle, Esq.*:

"SIR,—It is with feelings indescribably painful that I hasten to communicate to you, *for the information of the Board of Missions*, intelligence of a disastrous event which lately occurred at the mission station of Wailatpu. Our esteemed friend Dr. Whitman, his amiable and accomplished lady, and nine men and youths in the mission employ, were murdered on the 29th ultimo by the Cayuse Indians, with circumstances of the most revolting cruelty. The lives of the women and children, with the exception of the lamented lady already mentioned, were spared. The mission being situated in the Cayuse country, they had a peculiar interest in protecting it from harm, in gratitude for past favors, and for the blessings of religious instruction so assiduously dispensed to them and to their families; yet those very people, the objects of so much solicitude, *were alone concerned in effecting the destruction of the establishment* founded solely for their benefit.

"The Cayuses are the most treacherous and untractable of all the Indian tribes in this country [contradicted by Mr. Ogden], and had on many former occasions alarmed the inmates of the mission by their tumultuous proceedings and ferocious threats; but, unfortunately, these evidences of a brutal disposition were disregarded by their admirable pastor, and served only to arm him with a firmer resolution to do them good. He hoped that time and instruction would produce a change of mind,—a better state of feeling toward the mission,—and might have lived to see his hopes realized [had not the Hudson's Bay Company and the Roman priests determined otherwise], had not the measles and dysentery, following in the train of emigration from the United

States, made fearful ravages this year in the upper country, many Indians having been carried off through the violence of the disease, and others through their own imprudence.

"The Cayuse Indians of Wailatpu being sufferers in the general calamity, were incensed against Dr. Whitman, [by the tales of Joe Lewis, Stanfield, and the very Rev. Mr. Brouillet, who afterward found a vial of white powder and called it poison, and ordered the Indians to bury it, as per evidence in the case] for not exerting his supposed supernatural power in saving their lives. They carried this absurdity beyond that point of folly.

"Their superstitious minds becamed possessed with the horrible superstition that he was giving poison to the sick instead of wholesome medicine, with the view of working the destruction of the tribe; their former cruelty probably adding strength to their suspicions. Still some of the more reflecting had confidence in Dr. Whitman's integrity, and it was agreed to test the effect of the medicine he had furnished on three of their people, one of whom was said to be in perfect health."

The absurdity of this statement is so palpable, and so perfectly improbable in every respect, that, with all my study of Indian character, I am unable to understand why this statement is repeated by any of the parties concerned in bringing about that massacre. It can only be believed by the most stupid, as it has not the plausibility of truth in it; and Mr. Douglas showed a debasement of mind beyond comprehension in quoting it to his friend. We quote this whole letter, that it may be seen how low Sir James felt himself obliged to descend, to make an absurdity appear reasonable. The idea is started by Brouillet, increased by McBean, and completed by Douglas, who would give such accounts to the public to make others equally false appear probable. He continues:—

"*They unfortunately died, and from that moment it was resolved to destroy the mission.*"

But we have positive testimony that the destruction of that mission, with Mr. Spalding's, was determined upon, and so stated by McBean before an Indian was known to be sick in the tribe or at the station. Mr. Douglas says:—

"It was immediately after burying the remains of these three persons, that they repaired to the mission one after another, with their arms hid under their blankets. The Doctor was at the school with the children, the others were cutting up an ox which they had just killed. When the Indians were numerous enough to effect their object, they fell upon the poor victims, some with guns and others with hatchets, and their blood was soon streaming on all sides.

"Some of the Indians turned their attention toward the Doctor; he received a pistol-shot in the breast from one, and a blow on the head from another. He had still strength enough to reach a sofa, where he threw himself down and expired. Mrs. Whitman was dragged from the garret and mercilessly butchered at the door. Mr. Rogers was shot after his life had been granted to him.

"The women and children were also going to be murdered, when a voice was raised to ask for mercy in favor of those whom they thought innocent, and their lives were spared.

"It is reported that a kind of deposition made by Mr. Rogers incensed the fury of this savage mob. Mr. Rogers was seized, was made to sit down, and then told that his life would be spared if he made a full discovery of Dr. Whitman's supposed treachery. That person then told the Indians that the Doctor intended to poison them; that one night, when Mr. Spalding was at Wailatpu, he heard them say that the Indians ought to be poisoned, in order that the Americans might take possession of their lands; that the Doctor wished to poison them all at once, but Mr. Spalding advised him to do it gradually. Mr. Rogers, after this deposition, was spared, but an Indian, who was not present, having seen him, fired at and killed him.

"An American made a similar deposition, adding that Mrs. Whitman was an accomplice, and she deserved death as well as her husband.

"It appears that he concluded by saying that he would take the side of the Indians, and that he detested the Americans. An Indian then put a pistol into his hand, and said to him, 'If you tell the truth, you must prove it by shooting that young American;' and this wretched apostate from his country fired upon the young man shown to him, and laid him dead at his feet.

"It was upon the evidence of that *American* that Mrs. Whitman was murdered, or she might have shared in the mercy extended to the other females and children.

"*Such are the details, as far as known, of that disastrous event, and the causes which led to it.*

"Mr. Rogers' reported deposition, if correct, is unworthy of belief, having been drawn from him by the fear of instant death. The other American, who shed the blood of his own friend, must be a villain of the darkest dye, and ought to suffer for his aggravated crime."

There is no evidence that Sir James Douglas ever exerted the least influence to arrest or punish one of those murderers; on the contrary, there is evidence that the Hudson's Bay Company assisted them and facilitated their escape from justice, and supplied the Indians with arms and ammunition to carry on the war that followed. Particulars of the whole truth are given in another chapter. This letter of Sir James Douglas continues:—

"On the 7th instant, Mr. Ogden proceeded toward Wallawalla with a strong party of the Hudson's Bay Company's servants, to endeavor to prevent further evil.

"Accompanying, you will receive a copy of a letter which I addressed to Governor Abernethy immediately after the arrival of the melancholy intelligence at this place.

"All that can be collected will be considered important by the friends of Doctor and Mrs. Whitman in the United States, who will be anxious to learn every particular concerning their tragic fate. It will be a satisfaction for them to know that these eminent servants of God were faithful in their lives, though we have to deplore the melancholy circumstances which accompanied their departure from this world of trial.

"I am, sir, your obedient servant,

"JAMES DOUGLAS."

We now have before us the statements of all the parties concerned in the most inhuman and disgraceful tragedy that has darkened the pages of our history. The crime itself was most inhuman and brutal, but, being mixed with religious prejudice and sectarian hate, guided and brought about by foreign commercial influences under the direction of a British monopoly, it demands a national investigation.

That Sir James Douglas knew more of the inception and ultimate designs of that transaction is evident from the prompt and careful manner in which he answered Mr. Ogden's remark, that it was brought about from religious causes; he affirmed that "*there might be other causes;*" and when he had read the dispatches, he said, "*We must consider the poor man was in great perplexity, and might not know what to do.*" These two expressions of Sir James Douglas to Mr. Ogden and Mr. Hinman are the key that unlocks the whole mystery in this desperate arrangement to hold this whole country for the exclusive benefit of that monopoly.

As to the morality of the transaction, the great sympathy of Sir James and his conclave of bishops and priests, the church assumes all. The baptizing of three Indian children was of more importance to the church than all the suffering widows and orphans at that missionary settlement.

The particular account, as given by Sir James, was of more importance than punishing the murderers, or even casting a suspicion, such as Mr. Ogden, his associate, had done, upon his accomplices in crime.

These two letters show his duplicity, and the unblushing manner in which he gives one statement to Governor Abernethy, for Oregon, and another for the Board of Missions, and how careful he is to state circumstances and false impressions as to the facts he pretends to give with so much sympathy and apparent interest in the fate of the murdered dead.

There are but two other persons who have given us any information of this tragedy, on the part of the priests and the Hudson's Bay Company. One of those was, at the time, in charge of Fort Nez Percés. His account was sent to Sir James,—mutilated, and not as carefully prepared for the people of Oregon as was this one for the great world beyond. The other is prepared by the very Rev. Mr. Brouillet, vicar-general of Wallawalla, and given to the world to form an "*interesting and authentic chapter in the history of Protestant missions*," and contains all the imaginary circumstantial statements of the massacre, as given over the name of James Douglas, and officially in the report of J. Ross Browne, December 4, 1859.

If these statements had first appeared, as they now do, over the name and by the authority or affirmation of the very Rev. Mr. Brouillet, etc., all the world, as J. Ross Browne did, would have adopted the idea of Mr. Ogden, and said truly this was the result of *opposition in religion*. But Sir James Douglas proves, by his own statements and letters, and subsequent conduct all through the war that followed, that it was not "*opposition in religion* alone." It was a predetermined arrangement of the "*powerful company, the practical monopoly of the fur trade*," which, in 1865, he affirmed this company held over the country in 1846. The profits of that business were not to be lost to his powerful company by any missionary settlement in it.

Are we correct in these conclusions? The statements are given by the parties implicated. Were we to allow our personal feelings and sectarian preferences to influence our conclusions, we would join in the general conclusion of Mr. Ogden; but a full knowledge of the facts forces us to believe the statement of Mr. Douglas as being the most correct; nevertheless, we will not abate one iota of the scathing condemnation justly due to the foreign sectarianism brought into the country to effect the object of that corporation, nor of the scorn and infamy due to the immediate controlling actors—Bishop Blanchet and his priests—under the garb of religion.

We wish to keep as distinctly as possible before the mind the separate part each party has performed in this great drama of which we have been writing. As we have before said, there were four distinct parties or influences in the country, and the Indian formed the fifth. The Hudson's Bay Company and the Roman priests combined and formed one; the missionaries with the settlers formed another; and the Indian was between them. For a time, the American influence was the most prominent,—say in 1843, 1844, and 1845. In 1846, Bishop Blanchet was in Europe, making extensive preparations for missionary operations in Oregon, corresponding in extent with those made by the Rev. Jason Lee in 1839-40.

"On August 19, 1847, Bishop Blanchet arrived in the mouth of the Columbia River, in the *Morning Star*, Captain Menes, five and a half months from Brest, with five priests, three Jesuits, three lay brothers, two deacons, and seven nuns." In addition to these, we had, overland, eight priests and two nuns that same year. These, with the priests already in the country, gave us twenty-five of the Roman clerical order and fifteen nuns. This was a powerful and extensive effort to recover the lost foreign influence in the country. How well they succeeded is now a matter of history, and will enable the reader to understand the bold and defiant attitude of Mr. Douglas and his efficient co-laborers, Bishop Blanchet and his priests, among the Indians.

The missionary settlement at Wailatpu was the most important point in the whole upper country. The influence and position of those Indians were such, that special efforts were required to commence and carry on the destruction of all American settlements in the country.

We come now to the letter of Hon. A. Hinman, properly belonging to this chapter.

FORT VANCOUVER, December 4, 1847.

Mr. George Abernethy:

DEAR SIR,—A Frenchman, from Wallawalla, arrived at my place on last Saturday, and informed me that he was on his way to Vancouver, and wished me to assist in procuring him a canoe immediately. I was very inquisitive to know if there was any difficulty above. He said four Frenchmen had died recently, and he wished to get others to occupy their places.

I immediately got him a canoe, and concluded to go in company with him, in order to get some medicine for the Indians, as they were dying off with measles and other diseases very fast. I was charged with indifference. They said we were killing in not giving them medicines, and I found if we were not exposing our lives, we were our peace, and consequently I set out for this place. This side of the Cascades I was made acquainted with the horrible massacre that took place at Wailatpu last Monday. Horrid to relate! Dr. and Mrs. Whitman, Mr. Rogers, Mr. Osborn, Mr. Sanders, a school-teacher, the two orphan boys (John and Francis Sager), together with all the men at that place,—eleven in all. Some are living at the saw-mill, which is situated about twenty miles from the Doctor's. A party set out for that place to dispatch them; also a party for Mr. Spalding's, to dispatch them; and they are not satisfied yet, but a party is said to have started for my place, and has, if true, reached there before this time. Oh! had I known it when I was at home. I can neither sleep nor take any rest, on account of my family and those with them, viz., my wife and child, the Doctor's nephew, Dr. Saffron, and Mr. McKinney and wife. If I had ten men I could defend myself with perfect ease, by occupying the meeting-house, which is very roomy and close. You see my situation, as well as Mr. Spalding's. I have perfect confidence in your doing all you can to get a party to come up and spend the winter there, and likewise to go to the rescue of the women and children, and Mr. Spalding, if alive, which I think very doubtful.

Delay not a moment in sending a few men for my protection; a few moments may save our lives.

I expect to leave to-morrow for home, and perhaps the first salutation will be a ball. My family is there, and I must return if it costs my life.

We are in the hands of a merciful God, why should we be alarmed? I will close by saying again, send a small force immediately without the delay of one day. Farewell.

Yours truly,

ALANSON HINMAN.

It will be seen that the main facts are given by Mr. Hinman, with the designs of other Indian parties to cut off the Americans at Mr. Spalding's, the saw-mill, and at the Dalles, which Mr. Douglas omits in his letter to Governor Abernethy, but informs him of the Indians' threatened attack upon Fort Nez Percés (Wallawalla).

That part of Mr. Douglas's letter relating to Mr. Rogers' supposed statement to the Indians, the brother (still living) has requested Mr. Douglas to explain; but no explanation has been given. We know, from the depositions given, that Mr. Douglas made the statement without evidence of its truth; and it is evident he is too stubborn or proud to acknowledge or explain his error.

There is one other fact in connection with this transaction that looks dark on the part of Sir James Douglas.

It is shown in the dates of the several letters. Mr. Hinman's is dated December 4; Mr. Douglas's, December 7; that to the Sandwich Islands, December 9. Now, between the 4th and 7th are three days. In a case of so much importance, and professed sympathy,—as expressed in his letter,—how is it, that three, or even two days were allowed to pass without sending a dispatch informing Governor Abernethy of what had happened, and of what was expected to take place? which last he had left out of his letter, and the copy of McBean's; but does inform him of the threatened danger to Fort Nez Percés, as coming from McBean.

Mr. Douglas is prompt to urge the removal of Mr. Spalding, but unreasonably slow to send an express twenty or thirty miles to notify the American settlement of its danger.

We wish to say, once for all, that we are not giving the private history or character of any man or set of men. Their public conduct and proceedings are a part of our history. Mr. Douglas was, at the time we are writing, the acknowledged head of the Hudson's Bay Company, and, as such, acted and controlled the movements of its members. Bishop Blanchet was the acknowledged head of the Roman Church, and, as such, acted with Mr. Douglas; for while not one Roman priest, or a servant of either of these two parties were disturbed or harmed in the least, all Protestant missionaries and American citizens were either killed, or driven from the upper country by order of that company. As Robert Newell asserts, under date of October 25, 1866: "*And they could not have remained in the country a week* without the consent and aid of that company, nor could any mission, in my opinion, in those days have been established in this (Wallamet) or that (Wallawalla) valley, without the aid and influence of the Hudson's Bay Company, nor could the settlers have remained in the country as they did up to 1848, for the same reasons."

This statement is made by a gentleman who professes to know more of, and has been (without a question) more favored by the Hudson's Bay Company than any other American in the country. If his statement is true, which we have no doubt he believes it to be, then who is responsible for all the murders of American hunters, trappers, missionaries, immigrants, and settlers on their way to our country and in it. But we will not risk our conclusions upon the statement of an individual, who is totally ignorant of the policy of the company he undertakes to defend. We have, in addition, the sworn statement of Sir James Douglas as to the power and influence of his company, one year previous to the cutting off of the missionary settlement at Wailatpu.

He says, under oath: "Their posts were so arranged as to practically enjoy a monopoly in the fur trade, and they possessed an extraordinary influence with the nations west of the Rocky Mountains." (Answer to interrogatory in claim Hudson's Bay Company *v.* United States.)

That this influence was exerted to destroy that mission there can be no question; and that the same influence has since been exerted to spread, far and wide, statements originated by them and their associates to blast the character of the dead, and destroy the influence of the living in the cause of truth, is equally true.

We find it stated in Brouillet's narrative that the most friendly and cordial relations existed between the Hudson's Bay Company and his mission; so much so, that he is present by special invitation at Mr. Ogden's council for arranging the purchase of the captives. He informs us, on page 69, "Protestantism in Oregon," that Mr. Ogden told them that "the Hudson's Bay Company had never deceived them; that he hoped they would listen to his words; that the company did not meddle with the affairs of the Americans; that there were *three parties;* the *Americans* on one side, the *Cayuses* on the other, and the *French* people and the *priests* in the middle; the company was there to trade and the priests to teach them their duties; 'Listen to the priests,' said he, several times; 'listen to the priests; they will teach you how to keep a good life; the priests do not come to make war; they carry no arms,—they carry but their crucifixes,* and with them they can not kill.' He *insisted particularly*, and at several times, upon the *distinction necessary* to be made between the affairs of the company and those of the Americans."

The company's interests must not be interfered with. The professions of sympathy found in Mr. Douglas's letters are all explained, when the facts are fully developed. The complaint of the company, as stated in the memorial presented to the commissioners, April 17, 1865 (Hudson's Bay Company *v.* United States, page 19), states that "among these circumstances may be specified the aggressive acts and the general conduct of American citizens, and of persons acting under the authority of the United States, commencing shortly after the 15th of June, 1846, and continuing from year to year, by which the rights of the claimants under that treaty were violated and denied, and their property and possessions were, in some instances, usurped and taken from them, and, in others, were necessarily abandoned. This course of conduct was, perhaps, to be expected, from the anomalous position in which the company was placed,—a foreign corporation exercising a *quasi* sovereignty and exclusive rights over territory transferred to a power whose policy in dealing with such territory was diametrically opposed to that which the company pursued, and from which they derived their profits."

This complaint demands careful consideration at the present time.

* The Oblates, who constantly carry a crucifix on their breasts, were present.

The statements of Mr. Ogden to the Indians, the memorial of the company, and the testimony it has produced in support of its claims, the statements and correspondence of the Jesuit missionaries, all go to prove the settled policy of the company to maintain its "*quasi* sovereignty" and exclusive asserted claims to the country at the time of the Wailatpu massacre.

That company, with less than half its then powerful influence and capital, had compelled the more powerful and active French-Canadian Northwest Company, numerically stronger than itself, to yield and accept its terms of a union in 1821.

They had driven from the country all American traders. They had, as they vainly imagined, secured an influence in the provisional American government sufficient to control all danger from that source, while they were ready to let loose the Indians upon the settlers, and prepared to supply them with the means to destroy or drive them from the country.

CHAPTER LXI.

Preliminary events of the Cayuse war.—Message of Governor Abernethy.—Journal of the house.—Resolutions.—Assembling of the people at the call of the governor.—Enlisting of men.—Names of the volunteers.—Names of the officers.—Their flag.—Their departure.—Letter to Sir James Douglas.—His reply.—Commissioners return.—Address to the citizens.—Public meeting.—Report of commissioners to the Legislature.—Messenger sent to Washington.—Memorial to Congress.—Champoeg County tax.—Strength of the settlement called for.—Bishop Blanchet's letter to Governor Abernethy.

Message of Governor Abernethy.

OREGON CITY, December 8, 1847.

GENTLEMEN,—It is my painful duty to lay the inclosed communications before your honorable body. They will give you the particulars of the horrible massacre committed by the Cayuse Indians on the residents at Wailatpu. This is one of the most distressing circumstances that has occurred in our Territory, and one that calls for immediate and prompt action. I am aware that to meet this case funds will be required, and suggest the propriety of applying to the Hudson's Bay Company and the merchants of this place for a loan to carry out whatever plan you may fix upon. I have no doubt but the expense attending this affair will be promptly met by the United States government.

The wives and children of the murdered persons, the Rev. Mr. Spalding and family, and all others who may be in the upper country, should at once be proffered assistance, and an escort to convey them to places of safety. I have the honor to remain, gentlemen,

Your obedient servant,

GEORGE ABERNETHY.

To the Honorable Legislative Assembly, Oregon.

Journal of the House, December 8, 1847

At two o'clock the house met. The sergeant-at-arms announced a special communication from the governor, which was read by the clerk. It consisted of letters from Messrs. Douglas and McBean, of the forts on the Columbia, announcing the horrid murder of Dr. Whitman's family and others, accompanied by a letter from the governor, praying the immediate action of the house in the matter.

Mr. Meek moved the reference of the communications to a committee of the whole house, which was lost. Mr. Nesmith offered the following, which was adopted:—

"*Resolved*, That the governor be, and is hereby, authorized and required to raise, arm, and equip a company of riflemen, not to exceed fifty men, with their captain and subaltern officers, and dispatch them forthwith to occupy the mission station at the Dalles, on the Columbia River, and hold possession until re-enforcements can arrive at that point, or other means be taken, as the government thinks advisable."

Messrs. Nesmith, Reese, and Crawford were appointed a committee to wait on the governor and inform him of said resolution.

The communications concerning the Indian depredations were referred to a committee consisting of Messrs. Ford, Rector, and White.

The committee appointed to wait on the governor concerning the resolution for raising a company of riflemen, reported that they had discharged their duty, and received, in answer, that the governor will use his utmost endeavors to accomplish the object.

The governor called the people together in the evening, and, after the statements of the object of the meeting, some forcible and earnest remarks from Judge Nesmith and Messrs. Lee, Barlow, and others, the enrollment of the first company of Oregon riflemen commenced.

The following true and noble-hearted men sprang to arms, and, in fifteen hours from the time they had enrolled their names as defenders of Oregon, were on their way to protect their own and their countrymen's lives from Hudson's Bay Company, Jesuitical, and Indian savagism.

We will give the names of this noble little band a place in the history of the country they were so prompt and ready to defend. They are as follows:—

Joseph B. Proctor,
J. S. Rinearson,
H. A. G. Lee,
Thomas Purvis,
J. Magone,
C. Richardson,
J. E. Ross,
Isaac Walgamoutts,
John G. Gibson,
B. B. Rogers,
Benjamin Bratton,
Samuel K. Barlow,
Wm. Berry,
John Bolton,
George Moore,
Henry W. Coe,
William Buckman,
S. A. Jackson,
Jacob Witchey,
John Fleming,
A. C. Little,
A. J. Thomas,
George Westby,
Edward Robson,
Andrew Wise,
D. Averson,
J. H. McMellen,
John C. Danford,
W. M. Carpenter,
Lucius Marsh,
Joel McKee,
H. Levalley,
J. W. Morgan,
O. Tupper,
R. S. Tupper,
C. H. Devendorf,
John Hiner,
C. W. Savage,
G. H. Bosworth,
Jacob Johnson,
Stephen Cummings,
George Weston.

Forty-two as noble and true men as ever breathed. They were soon organized under a set of energetic and brave young officers, who feared no danger, and were ready to meet in open fight the combined enemies of their country's rights upon the shores of the Pacific, or in the mountains or valleys of Oregon. Their officers were:—

Captain, H. A. G. Lee.	*First Sergeant*, J. S. Rinearson.
First Lieutenant, J. Magone.	*Second Sergeant*, W. Savage.
Second Lieutenant, J. E. Ross.	*Third Sergeant*, Wm. Berry.
Commissary, C. H. Devendorf.	*First Corporal*, Stephen Cummings.
Surgeon, W. M. Carpenter, M. D.	*Second Corporal*, J. H. McMellen.

"At twelve o'clock on the afternoon of Tuesday, the company assembled at the City Hotel, where they were presented with an appropriate flag, by Judge Nesmith, in behalf of the ladies of Oregon City, with an appropriate address. (No record of that address or of the names of the donors can be found.) Captain Lee, on the part of the company, made an exceedingly happy reply upon receiving the beautiful token of the patriotism of the lovely donors."

In two hours after, the company started, amid the firing of cannon and the cheers of the assembled citizens. It speaks well for our city, that in less than twenty-four hours this detachment was raised and had started for the scene of action.

It is to be regretted that the editor of the Oregon *Spectator*, at the time these deeply-interesting events were occurring, should fill the only public journal on the coast with accounts of personal piques, and allow the remarks of Judge Nesmith and the reply of Captain Lee to pass with the meager notice we have quoted; that the deeply-stirring events respecting the murder of his countrymen should find so small a place in his editorial. He tells us in this same paper that he means to keep us posted in the war news, but the next paper is filled with a personal war between himself and the directors of the Printing Association, about some political resolutions that did no good or harm to anybody, except to show the party spirit then existing in the country, in which he is foolish enough to engage, and degrade his noble position as a journalist and editor, which compels us to look to other sources for facts relative to the history of those times.

Our little army of braves were accompanied by Governor Abernethy and three commissioners to Vancouver, where they completed their outfit before proceeding to the Dalles.

They arrived at Vancouver on the 10th of December. On the 11th, the commissioners addressed a letter to Mr. Douglas, requesting him to furnish supplies, as follows:—

FORT VANCOUVER, December 11, 1847.

To James Douglas, Esq.:

SIR,—By the inclosed document you will perceive that the undersigned have been charged by the Legislature of our provisional government with the difficult duty of obtaining the means necessary to arm, equip, and support in the field, a force sufficient to obtain full satisfaction of the Cayuse Indians for the late massacre at Wailatpu, and protect the white population of our common country from further aggression.

In pursuance of this object, they have deemed it their duty to make immediate application to the Honorable Hudson's Bay Company for the requisite assistance.

Though clothed with the power to pledge, to the fullest extent, the faith and means of the present government of Oregon, they do not consider this pledge the only security of those who, in this distressing emergency, may extend to the people of this country the means of protection and redress. Without claiming any especial authority from the government of the United States to contract a debt to be liquidated by that power, yet from all precedents of like character in the history of our country, the undersigned feel confident that the United States government will consider the murder of the late Dr. Whitman and lady as a national wrong, and will fully justify the people of Oregon in taking active measures to obtain redress for that outrage, and for their protection from further aggression.

The right of self-defense is tacitly accorded to every body politic in the confederacy to which we claim to belong, and in every case similar to our own, within our knowledge, the general government has promptly assumed the payment of all liabilities growing out of the measures taken by the constituted authorities to protect the lives and property of those residing within the limits of their districts.

If the citizens of the States and Territories east of the Rocky Mountains are justified in promptly acting in such emergencies, who are under the immediate protection of the general government, there appears no room to doubt that the lawful acts of the Oregon government will receive a like approval.

Should the temporary character of our government be considered by you sufficient ground to doubt its ability to redeem its pledge, and reasons growing out of its peculiar organization be deemed sufficient to prevent the recognition of its acts by the government of the United States, we feel it our duty, as private individuals, to inquire to what extent and on what terms advances may be had of the Honorable Hudson's Bay Company, to meet the wants of the force the authorities of Oregon deem it their duty to send into the field.

With sentiments of the highest respect, allow us to subscribe ourselves, Your most obedient servants,

JESSE APPLEGATE,
A. L. LOVEJOY,
GEO. L. CURRY,
} Commissioners.*

Captain Lee's company received their outfit as per arrangements through the governor, Mr. Applegate, and Mr. Lovejoy, and proceeded to the Dalles. The commissioners returned to Oregon City, and on the 13th December, 1847, addressed the merchants and citizens of Oregon as follows:—

GENTLEMEN,—You are aware that the undersigned have been charged by the Legislature of our provisional government with the difficult duty of obtaining the means necessary to arm, equip, and support in the field a force sufficient to obtain full satisfaction of the Cayuse Indians, for the late massacre at Wailatpu, and protect the white population of our common country from further aggression. In furtherance of this object, they have deemed it their duty to make immediate application to the merchants and citizens of the country for the requisite assistance. †

* * * * * * * *

Though the Indians of the Columbia have committed a great outrage upon our fellow-citizens passing through their country, and residing among them, and their punishment for these murders may, and ought to be, a prime object with every citizen of Oregon, yet, as that duty more particularly devolves upon the government of the United States, and admits of delay, we do not make this the strongest ground upon which to found our earnest appeal to you for pecuniary assistance. It is a fact well known to every person acquainted with the Indian character, that, by passing silently over their repeated thefts, robberies, and murders of our fellow-citizens, they have been emboldened to the commission of the appalling massacre at Wailatpu. They call us women, destitute of the hearts and courage of men, and if we allow this

* Mr. Douglas's reply to the above was, in substance, *a refusal to advance the means asked for in consequence of the stringent rules laid down for his government by the home company.* He, however, upon the security of the governor, and two of the commissioners, advanced the amount necessary to fit out the first company of Oregon riflemen, $999.59.—(See report of Loan Commissioners, *Oregon Archives*, p. 323.)

† The paragraphs here omitted are the same as those addressed to the Hudson's Bay Company.

wholesale murder to pass by as former aggressions, who can tell how long either life or property will be secure in any part of this country, or what moment the Wallamet will be the scene of blood and carnage?

The officers of our provisional government have nobly performed their duty. None can doubt the readiness of the patriotic sons of the West to offer their personal service in defense of a cause so righteous; so it now rests with you, gentlemen, to say whether our rights and our firesides shall be defended or not. Hoping that none will be found to falter in so high and so sacred a duty, we beg leave, gentlemen, to subscribe ourselves, your servants and fellow-citizens,

JESSE APPLEGATE,
A. L. LOVEJOY,
GEO. L. CURRY, } Commissioners.

On the evening of the 13th December, 1847, a public meeting of the citizens was called, and a public loan effected, and subscriptions commenced for the equipment and supply of the army, as will be seen by the following report of the commissioners:—

To the Honorable the Legislative Assembly of Oregon Territory:

The undersigned commissioners appointed by your honorable body for the purpose of negotiating a loan to carry into effect the provisions of an act entitled "An Act to authorize the governor to raise a regiment of volunteers," etc., have the honor to inform you, that, fully realizing the heavy responsibilities attached to their situation, and the peculiarly difficult nature of their duties, they at once determined to act with promptness and energy, and to leave no fair and honorable effort untried that might have a tendency to a successful termination of their undertaking.

They accordingly proceeded to Fort Vancouver on the 10th instant, and there addressed a communication to James Douglas, chief factor of the Hudson's Bay Company, a copy of which is already given. The commissioners had anticipated the unfavorable reply of Mr. Douglas, as agent of the Hudson's Bay Company, and its only effect was to heighten their zeal and to occasion them stronger hopes of a more satisfactory reliance upon the citizens generally of our common country.

However, two of the commissioners, with the governor, became responsible for the amount of the outfit for the first regiment of Oregon riflemen, being $999.59.

Not at all disheartened by the unsuccessful issue of their mission, the commissioners returned to this city on the 13th instant, and at once entered into negotiations, the revelation of which herewith follows.

The commissioners, through a public meeting held at Oregon City, on the night of the 13th instant, addressed the "merchants and citizens of Oregon," at which meeting, from citizens generally, a loan of about one thousand dollars was effected. * * * The commissioners are happy to state that they have succeeded in negotiating a loan of sixteen hundred dollars from the merchants of Oregon City, with, perhaps, a likelihood of a further advance. The commissioners feel well assured, from the interest manifested by our fellow-citizens in the matter, and the prompt action they have proposed to take in the several counties in the Territory to assist the commissioners in the successful discharge of their duties, that the government will ultimately succeed in negotiating an amount adequate to the present emergency of affairs.

The commissioners would beg your honorable body, with as little delay as possible, to appoint appraisers, whose duty it shall be to set a cash valuation upon produce and other property, which may be converted into means to assist government in its present operations.

Therefore, gentlemen, as we believe we can no longer be useful to our fellow-citizens as a Board, we hope to be permitted to resign our trust into the hands of the proper accounting officers of this government. We have the honor to remain,

JESSE APPLEGATE,
A. L. LOVEJOY,
GEO. L. CURRY,
Commissioners.

It will be seen by reference to this last report of the loan commissioners, and the answer to their letter of the 11th December, 1849, that Sir James Douglas had made up his mind to enforce "the *stringent rules* laid down for his government *by the home company*." In other words, the time had now arrived to allow the Indians and half-breeds in the country to destroy the missionary settlements that were beginning to extend beyond the Wallamet Valley; and in case they succeeded in defeating the provisional troops, the settlement in the Wallamet would become an easy prey to the combined Indian forces, while the Hudson's Bay Company would pursue its accustomed trade without any further interference from American settlements.

In addition to the proceedings above referred to, the Legislative Assembly, on the 10th of December, on motion of Hon. J. W. Nesmith,—

"*Resolved*, That in view of our critical situation with the powerful tribes of Indians inhabiting the banks of the Columbia, and with whom we are actually in a state of hostilities, it is the duty of this Legislature to dispatch a special messenger, as soon as practicable, to Washington

City, for the purpose of securing the immediate influence and protection of the United States government in our internal affairs."

On the 11th December, Cornelius Gilliam was elected by the Legislative Assembly, Colonel Commandant; James Waters, Lieutenant-Colonel; H. A. G. Lee, Major; and Joel Palmer, Commissary-General, in compliance with the bill passed on the 9th, authorizing the governor to call for one regiment of not to exceed five hundred men.

On the 13th, Mr. Nesmith presented a bill to provide for sending a special messenger to Washington.

On the 14th, on motion of Mr. Crawford, "*Resolved*, That a delegation of three persons be appointed by this house to proceed immediately to Wallawalla, and hold a council with the chiefs and principal men of the various tribes on the Columbia, to prevent, if possible, their coalition with the Cayuse tribe in the present difficulties."

On the 15th, it was "*Resolved*, That the commodore of the United States squadron in the Pacific Ocean be solicited to send a vessel of war into the Columbia River for our relief, and to send such other assistance as may be in his power."

A motion was adopted to appoint a committee of five to prepare a memorial to Congress.

On the 16th, an act was passed appropriating one thousand dollars to defray the expenses of J. L. Meek, special messenger to Washington.

On the 17th, Mr. Meek resigned his seat in the Legislative Assembly, preparatory to leaving for the United States with dispatches and a memorial to Congress.

As to what those dispatches were, we have no copy or public document that gives us any information, but we presume he carried a copy of Mr. McBean's mutilated letter, and one of Sir James Douglas's, such as we have already given; and also the following

Memorial to Congress.

"To the Honorable the Senate and House of Representatives of the United States in Congress assembled:

"Your memorialists, the Legislative Assembly of Oregon Territory, would respectfully beg leave once more to lay before your honorable body a brief statement of their situation and wants.

"Having called upon the government of the United States so often in vain, we have almost despaired of receiving its protection, yet we trust that our present situation, when fully laid before you, will at once satisfy your honorable body of the great necessity of extending the strong arm of guardianship and protection over this remote, but beautiful portion of the United States domain.

"*Our relations* with the proud and powerful tribes of Indians residing east of the Cascade Mountains, hitherto uniformly amicable and pacific, have recently assumed quite a different character. They have shouted the war-whoop, and crimsoned their tomahawks in the blood of our citizens. The Cayuse Indians, after committing numerous outrages and robberies upon the late immigrants, *have, without the semblance of provocation or excuse, murdered eleven* [seventeen] American citizens. Among the murdered were Dr. Marcus Whitman and his amiable wife, members of the American Board of Foreign Missions.

"Called upon to resent this outrage, we feel sensibly our weakness and inability to enter into a war with powerful tribes of Indians. Such outrages can not, however, be suffered to pass unpunished. It will be the commencement of future and more extensive murders, and our hitherto peaceful settlement will become the scene of fierce and violent warfare. We do not doubt the readiness of the people of this country to defend their lives and property, and to submit to all the privations incident to a state of war in a new and remote settlement like this. Circumstances warrant your memorialists in believing that many of the powerful tribes inhabiting the upper valley ot the Columbia have formed an alliance for the purpose of carrying on hostilities against our settlements. The number of white population in Oregon is alarmingly insignificant compared with the swarms of Indians which throng its valleys.

"To repel the attacks of so formidable a foe, and protect our families and property from violence and rapine, will require more strength than we possess. We are deficient in many of the grand essentials of war,—such as men, arms, and treasure; for them, our sole reliance is on the government of the United States; we have the right to expect your aid, and you are in justice bound to extend it. For although we are separated from our native land by ranges of mountains whose lofty altitudes are mantled in eternal snows; although three thousand miles, nearly two-thirds of which is a howling wild, lie between us and the federal capital, yet our hearts are unalienated from the land of our birth. Our love for the free and noble institutions, under which it was our fortune to be born and nurtured, remains unabated. In short, we are Americans still,—residing in a country over which the government of the United States have sole and acknowledged right of sovereignty, —and under such circumstances we have the right to claim the benefit of its laws and protection.

"Your memorialists would avail themselves of this opportunity to invite your attention to other subjects of deep and vital interest to the citizens of this Territory. The very nature of our compact formed between the citizens of a republic and the subjects and official representatives of a monarchy, is such that the ties of political union could not be drawn so closely as to produce that stability and strength sufficient to form an efficient government. This union between the democrats of a republic and wealthy aristocratic subjects of a monarchy could not be formed without reserving to themselves the right of allegiance to their respective governments. Political jealousy and strong party feeling have tended to thwart and render impotent the acts of government, from its very nature weak and insufficient."

The deep, dark, and infamous schemes of a foreign monopoly and religious bigots were but just developing themselves; but, thank God, there was strength enough in the provisional government, which was formed in the face of their combined opposition. They had yielded to its power, to gain time to organize their savage hosts to crush it; calculating, no doubt, that the Mexican war would prevent assistance reaching us from the United States. The Indians, let loose upon the settlements, would soon clear the country. That such was the general English idea, we know from two different English subjects. The one, a chief trader in the Hudson's Bay Company, who said all they had to do was *to organize the Indians, under the direction of their eight hundred half-breeds, to drive back any American force.* The other, a gold commissioner, a Mr. Saunders, direct from England, in speaking of the small number of troops the English government had in British Columbia, remarked to us, that if they had not troops enough to subdue the Americans in British Columbia, "*all they had to do was to let loose the Indians upon them.*"

Such being the facts, it is not surprising that our Legislative Assembly should be made to feel its weakness, under this powerful combination,—the British monopoly that had refused to furnish necessary supplies to the provisional troops sent to punish the murderers of our citizens. It was not yet apprised of the efforts made by Mr. Ogden to supply the Indians with munitions of war, and the determination of the company not to allow itself to be considered by the Indians as favoring the American settlement of the country. Mr. Hines' book, in which he says Dr. McLaughlin had announced to those Indians in 1843 "that in case the Americans did go to war with them, the Hudson's Bay Company would not assist them," had not yet been published. The memorial continues:—

"In establishing a regular form of government, creating tribunals for the adjustment of the rights of individuals, and the prevention and punishment of crime, a debt has accumulated, which, though an insignificant amount, your memorialists can devise no means of liquidating. The revenue laws, from not being properly executed, while they are burdensome to classes of our citizens and sections of country, are wholly disregarded by others, and whole counties, which for numerical strength are equal to any in the Territory, and fully participating in all the advantages of our compact, have never contributed any assistance in bearing the common burdens.*

"To coerce obedience to our temporary government would at once destroy the great object which called it into existence,—the peace and harmony of our country. Anxiously looking forward to that happy period when we should again be under the protection of our revered and parent republic, we have rather endeavored to maintain peace by forbearance, hoping that the dangers and difficulties to be apprehended from domestic discord and from the savages around us, would be postponed until we became an acknowledged people, and under the protection of our mother country.

"The action of your honorable body in regard to the land in Oregon would seem to justify the expectation that liberal grants would be made to our citizens; yet the uncertainty of our title, and the uneasiness which is felt upon this subject, urge to press this subject upon your attention. Our citizens, before leaving their homes in the United States for Oregon, have had the strongest inducements held out by Congress to settle in this country, and their just expectations will not be met short of liberal donations of land.

"On the subject of filling the offices that will be created in the event of the extension of the jurisdiction of the United States over this Territory, your memorialists would respectfully represent, that, as the pioneers of the American population in this country, the present citizens of this country have strong claims upon the patronage of the general government, and that it would be gratifying to have them filled by our fellow-citizens; but as few of them of an equally deserving number can enjoy this mark of the approbation of our parent republic, and in view of our peculiar and difficult situation, it is the opinion of your memorialists that it will be better for the future prosperity of our country, and that the great mass of the people will concur with them in requesting that important and responsible offices created here, such as the office of governor and the several judgeships, should be filled with men of the best talent and most approved integrity, without regard to their present location."

* Champoeg County being one, and represented by Dr. R. Newell, then Speaker of the house.

In relation to this last paragraph, emanating as it did from the Legislative Assembly of Oregon, it may appear strange that a body of men possessing the talent and ability there was in that Assembly, should be so liberal in requesting that most of the important federal appointments for the Territory should be filled from abroad, or with strangers to the condition and wants of the people; but the fact is plainly stated, and it becomes our duty to impart such information as will explain so strange a request. No one will contend for a moment that we did not have the men who were abundantly qualified to fill those offices, for they have since been filled with far better satisfaction to the country by men who were then in it, than by those sent by the federal government; hence we are led to inquire what was the reason for this request.

The general politics of the country, as intimated in the memorial, were *English aristocratic* and *American democratic*. The parties were nearly equally divided. At the same time, there was the pro-slavery influence laboring to so mold the Territory as to bring it in as a slave State, though it had started free, and upon the most liberal principles of a free government. The democratic pro-slavery influence was not strong enough to secure the federal appointments without cousining with the English aristocrats, who looked upon African slavery with abhorrence. Under these circumstances, the democrats of this assembly became liberal, and naturally sought aid from that party in the United States to which the anti-slavery influence yielded, and took their chances in the federal appointments. There was also in this Assembly a strong personal feeling against Judge Thornton, who was supposed to be in the federal capital seeking the organization of the Territory, as also its governorship; and, in that case, though Mr. Thornton was then acting with the democratic party, should he become the governor, or one of the judges, the pro-slavery influence would be the loser. Hence the "rule or ruin" party chose to make the strange request found in this memorial. The closing paragraph seems to be a flourish of rhetoric, and an appeal to *Uncle Samuel's* tender feelings. Notwithstanding, it took him till August 14, 1848, to say that Oregon should be a Territory under its protection. The remainder of the memorial is as follows:—

"If it be at all the intention of our honored parent to spread her guardian wing over her sons and daughters in Oregon, she surely will not refuse to do it now, when they are struggling with all the ills of a weak and temporary government, and when perils are daily thickening around them and preparing to burst upon their heads. When the ensuing summer's sun shall have dispelled the snow from the mountains, we shall look with glowing hopes and restless anxiety for the coming of your laws and your arms.

"The accompanying documents will afford additional information concerning some of the subjects of which we have spoken.

"To insure the speedy conveyance of these papers to the federal government, your memorialists have elected J. L. Meek, Esq., a special messenger to bear the same, and respectfully ask your honorable body to make him such compensation therefor as you may deem just. And your memorialists will ever pray, etc."

It will be seen by a reference to the first day's proceedings of this Legislative Assembly that Dr. Newell was chosen its Speaker. In tracing the history of events, we find this man always intimately in council with the English aristocratic party in the country. Although he sometimes favored unimportant American measures, he seemed always to guard carefully those in any way affecting the interests of this English monopoly. Champoeg, the county he in part represented, was the most numerous in population and wealth, and by reference to the *Spectator* of February 4, 1847, we find the following: "*Champoeg County tax.*—There has been no tax for the year 1846, received by the treasurer from Champoeg County. How is this? Who is to blame, and where is the honorable County Court of Champoeg County?" This note explains the critical relations of the country and the scheming policy of the enemy we had to contend with, as also the personal bickerings among the Americans. When Mr. Crawford, on the 14th of December, introduced his resolution for a delegation of three persons to endeavor to prevent a coalition with the Indians, we find this measure deferred till near the close of the session, and this Honorable Hudson's Bay Company Speaker of the Assembly is one of the commissioners, as we shall see hereafter.

On the 24th of December, Messrs. Nesmith, Rice, and Rector were appointed a committee to correspond with the American consul at the Sandwich Islands, and also with the commander-in-chief of the army and navy on this coast, in California, soliciting help from them. On the 25th, the house went into secret session for the purpose of conferring with the governor, colonel, lieutenant-colonel, and commissary-general, in relation to our Indian difficulties.

The result of that secret council was embodied in a resolution presented to the house by Mr. Nesmith.

"*Resolved*, That the executive, as commander-in-chief, has full power to adopt all measures necessary for the prosecution of the existing war, and that it is the opinion of this house, that it is expedient for the executive to issue orders for five hundred men, and trust to the patriotism of the citizens of Oregon for their support in the field."

It will be seen by this resolution that there was sufficient reason to justify the calling of the whole strength of the settlement into the field. The captives had reached the settlement, and his *Reverence Bishop Blanchet* had seen proper to inform the governor, "*that by going to war with the Cayuses to get redress for the murders committed at Wailatpu, he would have the whole Indian combination, or confederation, against him.* This, however, he must determine with his council," which we see was done, and the American settlement and Protestant missionaries gave them a cordial support. The Indian combination, which, the Jesuit Brouillet says, Dr. Whitman attempted to form, is here admitted by the bishop's letter to Governor Abernethy to have been formed, and ready to fight the American settlement. Who formed this confederation of Indian tribes is no longer a doubt.

But we have kept our readers too long from the proceedings of our little army, under the command of Captain H. A. G. Lee, which we left on its way to the Dalles, to save that station from falling into the hands of the Indians.

CHAPTER LXII.

The Cayuse war.—Letter of Captain Lee.—Indians friendly with the Hudson's Bay Company.—Conduct of Mr. Ogden.—His letters to Mr. Walker and Mr. Spalding.—Note of Rev. G. H. Atkinson.—Sir James Douglas's letter to Governor Abernethy.—A rumor.—The governor's reply.—Another letter from Sir James.—Mr. Ogden.—Extraordinary presents to the Indians of arms and ammunition.—Colonel Gilliam's campaign.—Indian fight.—Property captured.—The Des Chutes Indians make peace.—Captain McKay's company of British subjects join the army.—A nuisance.—"Veritas."—Nicholas Finlay gives the signal for battle.—Running fight.—Captain McKay's company.—Council held by the peace commissioners with the Indians.—Governor Abernethy's address.—Speeches of the Indians Camaspelo, Joseph, Jacob, Old James, Red Wolf, Timothy, Richard, and Kentuck.—Letters of Joel Palmer, R. Newell, James Douglas, and William McBean.—Who is responsible for the Cayuse war?

If the reader has carefully perused the foregoing pages, he will be able to understand the movements of our little army in the Cayuse war, as to the prime cause of which, the development of twenty-five years, and the monstrous claims of the Hudson's Bay Company, have relieved our present history from all mystery and doubt, and have enabled us to arrange and combine the facts, without fear of a truthful contradiction. Major H. A. G. Lee, in a letter dated at Wascopum, December 26, 1847, writes:—

To Governor Abernethy:

"Sir,—I reached this place on the evening of the 21st instant, with ten men, including Mr. Hinman, whom I met on his way to Wallamet at Wind River Mountain, thirty miles below. The boats being wind-bound, and hearing from Mr. Hinman that a party of the Cayuses and river Indians had been down and driven off some horses from the mission, and that he had left with his family soon after, thinking it unsafe to remain longer, I was induced to lead the few men that were with me (for we had been separated by the wind and could not get together), and press to this place by land with all dispatch, to save the houses from destruction; and I am very happy to inform you that we arrived just in time, and that all is now safe. The natives immediately about this place are friendly, and hailed our arrival with much joy. Seletsa professes friendship, but I shall keep an eye on him; his men have been killing cattle, and I suspect with his consent, though he promises to make them pay for them. We have been collecting the cattle and placing them below, in order to stop the slaughtering that has been carried on above. We have not yet learned the amount of mischief done at this place, but are getting things under way quite as well as I could have anticipated. Mr. Hinman has been of great service to me here; he leaves to-day to join his family, whom he left on the river.

"We have no intelligence from Wailatpu, except Indian report, which, if we may credit, is awful enough. It is said, after the murder of the whites at the place, a general council had been held, and that the Nez Percés were present by special invitation, *i. e.*, the chiefs; that it was determined to make '*a clean sweep*' of all the Bostons, including Messrs. Spalding, Eells, and Walker above, and Hinman here; that they had, in execution of that resolution, returned and murdered all the women and children who had been spared in the first place, with the exception of three females who had been reserved for wives. Remember this is but native news. I must refer you to Mr. Hinman for many other items which I dare not write.

"From all I can gather, the country east of the river Des Chutes is all an enemy's country, and our movements should be directed accordingly. Can you have us two or three small guns cast at the foundery? Each one would be equal in effect to fifty men. I am satisfied that the enemy is going to be much more formidable against an invading force than many in Wallamet are willing to believe. *The Indians are all friendly with the Hudson's Bay Company's men, and I am truly sorry to learn that Mr. Ogden paid them powder* and *ball* for making the portage at the Dalles. I hope this will be stopped, and their supplies of ammunition immediately cut off. Please take some measures to effect this without delay.

"Mr. Rogers and Mr. Savage return immediately from this place, feeling that the object for which they enlisted has been accomplished; and as they would have to return, according to promise, in the course of ten or twelve days, and there being no active employment for them, they are permitted to return now. You are aware that they are among my best men, and for their persevering energy, so far, they deserve the praise due to good soldiers, although they have not had the pleasure of a fight. They are therefore honorably discharged from service in the 1st company of Oregon riflemen.

"Sergeant McMellen will bear this to you and return to me as soon as possible. If he gets down in time to accompany the next party, he will be of much service to them on the river; he has few equals in the service.

"While writing the above, one horse which had been stolen from the immigrants has been brought in, and others reported on the way. I think most of the property stolen near this place will be returned; that above Des Chutes will probably be contended for. The Indians about this place are evidently terrified, and I shall avail myself of that fact, as far as possible, in furthering the object of our trip. I have no fears of an attack on this place, yet I shall be as vigilant as though an attack were certain. The boats which were windbound eight days arrived this morning all safe and well.

"I remain, your most obedient humble servant,

"H. A. G. LEE."

With the light that twenty-two years have shed upon the early history of Oregon, how shall we regard the policy and practice of the professedly kind and generous chief factors of the Hudson's Bay Company? The one, Sir James Douglas, attempting to deceive the American settlement and the world as to the real danger of the settlement and the cause of the massacre; the other, Mr. Ogden, supplying the Indians on his route, and at Wallawalla, with ammunition, and "*insisting*," while bargaining with the murderers for their captives, "*upon the distinction necessary to be made between the affairs of the company and those of the Americans.*"

We undertook, in our third position, to show the influences of this Hudson's Bay Company, as well as Romanism, upon our early settlements, and the causes of the Indian wars. These were backed by one of the most powerful nations then on the globe, while a handful of American pioneers found themselves involved in a savage war. *The Indians were advised, aided, and urged on by the teachings of Roman priests and this Hudson's Bay Company,* sustained by the British government, with assistance pledged to them by Bishop Blanchet and Chief-Factor Ogden, as he received the captives from their hands, and gave them more ammunition and guns than had ever before been given to them at any one time. He says, in a letter dated Fort Nez Percés, December 31, 1847, addressed to Rev. E. Walker, at Cimakain.

"I have been enabled to *effect my object without compromising myself or others,* and it now remains with the *American government* to take what measures they deem most beneficial to restore tranquillity to this part of the country, and this, I apprehend, can not be finally effected without blood being made to flow freely. So as not to compromise either party, I have made a *heavy sacrifice of goods;* but these, indeed, are of trifling value, compared to the unfortunate beings I have rescued from the hands of the murderous wretches, and I feel truly happy. Let this suffice for the present.

"On my arrival at the Dalles, Mr. Hinman's mission, the previous day, had been plundered of four horses in open day, and in presence of all the inmates of the mission; and on consulting me on the propriety of remaining or removing under the present distracted state of the country, *I advised him to move*, leaving a trusty Indian, on whom he could rely, and who speaks the English language, to remain in charge of the establishment; and he would have started the same day I left it. I trust this arrangement will meet with your approbation; under existing circumstances, could not consistently give any other."

"Yours truly, "P. S. OGDEN." *

With such powerful combinations, and such experienced, wise, and reverend advisers, it is not surprising that those Indians should feel themselves able to make, as Captain Lee says, "*a clean sweep of all the Bostons in the country.*" Mr. Ogden, in his letter to Mr. Walker, does not intimate that the provisional government will presume to attempt to seek any redress for the murders committed; but consoles himself with the "*happy*" thought that the difficulty is to be settled by the United States. Mr. Hinman he advises to leave, and to Mr. Spalding he sends the following letter:—

"FORT NEZ PERCÉS, December 23, 1847.

"*Rev. H. H. Spalding:*

"DEAR SIR,—I have assembled all the chiefs and addressed them in regard to the helpless situation of yourself and the rest at Wailatpu, and I have got them to consent to deliver them all to me: yourself and those with you, *save the two Canadians, who are safe enough among the Indians;* and have now to advise you to lose no time in joining me. At the same time, *bear in mind, sir, you have no promises to make them*, or payments to make. Once more, use all the diligence possible to overtake us. "Yours truly,

"P. S. OGDEN." *

We place a note of Rev. G. H. Atkinson, D. D., in this connection, to show the influences that have for a series of years been operating, and how careful that unscrupulous monopoly was to combine its influences, and to deal out its hospitalities, to secure a good word from a reverend Protestant divine, who was connected with the United States Home Missionary Board, whose character is unimpeachable, and to whom it refers for evidence of its generosity. We are not surprised to find

* Copied from the original letter.

Doctor Atkinson attempting to ease the weight of censure due to that overgrown monopoly, from the fact, that on his first arrival in the country (after the Cayuse war), on one of the company's ships, unusual attention and kindness were evidently shown to him and his family by the company's agents, to gain his favorable representations of their proceedings, and a name for *honorable* dealing and generous treatment of missionaries, as intimated in his note. Doctor Atkinson says:—

"The agents of the Hudson's Bay Company in Oregon furnished all the missionaries with supplies at the usual trade rates until they could supply themselves from home."

In this the doctor is mistaken, as we have shown in previous pages. He continues:—

"After the death of Mr. Whitman and family, Mr. Ogden, an agent of the company, brought the rest of the mission and the American families to the Wallamet Valley, at considerable risk and sacrifice to himself. The guilt of the plot to massacre Dr. Whitman and other Americans is understood to belong to the Jesuits."

The letters above quoted, from Mr. Ogden and Captain Lee, show the doctor's great mistake in this statement. Mr. Ogden ran no risk, and made no sacrifice, as the Hudson's Bay Company presented their bills, and have been paid every dollar they had the impudence to demand of our government, for transporting the captive women and children to a place of safety, and for all the supplies they so reluctantly furnished to our provisional troops. We do not believe it is good morals, or divinity, to say nothing of politics, to praise, encourage, or warm the serpent that improves every opportunity to sting us with his poisonous fangs. That company has enjoyed the monopoly of this vast country, and prevented its settlement too long, for any one to seek its praise or favor.

We have another letter from Sir James Douglas, which shows us more clearly the exact position of that monster monopoly. It is as follows:—

"FORT VANCOUVER, Dec. 31, 1847.

"*To Governor George Abernethy, Esq.:*

"SIR,—A rumor having been in circulation, for some days past, that it is General Gilliam's intention to levy contributions on the Hudson's Bay Company's property, for the purpose of completing the equipment of the troops ordered out in your late proclamation, for the intended operations against the Indians, I feel it my duty to communicate with you frankly on the subject, as it is most important, in the present critical state of our Indian relations, that there should be an entire absence of distrust, and that the most perfect unanimity should exist among the whites of every class. From my personal knowledge of General Gilliam, and his highly respectable character, I should be the last person to believe him capable of committing an outrage which may prove so disastrous in the immediate and remoter consequences to the peace and best interests of this country; *at the same time, as the representative of a powerful British association*, it becomes my duty to take instant measures for the protection of their property, until I receive, through you, a distinct disavowal of any such intention as herein stated. Difficulties of that nature were certainly not contemplated by us when we dispatched a large part of our effective force into the interior for the purpose of *receiving* the unfortunate women and children, the survivors of the massacre at Wailatpu, who remained in the hands of the Indians. It was never supposed that our establishment would be exposed to *insult or injury* from American citizens, while we are *braving the fury of the Indians* for their protection."

What a powerful and noble company, and how much "*fury of the Indians*" they had to contend with, when they were handing them *guns and ammunition* by the quantity; and all their servants and posts were unharmed by either whites or Indians, during all the Indian wars that have occurred on this coast. This letter continues:—

"Such a proceeding would, in fact, be so inconsistent with every principle of *honor and sound policy*, that I can not believe any attempt of the kind will be made; but I trust this explanation will satisfactorily account for any unusual precaution observed in the present arrangement of this establishment.

"Trusting that this note will be noticed at your earliest convenience, I have the honor to be, sir,

"Your most obedient, humble servant,

"James Douglas, C. F., H. B. Co."

Mr. Douglas, in this letter, has suddenly assumed a very honorable, as well as powerful position. As to his personal bravery, there is no question; but as to truth, there is. He says, "I can not believe any attempt of the kind will be made," and then tells us not to be alarmed; or, at least, as the "*rumor* having been in circulation," we must excuse him for his "unusual *precaution*" in his establishment, while he has deceived, and intends to continue to deceive, the governor and the settlers as to his real motives of caution, and the deep-laid schemes that he and his "*powerful British association*" are bringing about, not against the "*fury of the Indians*," but against the American settlements.

As was to be expected in those times, our governor and General Gilliam wilted right down, and the governor wrote:—

"OREGON CITY, January 3, 1848.

"SIR,—I received your favor of 31st ultimo yesterday evening, and, in answering it, would thank you for your frankness in communicating with me on the subject. Having had conversation with Colonel Gilliam on this subject, I can state that he has no intention of levying contributions on the Hudson's Bay Company's property for any purpose whatever. He will probably cross the Columbia River at the mouth of Sandy."

This was the information that Mr. Douglas wished to obtain, as we have since learned from one of the company's clerks, and also the extent of information received from Mr. Lee by his express.

"I trust nothing will occur that will in any way cause distrust among the whites during this crisis. The reports from above lead to the conclusion that Messrs. Spalding, Walker, and Eells have been cut off, and the women and children, spared in the first place, have since been murdered. Should these rumors prove true, we know that peace can not be restored between the Indians and whites without bloodshed."

As near as we can learn, Governor Abernethy was disposed to follow the counsels of a writer in the *Spectator*, signed "Veritas," which was, to wait till spring opened, and then make a decent demonstration in the summer to punish the murderers. The energy of the people overruled his tender spirit, to use no harsher term, and pushed their forces up in the winter, which allowed most of the men to return in time to secure the following harvest, and produced the desired effect upon the Hudson's Bay Company and the Indians. The governor says:—

"Captain Lee informs me that Mr. Ogden paid the Indians powder and ball for making the portage. The Legislature passed an act during their last session prohibiting the sale of powder, lead, caps, etc., to Indians. I trust you will see the necessity of complying with this act; it will be published in the next *Spectator*.

"I trust the disavowal in this letter will prove satisfactory to you. I have the honor to remain, sir,

"Your obedient servant,

"GEORGE ABERNETHY."

The next day, the 4th of January, Mr. Douglas returned a long letter, which is as follows:—

"FORT VANCOUVER, January 4, 1848.

"*George Abernethy, Esq.:*

"SIR,—I have to acknowledge yours of yesterday's date, and consider it perfectly satisfactory. I place little confidence in the late reports from the Dalles, and entertain sanguine hopes that they will prove unfounded.

"The Indians have been always paid with ammunition and tobacco by our traveling parties, for passing boats at the portages of this river, and *I can not see that Mr. Ogden had any reason to depart from the established practice on the occasion mentioned in your letter*, as these Indians have no fellow-feelings with the Cayuses."

This statement of Sir James is notoriously untrue; the Cayuses have always had more or less trade with the Dalles Indians, in dried salmon, horses, etc., and have always been the superiors, and treated them as they pleased. Mr. Douglas has invariably cautioned us, in passing those portages, not to give ammunition, as it was against the rules of the company to do so, *except to a very few*, and in small quantities, and *that* for packing goods by trusty Indians. This sudden change from tobacco to powder is only a part of the policy now being executed.

"These Indians behaved in the most friendly manner, and, I am convinced, will not enter into any combination against the whites, unless there be great mismanagement *on our part.*

"In fact, when we consider the object of Mr. Ogden's journey to Wallawalla [which we consider really to have been to inform the Indians, *as he did*, that the Hudson Bay Company would take no part in this quarrel between the Indians and Americans, and that the company would supply them with ammunition and aid them in the present war, we are not disposed to question but that the lives of some of the men that were left would have been taken, but we doubt if any more women would have been killed, unless the company had consented to it; but it answered for a plausible argument for Sir James, who says], and that the lives of sixty or seventy fellow-creatures were, under Providence, mainly dependent on the celerity of his movements, it can not be supposed he would allow any minor consideration to weigh one moment in his mind against the great object of their preservation. As he could not carry his boats over the portages of the falls without the assistance of the Indians, it would have been an act of great indiscretion on his part to have *excited alarm* and *created suspicion* in their minds."

Doctor Saffron, in answer to the interrogatory, "In what way did you become acquainted with the Whitman massacre?" makes the following reply: "I was residing at the Dalles mission when the Canadian, bearing an express from Fort Nez Percés to Vancouver, came to the station and ate dinner, and with whom Mr. Hinman went to the lodge, and secured a canoe to assist him on his way to Vancouver, and went to Vancouver with him. A very short time after they were off,—I did not think they had scarcely got off before the Indians came from the lodges, and told what they said the Frenchman had told them, that Doctor Whitman was killed. The next information was from an Indian lad from Des Chutes, who came on horseback, in great haste, and said that two Cayuses were at Des Chutes, and had told them that Dr. Whitman, his wife, and all his people were killed, except the women, who had been taken for wives for the chiefs. In giving the causes which the two Cayuses had given them, he spoke of the sickness, and *also that the priests had made known to them that the Doctor was a dangerous medicine man to have among them*, and said something of their having said about the Doctor's medicines being the cause of their dying; and also of what Mr. McBean had said of Dr. Whitman's determining to have all their spotted horses. I can be *certain as to the priests'* part, but not so certain as to McBean's part, being said by the young Indian at that time, or told me afterward by other Indians." Dr. Saffron states in this deposition that the Indians were very threatening about the station, and that he thinks the reason they did not commence the massacre of all at the station was the report that Mr. Ogden was just below with a party. "On Mr. Ogden's arrival, we stated to him these things, and he informed *Mr. Hinman* that we *had better get away as soon as possible*, which we did."

In this letter from Mr. Douglas, in answer to Governor Abernethy, about supplying the Indians with powder, etc., he says:—

"It would have been an act of great indiscretion on his part to have excited alarm and caused suspicion in their minds by withholding the compensation of two or three pounds of gunpowder and lead, which they had been *accustomed* to receive for such service, when it was certain that the omission would be regarded as evidence of a hostile intent, and induce them to put every possible obstacle in his way, whereby the object of the journey must have been entirely defeated, and the unfortunate women and children left to their cruel fate.

"To prohibit the sale of ammunition within certain districts in arms against the whites would be the proper course; but to extend the measure to every part of the country is to make the innocent suffer with the guilty, and a departure from the conciliatory course of policy which we have always found to answer best with Indians; and will, I much fear, drive them to the most desperate course. I am now only expressing an opinion on what the law is reported to be, and await the next issue of the *Spectator* with some impatience, to discover its real character and value.

"You may rest assured that we will do nothing improper, or which will, in any way, endanger the safety of the country.

"We have not yet heard from Mr. Ogden since he left the Dalles, but are now daily expecting to hear from him.

"I have the honor to be, sir,

"Your most obedient servant,

"JAMES DOUGLAS."

The careless reader, or one that is disposed to regard Sir James Douglas as an honorable, truthful, and upright man, will, on first reading this letter, in all probability, consider it a satisfactory reply to Governor Abernethy, and his reasons sufficient to justify Mr. Ogden's course at the Dalles and at Wallawalla.

Doctor Saffron tells us, under oath, "On Mr. Ogden's arrival, we stated to him these things," about the massacre, the priests, McBean, and the Indians threatening, which Mr. Ogden admits in his letter to Mr. Walker, when he advised them to leave. He then proceeds on up the river, and does a thing which Sir James says was *common*, which we know Mr. Douglas has said to us *was not common*, for the company to give ammunition to the Indians for making those portages.

On the present occasion, knowing all the facts, and the danger to the lives of all at the Dalles station, Mr. Ogden deliberately gave (Mr. Douglas says, "*as usual*") an unusual amount of war material; he then proceeds to Wallawalla, called the Indians together, and gave them "*twelve* common guns, *six hundred* loads of ammunition, twelve flints, thirty-seven pounds tobacco, sixty-two three-point blankets, sixty-three common cotton shirts."

And what was the service that these Indians had rendered, for which these goods were given by this "*powerful organization?*" Six years before, when a Hudson's Bay servant got into a drunken row, and was killed by an Indian at the mouth of the Columbia, the Americans and company went in a body, and demanded and hung the murderer; but now, when Dr. Whitman and fifteen other *Americans* are murdered, Mr. Ogden goes up and pays them more *guns*, *ammunition*, *blankets*, and *shirts*, than had ever before been given to them on any one occasion. Was that company weaker at this time than they had been before, that they could not manage or conquer the Cayuses? Sir James Douglas, under oath, says the company in 1846 "*practically enjoyed a monopoly of the fur trade, and possessed extraordinary influence with the natives.*" And we say, the Whitman massacre is the result of that influence.

Mr. Ogden, distinctly, and at several times, insisted upon the distinction necessary to be made between the affairs of the Americans and the company, and why? Simply, because the company had determined to suppress and crush the American settlements, if it could be done, by the Indians. They were now in a condition to furnish the Indians directly, or clandestinely, through their Jesuit missionaries, all the ammunition required. Hence the liberality of Mr. Ogden, and the care of Mr. Douglas to catch "*a rumor*" to defend Mr. Ogden's course; to manifest great sympathy for the sufferers, to deceive the settlement in every way possible; and refuse, under the plea of the "*stringent rules of the home department,*" to supply munitions to the provisional troops.

On the 23d of February, Colonel Gilliam, with fifty of his men, arrived at Wascopum, an express having been sent by Major Lee for him to hasten forward with his troops. On his arrival, he learned that the Des Chutes Indians were hostile. Was Mr. Douglas correct in his opinion?

The main body of his troops having arrived on the 27th, he started with 130 of his best mounted men, crossed Des Chutes, and ascended on its east or right bank. On the 28th, he sent forward Major Lee with twenty men to find the Indians, they all having fled from their usual encampments. At twelve o'clock at night, Major Lee returned, having found the Indians, and made the following report, which we give in Major Lee's own language. He says:—

"We proceeded this morning up the river some twenty miles, when we discovered a considerable party of Indians with their families, removing across the plains, and evidently to station themselves higher up the cañon, which was close by. We charged upon them, killed one, took two females prisoners, and several horses; the rest escaped into the cañon, which was close by. Expecting a large war party out immediately, we hastened toward camp with the prisoners, but had not proceeded far when we discovered a large party of mounted Indians making after us with all possible speed; we rode down into a small cañon, turned our horses loose below us, and prepared for battle,—the Indians by this time all around us on the hills, tumbling down huge stones in our midst, and annoying us much with their savage yells, some with their arms. We were fighting some two or three hours, killed and wounded, I suppose, some six or eight, as they took care to keep at a respectful distance. They drew no blood from us, and got only in return for their loss their horses which we had taken, with four or five of ours that went out with them, unperceived, through a small cañon, during the engagement. We have all returned safe, though much fatigued."

On the 29th of this month the whole of the camp moved to the mouth of the cañon, at the Meek crossing. On the 30th, ten A. M., as they entered the mouth of the cañon, the Indians appeared on the hills immediately above, drawn up in order of battle, to about their own number. The colonel ordered his horses and train to a safe position under a strong guard, dismounted his men, ascended the hill, drove and killed, as was supposed, some twenty or thirty Indians, with but one man (a Spaniard) slightly wounded, capturing forty horses, four head of cattle, and three hundred dollars' worth of personal property, which the colonel had sold to the regiment, and credited to the paymaster, amounting to fourteen hundred dollars. Mr. Brown, first lieutenant, 5th company, died at Vancouver. The skirmishing and battle with the Des Chutes Indians brought them to terms, and a treaty of peace was made with them. The army was re-enforced by the arrival of Captain McKay's company of *British subjects*, as claimed by a writer in the *Spectator*, of February 24, 1848, who says:—

"The party consisted of *two Canadians*, fifty or sixty half-breeds,—all *British subjects*,—and two or three American citizens, while there is not a single Frenchman in it. It is due to the *British subjects*, *Canadians*, *and half-breeds*, to state, that many more would have gone, but, they know well, that winter is not the time, in this country, to go to war, and that all that can be done at this season is, to rescue the prisoners, which could be effected only by negotiation, and acquire correct information, and make all preparations necessary, so as to be able to act with the *propriety*, *decorum*, and energy which the case required.

"VERITAS."

By the statements of "Veritas," the feelings of the *British subjects* in our midst, at that time, can be seen. He evidently wished to claim credit for the British and half-breed subjects, who, in the operations of the provisional army, were found to be, to use no harsher term, a nuisance in the American camp, keeping the Indians and murderers well informed as to all the movements of the army, so that while they were permitted to remain, no movement of the army produced any satisfactory results.

This statement is made upon the verbal information given to us at the time, as well as from personal knowledge, and a letter of Colonel Waters to Governor Abernethy, under date, Wailatpu, April 4, 1848, in the *Spectator*, April 20, 1848. The colonel says of the Indians, "They know our circumstances about as well as we do ourselves, both as regards ammunition and provisions, and it need not be thought strange if they act accordingly."

Soon after the re-enforcement of this provisional army by Captain T.

McKay's *British subjects*, there was a general engagement or battle. It commenced while the army was on the march in the open rolling prairie, between Mud Spring and the Umatilla. Nicholas Finlay, of the Whitman-massacre notoriety, met the scouts and officers, and while there was a consultation, or parley, it appears he prolonged it, to give time for the main body of the Indians to surround the troops; he then turned his horse, rode a short distance toward a party of Indians, and discharged his gun in the air, as a signal to commence the attack, while the peace commissioners were attempting to effect a compromise.

At Finlay's signal, from five to seven hundred Indian warriors appeared on the plains all about them, with from two to three hundred Indian camp-followers, as spectators, all on horseback, consisting of boys and women, who had come to see the slaughter, and gather up the property that the Americans were going to throw down and run from, as soon as Nicolas Finlay fired his gun, and the warriors raised the yell. But instead of this, Colonel Gilliam, as soon as Finlay made his appearance, and other Indians were seen in the distance, ordered a hollow square to be formed to protect his train and cattle, and by the time the Indians were ready, he was, and the fight commenced, a sort of running, dashing, and, on the part of the Indians, retreating performance. There being no water near the place where the attack was commenced, it became necessary to continue upon the march, and they drove the Indians before them, till they reached water at night. By this time the Indians found that the Bostons were not *all clochemen* (women), as they had been told by the "*British half-breeds*."

A stranger would naturally conclude from the accounts published in the *Spectator* at that time, that the company under Captain T. McKay did all the fighting on this occasion. They, we infer from the printed account as given in C. McKay's letter, made some gallant dashes in true Indian style, and as prudent retreats back to the protection of the "*Boston men*," making a great show of bravery and fight, without much effect. At the close of this demonstration, the Indians retired in their usual confused manner, while the Americans moved on to find water and a camp for the night. They continued their march till they reached Fort Waters, at Wailatpu.

At this place the commissioners called for the principal chiefs of all friendly tribes to meet them, to have a big talk. In this council, one Cayuse war-chief, Camaspelo, and two of the lower grade of the Nez Percés,—Joseph and Red Wolf,—with several prominent Indians of the Nez Percés, were present, and received the commissioners with the governor's letter, and made the speeches hereafter given.

Governor Abernethy's address to the Indians asserted the fact, that

Dr. Whitman was invited by the Indians themselves to remain in their country, and teach them the arts of civilization, agriculture, a knowledge of books and of religion; that the Indians had not regarded the Doctor's instructions, else they would not have stolen property belonging to the immigrants, and, on the 29th of November, murdered him and Mrs. Whitman. That the Doctor, in giving them medicine, was not poisoning them, but doing all he could to save their lives, and relieve their sick. That Americans died of the disease as well as the Indians. That if the Doctor was poisoning them, which they knew was not the case, why did they kill all the Americans at his place? That the Doctor was their best friend, and always trying to do them good; and now he required of them, that they should give up the murderers, and those who had taken and forced young women to be their wives, to be punished according to our laws. He named Tilokaikt and Tamsaky in particular. They were also required to restore or pay for the property stolen from the immigrants, while on their way to the Wallamet Valley.

Camaspelo (a Cayuse chief).—"My people seem to have two hearts. I have but one; my heart is as the Nez Percés. I have had nothing to do with the murder. Tamsaky came to me to get my consent to the murder, before it was committed. I refused. I pointed to my sick child, and told him my heart was there and not on murder; he went back and told his friends he had obtained my consent; it was false. I did not give my consent to the murder, neither will I protect or defend the murderers."

Joseph (a Nez Percé chief, half-brother of Five Crows).—"Now I show my heart. When I left my home I took the book (a testament Mr. Spalding had given him) in my hand and brought it with me; it is my light. I heard the Americans were coming to kill me. Still I held my book before me, and came on. I have heard the words of your chief. I speak for all the Cayuses present and all my people. I do not wish my children engaged in this war, although my brother (Five Crows) is wounded. You speak of the murderers; I shall not meddle with them; I bow my head; this much I speak."

Jacob.—This Indian had once been a celebrated medicine man among the Nez Percés. He said: "It is the law of this country that the murderer shall die. That law I keep in my heart, because I believe it is the law of God,—the first law. I started to see the Americans, and when on the way I heard the Americans were coming to kill all the Indians; still I came. I have heard your speech, and am thankful. When I left home I believed the Americans were coming for the murderers only. I thank the governor for his good talk."

James was an old Indian who was for a long time a pet of Mr. Spalding's; but, through the influence of Mr. Pambrun and the priest, he had been induced to receive a cross and a string of beads. He was the acknowledged owner of the land on which the Lapwai station was located, and, by the influence above referred to, caused Mr. Spalding considerable annoyance, though nothing of the difficulty asserted by Brouillet, page 14. He says: "The Indians then met together and kept all the whites who lived at the station blockaded in their houses for more than a month." Living at the station at the time, I know there was no quarrel or disturbance with the Indians, nor were any at the station confined to their houses for a moment at any time, as stated by this priest; it is one of a great number of just such statements made to cover their guilt in a great crime.

Old James said: "I have heard your words and my heart is glad. When I first heard of this murder, our white brother Spalding was down here; I heard the Cayuses had killed him also, and my heart was very sad. A few days after, when he returned, I met him as one arose from the dead. We spoke together; he said he would go to Wallamet. I told him to tell the chiefs there my heart. We have been listening for some word from him. All these chiefs are of one heart."

Red Wolf was connected by marriage with the Cayuses, and, it seems from his speech, was instructed as to the information he should give to the Americans. He says: "You speak of Doctor Whitman's body. When I heard of the Doctor's death, I came and called for the murderers. I wished to know if it was the work of the chiefs. I went to Tawatowe, and found it was not of all, but of the young men. I did not sleep. I went to Mr. Spalding and told him the chiefs were engaged in it. Mr. Spalding said, 'I go to Wallamet and will say the Nez Percés have saved my life, and I will go to Wallamet and save yours.' We have all been listening to hear from the white chief."

Timothy.—This Indian had always been a firm friend of the Americans, and of the mission, and was a consistent member of the mission church. He seems to have taken no decided part. He says: "You hear these chiefs; they speak for all. I am as one in the air. I do not meddle with these things; the chiefs speak; we are all of the same mind."

Richard was one of the Indian boys taken to the States by Doctor Whitman from the American rendezvous in 1835, and brought back in 1836, and was always more or less about the mission. He was an active and intelligent young Indian, and was basely murdered by a Catholic Indian after being appointed a chief by Indian Agent H. A. G. Lee. He said: "I feel thankful for the kind words of your chief.

My people will take no part in this matter. Our hearts cling to that which is good. We do not love blood. This is the way our old chief (Cut Nose) talked; his last words were: 'I leave you; love that which is good, be always on the side of right, and you will prosper.' His children remember his words. He told us, take no bad advice. Why should I take bad words from your enemies, and throw your good words away? Your chief's words are good; I thank him for them. My chief is in the buffalo country; he will be glad to hear I talk thus to you. They would be sorry should I talk otherwise. This much I tell you of the hearts of my people."

KENTUCK, a good-natured, sensible, and yet apparently crazy Indian, said: "The chiefs have all spoken; I have listened, and now I wish to speak a little. I have been much with the Americans and French; they know my heart, can any one tell any thing bad of me? In war with the Blackfeet, I and my father fought with the Americans, and my father was killed there. He (pointing to Mr. Newell) knows it. Last year I was in California at Captain Sutter's, and helped Captain Fremont,—not for pay, but from a good heart. I came home, and heard the Doctor was killed! We heard that the whites were told we were with the Cayuses. We have not such hearts. I and my people are from the furthermost part of our country. We had heard there that you were coming to kill off the last Indian west of the mountains. We have never shed the blood of the Americans. We are glad to hear that you want none but the murderers."

In the *Spectator* of March 23, 1848, we find the following letters:—

"WAILATPU, March 4, 1848.

"*William McBean, Esq.:*

"DEAR SIR,—I have been requested by Captain McKay to apprise you of the progress we have made in adjusting the difficulties between the whites and Cayuses, and I am happy to say that matters are assuming a favorable appearance. With your and his assistance, with that of a little forbearance on the part of the troops, I believe all that could be devised will be accomplished without further shedding of blood.

"*Captain McKay thinks that Captain Grant* (of the Hudson's Bay Company) *can travel through the country with perfect safety.* Mr. Meek will leave the first of the week. Doctor Newell will write to Captain Grant, according to your request. In haste, I have the honor to subscribe,

"Your humble servant,

"JOEL PALMER."

DEAR SIR,—I only have time to say a word. Stikas was here yesterday, and things look more favorable since Gervais arrived. *I wish to go down when your people go.* I will be ready in a few days and come to the fort; no time for particulars; *Mr. Meek leaves to-night.*

"With respects, yours, etc., "R. NEWELL."

"FORT VANCOUVER, March 15, 1848.

"*Governor Abernethy, Esq.:*

"DEAR SIR,—One of the company's servants has this moment arrived with dispatches from Wallawalla, of date the 7th instant; I hasten to communicate the intelligence received, for your information. The army had made its way to Wailatpu, and taken possession of the remains of the mission, the Cayuses having been defeated, with considerable loss, some days previously, in a pitched battle near the Umatilla River; and had since fallen back upon the Nez Percé country. Serpent Jaune, chief of the Wallawalla tribe, had visited the commissioners, and decided on remaining quiet; the Nez Percés had in part also decided for peace, and were expected in camp within a few days. The remaining part of the tribe appeared still undecided about the part they would take, and will, no doubt, be much influenced in their future conduct by the success which attends the operations of the army. *Their sympathies are with the Cayuses;* but fear may restrain them from taking an open part against the whites. The Cayuses remain, therefore, without any open support from the more powerful tribes in their neighborhood, and in such circumstances can not be expected to make a very protracted defense.

"The accompanying copy of a letter from Mr. Palmer possesses much of interest, and will put you in possession of further particulars.

"Our dates from Fort Colville are up to the 23d of January; the Indians were all quiet and well disposed, *though they had been severe sufferers from the measles and dysentery.* Their detestation of the brutal conduct of the Cayuses has been openly and generally expressed, as well as their determination to oppose the repetition of such atrocities in the country. Messrs. Walker and Eells have been induced, by the friendly protestations of the Indians about them, to continue their residence at the mission near Spokan.

"We have letters from Fort Hall up to the 30th of December. A city has sprung up, as if by enchantment, in the midst of the desert, near the southern extremity of great Salt Lake. It contains a population of 3,000, and numbers within its precincts 600 houses. One flour-mill was in operation, and four saw-mills were nearly finished.

"In haste, yours truly, "JAMES DOUGLAS."

As to the letter of General Palmer, he has informed us that, while he was attempting to effect an arrangement with the Indians, he was satisfied that McBean was using his influence against the Americans, and doing all he could to keep up the hostile feelings then existing, but, by humoring and flattering him, he would do less harm than by opposing his self-conceit.

As to Dr. Newell's note, it showed his disposition to crawl under the shade of McBean and the Hudson's Bay "*people*," and to give them information that would enable them to cut off the messenger sent to Washington.

General Palmer informed McBean that he would leave the first of the week. Newell says, "*Mr. Meek leaves to-night.*"

Mr. Douglas is all friendship and affection. He has just learned that a large body of American people are in Salt Lake Valley, and that the Indians about the Spokan station are friendly, notwithstanding the measles and dysentery have been severe among them.

The Indians had been defeated with considerable loss, but the "*sympathies of the Nez Percés are with the Cayuses.*" Whence did Sir James get this information? When he wished to convince Governor Abernethy that Mr. Ogden had done right in giving powder and ball for making the portages at Des Chutes, he said, "*These Indians have no fellow-feeling with the Cayuses.*" We will give *another remarkable letter*, in answer to the one Mr. Douglas refers to:—

"Fort Nez Percés, March 4, 1848.

"*To the Commissioners, Messrs. Palmer and Newell:*

"Gentlemen,—I have to acknowledge your esteemed favor of this date, which was handed me this evening.

"I am happy to learn that your success to effect peace has so far rewarded your endeavors, and that the Nez Percés *are on your side.* Previous to their visiting you, the most influential chiefs came to me, to know your real intention, which I fully explained, and addressed them at length. They left me well disposed, and, I am glad to learn, have acted up to their promise."

Put this statement of Mr. McBean by the side of that of Sir James Douglas, and how does it read? March 7, "*Their sympathies are with the Cayuses.*" What are we to understand by such information given to two different parties? Mr. McBean professes to know the views of the Nez Percés, and, on March 4, tells the American commissioners he is happy to learn they are on their side; and, three days after, writes to his superior, at Vancouver, "*Their sympathies are with the Cayuses.*" General Palmer, nor any one else, need mistake the character of such a man; and we will give the company credit for ability to select their men to perform their appropriate business, and at the proper time.

"I now forward letters to Fort Hall and Fort Boise, and have to request, in behalf of the company, that you be kind enough to get them forwarded by Mr. Meek. They are of importance. On their being delivered depends loss or gain to the company.

"WILLIAM McBEAN.

"P. S.—Please present my best respects to General Gilliam and Major Lee."

There are two remarkable facts in these two letters. The first, "the most influential chiefs" went to him, and he explained the real intentions of the Americans, which, according to his report to his superior, made them sympathize with the Cayuses; but to accomplish another object, he would have us believe he made them favorable to the Americans, and claims all the credit for doing so. This would have done very well, only it leaked out, in the speeches of the Indians, the part this agent of the company was playing.

Query 1. How came the Nez Percés, who had always been friendly with the Americans, and never had shed any of their blood, but always fought with and for them, to be at war—that it should require the consent or advice of McBean, or any other Hudson's Bay Company's servant or clerk, to go and make peace with friends?

Query 2. The importance of two letters to Forts Boise and Hall? The *loss or gain* to the company was of more importance to him than the lives of the missionaries and all at the Dalles, for he would not allow his messenger to inform them of their danger. We have in their communications a specimen of a high and a low agent of that company during the Cayuse war. *The Cayuse tribe* was always more dependent upon Fort Nez Percés for supplies than the Nez Percés, who have always had more or less intercourse with American traders. From the deposition of Mr. Geiger, we learn that this agent (McBean) of the company was in the habit of interfering with the affairs of the American Indians and missionaries, and from the deposition of Mr. Kimzey, that he was equally officious in favoring the Jesuit missions. And now, from his own officious letter, we learn his position in relation to the war then in progress; that he was attempting to deceive the commissioners, as to his operations and instructions to the Indians, is shown in the information he communicated to Mr. Douglas, and in the letter of Colonel Waters to Governor Abernethy.

Putting all these facts together, who is responsible for the massacre and the war with the Cayuses?

CHAPTER LXIII.

Letter to General Lovejoy.—Call for men and ammunition.—Yankama chief.—His speech.—Small supply of ammunition.—Letter of Joseph Cadwallader.—Claim and a girl.—Combined Indian tribes.—Ladies of Oregon.—Public meeting.—A noble address.—Vote of thanks.—Address of the young ladies.—Death of Colonel Gilliam.—His campaign.—Colonel Waters' letter.—Doubtful position of Indians.—Number at Fort Wallawalla.—Results of the war.—Jesuit letters.—Fathers Hoikin and De Smet.—The Choctaws.—Indian confederacy.—Last hope of the Indian.—Jesuit policy.—The Irish in the war of the Rebellion.—Father Hecker.—Boasts of the Jesuits.—Letter of Lieutenant Rogers.—Priests supply the Indians with arms and ammunition.—Ammunition seized.—Oregon *Argus*.—Discovery of gold.—No help for the Indian.—Withdrawal of the Hudson's Bay Company to Vancouver.—The smooth-tongued Jesuits yet remain.

LET us now turn our attention from scenes of baseness and treachery to such as can not fail to draw forth the more noble sentiments of the heart. We find in the *Old Spectator*, April 20, 1848:—

" *General A. L. Lovejoy:*

"SIR,—The following was written for the *Express*, but in the hurry and bustle of business, was omitted to be forwarded: To call the men (158) who fought on the Tukanon and Tuchet rivers brave were but common praise,—officers and privates fought with unequaled bravery and skill. Captains Hall, Owens, and Thompson behaved with all that deliberate judgment and determined bravery that was requisite to so hard-fought and long-continued a battle.

"The incomparable services of Sergeant-Major Birch, Quartermaster Goodhue, Judge-Advocate Rinearson, Sergeant Cook, Paymaster Magone, can not be passed unnoticed, and deserve their country's praises. Captains English and McKay were not in the engagement—the latter being sick, the former returning from the Tuchet with the wagons and the stock.

"H. J. G. MOXON,
"Commanding at Fort Wascopum."

"FORT WASCOPUM, April 7, 1848.

" *General A. L. Lovejoy:*

"SIR,—We received your letter of instructions, by express, on the 3d instant, and I assure you it gave me great satisfaction to make them known to the troops under my command. Since the promotion of Major Lee to the command, the boys have taken fresh courage; though some of them can hardly hide their nakedness, they are willing under your promises to stick it out like men.

"Give us five hundred men, and plenty of ammunition, with Colonel Lee at our head, and I think we will soon bring the war to an honorable close.

"*The Yankama chiefs* came over to see us a few days ago, and stated that they had written to the white chief but had received no answer. [Who was the writer for the Indians? No American dare remain in the country beyond the protection of the army.] Therefore they had come over to see him. They spoke to us as follows:—

"'We do not want to fight the Americans, nor the French; neither do the Spokans, a neighboring tribe to us. Last fall the Cayuses told us that they were about *to kill the whites at Dr. Whitman's*. We told them that was wrong, which made them mad *at* us; and when they killed them, they came and wished us to fight the whites, which we refused. We loved the whites; but they said, if you do not help us to fight the whites, when we have killed them we will come and kill you. This made us cry; but we told them we would not fight, but if they desired to kill us they might. We should feel happy to know that we die innocently.'

"I answered them as follows: 'We are glad you have come, because we like to see our friends, and do not like to make war on innocent people. The Great Spirit we love has taught us that it is wrong to shed innocent blood; therefore we wish everybody to be our friends. Our peace men long ago sent you word, that we did not come to make war on any but those murderers who shed the blood of our countrymen, and insulted our women. When we get those wicked men we will go home, but those we will have; if not now, we will fight until we do get them. We do not want to kill any but the murderers; but all who fight with them, we consider as bad as they are. All tribes which receive them we must make war upon, because their hearts are bad, and we know that the Great Spirit is angry with them. We hope your nation will not receive them. We hope that you will not let your young men join them, because we do not wish to kill innocent people. We hope, that if the murderers come among you, you will bring them to us; then the Great Spirit will not be angry with you. We that fight do not care how many bad people we have to fight. *The Americans and Hudson's Bay Company people are the same as one*, and you will get no more ammunition until the war is at a close.'

"I gave them a plow as a national gift, and told them that I gave that kind of a present because we thought tilling the ground would make them happy. They remained with us a day and night, and then left for their conntry with an assurance of friendship.

"The ammunition boats arrived here this evening, and I shall start to-morrow for Wailatpu with nine provision wagons and baggage wagons besides, and about one hundred men to guard them, leaving McKay's company to guard this place until Colonel Lee's arrival here.

"The *scanty supply of ammunition* sent us is almost disheartening. If the rumor that the Indians brought us this evening be true, I fear that we will have to shoot the most of it at the Indians before we can reach the boys. The Indians reported here this evening that the horse-guard at Wailatpu was killed by the Indians, and all the horses run off. I shall lose no time, I assure you, but will relieve them with all possible speed.

"Your obedient servant,

"H. J. G. Moxon, S. C. C. O. D."

We will not stop to comment on the facts and points stated in this letter relative to the Yankama Indians and Captain Moxon's remarks to them, but continue our narrative from a letter of Jesse Cadwallader from Fort Waters, April 4, 1848. At the time of writing, he did not know of Colonel Gilliam's death. He says:—

"At present we are not in a very pleasant fix for fighting, as we are but 150 in number, and nearly out of ammunition. Colonel Gilliam, with the rest of the men, left here on the 20th ult. for the Dalles for supplies. We look for them in a few days, and hope to see more men with them. We look for the Indians to come upon us every day. They say they will give us one more fight, and drive us from the country. We expect they will number 1,200. The Cayuses, Nez Percés, Walla-wallas, Spokans, and Paluces will all join and fight us, and you may expect a call for more men in a short time; we are preparing for an attack. We are killing beef and drying it to-day. I think we can defend this post; we shall do so or die in the attempt. * * *

"We can not complain of our living, so far; we have a plenty of beef and bread, nearly all the time. We have found several *caches* of wheat, peas, and potatoes. We have about thirty bushels of wheat on hand, and the mill fitted up for grinding.

"I wish you would see to my claim on Clear Creek, for I expect to return when this war is over, and occupy it, with some man's girl as a companion."

The following proceedings of the ladies of Oregon City and vicinity, which was responded to all over the country, showing how the ladies of Oregon and this Pacific coast can respond to the call of their country, found a welcome place in the columns of the *Spectator*. We understand that considerable clothing has been contributed by the ladies for the volunteers in the field. Such acts by ladies are highly commendable to them, and can not fail to have a favorable influence in the army:—

"At a meeting convened at the Methodist church, according to previous notice, on the 12th instant, to consult upon the best means to aid in relieving the necessities of the soldiers, the meeting was called to order by Mrs. Hood, when Mrs. Thornton was called to the chair, and Mrs. Thurston (the wife of our first delegate to Congress), was appointed secretary. Mrs. Thornton (whose husband was then in Washington, doing all he could for the country as a volunteer representative of its interests, while his noble wife was teaching school and ready to aid in sustaining our almost naked army) briefly stated the object of the meeting, when, on motion, it was resolved to form a society, the object of which should be to aid and assist in supporting the war (Sanitary Society). On motion, the meeting proceeded to choose officers, which resulted in the election of Mrs. Thornton, President; Mrs. Robb, Vice-President; Mrs. Leslie (second wife of Rev. D. Leslie), Treasurer; and Mrs. Thurston, Secretary.

"On motion, it was voted to appoint a committee of three, whose duty it should be to assist the society in raising funds, etc. The president appointed Mrs. Hood (an active, energetic old lady), Mrs. Crawford (the wife of our first internal revenue collector), and Mrs. Herford, said committee.

"Mrs. Robb then introduced the following address as expressive of the sense of the meeting, to be forwarded to the army with the clothing raised by the ladies, which, on being read, was unanimously adopted:—

"'OREGON CITY, April 12, 1848.

"'The volunteers of the first regiment of Oregon riflemen will please accept from the ladies of Oregon City and vicinity the articles herewith forwarded to them. The intelligence which convinces us of your many hardships, excessive fatigues, and your chivalrous bearing also satisfies us of your urgent wants.

"'These articles are not tendered for acceptance as a compensation for your services rendered; we know that a soldier's heart would spurn with contempt any boon tendered by us with such an object; accept them as a brother does, and may, accept a sister's tribute of remembrance—as a token, an evidence, that our best wishes have gone to, and will remain with you in your privations, your marches, your battles, and your victories.

"'Your fathers and ours, as soldiers, have endured privations and sufferings, and poured out their blood as water, to establish undisturbed freedom east of the Rocky Mountains; your and our mothers evinced the purity of their love of country, upon those occasions, by efforts to mitigate the horrors of war, in making and providing clothing for the soldiers. Accept this trifling present as an indorsement of an approval of the justice of the cause in which you have volunteered, and of your bearing in the service of our common country as manly, brave, and patriotic.

"'The war which you have generously volunteered to wage was challenged by acts the most ungrateful, bloody, barbarous, and brutal.

"'Perhaps the kindness which the natives have received at the hands of American citizens on their way hither, has, to some extent, induced a belief on the part of the natives, that all the Americans are "women" and dare not resent an outrage, however shameful, bloody, or wicked. Your unflinching bravery has struck this foolish error from the mind of your enemies, and impressed them with terror, and it is for you and a brotherhood who will join you, to follow up the victories so gloriously commenced, until a succession of victories shall compel an honorable peace, and insure respect for the American arms and name.

"'We have not forgotten that the soul-sickening massacre and enormities at Wailatpu were committed in part upon our sex. We know that your hardships and privations are great; but may we not hope, that through you these wrongs shall not only be amply avenged, but also that you inscribe, upon the heart of our savage enemies, a conviction never to be erased, that the virtue and lives of American women will be protected, defended, and avenged by American men.

"'The cause which you have espoused is a holy cause. We believe that the God of battle will so direct the destinies of this infant settlement, that she will come out of this contest clothed in honor, and her brave volunteers covered with glory.

"'The widows and orphans, made so by the massacre which called you to the field, unite with us in the bestowment of praise for the valuable service already rendered by you; and he who has already proclaimed himself the widow's God, Judge, and Husband, and a Father to the fatherless, will smile upon and aid your exertions. Fight on, then!—Fight as you have fought, and a glorious victory awaits you.'

"On motion, a vote of thanks was tendered to Mrs. Hood for her unwearied exertions in behalf of the suffering soldiers.

"Mrs. Robb moved, That when this society adjourn, it do so to meet at this place again on the 26th instant.

"On motion, it was then voted that the proceedings of this meeting, with the address adopted, be published in the Oregon *Spectator*.

"On motion, the meeting then adjourned.

"Mrs. N. M. THORNTON, President.
"Mrs. E. F. THURSTON, Secretary."

The thought and sentiment manifested in the above proceedings and address allow the reader to look right at the heart and soul of our people. No one who reads our history will have occasion to blush or be ashamed to know that his father or mother crossed the vast mountains and plains of North America, found a home in Oregon, and fought back the savages, and their more savage foreign leaders. *Oregonians*, the fact that your father or mother was a pioneer on this coast will redound to your honor,—as a reference to the deeds of our fathers and mothers, on the eastern part of our continent, strengthened and nerved our hearts, when the whole host of savage instruments of cruelty and barbarism were let loose upon us, and many of our dearest friends fell by their ruthless hordes! We know not who the author of that address is, but the sentiment—the soul—belongs alone to Oregon.

In the same paper we find the sentiment still further illustrated in a declaration of a number of young ladies. We only regret that we have not their names; the sentiment is too good to be lost, as it shows the finer and nobler sentiments of virtue and religion among the mothers and daughters of Oregon, in those trying times. The communication is as follows:—

"WALLAMET VALLEY, OREGON.

"Response by young ladies to the call of Captain Moxon for young men in the army.

"We have read with much interest the late report from the army, and feel ourselves under obligations to reply to the appeal made to us in that report. We are asked to evince our influence for our country's good, by withholding our hand from any young man who refuses to turn out in defense of our honor and our country's right.

"In reply, we hereby, one and all, of our own free good will, solemnly pledge ourselves to comply with that request, and to evince, on all suitable occasions, our detestation and contempt for any and all young men, who *can*, but *will not*, take up arms and march at once to the seat of war, to punish the Indians, who have not only murdered our friends, but have grossly insulted our sex. We never can, and never will, bestow our confidence upon a man who has neither patriotism nor courage enough to defend his country and the girls;—such a one would never have sufficient sense of obligations to defend and protect a *wife.*

"Do not be uneasy about your claims and your rights in the valley; while you are defending the rights of your country, she is watching yours. You must not be discouraged. Fight on, be brave, obey your officers, and never quit your posts till the enemy is conquered; and when you return in triumph to the valley, you shall find us as ready to rejoice with you as we now are to sympathize with you in your sufferings and dangers."

(Signed by fifteen young ladies).

Soon after the peace arrangements, as related in the previous chapter, the colonel and major left for the lower country. They arrived at the Dalles, where the colonel was accidentally shot by attempting to remove a rifle from the hind end of one of his wagons; the cap was burst, and he received the contents of the gun, which proved fatal in a few hours. In his death the country lost a valuable citizen, the army a good soldier, and his family a kind husband and affectionate father. As a commander of the provisional troops, he succeeded probably as well as any man could under the circumstances.

The deep schemes of the British fur monopoly, the baser schemes of the Jesuits, both working together, and in connection with the Indians and all the American dupes that they with their influence and capital could command, it is not surprising that, as a military man, he should fail to bring to justice the immediate or remote perpetrators of the crime he was expected to punish. In fact, but few at the present day are able to comprehend the extent and power of opposing influences. One of the commissioners informed us that from the time the colonel opened a correspondence with the priests, he appeared to lose his influence and power and control of the troops. He lacked an essential quality as a commander—promptness in action and decision to strike at the proper time, as was manifest in his whole campaign. Yet, for this he is to a certain extent excusable, as he had with his army the Indian peace commissioners, and was acting under the orders of a governor who was greatly deceived as to the prime movers in the war.

One of the commissioners was notoriously the dupe and tool of the foreign monopoly in our midst, as his own history before and since has proved. He claimed to know exactly how to deal with the difficulty. This influence was felt by the troops, and generally acknowledged, and, as we know from the best of authority, was the cause of the colonel's being ordered to report at head-quarters.

After lying at Fort Waters for a considerable time, his men becoming dissatisfied (as intimated in letters), he mounted his horse, and most of his men volunteered to follow him for a fight. He pursued what he supposed to be the correct trail of the murderers to a point on the Tukanon, and there fought a small party, and learned that the murderers were at the crossing of Snake River, some thirty miles distant. He continued his march all night. The next morning, the murderers having learned of his expedition in another direction, he came upon them and surprised their whole camp. An old man came out of the lodge and made signs of submission, and pretended that the murderers were not in his camp, but that their cattle were upon the hills. This induced the colonel to order his men to gather the cattle and return to Fort Waters (while Tilokaikt was then crossing the river), instead of attacking them, as he should have done. The Indians soon gathered their best horses, which were kept separate from the common band, and commenced an attack upon his cumbered, retreating column, till they came near the ford on the Tuchet, when a running fight was kept up, and an effort made to get possession of the ford by the Indians, which it required all the colonel's force to defeat; and like the crow and the fox in the fable, while the colonel was giving the Indians a specimen of American fighting, he neglected his cattle, and the Indians drove them off. But few were wounded on either side, though, in the struggle to gain the ford and bushes contiguous, there was swift running and close shooting, which continued till dark. The Indians retired with their cattle, and next day the colonel and his party, with the wounded, reached Fort Waters, and thence he obeyed the summons of the governor to return and report at head-quarters. While Major Lee is on his way with the body of Colonel Gilliam to the Wallamet, and to obtain recruits and supplies of arms and ammunition, we will see what Colonel Waters is about at Wailatpu, April 4, 1848.

In his letter of the above date, he says:—

"Since Colonel Gilliam's departure from this place, our relations with the *supposed friendly* Indians have undergone a material change; not seeing any, either friendly or hostile, for several days, I concluded to send an express to Fort Wallawalla, and if possible to gain some information concerning their movements, as I had reason to believe from their long silence that there was something wrong; I accordingly addressed a short note to Mr. McBean on the evening of the 1st of April, and dispatched two of my men with the same, charging them strictly to remain there during the day, and return, as they went, in the night. They returned yesterday in safety, and their narrative, together with Mr. McBean's written statements, fully confirms me in my previous views.

"The Wallawalla chief, notwithstanding his professions of friendship to Colonel Gilliam and the Bostons, now looks upon us as enemies. The law prohibiting the sale of ammunition appears to be his principal hobby. By refusing it to him and his people he says we place them on an equal footing with the guilty, and if this law is not abrogated, they will become murderers. This sentiment he expressed in the presence of our express bearers. [The sentiment of Sir James Douglas, as expressed in his letter to Governor Abernethy.]

"There were then at the fort some sixty lodges, and between two and three hundred warriors. Mr. McBean gave what purported to be information where the murderers had gone, stating that Ellis and sixty of his men had died in the mountains with the measles, and this had produced its effect upon our superstitious friends.

"The Cayuses and Nez Percés have had a big feast, which to my mind speaks in language not to be misunderstood. Mr. McBean further states, that the Paluce Indians, Cayuses, and part of the Nez Percés, are awaiting the American forces, to fight them on the Nez Percès, or Snake River; but the signs of the times justify the conclusion that we will be attacked nearer home, and much to our disadvantage, unless soon supplied with ammunition. They know our circumstances about as well as we do ourselves, both as regards ammunition and provisions, and it need not be thought strange if they act accordingly.

"Welaptulekt (an Indian chief) is at the fort, and has brought quite an amount of immigrant property with him, which he delivered to Mr. McBean; says he was afraid Colonel Gilliam would kill him, which was the reason of his not meeting him. This is the report of the men; Mr. McBean did not mention his name. My opinion is that we have nothing to hope from his friendship.

"I see by General Palmer's letter to Colonel Gilliam, that he (McBean) *refused to accept the American flag*, which was presented by his own Indians; he, of course, had nothing to fear from them.

"I have now given you the outlines of our unpleasant situation, and doubt not that you will make every exertion to forward us ammunition, and *men too of the right stripe*. I have exaggerated nothing, nor has any active cautiousness prompted me to address you upon this subject. If they do come upon us, be their numbers what they may, rest assured, while there is one bullet left, they will be taught to believe that the Bostons are not all *clochemen* (women).

"I have succeeded in getting the mill to work, and we are grinding up the little grain we found. Mr. Taylor died on the 24th of March. The wounded are doing well. I regret to say our surgeon talks strongly of leaving us the first opportunity. My impression is that a more suitable person could not be obtained in that capacity. His commission has not been sent on, which no doubt has its weight with him.

"I have the honor to remain,

"Your obedient servant,

"JAMES WATERS, Lieutenant-Colonel."

As to the propriety of Governor Abernethy's publishing this entire letter, there was at the time a question. With the facts since developed, it is plain that it should not have been given to the public; but, as we have before stated, the governor was one of those easy, confiding, unsuspecting men, that gave a wily and unprincipled enemy all the advantage he could ask. It was only the determined energy and courage of the settlers that enabled them to overcome their secret and open foes.

The evidence is conclusive, that Colonel Gilliam, through the influence and duplicity of Newell, McBean, and the Jesuits, was induced to withhold his men from punishing the Indians, and received and treated with bands as guilty as the murderers themselves, thus giving an impression to the Indians of weakness and cowardice on the part of the troops, as well as a want of the requisite qualities for a successful commander.

Major Lee returned to the settlement, obtained more troops and ammunition, and was appointed colonel of the regiment in place of Colonel Gilliam, deceased. This place he was justly entitled to fill by seniority in the service. He then returned to Fort Waters, and, finding the troops in the field satisfied with Colonel Waters, resigned at once, and filled a subordinate place in the army. The troops were soon put in motion. Captain McKay and his company of *British subjects* were disbanded, after being stationed a short time at Wascopum.

The troops soon drove the murderers off *to buffalo*, "*with the propriety, decorum, and energy which the case required*," as per "Veritas." They gathered up such of the murderers' cattle and horses as were not claimed by professed friendly Indians, and retired to the Wallamet, leaving a small garrison at Fort Waters and at Wascopum.

The war, though attended with little or no loss of life to the settlement or the Indians, was of incalculable value to the American cause. It taught the Indians, the British monopoly, and their allies, the Jesuits, that, notwithstanding they could drive from the upper country, or middle

Oregon, the missionaries of the American Board, they could not conquer and drive the settlements from the country.

While the main effort of the Hudson's Bay Company was to rid the country of American settlements, the Jesuits were working against American Protestantism, and endeavoring to secure the whole country, middle Oregon in particular, for their exclusive Indian mission. One of them, A. Hoikin, S. J., in a letter to the editor of the *Précis Historiques*, Brussels, dated "Mission of Flatheads, April 15, 1857" (this mission was established by Father De Smet as early as 1841 in opposition to that of the American Board at Spokan), says:—

"If the less well-intentioned Indians from the lower lands would keep within their own territory, and if the whites, the number of whom is daily augmenting in St. Mary's Valley, could act with moderation and conduct themselves prudently, I am convinced that soon the whole country would be at peace, and that not a single Indian would henceforward imbrue his hands in the blood of a white stranger.

"Were I authorized to suggest a plan, I would have all the upper lands *evacuated by the whites, and form of it a territory exclusively of Indians*; afterward, I would lead there all the Indians of the inferior portion, such as the Nez Percès, the Cayuses, the Yankamas, the Cœur d'Alênes, and the Spokans. Well-known facts lead me to believe that this plan, with such superior advantages, might be effected by means of a mission in the space of two or three years.

"For the love of God and of souls, I conjure you, reverend fathers, not to defer any longer. All the good that *Father De Smet and others have produced by their labors and visits will be lost* and forgotten if these Indians are disappointed in their expectation. They weigh men's characters in the balance of honesty; in their eyes, whosoever does not fulfill his promises is culpable; they do not regard or consider whether it be done for good reason, or that there is an impossibility in the execution.

"Some of them have sent their children to *Protestant schools*, and they will continue to do so as long as we form no establishments among them. From all this you may easily conclude that there is *apostasy and all its attendant evils.*"

In connection with the above, Father De Smet says:—

"These four letters of Rev. Father Hoikin show sufficiently, my dear and reverend father, the spiritual wants of these nations and their desire of being assisted. *Apostasy* is more frequent than is generally believed in Europe. Oh, if the zealous priests of the continent *know what we know*,—had they seen what we have witnessed, their generous hearts would transport them beyond the seas, and they would hasten to consecrate their lives to a ministry fruitful in salutary results.

"Time passes; already the *sectaries* of various shades are preparing to penetrate more deeply into the desert, and will wrest from those degraded and unhappy tribes their last hope,—that of knowing and practising the *sole* and *true faith.* Shall they, in fine, obtain the *black-gowns*, whom they have expected and called for during so many years.

"Accept, reverend father, the assurance of my sincere friendship.

"P. J. De Smet."

Would men entertaining the sentiments above expressed—sent among our American Indians, carried about, supplied and fed, by a foreign fur monopoly, who were seeking in every way possible, to hold the country themselves—be likely to teach the Indians to respect American institutions, American missionaries, or American citizens?

Let us look at another sentiment of this Father Hoikin; he says: "When, oh, when! shall the oppressed Indian find a poor corner of the earth on which he may lead a peaceful life, serving and loving his God in tranquillity, and preserving the ashes of his ancestors, without fear of beholding them profaned and trampled beneath the feet of an *unjust usurper.*" We can not discover in this sentiment any respect or love for the American people, or for their government, which is looked upon by this reverend priest, as an "*unjust usurper*" of Indian privileges;—something their own church and people have done the world over; but being done by a free American people, it becomes "*unjust*," profane, and horrible. We will make a few other quotations, which we find in the very extensive correspondence of these Jesuitical fathers, with their society in Brussels. The writer, Father P. J. De Smet, after enumerating the usual complaints against our government and its agents, makes his Indian complainingly to say, "The very contact of the whites has poisoned us." He then puts into the mouth of a Choctaw chief, a proposition from a Senator Johnson to establish three Indian territorial governments, "with the provision of being admitted later as distinct members of the *Confederate United States.*"

"On the 25th of last November, 1862," he says, "Harkins, chief among the Choctaws, addressed a speech on this subject to his nation assembled in council. Among other things he said: 'I appeal to you, what will become us, if we reject the proposition of Senator Johnson? Can we hope to remain a people, always separate and distinct? This is not possible. The time must come; yes the time is approaching in which we shall be swallowed up; and that, notwithstanding our just claims! I speak boldly. It is a fact; our days of peace and happiness are gone, and forever. * * * If we will preserve among us the rights of a people, one sole measure remains to us; it is to *instruct* and *civilize* the youth *promptly and efficiently*. The day of fraternity has arrived. We must act together, and, by common consent, let us attentively consider our critical situation, and the course now left us. One false step may prove fatal to our existence as a nation. I therefore propose that the council take this subject into consideration, and that a committee be named by it, to discuss and deliberate on the advantages and disadvantages of the proposition made to the Choctaws. Is it just and sage for the Choctaws to refuse a liberal and favorable offer, and expose themselves to the destiny of the Indians of Nebraska ?"

"According to news received recently, through a journal published in the Indian country, the speech of the chief has produced a profound impression, and was loudly applauded by all the counselors. All the intelligent Choctaws approve the measure.

"*The Protestant missionaries oppose the bill, and employ all their artifices and influence to prevent its success. Harkins proposes their expulsion.* 'It is our money' said he, 'that these missionaries come here to get. Surely, our money can get us better teachers. Let us therefore try to procure good missionaries, with whom we can live in harmony and good understanding; who will give us the assurance that their doctrine is based on that of the apostles and of Jesus Christ.'

"The Chickasaws are represented as opposed to Senator Johnson's measure. We trust, however, that the vote of the majority will prove favorable, and that the three territorial States will be established.

"It is, in my opinion, a last attempt, and a last chance of existence for the sad remnants of the poor Indians of America. It is, I will say, if I may here repeat what I wrote in my second letter in 1853, their only remaining source of happiness; *humanity and justice* seem to demand it. If they are again repulsed, and driven inland, they will infallibly perish. Such as refuse to submit, and accept the definite arrangement,—the only favorable one left,—must resume the nomad life of the prairies, and close their career with the vanishing buffaloes and other animals."

We have known this Father De Smet for many years, and have known of his connection as chaplain in the United States army, and of his extensive travels among the various Indian tribes of our country. We were well aware of his zeal and bigotry as a Jesuit; but we did not suppose he would take the first opportunity to combine all his associates, and the Indians under his influence, against the government that had favored him and his Indian missionary operations so readily. Yet perhaps we ought not to be surprised at this even, as the Roman hierarchy expressed more open sympathy and favor to the Southern rebellion than any other European power, by acknowledging the Southern Confederacy, and furnishing a man to assassinate President Lincoln.

We have introduced these quotations in our sketches of early history, in order to show to the reader the far-reaching policy, as also the determination of foreign powers, through the Jesuit missionaries, to accomplish the overthrow of our American institutions, and prevent the spread of them upon this coast. The following is copied from the *Christian Intelligencer*:—

"*Rome in the Field.*

"There are those who believe that Rome has an evil eye on this country, and that our next great battle will be with her hosts, rapidly mustering on these shores. We would not be alarmists, but we would not have our countrymen ignorant of matters which most nearly and vitally concern our country's welfare. If the policy of Rome is to rule or ruin, let us know it. If it be first to ruin, and then to rule, let us know that.

"We purpose to go no further back than the beginning of the war, and to let the facts which we shall name speak for themselves. If they have no other lesson, they will, at least, show that Rome, during our terrible struggle for national existence, was true to her ancient history and traditions, as the enemy of civil liberty and the friend of the oppressor the world over.

"It will not be forgotten how generally and enthusiastically our adopted citizens, the Irish, enlisted in the army when the call first came for men to put down rebellion. In the early part of the war, there were Irish battalions, and regiments, and brigades, but there were few, if any, at its close. The truth is, after the second year of the war, the Irish changed front, and suddenly became sympathizers with treason and rebellion. It was noticed that the girls in the kitchen began to roll their fierce gutturals against Mr. Lincoln; their brothers in the army began to curse the cause for which they fought; desertions were frequent; enlistments stopped; and the attitude of the Irish mind before Mr. Lincoln's second election was one of disloyalty and hostility to the government of the United States.

"And these facts can not be changed by the habit which these people have of boasting about fighting our battles, and saving our country. By actual examination of our muster-rolls, the simple truth appears to be, that only eight per cent. of our grand army were of foreign birth; the balance—ninety-two per cent.—were native Americans, who returned at length, worn and battle-scarred, to find their places on the farms, in the factories, and elsewhere, filled by Irish who had sought safety and profit at home, while our boys were courting danger and death in battle.

"It may be interesting to know when this change came over the Irish mind. What dampened their ardor, what quenched the glow of their patriotic impulse? The coincidence is so complete, that the cause is doubtless the same.

"It will be remembered that Bishop Hughes went abroad during the second year of the war, as was supposed, by authority of our government to interest the Catholic sovereigns of Europe in our favor. Instead of this, however, the archbishop went direct to Rome, and straightway the pope acknowledged the independence of the Confederate States. His insignificance gave him impunity, and purchased our silence. But the act had its influence; Biddy in the kitchen, Mike in the army, Patrick on the farm, and Mac in the factory, fell to cursing Mr. Lincoln as a tyrant and butcher. Enlistments among the Irish stopped from that time, unless it was bounty-jumpers and deserters. They banded together to resist the draft, as in New York, where they rioted in blood for three long days, and only yielded to the overwhelming power of United States troops. The spirit that actuated these human fiends came from Rome, and to Rome must be awarded the sole honor of welcoming to the family of nations a Confederacy whose first act was treason, and whose last was assassination. Indeed, it was Rome that furnished the assassin and his conspirators against the greatest life of modern times. And that assassin struck not againt the life of a man, but against the life of the Republic; and if guilt lies in the intent, then is Rome guilty of the nation's life.

"With such a record, Rome vainly puts herself among the friends of our free institutions. She misjudged, we think, but she no doubt thought the time had arrived to destroy what had come of Puritanism. And for this, she was willing to be the ally of a government whose corner-stone was negro slavery. Are we still dreaming that Rome is changed, or that she has surrendered the hope of supplanting Protestant freedom on these shores? Would not every Fenian lodge in the country rally to the help of the South, if there was a chance to restore the old negro-hating oligarchy to power.

"It can hardly have escaped every observing man that the Irish mind is expectant and exultant in regard to this country. They do not conceal their belief that the Catholic Church is to rise to the ascendant here, and that Protestantism is to do it reverence.

"But a few weeks since, Father Hecker, one of the lights of the Catholic Church in this country, said in a public lecture, in New

York, that his church had numbered eleven millions of our people, or one-third of our population; and that if the members of his church increased for the next thirty years as it had for the thirty years past, in 1900 Rome would have the majority, and would be bound to take the country and rule it in the interest of the church. 'And,' continued the reverend father, 'I consider it my highest mission to educate our people up to this idea, that America is ours, and belongs to the church.'

"It is all of a pattern. Rome during the war sought to ruin us in order to rule us. She failed in the first, but is no less tenaciously striving to accomplish the last. In a future number we will hope to show how she means to do this through the freedmen."

It appears that, when our government became apprised of the value of Oregon as a part of its domain, and was informed officially by the provisional government of the situation of affairs generally at the time of the Whitman massacre, at the same time the information was so arranged, and the circumstances so stated, that the government and people were generally deceived as to the cause and ultimate object of that transaction. It is clear that the Hudson's Bay Company designed to hold the country. It is also evident that British government expected that the arrangements of the company were such that their title to the Oregon Territory was secured beyond a question.

The far-seeing shrewdness of P. J. De Smet, S. J., in relation to his efforts and church influence, was in a measure superior to both; for he made use of both to secure his object and add to the numerical strength of his church, and by that means gain political consideration in the United States and in other countries. For instance, all the Indian children and adults they have ever baptized (as may be seen by their letters to their society in Brussels) are counted, numbering two hundred and ninety-four thousand,—nearly one-half of their American converts. This, with all their foreign population, as claimed by them, and improperly allowed in the United States census, gives to that sect a political influence they are not entitled to; and were the question agitated openly, as it was undertaken once secretly, the result would show their weakness. While that church professes the open Catholic faith, it still holds to its secret Society of Jesus, and through it has carried its missions and influence into every department of our American government, more especially into that of the Indians. General Grant seems to understand our Indian relations, and has advised the best plan for disposing of the Indian question, *i. e.*, place it under the exclusive control of the military department; and if an Indian becomes a settler, let him be protected as such.

After the greater portion of our provisional troops had been disbanded, Revs. Eells and Walker and their families were ordered out of the upper country, it not being deemed safe for them to remain, on account of hostile Indians who were notoriously friendly with every one claiming to belong to the Hudson's Bay Company or to the priests' party; as asserted by Father Hoikin, who says: "*The country is as safe for us as ever;* we can go freely wherever we desire. No one is ignorant that the black-gowns are not enemies; those at least who are among the Indians."

Notwithstanding the order had been given, by Indian Agent Major Lee, that all the missionaries among those Indians should leave the country till troops could be stationed to protect all alike, still not one of the Jesuit missionaries obeyed it. On the 21st of August, Lieutenant A. T. Rogers writes to Governor Abernethy, as follows:—

"FORT LEE, WASCOPUM, Aug. 21, 1848.

"Believing it to be my duty to let you know any thing of moment that transpires at this station, for this purpose I now address you.

"At about 2 o'clock, P. M., at this place, a boat arrived, consigned to the French priests who have taken up their residence here, loaded with eight casks of powder; six of them 150 pounds each, and two of them 90 pounds each, making 1,080 pounds. I also took fifteen sacks of balls, 100 pounds in each cask; three sacks of buck or goose shot, 100 pounds each, making 1,800 pounds of ball and buck-shot; counted one sack of the balls and found about 3,000 balls. I also took three boxes of guns; opened one box, and found twelve guns.

"The general conviction at the fort was, that not more than 500 pounds of powder in all had been forwarded for the army by the government, probably not even that amount. I was told by the priest from an interior station, as also by one at the Dalles, that the powder was for four stations, viz.: Cœur d'Alênes, Flatheads, Ponderays, and Okanagons; and this had been purchased at Vancouver the year before. I judged that at least one-third of their outfit was ammunition.

"Three days previous to the arrival of the ammunition, four Indians, embracing their chief from the Waiama village, near the mouth of Des Chutes, came into the fort, much alarmed, saying there had been Cayuses to them, declaring that the priests were going to furnish them plenty of ammunition, and that they were going to kill off all the Americans and all the Indians about that place, and the Cayuses wanted them to join them; said also that out of fear of the Cayuses they had sent away all their women and children. We had the best of evidence that they were frightened. Out of some four or five hundred souls along the river, between the fort and the Chutes of the Columbia, not a soul was to be seen on either side,—all, they said, were hid in the mountains. It was some ten days before the Indians came from their hiding-places.

"When the munitions came, Quartermaster Johnson swore he believed the priests designed them for the Cayuses; said also, a man in this country did not know when he was in a tight place.

"I must say I also believed it.

"A. T. ROGERS, Lieutenant Commanding Post."*

The following editorial notice of the above letter is copied from the Oregon *Spectator* of September 7, 1848:—

"By reference to the above letter by Lieutenant Rogers to Governor Abernethy, it will be seen that the arms and ammunition attempted to be taken into the upper Indian country by Catholic priests, have been seized by Lieutenant Rogers, and deposited in Fort Lee. Orders had been dispatched to Lieutenant Rogers to seize and detain those munitions. [A mistake of the editor. Lieutenant Rogers seized the ammunition, and wrote for orders.] Much credit is due to Lieutenant Rogers and the little garrison at Fort Lee for the promptness and efficiency with which they acted in the matter.

"We understand that there was no disposition on the part of the officers of the government to destroy or confiscate those munitions, but that they were detained to prevent their transportation into the Indian country under the present juncture of affairs.

"We had intended to have spoken upon the attempt by Catholic priests to transport such a quantity of arms and ammunition into the Indian country at this time, but as those munitions have been seized and are now safe, we abstain from present comment upon the transaction!"

The above notice of the transaction, as given by Lieutenant Rogers, is a fair specimen of the man who occupied the place of an editor at the time this infamous course was being carried on in Oregon by the two parties engaged in supplying the Indians with war materials. No one will suppose for a moment that these priests ever bought or owned the powder and arms; their own private supplies may have been in the cargo, but the ammunition and arms were on the way into the Indian country, under their priestly protection, for the benefit of their masters,

* From original letter.

the Hudson's Bay Company, who, as we have repeatedly proved, were acting in concert upon the prejudices and superstitions of the Indians.

Was it a great undertaking for that company to drive a thousand or twelve hundred American settlers from Oregon at that time?

Robert Newell, already known to our readers, says, in speaking of missionaries and settlers, "They could not have remained in the country a week without the consent and aid of that company, nor could the settlers have remained as they did up to 1848." We are willing to admit Mr. Newell's position only in part. We know that company's power and influence in Washington and London; we also know fully what they attempted to do from 1812 to 1821, and only succeeded by a compromise with their opponent. We also know all about their operations and influences in Oregon, and are ready to admit that they had the disposition to destroy the American settlements. We also know the extent of the effort made to establish a claim to the Oregon country by means of their French and Hudson's Bay half-breeds, and we are fully aware of their effort to procure witnesses to substantiate their monstrous claims for old rotten forts and imaginary improvements. Knowing all this, we deny that that company had the courage, or would have dared to molest a single American citizen or missionary, only as they could influence the Indians by just such means as they used to destroy *Smith's party on the Umpqua*, drive Captain Wyeth and the American Fur Company from the country, and destroy Dr. Whitman's settlement. Any other course would have involved the two countries in a war, and led to an investigation of their proceedings and of their charter.

"That company," says Mr. Fitzgerald, "have submitted to all manner of insult and indignity, and committed all manner of crime, and they dare not go before any competent tribunal for the redress of any real or supposed injury, or right they claim."

This brings us to the reason that Mr. Douglas gave in answer to Mr. Ogden, in the presence of Mr. Hinman, "*There might be other than sectarian causes*" *for the Whitman massacre*, and here we have the united effort of priests and Hudson's Bay Company to attribute the massacre to *measles* and *superstition*, while we have the positive testimony of Mr. Kimzey and others to show that the whole was determined upon before any sickness was among the Indians. From the testimony of General Palmer, the Donner party, Mr. Hines, and Mr. Ogden, we find but the one effort; which was, to prevent, or diminish as much as was possible, the settlement of the country. And why? To answer this question clearly, we have traced the early history of that *monster monopoly* in previous chapters, and given their proceedings in countries under their exclusive control. To illustrate more clearly the subject of the previous and present chapters, we will give an article we find in the Oregon *Argus* of February 9, 1856, eight years after the war. The article is headed:—

"*The Catholic Priests and the War—'A Catholic Citizen' attended to.*

"*To the Editor of the Oregon Argus:*

"SIR,—For the past month I have noticed several virulent articles in each issue of your paper, all tending to impress upon the minds of your readers the idea that the Catholic priests were the head and front of the present Indian difficulties; and being fearful that your constant harping upon that one subject might render you a monomaniac, I am induced to submit to your *Argus* eyes a few facts in relation to the conduct of the Catholic priests prior to and during the present war. In your issue of the 8th inst., I find an article based upon the following extract from the official report of Colonel Nesmith:—

"'With sundry papers discovered in the mission building, was a letter written by the priest, Pandozy, for Kamaiyahkan, head chief of the Yankama tribe, addressed to the officer in command of the troops, a copy of which is communicated with this report. There was also found an account-book kept by this priest Pandozy, which is now in the custody of Major Raines. This book contains daily entries of Pandozy's transactions with the Indians, and clearly demonstrates the indisputable fact that he has furnished the Indians with large quantities of ammunition, and leaving it a matter of doubt whether *gospel* or *gunpowder* was his principal stock in trade. The priest had abandoned the mission, but it gave unmistakable evidence of being cared for, and attended to, during his absence, by some Yankama Indian parishioners.'

"You then proceed with great *sang froid* to pride yourself upon the correct 'position' which you took about a month previous, relative to the above subject, and presuming upon the safe 'position' which you thus assumed, you say the priests have in a measure prompted the Indians to the late outbreak! A bold presumption, truly, when we find the puny evidence which you have to back your 'position.' You further assert as a fact, 'that in this, as in the Cayuse war, these priests have been detected in the very act of conveying large quantities of powder in the direction of the camp of the enemy.' This, sir, is a *fact* which emanated from your own disordered imagination, as during the Cayuse war no priest was ever detected in any such a position, and you *know* it; but then, it must be recollected that a little buncombe capital does not come amiss at this time, and if you can make it off of a poor priest by publishing a tissue of groundless falsehoods against him, why even that is 'grist to your mill.'"

"The foregoing is a portion of a communication which appeared in the *Standard* of December 13, over the signature of 'A Catholic Citizen.' The writer of that article, in endeavoring to blind the eyes of his readers, and his pretending to correct us in reference to certain statements we had made concerning a few things connected with the present Indian war, as also the Cayuse war of 1848, in which the Catholic priests had by their intercourse with the savages created more than a suspicion in the minds of the community that they were culpably implicated in the crimson character of these tragedies, wisely intrenched himself behind a fictitious signature. He has thereby thrown the responsibility of some three columns of pointless verbiage, flimsy sophistry, and Jesuitical falsehoods, upon the shoulders of an irresponsible, intangible, ghostly apparition, probably very recently dismissed from some sepulcher at Rome, or from the carcass of an Irishman just swamped in the bogs of Ireland.

"Seven or eight weeks have now elapsed since we called upon this Roman Catholic citizen to emerge from his hiding-place among the tombstones, and if he was really incarnate, with a body of flesh and bones, such as the rest of us have, to throw off the mask, and not only give us a full view of his corporeal developments, but also to send us a copy of the book by which he cleared Pandozy, and justified himself in issuing, from his sweat-house Vatican, his bull of excommunication against us.

"We have thus far 'harked' in vain for a sound 'from the tombs.' Like a true Jesuit, that loves darkness rather than light, he not only still persists in keeping his name in the dark, and keeping the 'book' we rightfully called for in the dark, but attempts to enshroud the whole subject in total darkness, by making up his own case from such parts of Pandozy's book as he chooses to have exposed, and then thrusting the whole manuscript into a dark corner of his dark-colored coat, and in order to darken what light we had already shed in upon the dark nest of Jesuits, among the dark-skinned and dark-hearted savages, he most solemnly denies as false the most important of the dark charges we made against them, and then, after 'darkening counsel' by a whole column of 'words without knowledge,' by which, like the cuttle-fish, he darkens the waters to elude the hand of his pursuer, and then, under cover of all this darkness, he dodges into his dark little sweat-house, and issues his terrible bull consigning us to a *very* dark place, where the multitudes of dark Jesuits that have gone before us have doubtless made it 'as dark as a stack of black cats.' But what makes the case still darker is, that while 'Catholic Citizen' refuses to expose his personal outlines to our 'Argus eyes,' but intimates that as he is a member of the Catholic Church, and of the Democratic party, if we let off a broadside upon either of these societies, and wound either of their carcasses, the one bloated on the blood of saints, and the other on the juice of corn, we shall of course inflict a material injury upon him, upon the principle that 'when one of the members suffers, all the members suffer with it;' we say, that in view of the fact that after 'Catholic Citizen' has claimed to be a member of both these organizations, the Corvallis organ of the Sag Nichts and Jesuits has whet the razor of authority, and lopped him off, as a heterodox member, and consigned him to the fires of damnation, because 'Catholic Citizen' has intimated that the two bodies were not identical, thus wisely enveloping him in a dark cloud, and translating him far beyond the reach of our guns, makes the case terribly dark indeed.

"'He (Catholic Citizen) displays the cloven foot of either direct opposition to the Democratic organization, or sore-head-ism and disaffection with that organization. * * * We can hardly conceive that the author of that communication is a Catholic, or a friend of the Catholic Church.'—*Statesman* of Dec. 25.

"Thus it will be seen that the editor of the 'organ' takes him by the top tuft, and applies the 'rapin hook' to his neck as a heretic, and not a genuine Catholic, because of his 'sore-head-ism and disaffection with the Democratic organization,' thus unequivocally asserting that the church and the clique are identical, or so closely identified that in placing himself in opposition to the one, he proves that he is not a friend of the other. Now whether the action of the organ has been from a malicious desire to 'bury him out of our sight' as an 'unfruitful branch' of the Catholic and Democratic trunk, or whether he intended in *mercy* to wrap him up in his Nessean shirt, and hide him from our view by denying to him the only earthly position he assumed, it matters not particularly to us. We shall probably teach him, or his ghost, in due time, a lesson which we long since whipped into the tough and slimy hide of the biped who controls the *Statesman*, and which he and his ilk would do well to read in the welts that checker his back, before they make their onslaughts upon us, viz., whenever we state a thing to be true, you may rest assured that it *is* so, and by calling it in question, you may be sure you will provoke the *proof*. We are not of that class of lying editors who make false charges which they are not able to sustain, and we have never yet vouched for the truth of a statement, and been afterward compelled to back out of it. Whenever we make a mistake, on account of bad information, we are sure to make the correction as soon as we are apprised of it, whether the statement affects the character or interest of friend or foe, or neither.

"Your vile innuendo, that we wished to make a little buncombe capital off a poor sniveling priest, is readily excused, knowing as we do your impressions from associating with political comrades who neither yield to nor expect justice or decency from their political opponents; and presuming also that the moment you stepped your foot upon American soil, with your little budget of Irish rags, some demagogue put a locofoco hook into your nose, and led you off to the political pound to learn your catechism, so fast that the remaining half of the nether extremity of your old swallow-fork made a right angle with your stalwart frame. We know very well what sort of lessons you have learned out of that catechism; how you have been duped to believe that the principles of Jefferson and other old sainted Democrats were still cherished by the designing demagogues who have taken you in tow; how we who oppose this office-hunting party are 'down upon Catholics and foreigners' simply because they are such; and how you had only to put in the 'clane dimocratthic ticket' to insure yourself great and glorious privileges. Under this sort of training, it is not surprising to us that you not only expect us to persecute you to the full extent that a priest is sworn to 'persecute' heretics, but that you are constantly in fear that the '*Noo Nothins*' will soon be ladling soup from a huge kettle that contains your quarters boiled up with Irish potatoes.

"We were not led to make the remarks we did in reference to the priests because they were *Papists*, but because we had reason to believe they were traitors to our government, and were identified with the savages in the present war. If Methodist, Presbyterian, or *any other Protestant clergymen* had rendered themselves equally obnoxious, we should probably have given our opinion at the time, that they deserved to be brought out of the Indian country, with all their 'traps,' to undergo a trial before a jury for their lives.

"But, sir, to one of your falsehoods:—

"'You further assert as a fact, "that in this, as in the Cayuse war, these priests have been detected in the very act of conveying large quantities of powder in the direction of the camp of the enemy." This, sir, is a *fact* which emanated from your own distorted imagination, as during the Cayuse war no priest was ever detected in any such a position, and you *know* it.'

"Now, sir, we did not suppose that there was a man green enough in all Oregon (excepting, perhaps, the *Statesman*) to call our statement in question. We happen to be an old Oregonian ourself, and profess to be pretty well posted in reference to many occurrences which will make up the future history of this lovely yet blood-stained land. The proof of our assertion we *supposed* could be come at by our file of the *Spectator*. The fact was still vivid in our memory. At the date of this transaction (August 21, 1848), there were three papers printed in the Territory: The *Free Press*, an 8 by 12 sheet, edited by G. L. Curry, present governor of Oregon, and the Oregon *Spectator*, a 22 by 32 sheet, edited by A. E. Wait, Esq., both published at Oregon City; besides a semi-monthly pamphlet, printed in the Tualatin Plains, and edited by Rev. J. S. Griffin. Although all of these papers at the time spoke of the transaction referred to, we believe none of them, excepting the *Spectator*, contained the official correspondence necessary to make out our case. We supposed, and so did many others, that all the old files of the *Spectator* were long since destroyed, excepting the imperfect one in our office. When 'A Catholic Citizen' called our statement in question, we, of course, referred to our 'file' for proof, but to our astonishment this particular paper was missing, although the immediate preceding and succeeding numbers were all there, embracing the whole summer of 1848. The missing number was *accidentally* (?) misplaced, of course, and the *proof* of that transaction supposed to be beyond our reach. By the kindness of a gentleman we have been furnished with the desired copy from his own file." (See official note and letter as previously quoted.)

"Now, will 'A Catholic Citizen' contend that our statement, in reference to the 'large quantities of powder,' is not fully covered by '*seven or eight hundred pounds of powder, fifteen hundred pounds of lead, and three boxes of guns.*'

"A man who can unblushingly utter such a falsehood as he has been guilty of, to create a public sentiment in favor of these priests, is below contempt, and we feel our task of exposing him to be truly humiliating We have branded this goat with an L***, which will stick to his hide as long as Cain carried *his* mark; and we now turn him out to browse for a while with B., who wears about a dozen of the same brands, under the pain of which we have sent him off howling. 'A Catholic Citizen' may feed on '*ferrin*' till we get time to clap the same brand to him again, when we shall tie him up to the post and again scorch his wool."

In reference to the article, as quoted from the Oregon *Argus*, it is not certainly known who "Catholic Citizen" is, but the impression is that the production is from the pen of Hon. P. H. Burnett or Sir James Douglas, and not impossible from Robert Newell, with such assistance as he could obtain.

If from either of those gentlemen, he may have been correctly informed as to the real owners of the munitions, but we can hardly believe

Mr. Douglas or Newell would lay themselves liable to the falsehood charged upon them, as they were in the country, and must have known of the facts in the case. Mr. Burnett was in California, and may have been misled by his informant. Be that as it may, the munitions were found on their way into the Indian country in charge of the priests, and the remarks of the editor of the *Argus*, W. L. Adams, Esq., shows the true history of the times, and the continued effort of the Jesuits and their neophytes to continue the Indian wars, to prevent the Protestant missionary stations from being reoccupied and the settlement of the country by the Americans, as intimated by Father Hoikin, in his letter to his society in Brussels.

Our provisional army did not capture a single murderer or prominent Indian engaged in the massacre, though many of them were known to have been frequently with the priests and at Fort Wallawalla. Neither the priests, McBean, nor the indescribably sympathizing Sir James Douglas made the least effort to bring the murderers to justice. A part of them were given up by the tribe,—tried and hung at Oregon City under the Territorial government of the United states, Judge Pratt presiding. In the trial, the same influence was used to get the murderers acquitted that had instigated and protected them in the commission of the crime.

The discovery of gold in California took place before our troops had all returned; the universal excitement in relation to it caused the desertion of a large portion of the Hudson's Bay Company's men, and almost an abandonment of the fur trade in the country for the time. They, however, still kept up the semblance of fur trade; and, at the expiration of their parliamentary license in 1858, withdrew to British Columbia and Vancouver Island to repeat upon their own people what they have practiced so successfully and so long upon the Americans.

There is, connected with this foreign company, a sort of Jesuitical suavity of manner and boasting propriety that naturally deceives all who come within its influence.

All its titles and little performances of charity are sounded forth with imperial pomposity. The man that does not acknowledge his obligations to it for being permitted to remain in the country previous to the expiration of its parliamentary license, is considered ungrateful by it, and by such as are blind to its infamous practices.

CHAPTER LXIV.

Missions among the Western Indians.—The Cœur d'Alêne Mission.—Protestant and Catholic missions compared.—What the American Protestant missionaries have done for the country and the Indians.—Extent of their influence, progress, and improvements.—Patriotism of Dr. Whitman.

Any person who has read the previous pages of this volume will not charge us with being ignorant of missionary operations on our western coast. Though we were but eight years connected in mechanical and business relations with them, still we have never lost sight of their labors, or their intellectual, moral, religious, political, or physical operations, nor of their personal conduct, or their adaptation to the work assigned them. We have spoken plainly our views, and impressions of the character, conduct, and influence of all prominent men in the country. Our main object has been to introduce the reader to the people of Oregon at the time in which they were acting in a public capacity. The private morals of the country have only been incidentally drawn out by reference to a petition sent to Congress, signed by the Rev. David Leslie, in 1840. In that document Mr. Leslie does himself and the country an injustice, by asserting that "theft, murder, infanticide, etc., are increasing among them to an alarming extent" (Senate Doc., 26th Congress, 1st Session, No. 514). Those charges Mr. Leslie no doubt sincerely thought to be true at that time, from the occurrence of the two most serious crimes about the time he wrote. But such crimes were by no means common.

It is often asked, *What good have the missionaries done to the Indians?* If this question applied alone to the Jesuit missionaries, brought to the country by the Hudson's Bay Company, we would say unhesitatingly, *None at all.* What few Indians there are now in the country that have been baptized by them, and have learned their religious catechisms, are to-day more hopelessly depraved, and are really poorer and more degraded than they were at the time we visited them twenty-two years since, looking carefully at their moral and pecuniary condition then and now. In proof of which we give the following article:—

"*Cœur d'Alêne Mission.*

"The old Mullan road from the Bitter Root or Missoula River to the Cœur d'Alêne Mission, shows to the traveler little evidence that it was once explored, laid out, and built by a scientific engineer. Decayed remnants of bridges are scattered all along the Cœur d'Alêne and St. Regis Borgia rivers; excavations have been filled up by the *débris* of fallen timber; huge bowlders that have rolled down the mountain side, constantly crumbling masses of slate, and huge chasms, worn or torn by the furious progress of the streams swollen by the melting snows and spring rains, obstruct entirely the passage of vehicles of all kinds, and render the passage of pack and saddle horses almost impossible. In the distance of eighty miles, you cross these two rivers one hundred and forty-six times, climb the precipitous sides of numerous mountains, continually jumping your horses over fallen timber, and filing to the right and left to avoid the impassable barriers which the mountain tornadoes have strewn in your way. The gorges, through which the road sometimes winds to avoid the mountains of rocks that close in even to the edge of the main stream, are narrow, and so completely shaded, that the rays of the sun have never penetrated, and one everlasting cold, chill dampness prevails. Our party were halted for an hour in one of those passes to allow the passage of a herd of two hundred Spanish cattle, and, although when we emerged from the cañon we found the sun oppressively hot, I do not remember ever to have suffered more from cold in any climate or in any altitude. The oppressiveness seemed to spring from something besides the mere temperature. We found but one living thing in those narrow cañons, and that was the most diminutive of the squirrel species. There was no song of birds or whir-r-r of partridge or grouse. It had the silence of the cold, damp grave.

"After arriving within six miles of the mission, the cañon of the Cœur d'Alêne opens out to about four miles in width, and you come suddenly to Mud Prairie,—a broad, open park, with here and there a solitary pine, and the ground covered with a heavy growth of swamp grass, which stock will only eat when nothing better can be obtained. Two hours more, and the mission, with its stately church (so it appears in the mountains), suddenly presents itself to view.

"Dilapidated fences are passed, rude Indian houses made of 'shakes,' fields of wheat and vegetables overrun with weeds, and at last, making the one hundred and forty-sixth crossing of the river, you halt your hungry and jaded horses in front of the rudest piece of architecture that ever supported a cross or echoed to the *Ave Maria* of the Catholic faith. Rude though it is, when we consider the workmen by whom it was constructed and the tools employed, the feeling of ridicule and smile of contempt will give way to admiration of the energy and (though I think mistaken) zeal which sustained the Jesuit fathers during what was to them, at that time, a most herculean labor. The building is 46 by 60 feet, and 30 feet posted, and was two years in process of construction. The workmen were two or three Jesuit priests, assisted by a few Indians, and the reverend fathers showed me a saw, an auger, an ax, and an old jack-plane, their only tools. It is situated on a little elevation from the main valley. On the left is the dwelling of the fathers, and still to the left is the storehouse, hospital, workshop, and building for the sick and crippled recipients of their benefactions. Around the slope of the elevation are scattered Indian huts and tepees, and at its base lies the resting-place of departed Indians who had died in the faith and gone to the hunting-grounds of the Great Spirit. In front of all, the Cœur d'Alêne, seemingly satisfied with the havoc which its furious progress had made, runs slowly and sluggishly along. The interior of the church is a curiosity. Here you see the marks of an unfortunate stroke from a clumsy axman; there a big Indian had sawed a stick of timber half off in the wrong place; in another spot, a little Indian had amused himself boring holes with the auger, while the joints 'broke' like a log-house before chinking. I was told that in its original construction there was not a nail used; but lately some efforts have been made to smooth down the rough exterior by the addition of cornice and corner-boards.

"The priests are very jealous of their claims to the territory around the mission, and regard the unlimited control of the Indians as a right which they have acquired by their self-sacrificing labors, and as a duty on the part of the Indians in return for the salvation of their souls and absolution from their sins. For my part, from an acquaintance with twelve tribes of Indians, among whom the gospel has been preached, and the forms, mysteries, and ceremonies of the Catholic Church introduced, I have failed to see a soul saved, or one single spark of Indian treachery, cruelty, or barbarism extinguished. The lamented General Wright thrashed the murdering propensities of the Cœur d'Alêne Indians out of them. The balance of their virtues—stealing, drinking, and supreme laziness—they possess in as large a share as they did before the heart of Saint Alêne was sent among them. I would like to give a favorable portrait of this mission and its occupants, if I could. I would like to say that the reverend fathers were neat, cleanly, intelligent, hospitable individuals, but there are too many who travel that road, and it would be pronounced false. I would like to say they were sowing the seed of civilization and cultivating it successfully in the untutored mind of the poor red man, but truth forbids. I would at least be glad that they urged upon the Indians to obey the laws of this government and respect the property of its citizens, but must leave that task to some one who has never bought of them horse meat for beef, and traveled for days on foot, because they would not, from pure deviltry, sell him one horse out of a band of two or three hundred. I say not these things with any reference to the Catholic Church or its belief, nor am I forgetful of what I have read of the Jesuits of St. Bernard and their acts of humanity; but for the filthy, worthless, superannuated relics of Italian ignorance, who have posted themselves midway between the extremes of Pacific and Atlantic civilization, acknowledging no law save that of their church, I have not the slightest particle of respect, and believe with an old packer, 'that it was a great pity General Wright had not carried his threat into execution, and blown the den over the range.'"*

These Indians were among the most honest, peaceable, and hopeful of any west of the Rocky Mountains. The mission here spoken of is the one represented by Fathers De Smet and Hôikin as their most successful one west of the mountains. We have reason to believe that Colonel Dow's statements are correct, from remarks made by other travelers, as also from Father Joset's own confession. On the 61st page of "Indian Sketches," he says: "I have been here nearly fifteen years; I am not yet master of the language, and am far from flattering myself with becoming so. My catechist remarked to me, the other day, 'You pronounce like a child learning to talk; when you speak of religion we understand you well, but when you change the subject it is another thing.' That is all I want. I have at last succeeded in translating the catechism; I think it is *nearly* correct. You can hardly imagine what it cost me to do it; I have been constantly at it since my arrival here; I finished it last winter; nevertheless it is short; it has but fourteen lessons; it is based upon the first part of the Catechism of Lyons. This catechism is printed, not on paper, but on the memory of the children."

According to Father Joset's own statement, it has taken him nearly fifteen years to learn their language sufficiently well to teach the children fourteen lessons in the catechism, about as much time as some of our Protestant missionaries have consumed in translating the whole of the New Testament, and a large part of the Old, into heathen languages, besides establishing schools, where they teach the people to read the pure word of God and practice its sacred principles, instead of following the traditions of men.

Father Joset continues: "From the end of November to Palm Sun-

* From the *Oregon Herald* of May 5, 1866.

day, on which day this ceremony (children's first communion) took place, they had catechism at the church three times a day, and it was rare that one missed the exercise; besides this, there was a repetition every day, either before the chief or the catechist. I give catechism three hundred times a year. I doubt whether there is a catechist in the world more utterly deprived of the means of encouraging his pupils. Some prayer beads would have been a great reward, but I could give them nothing but a medal to each, as a memorial of their first communion."

This reverend father, in speaking of the Church of the Sacred Heart, as it is called, says: "It is a magnificent monument to the faith of the Cœur d'Alênes, who have given the lie to their name by its erection. If it were finished, it would be a handsome church even in Europe. The design is by Father Ravalli; it is ninety feet long by forty wide; it has twenty-eight pillars, two and a half feet square by twenty-five feet in height; all the rest is of timber, and in proportion."

Compare this with Colonel Dow's description of the same building. It will be seen, by the quotations we have given, how these "*filthy, worthless, superannuated relics of Italian ignorance*" employ themselves and the Indians under their instruction. None but a bigot or a Jesuit will pretend that such instructions tend to enlarge, to elevate, or civilize the savage mind. We have only to look to countries grown old under just such teachings, to see its legitimate results.

From the Roman Catholic works before us, on the Oregon missions, embracing over eight hundred pages, one would conclude that over forty different tribes who have been visited by these Jesuits, in the territory of the United States, were all converted and Christian Indians, ready to shout, "Glory to God in the highest," and peace all over our Indian country. But Colonel Dow says he failed to see "one single spark of Indian treachery, cruelty, or barbarism extinguished" among the tribes he visited, who were taught by these priests.

De Smet, the prince and father of Jesuitism in the Indian country, as early as December 30, 1854, five years before the Southern rebellion commenced, communicated to his society in Brussels his approval and desire to have all these Indians join the confederate United States, as their last and only hope. This measure, he says, the Protestant missionaries strongly opposed. He says, also, that Harkins, the Choctaw chief, proposes the expulsion of the Protestant missionaries; we add, for their strong allegiance to their government, and their opposition to this Jesuitical confederate United States scheme (See his letter, "Western Missions," page 206). Such missionaries, we are forced to admit, have done no good to the Indians, and, we again repeat the question, *What good have the missionaries done?*

The writer will answer, that before he left the Whitman station in 1842, there were three hundred and twenty-two Indian families among the Cayuse and Nez Percé tribes that had commenced to cultivate, and were beginning to enjoy the fruits of their little farms. About one hundred of them were talking about locating, and were looking for places and material for building themselves more permanent houses. We have never doubted for a moment that the Cayuse, Nez Percé, and Spokan tribes would, in twenty-five years from the time the missions of the American Board were located among them (if let alone by the Hudson's Bay Company and Roman priests), have become a civilized, industrious, and happy Christian people, ready to have entered as honorable and intelligent citizens of our American Republic.

The unparalleled energy and success attending the efforts of the missionaries among these two powerful migratory tribes excited the jealousy, and aroused the extreme opposition of the Hudson's Bay Company, and caused them to encourage the largest possible number of Jesuits to come to the country and locate themselves immediately in the vicinity of those missions, and use every possible influence to dissuade the Indians from attending the missionary schools, cultivating their little farms, or attending in the least to any instruction, except such as was given by the priests when they came to the Hudson Bay Company's forts for trade, as they came at stated times to the fort, before the American missionaries came to the country. The Jesuit missionary teaching did not interfere with the roving and hunting life of the Indians, while the plan of settling and civilizing them proposed, and in a measure carried out, by the American missions, did directly interfere with the company's fur trappers and hunters. This at first was not so regarded, but a moment's reflection establishes the fact. Every Indian that became a settler, or farmer, had no occasion to hunt for furs to get his supplies.

The moral influence of those missions upon the Indians was good: the Nez Percé and the Protestant part of the Cayuses and Spokans have, through all the Indian wars, remained true and loyal to the American government, while, with perhaps a single exception, those who have been under the opposing religious teachings have been at war with our American people all over our territory. The Methodist missionary influence upon the natives was good, so far as they had an opportunity to exert any. At the Dalles it was certainly good and lasting, notwithstanding the Jesuits placed a station alongside of them. The Methodists were, from the commencement of their mission, interfered with in every way possible, in their efforts to improve the condition of the Indians, and induce them to cultivate their lands and leave the hunting of fur animals. As Rev. Mr. Beaver said of the Hudson's Bay Company, the life (and, we will add, the present condition and future happiness) of the Indian race had no influence upon that company when put in comparison with the few beavers they might hunt and sell to them. Still the Methodist influence was sufficient, up to the arrival of the French priests, and four years after, to keep up a flourishing native school, notwithstanding the French half-breed children were withdrawn from them, and placed under the tuition of the priests on French Prairie. The result of that Jesuitical teaching is embodied in the law disfranchising all half-breeds, except American, from the privileges of American citizens, for the course they took in the Indian wars against the American settlements and government. The larger portion of them, and especially those adhering to the company and the teachings of their priests, have gone into British Columbia, carrying with them an implacable hatred of our people and government. As to the good the American missionaries have done to the Indians on this coast, we can point to-day, more than thirty years from the commencement of their labors, to improvements, made and kept up by the Indians, that were commenced under the direction of those missionaries. We can point to Indian families who have strictly adhered to the Protestant religious forms of worship taught them by the American missionaries. We have the testimony of General Benjamin Alvord, of the United States army, on this point. After saying (September 10, 1854) that the Nez Percés never shared in the hostile feelings of the Cayuses, declined to join in the war of 1847 against the whites, and have since steadily and repeatedly refused to do so, he proceeds as follows: "In the spring of 1853 a white man, who had passed the previous winter in the country of the Nez Percés, came to the military post at the Dalles, and, on being questioned as to the manners and customs of the tribe, he said that he wintered with a band of several hundred in number, and that the whole party assembled every morning and evening for prayer, the exercises being conducted by one of themselves, and in their own language. He stated, that on Sunday they assembled for exhortation and worship. The writer of this communication made repeated inquiries, and these accounts have been confirmed by the statements of others who have resided among them. Thus, six years after the *forced* abandonment of the mission, its benign effects are witnessed among that interesting people."

In addition to the above, we would add our own observations made in 1861 among those Indians. That year they were more sorely tried than ever before. Gold had just been discovered in their country, and thousands of unarmed miners were passing and repassing all through it. The disaffected Cayuses were among them, urging them to join and rescue their country from the Bostons. We met some twenty-five of the chiefs and principal men, and conversed with them in the most friendly and familiar manner about their country and their situation; the old scenes of the mission; the killing of Dr. Whitman and those at his station; all the reasons assigned; the causes and the result of the Doctor's death, and its effect on the Cayuses. Having no disposition to deceive them, we inquired distinctly if there was gold in their country. They told us frankly there was, and that they had seen it, as the Americans had taken it away. They then asked what they had better do;—if it was not best for them to join the Cayuses, and drive the Americans from their country. They said the agent had told them to keep quiet, and in a few years the whites would get out the gold and leave the country, and their buildings and improvements would be their own. We replied: There are two things you can do. These miners *will* come to your country; they are bound to have the gold. Now, you can join the Cayuses, and go to killing them off if you choose, but you will soon find yourselves in the condition of the Cayuses,—roving about, without a home or country, and the more miners you kill, the sooner you will be cut off, and your country occupied by strangers. Our advice is, that you remain quiet and improve your farms; as fast as you can, educate your children; become like the Americans, and live in peace with all who come to settle, or dig gold in your country. This course will insure you protection from the American people.

We have reason to believe this advice was followed in a measure, at least, as no whites have been killed by them, and they remain peaceable and friendly. In this same meeting they wished to know if Mr. Spalding could come back as their teacher. We inquired particularly how many of them wished him to come back, and found that a majority of the tribe were in favor of his return. He went back as their teacher; but we have since learned that such influences were brought to bear upon him, as made him feel that he was compelled to leave the tribe. The mission right of the property, as we are fully assured, has since fallen into Jesuit hands, for the paltry sum of $500 in greenbacks. Who is responsible for the giving up of that mission, we are unable to say. No money consideration should ever have induced the American Board of Missions to relinquish their legitimate claim.

We have not recently been permitted to visit the Indians at Rev. Messrs. Walker and Eells' station; but we have the testimony of others in regard to the good effect of the teachings of their missionaries upon them. Major P. Lugenbeel, who was in command of New Fort Colville for years, and also acted as Indian agent, said to Mr. Eells in 1861, "Those Indians of yours are the best I ever saw. I wish you would go back and resume missionary labor among them."

Mr. Eells says, in the *Missionary Herald*, December, 1866 :—

"Some fifteen or twenty of these Indians spent a portion of last winter in Wallawalla. On the Sabbath a larger proportion of them than of the citizens of the place could be collected in a house of worship. I met them as my class in connection with the Sabbath school in the Congregational Church. As we were allowed our share of the time allotted to singing, we sang, in their tongue, the words which I arranged for them more than twenty-five years ago. So far as I have learned, their conduct in transactions with whites has been less objectionable than that of the superior race."

We have frequently met individual Indians from about all those early stations, and found a most cordial greeting from them, and always a regret that they have lost their Boston teachers.

We have always regretted the course pursued by the American Board, in allowing those missions to be given up, as unwise and injudicious. If the men who first commenced them had not the courage to return and continue their labors, others should have been sent to take their places.

The Whitman Institute has come up from the ashes of that noble and devoted martyred missionary, which to the writer looks like "whitewashing the sepulchers of the prophets" whose death we have seemed to approve, by our silence (not to say cowardice) in not ferreting out and exposing the authors of that crime.

Mr. Spalding has not been sustained in his recent efforts among the Nez Percés, but feels that he has been driven away from among his Indian brethren and disciples by Jesuit influence.

The cowardly, timid, hesitating, the half-God and half-mammon Christian may say, What will you have us do? We answer, Maintain the natural rights of men and Christians, and leave consequences to a higher power.

We have thus briefly summed up the labors of the Protestant and Roman missions, and shown the influence of each upon the Indians on the western portion of our American continent. In further proof that this Roman Jesuit influence tends only to the destruction of the Indian race, I might refer to California, Mexico, and other countries where they have had the exclusive religious teaching of the people ; the result is the same.

We know from long experience that it has always been the policy of the Hudson's Bay Company to place an opposing post or trader by the side of an opponent in the fur trade. The same policy was adopted, and carried out by the Jesuits in regard to the Protestant missions in American territory. We will be told that the Hudson's Bay Company people were principally of the English Episcopal Church. This is true, and they, to satisfy the Christian sentiment of the English people, brought an Episcopal minister to Vancouver, and allowed a few in the vicinity of Moose Factory, where they wished to renew their fur license, but dismissed them as soon as possible after their object was accomplished, for reasons already stated, and introduced these Jesuit missionaries for no other purpose than to facilitate their trade among the Indians, and destroy the American influence in the country. But, thank God and the energy of a free people, the country, with all its untold wealth and prospective grandeur, is ours, and to-day, as we hear the lightning tap of intelligence, from the Old World to Oregon, we have not one solitary regret that thirty of the best and most active years of our life have been spent, in contending publicly and privately, by day and by night, in season and out of season, against that influence. We know what it is to feel its power, as an assistant missionary, as a settler, as a representative and as an officer of the provisional, Territorial, and State governments. We have no complaint of personal unkindness to us, or ours; but we feel that the withering condemnation of every true American, and Englishman too, should rest upon the Hudson's Bay Company while that name is claimed by any association of men, for the unrighteous course they have been, and still are, pursuing.

It is obvious that to the American missionaries our nation owes an honorable record, and the names of Dr. Whitman, Rev. J. Lee, Mr. C. Shepard, Mr. C. Rogers, Rev. Harvey Clark, Mr. A. Beers, and Dr. Wilson, and Mrs. Whitman, Mrs. Spalding, Mrs. Lee, Mrs. Leslie, Mrs. Beers, and Mrs. Smith, among the dead, and many others still living, should find a prominent place in the catalogue of noble men and women who not only volunteered to civilize and Christianize the Indians, but did actually save this western golden coast, to honor and enrich the great Republic in the time of her greatest peril.

It would be ungenerous to confine the answer to our question alone to the good that the early American missionaries did to the Indians of our western coast. The whole country, now within the jurisdiction of the United States, is more indebted to them than most men are willing to admit.

The country, as all are aware, was first occupied by Astor's Company in 1811, followed by the Northwest Company in 1813, and by the Hudson's Bay Company in 1821. For twenty-three years the British

Hudson's Bay Company was scarcely disturbed by an American. No effort was made by it to comply with the conditions of its charter, in regard to the civil and religious instruction of the Indians, supposing that charter to have been valid.

In 1832, the Indians themselves asked for the American missionary. They had previously asked the Hudson's Bay Company for religious teachers, but they only allowed a few Indian boys to go to Red River, there to receive a very limited English education, and return to be employed by the company as interpreters or traders. This did not satisfy the Indian longing for light and knowledge. The tribes in middle Oregon resorted to the American rendezvous, and, although there was little or no moral influence there, they discovered a more liberal and generous spirit among the Americans than among the English or French. This led to further inquiry as to the cause, and by some means they concluded that it must arise from their religious notions or worship. They asked to see the Americans' sacred book, about which they had heard, as it was said that book told about the Great Spirit above. For a time they received packs of cards, but were not satisfied,—there must be something more. They sent some of their number to St. Louis, and as has been before stated, Mr. Catlin learned their object, and gave the information that started the missions.

While the American missionaries were going to the country, the American fur traders were being driven from it. Rev. Jason Lee and associate were allowed to locate in the Wallamet Valley. He labored, and measurably filled, gratuitously, the chartered stipulations of the company.

As there were no women in this first missionary party, no fears were excited as to the supremacy of the soil, or the future occupation of the country by the company's retired servants.

In 1836, Dr. Whitman and Mr. Spalding and their wives arrived, with cattle and other material for a distinct and independent mission. They at once commenced their labors, and sent for assistance by the overland route. Rev. Mr. Lee received a re-enforcement by sea, with which came a wife for himself and Mr. Shepard. Dr. Whitman and Mr. Spalding's associates arrived overland; more cattle were brought across the mountains, and, through the exertions and means of Mr. Lee and his associates, cattle were brought through from California.

Schools and farms were opened; mills, houses, and churches built; and more and better improvements made by the missionaries, than were then owned by the company, with the single exception of a farm at Vancouver.

The American missionaries did not stop with the mills and farms, nor with cattle and swine. Sheep and a printing-press were brought from the Sandwich Islands, and soon the Indian beholds the clean white paper made into a book, and his own thoughts and words placed before him, and he is taught to read for himself. In the Wallamet Valley an extensive building for an Indian boarding-school was erected, and one for whites and half-breed children, almost entirely by the American missionaries. A second school was started by the Rev. Harvey Clark and his friends at Forest Grove, which is now Pacific University. There were also private schools and churches all through the settlements, mostly under the Methodist influence; while the Hudson's Bay Company, with their priests, established three schools,—one for boys at Vancouver, one for girls at Oregon City, and one at French Prairie. These last institutions were particularly an opposition to the American schools.

The improvements spoken of above were accomplished within twelve years from the first arrival of the American missionaries. This laid the foundation for education and civilization, upon which the country has been steadily advancing. While the Legislative Assemblies refused to take action on the subject of education, the missionary influence was active, and strongly in favor of sectarian schools.

In the Legislature of 1845, an ineffectual effort was made to establish a common-school system for the country. In 1846, Mr. T. Vault, from the committee on education, made a report recommending a memorial to Congress on the subject of education. This is all that was done that year. In 1847–8, the Cayuse war, the liquor question, and the gold mines excitement, seem to have absorbed the whole attention of the Legislature; hence the subject of education was left to the direction and influence of the religious sects and individual effort, until the Territorial organization in 1849, in which we find a very imperfect school law; and the one at the present day, 1870, is no honor to our State. This, however, is wholly due to the influence of the various sects, each seeking to build up its own peculiar sectarian schools, thus dividing the whole educational interests of the country to promote sectarian education.

It is to be hoped that our next Legislature will adopt a system that will at once lay aside all sects, and place the education of our youth upon a national, instead of a sectarian basis, honorable alike to the State and nation. With all due credit and honor to all previous missionary and sectarian efforts, we say, give us a national standard of education that shall qualify our youth to become the honored sovereigns of a free, intelligent, industrious, virtuous, and forever united nation.

We have occupied much more space than we would, in giving quotations, knowing, as we do, the ignorance there is in relation to our early history, and the efforts of the British Hudson's Bay Company and Roman Church to secure the exclusive control of Oregon. We will here give an article which we find in the *Missionary Herald.* The writer says:—

"While it is apparent from the letters of Dr. Whitman at the missionary house, that, in visiting the Eastern States in 1842–3, he had certain missionary objects in view, it is no less clear that he would not have come at that time, and probably he would not have come at all [which we know to be the case], had it not been for his desire to save the disputed territory to the United States. It was not simply an American question, however,—it was at the same time a Protestant question. He was fully alive to the efforts which the Roman Catholics were making to gain the mastery on the Pacific coast, and *he was firmly persuaded that they were working in the interest of the Hudson's Bay Company,* with a view to this very end. The danger from this quarter had made a profound impression upon his mind. Under date of April 1, 1847, he said: 'In the autumn of 1842–3, I pointed out to our mission the arrangements of the Papists to settle in our vicinity, and that it only required that those arrangements should be completed to close our operations.'"

To the statement of Dr. Whitman as here quoted from his letter to the Board, we can bear positive testimony. He did point out to his associates all the dangers to which they were exposed.

"Dr. Whitman evidently regarded his visit to Washington, and his success in conducting the immigrants of 1843 [eight hundred and seventy-five souls] across the Rocky and Blue mountains, as settling the destiny of Oregon. In the letter just referred to, he said, 'It may be easily seen what would have become of American interests in this country, had the immigration of 1843 been as disastrous as were the immigrations of 1845 and 1846.' [In both those years the route which he had selected was abandoned for another.] In confirmation of this opinion, we find a writer in the *Colonial Magazine* using this language:—

"'By a strange and unpardonable oversight of the local officers, missionaries from the United States *were allowed* to take religious charge of the population; and these artful men lost no time in introducing such a number of their countrymen as reduced the influence of the British settlers to complete insignificance.'"

The above quotation from the *Colonial Magazine* is but a repetition of evidence already given from other English testimony, relative to their determination to hold the country. We also have the expectation of Chief-Factor A. McDonald, as expressed in 1842 to Rev. C. Eells: "He also gave it as his opinion that if England should obtain the desired portion of Oregon, it would be made over to the Hudson's Bay Company." He thought that fifty years from that time, the Hudson's Bay Company's descendants would be the only occupants of the country. Dr. Whitman, in expressing an opinion upon the same subject, thought that fifty years from that time they would not be found.

In the closing remarks of the article from which we have quoted the above, there is a strange mixture of truth and ignorance. The writer says: "It is not too much to say, perhaps, that Dr. and Mrs. Whitman lost their lives in consequence of the success of the endeavors already described. The immigrants of 1847 carried diseases into the Indian country, which proved very fatal to the aborigines. Some became suspicious of him; some were exasperated; and a few affirmed that he was poisoning them with his medicines, to get them out of the way. It is believed by many, moreover, that the Roman Catholics were in a measure responsible as directly or indirectly, for the catastrophe of Wailatpu. But it is inexpedient to discuss this question at the present time."

It is evident from this last quotation, that Sir James Douglas's letter for the information of the Board of Missions produced its desired effect; and it is only from the recent statements respecting that transaction, that the Board have allowed the subject to come before them; they have asked and received from the most cautious missionary they have ever sent to the country, a statement of the facts in the case. He has complied with their request, and the result is a repetition of the *slander* of the murdered dead. We are unwilling to believe that the Rev. Mr. Treat, D. D., in this closing paragraph, intended to give the impression that he believed the statement; yet we can not understand his object in reporting the statement made to blast the character of a good man, and to shield his murderers from the punishment due to their crime; leaving the impression upon the mind, that it was the *Indian superstitions* alone that were the cause of the massacre. Those who have read the foregoing pages will not be deceived as to those causes. Mr. Treat should have given us the benefit of his authority for that statement, as we are assured by the Indians themselves that there is not one of them that ever believed those reports till they were affirmed by the priests, and even then they doubted. We have been several times among the Indians of that tribe, and were present at the first consultation held with them by Indian Agent R. R. Thompson in 1853, and took particular pains to inquire as to their belief in that matter. I could not find one, even among the Roman Catholic Indians, that would say he believed that Dr. Whitman did as he is represented by the priests and the company to have done. The Indians invariably told me that the priests, Finlay, Stanfield, Joe Lewis, or Mr. McBean said so, but they believed Dr. Whitman was their friend, and their hearts had wept and cried because they had consented to his being killed.

It was to develop the facts and influences operating in our early history that we commenced to write. It does not matter to us whence a statement comes or by whom it is made, if it does not correspond with the facts in the case, we intend to give what we conceive and firmly believe to be the truth; letting such as are ignorant of the facts, or have been deceived by commercial, religious, or sectarian statements, judge as to the correctness or truth of our conclusions.

A great crime has been committed in our land;—a poor, ignorant, and harmless and comparatively innocent people, have been charged with committing it through "*superstitious prejudices*," which, if the very men who make the charge are to be believed, fixes the crimes upon their own heads, for they tell us that they were unharmed amid the scenes of blood and murder, while gathering up the remains of the first missionary victims and consigning them to a common grave. Their messengers pass and repass all through the country, and mingle freely, and "*rejoice*" that the ignorant murderers will come to them for advice, which is cheerfully given, and a pledge made to assist them to avoid its consequences; while the commercial party in this great crime is handing over to the murderers munitions for defense, and to continue the slaughter of American settlers, the Jesuitical party is confirming the doubtful mind of the Indians in the justness of the crime they have committed. Such were the parties seeking to control our destiny from 1834 to 1849, and such as we have quoted are the sentiments of men high in giving direction to truth and righteousness in a great nation in 1866–7.

We feel, and admit, that our task has been most difficult and arduous,—to seek out and bring to light the truth in relation to events so momentous, and consequences so important to the interests of this western part of our continent. It would be far more gratifying to us to dwell upon the pleasing and happy influences and incidents that float upon the surface of society; but these are commonplace and the natural growth of circumstances, such as the most careless could scarcely fail to observe.

Oregon was ours by right of discovery, exploration, and cession; as well as settlement by Astor in 1811–12. A foreign monopoly, having knowledge of the American Fur Company's weakness and danger, paid a nominal price for its goods and possessions, and has held and robbed the country, as by its own statements, of twenty million pounds sterling, in profits. As we have before stated, that company dared not use the same instruments at first, to drive out or destroy the missionaries, that it had used against fur traders and hunters. The Indians regarded the American missionaries as teachers sent from God, and received them, and protected them, till forced by the teachings and influence of their masters to attempt to cut off the American settlement.

The English people, as a whole, charge the American missionaries, *and justly*, with being the means of their losing Oregon. They also charge the Hudson's Bay Company, *wrongfully*, as favoring the American settlement of the country. Dr. John McLaughlin, all honor to his name and memory, told his superiors in London the truth, when he said to them, "Gentlemen, as a man of common humanity, I could not do otherwise than to give those naked and starving people to wear and to eat of our stores. They were not our enemies. I did what I thought was right, and must leave consequences to God and the government, and if you insist upon my compliance with your rules in this particular, *I will serve you no longer*."

Contrast this noble sentiment of Dr. McLaughlin, though a Canadian-born subject and supporter of the Roman Catholic faith in the country, with that of his successor, Sir James Douglas, who refused supplies to punish the murderers and protect the American settlements, he having been an officer under the provisional government, and taken an oath to protect and defend it.

Did it conflict with his duties as a British subject? The reason assigned by him for his refusal was, "*the stringent rules laid down for his government by the home company*," which the noble old Canadian said he would resign his position sooner than obey.

It is not difficult to see that Oregon, during the existence of the provisional government, was a country possessing peculiarly interesting relations to the two nations who were claiming its allegiance and sovereignty. Had the Hudson's Bay Company been true to its own country, and encouraged the settlement of loyal British subjects in it, there is no question but, with the facilities and capital at its command, it could have secured the country before an American settlement could have acquired any strength in it. The same was the case with California. One or two ships a year from 1835 to 1840, or even 1846, leaving out the Roman and Jesuit missionaries, could have brought substantial English families with their English chaplains, and formed their colonies and absorbed the American missionary settlements in it, and no one would have questioned their right, or attempted to defeat them; but the £7,000 or more of clear profits in the fur trade, and native associations, were too strong. The country becomes valuable in its estimation, as others have improved and developed its wealth. The natives with the furs of the country were the only source of wealth to it, and especially to the home company in London. If the least possible credit is due to it from any source, it is for its stupidity and ignorance as to the real value of the country, of which no one can give a true history without developing the avaricious character and degrading influences and proceedings of that company; for it had, as we remarked at the commencement of our history, and as every one knows, the absolute control of it up to the organization of the provisional government in 1843. Those influences were active and in full operation up to 1842, when it was discovered, by Dr. Whitman and a few others, that the whole country was about to pass into the hands of the English, as was asserted by the over-zealous priest at Wallawalla: "*The country is ours! America is too late! They may now whistle.*" An American heard, and to hear with him was to act. "*If the Board dismisses me, I will do what I can to save Oregon to my country,*" was his remark to us, as he gave his hand and mounted his horse, to see what could be done at Washington. The result of that trip was the delay of the boundary question and an immigration and settlement, that no Hudson's Bay and Jesuit exterminating combinations have been able to overcome or drive from the country.

CHAPTER LXV.

Description of the face of the country.—Agricultural and mining productions.—Timber.—The Wallamet.—Columbia.—Dalles.—Upper Columbia.—Mountains.—Rivers.—Mineral wealth.—Climate.—The Northern Pacific Railroad.—Conclusion.

Thus far I have confined myself to the history of the Hudson's Bay Company, the early settlement of the country, its public men, the provisional government, adverse influence, and the American and Jesuit missions. We will now proceed to describe its geographical and physical position and value.

Previous to the treaty of 1846, all that portion of country lying south of the Russian possessions, west of the Rocky Mountains, and north of California, was called Oregon. By that treaty the 49th parallel was constituted the boundary line between the United States and the British possessions.

In the act of Congress passed August 14, 1848, the boundaries were thus defined: "All that part of the territory of the United States which lies west of the summit of the Rocky Mountains, north of the 42d degree of north latitude, known as the Territory of Oregon, shall be organized into, and constitute a temporary government, by the name of The Territory of Oregon." Unfortunately, though our national Congress contained many noble, intelligent, and talented men, none of them knew any thing about the country they were defining as Oregon Territory.

Thomas H. Benton, about this time, made his famous Oregon speech. In it he declared that all north of the 49th parallel of latitude was only fit for the poorest and most meager animal existence; that it was the "derelict of all nations," not fit for the subsistence of civilized man.

This impression of Mr. Benton was received from high British—and no doubt he thought the most correct and reliable—authority. In fact, in the mind of this, and many other of our statesmen, the entire territory was of but little value. It is scarcely necessary to say whence this impression arose, and for what purpose it was so persistently kept before the minds of our most eminent statesmen. The immense fur trade of the country, carried on at a nominal expense, was too profitable to allow the truth to be told, or an experiment to be made, to show the value of the soil, or the amount or variety of its productions. The soil, like the furs and the natives, must be misrepresented, neglected, and slandered, that it may yield its silent income to avarice and idleness.

The American missionary arrives in the country, and is assured by the Hudson's Bay Company that but a very small portion of the country is susceptible of cultivation; that no extensive settlements can ever be formed in it. These statements are made by men who have spent their lives in the country, and say they have tested the qualities of the soil faithfully, and found it to be unproductive. The missionaries partially believe these statements, and communicate to their friends in the east their doubts as to the extent and richness of the arable land in the country. In the mean time they must provide for their own subsistence. The Missionary Boards that sent them out are not able to pay the prices demanded for a continual supply of such food as can be raised in the country. This they knew and were prepared for it, and at once commenced to experiment upon the soil for themselves. Their first effort astonishes and delights them. Instead of a hard, barren, unproductive soil, as they had been told, it proves to be a light rich clay loam all through the Wallamet Valley, and in the interior, a dark, mellow, inexhaustible alkali soil, of the richest kind, and, when properly cultivated, very productive.

The missionary experiments are continued and extended. They soon begin to send glowing accounts to their friends of the richness of the valleys of Oregon—eight hundred bushels of potatoes, or from thirty to sixty bushels of wheat, to the acre. The American trappers and hunters gather into the Wallamet Valley, around the Methodist Mission. The Canadian-French, British subjects, who have become worn out and unprofitable to the company, are permitted to locate in the same valley, but, with the clumsy and imperfect farming implements furnished them, and their ignorance of farming, they were not able to accomplish much, and are still referred to, as proof of the worthlessness of the country.

The American settler comes in, and proves the truth of the missionaries' large farming stories, and finds that he can do, with two yoke of oxen, what it required six to do in the Mississippi Valley—his labor producing double pay. He is more than satisfied—he is delighted—with the soil, the climate, and country, and reports his success to his friends.

By this time a few peaches and apples have been produced outside the inclosures and garden of Fort Vancouver, which convinces the American settler that fruit can be produced in Oregon; and soon we find every known variety to be profitably cultivated.

Timber.—The fir, spruce, and hemlock are superabundant, all along the coast range, from California to Puget Sound. The fir, pine, oak, ash, and maple are abundant in the valleys of the Wallamet and Cowlitz, and on the western slope of the Cascade range of mountains; there is also an abundance of pine, fir, oak, and maple on the eastern slope.

The Wallamet Valley is from forty to sixty miles wide, and one hundred and eighty long. It has less timber land than fine level prairie; through which winds with its tributaries the beautiful Wallamet, skirted all along its banks and level bottoms with cotton-wood, ash, alder, oak, fir, yellow pine, yew, and soft maple, with a small amount of cedar. This river has its source in the Umpqua Mountains; and its tributaries in the Coast and Cascade ranges,—the main river running north, or west of north, till it joins the majestic Columbia. Its meandering streams, and valleys composed mainly of prairie interspersed with groves of oak, pine, fir, and cotton-wood, make up a scenery which for beauty and loveliness can not be surpassed. The Cascade range on the east is dotted, at intervals of from a hundred to a hundred and fifty miles apart, with towering, snow-capped mountains from 15,000 to 18,600 feet high, and is cut at right angles, midway between the California Mountains on the south, and Mount Baker on the north, by the great river of Oregon, the noble Columbia, which forces its resistless current over its rocky bed, till it finds its way to the ocean.

Ascending this river from the ocean, for sixty miles, to the mouth of the Cowlitz, we find it lined on either bank with lofty and dense forests of spruce, hemlock, cedar, and fir, with scarcely a sign of prairie; from this up, the timber is interspersed with prairie, till we enter the Cascade Mountains, one hundred and twenty-five miles from the ocean, and ten below the Cascade portage, which is five miles long,—now made by railroad; thence to the Dalles is thirty-eight miles, making fifty miles of the roughest and grandest river and mountain scenery on our continent.

Old ocean in its mightiest heavings is but a placid lake, when compared with this fifty-five miles of mountain roughness, grandeur, and sublimity, from various points of which may be seen Mounts Baker, Rainier, St. Helens, Adams, Hood, and Jefferson, with others of less note, all raising their lofty heads above the regions of perpetual snow.

Prominent among them stands Mount Hood, about thirty miles south of the Columbia, towering to the height of 18,600 feet, with his everlasting white cap on, and overlooking the lovely valleys of the Wallamet to the south and west; the Columbia and Cowlitz to the west and north; and the great upper basin of the Columbia to the northeast, east, and southeast. From the Dalles we ascend this mighty river fourteen miles by rail, where the water has worn its crooked course amid solid basaltic rocks to unknown depths, not exceeding a hundred and fifty feet in width, causing the river, in discharging its annual floods, to rise at this point over eighty feet in perpendicular height.

At the end of the railroad the steamboat receives the traveler, when, as he ascends the river, the land on either side diminishes in height, till he reaches Castle Rock, seventy-one miles above the Dalles. This is a lone pile of basaltic rocks having the appearance of an old castle in the midst of a great plain to the east, south, and west of it.

A large portion of this plain, lying along the river, is of course gravel and sand, dry, and comparatively barren; yet producing the artemisia, sage, and a luxurious growth of wild mustard in the early spring; with but little grass, and abundance of the low sunflower.

The lands back from the river are high rolling prairie, covered with rich bunch grass, having a light soil composed of pulverized basaltic sandstone.

This soil, to the eye of the careless observer, though it is thickly set with the bunch grass, generally appears barren and worthless; yet, with irrigation, or with winter grains, or grasses adapted to the soil, it can not be exhausted.

Twenty-five miles above Castle Rock stands the thriving little town of Umatilla, at the mouth of the river of the same name, and nine miles above is Windmill Rock. In ascending the river fifteen miles from this place, the land on either side rises to some fifteen hundred feet above the level of the river which occupies the entire bottom from rocks to rocks on either side; when the land suddenly drops from this high plain which extends from the Blue Mountains on the east to the Cascade range on the west, forming, as it were, a great inland dam across the Columbia River, fifteen hundred feet high at the place where the river has broken through the dam. As you pass out of this gap, in looking to the north and east, the eye rests upon another vast, high, rolling plain, in the southeastern part of which lies the beautiful valley of the Wallawalla. At the upper or eastern end was situated the Whitman or Cayuse Mission. Some six miles above is the flourishing town of Wallawalla. The most of this vast, high, rolling plain, and especially the valleys, have more or less of alkali soil; the high plains are similar to those we have just passed,—destitute of all kinds of timber, except at the foot of the mountains, and small patches of willow and cotton-wood, in some little nook or corner, near some spring or stream.

Imagine Wallawalla a little east of the center of a great plain ~~ten~~ miles wide, east and west, one hundred and eighty long, north and south, situated just inside of this great mountain dam we have described; with the majestic Cascade range of mountains on the west, the Blue Mountains on the east, and this vast open plain covered with bunch grass, and no tree in sight, except upon the mountains; you can then form some idea of the middle Columbia plains. Ascending to the north one hundred miles, over the same high rolling plains, you begin to find the yellow pine and larch; not in dense forests, but scattering trees, the ground beneath being covered with a species of coarse, wild grass. These woods form a delightful change to the traveler after riding for days beneath the scorching rays of a summer sun. As you near the forty-ninth parallel, the timber increases in size, quantity, and quality. The soil is light, and, when the frosts of winter give place to the sleet and rain of early spring, forms a soft, deep mud, till the ground becomes settled, which is generally about the first of May; then all this vast country is in full bloom, with its myriads of beautiful wild flowers.

The northern portion of Oregon, now Washington Territory, is beautifully interspersed with timber and prairie, in good proportions, and has a rich clay soil.

The whole country abounds in trap-rock and granite, singularly mingled with basalt. Near the mouth of Spokan River is found a splendid variety of marble; some sections of it are of a pure white, while others are beautifully clouded with blue, brown, and green. The face of the country is not so uneven as that further south.

Some sixty miles south of the forty-ninth parallel, we come to the mouth of the Okanagon River, which is the outlet of a chain of lakes in British Columbia, from which it takes its name; it has an extensive and rich valley for settlement.

At Colville, in the vicinity of the Kettle Falls, on the Columbia, are a United States military post, the Hudson's Bay Company's post, and a considerable settlement. Some fifteen miles from the mouth of the Spokan, and sixty from Kettle Falls, was located the Cimakain—or Rev. Messrs. Walker and Eells'—Mission. About sixty miles in a southeasterly direction is the Cœur d' Alêne Italian Jesuit Mission.

Turning to the north, east, and southeast, we enter the gold and silver mountains of the Pacific Slope; this range is cut through by the Snake River, or south branch of the Columbia. Millions of dollars' worth of treasure is taken out of the mines within these desolate and barren-looking regions, and untold millions still await the miner's toil. The reader will remember that we are now traveling east. This range is, on the north of Snake River, called Salmon River Mountains, and on the south, the Blue Mountains; thence, on to the southern portions of Oregon, it joins the Sierra Nevada and Cascade ranges, bends to the west, and, near the forty-second parallel, runs into those vast promontories that jut into the Pacific Ocean.

Passing through this range of Salmon River and Blue Mountains, which are not as high as the Cascade range, we descend into the great basin of the Rocky Mountains, which is intersected by high, broken ranges running east and west for about three hundred miles, to what is usually called the top of the Rocky Mountains, and the eastern boundary of this vast basin. The principal rivers which flow into and through this immense plain, are the Boise, Snake, Portneuf, Owyhee, and their tributaries. On the north is Clarke's or Flathead River, which runs northwest into the Columbia, near the northern boundary of the United States.

In all the northern portion of this great inland mountain plain there is an extensive placer and quartz mining country, besides numerous rich farming valleys, with an abundance of timber for all practical uses; most of the rough, rocky ranges of mountains being covered about half-way up their sides with timber, till you reach the open prairies along the main valley.

To the south, and along Snake River, are the high barren sage plains, extending from the Rocky Mountains on the east to the Blue Mountains on the west.

There are large tracts of arable land in the region just described, though to the weary traveler coming from the green plains of Kansas or the valley of the Wallamet, every thing looks forbidding and desolate, especially during the dry season. But remove the sage from any of these dry, barren places, and the rich bunch-grass takes its place. As well might the farmer expect his wheat to grow in a hemlock wood or cedar swamp, as for any thing but sage to grow on these plains till that is destroyed. Hence, from the experiments we have made on the soils of which we have been speaking, we are confident that the greater portion of the country now and for years past pronounced barren and useless, will be found, with intelligent and proper cultivation, to rank among as good lands as any we have, and probably more desirable. As to timber, that must be cultivated till it becomes accustomed to the soil. Cotton-wood is found in small quantities all over this plain, in the vicinity of streams and springs. The northeastern part of this basin is Montana; the southwestern is Idaho. The mineral wealth of this country, especially that of north Idaho and Montana, is inexhaustible. Gold, silver, copper, iron, lead, cinnabar, and tin, are found in abundance in these Territories, and in eastern and middle Oregon.

" *Owyhee Bullion.*—John A. Post, internal revenue collector, furnishes the following *resumé* of the bullion product from January 1 to November 1, 1866, as assayed by different parties. The figures are greenback valuation:—

January	$36,632 81
February	62,874 00
March	15,640 85
April	11,959 25
May	34,570 34
June	46,224 44
July	46,456 26
August	177,704 15
September	293,921 53
October	371,173 13
Total	$1,073,256 78

"During the early part of the year, Mr. Post says, there was a great amount of treasure sent out in various shapes, of which he could get no account. To the foregoing must still be added the many tons of ruby silver, polybasite, etc., shipped just as it came from the Poorman mine, —enough, at a rough estimate, to increase the total to fifteen hundred thousand, at least. It is safe to say that the product of the present year will be two millions, and that of next year go beyond five millions." *

"*Treasure.*—There has been shipped from this city during the past year, the sum of $8,070,600 in treasure. The amount passing through private hands may be safely estimated at $3,000,000."†

We take the following from an official report to the Secretary of the Treasury, a copy of which has been sent to Congress:—

"From the best information available, the following is a near approximation to our total gold and silver product for the year ending January 7, 1867:—

California	$25,000,000
Nevada	20,000,000
Montana	12,000,000
Idaho	6,500,000
Washington	1,000,000
Oregon	2,000,000
Colorado	2,500,000
New Mexico	500,000
Arizona	500,000
Add for bullion derived from unknown sources within the States and Territories, unaccounted for by assessors and express companies, etc.	5,000,000
Total product of the United States	$75,000,000

"The bullion product of Washington is estimated by the surveyor-general at $1,500,000. That of Oregon is estimated at $2,500,000. In-

* From the *Oregonian*. † From the *Portland Herald.*

telligent residents of Idaho and Montana represent that the figures given in the above estimate, so far as these Territories are concerned, are entirely too low, and might be doubled without exceeding the truth. The product of Idaho alone, for this year, is said to be $15,000,000 to $18,000,000. That of Montana is estimated by the surveyor-general at $20,000,000. Similar exceptions are taken to the estimates of Colorado, New Mexico, and Arizona."

The climate varies in the three sections of country we have described, exactly in the ratio of soil and timber. On the coast, contiguous to the ocean, we have more rain than we require. Like our superabundance of the tallest and best of fir-timber, there is so much of it that we would be glad if we could divide with the second and third places we have described. We have enough rain and timber to supply all the country; and perhaps, when we can cut down our tall trees, that filter the rain out of the clouds, they may get more and we less. Be that as it may, our winters are mild and rainy, our summers cool and pleasant, with sufficient rain and ocean mist to supply the vegetable creation with abundant moisture.

In middle Oregon the winters are mild and frosty, with a small amount of snow—seldom severe; farmers should feed stock a month or six weeks; summers warm, and sometimes sultry in July and August; rains in the spring and late in the fall, scarcely enough for the farmers' use.

In the eastern plain or great mountain basin, the winters are cold and dry, snow and frost severe. Snow seldom falls to exceed two feet in depth,—average winters, eighteen inches,—but it falls deep upon the mountains and remains till it is melted by the warm winds and sun of early summer, causing the summer floods. The principal rise in the rivers is during the months of June and July. Less rain, spring and fall, than in middle Oregon; summers dry and hot. In the northern part, the country is better supplied with rain. This may arise from the ranges of the mountain currents of air and the winds from the South Pacific Ocean along the inland plains, and the cool atmosphere around our snow-clad mountains. We will leave further speculation on this point to those who have had more experience in such matters than ourselves.

Taking the country as a whole, with our inexhaustible gold, silver, and other minerals; our extensive farming valleys; our vast forests of timber upon the borders of an ocean comparatively destitute of this essential element of civilization; there is no plausible reason why this western portion of the United States may not in a few years become the abode of industrious and thriving millions.

The Northern Pacific Railroad.

The following article on the Northern Pacific Railroad is from the pen of Mr. Philip Ritz:—

"Having spent most of the last year in traveling through Washington, Idaho, and Montana Territories, and having crossed the continent in midwinter, partly on both of the great railroad routes, and at the earnest request of Ex-Governor Smith, of Massachusetts, who is president of the Northern Pacific Railroad Company, and of some members of Congress, I compiled, while in Washington, the following statistics, on the practicability of the Northern route:—

"On the first section of the country from Puget Sound, there are two routes, both practicable; one *via* the Columbia River, to the mouth of Snake River; the other *via* Snoqualmie Pass and Yakima River, to the same point. On either route there will not be much heavy grading. There is on this section an abundance of the finest timber, excepting on that part of the Columbia from the Dalles to Snake River, and a short distance of the route from Yakima to the mouth of Snake River.

"The second section, lying between the Columbia River and the Bitter Root Mountains, a distance of about two hundred and twenty miles, is over a rolling prairie country, with splendid grazing, and fine timber on the Spokan River, a distance of about one hundred miles.

"On the third section, which includes the mountainous part, a distance of two hundred and fifty miles, and lying between the 116th and 112th degrees of longitude, the grading will, in places, be heavy, and will require three or four short tunnels. This will include the entire Rocky Mountain district, the work on which will be heavy, but not more difficult than on the Baltimore and Ohio road, between the Ohio River and Harper's Ferry. On this entire section there is an abundance of the finest timber. On this section there is considerable good wheat land, as has been proven by the fine crops raised in Hell Gate Valley last season.

"This extends from the eastern slope of the Rocky Mountains to Lake Superior, a distance of about one thousand and ten miles. The route here passes over a rolling prairie, susceptible of settlement the entire distance.

"It will be seen that the entire distance on this route, between the head of Lake Superior and Puget Sound, is about 1,810 miles, and that there is scarcely a mile of the entire country but will eventually be settled. It is much shorter than any other route across the continent, connecting navigable waters. The mountains are much lower and the country much more fertile. It is really the only easy pass across the

American continent, for it is the only part of the continent where two large rivers rise immediately together and flow in opposite directions—the Columbia cutting its way entirely through the mountains on a water level to the Pacific; and the Missouri connecting with the great plains bordering on the lakes. The Rocky Mountains at this point are really so low, that the miners, last summer, actually took large streams in ditches from the waters of the Missouri, over the divide to the Pacific side for mining purposes. In consequence of the low passes through to the Pacific, the climate is warmer than it is in the mountains in the latitude of Salt Lake City, 400 miles due south. I crossed the summit of the Rocky Mountains near Deer Lodge Valley, in Montana, on the 17th of December. There was no snow; the roads dry and dusty, and the weather mild and pleasant, and none of the streams frozen over. When I reached Salt Lake City, the snow on the Wasatch and Rocky Mountain ranges was twenty-six inches deep, and the night we crossed the Wasatch range, the thermometer stood at ten degrees below zero, and Green River and all those streams in the mountains had been frozen over six weeks, so that the stage rolled over on the ice. Such was the difference in the climate of the two routes. The differences in the real wealth and resources of the two routes is perhaps even greater than that of climate. The central route, after it leaves the mining country of Nevada, around Virginia City, passes up the Humboldt country toward Salt Lake, for a distance of 500 or 600 miles, over the most desolate and barren country on the American continent. The country has neither mines, timber, nor any other redeemable quality about it. Salt Lake Valley is a small and rather fertile valley; the only fertile spot for hundreds of miles. From Salt Lake City to Denver, a distance of six hundred miles, the route lies over an alkali and sage plain. On the other hand, there is not one mile on the northern route that does not either furnish timber, grazing, agricultural lands, or minerals, and, in some instances, all together. Montana is just in its infancy; its mines scarcely prospected; and yet, last season, according to the report of the Treasury Department, Montana stood second on the list in the amount of gold produced; California producing $25,000,000; Montana, $18,000,000; Idaho and Colorado, $17,000,000 each; and Nevada, $16,000,000.

"The mountains of Montana are a perfect net-work of quartz ledges, immensely rich in gold and silver. Five years from this time, I believe there will be as much as $40,000,000 of gold and silver taken from the mines of Montana per year; more than one-fourth enough to build and equip the Northern Pacific Road, ready for use. There are also immense mines of coal, iron, copper, and lead, in the country. The northern route crosses but one range of mountains, and that at a point which, so far as the experience of white men have gone, is known to be as passable in winter as the Michigan Central Railroad. In deciding the question of relative distance, we must consider the entire distance between Liverpool and Canton. Say the mean latitude of the North Pacific route is 46 degrees, and of the Central 37¼, and a difference of nine degrees exists. Now a degree of longitude (longitude contracting as we approach the poles) is about six miles shorter on the former than the latter. There are 240 degrees of longitude between Liverpool and Canton; this makes the navigator's distance, on the line of the North Pacific, 1,440 miles less than the Central. This longitudinal difference is quite an item. This difference in distance is not the only item in favor of the northern route. It is an established fact that every sailing vessel, bound directly from San Francisco to Hong Kong, comes up to, and even beyond, the latitude of Puget Sound, before striking directly west, in order to take advantage of the wind currents of the Pacific Ocean. Time, these days, being an important consideration in commercial transactions, the argument would still be in favor of the North Pacific route, admitting rates of transportation to be equal on both lines. But these rates would not be the same, even if the distance of the two were equal, for the reason that the country would be self-supporting on nearly every mile of the Northern route, while on the Central, for hundreds of miles between Salt Lake and Nevada, not a tie for the track, nor a stick, nor a pound of coal for fuel can be had. All these things must be brought from abroad.

"Now, owing to adventitious circumstances,—the discovery of the precious metals in California, Nevada, and Colorado, and the settlement of Mormons in Utah,—the bulk of local business seems to be on the side of the Central route. But Montana will soon outstrip California in the yield of gold; besides, the route passes through a country susceptible of settlement all the way from Lake Superior to Puget Sound, and there is no doubt but that five years hence there will be as much local business through Minnesota, Dakota, Montana, Idaho, Washington, and Oregon, as through Nebraska, Colorado, Utah, Nevada, and California. Accident gives the Central route the present pre-eminence; nature insures the Northern the final victory.

"It is not generally known, the large amount of business that was done in Montana last season. From May, 1866, to October 1, 1866, C. C. Huntley carried, on his line of stages between Fort Benton and Helena, 2,500 passengers, and during the same period 9,500 tons of freight passed from Benton to Helena; 4,375 freight-wagons passed over the same route; 45 steamboats, with passengers and freight, arrived at Fort Benton from St. Louis and other points in the east, and this, be it remembered, is the first season that this trade has been carried on to any extent, and also, that this is but one point in the Territory. It is really the commencement of a great trade, that will require a vast capital, and employ the energy and industry of a large number of persons.

"There are no less than four lofty ranges of mountains to cross on the Central route, the Rocky Mountains, at Bridger's Pass, being the most passable crossing; the Wasatch, the Humboldt, and the Sierra Nevada are barely passable in summer. By the way of Pen d'Oreille Lake, on the Northern route, freight can be taken from the Columbia to the Missouri nearly all winter. Another advantage possessed by the Northern route is, that at present the distance is less than 600 miles between the head of steamboat navigation on the Missouri and Snake rivers, and when the boats are completed which are now building on the Pen d'Oreille Lake and Clarke's fork of the Columbia, the land travel will be reduced to about 390 miles.

"Did time and space permit, I might give further proof of the superiority of the Northern route. In my comparative reasoning, I have made these distinctions with no invidious feeling. The sooner San Francisco is connected by rail with New York, the better for Washington and Montana, in common with all the mountain regions. It is gratifying to see our friends to the southward prosecuting their enterprise with so much vigor. But I am perfectly satisfied in my own mind that the time will come when the trafficking wealth of Europe and Asia will be poured across the mountains and valleys of Washington and Montana Territories.

"Our prospects, it is true, look rather dull here at present, the whole energy of the Pacific coast being concentrated in building the Central road, and for a short time we may expect dull times. The attention of capitalists can not be diverted from this enterprise much longer, and when once fully examined, there will be millions of capital ready to invest in it.

"Let us open up the Mullan road and the lake route, and all other routes to the Missouri River, and invite travelers and emigrants to come this way and see the advantages of this northern country, and then we will have no trouble in getting money to build a railroad."

CONCLUSION.

As the reader will have discovered, we commenced our history with Oregon as it was in 1792. With the single exception of the feeble effort made by Mr. Astor in 1810–11, and Captain Wyeth in 1834–5, no one ever attempted any thing like an organized opposition to the British fur companies on the Pacific coast.

In regard to Captain Wyeth, we admit with Mr. Newell that he was driven from the country "not by fair and open competition in the trade," and that he is entitled to much credit for his discernment and forethought in leaving when he did, for if he had not accepted the terms offered to him by Dr. McLaughlin, that gentleman said to us that the company would have insisted on other means being used to relieve its trade from his competition, so that whatever credit or honor there is due in the case belongs to Captain Wyeth's judgment and decision in accepting such compensation as the company chose to give, and not to the company for giving it; for it was that, or a crime to be committed in getting rid of him and his party; and, as in the case of Smith and Dr. Whitman, to be charged upon the Indians.

As Americans, we must not conclude that it could do a dishonorable or mean act to our traders, hunters, missionaries, or even settlers. No one must presume to think that the Honorable Hudson's Bay Company would ever conduct any but an honorable trade, or engage in any but an honorable business, in the country; notwithstanding, its own countrymen charge it with having seized and sunk vessels belonging to them, by running them ashore in Hudson's Bay; robbed and fought with the Northwest Company before they combined their interests; and had its own Governor Semple killed in fighting for its interests, besides all its transactions with its own countrymen; this would be ungenerous and mean in the estimation of men unable to distinguish between a selfish and a generous act, or a cause and a crime of civilized and savage men.

Missionary efforts were first made in the country by Rev. Jason Lee. He, being a Canadian-born subject, was received with less objection than Rev. Messrs. Parker and Spalding, and Dr. Whitman; but, as has been shown, the English people expected to hold the country by the power and influence of their Hudson's Bay Company.

The company, as such, could not act against the American missionaries as it did against American traders and hunters; hence, the Episcopal or Established Church influence from London was made use of, and a clergyman sent to Vancouver. While missionary operations were confined to the Wallamet Valley this was sufficient, but when those efforts were extended to the Cayuses and Nez Percés, and efforts were being made to establish missions further north by another responsible religious society, the company became alarmed for its profits by the fur trade; and by one of its own unprincipled, dishonorable, as well as hypocritical arrangements, under the specious pretense of having religious teachers to look after the moral and religious instructions of its Canadian-French Catholic servants, it sent for, and continued in its service, the very religious order of the Roman Church that was at that time proscribed by the laws of the country from which it held its license. This showed the moral principle by which it was governed in relation to its own country. The interests of its trade were paramount to all moral principles or religious teachings; and while it was professing warm friendship for one religious sect, it was encouraging secretly and openly an opposite and strongly bigoted one, to divide and distract the moral and religious sentiments of the ignorant natives; claiming for itself an exclusive monopoly in trade, as being beneficial to the Indian race, which was admitted by all. This was the moral and religious condition of the whole country when the American settlers came to it. They, with the American missionaries, combined in forming a provisional government, and established a *quasi* independent American republic, with the condition that, whenever the United States government saw fit to extend its jurisdiction over the country, this temporary government should cease.

The English and French united with us in this organization, on condition that they should not be required to do any thing that would conflict with their duties as subjects of Great Britain.

The reader will perceive that, in carrying out the plan laid down in our preface, we have been obliged to give the Hudson's Bay Company a prominent place in our history, as we have had to meet them in every step of our progress.

No history of Oregon can be written, without acknowledging the immense influence that company held in the country, and the zeal and energy it put forth, in counteracting American ideas and influence. It was its original design to colonize and secure to the British crown all the countries which it might explore and occupy. And had it carried out that design, no American effort could have succeeded in securing the country to the government of the United States. But from a selfish, short-sighted, and mistaken policy; and a blind perception of its asserted commercial rights, privileges, and powers, it "*hunted up*" the country, and expected to secure to itself undisturbed possession of the northwestern part of the continent.

For this purpose, while it was destroying the valuable fur animals in what is now United States territory, it was protecting such as were to be found further north; and by this means continued the enormous profits of its trade, for a series of years longer than it otherwise could have done. The discovery of gold on the Frazer River in 1858, the rush of miners, and the organizing of British Columbia, partially checked this fur company, and led to the formation of a sickly colony strangled in the embrace of an avaricious monopoly. To counteract the American and Protestant missionary efforts, it brought to Oregon the Roman and French Jesuits. To compete with the Americans in stock and agricultural products, it originated the Puget Sound Company. To outnumber the American settlers, it brought on a colony of half-breeds from Red River.

While by the influence of its Jesuits it could destroy one branch of the Protestant missions, and bring on an Indian war, the settlement had gained strength sufficient to maintain independence without its aid.

While the country has increased in population and wealth, this English monopoly has been decreasing in power and influence.

While the Protestant religion has continued to widen and deepen its hold upon the American people, the Papal superstition has increased among the Indians, thus rendering them more hopelessly depraved, and consigning them and their descendants to unending superstition and ignorance, or to utter oblivion as a race, to be superseded by an enlightened Christian, American people.

With unfeigned thanks to all who have assisted us in this work, we take our leave, hoping the facts we have given will be useful, and abundantly reward the reader for his time and money.